George Finlay

History of the Greek revolution

George Finlay

History of the Greek revolution

ISBN/EAN: 9783741166723

Manufactured in Europe, USA, Canada, Australia, Japa

Cover: Foto ©ninafisch / pixelio.de

Manufactured and distributed by brebook publishing software (www.brebook.com)

George Finlay

History of the Greek revolution

HISTORY

OF THE

GREEK REVOLUTION

Καὶ παρὼν ἐρῶ
Οὐδὲν παρήσω τῆς ἀληθείας ἔπος
Τί γάρ σε μαλθάσσοιμ᾽ ἂν ὧν ἐς ὕστερον
Ψεῦσται φανούμεθ᾽; ὀρθὸν ἀληθεί᾽ ἀεί.

HISTORY

OF THE

GREEK REVOLUTION,

BY

GEORGE FINLAY, LL.D.

Hon. Member of the Royal Society of Literature, Member of the American Antiquarian
Society, Corresponding Member of the Archæological Institute at Rome
Knight Gold Cross of the Greek Order of the Redeemer

AUTHOR OF THE "HISTORY OF GREECE UNDER FOREIGN DOMINATION," ETC.

IN TWO VOLUMES

VOL. II.

WILLIAM BLACKWOOD AND SONS
EDINBURGH AND LONDON
MDCCCLXI

CONTENTS OF THE SECOND VOLUME.

BOOK THIRD.

THE SUCCESSES OF THE GREEKS.

CHAPTER IV.

THE CONDITION OF GREECE AS AN INDEPENDENT STATE.

	Page
Firmness of Sultan Mahmud,	2
He adopts a conciliatory policy,	4
Great fire destroys the Turkish armaments in 1823,	5
Plan of campaign for 1823,	6
Negligence of the Greek government,	7
Olympian armatoli plunder Skiathos and Skopelos,	7
Operations of the Turks,	9
Death of Marco Botzares,	10
Advance of the Othoman army,	12
Siege of Anatolikon,	13
Operations of the Greek and Turkish fleets,	14
Escape of eight Psarian sailors,	16
Violation of Ionian neutrality,	18
Misconduct of the sailors in the Greek fleet,	20
Surrender of the Turks in the Acrocorinth,	21
Lord Byron in Greece,	22
First Greek loan contracted in England,	26
First civil war,	28
Mohammed Ali engages to assist the sultan,	28
The political state of Greece in 1824,	30
Position of Kolettes,	32
Position of Mavrocordatos,	33
Second civil war,	34
Characters of Zaimes, Londos, and Sessini,	34
Evil effects of the two civil wars,	37
Wasteful expenditure of the two loans,	38
Anecdotes,	41
Military expenditure,	42
Naval expenditure,	43

BOOK FOURTH.

THE SUCCESSES OF THE TURKS.

CHAPTER I.

NAVAL SUCCESS.—IBRAHIM IN THE MOREA.

Destruction of Kasos,
Destruction of Psara,
Expedition of Mohammed Ali,
The Bairam at Makry,
Naval battles off Budrun,
Failure of the Turks at Samos,
Ibrahim driven back when off Crete,
He lands in Greece,
Greeks unprepared for defence,
Greek army defeated,
Egyptians take Sphakteria,
Escape of the brig Mars,
Capitulation of Pylos and Navarin,
Success of Miaoulis at Modon,
Kolokotrones appointed commander-in-chief,
Death of the archimandrite Dikaios,
Defeat of Kolokotrones at Makryplagi,
Ibrahim repulsed at Lerna,
Defeat of Kolokotrones at Trikorpha,
Ibrahim ravages the Morea,
Receives orders to aid in the siege of Mesolonghi,

CHAPTER II.

THE SIEGE OF MESOLONGHI.

Operations of Reshid Pasha,
State of Mesolonghi,
Number of the garrison and of the besiegers,
Arrival of the Othoman fleet,
Arrival of the Greek fleet,
Difficult position of Reshid,
The mound,
Treason of Odysseus,
Military operations in continental Greece,
Reshid withdraws to a fortified camp,
Operations of the Turkish and Greek fleets,
Ibrahim arrives before Mesolonghi,
Lethargy of the Greeks and of their government,

CONTENTS.

	Page
Turks take Vasiladi and Anatolikon,	101
Offers of capitulation rejected,	102
Turkish attack on Klisova repulsed,	103
Defeat of the Greek fleet under Miaoulis,	104
Final sortie,	106
Fall of Mesolonghi,	110

CHAPTER III.

THE SIEGE OF ATHENS.

Ibrahim's operations in the Morea during 1826,	112
Reshid's operations in continental Greece,	114
Athens invested, and battle of Khaidari,	116
Death of Goura,	118
Grigiottes throws himself into the Acropolis,	119
Karaiskaki's operations to raise the siege,	121
Fabvier throws himself into the Acropolis,	124
State of Greece during the winter of 1826-27,	126
Expeditions under Gordon, Burbaki, and Heideck,	131
General Sir Richard Church,	135
Lord Cochrane (Earl of Dundonald),	137
Election of Capodistrias as president of Greece,	138
Naval expedition under Captain Hastings,	139
Greek traders supply Reshid's army with provisions,	142
Operations of Church and Cochrane to relieve Athens,	143
Massacre of the garrison of the monastery of St Spiridion,	146
Karaiskaki's death,	148
Defeat of Sir Richard Church at the Phalerum,	149
Evacuation of the Acropolis,	152
Conduct of Philhellenes in Greece, England, and America,	154
Lord Cochrane's naval review at Poros,	157
Sufferings of the agricultural population,	158
Assistance sent from the United States,	159

BOOK FIFTH.

THE ESTABLISHMENT OF THE GREEK KINGDOM.

CHAPTER I.

FOREIGN INTERVENTION.—BATTLE OF NAVARIN.

Conduct of Russia,	160
Conduct of Great Britain,	161
Congress of Verona,	162

viii   CONTENTS.

	Page
Russian memoir relating to the pacification of Greece,	163
Effects of this memoir,	165
Turkey complains of the conduct of Great Britain,	167
Greece seeks the protection of Great Britain,	169
Protocol of 4th April 1826,	172
Destruction of the janissaries,	173
Treaty of 6th July 1827 for the pacification of Greece,	174
State of Greece in 1827,	174
Victory of Hastings at Salona,	176
Battle of Navarin,	178
Greek slaves carried to Alexandria,	183
Greek troops cross into Acarnania,	185
Hastings takes Vasiladi,	186
Death of Hastings,	188
Russia declares war with Turkey,	189
French troops compel Ibrahim to evacuate the Morea,	192

CHAPTER II.

PRESIDENCY OF COUNT CAPODISTRIAS.—JANUARY 1828 TO OCTOBER 1831.

Character of Count John Capodistrias,	195
First administrative measures of the president,	196
His opinions and policy,	198
Organisation of the army,	200
Fabvier's resignation,	205
Operations in Eastern and Western Greece,	206
Termination of hostilities,	207
Civil administration,	208
Viaro Capodistrias,	210
Financial administration,	213
Judicial administration,	216
Public instruction,	218
National assembly of Argos,	219
Protocols of the three protecting powers,	221
Prince Leopold of Saxe-Coburg sovereign of Greece,	224
Prince Leopold's resignation,	228
Capodistrias becomes a tyrant,	230
Hostility to the liberty of the press,	231
Tyranny of Capodistrias,	233
Affair of Poros,	235
Destruction of the Greek fleet,	238
Sack of Poros,	240
Family of Mavromichales,	242
Assassination of Capodistrias,	245

CHAPTER III.

ANARCHY.—9TH OCTOBER 1831 TO 1ST FEBRUARY 1833.

	Page
The governing commission refuses to grant a general amnesty after the murder of Capodistrias,	248
Second national assembly of Argos,	250
Romeliot military opposition,	252
Agostino Capodistrias president of Greece,	254
Romeliots expelled from Argos,	255
Sir Stratford Canning's memorandum,	255
Romeliots invade the Morea,	257
Conduct of the residents,	259
Agostino ejected from the presidency,	260
New governing commission,	261
State of Greece,	262
Anarchy,	266
French troops garrison Nauplia,	269
Djavellas occupies Patras,	270
Kolokotrones rallies the Capodistrians,	271
National assembly of Pronia,	272
Constitutional liberty in abeyance,	277
Intrigues of the senate,	278
Municipal institutions arrest the progress of anarchy in the Morea,	279
Condition of Messenia,	281
Position of Kolokotrones and Koletten,	283
True nature of the municipal institutions of Greece under the Turks not generally understood,	284
Attack on the French troops at Argos,	285
Establishment of the Bavarian dynasty,	287

CHAPTER IV.

BAVARIAN DESPOTISM AND CONSTITUTIONAL REVOLUTION.—FEBRUARY 1833 TO SEPTEMBER 1843.

Landing of King Otho,	290
The regency, its members and duties,	293
Royal proclamation—administrative measures,	300
Military organisation,	302
Civil administration—municipal institutions,	305
Financial administration—monetary system,	309
Judicial organisation,	312
The Greek church—reforms of the regency,	314
Synodal Tomos,	318
Monasteries,	319
Public instruction,	320

CONTENTS.

	Page
Restrictions on the liberty of the press,	321
Roads—Order of the Redeemer,	322
Quarrels in the regency,	324
Kolokotrones's plot and Armansperg's intrigue,	326
Armansperg's administration,	333
Bavarian influence,	336
Disputes with England,	341
Alarming increase of brigandage,	342
Insurrections in Maina and Messenia,	345
Brigandage in 1835,	350
General Gordon's expedition,	353
Insurrection in Acarnania,	357
Opinions of Lord Lyons and General Gordon on the state of Greece,	361
Brigandage continues,	363
King Otho's personal government,	365
Attacks on King Otho in the English newspapers,	367
Causes of the Revolution of 1843,	368
Revolution,	372
Observations on the constitution,	377
Conclusion,	381
Appendix—	
Hastings's memorandum on the use of steamers armed with heavy guns,	385
Napier's memorandum on military operations against Ibrahim Pasha,	390
Index,	393

HISTORY

OF THE

GREEK REVOLUTION.

BOOK THIRD.

THE SUCCESSES OF THE GREEKS.

CHAPTER IV.

THE CONDITION OF GREECE AS AN INDEPENDENT STATE.

" Τοιγαροῦν χωρὶς τῶν ἄλλων, οἱ τὰ κοινὰ χειρίζοντες παρὰ μὲν τοῖς Ἕλλησιν, ἐὰν ταλάντου μόνου πιστευθῶσιν, ἀντιγραφεῖς ἔχοντες δέκα, καὶ σφραγῖδας τοσαύτας καὶ μάρτυρας διπλασίους οὐ δύνανται τηρεῖν τὴν πίστιν."—POLYBIUS, vi. 56, 13.

Not to mention other defects, no Greek who is intrusted with public money can refrain from peculation, even if ten commissioners be appointed to watch over the expenditure, and though ten bonds be signed with twice as many witnesses as a security for his honesty.

FIRMNESS OF SULTAN MAHMUD—HE ADOPTS A CONCILIATORY POLICY—A GREAT FIRE AT CONSTANTINOPLE DESTROYS HIS ARMAMENTS IN 1823—PLAN OF CAMPAIGN FOR 1823—NEGLIGENCE OF THE GREEK GOVERNMENT—OLYMPIAN ARMATOLI PLUNDER SKIATHOS AND SKOPELOS—OPERATIONS OF THE TURKS—DEATH OF MARCO BOTZARIS—ADVANCE OF THE TURKISH ARMY—SIEGE OF ANATOLIKON—OPERATIONS OF THE GREEK AND TURKISH FLEETS—ESCAPE OF EIGHT PSARIAN SAILORS—VIOLATION OF IONIAN NEUTRALITY—MISCONDUCT OF THE SAILORS ON BOARD THE GREEK FLEET—SURRENDER OF THE TURKS IN THE ACROCORINTH—LORD BYRON IN GREECE—FIRST GREEK LOAN CONTRACTED IN ENGLAND—FIRST CIVIL WAR—MOHAMMED ALI ENGAGES TO ASSIST THE SULTAN—THE POLITICAL STATE OF GREECE IN 1824—POSITION OF KOLETTES—OF MAVROCORDATOS—SECOND CIVIL WAR—EVIL CONSEQUENCES OF THE TWO CIVIL WARS—WASTEFUL EXPENDITURE OF THE TWO LOANS—ANECDOTES—MILITARY EXPENDITURE—NAVAL EXPENDITURE.

THE successes of the Greeks during the year 1822 established Greece as an independent state, and forced even those who were hostile to the Revolution to acknowledge that the war was no longer a struggle of the Porte with a few rebellious rayahs. The importance of the Greek nation could no longer be denied, whatever might be the failings of the Greek government. The war was now the battle of an oppressed people against a powerful sovereign. The inhabitants of Greece, whether of the Hellenic or the Albanian race, fought to secure their religious liberty and the independence of their country. Sultan Mahmud fought to maintain Othoman supremacy and the divine right of tyranny. Both were supported by strong feelings of religious and national antipathy; but the strength of the Greek cause lay in the hearts of the people, and that of the Turkish in the energy of the sovereign. Between such enemies there could neither be peace nor truce.

To the friends of civil and religious liberty the cause of Greece seemed sure of victory. A nation in arms is not easily conquered. Holland established her independence, under greater difficulties, against a far greater power than the Othoman empire in the present time. Switzerland was another example of the success of patriotism when the people are determined to be free. The people in Greece had adopted that determination, and they neither counted the cost of their struggle, nor shrank from encountering any hardships to gain their end.

The noble resolution of the Greeks and of the Christian Albanians in Greece to live or die free, encountered a firm determination on the part of Sultan Mahmud to re-establish his authority even by the extermination of the inhabitants of liberated Greece. When his fleets were defeated and his armies destroyed; when Russia threatened his northern frontier, and Persia invaded his eastern provinces; when, to

meet his expenditure, he was cheating his subjects by
debasing his coinage; when the janissaries revolted in
his capital, and the timariots and spahis refused to
march against the rebellious infidels; when rival
pashas fought with one another instead of marching
against the Greeks; and when all Turkey appeared to
be a scene of anarchy, the inflexible sultan pursued
steadily his great object of preserving the integrity of
the Othoman empire. When European statesmen
treated him as a frantic tyrant, he was revealing to
Lord Stratford de Redcliffe the sagacious policy which
raised that skilful diplomatist to his profound mastery
of Eastern questions. The shattered fabric of the
falling empire was for some years upheld by the profound administrative views, the unwearied perseverance, and the iron character of Sultan Mahmud. He
was an energetic, if not a great man, and his calm
melancholy look was an index to his sagacious and
saturnine intellect.

The spectacle of a duel between such a sovereign
and the resuscitated Demos of Greece, was a spectacle
that deservedly excited the attention of civilised nations. Mohammedanism and Christianity, tyranny
and liberty, despotism and law, were all deeply compromised in the result. The massacres at Chios and
the defeat of Dramali were considered proofs that the
sultan could not reconquer the Greeks, and Christendom could not allow him to exterminate a Christian
people. Public opinion—the watch-dog whose bark
sounds as an evil omen in the ear of monarchs—began
to growl a warning to Christian kings not longer to
neglect the rights of Christian nations, and statesmen
began to feel that the sympathies of the people in
Western Europe were at last fairly interested in the
cause of Greece. But the friends of the holy alliance
still argued that anarchy was inflicting hourly more

misery in Greece than the sultan's government inflicted annually on the Greeks in Turkey; that the extortions of Kolokotrones and Odysseus, and the misgovernment of Mavrocordatos, produced greater evils than the faults of pashas and the errors of Sultan Mahmud; and that the power and resources of the Othoman empire rendered the success of the Greek Revolution hopeless. The friends of Greece, on the other hand, replied, that if the Greek chiefs were worthless, and the Greek government weak, the will of the people was strong, and the nation would prove unconquerable. The Greeks, they said, might yet find a government worthy of their cause, and the liberties of Greece might find a champion like William of Orange or Washington; or, if liberty produced no champion, war might give the nation a chief like Cromwell or Napoleon.

The animosity of the belligerents was never more violent than at the commencement of 1823, but the resources of both were for the time exhausted. The sultan, finding that his indiscriminate cruelty had only strengthened the Greeks in their determination to oppose his power, changed his policy, and began to treat them with mildness. Many who had been thrown into prison merely as hostages, were released, and the Greek communities generally were allowed to enjoy their old municipal privileges, and manage their own financial affairs. Strict orders were transmitted to all pashas to act equitably to the Greek subjects of the Porte. Some slight concessions were also made in order to conciliate Russia, and negotiations were opened with Persia, which eventually terminated the war with that power.[1] Even the sympathy of Western nations in the Greek cause was not overlooked. Sultan

[1] The treaty of peace between Turkey and Persia was signed on the 28th July 1823, but it was not published at Constantinople until the month of October, and not ratified by the Shah of Persia until January 1824.

Mahmud knew little of public opinion, but he was not ignorant of the power of popular feeling. The early events of his life, and the state of his capital, had taught him to fear insurrections. He was persuaded by his own judgment, as well as by foreign ambassadors and his own ministers, that Christian nations might force kings and emperors to defend the Greeks, and that it would be wise to avert a combination of the Christian powers for such a purpose. He therefore ordered the new capitan-pasha, Khosref Mehemet, called Topal, to assure the English ambassador and the Austrian internuncio, that the Othoman fleet would not lay waste the defenceless islands of the Archipelago, and that terms of submission would be offered to all Christians who had taken up arms.

The sultan's preparations for the campaign of 1823 were suddenly paralysed by a great disaster. The arsenal and cannon foundery at Tophana were destroyed by fire. An immense train of artillery had been prepared for the army of Thessaly; twelve hundred brass guns were ready to arm new ships in the port; an extraordinary supply of ammunition and military stores was packed up for service: all these materials were destroyed by one of the most terrible conflagrations ever witnessed, even by the inhabitants of Constantinople. Besides the artillery arsenal, fifty mosques and about six thousand houses were destroyed. A large part of Pera was reduced to ashes.

This fire was attributed by public rumour to the malevolence of the janissaries, and that rumour was believed by Sultan Mahmud. Fifteen ortas were under orders to march against the Greeks. They dared not refuse marching against infidels, but without the materials of war, destroyed by this conflagration, their departure was useless. They had now gained time to organise an insurrection, and their discontent alarmed the sultan to such a degree that, contrary to the established usage of the empire, he did not appear in public on several occasions. But neither his personal danger, nor the destruction of his artillery, abated his energy. A small fleet was fitted out, and, instead of making a decisive attack on the Greeks, it was resolved to harass them with desultory operations. The capitan-pasha hoisted his flag in a frigate, and his fleet was unencumbered by a single line-of-battle ship. The financial difficulties of the Turkish government were met by a new issue of debased money, which was at that time the substitute for a loan. By the old plan of debasing the coinage, the loss fell on the sultan's own subjects; by the new plan of borrowing money, it is sure to fall on strangers, and in all probability on the subjects of Queen Victoria.

The sultan's plan of campaign was as usual well devised. An army was destined to invade the Morea. Instead of entering the peninsula by the Isthmus of Corinth, it was to cross the gulf at Lepanto, and establish its headquarters at Patras. The garrison of Corinth was to be provisioned and strengthened by the Othoman fleet. Elis and Messenia offered facilities for the employment of the Turkish cavalry. Abundant supplies of all kinds might be obtained from the Ionian Islands to fill the magazines of the army at Patras, Modon, and Ceron.

Yussuf Berkoftzalee, who was well known to the Greeks by his exploits in Moldavia, was ordered to advance from Thessaly through Eastern Greece, with a strong body of cavalry. The main army, consisting of Guegs under Mustaï Pasha of Scodra, and Tosks under Omer Vrioni, pasha of Joannina, was ordered to advance through Western Greece. A junction was to be effected either at Lepanto or at Patras, where the Othoman fleet was to meet the army.

Mavrocordatos had been driven from office by his own mismanagement. His successors at the head of the Greek government were too ignorant to adopt measures for retarding the advance of the Turks, and too selfish to think of anything but their personal interests. The people stood ready to do their duty, but the popular energy was left without guidance. The captains and best soldiers were far from the frontier, collecting and consuming the national revenues. The Morea was filled with well-paid troops; but few were disposed to quit the flesh-pots of the districts in which they had taken up their quarters; so that, when the campaign opened, Greece had no army in the field.

Reshid Pasha (Kiutayhé) commenced the military operations of the year 1823, by treading out the ashes of the Revolution that still smouldered on Mount Pelion. He subdued Trikheri in conjunction with the capitan-pasha, and drove the Olympian armatoli from their last retreat in Thessaly.[1]

The Olympian armatoli escaped to Skiathos and Skopelos, where they maintained themselves by plundering the inhabitants, while Yussuf Berkoftzalee was laying waste Eastern Greece. In the month of July, the inhabitants of Skiathos were driven from their houses by these Greek troops, who took possession of the town, and consumed the grain, oil, and wine which they found stored up in the magazines. Parties of soldiers scoured the island, and seized the sheep and goats as if they had been in an enemy's country. The inhabitants fled to an ancient castle about five miles from the town, with as much of their property as they could save, and defended this strong position against their intrusive countrymen. The armatoli were so much pleased with their idle life, varied with goat hunts and skirmishes with the natives, that they re-

---

[1] See vol. i. p. 246.

fused to obey the orders they received from the Greek government, to join a body of troops in Eubœa. Admiral Miaoulis visited Skiathos on the 11th of October, and found the inhabitants in a state of destitution and distress. They were shut up in the castle, and their supplies were exhausted, while the soldiers were consuming the last remains of their property in the town. The authority, the solicitations, and the reproaches of Miaoulis, were employed in vain to expel the armatoli from the island, and the lawless soldiery did not quit Skiathos until they had consumed everything on which they could lay their hands.

While the Olympian armatoli were ruining Skiathos and plundering Skopelos, Yussuf Berkoftzalee was laying waste Phocis and Bœotia. Many villages, and several monasteries on Parnassus and Helicon, which had hitherto escaped devastation, were plundered and burned. Kastri, the village which occupies the site of Delphi, was pillaged; but instead of establishing himself at Salona, opening communications with Lepanto, and co-operating with the army of Mustaï Pasha, Berkoftzalee fixed his headquarters at Thebes, sent his infantry to Negrepont, and pushed forward his foraging parties into the plain of Athens.

Kolettes, like Mavrocordatos, was eager for military glory, and even more unfit for military command. He now persuaded the other members of the government to appoint him commander-in-chief of a Greek army which he was to assemble in Eubœa. He had no military qualifications but a portly frame and the Albanian dress; but these physical and artificial advantages induced the stout Zinzar Vallachian to despise the moral courage and the patriotic disinterestedness of his phanariot rival, whose frame, though smaller, was far more active. When the Turks appeared, Kolettes fled und abandoned Eubœa to its fate.

Odysseus, however, who commanded the Greek force in the southern part of the island, defeated the Mussulmans in a skirmish near Kanystos. As a trophy of his victory, he sent fifty heads and three living Turks to Athens. The modern Athenians deliberately stoned these three unfortunate prisoners to death.

Mustaï Pasha assembled his army at Ochrida. It consisted of five thousand Mohammedan Guegs, and three thousand Catholic Miridits. These Catholics, who speak the Guegh dialect of the Albanian language, boast of their descent from the Christians who fought against the Turks under their national hero Skanderbeg, or George Castriot. But their hatred of the orthodox Greeks has long since bound them in a closer alliance with the Mussulman tribes in their neighbourhood, than with any body of Christians. On the present occasion, the Miridits formed the advanced guard of Mustaï's army. They upheld the military glory of their race, and ridiculed the vanity of the Greeks, who attempted to filch from them the glory of Skanderbeg.

The Greeks made no preparations to oppose Mustaï. Mavrocordatos had quitted Mesolonghi. While he remained there, he concentrated in his own person the three offices of President of Greece, Governor-General of the Western Provinces, and Commander-in-Chief of the Etolian army; but when he departed he left three persons to execute the duties of commander-in-chief. This absurd arrangement would doubtless have created anarchy had it not already existed, and it tended to increase the disorders that already prevailed. Almost every chief, both in Etolia and Acarnania, engaged in quarrels with his neighbours. Sometimes they fought in order to decide who should march to encounter Mustaï's army, and the prize of victory was liberty to stay at home and plunder the peasantry. In most cases their proceedings were an inexplicable enigma; and their most intelligent countrymen could only tell strangers, what indeed was very evident without their communication, that the conduct of the captains and primates was ruining the people.

The advance of Mustai's army was signalised by one of the most brilliant exploits of the war. The first division of the Othoman force consisted of four thousand men, Catholics and Mussulmans, under the command of Djelaleddin Bey. It encamped in the valley of Karpenisi, near an abundant fountain of pure water, which forms a brook as it flows from its basin, shaded by a fine old willow-tree.

At midnight on the 21st of August 1823 the orthodox Tosks surprised the camp of the Catholic and Mussulman Guegs. Marco Botzares, at the head of three hundred and fifty Suliots, broke into the midst of their enemies and rushed forward to slay the bey. The Othoman troops, roused from sleep, fled with precipitation, leaving their arms behind. Had the Greek captains descended with the armatoli of Etolia and Acarnania from the villages in which they were idly watching the flashes of the Suliot arms, they might have annihilated the Turkish force. But Greek envy sacrificed the Albanian hero. The bey of Ochrida had pitched his tent in a mandra or walled enclosure, built to protect beehives or young lambs from badgers and foxes. Botzares reached this wall, and, not finding the entrance, raised his head to look over it, in order to discover a means of entering it with his followers. The alarm had now roused Djelaleddin's veterans, who were familiar with nocturnal surprises. Several were on the watch when the head of Botzares rose above the wall, and showed itself marked on the grey sky; a ball immediately pierced his brain, and the Suliots took up his body. Even then a few hand-grenades would have driven Djelaleddin's guard from the enclosure, and completed the defeat of the Turkish force; but the Suliots had learned nothing of the art of war during their long intercourse with the Russians, French, and English in the Ionian Islands. Like most warlike savages, they despised the improvements of science; and the consequence was, that their victorious career was now stopped by a rough wall, built as a defence against foxes and badgers. But before retiring with the body of their leader, they collected and carried off their booty. No attempt was made to interrupt their retreat to Mikrokherio, where they arrived accompanied by a train of mules caught in the camp, and laden with spoil. Horse-hair sacks filled with silver-mounted pistols, yataghans, and cartridge-cases, were fastened over pack-saddles like bags of meal, and long Albanian muskets were tied up in bundles like fagots of firewood. The booty was very great, but the death of Marco Botzares cast a gloom over their spirits. The Greek soldiers in the neighbouring villages of Tranakhorio and Nostimo, when it was too late, became ashamed of their inactivity, and reproached their captains for causing the death of the bravest chief in the Greek army. As the news of the loss spread, the whole nation grieved over the noble Suliot.

The affair at Karpenisi is one of the examples of the secondary part which the rival dominant races of Othomans and Greeks often bore in the war of the Greek Revolution. The Othomans who accompanied the army of Mustaï were still in the plain of Thessaly. The Greeks were encamped idly on the hills. The battle was fought between the Catholic Guegs and the orthodox Tosks.

The troops of Djelaleddin remained in possession of the field of battle, and buried their dead on the spot. Two English travellers who passed the place during the following summer saw a number of small wooden crosses fixed over the graves of the Miridits.

The Suliots who bore a part in this memorable exploit near the fountain and the old willow-tree, were long distinguished by the richly ornamented and strangely mounted arms they wore; but many regretted their dearly-purchased splendour, and thought the night accursed on which it was obtained, saying, that it had been better for them and for Greece had Markos still lived, and they had continued to carry the plain rifles of their fathers.

The success of the Suliots did not retard the advance of Mustaï. His Guegs pressed on, eager to avenge their losses and wipe off the stain on their military reputation. The Greeks abandoned their positions at Tranokhorio, and made an unsuccessful attempt to defend the valley between the two precipitous mountains of Khelidoni and Kaliakudi.

The road from Karpenisi to Vrachori runs through a succession of frightful passes and giant rocks. It may be compared with the most difficult footpaths over the Alps. The great mountain Kaliakudi closes the entrance by a wall of precipices, broken by one chasm, through which the river of Karpenisi forces its passage to join the Achelous. In this pass a skirmish took place, and the Greeks boast of an imaginary victory at Kaliakudi. To any one who has visited the monastery of Brusó, it must be evident that three hundred men, inspired with the spirit of Markos Botzares, might have stopped an army as numerous as that of Xerxes or of Brennus. But the Albanians of Mustaï drove the Greek armatoli before them through the sublime valleys which diverge from Brusó. It has been said that Mustaï sowed distrust among the Greek chiefs, by promising capitanliks to some venal leaders. He could hardly have ventured to march through the pass of Brusó had he not been assured that he should find no enemy to oppose him.

At Vrachori Mustaï found Omer Vrioni with an army of Mussulman Tosks. The dialects of the Guegs and Tosks do not afford a better means of communicating than those of the Irish and the Welsh. The dress of the two tribes is as dissimilar as their speech. The white kilt of the Tosk forms as strong a contrast with the red tunic of the Gueg, as the grey top-coat of Paddy with Sandy's checkered plaid. The followers of the two pashas quarrelled, and the pashas did not agree.

In October 1823 their united force attacked Anatolikon, a small town in the Etolian lagoons, about five miles west of Mesolonghi. The Greeks had only a mud battery, mounting six guns, to defend the place. In the hour of need they allowed William Martin, who had deserted with another seaman from an English ship, to constitute himself captain of a gun.[1] He dismounted the only piece of artillery the Turks placed in battery. The pashas found it impossible to do anything but bombard the place from a couple of mortars, which they planted out of reach of the fire of the Greeks. Their shells did little damage, and only about twenty persons were killed and wounded. On the 11th of December Mustaï raised the siege, and retired to Epirus, through the unguarded pass of Markynoros. Before commencing his retreat, he buried some guns which arrived too late to be of any use, and in order to conceal them from the Greeks, he surrounded them with a low wall of masonry, and ornamented the place like a Turkish cemetery. The Greeks showed the spot with pride, boasting of the beys who had fallen under

---

[1] Martin's companion died of typhus fever at Mesolonghi shortly after Mustaï's defeat. Martin was left without either pay or rations, and imprisoned by the Greeks for insubordination. From his own mouth the author learned that he must have died of want had he not been relieved by Mr Blackett.

their deadly fire; but when Kiutayhé besieged Mesolonghi in 1825, he commenced operations by digging up the brass guns in the tombs of the beys.

The new Othoman admiral Khosref, called Topal or the lame pasha, was a man of a courteous disposition and considerable ability—far better suited to be minister of foreign affairs than capitan-pasha. He was not more of a sailor, and quite as great a coward, as his unworthy predecessor Kara Mehemet, but he knew better how to make the officers of the fleet obey his orders. He issued from the Dardanelles at the end of May with a fine fleet, composed of fourteen frigates and twenty corvettes and brigs, attended by forty transports. On the 4th of June he landed three thousand Asiatic troops at Kargstos, and sent several transports laden with military stores to Negrepont. He then sailed past Hydra, threw supplies into Coron and Modon, and landed a body of troops and a large sum of money at Patras on the 20th of the same month. Instead, however, of remaining on the western coast of Greece, to support the operations of Mustaï, who was still at Ochrida, he hastened back to the Dardanelles.

The Albanians of Hydra and Spetzas displayed neither activity nor zeal during the year 1823. The Greeks of Psara, Kasos, and Samos, on the contrary, were never more active and enterprising. The Psarians made a descent on the Asiatic coast at Tchanderlik, on the site of Pitane in Æolis, where they stormed a battery, burned the town, and carried off the harem of a bey belonging to the great house of Kara Osman Oglou of Magnesia. The booty gained by plundering the town was increased by the receipt of ten thousand dollars as ransom for the bey's family. The shores of the gulf of Adrymetti were then plundered, and contributions were levied on the Greeks of Mytilene.

The ravages committed on the coast of Asia Minor caused the Mussulman population to break out into open revolt. The sultan was accused of sparing the Giaours to please the Christian ambassadors at Constantinople, and the people called on all true believers to avenge the slaughter of the Turks at Tchanderlik and other places by murdering the Greeks. In many towns the Christians were attacked by fanatical mobs, and at Pergamus several hundred Greeks perished before the Othoman authorities could restore order.

During the autumn Miaoulis sailed from Hydra with a small fleet. On his return he complained bitterly of the misconduct of those under his command. Some of the ships of Hydra delayed joining him. At Psara quarrels occurred between the Albanian and Greek sailors; and on the 5th of October the Psarians, in defiance of Miaoulis, seized some Turkish prisoners on board a Hydriot brig, and carried them on shore. Several were publicly tortured before the town hall of Psara, and the rest were murdered in the streets. When the fleet reached Skiathos fresh disorders broke out. The efforts of the admiral to expel the Olympian armatoli, who were plundering the island, proved ineffectual, as has been already mentioned, partly in consequence of the misconduct of the Albanian sailors. A fight took place on shore between the Hydriots and Spetziots, in which three Spetziots were killed and eight wounded. These dissensions rendered all co-operation between the ships of the three islands impossible, and Miaoulis returned to Hydra on the 16th of October almost in a state of despair.

The conduct of the sailors had been insolent and mutinous during the whole cruise. They landed at Lithi, on the west coast of Chios, without orders, robbed the poor Greek peasants of their oxen, plundered the men of their money, and violated the women. Complaints of these acts were laid before Miaoulis, but he was unable to punish the offenders.

Admiral Miaoulis and six brigs were exposed to great danger off Mount Athos on the 27th of September. A Turkish squadron, consisting of five frigates and four sloops-of-war, gained the wind of the Greeks while their ships lay in a calm. A cannonade of three hours and a half ensued, in which several thousand shot were fired; but as the Turks declined engaging their enemy at close quarters, the Hydriots escaped through the Turkish line with the loss of only eight men killed. The Turks declared that they did not lose a single man; and it is not improbable that they never ventured within range of the smaller guns of the Greek ships.

A romantic event during this cruise deserves to be recorded : On the 1st of October the Psarian admiral picked up a boat with eight of his countrymen on board, who were drifting about in the Archipelago without either provisions or water. They had encountered strange vicissitudes during the previous fortnight. An Austrian schooner had seized them in the gulf of Smyrna, where they were looking out for prizes without papers from the Greek government. They were delivered to the Turkish authorities as pirates, and put on board a small vessel bound for the Dardanelles. At the lower castles they were transferred to a boat manned by fifteen Turks, which was to convey them to the bagnio at Constantinople. They proceeded to Tchanek-akelcasi, where most of the Turkish boatmen slept ashore. The Psarians contrived to kill those who remained on board without noise, and, casting loose the moorings, they were carried by the current beyond the lower castles before daybreak. There they were met by a contrary wind, without provisions and with only one jar of water.

In this difficulty they were forced to put into a secluded creek in Tenedos, and two of their number, who were dressed like the Greek sailors who serve in the Turkish fleet, walked to the town to purchase bread and carry back two jars of water. One of them had fortunately succeeded in concealing a small gold coin in the upper leather of his slippers before he was searched by the lynx-eyed janissaries of Smyrna. The two Psarians remained all day in a Greek wine-shop kept by an Ionian, as the safest place of concealment, bought bread, and procured water. In the evening they walked back to their companions, who had found water, but were famished with hunger. At midnight they left Tenedos; but before they could reach any Greek island the wind became calm or contrary, and they had been rowing incessantly for thirty-six hours, endeavouring to reach Psara, when they were picked up by Admiral Apostoles.

A Greek squadron was sent to relieve Anatolikon, when it was besieged by Mustaï Pasha. Before the Hydriot and Spetziot sailors would embark they insisted on receiving a month's pay in advance. The primates made their mutinous behaviour during the previous cruise a pretext for refusing to make any advance. The Greeks of Psara, with more patriotism, immediately sent a few brigs and a fire-ship to Hydra, where their promptitude to serve the cause of their country was regarded as an offence. The Hydriots, who were intent only on the question of pay, attacked the Psarian sailors, in order to punish them for giving a bad example to the rest of the Greek navy. Several Psarians were cruelly beaten, and a civil war was on the point of breaking out. Shame, and the expectation of being speedily repaid by Lord Byron, at last induced the Hydriot primates to advance the sum required to fit out seven vessels and two fire-ships.

The fire-ships of Hydra were generally prepared as jobs, and were rarely of any service. One of these could not go farther than Navarin. The Hydriot squadron was joined by five Spetziot brigs and a fire-ship. Miaoulis, disgusted with the insubordination displayed in the preceding cruise, remained on shore, and the command was given to Captain Pinotzi, who hoisted a broad pennant, for the Greeks mimicked the external signs of naval organisation, though they neglected the essentials of discipline and tactics. Mavrocordatos embarked to resume his dictatorship in Western Greece, expecting to find a firm support in the influence of Lord Byron, who had recently arrived at Cephalonia.

On the 11th of December 1823 this squadron fell in with a Turkish brig off the Skrophes. Five Greek ships came up with her, and raked her with their broadsides until she was in a sinking state. None of these vessels ventured to run alongside and carry her by boarding, so that she was enabled to reach Ithaca, where the Turks expected to find protection under the English flag. This brig mounted twenty-two six-pounders, and carried a crew of eighty men, besides twenty passengers. She had sailed from Previsa the day before with a large sum of money for the garrison of Patras.

The Greeks had too often violated their most solemn treaties to care much about violating Ionian neutrality, when it appeared that they could do so with impunity. The sailors landed on Ithaca, and murdered the Turks who attempted to defend their ship. The brig was seized as soon as she was abandoned by her crew, and the treasure on board was transferred to the Greek ships. The captain, who refused to quit the deck, was slain. The brig presented a terrible spectacle to her captors. Upwards of forty

Turks had been killed during the action, and their dead bodies were found piled up between decks, in order that they might be taken ashore for burial. While some of the Greek sailors were plundering the stranded vessel, others were shooting down the Turks on shore, whose flight was impeded by the people of the island. The arrival of a company of English soldiers saved thirty-five men, who were carried to the lazaretto. Every one of these had received severe wounds.

The English government was justly indignant at this conduct on the part of a Greek claiming the rights of an organised force, and sailing under a broad pennant. It seemed intolerable that a navy which pretended to enjoy all the advantages accorded to Christian governments, should commit atrocities that would have disgraced Algerine pirates. The behaviour of the Greeks was on this occasion peculiarly offensive, for the neutrality of the Ionian Islands had been rendered by the British government extremely advantageous to Greece. Kalamos was at that very time serving as a refuge to the population of Acarnania and Etolia, which had fled from the armies of Omer Vrioni and Mustai. Karaiskaki, a distinguished captain, was receiving not only protection, but also medical assistance gratis, and hundreds of families of Greek armatoli were then fed by the British government; yet the newspapers of the Continent afford evidence that at this time the Greeks were calumniating England over all Europe from Marseilles to St Petersburg.

Among the wounded Turks who were carried into the lazaretto of Ithaca, there was one man of a noble aspect and of dignified manners, who had been left for dead all night on the beach. In the morning he was found breathing, and carried to the lazaretto to die. But after his wounds were dressed, his face and hands washed, and his green turban arranged on his head, he muttered a few words of thankfulness in Greek, and made signs for a pipe. He smoked one or two pipes, and the two English surgeons who were attending him thought it not improbable that he would die smoking. The pipes, however, appeared to restore him, and he gradually recovered. His convalescence was long; and during the time he remained in Ithaca, the fluency with which he spoke Greek, and the good sense he displayed in his conversation, made him a favourite. He had been cadi of Tripolitza just before the Revolution broke out, but had accompanied Khurshid's army to Thessaly. This man considered the Othoman empire on the verge of ruin; but he ridiculed the idea of its being replaced by a Greek kingdom. He feared a coalition of the Christian powers.

The Greek vessels returned to Mesolonghi with their booty, and quarrelled about the division of the spoil. A schooner, with several chests of treasure on board, attempted to escape, but was brought back by force, and anchored in the midst of the Hydriot brigs. Mavrocordatos, who was an involuntary spectator of these disgraceful scenes, attempted in vain to persuade the Hydriots to make an honourable division of their dishonest gains. On the 17th of December a scheme of division, modelled on the system of shares in the mercantile operations of the islanders, was adopted. The share of one of the Hydriot ships, which had sailed shamefully under-manned, with only forty-eight seamen on board, but which drew shares for seventy-one, amounted to 77 okas of paras, measured by weight, and 267 gold mahmudiés in coin, besides other plunder, estimated at 770 piastres.[1]

---

[1] An English gentleman, once a midshipman in the navy, was accidentally on board the Hydriot squadron as a volunteer, and witnessed the events above narrated.

No sooner was the division of the treasure terminated than the crews demanded pay for a second month in advance. Application was made to Lord Byron, but he considered it impolitic to purchase the service of such ill-manned ships, and hopeless to expect honourable service from such disorderly and mutinous crews. The Hydriots quitted Mesolonghi, and they so timed their voyage that they made Hydra on the 29th December, the very day on which the month paid in advance ended.

The Ionian government forgot its dignity in avenging the injury it had received. The Lord High Commissioner issued a violent proclamation, upbraiding Mavrocordatos in rather unseemly terms for calling himself a prince, which certainly was no violation of Ionian neutrality. The sultan called upon the Ionian government for indemnification for the loss he had sustained in consequence of their neglect to enforce neutrality, and his demand was immediately recognised. The Greek government foolishly refused to refund the money, until the British government, losing patience, ordered Captain Pechell in H.M.S. Sybille to enforce the claim. Several Greek ships were then seized, and not released until an indemnity of forty thousand dollars was refunded.

The Greeks had regained possession of the Acrocorinth before the Albanian pashas had raised the siege of Anatolikon. The Turks capitulated on the 7th November 1823. On this occasion the firmness and honourable conduct of Niketas, supported by the soldiers under his immediate orders, prevented Greece from being stained by another infamous massacre. But all the energy and activity of Niketas could not prevent four or five Turks from being murdered on the way from Corinth to Kenchries. The indifference shown by Kolokotrones to the disorderly conduct of the Greek troops under his command on this occasion, induced many to believe that he would have willingly seen a repetition of the massacres of Tripolitza.

In the autumn of 1823 Lord Byron directed the attention of all Europe to the affairs of Greece by joining the cause. He arrived at Mesolonghi on the 5th of January 1824. His short career in Greece was unconnected with any important military event, for he died on the 19th of April; but the enthusiasm he awakened perhaps served Greece more than his personal exertions would have done, had his life been prolonged. Wherever the English language was known, an electric shock was felt when it was heard that

> "The pilgrim of eternity, whose fame
> Over his living head like heaven was bent,
> An early but enduring monument,"

had died " where his young mind first caught ethereal fire."

The genius of Lord Byron would in all probability never have unfolded either political or military talent. He was not disposed to assume an active part in public affairs. He regarded politics as the art of cheating the people, by concealing one-half of the truth and misrepresenting the other; and whatever abstract enthusiasm he might feel for military glory was joined to an innate detestation of the trade of war. Both his character and his conduct presented unceasing contradictions. It seemed as if two different souls occupied his body alternately. One was feminine, and full of sympathy; the other masculine, and characterised by clear judgment. When one arrived the other departed. In company, his sympathetic soul was his tyrant. Alone, or with a single person, his masculine prudence displayed itself as his friend. No man could then arrange facts, investigate their causes, or examine their consequences, with more logical accuracy, or in a more practical spirit. Yet, in his most sagacious moment, the entrance of a third person would derange the order of his ideas,—judgment fled, and sympathy, generally laughing, took its place. Hence he appeared in his conduct extremely capricious, while in his opinions he had really great firmness. He often, however, displayed a feminine turn for deception in trifles, while at the same time he possessed a feminine candour of soul, and a natural love of truth, which made him often despise himself quite as much as he despised English fashionable society for what he called its brazen hypocrisy. He felt his want of self-command; and there can be no doubt that his strongest reason for withdrawing from society, and shunning public affairs, was the conviction of his inability to compress the sympathies which were in opposition to his judgment.

A.D. 1823.

No stranger estimated the character of the Greeks more correctly than Lord Byron. At Cephalonia he sometimes smiled at the enthusiasm of Sir Charles Napier, and pointed out where the soldier's ardour appeared to mislead his judgment. It may, however, be observed, that to nobody did the Greeks ever unmask their selfishness and self-deceit so candidly. Almost every distinguished statesman and general sent him letters soliciting his favour, his influence, or his money. Kolokotrones invited him to a national assembly at Salamis. Mavrocordatos informed him that he would be of no use anywhere but at Hydra, for Mavrocordatos was then in that island. Constantine Metaxa, who was then governor of Mesolonghi, wrote, saying that Greece would be ruined unless Lord Byron visited that fortress. Petrobey used plainer words. He informed Lord Byron that the true way to save Greece was to lend him, the bey, a thousand pounds. With that sum not three hundred but three thousand Spartans would be put in motion to the frontier, and the fall of the Othoman empire would be certain. Every Greek chief celebrated his own praises and Lord Byron's liberality, but most of them injured their own cause by dilating too eloquently on the vices and crimes of some friend or rival. Lord Byron made many sagacious and satirical comments on the *chiaroscuro* of these communications. He wrote: "Of the Greeks I can't say much good hitherto, and I do not like to speak ill of them, though they do of one another." He knew his own character so well, that he remained some time at Cephalonia, not venturing to trust himself among such a cunning and scheming set, fearing lest unworthy persons should exercise too much influence over his conduct. This feeling induced him to avoid familiarity with the Greeks, even after his arrival at Mesolonghi, and with Mavrocordatos his intercourse was not intimate. Business and ceremony alone brought them together. Their social and mental characteristics were not of a nature to create reciprocal confidence, and they felt no mutual esteem.

Lord Byron did not overlook the vices of the Greek leaders, but at the same time he did not underrate the virtues of the people. The determined spirit with which they asserted their independence received his sincere praise, even while the rapacity, cruelty, and dissensions of the military weighed heavily on his mind. Nothing, during his residence at Mesolonghi, distressed him more than the conduct of the Suliots whom he had taken into his pay. He saw that he had degraded himself into the chief of a band of personal followers, who thought of nothing but extorting money from their foreign leader. Three hundred Suliots were enrolled in his band; of these upwards of one hundred demanded double pay and triple rations, pretending

to be officers, whose dignity would not allow them to
lounge about the coffee-houses of Mesolonghi unless
they were attended by a henchman or pipebearer.
Lord Byron, annoyed by their absurd pretensions, remembered Napier's plans for the formation of a small
regular military force, and lamented his own inability
to carry them into execution. Colonel Leicester Stanhope (the Earl of Harrington) increased his irritation
by appearing as the agent of the Greek committee,
and giving in to all the pedantic delusions of the
literati. The typographical colonel, as Lord Byron
sarcastically termed him, seemed to think that newspapers would be more effectual in driving back the
Othoman armies than well-drilled troops and military
tactics.

The political information which Lord Byron extracted from Mavrocordatos in their personal interviews, and the proceedings of that statesman in the
conduct of the public administration, revealed the
thousand obstacles to the establishment of an honest
government in Greece. A mist fell from Lord Byron's
eyes. He owned that his sagacity was at fault, and he
abandoned all hope of being able to guide the Greeks, or
to assist them in improving their administration. Not
long before his death, he frequently repeated, that with
Napier to command and form regular troops, with
Hastings to arm and command a steamer, and with an
able financier, Greece would be sure of victory. Then,
too, he began to express doubts whether circumstances
had authorised him to recommend the Greek loan to
his friends in England. He was struck by the fact
that a majority of the Moreot captains and primates
opposed pledging the confiscated Turkish property as
a security to the lenders. He feared that the proceeds
of a loan might be misspent by one party, and the
loan itself disowned by another. Bowring and the

bankers, he said, would secure their commissions and their gains, but he feared many honest English families might lose their money by his Philhellenism.

Lord Byron's knowledge of the prominent defects of the Greek character, his personal experience of their rapacity, and his conviction that selfishness was the principal cause of a civil war in Argolis which broke out about the time of his arrival at Mesolonghi, made him an advocate for the formation of a strong central government. Order was, in his opinion, the first step to liberty. The Earl of Harrington talked as if he considered Lord Byron's desire for order a proof of his indifference to liberty. Lord Byron was, however, a far wiser counsellor than the typographical colonel, and, had he lived, might have done much to arrest the factious madness and shameless expenditure which rendered the English loans the prize and the aliment of two civil wars.

The first Greek loan was contracted early in 1824. The Greeks received about £300,000, and they engaged to pay annually £40,000 as interest, as the capital of the debt created was £800,000 at five per cent. The lenders risked their money to deliver Greece, and they have never received a shilling of interest or a syllable of gratitude from the thousands whom their money enriched. Indeed, the Greeks generally appear to have considered the loan as a small payment for the debt due by civilised society to the country that produced Homer and Plato. The modern Greek habit of reducing everything to a pecuniary standard, made Homer, Plato, & Co. creditors for a large capital and an enormous accumulation of unpaid interest.

A worse speculation, in a financial point of view, than the Greek loan, could not have been undertaken. Both the loan contractors and the members of the Greek committees knew that the revenues of Greece in

1823 fell short of £80,000. Yet with this knowledge they placed the absolute control of a sum equal to nearly four years' revenue of the country in the hands of a faction engaged in civil war. Foreigners were amazed at this display of financial insanity on the London Stock Exchange. Future years have proved that the disease returns in periodical fits, which can only be cured by copious bleeding.

Though the contractors of the Greek loan, when they paid over the money to a government engaged in civil war, could not be ignorant that the money would be diverted from carrying on hostilities against the Turks, in order to be employed in warring with domestic rivals, various attempts were made to check its wasteful expenditure during the year 1824. Sir Henry Lytton Bulwer, now her Majesty's ambassador at Constantinople, visited Greece, by request of the contractors of the loan, "to see if the nature of the Greek government warranted the payment of the portion not yet advanced." Sir Henry stated the following observations for the benefit of his countrymen, as the result of his experience: "We (the English) have generally busied ourselves about the government of Greece, which really was no business of ours; while the management of our money, in which we might be thought concerned, has been left entirely in the hands of the Greeks."[1] General Gordon was subsequently invited to return to Greece, which he had left shortly after the fall of Tripolitza, in order to watch over the expenditure of the second loan; but he wisely refused to have anything to do with the business when he read the instructions on which he was to act. He has recorded his deliberate opinion of the men who were intrusted with the expenditure of the English loans in very strong terms: "With, *perhaps*, the exception of

[1] *An Autumn in Greece.* By H. Lytton Bulwer, Esq. 8vo. London, 1826.

Zaimes, the members of the executive are no better than public robbers."[1] The internal history of Greece, from the defeat of Dramali to the arrival of King Otho, attests the truth of this severe sentence. The country was ruined by intestine broils, originating in private rapacity. Amidst these disorders, two civil wars stand out with disgraceful prominence, as having consumed the proceeds of the English loans, abandoned Psara and Kasos to be conquered by the Turks, and prepared the Morea to be subdued by Ibrahim Pasha.

The first of these civil wars was called the war of Kolokotrones, because that old chieftain was its principal author. It commenced in November 1823, and finished in June 1824. It was concluded as soon as the news reached the belligerents that an instalment of the first English loan had arrived at Zante. Panos, the eldest son of Kolokotrones, who held possession of Nauplia, immediately surrendered it to the executive body on receiving a share of the English money. This transaction took place on the 5th of June 1824.

While the Greeks were fighting among themselves, Sultan Mahmud was smoothing away the obstacles which impeded the co-operation of his powerful vassal, Mohammed Ali, pasha of Egypt, in attacking them. By his prudent arrangements he secured the zealous support of the Egyptian pasha. Mohammed Ali was already disposed to chastise the Greeks for the losses he had sustained from their cruisers. He also feared that a prolonged contest with the insurgent Christians might end in bringing a Russian fleet into the Mediterranean. He therefore received the proposals made to his political agent at Constantinople in the most conciliatory spirit. The sultan invested his son Ibrahim with the rank of vizier of the Morea, and wrote a flattering letter to the great pasha himself, calling him

[1] *History of the Greek Revolution*, ii. 72.

the champion of Islam. Mohammed Ali received this letter with the warmest expressions of pleasure, and engaged to send a powerful fleet and army to attack the Greeks. He had not yet been inspired by French intrigue with delusive visions of making himself the founder of an Arab empire.

A.D. 1824.

The Greeks heard with indifference of the preparations which were going on at the dockyards of Constantinople and Alexandria. They treated the rumoured co-operation of the sultan and the pasha as impossible. They insisted on supposing that Mohammed Ali reasoned like themselves. They thought that the pasha must want his own money for his own schemes, and deluded themselves with the idea that he was more likely to act against the sultan than for him. They argued that he must be more anxious to establish his own independence than to destroy theirs. Their whole souls were absorbed in party contests for wealth and power, until they were awakened from their delusive dreams by a series of terrible calamities.

It has been mentioned that the Kolokotrones's civil war embittered the last months of Lord Byron's life, by doubts of the propriety of intrusting the Greeks with large sums of money. He foresaw that selfishness would find more nutriment in foreign loans than patriotism.

The executive government which defeated the rebellion of Kolokotrones was supported by a majority in the legislative assembly. It cannot be said that the members of this assembly were freely chosen by the people; yet, on the whole, its feelings represented those of the best portion of the Greek population. Many were well-meaning men, who could clothe their thoughts in energetic and eloquent language, but few had any experience in legislation and politics. Their deliberations rarely conducted them to practical resolutions, and their incapacity prevented their exercising any control over the financial affairs of their country. The consequence of this inaptitude for business was, that George Konduriottes and Kolettes exercised absolute power in the name of the executive body.

The government which vanquished the faction of Kolokotrones was formed by a coalition of three parties: the Albanian shipowners of Hydra and Spetzas; the Greek primates of the Morea; and the Romeliot captains of armatoli. The chief authority was conceded to the Albanian shipowners; George Konduriottes of Hydra was elected president of Greece, and Botasses of Spetzas, vice-president. It is necessary to record the sad truth, that two more ignorant and incapable persons were never intrusted with the direction of a nation's affairs. The Greeks are the most prejudiced of all Europeans when there is a question of the purity of the Hellenic race, and no people regards education with more favour; yet with all this nationality and pedantry they intrusted their public affairs, in a period of great difficulty, to two men who could not address them in the Greek language, and whose intellectual deficiencies prevented them from expressing their thoughts with clearness even in the corrupt Tosk dialect which they habitually used. The descendants of Pericles and Demosthenes submitted tamely to these aliens in civilisation and race, because they were orthodox and wealthy.

The interest of the president and vice-president was identical with that of the shipowners of Hydra and Spetzas, and it was directly opposed to the formation of a national navy. The money placed at their disposal was wasted in paying inefficient ships, and hiring the support of mutinous sailors; and they refused to purchase and arm a single steamer at the recommendation of Captain Hastings, when such a vessel might have frustrated the operations of Mohammed Ali, and prevented Ibrahim Pasha from landing in the Morea. Had they possessed a very little naval knowledge and a small share of patriotism, they might have obtained the glory of initiating the change in naval warfare which is in progress throughout all maritime nations.[1]

The party of the Moreot primates was next in importance to that of the naval islanders; but this party soon forfeited its influence and fell into contempt, by the unprincipled selfishness of its leading members. Had the Moreot primates supported the just demands of the people for a system of publicity in financial business, they might have become the guardians of the liberties of Greece, and the founders of their country's constitution. They were, perhaps, the only persons capable, from their administrative experience, of placing the existing municipal institutions in harmony with the action of the central government.

The Romeliot captains of armatoli, though they already possessed great territorial and political influence when the government of Konduriottes entered on office, had not yet constituted themselves into a distinct party in the state. Kolettes now succeeded by his schemes in uniting them together, and allying them with himself by the ties of a common interest. He purchased their services by securing to them a large share of the English loans; and he taught them to maintain themselves in provincial commands, in imitation of the old system of armatoliks. Kolettes acted as their agent and representative in the executive body. That astute Vallach was the first to perceive how their political influence might be rendered supreme in liberated Greece, by imitating the administrative practice

[1] The memoir which Hastings laid before Konduriottes's government is subjoined in Appendix I.

of Ali of Joannina, with which he was well acquainted. He conducted their bargains for pay and rations with the central government; he assisted them in obtaining contracts for farming the taxes of the provinces of which they had obtained the military command; and he regulated with them the number of the personal followers they were to be permitted to charge on the public revenues as national troops.

The position which Kolettes created for himself by these arrangements rendered him the most influential politician in the government, and nothing but his want of personal courage and honesty prevented him from being the first man in Greece. It has been already said that he was a Zinzar Vallachian, and not a Greek, and all the moral and physical peculiarities of that race were strongly marked both in his mind and his personal appearance. Both contrasted with those of the Greeks and Albanians by whom he was surrounded. He exhibited neither the boorish pride of the Albanian islanders, nor the loquacious self-sufficiency of the Greek logiotati. With patience and stolid silence he profited by the blunders of his colleagues, always himself doing and saying as little as possible. He trusted that others, by their restless intrigues and precipitate ambition, would ruin their own position, and leave the field open for him. His policy was crowned with success. Hypsilantes, Mavrocordatos, Konduriottes, and Zaimes, all ruined their own personal position by exhibiting more ambition than capacity.

The second civil war, called the War of the Primates, constituted Kolettes the leader of the Romeliot military faction, and victory rendered that faction the most powerful party in Greece. During the period of Bavarian despotism, Kolettes was sent as minister to the court of Louis Philippe, and those who saw and conversed with him in Paris were surprised at the political reputation he had enjoyed in Greece. When they listened to the grave and portly Vallach, in his Albanian habiliments, uttering platitudes with an oracular air, they felt inclined to apply to him Fox's observation on Lord Thurlow's first appearance on the woolsack: "That fellow is a humbug; no man can be as wise as he looks." Kolettes, however, only acted a wise look, though it must be owned that he was not a bad actor.

In England, Mavrocordatos was supposed to be at the head of a powerful constitutional party. If this had ever been possible, he had destroyed that possibility by abandoning the presidency of Greece to play the commander-in-chief at Petta. The testimony of English Philhellenes and well-informed foreigners was, however, unavailing to undeceive the British public. The delusion appears to have originated among the Greeks settled in Western Europe, who believed that Mavrocordatos was the most disinterested statesman in Greece, and that a strong constitutional party ought to exist in a free country. But Mavrocordatos, by his grasping ambition, his schemes for governmental centralisation, his personal mismanagement, and his political indecision, had ruined his influence before the year 1824. Feeling his position changed, and ill satisfied unless he was the first man at the seat of government, he lingered at Mesolonghi during the whole of the important year 1824, and allowed all parties to learn that public business could go on perfectly well without him.

In Western Greece his administration, after Lord Byron's death, was neither honourable to himself nor advantageous to the country. A civil war broke out in the district of Vlochos between two rival captains, Staikos and Vlachopulos. Its continuance was ascribed to his imprudence and indecision. His civil administration was unpopular. He gave his support to John Soutzos, the eparch of Venetico, who was stigmatised as the most corrupt and rapacious phanariot in Greece.

Before quitting Mesolonghi to return to the seat of government, Mavrocordatos convoked an assembly of captains and eparchs, to concert measures for defending the country against the incursions of the Turks, and for reforming internal abuses. His dictatorial authority authorised him to take this step, but he ought to have perceived its imprudence. Its effect was to legalise the system of capitanlika, which had been tacitly revived, and to consolidate the personal independence of the military chiefs, who learned to act in concert whenever it was their interest to resist the central government. The peasants were not blind to the effect of Mavrocordatos's conduct. They saw that it would perpetuate a state of anarchy, and many were so alarmed that they fled to Kalamos, declaring that the prince, as they still called their governor-general, had assembled a pack of wolves to debate how the sheep could be preserved from the eagles and reserved for their own eating.

The second civil war, or war of the primates, was not of long duration. Zaimes was the principal author of this iniquitous movement, and his object was to deprive Konduriottes and those who supported his government of the wealth and influence they enjoyed, by disposing of the proceeds of the English loans.

In appearance and manners Andreas Zaimes was a perfect gentleman. His disposition was generous, and his private conduct upright; but his position as a hereditary primate made him ambitious, while nature had made him neither energetic nor courageous. He thrust himself forward as a statesman and military chief, but he was too weak for a political leader, and utterly unfit for a soldier. A.D. 1821.

Andreas Londos was next in rank and influence among the conspirators. He was a warm personal friend of Zaimes, and the constant affection which the two Andreas showed to one another in prosperity and adversity was most honourable to both. It proved that they had virtuous stuff in their hearts. Londos was brave and active. His personal courage, however, proved of no use to his party, for, instead of establishing order and enforcing discipline among his followers, he allowed them to commit as great depredations on the property of the Moreot peasants, as were committed by the most lawless chief of Romeliot armatoli. Londos was at this time addicted to riotous debauchery.[1]

Both Zaimes and Londos had assumed the position of Turkish beys, and the Greek government allowed them to collect the taxes and administer the greater part of the public affairs of their respective districts. They pretended to employ the revenues for the public service, and in maintaining troops to blockade Patras. But it was too evident that they surrounded themselves with bands of personal followers withdrawn from the armies of Greece, and that Patras was hardly blockaded at all.

Sessini of Gastuni was another influential man in the party of the primates. He was descended from a Venetian family, and had studied medicine in his youth. Shortly after the retreat of the Mussulmans

[1] Lord Byron used to describe an evening passed in the company of Londos at Vostitza, when both were young men, with a spirit that rendered the scene worthy of a place in Don Juan. After supper, Londos, who had the face and figure of a chimpanzee, sprang upon a table, which appeared to be a relic of the Venetian domination, and whose antiquity rendered the exploit a dangerous enterprise, and commenced singing through his nose Rhiga's Hymn to Liberty. A new cadi, passing near the house, inquired the cause of the discordant bubbuh. A native Mussulman replied, "It is only the young primate Londos, who is drunk, and is singing hymns to the new panaghia of the Greeks, whom they call Eleftheria."

from Lalla, he contrived to assume a position in Elis between that of a voevode and a pasha. He became receiver-general of taxes, paymaster of troops, and farmer-general of confiscated Turkish estates. He adopted the pride and many other vices of the Osmanlees. His household was maintained with considerable pomp. The courtyard was filled with well-caparisoned horses; the galleries were crowded with armed followers. He never quitted his dwelling without a suite of horsemen, armed guards on foot, and grooms leading Persian greyhounds. His sons were addressed as beys; and Ibrahim Pasha, when he occupied Gastuni, was much amused by the tales he heard from the peasantry, who said they had been compelled to fall down on their knees whenever they addressed a word to the medical primate, even in reply to the simplest question.[1]

Notaras, Deliyannes, and Kolokotrones, all joined the war of the primates, which broke out in November 1824.

[1] Many stories were current concerning the manner in which Sessini had collected his wealth; one may be mentioned, relating to the loss of a part of his ill-gotten riches. Whether true or false, it excited much amusement at Zante. Madame Sessini resided in that island, and acted as her husband's agent. Before the war of the primates commenced, he wished to place some of his treasure where it would be secure against the Greek government in case of defeat. He wished, however, to do this with great secrecy, for many valuable jewels had been deposited with him by Turkish families who had been obliged to escape in a hurry to Patras at the outbreak of the Revolution. His enemies accused him of intending to declare that these deposits were lost in the civil war. Sessini wrote to inform his wife that he would send the most valuable jewels in his possession to her in a cheese and skin of butter, with peculiar marks. The letter miscarried; and when the cheese and the skin of butter arrived, the lady, having a large supply of both, sold them to a bakal or grocer, who had often purchased previous consignments which she had received from old Sessini. A few days passed before the lost letter arrived. When it reached the lady she hastened to the bakal, but he denied all knowledge of the jewellery. He showed her a cheese with the mark for which she sought untouched, and a skin of butter unopened. The accounts of the customhouse showed that she had only imported cheese and butter. Lawyers and justice could not aid her. The bakal kept the treasure, and the world laughed at Madame Sessini and her rapacious husband. But it was said that the bakal proved himself a better man than the primate, and that he restored a valuable jewel to a Turkish family who had intrusted it to the keeping of Sessini, when that family passed by Zante on its way to Alexandria. The whole story may be the creation of an idle brain, but it deserves notice as a specimen of popular rumour. *Si non è vero è ben trovato.*

Kolettes was at this time the most active member of A.D. 1824. Konduriottes's government. In six weeks he marched an overwhelming force of Romeliot armatoli into the Morea, and crushed the rebels. Had the Greek government displayed similar energy in arraying the forces against the Turks during the years 1823 and 1824, the war might have changed its aspect. Panos Kolokotrones, the eldest son of the old klepht, after plundering the peasants of Arcadia like a brigand, was slain in a trifling skirmish. Old Kolokotrones and Deliyannes were made prisoners, and confined in a monastery at Hydra. Sessini sought safety at Zante; but the English government was determined to discountenance the unprincipled civil broils of the Greeks, and refused him permission to land. He had no resource but to submit to the clemency of the executive body, and join Kolokotrones in prison. Zaimes, Londos, and Niketas fled to Acarnania, where Mavrocordatos allowed them to hide themselves, and where they were protected by Zongas.

Konduriottes and Kolettes used their victory with impolitic barbarity. Their troops plundered innumerable Greek families who had taken no part in the civil war of everything they possessed. The working oxen of the peasantry were carried off, and in many villages the land remained unsown. The sheep and goats having been also devoured by the armatoli, the people were left to starve. The progress of Ibrahim Pasha in the following year was greatly facilitated by the misgovernment of Konduriottes, the barbarity of Kolettes, and the inhuman ravages of the Romeliot troops.

The two civil wars are black spots in the history of the Greek Revolution. No apology can be offered for those who took up arms against the government in either case, but in the second civil war the conduct of the primates was peculiarly blamable. Patriotism had certainly nothing to do with a contest in which Zaimes and Londos were acting in concert with Kolokotrones. Ambition and avidity were the only motives of action. The coalition of the primates and military chiefs was based on a tacit pretension which they entertained of forming a territorial aristocracy in the Morea. The leaders of the rebels knew that the great body of the people were discontented, and eager to constitute a national representation capable of controlling the executive body and enforcing financial responsibility. Zaimes and Kolokotrones attempted to make this patriotism of the people a means of binding them with fresh fetters. Had the primates given a thought to the interests of their country, they would have supported the demands of the people in a legal way, and there can be no doubt that they would have soon secured a majority in the legislative assembly, even as it was then constituted. Their rebellion inaugurated a long period of administrative anarchy, wasted the resources of Greece, and created a new race of tyrants as despotic as, and far meaner than, the hated Turks.

The victors in the civil wars were as corrupt as the vanquished had been rapacious. The members of the executive wasted the proceeds of the loans with dishonesty as well as extravagance; and the anomalous condition to which Greece was reduced by the stupidity of its government, cannot be exhibited in a clearer light than by tracing the way in which the money was consumed.

The first sums which arrived from England in 1824 were absorbed by arrears due on public and private debts. The payments made had no reference to the necessities of the public service, they were determined by the influence of individual members of the government. The greater part of the first loan was paid over to the shipowners and sailors of what was called the

Greek fleet; and the lion's share was appropriated to the Albanians of Hydra and Spetzas. The civil wars engulfed considerable sums. Romeliot captains and soldiers received large bribes to attack their countrymen. No inconsiderable amount was divided among the members of the legislative assembly, and among a large body of useless partisans, who were characterised as public officials. Every man of any consideration in his own imagination wanted to place himself at the head of a band of armed men, and hundreds of civilians paraded the streets of Nauplia with trains of kilted followers, like Scottish chieftains. Phanariots and doctors in medicine, who, in the month of April 1824, were clad in ragged coats, and who lived on scanty rations, threw off that patriotic chrysalis before summer was past, and emerged in all the splendour of brigand life, fluttering about in rich Albanian habiliments, refulgent with brilliant and unused arms, and followed by diminutive pipe-bearers and tall henchmen. The small stature, voluble tongues, turnspit legs, and Hebrew physiognomies of these Byzantine emigrants, excited the contempt, as much as their sudden and superfluous splendour awakened the envy, of the native Hellenes. Nauplia certainly offered a splendid spectacle to any one who could forget that it was the capital of an impoverished nation struggling through starvation to establish its liberty. The streets were for many months crowded with thousands of gallant young men in picturesque dresses and richly ornamented arms, who ought to have been on the frontiers of Greece.

To the stranger who saw only the fortress of Nauplia filled with troops, Greece appeared to be well prepared to resist the whole force of the Othoman empire. Veteran soldiers and enthusiastic volunteers were numerous. Military commands were distributed with a bountiful hand. Rhodios, the Secretary of State, who had studied medicine, was made colonel of the regular troops. It is needless to say that the appointment soon made them as irregular as any other troops in Greece. Military chiefs were allowed to enrol under their private banners upwards of thirty thousand men, and pay was actually issued for this number of troops from the proceeds of the English loans. But over these troops the Greek government exercised no direct control. No measure was taken even to verify the numbers of the men for whom pay and rations were furnished. Everything was left to the chiefs, who contracted to furnish a certain number of men for a certain amount of pay and a fixed number of daily rations. Amidst this lavish military expenditure, Modon, Coron, Patras, and Lepanto were left almost unwatched, and without any force to keep up a regular blockade.

The illegal gains made by drawing pay and rations for troops who were never mustered, quite as much as the commissions of colonel given to apothecaries, and of captain to grooms and pipe-bearers, demoralised the military forces of Greece. The war with the sultan seemed to be forgotten by the soldiers, who thought only of indulging in the luxury of embroidered dresses and splendid arms. This is the dominant passion of every military class in Turkey, whether Greeks, Albanians, or Turks. The money poured into Greece by the loans suddenly created a demand for Albanian equipments. The bazaars of Tripolitza, Nauplia, Mesolonghi, and Athens were filled with gold-embroidered jackets, gilded yataghans, and silver-mounted pistols. Tailors came flocking to Greece from Joannina and Saloniki. Sabres, pistols, and long guns, richly mounted, were constantly passing through the Ionian Islands as articles of trade between Albania and the Morea. The arms and dress of an ordinary palikari, made in imitation of the garb of the Tosks of Southern

Albania, often cost £50. Those of a chiliarch or strategos, with the showy trappings for his horse, generally exceeded £300. These sums were obtained from the loans, and were abstracted from the service of the country. The complaint that Greece was in danger of being ruined by this extravagant expenditure was general, yet everybody seemed to do his utmost to increase the evil by spending as much money as possible in idle parade. Strange stories were current at the time concerning the large sums of money which individuals contrived to amass. The Arabs, who took Sphakteria and slew the henchman of Mavrocordatos, were said to have found about £300 in his belt, in English sovereigns and Venetian sequins. This man had been appointed an officer in the Greek army, though he knew nothing of military service, and had only learned to carry a gun, as a municipal guard, when it was his duty to protect the vineyards of Vrachori from the hostilities of the dogs of the Turkish quarter and the invasions of the foxes of the neighbouring hills.

Makrys was for a time the hero of Mesolonghi, and the captain of the neighbouring district, Zygos. He was a brave man, but a lawless, and, consequently, a bad soldier. His early years were passed as a brigand, and he often recounted how he had lived for many days on the unbaked dough he had prepared from pounded Indian-corn. He first gained wealth by participating in the plunder and massacre of the Jews and Turks of Vrachori. The English loans increased his treasures, which the exaggerations of the people of Mesolonghi swelled to a fabulous amount. Yet, with all his wealth, he was in the habit of drawing pay and rations for five hundred men, when he had only fifty under arms.

Amongst the literary Greeks it has been the fashion to talk and write much concerning the patriotic spirit and the extraordinary military exploits of the klephts, as if these robbers had been the champions of Greek liberty. But the truth is, that these men were mere brigands, who, both before the Revolution, during the revolutionary war, and under the government of King Otho, have plundered the Greeks more than they were ever plundered by the Turks.

It is not to be supposed that military anarchy was established without some opposition on the part of many patriotic Greeks. But its opponents were civilians, and men generally without either practical experience or local influence. The treatment which the few who ventured to make any efforts to put some restraint on the frauds and peculations of the military chiefs received at the hands of the soldiery, prevented this kind of patriotism from finding imitators. Before the siege of Mesolonghi by the army of Reshid Pasha, a patriotic commissary made an attempt to force the chiefs in the Greek camp to muster their followers, in order that no more rations might be issued than were really required, as he found that a large sum was expended by the Greek government in transporting provisions to the camp, while the chiefs who received these provisions as rations for their soldiers compelled the peasants to carry them back to Mesolonghi. The soldiers of Makrys, instigated by their leader, declared that to muster troops was an arbitrary and despotic act, and pronounced that the reforming commissary was an enemy to constitutional liberty. The troops resolved that the rights of the military should not be violated by this undue assumption of power on the part of the central government, and they carried their resolution into effect by beating the patriotic commissary, and plundering the public magazine. The unfortunate man was confined to his bed for several days, and, if his patriotism was not diminished, we may be sure that he was more prudent and reserved in exhibiting a virtue which had proved so distasteful to the defenders of his country, and so calamitous to himself. His friends gave him no consolation during his convalescence. They reproached him with not commencing his reforms by cutting off the extra rations which were issued to Katzaro, the captain of the body-guard of Mavrocordatos, who drew fifty rations, and did duty with only seven armed followers; or with General Vlachopulos, who pretended to be the leader of four hundred soldiers, but who was said to be unable to muster more than about eighty. These abuses were universal. Mr Tricoupi informs the world that the veteran Anagnostaras, who fell at Sphakteria, marched against the enemy with only seventeen armed peasants, though he was paid by the Greek government to enrol seven hundred men.[1] Ghoura subsequently drew twelve thousand rations, when he commanded only from three to four thousand men.[2] It is vain for historians and orators to tell us that true patriotism existed in the hearts of men so wanting in common honesty. Men who combine heroism and fraud ought to be praised only in French novels.

The waste of money on the navy was even greater than on the army. Ill-equipped and dull-sailing vessels were hired to take their place in the Greek fleet, because their owners belonged to the faction of Konduriottes and Botasses. Fire-ships were purchased and fitted out at an unnecessary expense, because their proprietors wished to dispose of useless vessels. The great number of fire-ships belonging to the island of Hydra, which were consumed during the years 1824 and 1825 without inflicting any loss on the Turkish fleet, attest

---

[1] Tricoupi, iii. 206. Phrantzes considers Anagnostaras, the archimandrite Dikaois, and Odysseus, as the three principal corrupters of the Greek soldiery. —Vol. ii. p. 343, note.

[2] Gordon, ii. 231, 267. Phrantzes, ii. 403, note.

the maladministration which took place in this department of the naval service. The sailors, who were spectators of the jobs of the primates and captains, became every month more insolent and disorderly. During one cruise they landed at Santorin, and, not content with carrying off large supplies of grapes and figs, they deliberately plundered the cotton plantations, and sent boat-loads of cotton on board their ships, as if they had conquered a lawful prize in an enemy's territory.

Yet all these disorders, abuses, waste, and extravagance seem hardly sufficient to explain the rapidity with which the proceeds of the loans disappeared; and indeed it required the assistance of equal extravagance and similar jobbing in London and New York to empty the Greek treasury. But the thing was done quickly and effectually. Early in the year 1826, the government at Nauplia had spent every farthing it could obtain, and made a vain attempt to raise a loan of £800,000 among the Greeks themselves, which was to be immediately repaid from the proceeds of sales of national lands. This property had been pledged only a short time before by the same government to the English bondholders as a security for the second loan. The Greeks, who were better informed concerning the proceedings and bad faith of their countrymen than strangers, would not advance a single dollar. The dishonesty of the government, the rapacity of the military, and the indiscipline of the navy, were forerunners of the misfortunes of the nation.

BOOK FOURTH.

THE SUCCESSES OF THE TURKS.

CHAPTER I.

NAVAL SUCCESSES—IBRAHIM IN THE MOREA.

"Heaven's cause
Was as not victory where wisdom was not."

DESTRUCTION OF KASOS—DESTRUCTION OF PSARA—EXPEDITION OF MOHAMMED ALI—THE BAIRAM AT MARRY—NAVAL BATTLES OFF BUDRUN—FAILURE OF THE TURKS AT SAMOS—IBRAHIM DRIVEN BACK FROM CRETE—IBRAHIM LANDS IN GREECE—GREEKS UNPREPARED FOR DEFENCE—DEFEAT OF THE GREEK ARMY—EGYPTIANS TAKE SPHAKTERIA—ESCAPE OF THE BRIG MARS—CAPITULATION OF NAVARIN—SUCCESS OF MIAOULIS AT MODON—KOLOKOTRONES GENERAL IN THE PELOPONNESUS—DEFEAT OF THE GREEKS AND DEATH OF THE ARCHIMANDRITE DIKAIOS AT MANIAKI—DEFEAT OF KOLOKOTRONES AT MARRYPLAGI—IBRAHIM REPULSED AT LERNA—DEFEAT OF KOLOKOTRONES AT TRIKORPHA—IBRAHIM RAVAGES THE MOREA—RECEIVES ORDERS TO AID IN THE SIEGE OF MESOLONGHI.

THE tide of success which had hitherto borne the Greeks onward to glory and independence began to ebb in 1824. Sultan Mahmud studied the causes of the disasters of his fleets and armies, and laboured with stern industry to remedy their defects. He observed that his own resources were not diminished by his losses, while those of the Greeks were daily declining, and were sure to be utterly exhausted if he could prolong the contest for a few years. He therefore changed his plans. Instead of invading Greece, where the great mass of the population was determined to defend its liberty with desperate courage, he resolved to destroy all the outlying resources of his enemy before attempting to attack the centre of their power.

He saw that the first step to reconquering Greece was to recover the command of the sea. This, he soon discovered, was easier than was generally supposed. The Greeks were not in a condition to replace the loss of a few ships; the Othoman empire could rebuild a fleet every year. The destruction, therefore, of a single ship and a few sailors, was cheaply purchased by the conflagration of a line-of-battle ship or a frigate; the ruin of a Greek naval island by the sacrifice of an Othoman fleet. The sultan selected Psara and Kasos as the first objects of attack. They were the most exposed naval stations of the Greeks. Their cruisers inflicted the most extensive losses on the Turkish population, and their destruction would be more popular in the Othoman empire than any victory either by land or sea. Psara was the cause of intolerable evils to the Mussulmans in Thrace and Asia Minor; Kasos was an eyesore and a torment to Syria and Egypt. Mahmud and Mohammed Ali concerted their operations to attack the two islands suddenly and simultaneously with two fleets. Their plans were framed with skill and executed with vigour.

The commercial activity of Kasos adds another to the proofs already mentioned that the principles of the sultan's policy were better than the administration of his authority. Christians or Mussulmans, Yezidees and Nestorians, Druses and Maronites, were often prosperous and contented under the sultan's government, but rarely either the one or the other when their affairs were conducted by Othoman officials. Secluded valleys, like the valley of the river of Arta, were carefully cultivated; barren rocks, like Hydra, were peopled by active seamen. The Vallachs of Kalarites and Syrako, A.D. 1824. and the Albanians of Hydra, administered their own affairs without being controlled by a pasha or a voevode.

Kasos afforded a striking example of the advantages to be derived from the sultan's protection, when it could be obtained without the evils of the Othoman administration. This island is about twelve miles long, and in its aridity and iron-bound coast it resembles Hydra. It also has no secure port; yet at this time it contained seven thousand inhabitants, who owned fifteen square-rigged vessels and forty smaller craft, all of which had for three years been employed in plundering the islands of Crete, Rhodes, and Cyprus, and ravaging the coasts of Karamania, Syria, and Egypt. It was said that the Kasiots usually murdered their captives at sea; and there is reason to fear that the accusation is well founded, for few Turkish prisoners were ever brought to the island. Indeed, during the years 1821 and 1822 the inhabitants had difficulty in procuring bread for themselves, and could not feed their enemies. Mercy, it must be owned, was a virtue as little practised by the Christian as by the Mussulman combatants at the commencement of the Greek Revolution, and few lives were spared from motives of humanity.

Sultan Mahmud expected to paralyse the Greeks with terror, by destroying Kasos and Psara at the same time. But the Egyptian fleet was ready for action before that of the capitan-pasha could leave Constantinople. The force destined by Mohammed Ali to attack Kasos consisted of three frigates and ten sloops of war, under the command of Ismael Gibraltar Pasha. On board this squadron three thousand Albanians were embarked under Hussein Bey Djeritlee, an able officer, who fell afterwards at Mesolonghi.

DESTRUCTION OF KASOS.

Kasos was ill fortified, and the inhabitants neglected every precaution which common prudence ought to have suggested for preventing a landing. The Albanians effected their landing on the 19th of June 1824, during the night, not far from the usual landing-place, and they scaled the rocks that commanded the Kasiot batteries without encountering any resistance. The surprise was complete. The islanders dwelt in four villages situated high in the mountain. The troops of Hussein climbed the rugged ascent in silence, and fell unexpectedly on the villagers. The men capable of bearing arms were slain without mercy. The old women shared their fate, but the young women and children, who were deemed suitable for the slave-market of Alexandria, were carried on board the ships. The Kasiots posted in the batteries near the beach stood firm. But the Albanians, experienced in mountain warfare, occupied the higher grounds, and crept forward, under the cover of rocks and stones, until they could shoot the islanders at their guns. Fourteen square-rigged vessels and about thirty small craft were captured, and five hundred Kasiot seamen were slain. The Albanians lost only thirty killed and wounded. Upwards of two thousand women and children were enslaved. The Albanians were allowed twenty-four hours to plunder, and to collect booty and slaves. The instant that term was expired, Ismael Gibraltar and Hussein took effective measures to restore order, and gave protection to every Greek who submitted to the sultan's authority.

The news of this sad disaster spread consternation through all Greece. It was a forewarning of the vigour of their new enemy; but the admonition was given in vain.

A greater calamity followed. Khosreff Pasha sailed from the Dardanelles in the month of May, before the

Greeks had any cruisers out to watch his movements. A.D. 1824. After a feint attack on Skopelos, the Othoman fleet returned to Mytilene, where it was soon joined by transports carrying three thousand janissaries. The capitan-pasha then embarked four thousand Asiatic troops and sailed for Psara. His force consisted of thirty-eight frigates, corvettes, and brigs, and forty transports, with about eight thousand soldiers.

Psara is a high rocky island, smaller than Kasos. Its northern and eastern sides are precipitous and were considered unassailable. The town is situated in the south-western part. Below it, to the west, there is a good roadstead sheltered by a rocky islet, called Antipsara. A small port to the south of the town also affords shelter to a few vessels. The native Psarians amounted to seven thousand souls; but in the year 1824 there were so many refugees from Chios, Kydonics, and Smyrna, residing in the island, that the population exceeded twelve thousand. About a thousand of the Romeliot armatoli, who had plundered Skiathos, were now engaged to defend Psara. Every point where it was supposed that the Turks would attempt to land was fortified. The Psarians unfortunately overrated their own knowledge of military affairs, and greatly underrated the skill and enterprise of their enemy. Two hundred pieces of artillery were mounted in ill-constructed and ill-placed batteries.

Extraordinary success in privateering had rendered the Psarians presumptuous. They spoke of the Turks as cowards, and of Sultan Mahmud as a tyrant, a fool, and a butcher. Foreigners who possessed military knowledge in vain pointed out to them the defects of their batteries; their advice was treated with contempt. Their domineering conduct was insupportable to their countrymen in the Archipelago; they were the tyrants of the Greek islands on the Asiatic coast.

They seemed to emulate the insolence of the ancient Athenians. To complete the similarity, they commenced hostilities with the Samians, who refused to receive a Psarian governor and a Psarian tax-collector. Samos was blockaded, and the Turks of Asia Minor were relieved from the depredations of the Greeks, while the privateers of Psara were pursuing and plundering the privateers of Samos. The Psarians were also accused of neglecting to aid the brave inhabitants of Trikheri in their last struggle with the Turks, and of pillaging the Greeks of Mount Pelion, whom their neglect had compelled to acknowledge the sultan's authority.

Unlike the Athenians of old, the Psarians placed more confidence in their stone batteries than in their wooden walls. As sailors, they knew the inferiority of their ships; their utter ignorance of the art of war made them fancy that their batteries were impregnable. They laid up the greater part of their ships in the roadstead of Antipsara, and employed the crews as gunners on shore. The island was defended by four thousand well-armed men, but these men were without order and without a leader; they were consequently little better than an armed mob.

The safety of Psara depended on the activity of the Greek fleet, and on the skill of the Psarians in using fire-ships. Unfortunately for Greece, the plan of defence adopted by the local government threw away the best chance of success. Upwards of fifteen hundred seamen, who had acquired great naval skill, some degree of discipline, and some knowledge of marine artillery when embarked in small vessels, were rendered of little use by being mixed up with undisciplined armatoli in ill-constructed batteries without artillery officers.

The capitan-pasha consumed six weeks in making

preparations which ought to have been completed in A.D. 1824. as many days. The Greek government had, therefore, ample time to send a fleet to meet him in the narrow seas, to oppose his embarking troops at Mytilene, and to attack his transports when he attempted to effect a landing at Psara. The avarice of the Hydriot primates and the self-sufficiency of the Psarians prevented Greece from profiting by the delay.

The attack on Psara was skilfully conducted. Khosreff with ten ships opened a heavy cannonade on the batteries, while he detached a part of his fleet in a direction which rendered it visible from the town, and which induced the Psarians to expect that it intended to debark troops. The attention of the islanders was diverted by this simple stratagem. In the mean time a body of Arnaouts and Asiatics landed at a small open beach and stormed a battery manned by fifty armatoli. They then climbed the mountain, concealing themselves as much as possible from observation until they reached the heights above the town. On gaining that point they unfurled the Turkish flag, and announced their success to the capitan-pasha and the astonished Greeks by a discharge of firearms. At a signal from the Othoman flag-ship a hundred boats, filled with troops, immediately pushed off, and attacked simultaneously all the batteries at the roadstead. After a short engagement the Turks were everywhere victorious. Terror seized both the armatoli and the Psarians. All who saw a chance of escape fled. Those whose retreat was cut off made a desperate resistance, and no Psarian laid down his arms. What yesterday had been insolence and pride to-day was converted into patriotism. But the valour which, under the guidance of discipline and science, might have repulsed the Turks, could only secure an honourable death. Eight thousand persons were slain or reduced to slavery; about four thousand, chiefly Psarians, succeeded in getting on board vessels in the port and in putting to sea while their enemies were engaged in the sack of the town. The victorious Turks slew every male capable of bearing arms, and the heads of the vanquished were piled into one of those ghastly pyramidal trophies with which Othoman pashas then commemorated their triumphs. One hundred vessels of various sizes fell into the hands of the capitan-pasha. Only twenty vessels escaped.

The Turks of Asia Minor were frantic with joy, and their cruelty might have equalled that of the Greeks at Navarin and Tripolitza, had their avarice not induced them to spare the women and children for the slave-markets of Smyrna and Constantinople. Great were the festivities on the coasts of Thrace and Asia Minor when it was known that the dwellings of the Psarians were desolate, and the sailors who had plundered the true believers were slain.

The Albanians of Hydra and Spetzas had been slow to aid the Greeks of Kasos and Psara. This neglect was not caused by any prejudice of race, but by ignoble feelings of interest. When the terrible catastrophe of Psara was known at Hydra, fear for their own safety inspired the islanders with a degree of activity, which, if displayed a few weeks earlier, might have saved both Kasos and Psara. Both at Hydra and Spetzas, soldiers were hired to defend the islands during the absence of the sailors, who hastened on board their ships, and the whole Greek fleet put to sea.

The capitan-pasha had returned to Mytilene with the booty and slaves captured at Psara before Miaoulis appeared; so that the Greek fleet could only save a few of the fugitives who had concealed themselves in caverns and in secluded ravines. Two transports with some of the captives on board were also captured in the port. Khosreff celebrated the Courban Baïram at Mytilene. It was his intention to attack Samos, and, had he carried that project immediately into execution, it would have had a good chance of success. The blockade of Samos by the Psarians had thrown the affairs of that island into confusion, and the people were ill prepared for defence. But the month which the capitan-pasha wasted at Mytilene was not left unemployed. The fate of Kasos and Psara awakened all the energies of the Samians, and when the Greek and Turkish fleets appeared in the waters of Samos at the same time, the capitan-pasha did not venture to make an attempt to land troops. After some manœuvring, he bore up for Budrun, where he was to effect his junction with the Egyptian fleet.   A.D. 1824.

Mohammed Ali, having resolved to become the sultan's agent for reconquering the Morea, prepared for the enterprise with prudence and vigour. He had been previously engaged in forming a fleet, of which one of the finest ships, called the Asia, had been recently fitted out at Deptford. A fleet of twenty-five sail was now prepared for sea, and a hundred transports were collected in the port of Alexandria to receive troops, provisions, and military stores. Everything necessary for a long voyage was supplied in profusion, and eight thousand men and a thousand horses were embarked. An experienced English seaman who was present, declared that the stores were carefully packed, and that the transports could not have embarked the same number of men and the same amount of material in less time in most English ports, though the operation would of course be performed at home with less noise and fewer men. This service, like all other military and naval business in Egypt at this time, was organised and directed by French and Italian officers who had served in the armies of Napoleon I.

Ibrahim sailed from Alexandria on the 19th July 1824. The difficulty of getting clear of the Egyptian coast during the strong north winds which prevail in summer, forced the transports to beat up in small squadrons; and the whole sea between Egypt, Cyprus, and Crete was crowded with ships. A few Greek cruisers might have made great havoc, and secured valuable prizes—perhaps frustrated the expedition. But, at this time, the supineness and civil wars of the Greeks formed a discouraging contrast with the activity and harmony of the Turks.

On the 2d of August Ibrahim put into the Gulf of Makry, where he found two of his frigates repairing the damage they had sustained in a gale of wind. Many of the transports had already reached this rendezvous. The pasha landed the troops to celebrate the feast of Baïram, and the ceremonies of this great Mohammedan festival were performed in a very imposing manner. In the afternoon the whole army was drawn up on the beach. When the sun went down, bright-coloured lanterns were hoisted at the mastheads of all the ships, and a salute was fired from every gun in the fleet. The troops on shore followed the example, firing by platoons, companies, and battalions as rapidly as possible, until their fire became at last a continuous discharge of musketry along the whole line, which was prolonged in an incessant roar for a quarter of an hour. The spectacle was wild and strange, in a deserted bay, overlooked by the sculptured tombs of the ancient Telmessus. Ibrahim seemed to be rivalling the folly of Caligula. Suddenly, when the din of artillery and musketry had swelled into a sound like thunder, every noise was hushed, and, as the smoke rolled away, the thin silver crescent of the new moon was visible. A prolonged shout, repeated in melancholy cadence, rose from the army, and was echoed back from the fleet. A minute after, a hundred camp-fires blazed up as if by enchantment. The line was broken, and the busy hum of the soldiers hastening to receive their rations of pilaf, reminded the spectator that the pageant on which he had gazed with delight was only a transient interlude in a bloody drama.

The Egyptian fleet, after quitting Makry, proceeded to Budrun. In passing Rhodes it was ordered to bear up and come to anchor. The reason for this strange order was never known. Ibrahim's frigate gave the signal, and let go its anchor in sixty fathoms. Another frigate, in her zeal to obey the signal, let go her anchor in a hundred and fifty fathoms, and of course lost anchor and cable. A day or two after, Ibrahim's frigate drove into deeper water, and her crew being unable to get up the anchor, the pasha ordered her captain to be bastinadoed on the quarterdeck. There can be no doubt that if Miaoulis had possessed the power of applying the cat-o'-nine-tails to the backs of his mutinous sailors, the Greek fleet would have been a more dangerous adversary to the Egyptian than it proved.

Ibrahim joined the capitan-pasha at Budrun on the 1st of September. Their united fleets consisted of a seventy-four, bearing the flag of Khosreff, twenty frigates, twenty-five corvettes, and forty brigs and schooners, with nearly three hundred transports of all sizes and shapes. Great improvements had been made in the Othoman fleet during the preceding winter, but it was far from being in good order. The ships were in general so over-masted, and so heavily rigged, that they could not have carried their spars for an hour during a heavy gale in the Channel. Even in their own seas, the miltems, or summer gales, caused great confusion, and English seamen gave a good picture of the fleet in that condition, by speaking of the Othoman navy as being adrift in the Archipelago.

FIRST BATTLE OFF BUDRUN.

BOOK IV.
CHAP. I.

The Greek fleet, consisting of between seventy and eighty sail, mounting eight hundred and fifty guns, and manned by five thousand able seamen, appeared in the channel between Cos and the island of Kappari on the 5th of September. The Turkish fleet got under weigh and stood out to engage it. The capitan-pasha, though a man of some administrative capacity, was a coward. He fancied every Greek brig was a fire-ship prepared to blow him up, like his predecessor Kara Ali, and, to avoid that fate, he always contrived that some accident should prevent his ship from getting into danger. On this occasion, he carried away his maintop-sail and his topgallant-yard while in stays, and then ran behind Orak to refit.

The Greeks endeavoured to throw their enemies into confusion, hoping that when the ships were crowded together a favourable opportunity would occur for using their fire-ships. This object seemed nearly gained, when four frigates stood boldly on to gain the weather-gage of the Greeks. They were endeavouring to force Miaoulis and the leading ships of the Greek fleet under the guns of the fort of Cos. The naval skill of the Hydriots baffled this manœuvre. An Egyptian corvette at the same time engaged a Greek pretty closely for ten minutes, and did not haul off until her captain was killed. The frigates of Ibrahim and Ismael Gibraltar ran along the Greek line firing with steadiness, but at too great a distance to do much damage, and quite out of range of the smaller guns of their opponents. A fire-ship was directed against Ibrahim's frigate, but it drifted past, and consumed itself harmlessly in the midst of the Othoman fleet. The Egyptians succeeded in forcing another fire-ship under the guns of Cos, where it was abandoned by its crew with such precipitation, that it fell uninjured into the hands of the Turks, who examined its construction with the greatest interest. These two failures diminished the fear with A.D. 1824. which the Greek fire-ships had been hitherto regarded.

The first battle off Budrun was more favourable to the Turks than to the Greeks. A long day was spent by the hostile fleets in an incessant cannonade, and much powder was wasted beyond the range of any guns. To the Turks this was of use as practice; and if we take into account the number of ships engaged, the inexperience of the crews and officers, and the advantage which the narrow channel afforded to the light ships and naval skill of the Greeks, it appeared surprising that the Turks escaped with so little loss. Among the Constantinopolitan division of the fleet there was often considerable disorder. Several ships ran foul of each other. Most fired their broadsides as the guns were laid before getting under weigh, so that when the Greeks were to windward the shot were seen flying through the air like shells, and when the enemy was to leeward the broadsides lashed the sea into a foam at a hundred yards from the muzzles of the guns, while the Greeks were a mile distant. The day ended in a much greater loss of jib-booms and spars than of men on the part of the Turks. The Greeks lost two fire-ships. It is supposed that not twenty men were killed on both sides. Ibrahim was extremely proud of his exploits. It was his first naval engagement. He had baffled one Greek fire-ship and captured another. Half-a-dozen such battles would give him the command of the sea.

The Greek fleet anchored in the bay of Sandama. On the 10th of September the Turks again stood out of Budrun. Their object was to force a passage to Samos. Several ships endeavoured to get to windward of the Greeks by standing out to Leros, and for a time it seemed probable that Miaoulis, who lay becalmed near the rock Ataki with a dozen brigs, would be cut

SECOND BATTLE OFF BUDRUN.

BOOK IV.
CHAP. 1.

off from the rest of the fleet, and be surrounded by the enemy.[1] The breeze, which had hitherto only favoured the Turks, at last reached the Greeks, who knew how to employ it to the best advantage. A confused engagement ensued, in which both parties suffered several disasters. A Greek fire-ship was dismasted, but was burned by its own crew before it was abandoned. Three fire-ships, manned by Albanian islanders, were successively launched against an Egyptian brig, which disquieted the Greeks by the skill and daring of its manœuvres. For a moment the brig seemed to be enveloped in flames, and the report was spread through the Greek fleet that it was destroyed. This was a mistake. The little brig emerged from the flames uninjured, while the three fire-ships, drifting away, burned harmless to the water's edge. The sight of four fire-ships consumed in vain, inspired the Turks with unusual boldness. The Tunisian commodore led his squadron to attack the Greeks with more courage than caution. Two Hydriot fire-ships bore down upon him, and one grappled his frigate, which was blown up. The crew consisted of four hundred men, and she carried two hundred and fifty Arab regular troops. The commodore, the colonel of the troops, and about fifty men, were picked up by Greek boats. All the rest perished at the time, and most of those then saved were subsequently murdered at a massacre of Turkish prisoners in Hydra.[2]

---

[1] Gordon, ii. 154, by some mistake writes Zatalla instead of Ataki. Tricoupi, who habitually transposes the ancient and modern names of his authorities, misled by the word, supposes that the fleets were off Attaleia, which is at least two hundred miles distant.—Tricoupi, iii. 164. Gordon's information concerning the naval operations in 1824 was in part drawn from the journal of an Englishman in Ibrahim's fleet, which was lent to him by the author on his complaining that he had found great difficulty in obtaining accurate accounts of the movements of the Greek fleet from the Greek islanders.

[2] Sir James Emerson Tennent, in *A Picture of Greece* in 1825, by James Emerson, vol. i. 244, gives an account of this massacre, of which he was an eyewitness. Two hundred innocent and helpless prisoners were butchered like sheep in the public square of Hydra, and no primate or captain made an effort to save their lives. This unparalleled act of atrocity was caused by a mere rumour that a Hydriot vessel had been blown up by a Turkish slave, though it was as probable that it was destroyed by the carelessness of its crew.

A Turkish corvette was also destroyed by a Psarian fire-ship. These losses so terrified the Turks that they hauled off, and both fleets returned to their former anchorages.

In this second engagement the Egyptians remained almost inactive. Ibrahim and Gibraltar, who were neither of them deficient in courage, were not disposed to expose their ships to secure victory for a capitan-pasha who kept always at a distance from the enemy. Jealousy also prevailed between Ibrahim and Khosreff. The superior rank of the capitan-pasha had enabled him to assume airs of superiority, which had mortified the Egyptian. It was now necessary to secure the cordial co-operation of Ibrahim, since it was evident that it would be impossible for the Othoman fleet alone to effect a debarkation at Samos. After a few days had been passed in negotiations and ceremonious visits, Ibrahim consented to send all his frigates to assist the Turks, and encamped his own troops at Budrun until the capitan-pasha's operations should be finished.

It may be here observed, that if the Greeks had endeavoured to learn the truth concerning their enemies, they might easily have ascertained that they were now about to encounter a much more dangerous enemy than any who had previously attacked them. While the Egyptian regulars remained at Budrun they maintained strict discipline. Neither in the town nor in the neighbouring country were the Christians molested in any way by Ibrahim's soldiers, though two thousand Albanians, whose services had been transferred by the capitan-pasha to the Egyptian expedition, could hardly be prevented from plundering Mussulman and Christian alike. Ibrahim had accepted their services in order to keep them as a check on the Turks in the Cretan fortresses.

The Greek and Turkish fleets met again between

Icaria and Samos. Some severe skirmishing ensued, in which the Greeks compelled the capitan-pasha to abandon the project of landing on Samos. Heavy gales during the latter part of September dispersed both fleets, and the capitan-pasha returned to the Dardanelles early in October, leaving several Othoman frigates and corvettes with the Egyptian fleet.

The Greek fleet was about the same time weakened by the departure of the Psarians, but Miaoulis continued to harass the Egyptians. An engagement took place off Mytilene, in which Nicodemos, the only Psarian who remained with the Greek fleet, burned a Turkish corvette, and two other fire-ships destroyed an Egyptian brig. Again, however, a Hydriot fire-ship was burned uselessly in consequence of the timidity, the indiscipline, or the inexperience of the crew. Ibrahim was so dissatisfied with the conduct of his captains in this engagement, that he expressed his displeasure in strong terms. He ordered the captain of the brig which had been burned to be strangled for abandoning his ship too precipitately, and he ordered another captain to be bastinadoed on his own quarterdeck, for running foul of a frigate in order to escape a Greek fire-ship.

The season was far advanced before the Egyptians returned to Budrun. Most of the Greek ships, without waiting for orders, sailed for Hydra and Spetzas. Miaoulis remained with twenty-five sail, and continued to watch the enemy with indefatigable zeal. Ibrahim lost no time in embarking his army in order to reach Crete, where a considerable number of men and a large amount of military stores had already arrived direct from Alexandria.

On the 13th of November 1824, while the whole Egyptian fleet was approaching Crete, about twenty Greek brigs hove in sight, and bore down on the transports, which were far ahead of the men-of-war. A single frigate, which was much to windward of the others, was surrounded by five Greek brigs, and might easily have been carried by boarding her from stem and stern, had the Greek islanders ventured to come to close quarters. Their timid manœuvres allowed her to escape, which she did in the most unseamanlike way, by running towards the middle of the transports with all her studding-sails set. The Greeks, who outsailed her, passed successively under her stern, and raked her with their broadsides. A fire-ship was also sent down on her, and her studding-sails caught fire, but they were cut away, and the fire prevented from spreading to the other sails. The aversion of the Hydriots to encountering the Turks sword in hand, prevented their taking advantage of the confusion produced by the conflagration. A bold attack would have insured either the capture or the destruction of the frigate. In the afternoon all the transports had retired behind the men-of-war, and Ibrahim Pasha, his admiral Ismael Gibraltar, with nine more frigates, formed a line to protect them. The Greek force before night was increased to forty sail. Two fire-ships were directed against one of the Egyptian frigates, but she avoided them without much trouble. The night came on dark and squally, and the Egyptians were ordered to bear away between Crete and Kasos.

Next morning a number of transports assembled under the lee of Karpathos, where they found Ibrahim's frigate. They then made sail for Rhodes; but as that island affords no anchorage during the winter, the bay of Marmorice, on the opposite coast, was fixed on for the general rendezvous. In the engagement of the 13th the Greeks captured only seven or eight transports, but they dispersed the convoy so completely that many vessels bore away for Alexandria. A few, however, by holding on their course, gained Suda in safety. At Marmorice Ibrahim degraded eleven captains for neglecting to keep to windward of the transports, according to orders.

The Greeks allowed themselves to be deluded into a belief that Ibrahim would not dare to renew his voyage to Crete during the winter. They returned to Hydra with their prizes, and the persevering pasha sailed from Marmorice on the 5th of December, and before the end of the year 1824 he reached Suda, where he observed to one of the European officers of his suite, "As we have now outmanœuvred the Greeks at sea, we shall certainly find little difficulty in beating them on shore."

A calm survey of the campaign of 1824 at last convinced the Greeks that their navy was inadequate to obtain a decisive victory over the Turks. The expedition against Samos had indeed been frustrated, and seven Turkish ships had been destroyed. But to obtain these successes, twenty-two Greek fire-ships had been consumed. On the other hand, the Turks had to boast of the destruction of Kasos and Psara, and of having captured nearly a hundred and fifty Greek vessels, and slain about four thousand Greek seamen. The Greeks could only hope for ultimate success by changing their system of warfare. Captain Hastings urged them to purchase steam-ships, arm them with heavy guns, and make use of shells and hot shot. Had his proposition been promptly accepted, and its execution intrusted to his zeal and activity, Greece might still have been saved by her own exertions.

When Ibrahim Pasha quitted Alexandria in July 1824, he made a vow not to put his foot on shore until he landed in Greece. On the 24th of February 1825, he debarked at Modon with four thousand regular infantry and five hundred cavalry. His fleet immediately returned to Crete, and soon came back, bringing the second division of his army, consisting of six thou-

sand infantry, five hundred cavalry, and a strong A.D. 1825.
corps of field artillery. On the 21st of March the
Egyptian army encamped before Navarin.

After the unfortunate battle of Petta, the Greeks
banished every semblance of military discipline from
their armies in the field. At the beginning of 1825 no
words were strong enough to express their contempt
for the regular troops of the Egyptian pasha. They
said that the Arabs would run away at the sight of the
armatoli, who had always been victorious over the
bravest Mussulmans in the sultan's empire. This self-
confidence had prevented them taking any precautions
against an enemy they despised. For more than six
months the Greek government had known that Navarin would be the first fortress attacked, yet no measures
had been adopted for putting it in a state of defence.
Yet a small sum laid out at Navarin might have rendered it capable of a prolonged resistance, and nothing
was so likely to disgust Mohammed Ali with the war
in Greece as a long and expensive siege. Such an
enterprise would also have afforded the Greek navy
frequent opportunities of cutting off the supplies of the
besieging army.

At this crisis of the Revolution, the president of
Greece, George Konduriottes, showed himself utterly
unworthy of the high trust he had received from the
nation, and Kolettes proved himself ignorant and incapable. The Greek government had for several
months been paying thirty thousand men, who were
called soldiers; when it now became necessary to march
against the invaders of the Morea, ten thousand men
could not be collected. The sycophants who surrounded Konduriottes persuaded him to take the
command of the army. The president departed from
Nauplia with great pomp, mounted on a richly capari-
soned horse, which he hung over as if he had been a

sack of hay, supported by two grooms. His ungraceful exhibition of horsemanship was followed by a long train composed of secretaries, guards, grooms, and pipe-bearers. "As he passed under the lofty arched gateway of Nauplia on the 28th of March, the cannon from the ramparts and from the fortress above pealed out their loud salutations, and were answered by the batteries on the shore and the shipping in the harbour."[1] Mavrocordatos, whose presidency had been characterised by a similar attempt to play the generalissimo, accompanied Konduriottes as a cabinet counsellor. An old Hydriot sea-captain, named Skourti, who had displayed some skill as a sailor, and some courage on the quarterdeck, was named lieutenant-general of the Greek army. So little idea had the president of the real point where danger was to be apprehended, that he proposed besieging Patras. When he reached Tripolitza, he found that a storm had burst on another quarter. The natural imbecility of Konduriottes got the better of his pride, and he could not conceal his incapacity to form any resolution. He felt that he ought to hasten in person to Navarin, and he set out; but instead of taking the direct road, he turned off to Kalamata, lingered there a moment, and then regained the seat of government without ever seeing an enemy.

The simplicity with which Ibrahim Pasha took the field formed a striking contrast to the pomp affected by the Hydriot president and the Greek captains. The aspect of the two armies was equally dissimilar. The gold of the English loan glittered profusely in the embroidered jackets and richly ornamented arms of the Greek soldiers, while in the Egyptian army the dress and the arms were plain and simple. The Greek officers were equipped for show; the Egyptian for

[1] *Historical Sketch of the Greek Revolution*, by Dr S. G. Howe, who was an eyewitness, page 226.

service. The Greek camp seemed to contain an accidental crowd of armed men. The Egyptian camp exhibited strict discipline and perfect order. One half of the regular troops was engaged in constant exercise or unceasing labour, while the other half reposed. The artillery and material for a siege were brought up from Modon to the camp with order and celerity.

The first attempt of the Greeks to interrupt Ibrahim's operations was made by the veteran chieftain Karatassos, and it was defeated with severe loss. The armatoli found to their surprise that the Arab boys, who had been disciplined by Ibrahim, were more dangerous enemies than the bravest Arnaouts the Greeks had ever encountered. Karatassos stated that this was the case to the executive government. His opinion was disregarded. It was said that he praised the discipline of the Egyptians to excuse his defeat and he had conducted his attack carelessly because he was envious of the honour conferred on Captain Skourti, and wished to be named commander-in-chief.

Ibrahim formed the sieges of Navarin and of the old castle on the ruins of Pylos at the same time. Navarin contained a garrison of sixteen hundred men; Pylos of eight hundred. The flower of the Greek army advanced to relieve these two places, with the intention of falling on the rear of the besiegers, who were divided into two separate bodies, and compelled to keep up communications with Modon. The Greeks were commanded by Skourti. Their force exceeded seven thousand, and was composed of Romeliot armatoli, choice Moreot troops, and a band of Suliots. Ibrahim, who divined the plan of his enemy, did not allow him to choose his point of attack. On the 19th of April he attacked the Greek position at the head of three thousand regular infantry, four hundred cavalry, and four guns. The Suliots under Djavella and Constantine

Botzares, the armatoli under Karaïskaki, and the Albanians of Argolis under Skourti, received the Egyptians in positions which they had themselves selected for their encampment. They were supported by a body of irregular cavalry, consisting in great part of Servians and Bulgarians. The leader, Hadji Christos, made a gallant show. He was surrounded by a retinue in imitation of a pasha of three tails, with kettledrums, timbileks, and a topuz-bearer.

After a short halt, which Ibrahim employed in reconnoitring the Greek position, the first regiment of Arabs was ordered to charge the Suliots and armatoli with the bayonet. The regulars marched steadily up to the Greek intrenchments without wavering, though many fell. As they approached the enemy their officers cheered them on in double-quick time to the assault; but the best troops of Greece shrank from their encounter, and after a feeble resistance fled in every direction. A few round shot and a charge of cavalry dispersed the rest of the army and completed the victory. The vanquished Greeks fled in wild confusion, leaving six hundred men dead on the field. The Egyptians, particularly the cavalry, collected a rich booty; and silver-mounted arms, which had been thrown away by the Turks after their defeats at Valtetzi and Dervenaki, were now in like manner abandoned by the fugitive Greeks to insure their escape. This affair at Krommydi—for it cannot be called a battle—convinced every military friend of Greece that the best Greek irregular troops were unfit to encounter the most ordinary disciplined battalions in a pitched battle in the plain.

A few days after this victory, Husseïn Djeritlee, the conqueror of Kasos, arrived at the Egyptian camp with reinforcements. Husseïn had the eye of a soldier, and he immediately pointed out to Ibrahim that his engineer, Colonel Romey, had not selected the best A.D. 1825. position for the batteries he had constructed against Navarin. Without having read Thucydides, Husseïn also observed that the island of Sphakteria was the key of Navarin. It commanded the port, and its possession would render the defence of both Navarin and Pylos impracticable. He proposed to change the whole plan of attack. Ibrahim followed his advice, and intrusted him with the direction of the operations against Sphakteria.

When Ibrahim opened his trenches before Navarin, that fortress was ill supplied with provisions and ammunition. The neglect both of the government and the officers commanding in the place had been so great, that when the Egyptians cut off the water of the aqueduct half the cisterns were empty. Even Sphakteria had been left without defence. At last an effort was made to prevent the island from being occupied by the enemy. Eight brigs were at anchor in the harbour. Tsamados, who commanded one, the Mars, landed three eighteen-pounders, which he had embarked at Nauplia, and constructed a battery on the point of Sphakteria, in order to prevent the Egyptian ships from entering the port.[1] Though it was evident that this battery could oppose no obstacle to a landing of the Egyptians in other parts of the island, it was only with great difficulty that several foreign officers in Navarin could persuade the Greeks to take more effectual measures for the defence of Sphakteria. Mavrocordatos, who possessed more moral courage as well as more activity and ability than Konduriottes, fortunately visited Navarin to concert measures for its relief when the president fled back from Messenia. Mavrocordatos, Sakturi, the governor, and Tsamados, succeeded by their co-operation in getting four more

[1] These guns were intended by the Greek government for the siege of Patras.

guns in battery on the island, to protect the only spot where it was supposed that the Egyptians would attempt to land.[1]

On the 8th of May 1825, the Egyptian fleet, carrying three thousand troops, stood out from Modon, and on reaching Sphakteria opened a cannonade on the Greek batteries. Under cover of the smoke, a regiment of Arab regulars and a body of Moreot Turks, who had volunteered to lead the attack, effected a landing. Hussein Bey led them on to charge the Greeks who defended the guns, but Romeliots, Moreot klephts, and artillerymen, all fled at his approach, and abandoned the batteries without offering any resistance. The Arab bayonet swept all before it. Tsamados, who had landed with a few of his crew to assume the direction of a carronade belonging to his ship, stood his ground, and died bravely at his post. He was a member of the Hydriot aristocracy, and had shown himself more inclined to the introduction of discipline in the Greek fleet, and to avail himself of scientific improvements, than the rest of his countrymen. He commanded his own brig, and on several occasions he had displayed a degree of naval skill and personal courage which had obtained for him warm praise from Miaoulis. His amiable character, his youth, his enlightened views, and his true patriotism, rendered his death a national calamity at this moment.

The veteran Hetairist, Anagnostaras, who had forfeited a good name won at the siege of Tripolitza by his subsequent avarice and rapacity, was recognised by a Moreot Mussulman, and slain to avenge the blood of the slaughtered Turks. The victor carried the rich arms of Anagnostaras during the whole campaign of 1825.

[1] Collegno—*Diario dell' Assedio di Navarino*, p. 54—says there were twelve guns in battery on the 7th of May, but other authorities equally well informed agree in giving the number as only seven.

Count Santa Rosa, a Piedmontese exile, fell also in this affair. No man's death was more sincerely regretted, and none fell to whom death was so welcome. The Greek deputies at London, at the suggestion of some of the liberal counsellors by whom they were surrounded, invited Santa Rosa to serve in Greece. On his arrival at Nauplia he found the members of the Greek government turned from him with pride. Everything he said was treated with contempt, and he himself with neglect. Yet, as he understood much better than Mavrocordatos, Kolettes, and Rhodios the extent of the danger to which Greece was then exposed, he deemed it dishonourable to abandon her cause at such a crisis. His services not having been accepted, he was serving at Sphakteria as a volunteer. After receiving a severe wound, he refused to surrender, and was killed by an Arab soldier, who found a small sum of money and a seal in his possession. The sight of this seal enabled a friend in the Egyptian camp to learn his fate.[1]

Three hundred and fifty Greeks were killed, and two hundred taken prisoners, at Sphakteria. The victorious Arabs gained considerable booty, for the majority of the slain wore silver-mounted arms, and their belts were lined with English gold. Sovereigns soon circulated in the bazaar of Modon, and the war became extremely popular in the Egyptian army.

There were five brigs remaining in the harbour of Navarin when Hussein Bey stormed the island. They

---

[1] This seal was given to the author by a Philhellene who was taken prisoner a few days later. Collegno accompanied Santa Rosa to Greece. Like every foreigner, his feelings were wounded by the treatment his friend received, and he reproaches the Greeks with their ingratitude. Tricoupi gave a strong example of this national vice. His funeral oration in memory of those who fell at Sphakteria, amidst much hyperbole concerning Greek courage, omitted all mention of Santa Rosa's name, though he and many of his hearers knew well that Santa Rosa was one of the very small number who fell honourably fighting. The neglect was the more disgraceful, because the orator had known Santa Rosa personally, and knew his virtues.—Collegno, *Diario*, p. 118.

immediately stood out to sea, one only lingering at the entrance of the port. This was the Mars, which sent its boats to the shore to bring off the captain. Mavrocordatos and Sakturi escaped in these boats, and brought on board the news that Tsamados had refused to abandon his post, and had fallen doing his duty. Sakturi did not think of returning to his at Navarin. He left the governorship to anybody who wanted it, and remained on board the Mars, though there was both time and opportunity to return to his post. The Mars was obliged to pass through the Egyptian fleet, and receive the broadsides of several frigates, yet she lost only two men killed and seven wounded, so trifling was the danger in the severest naval engagement during this war, unless when fire-ships were successful. Lord Byron, who witnessed the firing of two Turkish men-of-war endeavouring to prevent the Greeks from taking possession of a stranded brig, quaintly observed, "These Turks, with so many guns, would prove dangerous enemies if they should happen to fire without taking aim."

Three days after the conquest of Sphakteria, Pylos capitulated. The garrison, consisting of seven hundred and eighty-six men, laid down its arms, and the Greeks were allowed to depart uninjured.

Navarin was feebly defended. The Romeliot troops in the place were eager to capitulate. George Mavromichales, who afterwards assassinated Capodistrias, displayed great determination, and urged his countrymen to defend the place to the last. He harangued the soldiers, and opposed all terms of capitulation. It was evident, however, that the fortress could not hold out many days. All hope of relief, both by land and sea, was cut off. Ibrahim offered honourable terms of capitulation. He was desirous of winning the Greeks to submit to his government, and for this purpose he was eager to exhibit proofs of his humanity. He had established his military superiority; he wished now to place his civil and financial administration in contrast with that of the Greek government. He expected by his treatment of the garrison of Navarin to facilitate his future conquests. The Greeks laid down their arms and surrendered all their property. The field-officers alone were allowed to retain their swords. The whole garrison was transported to Kalamata in neutral vessels, under the escort of a French and Austrian man-of-war. Ibrahim, who thought that the British government showed undue favour to the Greek cause, refused to allow any mention of an English escort to be inserted in the capitulation.

On the 21st of May the Greeks marched out of Navarin to embark in the transports prepared for their reception. A crowd of Moreot Turks from Modon and Coron, excited by a few survivors of the massacre of Navarin, assembled to waylay the Greeks as they were embarking. But Ibrahim was a man of a firmer character and more enlarged political views than the primates and chieftains of Greece. He had foreseen the attempt, and he adopted effectual measures for preventing any stain on his good faith. A body of regular cavalry prevented the Turks from approaching the ground; and the unarmed Greeks marched securely to the ships between lines of Arab infantry with fixed bayonets. George Mavromichales and Iatrakos of Mistra were detained as hostages for the release of the two pashas who were detained by the Greeks after the capitulation of Nauplia. George Mavromichales, like Ali of Argos, had refused to sign the capitulation. The exchange was soon effected.

We have often had occasion to observe that the Greek fleet arrived too late to avert disaster. It mattered little whether the Greek government was destitute of money or rolling in wealth, whether the scene of danger was near or far off, the same supineness and selfishness always characterised the proceedings of the Albanian islanders. At Chios, at Kasos, at Psara, at Sphakteria, and at Mesolonghi, the neglect of the Greek government and the sordid spirit of the Hydriots were equally conspicuous. A small squadron put to sea when the news of Ibrahim's landing in the Morea reached Hydra, but it was so weak that Miaoulis could not prevent Hussein Bey from conquering Sphakteria, and gaining possession of the magnificent harbour of Navarin, where the Egyptian fleet was anchored in safety, even before the fortress capitulated. But when Miaoulis reached Modon, he observed that a part of the Egyptian fleet was still at that place, and by instant action he hoped to inflict such a loss on Ibrahim as might delay the fall of Navarin, and perhaps save the place.

On the 12th of May he sent six fire-ships simultaneously into the midst of the Egyptian squadron as it lay at anchor. The attack was well planned and promptly and boldly executed. The conflagration was terrible, and accident alone prevented it from being more extensive. A fine double-banked frigate, the Asia, which, it has been mentioned, was fitted out at Deptford, three sloops of war, and seven transports, were destroyed; but on shore the fire was prevented from destroying anything but a magazine of provisions.[1] The explosion of the powder-magazines of the ships of war was heard both in Ibrahim's camp and in Navarin; and for some time a report prevailed that all the transports and military stores had been destroyed. Successive couriers soon brought exact accounts of the real loss sustained. Ibrahim was satisfied that it was not sufficient to interrupt his operations for a single

---

[1] The Egyptians reported their loss as one frigate, two brigs, and eight transports.—Collegno, *Diario*, 75.

hour. The Greeks considered this affair of Modon as a brilliant achievement; with equal justice, the Egyptians regarded it as an insignificant disaster.[1]

A. D. 1825.

Even the fall of Navarin did not entirely awaken the Greeks from the lethargy and corruption into which they had sunk. The government did everything in its power to conceal the disgrace sustained by the Greek army, and the people were willing to be deceived. The news of the capitulation spread slowly, and was in some degree neutralised by fabricated reports of imaginary successes.[2]

Ibrahim advanced towards the centre of the Peloponnesus before the Moreots made any national effort to repel his invasion. Selfishness and party animosity were more powerful than patriotism. But the timid Konduriottes observed with alarm many signs of his own declining influence, and of the reviving power of the Peloponnesian primates and chieftains. The departure of the Romeliot troops, who had quitted the Morea when they heard of the invasion of Western Greece by Kiutayhé, left the executive body without a strong military force on which it could depend. The nullity of Konduriottes, the administrative ignorance of Kolettes, the licentiousness of the archimandrite Dikaios, and the shallow presumption of Rhodios, added to the fiscal corruption of the civil officials and the rapacity and dissensions of the military, enabled the municipal authorities to recover some portion of their former power. They raised a cry for the deliverance of Kolokotrones and the other primates and chiefs imprisoned at Hydra; and the people soon sup-

[1] Two eyewitnesses give accurate information concerning the siege of Navarin—Collegno in his *Diario*, and Dr Millingen in *Memoirs of the Affairs of Greece*.
[2] Some time elapsed before the Greek newspapers alluded to the fall of Navarin, and the private journals of many Philhellenes which the author has examined record reports of victories which, though generally circulated, were entirely without foundation.

ported their demand in a voice which the government did not dare to disobey.

It was necessary to raise a new army in order to replace the armatoli who had abandoned the defence of the Peloponnesus. Kolokotrones was the only man whom the Moreots were inclined to follow to the field. There was therefore no alternative but to reinstate him in his former position as general-in-chief of the Peloponnesian forces, to release all who were in prison for their share in the second civil war, and to conciliate the two primates, Zaimes and Londos, who had returned from exile, and declared their wish to serve their country and forget past dissensions. Konduriottes's government proclaimed a general amnesty: thanksgivings were offered up in the churches of Nauplia for the happy change which had taken place in the hearts of the rulers of Greece; harangues in praise of forgiveness and concord were now uttered by men who had hitherto been the most violent instigators of discord and vengeance. By these timely and politic concessions, Konduriottes, Kolettes, and Rhodios purchased immunity for the violence and peculation which had characterised their public administration. Kolokotrones resumed his former power and his old habits. The severe lesson he had learned, and the calamities he had brought on his country, had not moderated the egoism of his ambition. His administrative and military views were as confined as ever, and his avarice remained insatiable.

The archimandrite Dikaios (Pappa Phlesas) was still Minister of the Interior. He was the most unprincipled man of his party, and had been, with Kolettes, the most violent persecutor of the Moreot chiefs. The universal indignation now expressed at his conduct convinced him that it would be dangerous for him to remain at Nauplia, where his licentious life and gross peculation

pointed him out as the first object of popular ven- A.D. 1825.
geance, and the scapegoat for the sins of his colleagues.
The archimandrite was destitute of private virtue and
political honesty, but he was a man of activity and
courage. Perhaps, too, at this decisive moment a
sense of shame urged him to cancel his previous misdeeds by an act of patriotism. He asked permission
of the government to march against the Egyptians,
boasting that he would vanquish Ibrahim or perish
in the combat. The permission was readily granted,
though little confidence was felt in his military conduct. He quitted Nauplia with great parade, attended
by a body of veteran soldiers; and when he reached
the village of Maniaki, in the hills to the east of Gargaliano, his force exceeded three thousand men.

The bold priest possessed no military quality but
courage. He posted his troops in an ill-selected position, and awaited the attack of Ibrahim, who advanced
in person to carry the position at the head of six
thousand men on the 1st of June. Many of the archimandrite's troops, seeing the superior force of the
Egyptians, deserted during the night, and only about
fifteen hundred men remained. The pasha's regulars
were led on to storm the Greek intrenchments in
gallant style, and a short and desperate struggle ensued. The Greeks were forced from their position
before they fled. The affair was the best contested
during the war, for a thousand Greeks perished by the
Arab bayonets, and four hundred Arabs lay dead on
the field.[1] In spite of the defeat and the severe loss
sustained by the Greeks, they gained both honour and
courage by the battle of Maniaki. The national spirit,
which had been greatly depressed by the flight of the
Romeliots, and by the ease with which the Egyptians
had taken Sphakteria, again revived at seeing so great

[1] Phrantzes, ii. 347-351.

a loss inflicted on Ibrahim's army by a body of men consisting in great part of armed Moreot peasants. Very little had been expected from Dikaios as a military leader. He had selected his position ill, and he had not known how to construct proper intrenchments, but he had given his followers an example of brilliant courage, and died nobly at his post. The result induced the Greeks to expect a great victory when the Moreot soldiery took the field under their tried champion Kolokotrones.

The indefatigable Ibrahim lost no time in profiting by his victory. After allowing his troops to plunder the town of Arcadia, he marched to occupy Nisi and Kalamata, which the Maniats, who called themselves Spartans, abandoned at his approach. On the 10th of June he made a short incursion into Maina, but, seeing the mountaineers prepared to dispute his progress, he advanced no farther than Kytries.

Kolokotrones was now in the field. It is said that he wished to destroy the walls and citadel of Tripolitza, but that the executive body refused to sanction this measure, fearing lest it should tend more towards rendering Kolokotrones master of the Morea than towards defending the country against Ibrahim Pasha.[1] Kolokotrones made his dispositions for defending the passes between Messenia and Arcadia by establishing magazines at Leondari, and fixing his headquarters at Makryplagi, where his troops constructed their tambouria or stone intrenchments to cover the defile. His force was considerable, but he was incompetent to employ it to advantage. A thousand Greeks were posted at Poliani, a village which commands a difficult passage over the northern slopes of Mount Taygetus. But in spite of the advantage of the ground, Kolokotrones made his dispositions so ill that he allowed the

[1] Phrantzes, ii. 356.

Egyptians to turn his flank. The general-in-chief of the Peloponnesus always appeared to be more ignorant of Greek topography than the Egyptian pasha. The troops at Poliani were left without provisions. Their officers, who usually derive a considerable profit from the extra rations they draw, hastened to Makryplagi to upbraid Kolokotrones with his neglect, which they ascribed to his avarice. Ibrahim profited by this misconduct. Advancing along an almost impracticable mountain track, he gained possession of Poliani, and on the 16th June compelled the Greeks to abandon the pass of Makryplagi. The superiority of Ibrahim to Kolokotrones as a general, and the inferiority of the irregular Greek troops to the regular Arab battalions, were never exhibited in a more decisive manner. The Greeks had selected their own positions in an almost impracticable country, with which they were well acquainted. They were routed by a foreign force which could make no use of its cavalry and artillery, and on ground where even regular infantry was compelled to act almost as irregulars. Kolokotrones was perhaps a better military chief than Dikaios, but he wanted his bravery and patriotism.

The Greek army fled to Karitena, leaving the road to Tripolitza without defence; and Ibrahim on reaching that city found it abandoned by its inhabitants and garrison. He found in it large stores of provisions, which the officers commanding in the place had neglected to destroy. Without losing a moment, the pasha pushed on to the plain of Argos with about five thousand men, hoping to gain possession of Nauplia either by surprise or treachery.

On the 24th of June he reached the mills of Lerna. Nauplia was thrown into a state of the wildest confusion by his unexpected appearance. A report of treason spread among the citizens, and several persons were accused of holding treasonable correspondence with the enemy. Among these was George Orphanides, a friend of Kolettes, who was tried and acquitted.[1] The patriotism of the people awakened with a sense of the magnitude of the danger to which their country was exposed. Captain Makryannes and Constantine Mavromichales, who afterwards assassinated Capodistrias, with about three hundred and fifty soldiers, hastened over to defend the mills of Lerna as soon as the Egyptians were descried on the hills. Prince Demetrius Hypsilantes and several Philhellenes followed as volunteers. A large quantity of grain for the supply of Nauplia was stored at Lerna. Its loss would have endangered the safety of that fortress.

The mills of Lerna were surrounded by a stone wall, flanked by the celebrated marsh and a deep pond. The garrison was supported by two gunboats anchored within musket-shot of the shore. There was, however, a small break in the wall, which the Greeks, with their usual carelessness, had neglected to repair. Through this space a company of Arabs attempted to force an entrance into the enclosure. They crowded over the breach, and attempted to form in the court; but before they could get into order, they were charged by Makryannes and a band of Greeks and Philhellenes sword in hand, who cut down thirteen on the spot, and drove the rest back over the breach. The Greeks then occupied the wall of the enclosure, and opened loop-holes. Ibrahim, finding that the garrison was prepared for a desperate defence, and was constantly receiving reinforcements, did not venture to renew the attack. He marched on to Argos to pass the night; and after remaining there a day or two, and reconnoitring the environs of Nauplia, he returned with his little army

[1] Tricoupi, III. 221.

to Tripolitza on the 29th of June, without the Greeks venturing to attack him on the way.

As Ibrahim carried with him no provisions on this expedition, it has been inferred that he trusted to some secret intelligence, and expected to gain an entrance into Nauplia by treachery. It seems, however, that he counted rather on surprise and intimidation. The arrival of Captain Hamilton in the Cambrian, accompanied by another frigate and a sloop of war, appears to have hastened his departure. Hamilton landed at Nauplia with a number of his officers, and held a private conference with the members of the Greek government. He encouraged them, and every person with whom he spoke, to put the place in the best state of defence; and he took up such a position with his ships as induced both the Greeks and the Egyptians to infer that he proposed aiding in the defence of the fortress. A report was spread and generally believed at the time, that, in case of an attack, the Greeks were authorised to hoist the English flag, and place their country under British protection.[1] Ibrahim, who was informed of all that passed, retired immediately; but he drew off his troops without precipitation, and took such precautions to secure his flanks that Kolokotrones, with the whole forces of the Morea, did not attempt to make the Kakeskala of Mount Parthenius a scene of triumph to the Greeks like the defile of Dervenaki. The army of Ibrahim received considerable reinforcements shortly after his return to Tripolitza.

Early in July Kolokotrones had assembled upwards of ten thousand men on the hills overlooking the great Arcadian plain.[2] He then occupied Trikorphas, and began to make preparations for blockading Tripolitza.

[1] Tricoupi, iii. 224.
[2] Phrantzes, II. 367; and Tricoupi, III. 226.

Ibrahim, on the 6th of July, anticipated his design by making a simultaneous attack on all his positions. The pasha directed the attack on Trikorphas in person. Kolokotrones made a feeble resistance, but the Greeks lost two hundred men, most of whom were killed in their flight after they had abandoned their intrenchments.[1] The Greek army was completely defeated, but the soldiers felt that they had been worsted in consequence of the bad dispositions of their chiefs, and they did not disperse. They rallied in the mountain passes that lead into the great Arcadian plain, and showed by their activity and perseverance that they only required an abler chief to keep Ibrahim blockaded in Tripolitza. After his defeat, Kolokotrones invited the Mauiats to hasten to his assistance, declaring that he had still four thousand men under arms at Karitena and three thousand at Vervena.[2]

Kolokotrones, with his usual military incapacity, neglected to fortify the mills of Piana, Zarakova, and Davia, from which the garrison of Tripolitza obtained the necessary supplies of flour. The siege of Tripolitza by the Greeks ought to have taught him the importance of keeping possession of these mills; but even experience could not teach him foresight where his own personal interests were not directly and immediately concerned. The Egyptian pasha profited by his enemy's neglect. He seized and fortified these mills, and secured their communications with Tripolitza by a line of posts which he established in the mountains. His foraging parties then covered the plains of Arcadia from Mantinea to Megalopolis, and collected large quantities of grain.

On the 8th of August Ibrahim drove Hypsilantes and

---

[1] Phrantzes, ii. 370.
[2] Phrantzes, ii. 372, who gives Kolokotrones's letter. It proves that Phrantzes assigns an erroneous date to the affair of Trikorphas.

Mavromichales from the camp at Vervena, established A.D. 1825. a strong garrison at Leondari, and returned to Modon on the 13th. Soon after his departure from Arcadia, the Greeks surprised the post at Trikorpha, and recovered possession of the mills of Piana and Zarakova; but when Ibrahim returned to Tripolitza, before the end of the month they were again driven from their conquests.

Ibrahim then led his troops through Tzakonia to Monemvasia, laying waste the country in every direction. The Greeks nowhere opposed him with vigour. Their spirit seemed broken, and they contented themselves with following on his flanks and rear to waylay foragers and recapture small portions of his plunder.[1] He was now intent on destroying the resources of the population. The Egyptians carried on a war of extermination; the Greeks replied by a war of brigandage. The ultimate result of such a system of warfare was inevitable. The invaders were fed by supplies from abroad; the country could not long furnish the means of subsistence to its defenders. Famine would soon consume those who escaped the sword.

During the expedition to Tzakonia, Colonel Fabvier, who had been appointed to command a body of Greek regulars, made an attempt to surprise Tripolitza. It failed, in consequence of the irregulars under Andreas Londos not making the concerted diversion.

On returning to Tripolitza, and finding everything in good order, Ibrahim marched to Arcadia (Cyparissia), carrying off all the provisions from the districts through which he passed, and laying waste the towns of Philiatra and Gargaliano. The campaign

---

[1] Tricoupi says, "τοὺς ἐχθροὺς ἐβλαπταν ἀληστοπολεμοῦντες" (iii. 233); and no great injury could they inflict by such contemptible warfare.

of 1825 terminated when he reached Modon on the 30th of September.

Mohammed Ali was induced by the sultan to send large reinforcements to Ibrahim about this time, and to order him to co-operate with Reshid Pasha in the siege of Mesolonghi.

CHAPTER II.

THE SIEGE OF MESOLONGHI.

"Pride points the path that leads to liberty.
Back to the struggle, baffled in the strife,
War, war is still their cry—war even to the knife."

OPERATIONS OF RESHID PASHA—STATE OF MESOLONGHI—NUMBER OF ITS GARRISON AND OF ITS BESIEGERS—ARRIVAL OF THE OTTOMAN FLEET—ARRIVAL OF THE GREEK FLEET — DIFFICULT POSITION OF RESHID—HE CONSTRUCTS A MOUND—TREASON OF ODYSSEUS—MILITARY OPERATIONS IN CONTINENTAL GREECE—RESHID WITHDRAWS TO A FORTIFIED CAMP—OPERATIONS OF THE TURKISH AND GREEK FLEETS—IBRAHIM ARRIVES BEFORE MESOLONGHI—LETHARGY OF THE GREEKS AND OF THEIR GOVERNMENT—THE TURKS TAKE VASILADI AND ANATOLIKON—OFFERS OF CAPITULATION REJECTED—TURKISH ATTACK ON KLISSOVA REPULSED — DEFEAT OF THE GREEK FLEET UNDER MIAOULIS—FINAL SORTIE—FALL OF MESOLONGHI.

THE second siege of Mesolonghi is the most glorious military operation of the Greek Revolution : it is also one of the most characteristic of the moral and political condition of the nation, for it exhibits the invincible energy of the people in strong contrast with the inefficiency of the military chiefs, and the inertness and ignorance of the members of the government. Never was greater courage and constancy displayed by the population of a besieged town ; rarely has less science been shown by combatants, at a time when military science formed the chief element of success in warfare.

Greek patriotism seemed to have concentrated itself within the walls of Mesolonghi. Elsewhere hostilities languished. While the citizens of a small town, the fishermen of a shallow lagoon, and the peasants of a desolated district, sustained the vigorous attack of a determined enemy, the fleets and armies wasted their time and their strength in trifling and desultory operations. An undisciplined population performed the duty of a trained garrison. Here, therefore, the valour of the individual demands a record in history. Yet, though private deeds of heroism were of daily occurrence, the historian shrinks from selecting the acts of heroism, and the names of the warriors that deserve pre-eminence. All within the town seemed to be inspired by the warmest love for political liberty and national independence, and all proved that they were ready to guarantee the sincerity of their feeling with the sacrifice of their lives.

Reshid Pasha of Joannina, who, it has been already said, was generally called Kiutayhé by the Greeks and Albanians, had distinguished himself at the battle of Petta. When he assumed the command of the Othoman forces destined to invade Western Greece in the year 1825, much was expected by the sultan from his known firmness and ability. On the 6th of April he seized the pass of Makrynoros, which the Greek chieftains neglected to defend, and where the Greek government had only stationed a few guards under the command of Nothi Botzares, a veteran Suliot. No three hundred Greeks were now found to make an effort for the defence of these Western Thermopylæ.[1] Reshid advanced through Acarnania without encountering any opposition. The inhabitants fled before him. Many, with their flocks and herds, found shelter under the English flag in Calamo, where the poor were maintained by rations from the British government; others retired to Mesolonghi, and formed part of the garrison which defended that place. On the 27th of April,

[1] Tricoupi, iii. 281.

Reshid established his headquarters in the plain, and A.D. 1825. two days afterwards he opened his first parallel against Mesolonghi, at a distance of about six hundred yards from the walls.[1] His force then consisted of only six thousand men and three guns.

Mesolonghi was in a good state of defence. An earthen rampart of two thousand three hundred yards in length extended from the waters of the lagoon across the promontory on which the town was built. This rampart was partly faced with masonry, flanked by two bastions near the centre, strengthened towards its eastern extremity by a lunette and a tenaille, and protected where it joined the lagoon to the west by a battery on an islet called Marmaro, distant about two hundred yards from the angle of the place. In front of the rampart a muddy ditch, not easy to pass, separated the fortress from the adjoining plain. Forty-eight guns and four mortars were mounted in battery. The garrison consisted of four thousand soldiers and armed peasants, and one thousand citizens and boatmen. The place was well supplied with provisions and ammunition at the commencement of the siege, but there were upwards of twelve thousand persons to feed within the walls.

The army of Reshid never exceeded ten thousand troops, and a considerable part of it never entered the plain of Mesolonghi, for he was obliged to employ about two thousand men in guarding a line of stations from Makrynoros and Karavanserai, on the Ambracian Gulf, to Kakiscala on the Gulf of Patras, in order to keep open his communications with Arta, Previsa, Lepanto, and Patras. But in addition to his troops, Reshid was accompanied by three thousand pioneers, muleteers, and camp-followers.[2] It was not until the

---

[1] Gordon, ii. 283. Tricoupi, iii. 267.
[2] Compare Gordon, ii. 233, and Tricoupi, iii. 281. Reshid's commissariat

commencement of June that the besiegers obtained a supply of artillery from Patras, which increased their force to eight guns and four mortars. For several weeks, therefore, Reshid trusted more to the spade than to his fire, and during this time he pushed forward his approaches with indefatigable industry. Early in June he had advanced to within thirty yards of the bastion Franklin, which covered the western side of the walls. But his ammunition was then so much reduced that he was compelled to fire stones from his mortars instead of shells.[1]

While the Turks were working at their approaches, the Greeks constructed traverses and erected new batteries.

Little progress had been made in the active operations of the siege, when a Greek squadron of seven sail arrived off Mesolonghi on the 10th of June. It encouraged the besieged by announcing that Miaoulis would soon make his appearance with a large fleet, and by landing considerable supplies of provisions and ammunition. The garrison, confident of success, began to make frequent and vigorous sorties. In one of these, Routsos, a native of Mesolonghi, was taken prisoner by the Turks, and was terrified into revealing to the enemy the position of the subterraneous aqueducts which supplied the town with water. The supply was immediately cut off, but fortunately the besieged found fresh water in abundance by digging new wells, so that very little inconvenience was felt, even during the

---

distributed twenty-five thousand rations at the commencement of this campaign. A deduction of one-third must be made in estimating the number of men then actually under arms. A few weeks of actual service usually reduced a Turkish army to one-half of the number of the rations issued. It must also be observed that Reshid detached two thousand men under his kehaya to dislodge the Greeks from Salona.

[1] Gordon, Fabvier, and Tricoupi, all indicate the position and nature of the defensive works of Mesolonghi with sufficient accuracy. The bastion Franklin to the west, and the bastion Botsares to the east, formed the centre. Between them was the battery Korais. Against these the principal attack of Reshid was directed.

greatest heat of summer, from the destruction of the aqueducts. The besiegers, who had pushed on their operations with great activity, at last made an attempt to carry the islet of Marmoras by assault, which was repulsed, and entailed on them a severe loss.

On the 10th of July the Greeks met with their first great disappointment. The defenders of Mesolonghi were looking forward to the arrival of the fleet, which they fondly expected would compel Reshid to raise the siege. Several vessels were descried in the offing. Their joy reached the highest pitch, and they overwhelmed the advanced-guard of the besiegers, which consisted of Albanians, with insulting boasts. Soon, however, fresh ships hove in sight, and it was evident that the fleet was too numerous and the ships too large to be Greek. The red flag became visible both to Turks and Greeks, and gradually the broad white streaks on the hulls and the numerous ports showed that the fleet was that of the capitan-pasha. The besieged were greatly depressed, but their constancy was unshaken.

Reshid now assumed the offensive with great vigour. He introduced a number of flat-bottomed boats into the lagoon, gained possession of the islands of Aghiosostis and Prokopanistos, which the Mesolonghiots had neglected to fortify, and completely invested the place both by sea and land. On the 28th of July he made a determined attack on the bastion Botzares, and on the 2d of August he renewed the assault by a still more furious attempt to storm the bastion Franklin, in which a breach had been opened by his artillery; but both these attacks were gallantly repulsed.

Before the assault on the bastion Franklin, Reshid offered terms of capitulation to the garrison of Mesolonghi. His offers were rejected, and, to revenge his defeat, he ordered Routsos and some other prisoners to be beheaded before the walls. Reshid had expected to carry Mesolonghi by assault before the arrival of the Greek fleet, of whose approach he had been informed by the cruisers of the capitan-pasha before it was known to the besieged.

The Greek fleet, consisting of forty sail of the best ships which Greece still possessed, under the command of Miaoulis, Sakturcs, Kolandrutzos, and Apostales, was descried from Mesolonghi on the 3d of August. Next day the Othoman fleet manœuvred to obtain an advantageous position. The Hydriot squadron in the end succeeded in getting the weather-gage of the advanced ships of the Turks; but the Greeks, in spite of this success, could not break the line of the main division, which consisted of twenty-two sail. Three fire-ships were launched in succession against the capitan-pasha's flag-ship; but the Turks no longer entertained a senseless fear of these engines of attack, and they manœuvred so well that the blazing vessels drifted harmless to leeward without forcing them to break their line of battle. Khosreff was, nevertheless, so intimidated by the determined manner in which the Greeks directed their attacks against his flag, that he avoided a second engagement. He claimed the victory in this indecisive engagement merely because he had escaped defeat, and he made his orders to effect a prompt junction with the Egyptian fleet a pretext for sailing immediately for Alexandria. His cowardice left the flotilla of Reshid in the lagoon without support, and as the Greeks had captured one of the transports laden with powder and shells for the army before Mesolonghi, the besiegers were again inadequately supplied with ammunition for their mortars.

Miaoulis aided the Mesolonghiots in driving the Turks from all the posts they occupied in the lagoons, and in destroying their flotilla. Five of the flat-bottomed boats were captured by the Greeks, who recovered the command of the whole lagoon.¹ The Greek fleet then sailed in pursuit of the capitan-pasha, leaving eight ships to keep open the communications between the besieged and the Ionian Islands, and to prevent any supplies being sent by sea to the besieging army.

Reshid was now placed in a very difficult position. He received his supplies of provisions with irregularity, and his stores of ammunition were so scanty that he could not keep up a continuous fire from his guns, and was compelled to abandon the hope of carrying the place by an artillery attack. He had no money to pay his troops, and was unable to prevent the Albanians from returning home, though he allowed all who remained double rations.² The besieged daily expected to hear that a Greek army had occupied the passes in the rear of Reshid, and felt confident that he would be forced to raise the siege at the approach of winter. If he persisted in maintaining his position, it was thought that his army must perish of want and disease. The armatoli of Romelia, who had quitted the Peloponnesus after their defeats at Navarin, were said to be marching into the mountains behind Lepanto, whose rugged surface is familiar to classic readers from the description which Thucydides has left us of the destruction of the Athenian army under Demosthenes.

Reshid weighed his own resources and estimated the activity of the Greek irregulars with sagacity. His guns could not render him much service, but he still believed that the spade would enable him to gain possession of Mesolonghi before winter. He set his

---

[1] Tricoupi, iii. 303, says seven.
[2] Tricoupi, iii. 305. Yet only twelve thousand rations were now issued daily in Reshid's camp.

army to raise a mound by heaping up earth, and this primitive work was carried forward to the walls of the place in defiance of every effort which the besieged made to interrupt the new mode of attack. So strange a revival of the siege operations of the ancients excited the ridicule of the Greeks. They called the work "the dyke of union," in allusion to the mound which Alexander the Great constructed at the siege of Tyre. The mound was commenced at about a hundred and sixty yards from the salient angle of the bastion Franklin, and it made an obtuse angle as it approached the place. It was from five to eight yards broad at the base, and so high as to overlook the ramparts of the besieged. By indefatigable perseverance, and after much severe fighting in the trenches, the Turks carried the mound to the ditch, filled up the ditch, and stormed the bastion Franklin. Even then they could not effect an entry into the place, for the Greeks had cut off this bastion from all communication with the rest of the defences, and they soon erected batteries which completely commanded it. The besieged then became the assailants, and after a desperate struggle they drove the Turks from their recent conquest. On the 31st of August all the ground they had lost was regained, and they prepared for a great effort against the mound. Several sorties were made in order to obtain exact knowledge of the enemy's trenches. At last, on the 21st of September, a great sortie was made by the whole garrison. The Turkish camp was attacked in several places with such fury that Reshid was unable to conjecture against what point the principal force was directed. He was in danger of seeing his batteries stormed and his guns spiked. The fighting was severe, but the Greeks carried the works that protected the head of the mound, and maintained possession of their conquest until they had levelled that part of it which threatened their defences. While A.D. 1825. every spade in Mesolonghi was destroying the mound, bodies of troops cleared the trenches, and prevented the enemy from interrupting the work. As the Greeks had foreseen, rain soon rendered it impossible for Reshid to repair the damage his works had sustained.

The garrison of Mesolonghi received considerable reinforcements after the capitan-pasha's departure. At the end of September it still amounted to four thousand five hundred men, and was much more efficient than at the commencement of the siege. Hitherto the fire of the Turkish artillery had been so desultory and so ill directed, that not more than one hundred persons had been killed and wounded in the place. This trifling loss during a six months' siege induced the Greeks to form a very erroneous idea of the efficiency of siege-artillery, while the facility with which provisions and ammunition had been introduced inspired them with a blind confidence in their naval superiority. The only severe loss they had suffered had been in their sorties, and in these they had hitherto been almost invariably the victors.

The operations of the Greek army to the north of the Isthmus of Corinth were feeble, desultory, and unsuccessful. The leaders could not be prevailed upon to act in concert. Party intrigues, personal jealousies, and sordid avidity, prevented them from combining at a time when it was evident that a vigorous effort would have delivered Mesolonghi. Northern Greece was then occupied by a numerous body of armatoli. Even in the year 1830, after the losses sustained at Mesolonghi and Athens, Capodistrias assembled six thousand veterans belonging to this army.[1] By a

---

[1] Parliamentary Papers: Communications with Prince Leopold relating to the sovereignty of Greece; Count Capodistrias to Prince Leopold, 25th March (6th April) 1830, p. 42.

bold advance, the communications of Reshid with his resources in Arta, Previsa, and Joannina might have been cut off. The treason of Odysseus has been urged as an apology for the inactivity of the Romeliots at the opening of the campaign of 1825, but it ought to have excited them to increase their exertions, as it rendered their services more necessary. But very little patriotism was displayed this year by the armatoli, either before or after the treason of Odysseus.

Odysseus was a man of considerable ability, but he was too selfish to become a dangerous enemy to a national cause; and when he became openly a traitor, his career was soon terminated. He would not trust himself in the power of the Turks, and the Turks knew him so well that they would afford him no assistance unless he openly joined their army. In trying to overreach everybody he overreached himself, and was easily overpowered. On the 19th of April 1825 he surrendered himself a prisoner to Goura at Livanates.

The treason of Odysseus is the most celebrated instance of treachery among the Greeks during their Revolution. But it derives its importance more from the previous fame of the traitor, and from his tragic end in the Acropolis of Athens, than from the singularity and baseness of his conduct. Many chiefs of armatoli, who, like Odysseus, had been bred up in the service and imbibed the moral corruption of Ali of Joannina, felt like Albanian mercenaries rather than Greek patriots. Several committed acts of treason—Gogos, Varnakiottes, Rhangos, Zongas, Valtinas, and the Moreot captain Nenekos, were all as guilty as, some of them even more guilty than, Odysseus. Gogos was a far greater criminal, and his treachery on the field of Petta inflicted a deeper wound on Greece.

Odysseus never attached any importance to political independence and national liberty. His ambition was to ape the tyranny of Ali in a small sphere. His conduct from the commencement of the Revolution testified that he had no confidence in its ultimate success. He viewed it as a temporary revolt, which he might render conducive to his own interests. He attempted at times to make use of popular feelings which he did not understand, and whose strength he was of course unable to estimate. His opinions prepared him to act the traitor, but he was so far from being a man of a daring character, that a prudent government might have retained him in its service, and found in him a useful instrument, for he possessed more administrative capacity than most of the Romeliot chiefs. Kolettes's influence caused Konduriottes's government to leave him without employment, and to stop the pay and rations of the soldiers who followed his banner. When he saw chiefs of inferior rank, who had previously served under his orders, named captains of districts, and observed that every soldier who quitted his band received a reward, he became alarmed for his personal safety. He believed that Kolettes designed to treat him as he had treated Noutzas and Palaskas, and fear made him a traitor. He opened a negotiation with the Turks, with the hope of securing to himself a capitanlik in Eastern Greece like those held by Gogos and Varnakiottes in Western Greece, but the Turks would not trust him unless he joined them openly. When forced to choose his side, it was fear of Kolettes which decided his conduct. A small body of Mussulman Albanians was then sent to his aid, but his movements had been long watched, and he was quickly surrounded by superior numbers. Goura, his former lieutenant, commanded his assailants, and to him he surrendered himself a prisoner. Goura did not deliver him up to the vengeance of the members of the government. He was kept prisoner in the Acropolis until the disastrous measures of Konduriottes and Kolettes roused general indignation. Goura then feared that Odysseus might escape, and regain his former power. Interest prevailed over gratitude, and Odysseus was murdered on the night of 16th July. After the murder, his body was thrown from the Frank tower in the southern wing of the Propylæa, in order to give credit to the assertion that he perished by a fall in attempting to escape. Thus one of the most astute of the Greek chiefs fell a victim to the policy of a rude Albanian soldier whom he had raised to a high rank.[1] And the son of that Andrutsos, who first raised the standard of revolt against the Othomans in 1769, is the traitor at whose name the finger of scorn is pointed by every Greek. Odysseus perished like his patron and model, Ali of Joannina, a sacrifice to his own selfishness; and he will be execrated as long as the memory of the Greek Revolution shall endure.

On the 17th April 1825, Abbas Pasha crossed the Sperchius with two thousand men and two guns. The surrender of Odysseus, who had been expected to make a vigorous diversion, prevented this small force from advancing southward until the kehaya of Reshid marched into the heart of Etolia with about the same number of chosen Albanians. The kehaya routed the Greek captain Saphaka, who attempted to oppose his progress, occupied Vetrinitza, defeated the Greeks a second time at Pentornea, and entered Salona in triumph, where he was joined by Abbas Pasha at the end of May.

About the same time, the Romeliot troops, who had

---

[1] Tricoupi mentions that Goura tortured his benefactor to learn where his treasures were concealed, iii. 240. Odysseus fortified a cavern near Vellitza (Tithorea), of which Trelawney, who married his sister, kept possession until he was severely wounded by Fenton and Whitcombe, who were suborned by agents of the Greek government to assassinate him. Tricoupi erroneously supposes this cavern to be the Corycian Cave, and quotes Pausanias, who proves the contrary.

abandoned the Morea after their defeat by Ibrahim, formed a camp at Dystomo, round which large bodies of Greek troops rallied. This force arrested the advance of the Turks, who were inferior in number. But anarchy prevailed among the Greek leaders, and prevented them from availing themselves of their superiority. Abbas Pasha was allowed to establish himself at Salona, and no attempt was made to raise the siege of Mesolonghi. The military operations of the Greeks in continental Greece during the whole campaign of 1825 were conducted in the same desultory and feeble manner as in the Peloponnesus.

Goura was commissioned by the Greek government to enrol six thousand veteran soldiers. He assumed the chief command at Dystomo, where the troops under his orders drew daily eleven thousand six hundred rations, though their number hardly ever exceeded three thousand men.[1] A trade in provisions was openly carried on both by the officers and the soldiers. They sold their surplus rations to the families of the peasants, whom patriotism had induced to abandon their villages rather than submit to the Turks.

While the advanced-guard of the army of Eastern Greece skirmished with the Turks at Salona, a body of troops under Karaïskaki and Djavellas marched into Western Greece. Karaïskaki threw himself into the rear of Reshid's position. Djavellas forced his way into Mesolonghi on the 19th of August.[2] The summer was consumed in trifling skirmishes, in struggles for booty, or in contests of military rivalry. The country was laid waste, and truth compels the historian to record that the cultivators of the soil suffered quite as much from the rapacity of their countrymen

---

[1] Compare Tricoupi, iii. 219, with Captain Humphrey's Journal, p. 812.
[2] Gordon, II. 240, mentions that Djavellas entered Mesolonghi with only twenty-five men, yet he drew rations for one thousand.

who came to defend them, as from the Turks who came to plunder them.¹ The Turks occupied Salona until the 6th of November, when it is the immemorial custom of the Albanian and Turkish militia to return home, for the habits of the timariot system are still preserved.²

The victory which the garrison of Mesolonghi obtained over the besiegers on the 21st of September, convinced Reshid that he must think rather of defending his own position from the sorties of the Greeks than of prosecuting the siege. He had almost matured his plan when a vigorous sortie of the besieged, on the 13th of October, inflicted a severe loss on his army, and accelerated his retreat from the trenches. He immediately fortified the position which he had selected for his camp at the foot of Mount Zygos, and on the 17th of October withdrew the remains of his army to this new station. His cavalry enabled him to keep open his communications with Krioneri, where his supplies of provisions were usually landed. He now anxiously awaited the return of the capitan-pasha, and the reinforcements which Ibrahim Pasha was about to bring. But with all his vigour and ability, had the Greeks employed the superiority which they possessed at this time with skill, courage, and unanimity, his position might have been rendered untenable long before assistance could arrive. He had not now more than three thousand infantry and six hundred cavalry fit for service. The garrison of Mesolonghi was more numerous, and a considerable body of Greek troops under Karaïskaki and other captains had occupied

---

¹ The armatoli were truly ἄνδρες ἐφ' ἑαυτῶν ἐπιτάσσοντες τριάκοντα δρεπανηφόροι.
² The troops of the Othomans then took the field on St. George's Day (5th May), after the horses of the spahis had eaten their green barley, and broke up their camp to return home on St. Demetrius's Day (7th November), in order to superintend the cultivation of their property by their Christian tenants. It deserves notice that the spring is much later in Macedonia and Greece than in corresponding latitudes in Italy and Spain.

strong positions in his rear. Nothing but the irreconcilable jealousies of the Greek chieftains and their military ignorance, which prevented their executing any combined operations, saved Reshid's army from destruction. The pasha remained for a month in this dangerous situation, liable to be attacked by an overwhelming force at any moment, but determined to persist in his enterprise—to take Mesolonghi, or perish before its walls.

The Greeks amused themselves with destroying the works of the besiegers; but their confidence in their ultimate success was so great that they executed even this triumphant labour with extreme carelessness. They also committed a blamable oversight in not transporting to Mesolonghi a supply of grain which had been collected in magazines on the western coast of the Morea, consisting of the produce of the land-tax from the rich plains of Elis and Achaia. The sea was open, and these supplies might have been removed without difficulty.

The Othoman fleet returned to Patras on the 18th of November, saved Reshid's army from starvation, and furnished him some reinforcements and ample supplies of ammunition. The Greek fleet, which ought to have engaged the Othoman in the waters of Patras, did not reach the entrance of the gulf until the capitan-pasha had terminated the delicate operation of landing stores at Krioneri.

A series of naval engagements took place, in which the Turks succeeded in baffling the attempts of the Greeks to cut off their straggling ships and to capture their transports. Both parties boasted of their success. The capitan-pasha kept open his communications with Patras and Krioneri. Miaoulis threw supplies into Mesolonghi, and kept open its communications with the Ionian Islands. The real victory remained with the Turks; their fleet kept its station at Patras. The Greek fleet quitted the waters of Mesolonghi on the 4th December 1825, and returned to Hydra.

A new and more formidable enemy now appeared before Mesolonghi. The campaign in the Peloponnesus had proved that neither the courage of the armatoli nor the stratagems of the klephts were a match for the discipline and tactics of the Egyptians; and Ibrahim now advanced to attack the brave garrison of Mesolonghi, confident of success. He encountered no opposition in his march from Navarin to Patras. The pass of Kleidi was left unguarded, and he captured large magazines of grain which the collectors of the tenths had stored at Agoulinitza, Pyrgos, and Gastouni, and which ought either to have been previously transported to Mesolonghi or now destroyed. These supplies proved of great use to Ibrahim's army during the siege.[1]

On the 29th of November a council of war was held by the Othoman pashas at Lepanto, to settle the plan of their operations. The capitan-pasha, Ibrahim, Reshid, and Yussuf were present, and they engaged mutually to support one another as much as lay in their power, to act always with unanimity, and to prosecute the siege with vigour. They kept their promises better than the Greek chiefs usually kept theirs. Yussuf at this meeting pointed out the measures which had enabled him to defend Patras for nearly five years. He soon after quitted Greece, being raised to the rank of pasha of Magnesia as a reward for his prudence and valour.[2]

The month of December was employed by Ibrahim in forming magazines at Krioneri, and bringing up ammunition to his camp before Mesolonghi. Heavy

---

[1] Phrantzes, ii. 358, note.
[2] Gordon, ii. 244. Tricoupi, iii. 325.

rains rendered it impossible to work at the trenches. The whole plain, from the walls of the town to the banks of the Fidari, was under water, or formed a wide expanse of mud and marsh. The Egyptian soldiers laboured indefatigably, and the order which prevailed in their camp astonished Reshid, who was said to have felt some irritation when he found that Ibrahim never asked him for any assistance or advice, but carried on his own operations with unceasing activity and perfect independence. A horrid act of cruelty, perpetrated by Reshid, was ascribed to an explosion of his suppressed rage. A priest, two women, and three boys, were impaled by his order before the walls of Mesolonghi, because they had conveyed intelligence to their relatives in the besieged town.[1]

The Greek government became at last sensible that it had too long neglected the defence of Mesolonghi. It had often announced that Reshid was about to raise the siege, and, believing its own sayings, it had neglected to do anything to force him to retreat. It now learned with surprise that Reshid's camp was well supplied with provisions; that the garrison of Mesolonghi was in want of ammunition; and that the Greek troops sent to cut off the supplies of the Turks were in danger of starvation. An attempt was made to raise money by selling national lands; but as these lands were already mortgaged to the English bondholders, and the sale of national lands was expressly prohibited by national assemblies, the bad faith of the members of the government was too apparent for Greeks to part with their money on such security. The conduct of the members of the executive body

---

[1] Gordon, ii. 253, and Tricoupi, iii. 331, both say that several children suffered. They were boys above twelve years of age. Children under that age would have been compelled to embrace Mohammedanism. Reshid, who was religious as well as inhuman, would have seized the opportunity of making forced converts had the law of Mohammed allowed it.

was in this case both impolitic and dishonest. It proved that they were dishonourable enough to violate every national engagement, and so incapable that they made a display of their bad faith without any profit. A sum sufficient to enable a Greek fleet to put to sea was soon raised by private subscription. Individual patriotism has generally displayed itself on every emergency in Greece, when not thwarted by the action of the government. Many Greeks who were not wealthy subscribed largely; ministers of state, shipowners, chieftains, and officials, who had enriched themselves with the produce of the English loans, or by farming taxes, endeavoured to conceal their wealth by their illiberality.[1]

The sums collected equipped twenty Hydriot and four Psarian ships. On the 21st of January 1826 these vessels, reinforced by three Spetziot brigs which had remained in the waters of Mesolonghi, forced the Turkish cruisers to retire under the guns of Patras, and enabled the besieged to communicate directly with the Ionian Islands, and lay in stores of provisions and ammunition for two months. The crews of the Greek ships were only paid in advance for a single month. The spirit of patriotism was not then powerful in the Albanian islands; and the Hydriot sailors, in order to escape being obliged to give their services to their country for a single hour gratuitously, sailed from

[1] Dr Howe, the well-known philanthropist of Boston, Mass., who was present, records the manner in which the people expressed their feelings when Professor Gennadios addressed an appeal to their patriotism at a public meeting in the square of Nauplia (*Historical Sketch of the Greek Revolution*, p. 329):—"Gennadios threw down his purse. 'There is my all; I give it to my country as freely as I would to my child. I am ready to serve in any occupation for a year, and pay the whole salary I receive into the public treasury.' The crowd was moved to tears. Many voices were raised offering money. The public excitement forced the chiefs and rich men to come forward, though unwillingly, and a scornful laugh was raised as their names were called out." Compare the vauntings of Tricoupi, iii. 332. The letter of the President soliciting subscriptions is given in the Hydriot newspaper, 'Ο Φίλος τοῦ Νόμου, December 14 (26), 1825.

Mesolonghi, after remaining in its waters only a fortnight.[1]

Three weeks after the departure of the Greek ships, Ibrahim commenced active operations. On the 25th of February he opened his fire from batteries mounting forty pieces of artillery, and on the 27th and 28th two unsuccessful attempts were made to storm the walls by the united forces of the Turks and Egyptians. The gallant resistance of the besieged convinced Ibrahim that it would cost too much to take the place by storm, unless he could attack it by sea as well as by land. He soon launched a flotilla of thirty-two flat-bottomed boats, and obtained the complete command of the lagoon. Vasiladi, the fort which commanded the entrance of the lagoon which leads from the sea directly to the town, was taken by storm on the 9th of March 1826, and Anatolikon capitulated on the 13th.

The Greeks now perceived that the progress of the besiegers, although not very rapid, would soon render the place untenable. The supplies of provisions received in January, added to what was then in the public magazines, ought to have furnished abundant rations to the whole population until the end of April; but these stores were wasted by the rapacity of the soldiery.[2] Ibrahim and Reshid contrived to be well informed of everything that was said or done within the walls of Mesolonghi, and they learned with pleasure that watchfulness and patience would soon force the Greeks to surrender the place or to die of hunger.

The moment appeared favourable for offering a cap-

---

[1] It is curious to read the accounts which were given of the deplorable condition of the Egyptians and Turks before Mesolonghi at this time in the Greek newspapers, and in the MS. journals of Philhellenes. The Arab regulars of Ibrahim's army in particular were supposed to be then enduring a series of calamities which would exterminate them in a few weeks.

[2] Gordon, ii. 267, states this in his usual candid manner:—"We have one reproach to address to the Suliot chiefs, and particularly to Nothi Botsares; it is, that, whenever things wore a favourable aspect, they did not bridle their incurable improvidence and love of peculation."

itulation, but the besieged rejected all negotiation with disdain. Sir Frederic Adam, the Lord High Commissioner in the Ionian Islands, convinced that the loss of Vasiladi and Anatolikon rendered the fall of Mesolonghi inevitable, endeavoured to prevent farther bloodshed. He visited Krioneri in a British ship-of-war, and offered his mediation. But the two pashas were now sure of their prey, and as the Greeks refused to treat of a capitulation directly with their enemies, Sir Frederic was obliged to retire without effecting anything—an example of the folly of too much zeal in other people's business. As soon as he was gone, Ibrahim and Reshid sent a written summons to the garrison, pretending that the Greeks had expressed a wish to negotiate terms of capitulation. They offered to allow all the Greek troops to quit Mesolonghi on laying down their arms, and they engaged to permit the inhabitants who desired to leave the town to depart with the garrison; but they declared also, that all those who wished to remain should be allowed to retain possession of their property, and should enjoy ample protection for themselves and their families. To this summons the Greeks replied, that they had never expressed any wish to capitulate; that they were determined to defend Mesolonghi to the last drop of their blood; that if the pashas wanted their arms they might come to take them; and that they remitted the issue of the combat to the will of God.[1]

The only post in the lagoon of which the Greeks held possession, was the small islet of Klissova, about a mile from Mesolonghi, to the south-east. This post was defended by a hundred and fifty men under Kitzo Djavellas. The Greeks were advantageously posted,

[1] The summons was dated the 2d of April 1826. Both it and the reply of the Greeks are curious and characteristic documents. They are printed by Tricoupi, iii. 401, 402.

and protected by a low rampart of earth from the artillery of their assailants; while a low chapel, with an arched roof of stone, served them as a magazine and citadel. On the 6th of April the Albanians of Reshid attacked Klissova. The shallow water prevented even the flat-bottomed boats of the Turks from approaching close to the shore, so that the attacking party was compelled to jump into the sea and wade forward through the deep mud. While the gunboats fired showers of grape, the Greeks kept themselves hid under their earthen rampart; but as soon as the Albanians were in the water, they rose on their knees, and, resting their long guns on the parapet, poured such a well-directed volley on their enemies, that the foremost fell dead or wounded, and the rest recoiled in fear. Several officers were standing up in the boats directing the landing: they offered a conspicuous mark to the best shots among the Greeks, and most of them fell mortally wounded. The Albanians retired in confusion.

Ibrahim then ordered his regular troops to renew the attack. The result was similar; but the Egyptians were led back a second time to the attack, and again retreated under the deadly fire of the Greeks. Seeing the advantage which the defenders of Klissova derived from their position, Ibrahim ought to have abandoned the assault and kept the islet closely blockaded until he could bring up a few mortars. But he was eager to prove that his regulars were superior to the Albanians of Reshid. He therefore ordered Hussein, the conqueror of Kasos, Sphakteria, and Vasiladi, to make a third attack. Hussein led his men bravely on, but as he stood up in his boat giving orders concerning the formation of the storming parties, he was struck by a musket-ball, and fell down mortally wounded. The steady fire of the Greeks prevented the regulars from completing their formation. The men turned and scrambled back into the boats in complete disorder. After this repulse the pashas drew off their troops. Five hundred men were killed or wounded in this vain attempt to storm a sandbank defended by a hundred and fifty good marksmen.

The victory of Klissova was the last success of the Greeks during the siege of Mesolonghi. Provisions began to fail, and rations ceased to be distributed to any but the men who performed service. Yet as relief by sea was hourly expected, the garrison remained firm. At last the Greek fleet made its appearance, but the hope it inspired was soon disappointed. The Turks were in possession of the lagoon, and Miaoulis arrived without any flat-bottomed boats to enable him to penetrate to Mesolonghi. A feeble attempt was made by the Hydriots on the 13th of April to penetrate into the lagoon by the channel of Petala; but it was easily repulsed, and never renewed. The naval skill of the Greeks no longer insured them the command of the sea, nor did they now possess the heroic enterprise which they had often displayed during the first years of the Revolution. They had refused to adopt any scientific improvements either in their ships or their artillery; the Turks had done both. Miaoulis entered the waters of Mesolonghi with the same ships as those with which he had combated Kara Ali; the Turkish fleet, which stood out of the Gulf of Lepanto to engage him, was very different in construction and armament from the fleets that sailed from Constantinople in 1821 and 1822. The Turks kept their line of battle, and held their position to windward of the Greeks, exchanging broadsides, and frustrating all the manœuvres of their enemy to bring on a general action or cut off straggling ships.

On the 15th of April Miaoulis found that the Turks had completely closed the communication with the lagoon, and held their position between him and the shore. He attempted to throw their line into confusion by sending down a fire-ship on two frigates; but the exposed vessels tacked, kept the weather-gage, and allowed the blazing brulot to drift away to leeward and consume itself ineffectually. Fire-ships had ceased to be a terror to the Turks. The Greek fleet at this time consisted of only thirty sail, and the Turkish of sixty; but at the commencement of the war this disparity would have hardly enabled the Othomans to keep the sea. It now insured them a decided victory. Miaoulis, baffled and cut off from all communication with the besieged, was driven out to sea, and the besieged town was abandoned to its fate. The glory of the Greek navy was tarnished by the tameness with which it declined to close with the enemy, and retreated without an effort to emulate the heroism of the defenders of Mesolonghi.

When the Greek fleet departed, the magazines of Mesolonghi did not contain rations for more than two days. The garrison had now to choose whether it would perish by starvation, capitulate, or cut its way through the besiegers. It resolved to face every danger rather than surrender. The inhabitants who were unable to bear arms, the women, and the children, showed as much patience and courage in this dreadful situation as the veteran soldiers hardened in Turkish warfare. A spirit of Greek heroism, rare in the Greek Revolution—rare even in the history of mankind—pervaded every breast. After deliberate consultation in a numerous assembly, it was resolved to force a passage for the whole population through the besiegers. Many would perish, some might escape; but those who fell and those who escaped would be alike free. The plan adopted for evacuating the town was well devised; but its success was marred by several accidents.

About sunset on the 22d of April 1826 a discharge of musketry was heard by the besieged on the ridge of Zygos. This was a concerted signal to inform the chiefs in Mesolonghi that a body of fifteen hundred armatoli, detached from the camp of Karaiskaki at Platanos, was ready to attack the rear of the Turks and aid the sortie of the besieged. The garrison was mustered in three divisions. Bridges were thrown across the ditch, and breaches were opened in the walls. There were still nine thousand persons in the town, of whom only three thousand were capable of bearing arms. Nearly two thousand men, women, and children were so feeble from age, disease, or starvation, that they were unable to join the sortie. Some of the relations of these helpless individuals voluntarily remained to share their fate. The non-combatants, who were to join the sortie, were drawn up in several bodies, according to the quarters in which they resided, or the chiefs under whose escort they were to march. The Mesolonghiots formed themselves into a separate band. They were less attenuated by fatigue than the rest; but being collected from every quarter of the town, their band was less orderly than the emigrants from the country, who had been disciplined by privation, and accustomed to live and act together during the siege. Most of the women who took part in the sortie dressed themselves in the fustinello, like the Albanians and armatoli, and carried arms like soldiers; most of the children had also loaded pistols in their belts, which many had already learned how to use.

At nine o'clock the bridges were placed in the ditch without noise, and a thousand soldiers crossed and ranged themselves along the covered way. Unfortunately a deserter had informed Ibrahim of the projected sortie, and both he and Reshid, though they gave little credit to the information that the whole population would attempt to escape, adopted every precaution to repulse any sortie of the garrison. When the non-combatants began to cross the bridges the noise revealed to the Turks the positions in which crowds were assembled, and on these points they opened a terrific fire. Crowds rushed forward to escape the shot. The shrieks of the wounded and the splash of those who were forced from the bridges were unnoticed; and in spite of the enemy's fire the greater part of the inhabitants crossed the ditch in tolerable order. The Mesolonghiots still lingered behind, retarded by their interests and their feelings. It was no easy sacrifice to quit their property and their relations. For a considerable time the garrison waited patiently for them under a heavy fire. At last the first body of the Mesolonghiots crossed the ditch, and then the troops sprang forward with a loud shout and rushed sword in hand on the Turks.

Never was a charge made more valiantly. The eastern division of the garrison, under Nothi Botzares, struggled forward to gain the road to Bochori; the central division, under Kitzos Djavellas, pushed straight through the enemy's lines towards the hills; and the western division, under Makry, strove to gain the road to the Kleisura. All three intended, when clear of the Turks, to effect a junction on the slopes of Zygos, where the road ascends to the monastery of St Simeon.

Almost at the moment when the garrison rushed on the Turks, that portion of the Mesolonghiots which was then on the bridges raised a cry of "back, back." Great part of the Mesolonghiots stopped, fell back, and returned into the town with the military escort which ought to have formed the rearguard of the sortie. The origin of this ill-timed cry, which weakened the force of the sortie and added to the victims in the place, has excited much unnecessary speculation. It evidently rose among those who were in danger of being forced into the ditch. It was repeated so loudly that it created a panic.

The three leading divisions bore down all opposition. Neither the yataghan of Reshid's Albanians, nor the bayonet of Ibrahim's Arabs, could arrest their impetuous attack; and they forced their way through the labyrinth of trenches, dykes, and ditches, with comparatively little loss. Only some women and children, who could not keep up with the column as it rushed forward over the broken ground, were left behind. But for the information which had been given by the traitor, the greater part of the defenders of Mesolonghi would have escaped. In consequence of that information, Ibrahim and Reshid had taken the precaution to send bodies of cavalry to watch the roads leading to Bochori, St Simeon, and Kleisura. The horsemen fell in with Greek columns when they were about a mile beyond the Turkish lines, and were beginning to feel secure. The division of Makry was completely broken by the first charge of the cavalry. The others were thrown into confusion. All suffered severely, yet small bands of the garrison still kept together, and, by keeping up a continuous fire, enabled numbers of women and children to rally under their protection. At last the scattered remnants of the three divisions began to recover some order on reaching the slopes of Zygos, where the irregularities of the ground forced the cavalry to slacken the pursuit.

The fugitives prepared to enjoy a short rest, and endeavoured to assemble the stragglers who had eluded the swords of the horsemen. They thought that the fire they had kept up against the cavalry would draw down the fifteen hundred men of Karaïskaki's corps to

their assistance. While they were thus engaged in A.D. 1826.
giving and expecting succour, a body of Albanians,
placed in ambuscade by Reshid to watch the road to
the monastery of St Simeon, crept to their vicinity un-
perceived, and poured a deadly volley into their ranks.
Instead of friends to assist them, they had to encounter
one thousand mountaineers, well posted, to bar their
progress. The Greeks, surprised by unseen enemies,
could do nothing but get out of the range of the rifles
of the Albanians as far as possible. The Albanians followed and tracked them in order to secure their heads,
for which the pashas had promised a high price. The loss
of the Greeks was greater at the foot of the hills, where
their own troops ought to have insured their safety,
than it had been in forcing the enemy's lines and in
resisting the charges of the cavalry. Most of the
women and children who had dragged themselves thus
far, were so exhausted that they were taken prisoners.

About midnight small parties of the garrison of
Mesolonghi, and a few women and children, succeeded
in reaching the post occupied by the Greek troops;
but instead of fifteen hundred men they found only
fifty, and only a very small supply of provisions to
relieve their wants. Here they learned also, with dismay, that the camp at Platanos was a prey to the
ordinary dissensions and abuses which disgraced the
military classes of Greece at this period. The weary
fugitives, in order to escape starvation, were soon compelled to continue their march to Platanos. Even there
they obtained very little assistance from the chiefs of
the armatoli; and when they had rested about a week,
they resumed their journey to Salona. Many perished
from wounds, disease, and hunger on the road. About
fifteen hundred reached Salona during the month of
May, straggling thither generally in small bands, and
often by very circuitous roads, which they had followed

in order to procure food. Of these about thirteen hundred were soldiers; there were several girls in the number of those who escaped, and a few boys under twelve years of age.

As soon as Ibrahim and Reshid found that the greater part of the garrison had evacuated Mesolonghi, they ordered a general assault. Their troops occupied the whole line of the walls without encountering resistance. The Greek soldiers whom wounds or disease had prevented from marching, had established themselves in different buildings. The party which occupied the principal powder-magazine, when surrounded by the Turks, and summoned to surrender, set fire to the powder and perished in the explosion.

It was not until morning dawned that the Turkish officers allowed their men to advance into the interior of the town, though several houses near the walls had been set on fire during the night. A whole day was spent by the conquerors in plundering Mesolonghi. A second powder-magazine was exploded by its defenders, who perished with their assailants. A windmill, which served as a central depot of ammunition, was defended until the 24th of April, when its little garrison, having exhausted their provisions, set fire to the powder, preferring death to captivity.

The loss of the Greeks amounted to four thousand. Ibrahim boasted that the Turks had collected three thousand heads; and it is probable that at least one thousand perished from wounds and starvation beyond the limits which the besiegers examined. The nearest points where the fugitives could find security and rest, were Petala, Kalamos, and Salona. The conquerors took about three thousand prisoners, chiefly women and children. About two thousand escaped; for besides those who reached Salona, a few found refuge in the villages of Etolia, and some of the inhabitants of

Mesolonghi and of the surrounding country evaded the Turkish pursuit by wading into the lagoon, and ultimately reached Petala and Kalamos, where they received protection and rations from the British government.

Many deeds of heroism might be recorded. One example deserves to be selected. The Moreot primates have been justly stigmatised as a kind of Christian Turks; and, as a class, their conduct during the Greek Revolution was marked by ambition and selfishness. Yet a Moreot primate displayed a noble example of the purest patriotism at the fall of Mesolonghi. Papadiamantopulos of Patras, a leading Hetairist, was one of the members of the executive commission intrusted with the administration of Western Greece. In the month of February he visited Zante to hasten the departure of supplies. His friends there urged him to remain. They said that as he was not a soldier he could assist in prolonging the defence of Mesolonghi more effectually by remaining at Zante, to avail himself of every opportunity of sending over supplies, than by serving in the besieged town. But the noble old gentleman silenced every entreaty by the simple observation: " I invited my countrymen to take up arms against the Turks, and I swore to live and die with them. This is the hour to keep my promise." He returned to Mesolonghi, and died the death of a hero in the final sortie.[1]

The conduct of the defenders of Mesolonghi will awaken the sympathies of freemen in every country as long as Grecian history endures. The siege rivals that of Platæa in the energy and constancy of the besieged; it wants only a historian like Thucydides to secure for it a like immortality of fame.

[1] Gordon, L 206, and Tricoupi, iii. 356, both mention the conduct of Papadiamantopulos with just praise.

CHAPTER III.

THE SIEGE OF ATHENS.

"August Athens! where,
Where are thy men of might, thy grand in soul?"

IBRAHIM'S OPERATIONS IN THE MOREA DURING 1826—RESHID'S OPERATIONS IN CONTINENTAL GREECE—COMMENCEMENT OF THE SIEGE OF ATHENS, AND BATTLE OF KHAIDARI—DEATH OF GOURA—GRIGIOTTES THROWS HIMSELF INTO THE ACROPOLIS—KARAISKAKI'S OPERATIONS TO RAISE THE SIEGE—FABVIER THROWS HIMSELF INTO THE ACROPOLIS—STATE OF GREECE DURING THE WINTER 1826-27—EXPEDITIONS FOR THE RELIEF OF ATHENS UNDER GORDON, BURBAKI, AND HEIDECK—GENERAL SIR RICHARD CHURCH—LORD COCHRANE (EARL OF DUNDONALD)—ELECTION OF COUNT CAPODISTRIAS TO BE PRESIDENT OF GREECE—NAVAL EXPEDITION UNDER CAPTAIN HASTINGS—GREEK TRADERS SUPPLY RESHID'S ARMY WITH PROVISIONS—OPERATIONS OF CHURCH AND COCHRANE BEFORE ATHENS—MASSACRE OF THE GARRISON OF THE MONASTERY OF ST SPIRIDION—KARAISKAKI'S DEATH—DEFEAT OF SIR RICHARD CHURCH AT THE PHALERUM—EVACUATION OF THE ACROPOLIS—CONDUCT OF PHILHELLENES IN GREECE, ENGLAND, AND AMERICA—LORD COCHRANE'S NAVAL REVIEW AT POROS—SUFFERINGS OF THE GREEKS—ASSISTANCE SENT FROM THE UNITED STATES.

AFTER the conquest of Mesolonghi, the Othoman fleet returned to Constantinople, and the Egyptian to Alexandria. The Greeks, with their reduced naval strength, were therefore again left masters of the sea.

Ibrahim Pasha returned to the Morea in order to complete the conquest of his own pashalik. After reviewing his troops at Patras, he found himself compelled to open the campaign of 1826 at the head of only four thousand infantry and six hundred cavalry. With this insignificant army he marched against the Greeks, laid waste the fields of that part of the population of Achaia which had not submitted to his authority, and drove the inhabitants into the inaccessible regions of Mount Chelmos, where the snow still lay thick on the ground. During this foray he captured many prisoners, and carried off large herds of cattle and innumerable flocks of sheep.

A small detachment was sent to reconnoitre the monastery of Megaspelaion; but at this time no attack was made on it. The monks imagined a miracle. They recounted that a high wall stood up before the Egyptian troops, and closed the road by which they endeavoured to reach the holy building. Terrified by this proof that God opposed their undertaking, they marched back to Kalavryta.[1]

From Kalavryta Ibrahim marched to Tripolitza. Near Karitena he was joined by considerable reinforcements from Modon. The summer was employed in a series of expeditions for laying waste the country and starving the population into submission. The crops being generally ready for the sickle, or already reaped, were either destroyed or carried off. Great quantities of grain were burned, and great quantities were transported to Tripolitza. From the 15th of May to the 14th of November 1826 the Egyptian troops carried on the work of destruction almost without interruption. Achaia, Elis, Arcadia, Messenia, and Laconia were devastated, villages were burned to the ground, cattle were driven away, and the inhabitants, when captured, were either shot or sold as slaves. The desolation produced was so complete, that during the following winter numbers of the peasantry, particularly women and children, died of actual starvation.

---

[1] The ecclesiastic Phrantzes boasts of his own belief in this miracle, which took place on the 7th May 1826. On the 6th July 1827, Ibrahim reconnoitred the monastery in person, and made an attack on it. The monks were prepared, and the monastery was garrisoned by Greek troops, who repulsed the attack, which Ibrahim did not renew. The monks were generally suspected of having entered into a secret arrangement with the Egyptian pasha, but Phrantzes assures us that this was not the case.—Phrantzes, ii. 441, note 1, and 495.

During the summer Ibrahim made two attempts to penetrate into Maina—the first from the pass of Armyros on the west side, the other from Marathonesi on the east coast. Both were repulsed by the Maniats, who availed themselves of the natural difficulties which the precipitous gorges of Mount Taygetus offer to the advance of an invader.

The military operations of Kolokotrones and the other Peloponnesian chiefs were conducted without union, vigour, or judgment. An abortive attempt had been made to surprise Tripolitza, while Ibrahim was absent besieging Mesolonghi.[1] After Ibrahim returned to the Morea, the faculties of Kolokotrones appeared to have been paralysed. The only success he obtained was carrying off a few mules from the Egyptian convoys, and recovering a small portion of the booty taken from the peasantry, which he employed to feed his own followers.

At the end of the year Ibrahim found his troops so worn out by fatigue and disease, that he was compelled to suspend his operations until he received fresh reinforcements from Egypt.[2] Mohammed Ali showed some hesitation in prosecuting the war against the Greeks at this time. He was watching the progress of the negotiations between the sultan and the courts of Great Britain and Russia, and he wished to learn whether his son would be allowed to complete the conquest of the Morea, and retain permanent possession of it, before expending more money in the undertaking.

In the mean time Reshid Pasha laboured strenuously to re-establish the sultan's authority in continental

---

[1] See a boasting extract from a despatch of Kolokotrones in Fabvier, *Histoire du Siège de Mesolonghi*, 331. The disorder that prevailed in the Greek armies is well described in the graphic dialect of the old klepht, as reported in Αρτγροτι Συμβάντων τῆς Ἑλληνικῆς Φυλῆς, Ἀθῆν., 1846.

[2] See the plan of campaign proposed by Sir C. Napier in Appendix.

Greece. His road to fame and power lay in his absolute devotion to Sultan Mahmud's interests, and his faithful execution of the orders he received from the Porte.

A. D. 1826.

During the month of June 1826 he fixed his headquarters at Mesolonghi, and many of the Greek chieftains submitted to him, and publicly recognised the sultan's authority. Rhangos, Siphakas, Dyovuniattes, Kontoyannes, and Andreas Iskos all owned allegiance to the Porte, accepted the rank of captains of armatoli, and forgot the heroism of the defenders of Mesolonghi.

As soon as the affairs of Western Greece were settled on a footing that promised at least a temporary security for the restoration of order, Reshid marched into Eastern Greece, occupied the passes over Œta, Knemis, Parnassus, and Parnes, strengthened the garrison of Thebes, and organised regular communications by land between Larissa and Chalcis in Euboea. He entered Attica before the crops of 1826 were gathered in.

The exactions of Goura had exceeded those of Odysseus, for Odysseus, like his patron, Ali of Joannina, allowed no extortions but his own, while Goura permitted his mercenaries to glean after the harvest of his own rapacity had been gathered in. A great proportion of the Attic peasantry was driven to despair, and the moment Reshid's forces appeared in the Ratadema, or hilly district between Parnes and the channel of Euboea, they were welcomed as deliverers. On advancing into the plain of Athens, they were openly joined by the warlike inhabitants of Menidhi and Khasia, who vigorously supported Reshid's government as long as he remained in Attica.

The contributions which Goura levied under the pretext of preparing for the defence of Attica were exclusively employed for provisioning the Acropolis, and in garrisoning that stronghold with four hundred chosen mercenaries in his own pay. These men were selected from those whom the civil war in the Morea had inured to acts of tyranny, and they were taught to look to Goura and not to the Greek government for pay and promotion. The citizens of Athens were not allowed to form part of the garrison of their own citadel.

The Turks took possession of Sepolia, Patissia, and Ambelokepos without encountering serious opposition. On the 28th of June, Reshid arrived from Thebes, and established his headquarters at Patissia. His army did not exceed seven thousand men, but his cavalry, which amounted to eight hundred, were in a high state of efficiency, and he had a fine train of artillery, consisting of twenty-six guns and mortars. The siege of Athens was immediately commenced. The hill of the Museion was occupied, and batteries were erected at the little chapel of St Demetrius, and on the level above the Pnyx.

He soon obtained a brilliant victory over the Greeks. About four thousand armatoli had been concentrated at Eleusis. The Greek chiefs who commanded this army proposed to force their way into the town of Athens, and expected to be able to maintain themselves in the houses. Reshid divined their object, and forestalled them in its execution. On the night of the 14th of August he stormed the town, and drove the Athenians into the Acropolis, into which Goura could not refuse to admit them.

The Greek troops persisted in advancing from Eleusis, though they seem to have formed no definite plan. Their numbers were insufficient to hold out any reasonable probability of their being able to recover possession of Athens. The irregulars amounted to two

thousand five hundred under the command of Karaïs- A.D. 1826.
kaki, the regulars to one thousand five hundred under
Fabvier. The Greek force crossed the mountains by
a pathway which leaves the Sacred Way and the
monastery of Daphne to the right, and took up a
position at a farmhouse with a small tower called
Khaïdari. Instead of pushing on to the Olive Grove,
and stationing themselves among the vineyards, where
the Turkish cavalry and artillery would have been
useless, they awaited Reshid at Khaïdari. On the 20th
of August the attack was made, and the Greeks were
completely defeated. The two leaders endeavoured to
throw the whole blame of the disaster on one another,
and they succeeded in convincing everybody who paid
any attention to their proceedings that both of them
had displayed great want of judgment. Nobody suspected either of them of want of personal energy and
daring, but both were notoriously deficient in temper
and prudence.[1]

Karaïskaki soon regained his reputation with his
own soldiers, by sending a large body on a successful
foray to Skourta, where they captured a numerous
herd of cattle destined for the use of the Turkish
army.

Fabvier withdrew his corps to Salamis.

Reshid bombarded the Acropolis hotly for some
time, but seeing that his fire did the besieged little
injury, he attempted to take the place by mining.
Though he made little progress even with his mines,
he persisted in carrying on his operations with his
characteristic perseverance.

A body of Greek troops, consisting of Ionians and
Romeliots, made two unsuccessful attempts to relieve
the besieged. The summer dragged on without anything

---

[1] The best account of this affair is by Friedrich Müller, *Denkwürdigkeiten aus Griechenland*, 17. See also Gordon, ii. 336.

decisive, when the death of Goura drew public attention to the dangerous position of the garrison and the neglect of the Greek government. The soldiers in the Acropolis manifested a mutinous spirit in consequence of the ineffectual efforts made to relieve them. Many succeeded in deserting during the night, by creeping unobserved through the Turkish lines. To prevent these desertions Goura passed the night among the soldiers on guard, and in order to secure the assistance of the enemy in preventing the escape of his men, he generally brought on a skirmish which put them on the alert. On the 13th of October, while exchanging shots with the Turkish sentinels, he was shot through the brain. His opponent had watched the flash of the powder in the touch-hole of Goura's rifle.[1]

A cry of indignation at the incapacity and negligence of the members of the Greek government was now raised both in Greece and the Ionian Islands. Greece had still a numerous body of men under arms in continental Greece, yet these troops were inactive spectators of the siege of Athens. General Gordon, who had recently returned to Greece, records the general opinion when he states that these troops were condemned to inaction by the bickerings of their leaders.[2] Some attempts were at last made to interrupt Reshid's operations. Fabvier advanced into Bœotia with the intention of storming Thebes; but being deserted by his soldiers, he was compelled to fall back without attempting anything. Reshid, who was well informed of every movement made by the Greeks

---

[1] Sourmeles, 164; Tricoupi, iv. 74. Goura's widow was killed, with ten female companions and attendants, three months later, by the roof of the Erechtheion falling in. The Athenian historian Sourmeles says that she was already betrothed to Grigiottes, by the persuasion of her intriguing brother Anastasios Loidorikes, who had induced her to lay aside her widow's weeds. He exclaims, 'Ἰδοὺ ἀπιστία γυναικὸς καὶ ἀπαιδεία, p. 189.

[2] Gordon, ii. 313.

through the Attic peasants who acted as his scouts, sent forward a body of cavalry, which very nearly succeeded in occupying the passes of Cithæron and cutting off Fabvier's retreat to Megara. On his return, Fabvier was left by the Greek government without provisions; and attempts being made in the name of Karaïskaki and Niketas, perhaps without their authority, to induce his men to desert, he found himself obliged to withdraw the regular corps to Methana in order to prevent its dissolution.[1]

Karaïskaki advanced a second time to Khaïdari. This movement enabled Grigiottes to land unobserved in the Bay of Phalerum, near the mouth of the Cephissus, and to march up to the Acropolis, into which he introduced himself and four hundred and fifty men without loss.

As Athens was now safe for some time, Karaïskaki moved off to Mount Helicon, where a few of the inhabitants still remained faithful to their country's cause. He expected to succeed in capturing some of the Turkish magazines in Bœotia, and in intercepting the supplies which Reshid drew from Thessaly by the way of Zeituni.

The Acropolis was now garrisoned by about one thousand soldiers, but it was encumbered by the presence of upwards of four hundred women and children. The supply of wheat and barley was abundant, but the clothes of the soldiers were in rags, and there was no fuel to bake bread. Reshid, who determined to prosecute the siege during the winter, made arrangements for keeping his troops well supplied with provisions and military stores, and for defending the posts which protected his communications with Thessaly.

The Turks neglected to keep a naval squadron in the channel of Eubœa, though it would always have

[1] Friedrich Müller, 22.

found safe harbours at Negrepont and Volo. The Greeks were therefore enabled to transport a large force to attack any point in the rear of Reshid's army. It was in their power to cut off all the supplies he received by sea, and, by occupying some defensible station in the northern channel of Euboea, to establish communications with Karaïskaki's troops on Mount Helicon, and form a line of posts from this defensible station to another of a similar kind on the Gulf of Corinth. Talanta and Dobrena were the stations indicated. But instead of attempting to aid the army, the Greek navy either remained idle or engaged in piracy. Faction also prevented a great part of the Greek army from taking the field, and the assistance which the Philhellenic committee in Paris transmitted to Greece was employed by its agent, Dr Bailly, in feeding Kolokotrones's soldiers, who remained idle in the Morea, without marching either against the Egyptians or the Turks. Konduriottes and Kolokotrones, formerly the deadliest enemies, being now both excluded from a place in the executive government, were banded together in a most unpatriotic and dishonourable opposition to a weak but not ill-disposed government, composed of nearly a dozen members, many of whom were utterly unfit for political employment of any kind.[1] Some feeble attempts were made to organise attacks on Reshid's rear; but each leader was allowed to form an independent scheme of operations, and to abandon his enterprise when it suited his convenience.

[1] General Gordon, who served under this executive, thought more favourably of it than the author of this work, who watched its proceedings as a volunteer under Captain Hastings. The General says, "The president, Zaïmes, had considerable merit, and the government contained several men of fair talent and business-like habits," ii. 300. Their names were:—Zaïmes, president, Petrobey of Maina, A. Dellyannes, Tzamados, Hadji, Anargyros, Monarchides, Tricoupi, Vlachos, Zotos, Demetrakopolos. This government removed from Nauplia, where it fell too much under the control of the Moreot military faction, to Egina, on the 23d of November 1826.

The command of one expedition was intrusted to Kolettes, a man destitute both of physical and moral courage, though he looked a very truculent personage, and nourished a boundless ambition. The feeble government was anxious to prevent his allying himself with Konduriottes and Kolokotrones, and to effect that object he was placed at the head of a body of troops destined to destroy the magazines of the Turks in the northern channel of Eubœa. Nobody expected much from a military undertaking commanded by Kolettes, but the selfish members of the executive body, as usual, consulted their personal and party interests, and not their country's advantage, in making the nomination.

Kolettes collected the Olympian armatoli who had been living at free quarters in Skiathos, Skopelos, and Skyros for two years. The agents of the French Philhellenic committees supplied the expedition with provisions and military stores, and Kalergy, a wealthy Greek in Russia, paid a considerable sum of money into its military chest. Kolettes's troops landed near Talanti in order to gain possession of the magazines in that town, but the Turks, though much inferior in number, defeated them on the 20th November 1826. The armatoli escaped in the ships, and Kolettes abandoned his military career, and returned to the more congenial occupation of seeking importance by intriguing at Nauplia.

Karaïskaki about the same time began active operations at the head of three thousand of the best troops in Greece. Though he was compelled to render all his movements subordinate to the manner in which his troops could be supplied with provisions, he displayed both activity and judgment. His object was to throw his whole force on the rear of Reshid's army, master his line of communications, and destroy his magazines. The diversion, which it was expected would be made by Kolettes's expedition, would enable Karaïskaki's troops to draw supplies of provisions and ammunition from the channel of Euboea through Eastern Locris, as well as from Megara and the Gulf of Corinth. The victory of the Turks at Talanti occurring before the Greek troops had entered Phocis, Karaïskaki determined to cut off the retreat of Mustapha Bey, who had defeated Kolettes, and proposed falling back on Salona. Both Turks and Greeks were endeavouring to be first in gaining possession of the passes between Mounts Cirphis and Parnassus. Karaïskaki sent forward his advanced-guard with all speed to occupy Arachova, and his men had hardly established themselves in the village before they were attacked by a corps of fifteen hundred Mussulman Albanians. Mustapha Bey had united his force with that of Elmas Bey, whom Reshid had ordered to occupy Arachova and Budunitza, in order to secure his communications with Zeituni.

The beys endeavoured to drive the advanced-guard of the Greeks out of Arachova before the main body could arrive from Dystomo to its support, but their attacks were repulsed with loss. When Karaïskaki heard of the enemy's movements, he took his measures with promptitude and judgment. He occupied the Triodos with a strong body of men, to prevent the Albanians falling back on Livadea; and he sent another strong body over Mount Cirphis to take possession of Delphi, and prevent them from marching on to Salona. While the beys lingered in the hope of destroying the advanced-guard of the Greeks, they found themselves blockaded by a superior force. They were attacked, and lost the greater part of their baggage and provisions in the engagement. During the night after their defeat they made a bold attempt to escape to Salona by climbing the precipices of Parnassus, which the Greeks left unguarded. The darkness and their experience in ambuscades enabled them to move off from the vicinity of Arachova unobserved, but a heavy fall of snow surprised them as they were seeking paths up the rocks. At sunrise the Greeks followed them. Escape was impossible, for the only tracks over the precipices which the fugitives were endeavouring to ascend, were paths along which the shepherd follows his goats with difficulty, even in summer. They were all destroyed on the 6th of December. Their defence was valiant, but hopeless; quarter was neither asked nor given. Many were frozen to death, but three hundred, protected by the veil of falling snow, succeeded in climbing the precipices and reaching Salona. The heads of four boys were sent to Egina as a token of victory.

Karaïskaki was unable to follow up this success; want of provisions, more than the severity of the weather, kept his troops inactive. Reshid profited by this inaction to strengthen his posts at Livadea and Budunitza. Part of the Greek troops at last moved northward to plunder his convoys, while the rest spread over the whole country to obtain the means of subsistence which the Greek government neglected to supply. The Turks intrenched themselves at Daulis. Omer Pasha of Negrepont at last attacked the Greek camp at Dystomo, and this attack compelled Karaïskaki to return and recall the greater part of his troops. After many skirmishes the Turks made a general attack on the Greeks at Dystomo on the 12th of February 1827, which terminated in their defeat. But the country was now so completely exhausted that Karaïskaki was compelled to abandon his camp and fall back on Megara and Eleusis, where the presence of his army was deemed necessary to co-operate in a direct attack on Reshid's force before Athens.

After Goura's death, several officers in the Acropolis

pretended to equal authority. Grigiottes was the chief who possessed most personal influence. All measures were discussed in a council of chiefs, and instability of purpose was as much a characteristic of this small assembly of military leaders as it was of the Athenian Demos of old. One of the chiefs, Makriyannes, who distinguished himself greatly when Ibrahim attacked the mills at Lerna, was charged to pass the Turkish lines, in order to inform the Greek government that the supply of powder was exhausted, and that the garrison was so disheartened that succour must be sent without delay. Makriyannes quitted the Acropolis on the 29th November 1826, and reached Egina in safety. His appearance awakened the deepest interest. He had distinguished himself in many sorties during the siege, and he was then suffering from the wounds he had received. His frank and loyal character inspired general confidence. The members of the executive government again felt the necessity of immediate action.

Colonel Fabvier, who had brought the regular corps into some state of efficiency at Methana, was the only officer in Greece at this time capable of taking the field with a force on which the government could place any reliance. He was not personally a favourite with the members of the executive body. They feared and distrusted him, and he despised and distrusted them. Fortunately the news of Karaïskaki's victory at Arachova rendered him extremely eager for immediate action. The fame of his rival irritated his jealous disposition and excited his emulation. He therefore accepted the offer to command an expedition for the relief of Athens with pleasure, and prepared to carry succour to the Acropolis with his usual promptitude, and more than his usual prudence.

Fabvier landed with six hundred and fifty chosen men of the regular corps in the Bay of Phalerum, about midnight on the 12th December 1826.[1] Each man carried on his back a leather sack filled with gunpowder. The whole body reached the Turkish lines in good order and without being observed. They were formed in column on the road which leads from Athens to the Phalerum, a little below its junction with the road to Sunium, and rushed on the Turkish guard with fixed bayonets, while the drums sounded a loud signal to the garrison of the Acropolis to divert the attention of the besiegers by a desperate sortie. Fabvier cleared all before him, leading on his troops rapidly and silently over the space that separated the enemy's lines from the theatre of Herodes Atticus, under a shower of grape and musket-balls. To prevent his men from delaying their march, and exchanging shots with the Turks, Fabvier had ordered all the flints to be taken out of their muskets. A bright moon enabled the troops of Reshid to take aim at the Greeks, but the rapidity of Fabvier's movements carried his whole body within the walls of the Acropolis, with the loss of only six killed and fourteen wounded. In such enterprises, where the valour of the soldier and the activity of the leader were the only qualities wanted to insure success, Fabvier's personal conduct shone to the greatest advantage. His shortcomings were most manifest when patience and prudence were the qualities required in the general.

His men carried nothing with them into the Acropolis but their arms, and the powder on their backs. Even their greatcoats were left behind, for Fabvier proposed returning to the vessels which brought him on the ensuing night. The garrison of the Acropolis was sufficiently strong, and any addition to its numbers would only add to the difficulties of its defence by increasing the number of killed and wounded, and exhausting the provisions. Unfortunately, most of the

[1] Friedrich Müller, 25.

chiefs of the irregular troops wished to quit the place and leave the regular troops in their place, and they took effectual measures to prevent Fabvier's departure by skirmishing with the Turks, and putting them on the alert whenever he made an attempt to pass their lines. It is also asserted with confidence, by persons who had the best means of knowing the truth, and whose honour and sagacity are unimpeachable, that secret orders were transmitted from the executive government at Egina to Grigiottes, to prevent Fabvier from returning to Methana.[1] This unprincipled conduct of the Greek government and the military chiefs in the Acropolis caused great calamities to Greece, for Fabvier's presence hastened the fall of Athens, both by increasing the sufferings of the garrison, and by his eagerness to quit a fortress where he could gain no honour. After the nomination of Sir Richard Church as generalissimo of the Greek troops, Fabvier's impatience to quit the Acropolis and resume his separate command at Methana was immoderate; and Gordon asserts that, had only Greeks been in the Acropolis, it might have held out until the battle of Navarin saved Greece.

Greece fell into the chronic state of political anarchy during the latter part of the year 1826, which perpetuated the social demoralisation that continued visibly to influence her history during the remainder of her struggle for independence. The executive body, which retired from Nauplia to Egina in the month of November, was the legal government; but its members were numerous, selfish, and incapable, and far more intent on injuring their rivals in the Peloponnesus, who established a hostile executive at Kastri (Hermione), than on injuring the Turks who were besieging Athens.

[1] This accusation is repeated by Gordon, ii. 400, who was on terms of intimacy with several members of the government.

Kolokotrones, who was the leader of the faction at A.D. 1826.
Kastri, formed a coalition with his former enemy Konduriottes, and this unprincipled alliance endeavoured
to weaken the influence of the government at Egina,
by preventing Greece from profiting by the mediation
which Great Britain now proposed as the most effectual
means of saving the Greek people from ruin, and the
inhabitants of many provinces from extermination.

The Treaty of Akerman, concluded between Russia
and Turkey on the 6th of October 1826, put an end
to the hopes which the Greeks long cherished of seeing
Russia ultimately engaged in war with the sultan.
But this event rather revived than depressed the
Russian party in Greece, whose leading members believed that the emperor would now interfere actively
in thwarting the influence of England. At the same
time, the agents of the French Philhellenic committees
displayed a malevolent hostility to British policy, and
seized every opportunity of encouraging faction, by
distributing supplies to the troops of Kolokotrones,
who remained idle, and withholding them from those
of Karaiskaki, who were carrying on war against the
Turks in the field.[1]

The active strength both of the army and navy in
Greece began to diminish rapidly about this time. The
people in general lost all confidence in the talents and
the honesty both of their military and political leaders.
The bravest and most patriotic chiefs had fallen in
battle. Two names, however, still shed a bright light
through the mist of selfishness, Kanaris and Miaoulis,
and these two naval heroes belonged to adverse parties
and different nationalities. The Greek navy was unemployed. A small part of the army was in the field
against the Turks; the greater part was engaged in
collecting the national revenues, or extorting their

[1] Gordon, ii. 356.

subsistence from the unfortunate peasantry. The shipowners and sailors, who could no longer find profitable employment by serving against the Turks, engaged in an extensive and organised system of piracy against the ships of every Christian power, which was carried on with a degree of cruelty never exceeded in the annals of crime. The peasantry alone remained true to the cause of the nation, but they could do little more than display their perseverance by patient suffering, and never did a people suffer with greater constancy and fortitude. Many died of hunger rather than submit to the Turks, particularly in the Morea, where they feared lest Ibrahim should transport their families to Egypt, educate their boys as Mohammedans, and sell their girls into Mussulman harems.

The Philhellenic committees of Switzerland, France, and Germany redoubled their activity when the proceeds of the English loans were exhausted. Large supplies of provisions were sent to Greece, and assisted in maintaining the troops who took the field against the Turks, and in preventing many families in different parts of the country from perishing by starvation. The presence of several foreigners prevented the executive government at Egina from diverting these supplies to serve the ambitious schemes of its members, as shamelessly as Konduriottes's government had disposed of the English loans, or as Kolokotrones's faction at this very time employed such supplies as it could obtain. Colonel Heideck, who acted as the agent of the King of Bavaria; Dr Goss of Geneva, who represented the Swiss committees and Mr Eynard; Count Porro, a noble Milanese exile; and Mr Koering, an experienced German administrator,[1] set the Greeks an example of

---

[1] This singular man came to Greece with Dr Goss, who assisted him in escaping from the Continent on receiving his word of honour that he was not flying from any fear of criminal law: yet even Dr Goss never knew his real name. He was of great use to Dr Goss in organising the manner of distributing

prudence and good conduct by acting always in concord.

Two Philhellenes, General Gordon and Captain Frank Abney Hastings, had also some influence in preventing the executive government at Egina from completely neglecting the defence of Athens.

General Gordon returned to Greece at the invitation of the government with £15,000, saved from the proceeds of the second loan, which was placed at his absolute disposal. He was intimately acquainted with the military character and resources of both the belligerents. He spoke both Greek and Turkish with ease, and could even carry on a correspondence in the Turkish language. His *History of the Greek Revolution* is a work of such accuracy in detail, that it has served as one of the sources from which the principal Greek historian of the Revolution has compiled his narrative of most military operations.[1] Gordon was firm and sagacious, but he did not possess the activity and decision of character necessary to obtain commanding influence in council, or to initiate daring measures in the field.

Captain Hastings was probably the best foreign officer who embarked in the Greek cause. Though calm and patient in council, he was extremely rapid and bold in action. He brought to Greece the first steam-ship, which was armed with heavy guns for the use of shells and hot shot; and he was the first officer who habitually made use of these engines of war at

---

the stores sent by the various committees, and he displayed a degree of administrative experience, and an acquaintance with governmental business, which could hardly have been acquired by service in an inferior position. To wealth or rank, even to the ordinary comforts of life, he seemed to have resigned all claim. Though of some use to Capodistrias, he was neglected by that statesman, who feared him as a Liberal; and he died of fever during the president's administration.

[1] Compare Gordon's *History of the Greek Revolution*, 2 vols. 8vo, 1832, with Σ. Τρικούπη Ἱστορία τῆς Ἑλληνικῆς Ἐπαναστάσεως, 4 vols., 1853. Any portion of the military operations of the Turkish armies will afford proof.

sea. At this time he had brought his ship, the Karteria, into a high state of discipline.

Mr Gropius, the Austrian consul at Athens, who then resided at Egina, was also frequently consulted by individual members of the executive body. His long residence in the East had rendered him well acquainted with the character and views of the Greeks and Turks, but his long absence from Western Europe had prevented him from acquiring any profound political and administrative views.

Mavrocordatos and Tricoupi were generally the medium through which the opinions of the foreigners who have been mentioned were transmitted to the majority of the members of the executive body. Mavrocordatos possessed more administrative capacity than any of his countrymen connected with the government at Egina; but the errors into which he was led by his personal ambition and his phanariot education had greatly diminished his influence. Tricoupi was a man of eloquence, but of a commonplace mind, and destitute of the very elements of administrative knowledge. These two men served their country well at this time, by conveying to the government an echo of the reproaches which were loudly uttered, both at home and abroad, against its neglect; and they assisted in persuading it to devote all the resources it could command to new operations for the relief of Athens.

It has been already observed, that the simplest way of raising the siege of Athens was by interrupting Reshid's communications with his magazines in Thessaly. The Greeks could easily bring more men into the field than Reshid, and during the winter months they commanded the sea. An intelligent government, with an able general, might have compelled the army before Athens to have disbanded, or surrendered at discretion, even without a battle; for with six thousand men on Mount Parnassus, and a few ships in the northern and southern channels of Eubœa, no supplies, either of ammunition or provision, could have reached Reshid's army. The besiegers of Athens might also have been closely blockaded by a line of posts, extending from Megara to Eleutheræ, Phyle, Deceleia, and Rhamnus. This plan was rejected, and a number of desultory operations were undertaken, with the hope of obtaining the desired result more speedily.

The first of these ill-judged expeditions was placed under the command of General Gordon. Two thousand three hundred men and fifteen guns were landed on the night of the 5th February 1827, and took possession of the hill of Munychia. Thrasybulus had delivered Athens from the thirty tyrants by occupying this position, and the modern Greeks have a pedantic love for classical imitation.[1] In spite of this advantage, Reshid secured the command of the Piræus by preventing the Greeks from getting possession of the monastery of St Spiridion, and thus rendered the permanent occupation of Munychia utterly useless.

While Gordon was engaged in fortifying the desert rock on which he had perched his men, the attention of the Turks was drawn off by another body of Greeks. Colonel Burbaki, a Cephaloniot, who had distinguished himself as a cavalry officer in the French service, offered to head a diversion, for the purpose of enabling Gordon to complete his defences. Burbaki descended from the hills that bound the plain of Athens to the west, and advanced to Kamatero near Menidi. He was accompanied by eight hundred irregulars; and Vassos and Panayotaki Notaras, who were each at the head of a thousand men, were ordered to support him, and promised to do so. Burbaki was brave and enthu-

A.D. 1827.

[1] "Ὁ Θρασύβουλος κατελάβετο τὴν Μουνυχίαν ἄφρων ἱππομενεὶ πέφυσει."—Diodorus, xiv. 33.

siastic; Vassos and Notaras selfish, and without military capacity. Burbaki pushed forward rashly into the plain, and before he could take up a defensive position in the olive grove, he was attacked by Reshid Pasha in person at the head of an overwhelming force. Burbaki's men behaved well, and five hundred fell with their gallant leader. The two chiefs, who ought to have supported him with two thousand men, never came into action: they and their followers fled in the most dastardly manner, abandoning all their provisions to the Turks.

After this victory Reshid marched to the Piræus, hoping to drive Gordon into the sea. On the 11th of February he attacked the hill of Munychia. His troops advanced boldly to the assault, supported by the fire of four long five-inch howitzers. The attack was skilfully conducted. About three thousand men, scattered in loose order round the base of the hill, climbed its sides, covered by the steep declivities which sheltered them from the fire of the Greeks who crowned the summit. Several gallant attempts were made to reach the Greek intrenchments; but as soon as the Turks issued from their cover, they were received with such a fire of musketry and grape that they fled back to some sheltered position. A diversion was made by Captain Hastings, which put an end to the combat. He entered the Piræus with the Karteria under steam, and opened a fire of grape from his 68-pounders on the Turkish reserves and artillery. The troops fled, one of the enemy's guns was dismounted, and the others only escaped by getting under cover of the monastery. The Turkish artillerymen, however, nothing daunted, contrived to run out one of the howitzers under the protection of an angle of the building, and opened a well-directed fire of five-inch shells on the Karteria. Every boat belonging to the ship was struck, and several shells exploded on board, so A.D. 1827. that Hastings, unable to remain in the Piræus without exposing his ship to serious danger, escaped out of the port. His diversion proved completely successful, for Reshid did not attempt to renew the attack on Gordon's positions.

Reshid had some reason to boast of his success; and in order to give the sultan a correct idea of the difficulties with which he was contending, he sent to Constantinople the 68-lb. shot of the Karteria which had dismounted his gun, and a bag of the white biscuits from Ancona, which were distributed as rations to the Greek troops. At the same time he forwarded to the Porte the head of the gallant Burbaki and the cavalry helmet he wore.

The failure of the double attack on Reshid's front persuaded the Greek government to recommence operations against his rear. General Heideck was appointed to command an enterprise similar to that in which Kolettes had failed in the disgraceful manner previously recounted. But Oropos was selected as the point of attack instead of Talanti.[1] Oropos was the principal magazine for the supplies which the army besieging Athens received by sea. These supplies were conveyed to Negrepont by the northern channel, and sent on to Oropos in small transports. Heideck sailed from the Bay of Phalerum with five hundred men. The naval force, consisting of the Hellas frigate, the steam corvette Karteria, and the brig Nelson, was commanded by Miaoulis. On arriving at Oropos, the Hellas anchored about a mile from the Turkish battery; and Hastings, with the Karteria,

---

[1] An anecdote proving the folly of the Greek government deserves notice. Ten days before Heideck's expedition sailed, it was announced in the government Gazette that the executive body had resolved to send a body of troops to *surprise* the Turks at Oropos. Yet, after all, the Turks allowed themselves to be surprised.— Γενική Εφημερίς τῆς Ἑλλάδος, 23 Φεβ. (6 March) 1827, p. 122, and MS. journal.

steamed to within musket-shot of the Turkish guns, silenced them with a shower of grape, and took possession of two transports laden with flour. One of the carcass shells of the Karteria's 68-pounders set fire to the fascines of the Turkish battery, destroyed the carriage of a gun, and exploded the powder-magazine. The evening was already dark, but Miaoulis urged Heideck to land the troops immediately and storm the enemy's position, or at least endeavour to burn down his magazines, while his attention was distracted by the fire in his battery. Heideck declined to make the attempt on account of the darkness, which the admiral thought favoured his attack. Next day the Greek troops landed in a disorderly manner, nor did Heideck himself put his foot on shore, or visit the Karteria, which remained at anchor close to the enemy's battery. The Turks, however, contrived to remove a gun, which they placed so as to defend their position from any attack on the side where the Greeks had landed. Nothing was done until, a body of cavalry arriving from Reshid's camp, Heideck ordered his men to be re-embarked, and sent them back to the camp at Munychia.

The conduct of Heideck on this occasion fixed a stain on his military reputation which was extremely injurious to his future influence in Greece. It furnished a parallel to the generalship of Kolettes, and encouraged the enemies of military science to express their contempt for the pedantry of tactics, and to proclaim that the maxims and rules of European warfare were not applicable to the war in Greece. It was in vain to point out to the Greeks, immediately after this unfortunate exhibition of military incapacity, that it was by gradually adopting some of the improvements of military science, and establishing some discipline, that the Turks were steadily acquiring the superiority both by sea and land.

Immediately after Heideck's failure, the affairs of Greece assumed a new aspect by the arrival of Sir Richard Church and Lord Cochrane. A.D. 1827.

Sir Richard Church had commanded a Greek battalion in the British army, but had not risen to a higher rank than lieutenant-colonel in the service.[1] After the peace he had entered the Neapolitan service, where he attained the rank of lieutenant-general. He now came to Greece, at the invitation of the Greek government, to assume the command of the army. His popularity was great among the military chiefs, who connected his name with the high pay and liberal rations which both officers and men had received while serving in the Anglo-Greek battalion.

The prominent political as well as military position which Sir Richard Church has occupied for many years in Greece, and the influence which his personal views have exercised on the public affairs of the country, render it necessary for the historian to scrutinise his conduct more than once, both as a statesman and a general, during his long career. The physical qualities of military men exert no trifling influence over their acts. Church was of a small, well-made, active frame, and of a healthy constitution. His manner was agreeable and easy, with the polish of great social experience. The goodness of his disposition was admitted by his enemies, but the strength of his mind was not the quality of which his friends boasted. In Greece he committed the common error of assuming a high position without possessing the means of performing its duties: and it may be questioned whether he possessed the talents necessary for performing the duties well, had it been in his power to perform them at all.

---

[1] His services are thus given in *Hart's Army List* for 1859: Ferrol, 1800; Egyptian campaign, 1801; battle of Maida; Sicily and Calabria, and wounded at defence of Capri; capture of Ischia, 1809; severely wounded at St Maura.

As a military man, his career in Greece was a signal failure. His plans of operations never led to any successful result; and on the only occasion which was afforded him of conducting an enterprise on a considerable scale, they led to the greatest disaster that ever happened to the Greek army. His camps were as disorderly as those of the rudest chieftain, and the troops under his immediate command looked more like a casual assemblage of armed mountaineers than a body of veteran soldiers.

Shortly after his arrival, Sir Richard Church obtained from a national assembly the empty title of Archistratcgos, or Generalissimo; and often, to win over independent chiefs to recognise this verbal rank, he sacrificed both his own personal dignity and the character of the office which he aspired to exercise. He succeeded in attaching several chiefs to his person, but he did so by tolerating abuses by which they profited, and which tended to increase the disorganisation of the Greek military system.

As a councillor of state, the career of Church was not more successful than as a general. His name was not connected with any wise measure or useful reform. Even as a statesman he clung to the abuses of the revolutionary system which he had supported as a soldier.

Both Church and the Greeks misunderstood one another. The Greeks expected Church to prove a Wellington, with a military chest well supplied from the British treasury. Church expected the irregulars of Greece to execute his strategy like regiments of guards. Experience might have taught him another lesson. When he led his Greek battalion to storm Santa Maura, his men left him wounded in the breach; and had an English company not carried the place, there he might have lain until the French could take him prisoner. The conduct of the Greek regiments had been often disorderly; they had mutinied at Malta, and behaved ill at Messina. The military chiefs who welcomed him to Greece never intended to allow him to form a regular army, if such had been his desire. They believed that his supposed influence with the British Government would obtain a new loan for Greece, and for them high pay and fresh sources of peculation.

Sir Richard Church arrived at Porto Kheli, near Kastri, on the 9th of March, and was warmly welcomed by Kolokotrones and his faction. After a short stay he proceeded to Egina, where he found the members of the executive dissatisfied with his having first visited their rivals.

Lord Cochrane (Earl of Dundonald) arrived at Hydra on the 17th March. He had been wandering about the Mediterranean in a fine English yacht, purchased for him out of the proceeds of the loan in order to accelerate his arrival in Greece, ever since the month of June 1826.

Cochrane was a contrast to Church in appearance, mind, character, and political opinions. He was tall and commanding in person, lively and winning in manner, prompt in counsel, and daring but cool in action. Endowed by nature both with strength of character and military genius, versed in naval science both by study and experience, and acquainted with seamen and their habits and thoughts in every clime and country, nothing but an untimely restlessness of disposition, and a too strongly expressed contempt for mediocrity and conventional rules, prevented his becoming one of Britain's naval heroes. Unfortunately, accident, and his eagerness to gain some desired object, engaged him more than once in enterprises where money rather than honour appeared to be the end he sought.

Cochrane, with the eye of genius, looked into the thoughts of the Greeks with whom he came into close contact, and his mind quickly embraced the facts that marked the true state of the country, and revealed the extent of its resources. To the leading members of the executive body he hinted that the rulers of Greece ought to possess more activity and talent for government than they had displayed. To the factious opposition at Kastri he used stronger language. He recommended them, with bitter irony, to read the first philippic of Demosthenes in their assembly.[1] His opinions and his discourse were soon well known, for they embodied the feelings of every patriot, and echoed the voice of the nation. His influence became suddenly unbounded, and faction for a moment was silenced. All parties agreed to think only of the nation's interests. The executive body removed from Egina to Poros, and a congress was held at Damala, called the National Assembly of Trœzene.

The first meetings of the national assembly of Trœzene were tumultuous. Captain Hamilton fortunately arrived at Poros with his frigate the Cambrian. His influence with Mavrocordatos and the executive, the influence of Church with Kolokotrones and the Kastri faction, and the authority of Lord Cochrane over all parties, prevented an open rupture. Matters were compromised by the election of Count Capodistrias to be president of Greece for seven years. Lord Cochrane was appointed arch-admiral, and Sir Richard Church arch-general. As the national assembly could not invest them with ordinary power, it gave them extraordinary titles. As very often happens in political compromises, prospective good government was secured by the resolution to remain for a time without anything more than the semblance of a government.

[1] Tricoupi, iv. 122, gives a Greek translation of Cochrane's letter.

A commission of three persons was appointed to conduct the executive until the arrival of Capodistrias; and three men of no political talent and no party influence, but not behind any of their predecessors in corruption and misgovernment, were selected.[1]

The election of Capodistrias was proposed by Kolokotrones and the Russian party, in order to counterbalance the influence which England then exercised in Greece in consequence of the enlightened zeal which Captain Hamilton displayed in favour of Greek independence, and the liberal policy supported by the two Cannings.[2] A few men among the political leaders, whose incapacity and selfishness had rendered a free government impracticable, endeavoured to prevent the election of Capodistrias without success. Captain Hamilton observed a perfect neutrality, and would not authorise any opposition by an English party. Gordon's description of the scene on the day of the election is correct and graphic. He says the Anglo-Greeks hung down their heads, and the deputies of Hydra, Spetzas, and Psara walked up the hill to Damala with the air of criminals marching to execution.

It has been said already that the Turkish army before Athens drew the greater part of its supplies from Thessaly. These supplies were shipped at Volo during the winter, and forwarded by sea to Negrepont and Oropos. It was at last decided that an expedition should be sent to destroy the Turkish magazines and transports at Volo, and the command of the expedition was given to Captain Hastings. He sailed from Poros with a small squadron to perform this service.[3]

[1] Gordon gives an able and accurate account of the proceedings at Trœzena, ii. 364.
[2] George Canning, Prime Minister of England from March to August 1827, and Sir Stratford Canning (Lord Stratford de Redcliffe), Ambassador at Constantinople from 1825 to 1858.
[3] The steamer Karteria, the corvette Themistocles, Captain Raphael, the brig Aros, Captain (Admiral) Kriesis, and the schooners Panaghia and Aspasia.

The Gulf of Volo resembles a large lake, and few lakes surpass it in picturesque beauty and historical associations. Mount Pelion rises boldly from the water on its eastern side. The slopes of the mountain are studded with many villages, whose white dwellings, imbedded in luxuriant foliage, reflected the western sun as the Greek squadron sailed up the gulf on the afternoon of the 20th April 1827.

The fort of Volo lies at the northern extremity of the gulf, where a bay, extending from the ruins of Demetrius to those of Pagasæ, forms a good port. At the point near Pagasæ, on the western side of the bay, the Turks had constructed a battery with five guns. These guns crossed their fire with those of the fort, and commanded the whole anchorage. Eight transports were moored as close to the fort as possible. The Karteria anchored before the fort at half-past four in the afternoon, while the corvette and brig anchored before the five-gun battery. The Turks were soon driven from their guns. A few rounds of grape from the Karteria compelled them to abandon the transports, which were immediately taken possession of by the Greeks. Five of these vessels, which were heavily laden, were towed out of the port, but two, not having their sails on board, were burned; and the eighth, which the Turks contrived to run aground within musket-shot of their walls, was destroyed by shells. About nine o'clock a light breeze from the land enabled the Greek squadron to carry off its prizes in triumph.

After carefully examining every creek, Hastings quitted the Gulf of Volo on the 22d. On entering the northern channel of Eubœa he discovered a large brig-of-war and three schooners in a bight near the scala of Tricheri. This brig mounted fourteen long 24-pounders and two mortars. It was made fast head and stern to the rocks, and planks were laid from its deck to the shore. A battery of three guns was constructed close to the bows, and several other batteries were placed in different positions among the surrounding rocks, so that the brig was defended not only by her own broadside and four hundred Albanian marksmen, but also by twelve guns well placed on shore. Hastings attempted to capture it by boarding during the night. The Greek boats moved silently with muffled oars, but when they had approached nearly within musket-shot, heaps of faggots blazed up at different places, casting long streams of light over the water, while at the same time a heavy fire of round-shot and grape proved the strength and watchfulness of the enemy. Fortunately the Turks opened their fire rather too soon, and Hastings was enabled to regain the Karteria without loss.

On the following day the attack was renewed from a distance in order to destroy the brig with hot shot, for the dispersed positions of the batteries, and the cover which the ground afforded to the Albanian infantry, rendered the grape of the Karteria's guns useless. Seven 68-pound shot were heated in the fires of the engine, brought on deck, and put into the guns with an instrument of the captain's own invention; and as the Karteria steamed round in a large circle about a mile from the shore, her long guns were discharged in succession at intervals of four minutes. When the seven shot were expended, the Karteria steamed out of range of the enemy's fire to await the result. Smoke soon issued from the brig, and a great movement was observed on shore. Hastings then steamed near the land, and showered grape and shells on the Turks to prevent them from extinguishing the fire. A shell exploding in the brig gave him the satisfaction of seeing her abandoned by her crew. Fire at last burst from her deck, and she burned gradually to the water's edge. Her guns towards the shore went off in succession, and caused no inconsiderable confusion among the Albanians; the shells from her mortars mounted in the air, and then her powder-magazine exploded. The Karteria lost only one man killed, a brave Northumbrian quartermaster, named James Hall, and two wounded.

Experience thus confirmed the soundness of the views which Hastings had urged the Greek government to adopt as early as the year 1823. It was evident that he had practically introduced a revolution in naval warfare. He had also proved that a Greek crew could use the dangerous missiles he employed with perfect security. Sixty-eight pound shot had been heated below, carried on deck, and loaded with great ease, while the ship was moving under the fire of hostile batteries. The Karteria herself had suffered severely in her spars and rigging, and it was necessary for her to return to Poros to refit.

In passing along the eastern coast of Euboea, Hastings discovered that Reshid Pasha did not depend entirely on his magazines in Thessaly for supplying his army before Athens with provisions.

Several vessels were observed at anchor off Kumi, and a number of boats were seen drawn up on the beach. Though the place was occupied by the Turks, it was evidently the centre of a considerable trade. It was necessary to ascertain the nature of this trade. Hastings approached the shore, and a few Turks were observed escaping to the town, which is situated about two miles from the port. The vessels at anchor were found to be laden with grain, shipped by Greek merchants at Syra; and it was ascertained that both Reshid and Omar Pasha of Negrepont had, during the winter, purchased large supplies of provisions, forwarded

to Kumi by Greeks. Hastings found a brig under
Russian colours and a Psarian schooner just beginning
to land their cargoes of wheat. A large magazine was
found full of grain, and other magazines were said to
be well filled in the neighbouring town. About one-
third of the grain on shore was transferred to the
prizes taken at Volo. The Russian brig was not molested, but two vessels, fully laden with wheat, were
taken to Poros, where they were condemned by the
Greek admiralty court. On his return Hastings urged
both Lord Cochrane and the Greek government to
adopt measures for putting an end to this disgraceful
traffic; but the attention of Lord Cochrane was called
off to other matters, and there were some scoundrels
who possessed considerable influence with the Greek
government, and who profited by licensing this nefa-
rious traffic.

Military operations were now renewed against the
Turkish army engaged in the siege of Athens. Karaïskaki, after his retreat from Dystomo, established his
force, amounting to three thousand men, at Keratsina,
in the plain to the west of the Piræus. Repeated
letters had been transmitted from the Acropolis, written
by Fabvier and the Greek chiefs, declaring that the
garrison could not hold out much longer.[1]

Sir Richard Church commenced his career as generalissimo by assembling an army at the Piræus of more
than ten thousand, with which he proposed driving
Reshid from his positions.[2] He caused, however, considerable dissatisfaction by hiring a fine armed schooner
to serve as a yacht, and establishing his headquarters
in this commodious but most unmilitary habitation.[3]

---
[1] Gordon, ii. 387.
[2] Church gives this number in his report on the massacre of the Turks who capitulated in the monastery of St Spiridion.—Lesur, *Annuaire Historique*, 1827.
[3] Gordon blames Church for remaining too much on board this schooner, and not exhibiting himself sufficiently to the troops, and also of being too fond

It was decided that the navy should co-operate with the army, so that the whole force of Greece was at last employed to raise the siege of Athens.

Lord Cochrane hoisted his flag in the Hellas, but continued to reside on board his English yacht, not deeming it prudent to remove his treasure, which amounted to £20,000, from under the protection of the British flag. He enrolled a corps of one thousand Hydriots to serve on shore, and placed them under the command of his relation, Lieutenant Urquhart, who was appointed a major in the Greek service. The enrolment of these Hydriots was a very injudicious measure. They were unable to perform the service of armatoli, and they were quite as undisciplined as the most disorderly of the irregulars. When landed at Munychia they excited the contempt of the Romeliot veterans, strutting about with brass blunderbusses or light double-barrelled guns. The army had also reasonable ground for complaint, for these inefficient troops received higher pay than other soldiers.

Lord Cochrane's own landing at the Piræus was signalised by a brilliant exploit. On the 25th of April, while he was reconnoitring the positions of the two hostile armies, a skirmish ensued. He observed a moment when a daring charge would insure victory to the Greeks, and, cheering on the troops near him, he led them to the attack with nothing but his telescope in his hand. All eyes had been watching his movements, and when he was seen to advance, a shout ran through the Greek army, and a general attack was made simultaneously on all the positions occupied by the Turks at the Piræus. The fury of the assault per-

of employing his pen, which was a very useless instrument with armatoli. Gordon himself set the fashion of generals keeping yachts in Greece; but Gordon lived on shore while he commanded at Munychia, and sent his yacht to Salamis. The inaccuracies contained in the published despatches of Sir Richard Church were caused by his isolation on board.

suaded the Mohammedans that a new enemy had taken A.D. 1827. the field against them, and they abandoned nine of their small redoubts. Three hundred Albanians threw themselves into the monastery of St Spiridion; the rest retired to an eminence beyond the head of the port.

The troops in the monastery were without provisions, and only scantily supplied with water. In a short time they must have attempted to cut their way through the Greek army, or surrendered at discretion. Unfortunately, it was determined to bombard the building and carry it by storm. In order to breach the wall of the monastery, the Hellas cannonaded it for several hours with her long 32-pounders. The building looked like a heap of ruins, and the Greek troops made a feeble attempt to carry it by storm, which was easily repulsed by the Albanians, who sprang up from the arched cells in which they had found shelter from the fire of the frigate.

Attempts were made next day to open negotiations with the Albanians, who it was supposed would be now suffering from hunger; but a Greek soldier who carried proposals for a capitulation was put to death, and his head was exposed from the wall; and a boat sent from Lord Cochrane's yacht with a flag of truce, was fired on, and an English sailor dangerously wounded. The frigate then renewed her fire with no more effect than on the previous day. The garrison found shelter in a ditch, which was dug during the night behind the ruins of the outer wall, and its courage was increased by observing the trifling loss which was caused by the tremendous fire of the broadside of a sixty-four gun frigate. The Turks, having now placed four guns[1] on the height to which they had retired on the

---

[1] Gordon, II. 389. My own journal says only three. We both paid particular attention to the effect of the artillery. The hill is named Xypete in Colonel Leake's plan of Athens and its harbours.

25th, opened a plunging fire on the ships in the Piræus, and by a chance shot cut the main-stay of the Hellas.

There was little community of views between the lord high admiral and the generalissimo. Cochrane objected to granting a capitulation to the Albanians in the monastery, as tending to encourage obstinate resistance in desperate cases, and he reproached the Greek chiefs with their cowardice in not storming the building. The irregulars refused to undertake any operation until they gained possession of the monastery. There could be no doubt that a storming party, supported by a couple of howitzers, ought to have carried the place without difficulty. Church determined to make the attempt, and Gordon, who commanded the artillery, was ordered to prepare for the assault on the morning of the 28th of April.

In an evil hour the generalissimo changed his plans. Surrounded by a multitude of counsellors, and destitute of a firm will of his own, he concluded a capitulation with the Albanians, without consulting Lord Cochrane or communicating with General Gordon. Karaïskaki was intrusted with the negotiations. The Albanians were to retire from the monastery with arms and baggage. Several Greek chiefs accompanied them as hostages for their safety. But the generalissimo took no precautions for enforcing order, or preventing an undisciplined rabble of soldiers from crowding round the Mussulmans as they issued from the monastery. He must have been grossly deceived by his agents, for his report to the Greek government states "that no measures had been neglected to prevent the frightful catastrophe that ensued." Nothing warranted this assertion but the fact that Karaïskaki Djavellas, and some other chiefs, accompanied the Albanians as hostages.

As soon as Lord Cochrane was aware that the commander-in-chief of the army had opened negotiations with the Albanians, he ordered Major Urquhart to withdraw the Hydriots from their post near the monastery to the summit of Munychia.

The Albanians had not advanced fifty yards through the dense crowd of armed men who surrounded them as they issued from St Spiridion's, when a fire was opened on them. Twenty different accounts were given of the origin of the massacre. It was vain for the Mussulmans to think of defending themselves; their only hope of safety was to gain the hill occupied by the Turkish artillery. Few reached it even under the protection of a fire which the Turks opened on the masses of the Greeks. Two hundred and seventy men quitted the monastery of St Spiridion, and more than two hundred were murdered before they reached the hill. "The slain were immediately stripped, and the infuriated soldiers fought with each other for the spoil," as we are told by a conscientious eyewitness of the scene.[1]

This crime converted the Greek camp into a scene of anarchy. General Gordon, who had witnessed some of the atrocities which followed the sack of Tripolitza, was so disgusted with the disorder that prevailed, and so dissatisfied on account of the neglect with which he was treated, that he resigned the command of the artillery and quitted Greece. Reshid Pasha, on being informed of the catastrophe, rose up and exclaimed with great solemnity, "God will not leave this faithlessness unpunished. He will pardon the murdered, and inflict some signal punishment on the murderers."[2]

[1] Gordon, ii. 391.
[2] The author was serving as a volunteer on the staff of General Gordon, and accompanied him to join the storming-party on the 28th of April. It had been observed from Gordon's yacht, which was anchored in the Piræus, that communications passed between the Albanians and the Greeks during the whole morning. The Hydriots were also seen retiring to the summit of Munychia. As Gordon passed in his boat under the stern of Lord Cochrane's yacht, the

Nothing now prevented the Greeks from pushing on to Athens but the confusion that prevailed in the camp and the want of a daring leader. Some skirmishing ensued, and in one of these skirmishes, on the 4th of May, Karaïskaki was mortally wounded. His death increased the disorder in the Greek army, for he exercised considerable personal influence over several Romeliot chiefs, and compressed the jealousies of many captains, who were now thrown into direct communication with the generalissimo.

Karaïskaki fell at a moment favourable to his reputation. He had not always acted the patriot, but his recent success in Phocis contrasted with the defeats of Fabvier, Heideck, and Church in a manner so flattering to national vanity, that his name was idolised by the irregular troops. He was one of the bravest and most active of the chiefs whom the war had spared, and his recent conduct on more than one occasion had effaced the memory of his unprincipled proceedings

---

author prevailed on him to seek an explanation of what was going on. Cochrane said that he, as admiral, had refused to concur in a capitulation, unless the Albanians laid down their arms, and were transported as prisoners of war on board the fleet. He added, that he feared Church had concluded a capitulation. While this conversation was going on, the author was watching the proceedings at the monastery with his glass, and, seeing the Albanians issue from the building into the armed mob before the gates, he could not refrain from exclaiming, "All those men will be murdered!" Lord Cochrane turned to Gordon and said, "Do you hear what he says?" to which the general replied, in his usual deliberate manner, "I fear, my Lord, it is too true." The words were hardly uttered when the massacre commenced.

The author landed immediately to examine the effect of the frigate's fire on the monastery. He witnessed a strange scene of anarchy and disorder, and while he remained in the building two Greeks were killed by shot from the guns on the hill.

The Hydriots under Major Urquhart mutinied at being deprived of their share of the spoil. Lord Cochrane sent Mr Masson to pacify them with this message, "My reason for ordering the Hydriots to muster on Munychia was to remove the forces under my command from participating in a capitulation, unless the Turks surrendered at discretion. My objects were to preserve the honour of the navy unsullied, and at the same time to secure an equal distribution of the prize-money."

The author visited the yacht of the generalissimo shortly after, and found the staff on board in high dudgeon at what they called the treachery of the Greeks. He did not see the generalissimo. The feeling among the Philhellenes in the camp, and there were many officers of many nations, was amazement at the neglect on the part of the generalissimo.—*MS. Journal*, 28th April 1827.

during the early years of the Revolution; indeed, it seemed even to his intimate acquaintances that his mind had expanded as he rose in rank and importance. His military talents were those which a leader of irregular bands is called upon to employ in casual emergencies, not those which qualify a soldier to command the numerous bodies required to compose an army. He never formed any regular plan of campaign, and he was destitute of the coolness and perseverance which sacrifices a temporary advantage to secure a great end. In personal appearance he was of the middle size, thin, dark-complexioned, and haggard, with a bright expressive animal eye, which, joined to the cast of his countenance, indicated that there was gypsy blood in his veins. His features, while in perfect repose, wore an air of suffering, which was usually succeeded by a quick unquiet glance.[1]

Sir Richard Church now resolved to change his base of operations from the Piræus to the cape at the eastern end of the Bay of Phalerum. Why it was supposed that troops who could not advance by a road where olive-trees, vineyards, and ditches afforded them some protection from the enemy's cavalry, should be expected to succeed better in open ground, has never been explained.

On the night of the 5th May the generalissimo transported three thousand men, with nine field-pieces, to his new position, but it was nearly daybreak before the whole were landed. It was then too late to reach the Acropolis before sunrise, and the road lay over open downs. Gordon calls the operation "an insane project," and says that "if the plan deserves the severest censure, what shall we say to the pitiful method in which it was executed?"[2]

[1] Compare the characters of Karaïskaki by Gordon, ii. 393, and Tricoupi, iv. 151.
[2] A Philhellene who arrived from Ambelaki just in time to take part in the

BATTLE OF THE PHALERUM.

BOOK IV.
CHAP. III.

Early dawn found the Greek troops posted on a low ridge of hills not more than half-way between the place where they had landed and the Acropolis. A strong body of Othoman cavalry was already watching their movements, and a body of infantry, accompanied by a gun, soon took up a position in front of the Greek advanced-guard. The position occupied by the Greeks was far beyond the range of any guns in the Turkish lines, but Sir Richard Church, who had not examined the ground, was under the erroneous impression that his troops had arrived within a short distance of Athens, and counted on some co-operation on the part of the garrison of the Acropolis. Had he seen the position, he could not have allowed his troops to remain on ground so ill chosen for defence against cavalry, with the imperfect works which they had thrown up. The advanced-guard had not completed the redoubt it had commenced, and the main body, with the artillery, could give no support to the advanced-guard.[1]

Reshid Pasha made his dispositions for a cavalry attack. They were similar to those which had secured him the victory at Petta, at Khaidari, and at Kamatero. He ascertained by his feints that his enemy had not a single gun to command the easy slope of a ravine that led to the crest of the elevation on which the advanced redoubt was placed. Two successive charges of cavalry were repulsed by the regular troops and the Suliots,

action, and who was one of the four who escaped, wrote a few days after :—
" Believing that the object was to reach Athens by a coup-de-main, I was much surprised to find that the troops did not quit the seaside until near morning. Nevertheless they had some time to fortify themselves before they were attacked. Unfortunately, no disposition had been made, and the troops were dispersed without order."—*Letter of Lieut. Myhrbergh to Gen. Gordon,* dated 9th May 1827.

[1] The report of Sir Richard Church, printed in Lesur, *Annuaire Historique pour 1827,* App. 127, contains many inaccuracies. The author not only witnessed the engagement from his tent on the summit of Munychia, but he rode over the ground with Mr Gropius, the Austrian consul-general in Greece, who had also seen the battle, while the bones of the slain still remained unburied, and the imperfect intrenchments of the Greeks were exactly in the same state as on the morning of the attack. He then compared his notes and recollections with the known facts and the configuration of the ground.

who formed the advanced-guard of the Greek force. But this small body of men was left unsupported, while the Turks had collected eight hundred cavalry and four hundred infantry in a ravine, by which they were protected until they charged forward on the summit of the ridge. The third attack of the Turks decided the contest. The cavalry galloped into the imperfect redoubt. A short struggle ensued, and completed Reshid's victory. The main body of the Greeks fled before it was attacked, and abandoned the guns, which remained standing alone for a short interval before the Turkish cavalry took possession of them, and turned them on those by whom they had been deserted. The fugitives endeavoured to reach the beach where they had landed. The Turks followed, cutting them down, until the pursuit was checked by the fire of the ships.

Sir Richard Church and Lord Cochrane both landed too late to obtain a view of the battle. The approach of the Turkish cavalry to their landing-place compelled them to regain their yachts. Reshid Pasha, who directed the attack of the Turkish cavalry in person, was slightly wounded in the hand.

Fifteen hundred Greeks fell in this disastrous battle, and six guns were lost. It was the most complete defeat sustained by the Greeks during the course of the war, and effaced the memory of the rout at Petta, and of the victories gained by Ibrahim Pasha in the Morea. The Turks took two hundred and forty prisoners, all of whom were beheaded except General Kalergy, who was released on paying a ransom of 5000 dollars,[1] and who lived to obtain for his country

[1] Kalergy's leg was broken, and he was made prisoner by an Albanian bey. Reshid wished his head to be piled up with those of the other prisoners, but his captor insisted on receiving 5000 dollars before he would part with it, as Kalergy had promised him that sum. Fortunately the Turkish military chest was not in a condition to allow the pasha to purchase a single head at so high a price. The money was immediately raised among Kalergy's friends, and was remitted from St Petersburg as soon as Kalergy's uncle heard of his nephew's misfortune.

the inestimable boon of representative institutions by the Revolution of 1843, which put an end to Bavarian domination, and completed the establishment of the independence of Greece.

The battle of Phalerum dispersed the Greek army at the Piræus. Upwards of three thousand men deserted the camp in three days; and the generalissimo was so discouraged by the aspect of affairs, that he ordered the garrison of the Acropolis to capitulate.[1] Captain Leblanc, of the French frigate Junon, was requested to mediate for favourable terms, and was furnished with a sketch of the proposed capitulation. This precipitate step on the part of Sir Richard Church drew on him a severe reprimand from the chiefs in the Acropolis, who treated his order with contempt, and rejected Captain Leblanc's offer of mediation with the boast, that "we are Greeks, and we are determined to live or die free. If, therefore, Reshid Pasha wants our arms, he may come and take them." These bold words were not backed by deeds of valour.

Church abandoned the position of Munychia on the 27th of May, and the garrison of the Acropolis then laid aside its theatrical heroism. Captain Corner, of the Austrian brig Veneto, renewed the negotiations for a capitulation, and the arrival of the French admiral, De Rigny, brought them to a speedy termination. The capitulation was signed on the 5th of June. The garrison marched out with arms and baggage. About fifteen hundred persons quitted the place, including four hundred women and children. The Acropolis still contained a supply of grain for several months' consumption, and about two thousand pounds of powder, but the water was scarce and bad. There was no fuel

---

[1] Jourdain, *Mémoires Historiques et Militaires sur les Evénements de la Grèce depuis 1822 jusqu'au Combat de Navarin*. See also Tricoupi, iv. 160. Not much reliance can be placed either on the accuracy or the judgment of Jourdain, but he prints a few documents.

for baking bread, and the clothes of the soldiers were A.D. 1827.
in rags.

The surrender of the Acropolis, following so quickly after the bombastic rejection of the first proposals, caused great surprise. The conduct of Fabvier was severely criticised, and the behaviour of the Greek chiefs was compared with the heroism of the defenders of Mesolonghi. The sufferings of those who were shut up in the Acropolis were undoubtedly very great, but the winter was past, and had they been inspired with the devoted patriotism of the men of Mesolonghi, they might have held out until the battle of Navarin.

The conduct of Reshid Pasha on this occasion gained him immortal honour. He showed himself as much superior to Sir Richard Church in counsel, as he had proved himself to be in the field. Every measure that prudence could suggest was adopted to prevent the Turks from sullying the Mohammedan character with any act of revenge for the bad faith of the Greeks at the Piræus. The pasha patrolled the ground in person, at the head of a strong body of cavalry, and saw that his troops who escorted the Greeks to the place of embarkation performed their duty.

The fall of Athens enabled Reshid to complete the conquest of that part of continental Greece which Karaïskaki had occupied; but the Turks did not advance beyond the limits of Romelia, and the Greeks were allowed to remain unmolested in Megara and the Dervenokhoria, which were dependencies of the pashalik of the Morea, and consequently within the jurisdiction of Ibrahim Pasha. Many of the Romeliot chiefs now submitted to the Turks, and were recognised by Reshid as captains of armatoli. In his despatches to the sultan he boasted with some truth that he had terminated the military operations with which he was intrusted, and re-established the sultan's authority in all that part of continental Greece placed under his command, from Mesolonghi to Athens.

The interference of foreigners in the affairs of Greece was generally unfortunate, often injudicious, and sometimes dishonest. Few of the officers who entered the Greek service did anything worthy of their previous reputation. The careers of Norman, Fabvier, Church, and Cochrane, were marked by great disasters. Frank Hastings was perhaps the only foreigner in whose character and deeds there were the elements of true glory.

But it was by those who called themselves Philhellenes in England and America that Greece was most injured. Several of the steam-ships, for which the Greek government paid large sums in London, were never sent to Greece. Some of the field-artillery purchased by the Greek deputies was so ill constructed that the carriages broke down the first time the guns were brought into action. Two frigates were contracted for at New York; and the business of the contractors was so managed that Greece received only one frigate after paying the cost of two.

The manner in which the Greeks wasted the money of the English loans in Greece has been already recorded. It is now necessary to mention how the Greek deputies, and their English and American friends, misappropriated large sums at London and New York. It will be seen that waste and peculation were not monopolies in the hands of Greek statesmen, Albanian shipowners, and captains of armatoli and klephts. English politicians and American merchants had also their share.[1]

[1] Dr Howe, *Historical Sketch of the Greek Revolution*, 376, says, " The shameful waste of a large part of the loan, and the numerous peculations which were committed upon it, have not been fully exposed to the world; but enough has been exposed to show that the London Greek committee shamefully neglected its duty; that some of its members meanly speculated on the miseries of Greece; that others committed, what in men of lesser note would have been called

The grandest job of the English Philhellenes was A.D. 1827. purchasing the services of Lord Cochrane to command a fleet for the sum of £57,000, and setting apart £150,000 to build the fleet which he was hired to command. Lord Cochrane was engaged to act as a Greek admiral in the autumn of 1825. He went to reside at Brussels while his fleet was building, and arrived in Greece in the month of March 1827, as has been already mentioned, before any of the steam-ships of his expedition. Indeed, the first vessel, which was commenced at London by his orders, did not arrive in Greece until after the battle of Navarin.

The persons principally responsible for this waste of money and these delays were Mr Hobhouse, now Lord Broughton; Mr Edward Ellice; Sir Francis Burdett; Mr Hume; Sir John Bowring, the secretary of the Greek Committee; and Messrs Ricardo, the contractors of the second Greek loan. Sir Francis Burdett was floating on the cream of Radicalism, and Lord Broughton was supporting himself above the thin milk of Whiggery by holding on vigorously at the baronet's coat-tails. Both these gentlemen, however, though they were guilty of negligence and folly, kept their hands pure from all money transactions in Greek bonds. The Right Honourable Edward Ellice was a contractor for the first Greek loan, but was not a bear, at least of Greek stock. In a letter to the *Times* he made a plain statement of his position in Greek affairs, and owned candidly that he had been guilty of "extreme indiscretion in mixing himself up with the Greek deputies and their affairs." What he said was no doubt perfectly true; but we must not overlook

fraud; and it is well known too that Orlando and Luriottis, the Greek deputies, proved themselves fools and knaves." A pamphlet, however, was published defending the Greek deputies, written by an Italian lawyer, Count Palma, who was afterwards a judge in Greece.—*Summary Account of the Steamboats for Lord Cochrane's Expedition:* London, 1826.

that it was not said until Greek affairs had ceased to discount the political drafts of the Whigs, and a less friendly witness might perhaps have used a stronger word than "extreme indiscretion." The conduct of Mr Hume and Sir John Bowring was more reprehensible, and their names were deeply imbedded in the financial pastry which Cobbett called "the Greek pie," and which was served with the rich sauce of his savoury tongue in the celebrated *Weekly Register*.[1] Where there was both just blame and much calumny, it is difficult and not very important to apportion the exact amount of censure which the conduct of each individual merited. The act which was most injurious to Greece, and for the folly of which no apology can be found, was intrusting the construction of all the engines for Lord Cochrane's steamers to an engineer (Mr Galloway), who failed to construct one in proper time. He contracted to send Captain Hastings' steamer, the Perseverance (Karteria), to sea in August 1825. Her engines were not ready until May 1826.[2]

When the Greeks were reduced to despair by the successes of Ibrahim Pasha, the government ordered the deputies in London to purchase two frigates of moderate size. With the folly which characterised all their proceedings, they sent a French cavalry officer to build frigates in America. The cavalry officer fell into the hands of speculators. The Greek deputies neglected to perform their duty. The president of the Greek Committee in New York, and a mercantile house also boasting of Philhellenic views, undertook the construction of two leviathan frigates.[3] The sum of £150,000 was expended before any inquiry was made.

---

[1] *Cobbett's Weekly Register*, vol. lx. Nos. 7, 8, and 10, Nov. and Dec. 1826.
[2] Compare Gordon, ii. 275.
[3] Gordon, ii. 275, says, On the western side of the Atlantic the Greeks were yet more infamously used by some of their pretended friends than on the eastern.

It was then found that the frigates were only half finished. The American Philhellenes who had contracted to build them became immediately bankrupts, and the Greek government, having expended the loans, would have never received anything for the money spent in America, had some real Philhellenes not stepped forward and induced the government of the United States to purchase one of the ships. The other was completed with the money obtained by this sale, and a magnificent frigate, named the Hellas, mounting sixty-four 32-pounders, arrived in Greece at the end of the year 1826, having cost about £200,000.

Shortly after the defeat of Sir Richard Church at the Phalerum, Lord Cochrane assembled the Greek fleet at Poros. His first naval review was a sad spectacle of national disorganisation, and presented an unlucky omen of his future achievements. The ships of Hydra and Spetzas were anchored in the port; but before their Albanian crews would get their vessels under weigh, they sent a deputation to the arch-admiral asking for the payment of a month's wages in advance. They enforced their demand by reminding Lord Cochrane, with seamanlike frankness, that he had received funds on board his yacht for the express purpose of paying the fleet. His lordship replied, that he had already expended so much of the money intrusted to him in the abortive attempt to raise the siege of Athens, that he could only now offer the sailors a fortnight's wages in advance. This proposal was considered to be a violation of the seaman's charter in the Albanian Islands, and it was indignantly rejected by the patriotic sailors. In vain the arch-admiral urged the duty they owed to their country. No seaman could trust his country for a fortnight's wages. Without waiting for orders, the crews of the ships ready for sea weighed anchor and returned to Hydra and

Spetzas, from whence some of them sailed on privateering and piratical cruises. The spectacle of this dispersal of the Greek fleet, though humiliating, was impressive. The afternoon was calm, the sun was descending to the mountains of Argolis, and the shadows of the rocks of Methana already darkened the water, when brig after brig passed in succession under the stern of the Hellas, from whose lofty mast the flag of High Admiral of Greece floated, unconscious of the disgraceful stain it was receiving, and in whose cabin sat the noble admiral steadily watching the scene.

The whole of Greece was now laid waste, and the sufferings of the agricultural population were so terrible, that any correct description even by an eyewitness would be suspected of exaggeration. In many districts hundreds died of absolute starvation, and thousands of the diseases caused by insufficient nourishment. The islands of the Archipelago, which escaped the ravages both of friends and foes, did not supply grain in sufficient quantity for their own consumption. Poverty prevented the people from obtaining supplies of provisions under neutral flags.

During this period of destitution, which commenced towards the end of 1826, and continued until the harvest of 1828, the greater part of the Greeks who bore arms against the Turks were fed by provisions supplied by the Greek committees in Switzerland, France, and Germany. The judicious arrangements adopted by Mr Eynard at Geneva and Paris, and the zeal of Dr Goss, General Heideck, and Mr Koering in Greece, caused the limited resources at their disposal to render more real service than the whole proceeds of the English loans.

While the Continental committees were supporting the war, the Greek committees in the United States directed their attention to the relief of the peaceful population. The amount of provisions and clothing sent from America was very great. Cargo after cargo arrived at Poros, and fortunately there was then in Greece an American Philhellene capable, from his knowledge of the people, and from his energy, honour, and humanity, of making the distribution with promptitude and equity. Dr Home requires no praise from the feeble pen of the writer of this History, but his early efforts in favour of the cause of liberty and humanity in Greece deserve to be remembered, even though their greatness be eclipsed by his more mature labours at home. He found able coadjutors in several of his countrymen, who were guided by his counsels.[1] Thousands of Greek families, and many members of the clergy and of the legislature, were relieved from severe privations by the food and clothing sent across the Atlantic. Indeed, it may be said without exaggeration that these supplies prevented a large part of the population from perishing before the battle of Navarin.

In the summer of the year 1627 Greece was utterly exhausted, and the interference of the European powers could alone prevent the extermination of the population, or their submission to the sultan.

[1] Mr or Colonel Miller, Dr Rum, and Mr Stayvesant.

BOOK FIFTH.

FOUNDATION OF THE GREEK KINGDOM.

CHAPTER I.

FOREIGN INTERVENTION—BATTLE OF NAVARIN.

> "Earth is sick,
> And Heaven is weary of the hollow words
> Which states and kingdoms utter when they talk
> Of truth and justice."

CONDUCT OF RUSSIA—CONDUCT OF GREAT BRITAIN—CONGRESS OF VERONA—RUSSIAN MEMOIR ON THE PACIFICATION OF GREECE IN 1823—EFFECT OF THIS MEMOIR—TURKEY COMPLAINS OF THE CONDUCT OF THE BRITISH GOVERNMENT—GREECE PLACES HERSELF UNDER THE PROTECTION OF ENGLAND—PROTOCOL OF THE 4TH APRIL 1826 FOR THE PACIFICATION OF GREECE—DESTRUCTION OF THE JANISSARIES—TREATY OF THE 6TH JULY 1827 FOR THE PACIFICATION OF GREECE—STATE OF GREECE IN 1827—VICTORY OF HASTINGS AT SALONA—BATTLE OF NAVARIN—GREEK SLAVES CARRIED OFF TO ALEXANDRIA—GREEK TROOPS CROSS INTO ACARNANIA—HASTINGS TAKES VASILADI—DEATH OF HASTINGS—RUSSIA DECLARES WAR WITH TURKEY—FRENCH TROOPS COMPEL IBRAHIM TO EVACUATE THE MOREA.

WHEN the Greeks commenced the Revolution, they were firmly persuaded that Russia would immediately assist them. Many acts of the Emperor Alexander I. authorised this opinion, which was shared by numbers of well-educated men in Western Europe. But whatever might have been the wish of the emperor personally, policy prevailed over feeling. The sovereigns of Europe feared a general rising of nations. Monarchs were alarmed by a panic fear of popular movements, A.D. 1827. and the judgment of statesmen was disturbed by the conviction that cabinets and nations were pursuing adverse objects. There was a strong desire among a part of the Russian population to take up arms against the sultan in order to protect the Greeks, because they belonged to the same Oriental Church. But the conservative policy of the emperor, the selfishness of his ministers, and the power of his police, prevented any active display of Philhellenism in Russia.

Time rolled on. Year after year the Greeks talked with laudable perseverance of the great aid which Russia was soon to send them. Philhellenes from other nations arrived and fought by their side; large pecuniary contributions were made to their cause by Catholics and Protestants, but their coreligionaries of orthodox Russia failed them in the hour of trial. The cabinet of St Petersburg coolly surveyed the struggle, weighed the effect of exhaustion on the position of both the combatants, and watched for a favourable moment to extend the influence of Russia towards the south, and for an opportunity of adding new provinces to the empire.

The conduct of Great Britain was very different. The British cabinet was more surprised by the Greek Revolution, and viewed the outbreak with more aversion than any other Christian government. The events in Vallachia, and the assertions of the Hetairists in the Morea, made the rising of the Greeks appear to be the result of Russian intrigue. The immediate suppression of the revolt seemed therefore to be the only way of preventing Greece from falling under the protection of the Emperor Alexander, and of hindering Russia from acquiring naval stations in the Mediterranean. The British government consequently opposed the Revolution; but it had not, like that of Russia, the power to coerce the sympathies of Britons. British Philhellenes were among the first to join the cause, and in merit they were second to none. The names of Gordon, Hastings, and Byron will be honoured in Greece as long as disinterested service is rewarded by national gratitude.

The habits of the English people, long accustomed to think and act for themselves in public affairs, enabled public opinion to judge the conduct of the Greeks without prejudice, and to separate the crimes which stained the outbreak from the cause which consecrated the struggle.

It is necessary, however, to look beyond the East in order to form a correct judgment of the policy of the cabinets of Europe with regard to the Greek Revolution. The equilibrium of the European powers was threatened with disturbance by a war of opinion. Two camps were gradually forming in hostile array, under the banners of despotism and liberty. The Greek question was brought prominently forward by the Continental press, because it afforded the means of indulging in political discussion without allusion to domestic administration, and of proclaiming that principles of political justice were applicable to Greeks and Turks which they dared not affirm to be applicable to the subjects and rulers in Christian nations.

The affairs of Greece were brought under discussion at the Congress of Verona in 1822. A declaration of the Russian Emperor, and the protocols of the conferences, proclaimed that the subject interested all Europe; but the view which the Congress took of the war in Greece showed more kingcraft than statesmanship. It was identified too closely with the democratic *revolutions of Naples, Piedmont, and Spain. Yet so great was the fear of any extension of Russian influence in the East, that even the members of the

Holy Alliance preferred trusting to the chance of its A.D. 1827.
suppression by the sultan rather than authorise the
czar to interfere.

In the mean time, Russia persuaded France to undertake the task of suppressing constitutional liberty in Spain, as a step to a general concession of the right of one nation to interfere in the internal affairs of another when it suspects danger from political opinions.

The march of the French armies beyond the Pyrenees placed the cabinets of France and England in direct opposition. England replied to the destruction of constitutional liberty in Spain by acknowledging the right of the revolted Spanish colonies in America to establish independent states. George Canning delighted the liberals and alarmed the despots on the Continent by boasting in parliament that he had called a new political world into existence to redress the balance of the old. The phrase, though somewhat inflated, has truth and buoyancy enough to float down the stream of time. At the same time the British government adopted the energetic step of repealing the prohibition to export arms and ammunition, in order to afford the Spanish patriots the means of obtaining supplies and of resisting the French invasion.[1]

While the English cabinet was thus incurring the danger of war in the West, it exerted itself to prevent hostilities in the East. The ambassadors of England and Austria induced the sultan to take some measures to conciliate Russia in 1823. A note of the reis-effendi was addressed to the Russian government, announcing the speedy evacuation of the transdanubian principalities, and a desire to renew direct diplomatic relations between the sultan and the czar. After much tergiversation in the usual style of Othoman diplomacy, the Porte opened the navigation of the

[1] By an order in council, 26th February 1823.

Bosphorus to the Russian flag, and the Emperor Alexander sent a consul-general to Constantinople.[1]

From this time Russia began to take a more active part than she had hitherto taken in the negotiations relating to Greece. The activity of the Philhellenic committees alarmed the Holy Alliance. The success of the French in Spain encouraged the despotic party throughout Europe. Russia, availing herself adroitly of these feelings, seized the opportunity of resuming her relations with Turkey, and of laying before the European cabinets a memoir on the pacification of Greece.

The principal object of this document was the dismemberment of Greece, in order to prevent the Greek Revolution from founding an independent state. The statesmen of Russia, having watched dispassionately the progress of public opinion in the West, had arrived at the conclusion that if monarchs delayed much longer assuming the initiative in the establishment of peace between the Greeks and Turks, Christian nations might take the matter in their own hands. Russia naturally wished to preserve her position as protector of the Greeks, and to retain the honour of being the first Christian government that covered her coreligionaries with her orthodox ægis.

The Russian plan of pacification was calculated to win the assent of the Holy Alliance, by suppressing everything in Greece that appeared to have a revolutionary tendency. It proposed to retain the Greeks in such a degree of subjection to Turkey that they would always stand in need of Russian protection. It contemplated annihilating the political importance of the Greeks as a nation, by dividing their country into three separate governments. By creating powerful

---

[1] The notes relating to these negotiations are printed in *Archives Diplomatiques*, vi. 31, and Lesur, *Annuaire Historique*, 1823.

classes in each of these governments with adverse interests, it hoped to render any future national union impossible; and by allowing the sultan to keep Othoman garrisons in the Greek fortresses, the hostile feelings of the Greeks would be kept in a state of irritation, and they would continue to be subservient to Russia in all her ambitious schemes in the Turkish empire. The three governments into which Russia proposed to divide Greece, were to be ruled by native hospodars, and administered by native officials chosen by the sultan. The islands of the Egean Sea were to be separated from the rest of their countrymen, and placed under the direct protection of the Porte, with such a guarantee for their local good government as could be obtained by the extension of a municipal system similar to that which had existed at Chios, at Hydra, or at Psara.[1]

As a lure to gain the assent of the members of the Holy Alliance to these arrangements, Russia urged the necessity of preventing Greece from becoming a nest of democrats and revolutionists, by paralysing the political energy of the nation, which could easily be effected by gratifying the selfish ambition of the leading Greeks. Personal interest would extinguish national patriotism in Greece, as it had done at the Phanar, and in Vallachia and Moldavia.[2]

When the contents of this memoir became known, they caused great dissatisfaction both in Greece and Turkey.

[1] An extract from this memoir was published in 1824, and this extract is translated by Tricoupi, III. 385; but a complete copy was printed in the *Courier de Smyrne*, 1828, Nos. 37 and 38. The hospodarats were — 1. Thessaly, with Eastern Greece; 2. Epirus and Western Greece; 3. The Morea with Crete. The islands which were to enjoy municipal governments are not enumerated.

[2] The expressions deserve to be quoted:—" Paralyser l'influence des revolutionnaires dans toute la Grèce;" and " que la création de trois principautés Grecques, en diminuant l'étendue et les forces respectives de chacune de ces provinces, offre une nouvelle guarantée à la Porte: qu'elle offre enfin un puissant appât aux principales familles de la Grèce; et qu'elle pourra servir à les détacher des intérêts de l'insurrection."

The sultan was indignant that a foreign sovereign should interfere to regulate the internal government of his empire, and propose the dismemberment of his dominions as a subject of discussion for other powers. He naturally asked in what manner the Emperor Alexander would treat the interference of any Catholic sovereign in favour of Polish independence, or of the sultan himself in favour of Tartar Mohammedanism.

The Greeks were astonished to find the Emperor Alexander, whom they had always believed to be a firm friend, coolly aiming a mortal blow at their national independence. Their own confused notions of politics and religion had led them to infer that the orthodoxy of the czar was a sure guarantee for his support in all measures tending to throw off the Othoman yoke both in their civil and ecclesiastical government. They were appalled at the Machiavelism of a cabinet that sought to ruin their cause under the pretext of assisting it.[1]

Great Britain was now the only European power that openly supported the cause of liberty, and her counsels bore a character of vigour that commanded the admiration of her enemies. To the British government the Greeks turned for support when they saw that Russia had abandoned their cause. In a communication addressed to the British Foreign Secretary, dated the 24th August 1824, they protested against the arrangements proposed in the memoir, and adjured England to defend the independence of Greece and frustrate the schemes of Russia. This letter did not reach George Canning, who was then at the Foreign Office, until the 4th November, and he replied on the 1st of December. By the mere fact of replying to a

---

[1] The unpopularity of Russia was greatly increased by the expulsion of many Greek families from the dominions of the Emperor Alexander at this time. Some of these families were conveyed to Greece at a considerable expense by the Phillhellenic committees of Switzerland.—Gordon, ii. 83.

communication of the Greek government, he recognised the right of the Greeks to secure their independence, and form a new Christian state.

Mr Canning's answer contained a distinct and candid statement of the views of the British cabinet. Mediation appeared for the moment impossible, for the sultan insisted on the unconditional submission of the Greeks, and the Greeks demanded the immediate recognition of their political independence. Nevertheless, the English minister declared that, if at a future period Greece should demand the mediation of Great Britain, and the sultan should accept that mediation, the British government would willingly co-operate with the other powers of Europe to facilitate a treaty of peace, and guarantee its duration. In the mean time Great Britain engaged to observe the strictest neutrality, adding, however, that as the king of England was united in alliance with Turkey by ancient treaties, which the sultan had not violated, it could not be expected that the British government should involve itself in a war in which Great Britain had no concern.[1]

The moderate tone of this state-paper directed public opinion to the question of establishing peace between the Greeks and the sultan. It also convinced most thinking men that the object of Russian policy was to increase the sultan's difficulties, not to establish tranquillity in Turkey. The British Parliament, in particular, began to feel that the English ambassador at Constantinople must cease to support many of the demands of Russia. The memoir of 1820, therefore, though able and well devised as a document addressed to cabinets and diplomatists, became a false step by being subjected to the ordeal of public opinion. The morality of nations was already better than that of

[1] For the letter of the Greek government, and Canning's answer, see Lesur, Ann. Hist., 1824, p. 627. Tricoupi gives Canning's letter a wrong date, iii. 390.

emperors and kings. For a time all went on smoothly, and meetings of the ambassadors of the great powers were held at St Petersburg in the month of June 1824, to concert measures for the pacification of the East.

Early in the year 1824, the influence of England at Constantinople diminished greatly, in consequence of the public manifestations of Philhellenism. The sultan heard with surprise that the Lord Mayor of London had subscribed a large sum to support the cause of the Greeks; that Lord Byron, an English peer, and Colonel the Honourable Leicester Stanhope (Earl of Harrington), an officer in the king's service, had openly joined the Greeks; that the British authorities in the Ionian Islands granted refuge to the rebellious armatoli; and that English bankers supplied the insurgents with money. The sultan attributed these acts to the hostile disposition of the government. Neither Sultan Mahmud nor his divan could be persuaded that in a free country public opinion had a power to control the action of the executive administration in enforcing the law. The sultan could not be expected to appreciate what Continental despots refuse to understand—that Englishmen legally enjoy and habitually exercise a right of political action for which they are responsible to society and not to government. In the year 1823, the sympathies of Englishmen, with all those engaged in defending the inalienable rights of citizens, were so strong, that the British government feared to act in strict accordance with the recognised law of nations. The people considered that the duties of humanity were more binding than national treaties. But as the ambassador at Constantinople could not urge popular feelings as an excuse for violating national engagements, the sultan had the best of the argument when he formally complained to the cabinets of Europe of the conduct of England to Turkey.

five years to elapse without doing much to fulfil them.

Death arrested the vacillating career of Alexander I. in November 1825. For a moment Russia was threatened with internal revolution, but Nicholas was soon firmly seated on the throne by his energetic conduct. His stern and arrogant disposition soon displayed itself in his foreign policy; but his personal presumption and despotic pretensions encountered the petulant boldness and liberal opinions of George Canning, and an estrangement ensued between the Russian and British cabinets, greater than would have resulted solely from the divergency of their national interests.[1]

Mr Stratford Canning (Lord Stratford de Redcliffe), one of England's ablest diplomatists, arrived at Constantinople, as ambassador to the Porte, early in 1826, with the delicate mission of inducing the sultan to put an end to the war in Greece, and of preventing war from breaking out between Russia and Turkey. On his way to the Dardanelles he conferred with Mavrocordatos concerning the basis of an effectual mediation between the belligerents.[2] The result of this interview was that the National Assembly of Epidaurus passed a decree, dated 24th April 1826, authorising the British ambassador at Constantinople to treat concerning peace, on the basis of independent self-government for Greece, with a recognition of the sultan's suzerainty, and the payment of a fixed tribute.[3]

The pacification of Greece was now the leading object of British policy in the Levant. The Emperor Nicholas had rejected all mediation in his differences

[1] An instance of the haughty tone assumed by the Emperor Nicholas towards the British government, will be found in a despatch from Nesselrode to Lieven, dated 9th January 1827, printed in the *Portfolio*, iv. 267.
[2] The meeting took place at Hydra, 9th January 1826.
[3] The decree and instructions to the committee of the Assembly are given by Mamouka, iv. 94; the letter to Canning, iv. 132.

with Turkey, but the British cabinet was still anxious to secure unity of action between England and Russia on the Greek question. The Duke of Wellington was sent to St Petersburg for this purpose, and on the 4th April 1826 a protocol was signed, stating the terms agreed on by the two powers as a basis for the pacification of Greece. This protocol acknowledged the right of the Greeks to obtain from the Porte a solemn recognition of their independent political existence, so far as to secure them a guarantee for liberty of conscience, freedom of commerce, and the exclusive regulation of their internal government. This was a considerable step towards the establishment of national independence on a solid foundation.[1]

Unfortunately, the relations of the British government with the members of the Holy Alliance, and the Continental princes under their influence, were far from amicable during the year 1826. No progress could therefore be made in a negotiation in which the Porte could only be induced to make concessions by fear of a coalition of the Christian powers, and their determination to act with unity and vigour.

The royalists in Spain, under the protection of the French army of occupation, began to aid the despotic party in Portugal. The princess-regent at Lisbon, alarmed at the prospect of a civil war, claimed the assistance which England was bound to give to Portugal by ancient treaties. The occupation of Spain by foreign troops threatened Portugal with war; foreign assistance could alone prevent hostilities. A French army had destroyed liberty in Spain; an English army could alone preserve it in Portugal. Canning did not hesitate, and in December 1826 he announced in Parliament that six thousand British troops were ordered to Lisbon. All Europe was taken by surprise.

[1] *Parliamentary Papers;* and *Portfolio,* iv. 516.

The Emperor Nicholas, who had placed himself at the head of the despotic party on the Continent, was extremely irritated at this bold step in favour of constitutional liberty. A coolness ensued between the English and Russian cabinets, and the negotiations for the pacification of Greece were allowed to lag. On the other hand, the attitude assumed by the czar towards Turkey had previously become so menacing, that Sultan Mahmud yielded the points he had hitherto contested, and concluded the convention of Akermann on the 7th October 1826.[1]

But Sultan Mahmud had not trifled away his time during the year 1826. In the month of May he promulgated an ordinance reforming the corps of janissaries. His reforms were so indispensable for the establishment of order, that the great body of the Mohammedans supported them. But in the capital several powerful classes were interested in the continuance of the existing abuses. The janissaries took up arms to defend their privileges, which could only be maintained by dethroning the sultan. A furious contest ensued on the 14th June, but it was quickly terminated. Sultan Mahmud had foreseen the insurrection, and was prepared to suppress it. The sacred banner of Mohammed was unfurled, the grand mufti excommunicated the janissaries as traitors to their sovereign and their religion, and an overwhelming force was collected to crush them. Their barracks were stormed, the whole quarter they inhabited was laid in ashes, their corps dissolved, and the very name of janissary abolished. On the 13th of September 1826, tranquillity being completely restored at Constantinople, the sandjaksherif was furled and replaced in its usual sanctuary.

The convention of Akermann re-established Russian

[1] Lesur, *Ann. Hist.*, 1826, p. 100.

influence at the Porte. On the 5th of February 1827, Great Britain and Russia made formal offers of their mediation in the affairs of Greece, and proposed a suspension of hostilities. After many tedious conferences, the reis-effendi, in order to terminate the discussion, delivered to the representatives of the European powers at Constantinople a statement of the reasons which induced the sultan to reject the interference of foreign states in a question which related to the internal government of his empire.[1]

France was at this time engaged in a dispute with the dey of Algiers, which led to the conquest of that dependency of the sultan's empire. She now joined Great Britain and Russia in common measures for the pacification of Greece, and a treaty between the three powers was signed at London on the 6th July 1827.

This treaty proposed to enforce an armistice between the Greeks and Turks by an armed intervention, and contemplated securing to the Greeks a virtual independence under the suzerainty of the sultan.[2] An armistice was notified to both the belligerents. The Greeks accepted it as a boon which they had solicited; but the sultan rejected all intervention, and referred the Allies to the note of the reis-effendi already mentioned.

After the disastrous battle of Phalerum, it required no armistice to prevent the Greeks from prosecuting hostilities by land. Their army was broken up, and no military operations were attempted during the summer of 1827. Sir Richard Church moved about at the head of fewer troops than some chieftains, and many captains paid not the slightest attention to his orders. Fabvier shut himself up in Methana, sulky and discontented. The greater part of the Greek

---

[1] This document, dated 9th and 10th June 1827, is given in Lesur, *Ann. Hist.*, 1827, p. 99.
[2] For the treaty, see *Parliamentary Papers*.

chiefs, imitating the example of Kolokotrones, occupied themselves in collecting the public revenues in order to pay the personal followers they collected under their standard. The efforts of the different leaders to extend their territory and profits caused frequent civil broils, and the whole military strength of the nation was, by this system of brigandage and anarchy, diverted from opposing the Turks. While Greece was supporting about twenty thousand troops, she could not move two thousand to oppose either the Egyptians or the Turks in the field. The best soldiers in Greece were dispersed over the country collecting the means of subsistence, and the frontiers and the fortresses were alike neglected. Famine was beginning to be felt, and the soldiery, accustomed to waste, acted towards the peasantry in the most inhuman manner. The beasts of burden were carried off, and the labouring oxen devoured before the eyes of starving families.[1] Some districts of the Peloponnesus had submitted to Ibrahim Pasha during the winter of 1826, and one of the chiefs in the vicinity of Patras, named Demetrius Nenekos, now served actively against his countrymen.[2]

The exploits of the Greek seamen were not more patriotic than those of the Greek soldiers. Only a few, following the example of Miaoulis and Kanaris, remained indefatigable in serving their country; but the best ships and the best sailors of the naval islands were more frequently employed scouring the sea as pirates than cruising with the national fleet.[3] Lord Cochrane kept the sea with a small force. On the

[1] Admiral de Rigny tells us that the peasants were "chassés, dépouillés, pillés alternativement par les Turcs et par les palikares;" and he mentions " îles de l'Archipel, où, dans chacune, une bande de pirates de terre et de mer font la loi."—*Parliamentary Papers,* B, *Protocols at Constantinople,* p. 37.
[2] Compare Tricoupi, iv. 182.
[3] For the extent to which piracy was carried on, see Gordon, ii. 475; and Tricoupi confesses, iv. 248, that it was μεγάλιστον καὶ αἰσχιστον φαιδρύρημα ἐν τῇ ἱστορίᾳ τῶν ἐθνῶν.

16th of June he made an ineffectual attempt to destroy the Egyptian fleet at Alexandria. On the 1st of August, the high admiral in the Hellas, and Captain Thomas in the brig Soter, took a fine corvette and a large Tunisian schooner after a short engagement, and brought their prizes in safety to Poros, though pursued by the whole Egyptian fleet. On the 18th of September Lord Cochrane anchored off Mesolonghi with a fleet of twenty-three sail; but after some feeble and unsuccessful attempts to take Vasiladi, he sailed away, leaving Hastings to enter the Gulf of Corinth with a small squadron.

On the 29th of September Hastings stood into the Bay of Salona to attack a Turkish squadron anchored at the Scala, under the protection of two batteries and a body of troops. The Greek force consisted of the steam-corvette Karteria, the brig Soter, under the gallant Captain Thomas, and two gunboats, mounting each a long 32-pounder. The Turkish force consisted of an Algerine schooner, mounting twenty long brass guns, six brigs and schooners, and two transports. The Turks were so confident of victory that they prepared to capture the whole Greek force, and did not fire until the Karteria came to an anchor, fearing lest the attack might be abandoned if they opened their destructive fire too soon. Hastings anchored about five hundred yards from the enemy's vessels. While the Karteria was bringing her broadside to bear, the batteries on shore and the vessels at anchor saluted her with a heavy cannonade. When the Soter and the gunboats came up, they were compelled to anchor about three hundred yards further out than the Karteria. Hastings commenced the action on the part of the Greeks by firing his guns loaded with round-shot, in slow succession, in order to make sure of the range. He then fired hot shells from his long guns, and carcass-shells from his carronades. The effect was terrific.[1] A.D. 1827. One of the shells penetrated to the magazine of the Turkish Commodore, who blew up. A carcass-shell exploded in the bows of the brig anchored astern the Commodore, and she settled down forward. The next broadside lodged a shell in the Algerine, which exploded between her decks, and she was immediately abandoned by her crew. Another schooner burst out in flames at the same time, and a hot shell, lodging in the stern of the brig which had sunk forward, she also was soon on fire. Thus, before the guns of the batteries on shore could inflict any serious loss on the Karteria, she had destroyed the four largest ships of the enemy. Captain Thomas and the gunboats soon silenced the batteries, and took possession of the Algerine schooner, which, however, the Greeks were unable to carry off, as she was discovered to be aground, and her deck was within the range of the Albanian riflemen on shore. Hastings steamed up, and endeavoured to tow her out to sea, but his hawsers snapped. The crews of the Soter and the gunboats succeeded by great exertion, and with some loss, in carrying off her brass guns, and in setting her and the remaining brig on fire. The other vessels, being aground close to the rocks which concealed the Albanian riflemen, could not be boarded, but they were destroyed with shells.

This victory at Salona afforded fresh proof of the value of steam and large guns in naval warfare. The terrific effect of hot projectiles, and the ease with which they were managed, astonished both friends and foes.

Ibrahim Pasha was at Navarin when he heard of

---

[1] Hot shells were used, though liable to greater deviation than shot, because it was feared that solid 68-lb. shot might pass through both sides of the enemy's ships.

the destruction of the squadron at Salona. He considered it a violation of the armistice proposed by the Allies and accepted by the Greeks, and he resolved to take instant vengeance on Hastings and Thomas, whose small force he hoped to annihilate with superior numbers.

Mohammed Ali was not less averse to an armistice than the sultan, but Ibrahim could not refuse, when the Allied admirals appeared in the Levant, to consent to an armistice at sea. Hastings's victory at Salona now, in his opinion, absolved him from his engagement, for it could not be supposed that the Allies would allow one party to carry on hostilities and hinder the other. Ibrahim therefore sent a squadron from Navarin with orders to enter the Gulf of Corinth and attack Hastings, who had fortified himself in the little port of Strava, near Perakhova. Sir Edward Codrington, the English admiral, compelled this squadron to return, and accused Ibrahim of violating the armistice. Candour, however, forbids us to overlook the fact that Ibrahim gave his consent to a suspension of hostilities by sea under the persuasion that the Greeks would not be allowed to carry on hostile operations any more than the Turks.

The measures adopted by the Allies to establish an armistice were, during the whole period of their negotiations, remarkable for incongruity. The Greeks accepted the armistice, and were allowed to carry on hostilities both by sea and land. The Turks refused, and were prevented from prosecuting the war by sea. Ibrahim avenged himself by burning down the olive-groves and destroying the fig-trees in Messenia. The Allied admirals kept his fleet closely blockaded in Navarin, where it had been joined by the capitan-pasha with the Othoman fleet. Winter was approaching, and the Allies might be blown off the coast, which would afford the Turkish naval forces in Navarin an opportunity of slipping out and inflicting on Hydra the fate which had overwhelmed Galaxidi, Kasos, and Psara. To prevent so great a calamity, the Allied admirals resolved to bring their fleets to anchor in the great bay of Navarin, alongside the Egyptian and Othoman fleets. This resolution rendered a collision inevitable.

The bay of Navarin is about three miles long and two broad. It is protected from the west by the rocky island of Sphakteria, but is open to the southwest by an entrance three-quarters of a mile broad. The northern end of Sphakteria is separated from the cape of the mainland, crowned with the ruins of Pylos, by a channel only navigable for boats.[1] A small island called Chelonaki is situated near the middle of the port, about a mile from the shore.

The Turkish fleets were anchored in a line of battle forming two-thirds of a circle, facing the entrance of the port, and with the extremities resting on and protected by the fortress of Navarin and the batteries on Sphakteria. The ships were stationed three deep, so as to command every interval in the first line by the guns of the ships in the second and third lines. The first consisted of twenty-two heavy ships, with three fire-ships at each extremity. The second of twenty-six ships, including the smaller frigates and the corvettes. The third consisted of a few corvettes, and of the brigs and schooners which were ordered to assist any of the larger ships that might require aid. The whole force ranged in line of battle to receive the Allies amounted to eighty-two sail, and in this number there were

[1] Old Navarin, built on the ruins of Pylos, and called Avarinos, is said to have been built by the Avars when they ruled the Sclavonians, who colonised the Morea in the seventh century. For the ancient and modern topography of this district, see Leake's *Travels in the Morea*, Arnold's *Thucydides*, and the article Pylos, in Smith's *Dictionary of Greek and Roman Geography*.

three line-of-battle ships and five double-banked frigates.[1]

The Allied force consisted of twenty-seven sail, and of these ten were line-of-battle ships and one a double-banked frigate.[2]

About half-past one o'clock, on the afternoon of the 20th October 1827, Sir Edward Codrington entered the harbour of Navarin, leading the van of the Allies in his flag-ship the Asia. A favourable breeze wafted the Allied ships slowly forward; while twenty thousand Turkish troops, encamped without the fortress of Navarin, were ranged on the slopes overlooking the port, like spectators in a theatre. The Turkish admirals, seeing the Allies advancing in hostile array,

---

[1] The Othoman and Egyptian fleets united comprised—
    3 line-of-battle ships.
    5 double-banked frigates.
    21 frigates.
    33 corvettes.
    13 brigs and schooners.
    6 fire-ships.
    ——
    82 sail, mounting about 2000 guns.

A Tunisian squadron of three frigates and a brig anchored behind Chelonaki, but neither it nor the armed transports in the upper part of the bay took any share in the battle.

[2] The Allied fleet was thus composed—

ENGLISH DIVISION, 11 sail,   Guns. 456

Line-of-battle		Frigates.		Sloops of war.	
Asia,	84	Glasgow,	50	Rose,	18
Genoa,	74	Cambrian,	48	Brisk,	10
Albion,	74	Dartmouth,	44	Philomel,	10
		Talbot,	28	Mosquito,	10
				Stag (tender to Asia),	6

FRENCH DIVISION, 7 sail,   362

Scipion,	74	Sirène,	60	Alcyone,	18
Breslau,	74	Armide,	44	Daphne,	18
Trident,	74				

RUSSIAN DIVISION, 8 sail,   452

Azof,	74	Constantine,	48
Hanhoute,	74	Provenay,	44
Ezekiel,	74	Elene,	33
Alexander Nevsky,	74	Castor,	32

                                                                        Total guns, 1270

made their preparations for the battle, which they A.D. 1827. knew was inevitable. Their great superiority in number gave them a degree of confidence in victory, which the relative force of the two fleets, in the character of the ships, did not entirely warrant. The greatest disadvantage of the Allies was that they were compelled to enter the port in succession, exposed to a cross-fire of the Turkish ships and the batteries of Sphakteria and Navarin. Fortunately for them, the guns on shore did not open their fire until the English and French admirals had taken up their positions. The imperfect artillery of the Turkish fleet, and the superiority of the Allies in the number of line-of-battle ships, as well as in discipline and science, were the grounds which were supposed to authorise the bold enterprise of the admirals. But there can be no doubt that a well-directed fire from the Turkish guns on shore might have destroyed the English and French flag-ships before the great body of the Allied fleet arrived to their assistance.

The first shot was fired by the Turks. The Allied admirals would willingly have delayed the commencement of the engagement until all their ships had entered the port, and ranged themselves in line of battle. But the breeze died away after a part of their squadrons anchored, and it was more than an hour before the first ship of the Russian division could reach its station. The battle was remarkable for nothing but hard fighting, which allowed a display of good discipline, but not of naval science. The fire of the Allies was steady and well directed; that of the Othomans and Egyptians irregular and ill directed, but kept up with great perseverance. The most difficult operation of the day was taking possession of and turning aside the Turkish fire-ships stationed at the extremities of the line. When the English and French admirals anchored, these fire-ships were to windward, and a favourable opportunity was offered for using them with effect. The attempt was made to bear down on the flag-ships of the Allies, but it was frustrated by the skill and courage of Sir Thomas Fellowes of the Dartmouth, and of the officers and men of the brigs which were ordered on this duty. This battle, therefore, confirms the experience of the Othoman and Egyptian fleets in 1824, that fire-ships constructed on the Greek model require favourable circumstances and skill on the part of their crews, and some mismanagement or ignorance on the part of those assailed, to render them very efficient engines in naval warfare.

For about two hours the capitan-bey and the Egyptian admiral, Moharrem Bey, sustained the fire of the Asia and Sirène, but they then cut their cables and drifted to leeward. The victory was soon after secured by the Russian division under Count Heyden engaging the capitan-pasha, Tahir, whose squadron formed the starboard division of the Turkish line. The fire of the Allies now became greatly superior to that of their enemies, and the Turks abandoned several of their ships, and set them on fire. As evening approached, the scene of destruction extended over the whole port.

The Allies took every precaution to insure the safety of their ships during the night, which they were compelled to pass in the port amidst burning vessels drifting about in every direction. Every now and then fresh ships burst out into a mass of flames, and cast a lurid light over the water. The crews who had been fighting all day to destroy the ships of their enemies were compelled to labour all night to save their own.

Of the eighty-two sail of Turkish ships anchored in line of battle at noon, on the 20th of October 1827, only twenty-nine remained afloat at daylight on the following morning.[1]

[1] An Austrian officer, who visited Navarin shortly after the battle, reported

The loss of the Allies amounted to 172 killed, and 470 wounded. Several ships suffered so severely in their hulls and rigging as to be unfit to keep the sea. The greatest loss was sustained on board the flag-ships of the three admirals.

The English and Russian line-of-battle ships sailed to Malta to refit. The French returned to Toulon. Only the smaller vessels remained in the Levant to watch the proceedings of Ibrahim, whose courage was not depressed by his defeat.[1]

Ibrahim resolved not to abandon his position in the Morea. In order to relieve his force of the wounded, the supernumerary sailors, and the invalided soldiers, as well as to remove the Turkish families and Greek slaves who encumbered the fortresses, he embarked all these classes in the ships which escaped destruction. A fleet of fifty-two sail was prepared for sea, of which twenty-four were men-of-war present at the battle of Navarin. This fleet quitted Greece on the 22d December, and arrived safely at Alexandria, where it landed two thousand Greek slaves captured in the Morea.

Sir Edward Codrington was severely blamed for allowing this deportation of Christians, as he had been warned that Ibrahim contemplated the gradual removal of the whole Greek population from the Peloponnesus, and its colonisation by Mussulman Albanians and Arabs. This was indeed the only way in which the

---

the vessels then afloat to be—two line-of-battle ships, one double-banked frigate, five frigates, nine corvettes, and twelve brigs.

[1] The best accounts of the battle of Navarin are the official reports of the three admirals, published in the *London Gazette*, *Le Moniteur*, and the *Gazette of St Petersburg*. They may be compared with one another, and with a complete account of the battle, published at Naples, with a good plan—*Memoria intorno alla Battaglia di Navarino;* Napoli dalla Reale Tipografia della guerra : 1833. There is an account of what was seen by an officer on board the Talbot, in the *United Service Journal*, 1829, pt. I. 117. There is a plan of the port of Navarin, by Sir Thomas Fellowes. A MS. plan of the battle prepared by an English officer, was frequently copied in the Levant: it agrees very nearly with that published at Naples.

Egyptian pasha could complete and maintain his conquest. Sir Edward Codrington, considering that it was his duty to accelerate the evacuation of the Morea, did not think that his instructions warranted his assuming the responsibility of searching Turkish men-of-war as they were returning home. This, indeed, could not be done without a declaration of war; and even after the battle of Navarin, England did not declare war with the sultan, nor the sultan with England. The truth seems to be, that the naval force of the admiral was inadequate both to blockade the Egyptians and to protect British ships from the Greek pirates, who now attacked every merchantman that passed to the eastward of Cape Matapan. But it was the general opinion that Sir Edward Codrington fell into a very usual error of commanders-in-chief in the Mediterranean at that time, and both remained too much at Malta himself, and kept too many of his ships there. His judgment appears to have been misled by the severe censure cast on his conduct at Navarin, in the king's speech at the opening of parliament, in which his victory was termed "an untoward event."[1]

The destruction of the Othoman fleet made no change in the determination of Sultan Mahmud. The ambassadors at Constantinople again offered their mediation in vain, and, after reiterated conferences, they quitted the Turkish capital in December 1827.

The Greeks were allowed by the Allies to make every effort in their power to regain possession of the territory conquered by Reshid since the year 1825.

---

[1] Sir Edward Codrington was recalled for misapprehending his instructions, and for not disposing of his force so as to watch the movements of the Egyptian ships in Greece from the 21st November 1827 to 26th February 1828. See the Earl of Aberdeen's Letter, May 1829, with P.S., 4th June, in *Parliamentary Papers*, and *Documents relating to the Recall of Sir Edward Codrington in June 1828*, printed for private distribution, p. 21. See also the Instructions addressed to the admirals, annexed to the protocol of 15th October 1827, particularly the separate Instructions relative to the Egyptian forces, in the *Parliamentary Papers*.

But anarchy had reached such a pitch that the Greek government was powerless, and no army could be assembled. Sir Richard Church resolved, however, to establish himself at some harbour on the coast of Acarnania with the small body of men he could assemble, trusting to his being joined by the armatoli in continental Greece, whom the hostile demonstrations of the Allied powers might induce to throw off the Turkish yoke. At Church's invitation, Hastings sailed out of the Gulf of Corinth in the daytime, exposing the Karteria to the fire of the castles of Morea and Romelia, that he might transport the Greek troops to Acarnania. When he reached Cape Papas, after having exposed his ship to great danger in order to be in time at the rendezvous, he was obliged to wait ten days before the generalissimo made his appearance.[1] Church's movements had been retarded by the news that Achmet Pasha was on his march from Navarin to Patras with a reinforcement of two thousand men. The army of the generalissimo did not exceed fourteen hundred men, and it reached the coast in a state of destitution. The embarkation of this phantom of a military force was effected under the immediate superintendence of the officers of the Karteria, without any assistance from those of the army. The Greek troops were landed at Dragomestre, where they remained inactive, drawing their supplies from abroad.

Shortly after, another body of Greek troops crossed the Gulf of Corinth, and occupied the site of a Hellenic fortress on the mainland opposite the island of Trisognia, but remained as inactive as the division at Dragomestre. The peasantry showed themselves in

---

[1] Hastings lost two men killed and two wounded in passing the castles, but he succeeded in sinking an Austrian brig laden with flour, which had just broken the blockade, and was already under the guns of the batteries at Patras. Hastings passed the castles on the 15th of November, and Church arrived at Cape Papas on the 26th.

general to be hostile to the Greek soldiery, and kept the Turks well informed concerning every movement of the land and naval forces of Greece.

Hastings had no sooner transported the troops to Dragomestre than he resolved to attack the fort of Vasiladi, hoping that its conquest would enable the Greek army to besiege Mesolonghi. Ever since Lord Cochrane's failure in September, he had sought in his mind the best means of gaining possession of this key of the lagoons of Mesolonghi. Vasiladi is not more than one hundred yards in circumference, and its works rose only six feet above the water. The Karteria could not approach nearer than a mile and a quarter. Two attempts to throw shells into the place on different days failed, but on the 29th December 1827, the day being perfectly calm, the firing was renewed. The long guns of the Karteria threw shells at an elevation of 23°, and the third gun, pointed by Hastings himself, pitched its shell into the Turkish powder-magazine.[1] The explosion rendered the place untenable, and the boats of the Karteria arrived before the Turks could offer any resistance. The bodies of twelve men were found in the fort, and thirty-nine were taken prisoners.

These prisoners were taken on board the Karteria, but Hastings, who had been feeding his crew at his own expense for some time, resolved to put them on shore as soon as possible. He therefore informed the commandant of Vasiladi that a monoxylon (canoe of the lagoon) would convey him to Mesolonghi, to enable him to make arrangements for sending off flat-bottomed boats to land the prisoners without loss of time. The Mussulman, remembering the manner in which both Turks and Greeks had generally disposed of their cap-

[1] Memoir on the use of Shells, Hot Shot, and Carcass-Shells, from Ship Artillery, by Frank Abney Hastings, published by Ridgway in 1828, page 18.

tives, considered this to be a sentence to an honourable death. He supposed that he was to be taken to the nearest shore where he could receive burial after being shot, and he thanked Hastings like a brave man, saying that he was ready to meet death in any way his victor might order. The conversation passed through an interpreter, and Hastings being the last man on the quarter-deck to perceive that it was supposed to be his intention to murder his prisoner, the scene began at last to assume a comic aspect. The Turk was conducted to the gangway, where, seeing only a monoxylon, with one of his own men to receive him, he became conscious of his misunderstanding. He then turned back to Hastings, and uttered a few expressions of gratitude in the most dignified and graceful manner. The rest of the prisoners were landed on the following morning, and an interchange of presents took place. The Turk sending some fresh provisions on board the Karteria, and Hastings sending back some coffee and sugar.

Shortly after the battle of Navarin, Fabvier undertook an expedition to Chios, which ended in total failure.[1] The Greeks also made an effort to renew the war in Crete, but without success.[2]

After the arrival of Capodistrias in Greece, an attempt was made to revive the spirit of the irregular troops, but even the camp of Sir Richard Church continued to be a scene of disorganisation. The chieftains were everywhere intent on drawing as many rations as possible, and several of them made illicit gains by selling the supplies, which were furnished to Greece by Philhellenic societies, to men in the Turkish service. Sir Richard Church having imprudently given pass-

[1] Fabvier left Methana in October 1827, and raised the siege of Chios in March 1828. Gordon, ii. 450-473.
[2] The termination of the insurrection in Crete, and the gallant death of Hadji Mikhali on the 28th May 1828, are well recounted by Gordon, ii. 499.

ports to boats engaged in carrying on this trade in provisions with the districts in the vicinity of Patras, occupied by the troops of Ibrahim, became involved in an acrimonious correspondence with Captain Hastings, who, as the naval commander on the station, considered the proceeding as a gross violation of the rules of service, as well as of a naval blockade. It induced Hastings to get himself removed from the station, in order to make room for somebody who could agree better with the generalissimo. But in the month of May, Capodistrias induced him to accept the command of a small squadron in Western Greece, and he immediately resumed his former activity. His career was soon cut short. On the 25th of May he was mortally wounded in an attack on Anatolikon, and expired on board the Karteria. No man ever served a foreign cause more disinterestedly.[1]

Before delivering up the command of the Mediterranean fleet to his successor, Sir Pulteney Malcolm, Sir Edward Codrington concluded a convention with Mohammed Ali for the evacuation of the Morea by Ibrahim Pasha.[2] Before that convention was executed, the alliance of the three powers was threatened with

---

[1] The difficulties under which Hastings laboured during his career in Greece, belong rather to his biography than to Greek history; but a few words may be extracted from his correspondence to show how great they were. On the 7th January 1828 he wrote, "I am full of misery. I have not a dollar. I owe my people three months' pay, and five dollars a-head gratuity for the taking of Vasiladi. I have no provisions, and I have lost an anchor and chain." On the 16th he wrote again: "It has become an established maxim to leave this vessel without supplies. Dr Goss (agent of the Swiss committees) has just been at Zante, and has left three hundred dollars for the gunboat Helvetia, now serving under my orders, but not one farthing, no provisions, and not even a single word for me. Five months ago I was eight thousand dollars in advance for the pay of my crew, and since that time I have only received a thousand dollars from the naval chest of Lord Cochrane, and six hundred dollars from the military chest of Sir Richard Church, and this last sum is not even sufficient to pay the expenses incurred by the detention of our prizes to serve as transports for his army." See Biographical Sketch of Frank Abney Hastings in *Blackwood's Magazine*, October 1845. Both Gordon and Tricoupi have done justice to the memory of Hastings, who was as distinguished for sincerity and truth in private life, as for ability and daring in war.

[2] *Parliamentary Papers*, C, Convention of Alexandria, 6th August 1828.

dissolution. England and France wished to preserve the sultan's throne, as well as to establish the independence of Greece. Russia was even more eager to destroy the Othoman empire than to save Greece. Nicholas proposed to employ coercive measures by land, as the battle of Navarin had produced no effect. He wished to occupy Moldavia and Vallachia, and to invade Bulgaria, while the English and French fleets forced the Dardanelles. England and France rejected this proposal on the ground that it was more likely to involve Europe in a general war than to establish peace in the Levant. Russia then took advantage of some arbitrary conduct on the part of the sultan's government relative to the Black Sea trade, and of some violent expressions in an imperial proclamation of the Porte, to declare war with Turkey on the 26th April 1828.[1]

The alliance would have been dissolved had the Emperor Nicholas not retracted so much of his separate action as to consent to lay aside his character of a belligerent in the Mediterranean, and engage to act in that sea only as a member of the alliance, and within the limits traced by the treaty of the 6th July 1827.

The death of George Canning deprived British counsels of all their energy, and the measures adopted to coerce the sultan were timid, desultory, and dilatory.[2] A bold and prompt declaration of the concessions which the Allies were determined to exact in favour of the Greeks, would have been the most effectual

---

[1] The Hatt-sherif, dated 20th December 1827, announcing sentiments of bitter animosity against Russia, is given in the *Parliamentary Papers*. Annex D, No. 2, to the protocol of the 12th March 1828.

[2] In the protocol of the 15th June 1828, Lord Aberdeen, with the diplomatic inaptitude which characterises the proceedings of Great Britain at this period, allowed the clauses to be inverted, and by this inversion the claim of Russia to an exceptional position with regard to Turkey was in some measure ratified. England, as protector of a Greek population in the Ionian Islands, ought to have insisted on equal rights. Russia was not driven from the claim she set up to an exceptional position until Sevastopol fell.

mediation. When Russia delared war with Turkey, England ought instantly to have recognised the independence of Greece, and proceeded to carry the treaty of the 6th July into execution by force. As France would in all probability have acted in the same manner, the consent of the sultan would have been gained, and a check might have been placed on the ambition of Russia by occupying the Black Sea with an English and French fleet.

The weakness of the British Cabinet allowed Russia to assume a decided political superiority in the East. On the Danube, where discipline gave her armies an immense advantage, and in the Black Sea, where the battle of Navarin had left the sultan without a fleet, she acted as a belligerent. But in the Mediterranean, where she was weak, and where she could only carry on hostilities at an enormous expense, she was allowed to conceal her weakness and economise her treasure by acting as a mediator.

With all the diplomatic successes of the Russian cabinet, the war of 1828-29 reflected little honour on the armies of the Emperor Nicholas. Though Turkey was suffering from a long series of rebellions and revolutions, which had in turn desolated almost every province of the Othoman empire; though the sultan had destroyed the janissaries, and had not yet formed a regular army; though his fleet had been annihilated at Navarin, and his finances ruined by the blockade of the Dardanelles, still under all these disadvantages Sultan Mahmud displayed an unexpected fertility of resources, and the Mussulmans in European Turkey something of their ancient energy. The desperate resistance the Russians met with at Silistria and Varna covered the Turks with glory. Two campaigns were necessary to enable the Russian armies to advance to Adrianople; and they reached that city so weak in number that they did not venture to push on to Constantinople and dictate peace to Sultan Mahmud before the walls of his capital. Nevertheless, the victories of the Russians in Asia, and their complete command of the Black Sea, convinced the sultan that an attack on his capital would not be long delayed ; and as Constantinople was inadequately supplied with provisions, and no troops could be assembled to fight a battle for its defence, Sultan Mahmud submitted to the terms of peace imposed on him. The treaty was signed on the 14th September 1829.[1]

The army of Ibrahim Pasha suffered great privations during the winter of 1827-28. Though no regular blockade of the ports in his possession was maintained either by the Greeks or the Allies, his army would have starved, or he would have evacuated the Morea, had he not succeeded in obtaining large supplies of provisions from the Ionian Islands, and particularly from Zante. About fifty Ionian boats, entirely manned by Greeks, were almost constantly employed for several months in carrying provisions to Ibrahim's troops in Greece.[2] But even with all the assistance supplied by the Ionians, the price of provisions was high, and the sufferings of the soldiers were great in the fortresses of Navarin, Modon, and Coron. At last these sufferings became intolerable.

In June 1828 about two thousand Albanians in garrison at Coron broke out into open mutiny, and after plundering the place marched out to return home. They concluded a convention with the Greek government, and Capodistrias ordered a body of Greek troops to escort them to the Isthmus of Corinth, from whence they marched along the coast of the Morea to the castle of Rhion. On entering that fort they murdered

[1] Lesur, *Annuaire Historique*, 1829.
[2] Codrington's despatch. *Documents relating to the Recall of V. A. Codrington*, p. 35.

the governor, and after resting a few days crossed the straits, marched hastily through the desolate plains of Etolia, and reached the frontier of Turkey in safety.

The utter exhaustion of Greece prevented even the government of Capodistrias from making any effort to expel the Egyptians from the Peloponnesus. The direct agency of the Allies could alone deliver the country.

The French government undertook to send an army to expel Ibrahim, for the mutual jealousies of England and Russia threatened otherwise to retard the pacification of Greece indefinitely. On the 19th July 1828 a protocol was signed, accepting the offer of France; and on the 30th August an army of fourteen thousand men, under the command of General Maison, landed at Petalidi in the Gulf of Coron. The convention concluded by Codrington at Alexandria had been ineffectual. It required the imposing force of the French general to compel Ibrahim to sign a new convention for the immediate evacuation of the Morea. The convention was signed on the 7th of September 1828, and the first division of the Egyptian army, consisting of five thousand five hundred men, sailed from Navarin on the 16th. Ibrahim Pasha sailed with the remainder on the 5th October; but he refused to deliver up the fortresses to the French, alleging that he had found them occupied by Turkish garrisons on his arrival in Greece, and that it was his duty to leave them in the hands of the sultan's officers.

After Ibrahim's departure, the Turks refused to surrender the fortresses, and General Maison indulged their pride by allowing them to close the gates. The French troops then planted their ladders, scaled the walls, and opened the gates without any opposition. In this way Navarin, Modon, and Coron fell into the hands of the French. But the castle of Rhion offered some resistance, and it was found necessary to lay siege to it in regular form. On the 30th October the A.D. 1828 French batteries opened their fire, and the garrison surrendered at discretion.

France thus gained the honour of delivering Greece from the last of her conquerors, and she increased the debt of gratitude due by the Greeks by the admirable conduct of the French soldiers. The fortresses surrendered by the Turks were in a ruinous condition, and the streets were encumbered with filth accumulated during seven years. All within the walls was a mass of putridity. Malignant fevers and plague were endemic, and had every year carried off numbers of the garrisons. The French troops transformed themselves into an army of pioneers; and these pestilential medieval castles were converted into habitable towns. The principal buildings were repaired, the fortifications improved, the ditches of Modon were purified, the citadel of Patras reconstructed, and a road for wheeled carriages formed from Modon to Navarin. The activity of the French troops exhibited how an army raised by conscription ought to be employed in time of peace, in order to prevent the labour of the men from being lost to their country. But like most lessons that inculcated order and system, the lesson was not studied by the rulers of Greece.

CHAPTER II.

PRESIDENCY OF COUNT CAPODISTRIAS. JANUARY 1828 TO OCTOBER 1831.

"Unlimited power corrupts the possessor; and this I know, that where law ends, there tyranny begins."—LORD CHATHAM.

CHARACTER OF COUNT JOHN CAPODISTRIAS—FIRST ADMINISTRATIVE MEASURES AS PRESIDENT—HIS OPINIONS AND POLICY—ORGANISATION OF THE ARMY—FABVIER'S RESIGNATION—OPERATIONS IN EASTERN AND WESTERN GREECE—TERMINATION OF HOSTILITIES—CIVIL ADMINISTRATION—VIARO CAPODISTRIAS—FINANCIAL ADMINISTRATION—JUDICIAL ADMINISTRATION—PUBLIC INSTRUCTION—NATIONAL ASSEMBLY OF ARGOS—PROTOCOLS OF THE THREE PROTECTING POWERS—PRINCE LEOPOLD OF SAXE-COBURG SOVEREIGN OF GREECE—HIS RESIGNATION—CAPODISTRIAS BECOMES A TYRANT—HOSTILITY TO THE LIBERTY OF THE PRESS—TYRANNY OF CAPODISTRIAS—AFFAIR OF POROS—DESTRUCTION OF THE GREEK FLEET—SACK OF POROS—FAMILY OF MAVROMICHALES—ASSASSINATION OF CAPODISTRIAS.

THE struggle for independence unfolded some virtues in the breasts of the Greeks which they were not previously supposed to possess. But a few years of a liberty that was mingled with lawlessness could not be expected to efface the effects of old habits and a vicious nurture. National energies were awakened, but no national responsibility was felt by individuals, so that the vices of modern Greek society were in each class stronger than the popular virtues which liberty was endeavouring to nourish. The mass of the people had behaved well; but the conduct of political and military leaders, of primates and statesmen, had been selfish and incapable. This was deliberately proclaimed by the National Assembly of Trœzene in 1827, when public opinion rejected all the actors in the Revolution as unworthy of the nation's confidence, and elected Count Capodistrias president of Greece on the 14th April 1827 for a period of seven years.[1]

The decree which conferred the presidency on Capodistrias declared that he was elected because he possessed a degree of political experience which the Othoman domination had prevented any native Greek from acquiring. Much was therefore expected at his hands. It is the duty of the historian not only to record his acts, but to explain why his performances fell short of the expectations of the Greek nation.

Capodistrias was fifty-one years of age when he arrived in Greece. He was born at Corfu. His ancestors had received a title of nobility from the Venetian republic, but the family was not wealthy, and the young count, like many Corfiot nobles, was sent to Italy to study medicine, in order to gain his livelihood.[2] In 1803 he commenced his political career, being appointed secretary to the newly created republic of the Ionian Islands; in 1807, when Napoleon I. annexed the Ionian Islands to the French empire, he transferred his services to Russia, where accident gained him the favour of the Emperor Alexander I.; and in 1815 he was employed in the negotiations relating to the treaty of Paris. At that time he exerted himself, and was allowed to employ all the influence of the Russian cabinet, to re-establish the Ionian republic; but Great Britain insisted on retaining possession of these islands, and of holding complete command over their government, as a check on Russian intrigues among the orthodox population of the Othoman empire. Capodistrias was consequently

---

[1] Mamouka, vii. 132, and ix. 97. The decree is sometimes dated 3d (15th) April, which was Easter Sunday. It was adopted on Saturday, but signed by many members on Sunday.

[2] Kolettes, Glarakes, Zographos, Rhodios, and many other Greeks who acted a prominent part during the Revolution, were doctors.

obliged to rest satisfied with the concession that the Ionian Islands were to be formed into a separate, but not an independent, state under the British crown, instead of being, like Malta, declared a dependency of the British empire. Capodistrias hoped that even this might be rendered subservient to his ambitious schemes. He affected great contempt for English dulness, and he hoped that English dullards might be inveigled into favouring his views in the East. He never forgave English ministers for foiling his diplomatic projects, and the rancorous malevolence of his nature led him into several grave political errors. He hated England like an Ionian, but he indulged and exhibited his hatred in a way that was very unlike a statesman.

The patriotism of Capodistrias was identified with orthodoxy and nationality, not with civil liberty and political independence. To the social progress of the bulk of the population in Western Europe during his own lifetime, he paid little attention, and this neglect prevented his observing the influence which public opinion already exercised on the general conduct of most cabinets. He overrated the influence of orthodoxy in the Othoman empire, and the power of Russia in the international system of Europe. All this was quite natural, for his experience of mankind had been acquired either in the confined and corrupt society of Corfu, or in the artificial atmosphere of Russian diplomacy.

Yet with all his defects and prejudices, Capodistrias was immeasurably superior to every Greek whom the Revolution had hitherto raised to power. He had many virtues and great abilities. His conduct was firm and disinterested; his manners simple and dignified. His personal feelings were warm, and, as a consequence of this virtue, they were sometimes so strong as to warp his judgment. He wanted the equanimity and imparti-

ality of mind and the elevation of soul necessary to A.D. 1828.
make a great man.

The father of Capodistrias was a bigoted aristocrat, and his own youthful education was partly Venetian and partly Greek. His instruction was not accurate, nor was his reading extensive, so that, through the cosmopolite intellectual cultivation of his later years, his provincial ideas often peeped out. He generally used the French language in writing as well as speaking. He was indeed unable to write Greek, though he spoke it fluently. Italian was of course his mother tongue. For a statesman he was far too loquacious.[1] He allowed everybody who approached him to perceive that on many great political questions of importance in Greece, his opinions were vague and unsettled. At times he spoke as a warm panegyrist of Russian absolutism, and at times as an enthusiastic admirer of American democracy.

Before accepting the presidency of Greece, Capodistrias visited Russia, and obtained the approbation of the Emperor Nicholas. He arrived in Greece in the month of January 1828, and he found the country in a state of anarchy. The government had been compelled to wander from one place to another, and had rendered itself contemptible wherever it had appeared. In November 1826 it fled from Nauplia, and soon after established itself at Egina. In 1827 it removed to Poros. In consequence of a decree of the National Assembly of Trœzene, it returned to Nauplia, but its presence caused a civil war, and it went back to Egina.

The first measures of Capodistrias were prompt and judicious. He could not put an immediate stop to

---

[1] General Pellion says, "Tous ceux qui ont connu particulièrement Capodistrias avouent que, parlant avec une étonnante facilité et parlant beaucoup, il se laissait parfois aller à des indiscrétions fort extraordinaires."—*La Grèce et les Capodistrias pendant l'Occupation Française de 1828 à 1834.* Tricoupi, who was the president's secretary, says, Ἑλληνι ἀλλὰ δὲν ἔγραφεν Ἑλληνιστί, iv. 217.

some of the grossest abuses in the army, navy, and financial administration, without assuming dictatorial power. The necessity of his dictatorship was admitted; and the manner by which he sought its ratification from the existing government and the representative body, was generally approved. To give his administrative changes a national sanction without creating any check on his own power, he established a council of state, called Panhellenion, consisting of twenty-seven members, divided into three sections, for the consideration of administrative, financial, and judicial business. Decrees of the president were to be promulgated on reports of the whole Panhellenion, or of the section to which the business of the decree related. Capodistrias announced that he would convoke a national assembly in the month of April, and the warmest partisans of representative institutions allowed that the state of the country rendered an earlier convocation impracticable.[1]

But after making these concessions to public opinion, Capodistrias began to display his aversion to any systematic restraint on his arbitrary powers. He violated the provisions of the constitution of Trœzene without necessity, and by his proceedings soon taught the liberal party to regard him as the representative of force and not of law. Yet a clear perception of his position and his interest would have shown him that his power could have no firm foundation unless it was based on the supremacy of right.

The opinions and the policy of Capodistrias during his presidency are revealed by Count Bulgari, another Greek, who was Russian minister in Greece, and who was understood to echo the president's sentiments, even if he did not, as was generally reported, write under his dictation. In a memoir on the state of

---

[1] Proclamation, dated 20th January 1828. *Γενικὴ Ἐφημερίς*, 25th January 1828.

Greece in 1828, the views of Capodistrias are thus stated: " It would be a strange delusion to believe seriously in the possibility of organising any government whatever in Greece upon purely constitutional principles, which require a general tendency of the people to political forms, as well as elements of civilisation which exist only in a few individuals. The president of Greece thought that it was the duty of the three powers to destroy the Greek Revolution by establishing a monarchical government, in order to put an end to the scandalous and sanguinary scenes which made humanity shudder."[1] These sentiments were repeated by the president both to foreigners and Greeks, and showed on many occasions his want of sympathy with the cause of national independence, as well as his aversion to political liberty. His language constantly insinuated, though he perhaps never directly asserted, that he was the only fit sovereign for Greece. He harped incessantly on the theme, that all the men previously engaged in public business were demoralised either by the Turkish yoke, or by revolutionary anarchy; and he asserted that no permanent improvement could take place in the condition of the Greeks until the living generation had passed away. He called the primates, Christian Turks; the military chiefs, robbers; the men of letters, fools; and the phanariots, children of Satan; and he habitually concluded such diatribes by adding, that the good of the suffering people required that he should be allowed to govern with absolute power. And perhaps nothing better could have happened to Greece, had it been possible for him to forget that he was a Corfiot, and that he had two or three stupid brothers at Corfu.[2]

The presidency of Capodistrias lasted more than three

[1] *Parliamentary Papers.* Protocol of 22d March 1829, enclosure in annex C.
[2] Compare Tricoupi, iv. 285.

years and a half. It was not, therefore, want of time which prevented his laying the foundations of an administrative system, and adopting a judicial organisation. The Greeks possessed local institutions of great administrative value; but instead of making use of these institutions, he wasted much time in striving to undermine them. He argued that no political good could rest on a democratic foundation. To the reign of law he had a passionate antipathy. He sometimes spoke of the law as a kind of personal enemy to his dictatorship. He insisted that, to govern Greece well, his power must be exercised without limit or restraint, and that the law which subjected his arbitrary authority to systematic rules was in some degree a mere constitutional delusion. He forgot that he required the assistance of the law to prevent his own creatures from robbing him of the power he had assumed. Unfortunately for Greece, Capodistrias was a diplomatist and not a statesman. His plans of government were vaguely sketched in provisional laws. He never framed a precise code of administrative procedure, and, as a natural consequence of the provisional nature of his government, his ordinances were nullified by the agents charged to carry them into execution. While he ridiculed the liberal theories of the constitutions of Epidaurus and Trœzene, he did not perceive that his own acts were those of an administrative sciolist.

The president's attention was early directed to the anarchy that prevailed in the military forces of Greece. The extortions of the soldiery were wasting all those districts into which the Egyptians had not penetrated. The agricultural population was in danger of extermination. The armed men who extorted pay and provisions from the country were now the followers of military chiefs, not the soldiers of the Greek government. In order to form an army, it was necessary to break the connection between the soldiers and their leaders, and to form corps in which both the inferior and superior officers should depend directly on the president for their authority, and in which the soldiers should look to him for their pay, subsistence, reward, and punishment. Of military affairs Capodistrias was utterly ignorant, and, as usual, he allowed his suspicious nature to neutralise the effect of his sagacity. From excessive jealousy of his personal authority, he refused to employ experienced soldiers in organising his army, and he made a vain attempt to direct the enterprise himself.

Demetrius Hypsilantes had proved his inability for organising an army, and Sir Richard Church had never been able to introduce any discipline in his camps. Capodistrias appointed the first to command an army destined to reconquer Eastern Greece, and left the second at the head of the disorganised bands in Western Greece. Fabvier, who had proved himself a good disciplinarian, and had formed regular battalions under circumstances of great difficulty, was neglected and driven from Greece. Capodistrias had the weakness or the misfortune to name always the wrong man for every important place. His enemies accused him of fearing the right man in any office.

The consequence of the unmilitary president attempting to regulate the details of military organisation, was that the Greek army remained without either order or discipline. A few reforms were introduced, tending to enable the president to know how many men Greece had in the field, and to diminish the frauds committed in the distribution of rations; and this introduction of a regular system of mustering, paying, and provisioning the troops by the central government deserves praise, though it was a very small step towards the formation of a Greek army.

The circumstances in which the Greek soldiery were placed at this epoch of the Revolution afforded great facilities for the introduction of military discipline, and for the formation of an efficient national army of veteran troops. The soldiers had eaten up the substance of the agricultural population, and were themselves in danger of starvation. Capodistrias, holding in his hands the absolute disposal of all the supplies from abroad on which the troops were dependent for pay and rations, could command their obedience to any terms he might impose. The most powerful chieftains only maintained a few followers by seizing the public revenues. They were hated by the people for their extortions, envied by the mass of the soldiery for the benefits they conferred on a few, and in open hostility with the public interests. The arrival of Capodistrias annihilated their usurped power, and the chieftains who kept possession of the fortresses of Corinth, Nauplia, and Monemvasia, in defiance of the preceding government, were compelled to surrender those places into his hands.

A camp was formed at Trœzene, to which all the troops of continental Greece in the Morea were summoned, in order that they might receive their new organisation. The president appeared and promulgated his scheme for the formation of a national army. About eight thousand men, consisting in great part of the armatoli who had remained faithful to the Greek cause, were divided into eight regiments or chiliarchies. The chiliarchs or colonels, and the other officers of these regiments, were named by the president. Paymasters were also appointed, and a regular commissariat formed, so that an end was put to the previous system of trading in rations. The facility with which every reform was adopted by the soldiers, and their alacrity in preferring the position of government troops to that of personal followers of individual chieftains, proved that the president might easily have effected much more than he attempted.

The new regiments were inspected by the president at Trœzene in February 1828. The men had the aspect of veteran soldiers; still the review presented a very unmilitary spectacle. The chiliarchies were only distinguished by being separate groups of companies. The different companies were ranged in various forms and figures, according to the fancies of their captains—some were spun out in single files, some were drawn up four deep, some seemed to form circles, and some attempted to form squares. At last the whole army was ranged in lines, straggling in disorder, and undulating in unmeaning restlessness. The review, if such a spectacle can be called by a military term, was a parade for the purpose of enabling the inexperienced eye of the president to count the companies and examine the men of whom they were composed.

At a later period Capodistrias attempted to carry his organisation a step farther. In the autumn of 1829, after the termination of the war against the Turks in continental Greece, he again mustered the chiliarchies at Salamis. His military counsellor was Colonel Gerard, a French officer, whom he had appointed inspector of the Greek army. The troops present did not exceed five thousand men, who were divided into twenty battalions, and each battalion was composed of four companies. The commanders of the new battalions were called taxiarchs, and the chiliarchs were now ranked as generals. Paymasters were appointed to each battalion, and commanders were deprived of all control over the military chests. Had Capodistrias, when he introduced this new organisation, settled the supernumerary officers who were willing to become agriculturists on national lands, he might have broken up the system of farming the revenues of the country to military men, which the chieftains had introduced, and saved Greece from the calamity of nourishing in her breast a second generation of these vipers.

Demetrius Hypsilantes was appointed to command the chiliarchies formed at Trœzene, and he established a camp at Megara. But though he was at the head of eight thousand armatoli, and the Turks had not four thousand men in Eastern Greece, he remained for seven months in utter idleness. No attempt was made to drill the men, to instruct the companies in the manœuvres of light infantry, nor to teach the chiliarchies the tactics of an army. Capodistrias justly reproached Hypsilantes with his inactivity and incapacity; but he forgot that it was his own duty to frame systematic regulations for the discipline of the whole Greek army, and to transmit both to Hypsilantes and Church precise orders to carry these regulations into effect.

Amidst the military reforms of Capodistrias he neglected the regular troops. Yet he was well aware that this body formed the only corps on which the government could always rely. Indeed this fact contains the true explanation of his neglect. The regular corps was a body that from its nature would identify itself with the executive government of Greece. The semi-organised battalions of regulars were held in dependence on the personal will and favour of Count Capodistrias. The president wished everything in Greece to be provisional until he should be appointed president for life, or sovereign of the country. That he might have it in his power to revive the regular corps when he required its services, he revived the law of conscription passed by the Greek government in 1825, and applied it to the islands of the Archipelago. The pay of Fabvier's corps had fallen ten months into arrear after the unfortunate expedition to Chios. Instead of paying these arrears, and retaining Fabvier's veterans under arms, he allowed them to disband themselves. These men were attached to Fabvier, and Capodistrias was jealous of Fabvier's influence. But as it was necessary to gain credit in Western Europe for a wish to form a regular army, the president pretended that it was necessary to apply the law of conscription in order to obtain men. In this case the conduct of the president was marked by excessive duplicity, for he knew well that it would have been more economical to retain the veterans of the regular corps by paying the ten months' arrears which were due to them, than to enrol new recruits; and he was not insensible to the folly of withdrawing active labourers from the cultivation of the soil in the only part of Greece where agriculture was pursued in security and with profit. As soon as Fabvier perceived that the military plans of the president were subordinated to personal schemes of ambition, he resigned his command, as has been already mentioned, and quitted Greece in May 1828.[1]

Hypsilantes, as has been said, passed the summer of 1828 at Megara. The Russian war compelled Reshid Pasha to leave continental Greece and Epirus almost destitute of troops, and he was threatened with an insurrection of the Albanian chieftains in his own pashalik of Joannina. In autumn the Greeks advanced to Lombotina, famous for its apples, and drove the Turks into Lepanto. Hypsilantes about the same time occupied Bœotia and Phocis, and on the 29th of November

[1] The law of conscription was put in operation by a circular addressed to the municipalities, Γενικὴ 'Εφημερὶς, 25th April 1828; yet in March 1830 the number of Capodistrias's regulars only amounted to two thousand two hundred and fifty.

the Turks in Salona capitulated, and the capitulation was faithfully observed by the Greeks. On the 5th of December Karpenisi was evacuated. A few insignificant skirmishes took place during the winter. The Turks were too weak to attempt anything, and the anarchy that still prevailed among the Greek chiefs prevented the numerical superiority of the Greek forces from being available.[1]

The army of Western Greece was not more active than that of Eastern during the summer of 1828. Capodistrias visited the camp of Sir Richard Church near Mytika, and he declared that, on inspecting the troops in Acarnania, he found less order than in those he had reviewed at Trœzena. This visit gave the president a very unfavourable opinion of the generalissimo's talents for organisation. In September the Greeks advanced to the Gulf of Arta, and occupied Loutraki, where they gained possession of a few boats. Capodistrias named Pasano, a Corsican adventurer, to succeed Hastings as commander of the naval forces in Western Greece. Pasano made an unsuccessful attempt to force the passage into the Gulf of Arta, but some of the Greek officers under his command, considering that he had shown both cowardice and incapacity in the affair, renewed the enterprise without his order, and passed gallantly under the batteries of

---

[1] Two examples of the condition of the Greek army may be cited:—"Dr Howe gave 12,000 lb. of beans to the Megarians to sow their fields. To-day a deputation informed him that the troops who had returned to Megara were cutting down all the young plants for salad, and the officers were feeding their horses on them. They solicited Howe to use his influence with the president to prevent the entire destruction of their crop."—MS. Journal, 20th February 1829. Captain Hane reports that a regular trade in provisions was carried on by some men with the Turks, and the supplies were drawn from Sir Richard Church's camp. Fabricius, who commanded the Helvetia, stopped a vessel laden with provisions attempting to reach Previsa, and as she had a passport signed by the generalissimo, he sent her to Dragomestre, where Sir Richard Church released her without waiting for a decision of the Admiralty Court. Hastings, on returning from Western Greece in 1828, complained of similar conduct. He wrote: "To conciliate the unprincipled chieftains, Church ruins the army."

Previsa.[1] This exploit secured to the Greeks the command of the Gulf of Arta. Pasano was recalled, and Admiral Kriezes, a Hydriot officer of ability and courage, succeeded him. The town of Vonitza, a ruinous spot, was occupied by the Greek troops on the 27th December 1828; but the almost defenceless Venetian castle did not capitulate until the 17th March 1829. The passes of Makrynoros were occupied in April.

A.D. 1829.

Capodistrias, who had blamed both Hypsilantes and Church for incapacity, now astonished the world by making his brother Agostino a general.[2]

Count Agostino Capodistrias, besides not being a military man, was really little better than a fool; yet the president, blinded by fraternal affection, named this miserable creature his plenipotentiary in Western Greece, and empowered him to direct all military and civil business. The plenipotentiary arrived in the Hellas. On the 30th April 1829, the garrison of Naupaktos (Lepanto) capitulated, and was transported to Previsa. On the 14th May, Mesolonghi and Anatolikon were evacuated by the Turks.

Reshid Pasha escaped the mortification of witnessing the loss of all his conquests in Greece. His prudence and valour were rewarded with the rank of grand vizier, and he quitted Joannina to assume the command of the Othoman army at Shumla before the Turks evacuated continental Greece.

The war terminated in 1829. The Allied powers fixed the frontier of Greece by a protocol in the month of March. Yet the Turks would not yield possession of the places they still held in Eastern Greece, and some skirmishes ensued, in which a great deal of

---

[1] The Greeks lost one killed and three wounded.
[2] Tricoupi says, 'Ο κυβερνήτης ἐνέμφετο τὸν ἀρχιστράτηγον καὶ τὸν στρατάρχην ὡς ἀναξίους τῆς ὑψηλῆς θέσεώς των, iv. 342.

CIVIL ADMINISTRATION

powder was wasted, and very little blood was shed.[1] A body of Albanians, under Aslan Bey, marched from Zeituni by Thermopylæ, Livadea, and Thebes, and reached Athens without encountering opposition. After leaving a small and select garrison in the Acropolis, Aslan Bey collected all the Turks in Attica and Bœotia, and commenced his retreat. But on arriving at the pass of Petra, between Thebes and Livadea, he found a body of Greek troops strongly posted to dispute the passage. The Turks, unable to advance, concluded a capitulation on the 25th of September 1829, by which they engaged to evacuate all Eastern Greece, except the Acropolis of Athens and the fort of Karababa on the Euripus. Thus Prince Demetrius Hypsilantes had the honour of terminating the war which his brother had commenced on the banks of the Pruth; and this action cherished in his mind the delusion that, as the representative of his brother Alexander, he was the right sovereign for Greece. As a military man, he was deficient in tactical knowledge and strategic capacity; as a statesman, he was utterly destitute of judgment; but his personal courage and private virtues command respect.

The civil administration of Capodistrias was founded on no organised system. He found the Greeks enjoying a degree of individual liberty, and exercising in their municipalities more independent political action than he had supposed existed on the continent of Europe; for his opinions concerning the internal administration of Switzerland, though he had resided there for some time, and laboured as a Russian diplomatist to secure its existence as an independent state, were very crude. In Greece he mistook the liberty he found existing for the cause of the anarchy that desolated the country, and this anarchy he considered to be a

[1] Tricoupi, iv. 365: Πολλὴ πυρόκαυσις ἐγένη, ἀλλ᾽ ὀλίγον αἷμα ἐχύθη.

necessary consequence of the sovereignty of the people. A.D. 1828.
He determined to eradicate the municipal system,
which appeared to him to have transfused the elements
of revolutionary action into the frame of society; and
he began to weaken the power of the municipalities,
by converting the demogeronts into agents of the
executive authority. To complete the destruction of
revolutionary principles, he created a governmental
police, and rendered its members responsible to him
alone for the exercise of their powers. His plan of
government was very simple, but really impracticable.
He retained in his own hands the absolute direction
of every branch of the public administration, declaring
that nothing could be permanently settled concerning
the internal organisation of the country until the three
powers had decided its external position as an independent
state. The real object was to render his services
indispensable either as prime minister, hospodar,
prince, or king.

Capodistrias divided the Morea into seven provinces,
and the islands into six. These provinces were governed
provisionally by thirteen extraordinary commissioners,
to whom he intrusted great and ill-defined
authority.[1] Immemorial usages, and old as well as
new political institutions, were suspended, and the
despotism of these Greek pashas was restrained by no
published instructions, no fixed forms of proceeding,
and by no judicial authority.

The evil effects of arbitrary power were soon visible.
Ibrahim's conquests, the financial corruption of Konduriottes's
government, and the military anarchy that
succeeded, had paralysed the action of the municipalities.
Instead of removing abuses and restoring their
vigour, they were robbed of all independent action,
even in the direction of their local affairs. The com-

[1] Γενικὴ 'Εφημερίς, 18th and 21st April 1828.

missioners of Capodistrias presided at the election of new demogeronts; and these newly-elected municipal magistrates were converted into subordinate agents of the president's minister of the interior. By this change in the local institutions of Greece, the way was prepared for their complete nullification by the Bavarians.

The operation of Capodistrias's government may be exemplified by citing the proceedings of Viaro Capodistrias, who was considered the most energetic of the extraordinary commissioners, and who governed the Western Sporades, which was the most important province in the islands. Viaro was the president's elder brother: he was a Corfiot lawyer. The confined experience gained in a corrupt semi-Venetian society was not counteracted by good sense and a benevolent heart: Viaro was sulky, obstinate, and insolent. Capodistrias cannot have been entirely blind to his brother's defects, for he drove him away from Russia, though he invited him to Greece.

While Capodistrias was a favourite minister of the Emperor Alexander, Viaro visited Russia, where he met with a very kind reception. For a moment the Corfiot lawyer indulged in visions of wealth and splendour, which were very soon dispelled by his diplomatic brother. One evening, after Capodistrias had waited on some members of the imperial family, he came back to Viaro, and addressed him to the following purport: "I have seen the emperor to-day, and I have just quitted several members of the imperial family. The emperor is ready to appoint you to an honourable place in his service; but I must tell you beforehand, that if you accept the offer, I shall immediately resign my place and return to Corfu. We are foreigners, and we could not both long retain office here. It is for you to decide which of us ought to remain."[1] Viaro believed that he was capable of ruling an empire, but he felt that he could not instantly move with an unembarrassed step among the statesmen and princes of Russia if deprived of his brother's countenance. He therefore returned to Corfu.

A.D. 1828.

A more confined sphere of action was opened to him in 1828, but he was intrusted with absolute power over the islands of Hydra, Spetzas, Poros, and Egina. The elevation was sufficient to turn his head. He arrogated to himself both legislative and judicial, as well as merely administrative, authority, within the bounds of his province, and he exercised the sovereign power he assumed in a very capricious manner. In virtue of his legislative power he fixed the rate of interest, and in virtue of his judicial he inflicted the penalty of confiscation for the violation of this provincial law. He arrested Greek citizens, and retained them in prison, without accusing them of any offence except dissatisfaction with his conduct. He appointed demogeronts without even going through the formality of a popular election; he superseded those elected by the people whenever they opposed his measures, and replaced them by his own nominees. He named judges without any warrant from the president; and when a primate of Livadea refused to obey a decision of these judges, he sent the primate to prison. He imposed taxes when he was in want of money, without any vote of the municipalities, or any authority from the central government. He ordered private letters to be stopped and opened; and he carried his imprudence and folly so far as to break open and read despatches addressed to the English naval

[1] This well-known anecdote will be found in *Mémoires Biographiques Historiques sur le Comte Jean Capodistrias*, par A. Papadopoulos Vretos, vol. I. p. 37.

officer on the station, though he was assured by Mr Gropius, the Austrian consul, that these despatches were official orders passing from one ship on the station to another, and which ought not to be passed through the health-office.

The friends of Capodistrias declared that many of the arbitrary acts of Viaro's administration proceeded from the misconduct of his subordinates. The inhabitants of Egina, believing this, appealed to the sense of justice of their extraordinary commissioner. They transmitted to him a petition complaining of the oppressive and corrupt conduct of the health-officer he had appointed. Viaro received the document at Poros, and immediately ordered his secretary, who remained at Egina, to call a meeting of the inhabitants to receive his answer. When the Eginetans were assembled, the secretary produced the petition, and asked them if that was the paper they had signed and transmitted to Viaro. They replied that it was. The secretary then announced to them that they were convoked to see their petition burned by order of Count Viaro Capodistrias, extraordinary commissioner of the president of Greece in the Western Sporades; and when the document was consumed, they were told that they had received a milder reply than they merited.

The acts of Viaro rendered him unpopular; his proclamations rendered him ridiculous. The Hydriots resisted some of his quarantine regulations, and when the quarantine to which he had subjected them expired, he addressed them thus—" Place your confidence in the providence of God and the forethought of your government; but beware of examining the acts or criticising the conduct of your rulers, for you may be led into error, and error may bring down calamity on your heads."

The folly of Agostino, and the tyranny of Viaro, would have ruined the president without the assistance of any other Corfiots, but he brought over Mustoxidi, A.D. 1829. a literary man of some merit, and Gennatas, a lawyer in good practice, to aid in exciting the jealousy of the Greeks, who had borne an active part in the Revolution, and considered themselves entitled to all the spoils of official employment.

Public opinion generally verifies the value of modern governments by the touchstone of finance. The presidency of Capodistrias was not remarkable either for the ability or the honesty of its financial administration. He found the collection and expenditure of the public revenues a mass of fraud and peculation. His overweening self-sufficiency prompted him to assume the whole task of cleansing the Augean stable, and he retained the supreme direction of the finance department in his own hands. His hostility to all constitutional forms prevented him from making use of publicity as a means of controlling subordinate and distant officials, over whose proceedings he could exercise no direct inspection. His admiration of the autocratic system of administration blinded him to the impossibility of applying it without a well-organised body of officials. His want of practical acquaintance with the details of financial business rendered all his schemes for reforming abuses unavailing; and, as in every other department, his extreme jealousy prevented him from employing men who possessed the practical knowledge in which he was deficient. The general conduct of the finance department was intrusted to a board composed of three members. But they were men who possessed little knowledge beyond that of experienced accountants. No payments were made for the service of any ministerial department without an order under the president's sign-manual. He reserved to himself the task of framing a new financial system for Greece. The consequence of this determination to do everything was, that he neither effected any improvement, nor allowed others to propose any extensive reform.

The principal branch of the Greek revenues was the tenth of the annual produce of all cultivated land, and an additional rent of fifteen per cent on all Turkish property which had been declared national.[1] The Othoman system of farming the taxes was adhered to, and the revolutionary practice of letting large districts to primates and military chiefs, instead of committing the collection to the municipal authorities.

Capodistrias did not restrain the abuses of the farmers of the tenths.[2] He even employed the farming system as a means of strengthening his power. He favoured the chieftains whom he considered to be his personal partisans, and increased their influence by allowing them to farm large districts. By this means they maintained large bodies of military followers as tax-collectors, and the president considered these men as more completely under his personal influence than the soldiers of the government. This policy often led him to sacrifice national advantages to the tortuous schemes of personal ambition.

The receipts of the year 1829 exceeded 4,000,000 drachms, and the expense of three thousand regular troops amounted to only about 1,000,000. The sum of 3,000,000 would have been amply sufficient to

---

[1] The Greek revenues at this time were derived from the following sources:—
    1°, The tenth of cultivated land, and 25 per cent on national property.
    2°, The custom duties.
    3°, The farming of salt-works and fisheries.
    4°, Cattle-tax.
    5°, Duties on houses, shops, and mills, on passports, and from quarantines.

[2] The Island of Egina enjoyed more direct protection from Capodistrias than any part of Greece, yet the proprietors were often forced to leave ripe figs and grapes ungathered until they bribed the farmer of the taxes for permission to gather them. Cases often occurred in which a part of the crop was lost by the tax-gatherer delaying to visit any garden of which the proprietor refused to pay the composition which was demanded.

maintain an army of five thousand regulars, with a A.D. 1829. due proportion of cavalry and artillery. Now, as the expenditure of the civil government was only estimated at 300,000 drachms, it is evident that an able and honest administration might have laid the foundations of order in the army, and secured an impartial administration of justice by appointing well-paid judges. A man less occupied with diplomatic intrigues, Holy-Alliance policy, and foreign protocols, than Capodistrias, even though of far inferior ability, might, by giving his principal attention to the improvement of the condition of the agricultural population, have soon raised Greece to a flourishing position, and secured to himself a great historic name.

The administration of the customs was greatly improved. Under the inspection of Colonel Heldeck, those of the Gulf of Argolis were raised from 20,000 to 336,000 drachms annually, without any increase of duties, and those of Syra were greatly increased.

A new monetary system was introduced, but it was unfortunately based on an erroneous theory, and carried into execution with a defective assay. The monetary relations of Greece indicated that the currency either of France or Austria ought to have been adopted as the standard of the Greek coinage, and there were strong theoretic and practical reasons for preferring the franc as the unit. Capodistrias, influenced by old commercial associations of Levant merchants, struck a new coin called a phœnix (which was afterwards termed a drachma by the Bavarian regency), as the unit of the Greek monetary system; but in place of making it equal in value to a franc, he made it one-sixth of the metallic value of a Spanish pillar dollar. Now, as the Spanish pillar dollar was a coin circulating in Levant for commercial purposes at an agio, it was clearly an error to base the monetary system on such a standard.

A defective assay also caused an error in the metallic value of the coinage issued by Capodistrias, and the phœnix was issued in small quantity.

A national bank was also established in name, but the title was intended to deceive Western Europe, not to facilitate banking operations in Greece. The so-called national bank was nothing more than a loan, opened at first by voluntary subscription. The misapplication of the name caused distrust in a mercantile society like that of Greece; and the president, finding his persuasion insufficient to induce many wealthy Greeks to deposit money in the national bank, used his political power to compel them to advance money to it. Government took possession of all the sums received; and before two months elapsed, Capodistrias himself candidly admitted to Captain Hastings that for the time the national bank was only a forced loan.

At a later period the president proposed an excellent financial measure to the national assembly of Argos, but, like too many of his good intentions, it was never carried into execution. The public accounts were ordered to be submitted to the supervision of a court of control at the end of every quarter.

The absence of any systematic administration of justice was the cause of great national demoralisation during the course of the Greek Revolution. Honest men ruined themselves by fulfilling their obligations; dishonest men repudiated even those pecuniary debts which they could have paid without inconvenience. To the people it appeared that honesty was not the best policy in pecuniary affairs, and the general tendency to financial dishonesty is, as the preceding pages have shown, deeply marked on the history of the Greeks. When Capodistrias arrived, the insecurity of life and property among the agricultural classes threatened the dissolution of society, and the Greeks seemed in danger of becoming a nation of traders in towns and cities like the Jews. The desire to see the supremacy of justice firmly established was one cause of the election of Capodistrias to the presidency, and to the fervour with which he was welcomed on his arrival. He was selected by the almost unanimous voice of his countrymen as the only Greek capable of putting an end to the reign of injustice. Nothing in his political career exhibits his deficiencies as a statesman so strikingly as his failure to appreciate the value of a firm and impartial administration of justice. The career of a legislator lay before him. Had he seized the sword of justice and walked boldly forward, he would have soon marched at the head of the Greek nation; and courts, cabinets, and protocols would have found some difficulty in contesting his right to be the ruler of Greece. But he loved power more than justice; and yet by not loving justice he lost his hold on power.

The indifference of Capodistrias to the establishment of legal tribunals can only be explained by his love of absolute power. Soon after his arrival, he created a few justices and some minor courts to decide trifling questions. But no legal tribunals were established, and his extraordinary commissioners were allowed to exercise an exceptional and extensive legal jurisdiction, of which his brother Viaro took every possible advantage, and used with unrestricted licence. A decree organising civil and criminal tribunals, and establishing a court of review, at last appeared on the 27th August 1830.[1] Capodistrias attempted to excuse his delay by declaring that he had avoided doing anything to circumscribe the authority of the future sovereign of Greece—a futile assertion; for he well knew that by prolonging anarchy he had increased the difficulties in the way of

[1] Supplement to No. 73 of the Γενικὴ 'Εφημερίς, 10th September 1830.

establishing order. As long as Capodistrias had any prospect of retaining the government of Greece in his own hands, he wished to retain all judiciary authority in direct subordination to the executive, as in Russia; and he was adverse to the promulgation of fixed rules of procedure, and to the constitution of independent courts of law. The Corfiot lawyer, Gennatas, whom he appointed minister of justice, and to whom he intrusted the task of preparing the judicial organisation, was the instrument of his views rather from defective judgment than from malevolent intentions. The assembly of Argos declared that the president ought to render the judges irremovable, but neither Capodistrias nor Gennatas were of this opinion.[1] This good advice was rejected by Capodistrias, as it has been for more than a quarter of a century by King Otho. But Capodistrias, in the true spirit of despotism, conferred arbitrary powers on the police authorities, and created exceptional tribunals to judge political offences.[2]

Capodistrias made a great show of promoting education, but he did very little for facilitating public instruction, and nothing for improving the intellectual condition of the Greek clergy. Yet he affected to be a friend to knowledge, and he was sincerely devout. Political intrigue seems to have occupied all his thoughts, absorbed his time, and inspired all his actions during his presidency.

He built an immense orphan asylum at Egina, which was filled with children delivered from slavery and brought back from Egypt. It was from no fault of Capodistrias, perhaps, but the internal management of this establishment was ill regulated, and it did not prosper. The president ordered many schoolhouses to

---

[1] Decrees of the Assembly of Argos, No. 11, art. 7, 22d June 1829.
[2] See Πολιτικὴ καὶ Ἐγκληματικὴ Διαθέσεις, published at Egina in 1830 pp. 11 and 110.

be built in different parts of Greece, but he had shown so little forethought in the business, that many were soon converted into barracks for soldiers. In the towns, government did very little to promote public education, and the governors named by the president more than once prevented teachers from opening private schools. The education of the clergy was utterly neglected, and a race of priests remained, whose ignorance was a disgrace to the Orthodox Church, and who increased the national corruption. Capodistrias succeeded in deceiving the Liberals in France, Germany, and Switzerland, into a belief that he was labouring sincerely to improve public instruction, but his personal views are exemplified by two acts. He ordered the professor of Greek literature at Egina not to read the Gorgias of Plato with his pupils, and he made war on the press at Nauplia.[1]

The arbitrary conduct of the president created a constitutional opposition to his administration, and he found himself obliged to convoke a national assembly, in order to give a sanction to his dictatorial power. His popularity with the people in the Morea was very great, for his government had delivered them from the Egyptians, and established some better guarantees for the protection of life and property than had previously existed. In a freely-elected chamber of deputies he would have been sure of a large majority, but he wished to silence all opposition, and he adopted many violent and illegal measures to exclude every man whom he deemed a Liberal. In a number of districts where the character of his opponents seemed likely to insure their election, he proposed himself as a candidate; and after securing his own election, it was generally not difficult to obtain the nomination of one of his own partisans in his place.

[1] Thiersch, *De l'Etat Actuel de la Grèce*, I. 22 and 54; Tricoupi, iv. 291.

The national assembly of Argos was opened by Capodistrias in a Russian uniform on the 23d July 1829. The assembly ratified everything the president had done, and intrusted him with all the additional power he desired. Only the laws which he approved and recommended were passed. He did not venture to obtain his nomination to the presidency for life, for it would have been imprudent to take so important a step in the settlement of the government of Greece without the previous consent of the three allied powers. But he obtained an act of the assembly, declaring that the decisions of the conferences of London should not be held to be binding on Greece until they were ratified by the Greek legislature.[1] He trusted to his own diplomatic skill for rendering this law subservient to his schemes concerning the sovereignty of Greece.

The Panhellenion was replaced by a senate, but the organisation of this senate was left by the assembly entirely in the hands of the president. It was a consultative and not a legislative council, and its consent was not indispensable to any laws except those relating to the permanent disposition of the national lands.

Capodistrias was also empowered to name a regency in case of his death, which was to conduct the government until the meeting of a national assembly.

The proceedings of the national assembly of Argos were opposed to the free spirit of the national assemblies of the earlier period of the Greek Revolution. The principle of government nomination too often replaced the old usage of popular election, and tortuous ways were adopted instead of direct courses. Thus, in appointing the senate, sixty-eight names were submitted by the assembly to the president, who selected twenty-one of these candidates to be senators. The

---

[1] Γενικὴ Ἐφημερίς, No. 53, 30th July 1829.

senate was then completed by the addition of six members named by the president.

The establishment of two chambers to share the legislative power, was contemplated by the assembly, but the president was intrusted with the arrangements necessary for calling the legislature into existence.[1]

The excessive confidence of the deputies misled Capodistrias into the conviction that his power was irresistible, and from this time his conduct became more arbitrary, and his personal partisans more insolent.

The proceedings of the three protecting powers gave him great anxiety. He detested England, mistrusted France, and doubted the sentiments of the Russian cabinet, for he felt that he was not admitted to its secrets. The nomination of Prince Leopold of Saxe-Coburg (Leopold, king of the Belgians) to be sovereign of Greece, disappointed his hopes and irritated his feelings. He had laboured to convince Europe that he was the only man capable of organising a state in Greece. His ambition was legitimate. But his own double-dealing had prevented even Russia from assuming the responsibility of advocating his cause. Had his conduct not been marked by duplicity, and had he sought to attain his object by honest and legal measures, it is probable that he would have succeeded. Diplomacy is not in the habit of working miracles, and neither an Epaminondas nor a Washington was likely to arise among the semi-Venetian aristocracy of Corfu.

The three powers conducted their conferences at London in a slow and vacillating manner. The principles which ought to have regulated their proceedings were lucidly announced in a report drawn up by their representatives at Poros, on the 12th December 1828.[2]

[1] Γενικὴ 'Εφημερίς, No. 53. The decree is dated 22d July (3d August) 1829
[2] *Parliamentary Papers* — Protocol of a conference of the representatives of Great Britain, France, and Russia, held at Poros 12th December 1828.

The measures then recommended were embodied in a protocol signed at London on the 22d March 1829, and were not very dissimilar from those which were ultimately adopted when Greece was declared a kingdom in 1832.[1] The frontier of the Greek state was drawn from the Gulf of Volo to the Gulf of Arta. The annual tribute to the sultan was fixed at about £30,000. The Turks who had possessed land in Greece were allowed to sell their property. An hereditary sovereign was to be chosen by the three protecting powers, who, though he acknowledged the suzerainty of the Porte, was to enjoy complete independence in all business relating to the political government and the internal administration. This plan, warmly supported by Sir Stratford Canning (Lord Stratford de Redcliffe), might have been carried into execution without delay, had the Earl of Aberdeen, who was then Foreign Secretary, been as well acquainted with the state of Turkey and Greece as Sir Stratford. Unfortunately the Earl of Aberdeen treated the question with diplomatic pedantry. While Capodistrias was intriguing, while Sultan Mahmud was fuming with rage, and while the population of Greece was perishing from misery, the English Foreign Secretary insisted on reserving to each of the Allied courts the right of weighing separately the objections which the indignant sultan might make to the proposed arrangements; and England and France sent ambassadors to Constantinople to open negotiations with the Othoman government.

In the mean time the success of Russia compelled the sultan to sign the treaty of Adrianople on the 14th September 1829; and an article in this treaty bound the sultan to adhere to the treaty of 6th July 1827 for the pacification of Greece, and to adopt the provisions

---

[1] Compare the Protocol of the 22d March 1829 with Annex A to the Protocol of the 26th April 1832.

of the protocol of the 22d March 1829.¹ The alarm of the sultan at the progress of the Russian army had induced him to make this concession a few days sooner to the ambassadors of England and France. On the 9th September the reis-effendi notified to them the sultan's adhesion to the treaty, and pledged himself to adopt all the decisions of the powers for carrying it into execution.² The Russians took advantage of the vagueness of this communication to exact a precise recognition of the protocol of the 22d of March in their treaty of peace, and in order to prevent the Porte from making use of its habitual tergiversations and delays, they bound the sultan to name a plenipotentiary for executing the stipulations of the protocol in conjunction with commissioners of the Allied powers.

The policy of the British cabinet received a severe rebuke. Great Britain had prevented France from establishing the pacification of Greece, by sending the French troops in the Morea to compel the Turks to evacuate continental Greece. France yielded to the counsels of Lord Aberdeen, and Russia profited by his lordship's blunder.

The courts of England and France felt humiliated by the position in which Russia had placed them. The sultan was obsequious; the Greeks were grateful. Capodistrias perhaps expected with secret tremulation to hear that he was named hospodar of the Morea. To give the negotiations a new turn, and neutralise the credit of Russia, a decisive step was taken in a different direction. By the protocol of 3d February 1830, Greece was declared an independent state, but the boon of independence was rendered a punishment by diminishing the extent of the country. A new frontier was drawn from the mouth of the Achelous to the mouth

---

¹ Lesur, *Annuaire Historique*, 1829. See the 10th article of the treaty.
² *Parliamentary Papers*, Annex B to Protocol of 3d February 1830.

of the Sperchius. Diplomatic ignorance could hardly have traced a more unsuitable line of demarcation. All Acarnania and a considerable part of Etolia were surrendered to the sultan. That part of the continent in which Greek is the language of the people was annexed to Turkey, and that part in which the agricultural population speaks the Albanian language was attached to Greece. With such a frontier it was certain that peace could only be established by force; yet the protocol declared that no power should send troops to Greece without the unanimous consent of the Allies. Lord Aberdeen's injudicious protocol concluded with a foolish paragraph, congratulating the Allied courts on having reached the close of a long and difficult negotiation.

The sovereignty of the diminished state was offered to and accepted by Prince Leopold of Saxe-Coburg.[1] The Porte immediately accepted these arrangements. It was not blind to the advantage of retaining possession of Acarnania and great part of Etolia. On the other hand, Capodistrias availed himself of the unsuitable frontier to thwart the execution of the protocol. He was so sure of the nation's support, that he did not give himself any trouble to conceal his duplicity. He declared that the decree of the national assembly of Argos deprived him of the power of giving a legal sanction to the provisions of the protocol signed by the Allied powers. He pretended that he was placed in a position of great difficulty; that he feared to convoke a national assembly, as the deputies would either protest against the proceedings of the Allies, or violate their duty to their country and their instructions from their electors; but that he would accept the protocol on his own responsibility.[2] The

[1] *Parliamentary Papers.* Prince Leopold accepted the sovereignty on the 11th February 1830.
[2] *Parliamentary Papers*, Annex F, Protocol, 14th May 1830; Lesur, *Ann. Hist.*, 1829 — Documents, p. 111.

ministers of Great Britain, France, and Russia knew that he had drawn up the instructions of the electors to the deputies with his own hand, and they could not overlook the fact, that while he manifested extreme tenderness for the consciences of the deputies, he showed no hesitation in violating his own duty as president of Greece by setting aside a national decree, and accepting the protocol in an illegal manner, in order to obtain its repudiation, if it suited his convenience, at a later period.

Greece was so tortured by her provisional condition that the nomination of Prince Leopold was accepted by the people as a boon. Addresses of congratulation were spontaneously prepared. There was an outbreak of national enthusiasm; and many officials, believing that Capodistrias was sincere in the assurance which he gave in public, that he was anxious to give the new sovereign a cordial reception, signed these addresses. At first the president did not venture to oppose the general feeling, but he announced that previous approval of the government was necessary in order to give the addresses a legitimate character. Shortly after, he ventured to proclaim that every address which had not been submitted to the revision of the agents of his government previous to signature, emanated from obscure emissaries of the opposition. He was seriously alarmed at the eagerness to welcome the new sovereign in order to put an end to his own provisional administration. His devoted partisans alone knew his private wishes, and they endeavoured to prevent the spontaneous addresses from being signed, and delayed their transmission to the prince.[1] After the resignation of Prince Leopold, Capodistrias treated the signature of the spontaneous addresses as an act of

---

[1] *Parliamentary Papers*, Annex C, Protocol, 26th July 1830; Circular to Civil Governors of Greece, dated 2d June 1830.

hostility to his government, and dismissed many officials who were innocent of any wish to join the opposition, but who had been misled by his own assurance into a belief that he wished the prince to receive a hearty welcome. In order to neutralise the effect of the popular demonstrations in the prince's favour, the civil governors in the provinces were ordered to prepare other addresses. Many of these were not circulated for signature until the resignation of Prince Leopold was known to Capodistrias, and several of them were antedated.[1]

From this period, the secret police, which had been gradually formed under the direction of Viaro and Gennatas, acquired additional power. It became, as in many countries on the continent of Europe, a terrible social scourge.[2] The preference which the great body of the people had shown for a foreign sovereign filled the heart of Capodistrias with rage. He could not repress his feelings, and even to strangers he often inveighed bitterly against the ingratitude of his countrymen.

Yet he endeavoured to persuade the world that the Greeks viewed the nomination of Prince Leopold with dissatisfaction, if not with absolute aversion, and he succeeded so far as to create an impression that the Greeks were at least divided in opinion. He alarmed Prince Leopold with the fear of meeting an unfavourable reception. He attempted to disgust the prince by suggesting the necessity of his changing his religion, though it was well known that the Greek clergy were as eager to welcome a Protestant sovereign as the laity.

---

[1] The address of the Psarians was signed at Egina on the 20th July, but it was dated 7th June. Capodistrias did not inform the prince that the addresses were ready to be transmitted to England until the 26th of July. He was then aware that the prince had resigned on the 21st of May.

[2] Thiersch, L 27; Pallion, 177.

The condition of Greece at the time of Prince Leo- A. D. 1830. pold's nomination explains the proceedings of Capodistrias. Most of the ablest and most influential men had been driven from the public service, and excluded from the assembly of Argos. The senate was composed of the president's creatures. The government had not received a permanent organisation. No administration of justice gave a sure guarantee for life and property to private individuals. The people suspected that the country was retained in this provisional state to further the president's schemes of personal ambition. The nomination of Prince Leopold took Capodistrias by surprise, while he was preparing to convince Europe that the Greeks would not accept a foreign sovereign, and to persuade Liberals that the constitutional governments of England and France ought to admit the principle of popular election. He knew how to manage that universal suffrage should elect him sovereign of Greece. When he found his hopes baffled, and saw himself without any national support, he acted like a diplomatist, and not like a statesman. Instead of convoking a national assembly and adopting a national policy, he played a game of personal intrigue. He accepted the protocol to thwart its execution. He violated the law of Greece to keep the conduct of the negotiations in his own hands, and he deceived the prince with false representations.

Prince Leopold, on the other hand, acted imprudently in accepting the sovereignty of Greece before he had made up his mind to assume the immediate direction of the government. And his resignation, after having accepted the sovereignty, deserves severe reprobation. Princes can only be punished for trifling with the fortunes of nations by the judgment of history. The British government also acted most injudiciously, both in pressing him to accept, and in permitting him to double about after accepting. The objections he made to the arrangements of the protocol ought to have warned Lord Aberdeen that the prince was not the man suitable for the contingency. Indeed, it seems strange that the unfriendly correspondence which preceded Prince Leopold's nomination did not awaken a deeper sense of the responsibility due to the suffering inhabitants of Greece in the breasts both of the prince and of the British ministers.

If Prince Leopold really believed, as he wrote to Lord Aberdeen on the 3d February 1830, "that he could imagine no effectual mode of pacifying Greece without including Candia in the new state," it was his duty to refuse the government of Greece until Candia formed part of his sovereignty. Yet he was content to give up Candia and accept the sovereignty on the 11th of the month. The Allies were fairly warned not to permit ulterior negotiations on questions concerning which they were determined to make no concessions, but they neglected the warning. In the correspondence between the British government and Prince Leopold, which was laid before parliament, the prince appears as a rhetorician and not a statesman, and as a diplomatist and not an administrator.[1]

Even the dark picture Capodistrias drew of the state of Greece, and the difficulties likely to await the prince on his arrival, did not warrant Prince Leopold's retiring from his engagement. But Prince Leopold all along trifled with the awful responsibility he had assumed. It was his duty, the moment he accepted the sovereignty of Greece, to invite some Greek who had acquired practical experience in public business during the Revolution, to attend his person and act as

---

[1] *Parliamentary Papers*—Communications with Prince Leopold relating to the sovereignty of Greece, particularly letters of Lord Aberdeen to Prince Leopold, 31st January 1830, and Prince Leopold to Lord Aberdeen, 3d February 1830.

secretary of state. He ought immediately to have summoned a council of state, of which he might have invited Capodistrias to name a few members. With constitutional advisers, Prince Leopold would have found all his difficulties vanish. The bad faith of Capodistrias in his dealings with the prince is proved by the simple fact that he did not immediately send to London such men as Glarakes, Rizos, Psyllas, and Tricoupi, for he had employed them all in high office, and knew that, whatever might be their deficiencies, they were men of education and personal integrity. The president may be excused for trusting party leaders like Mavrocordatos, Metaxas, or Kolettes; but when the prince asked for a confidential adviser, it was insulting Greece to send Prince Wrede, a young Bavarian, who had arrived in the country after the termination of the war, and who knew very little more of the social and political condition of Greece than the Greeks knew of his existence. Indeed, Capodistrias himself knew only that the man he sent was called Prince Wrede, and had been recommended to General Heideck. It would have been almost impossible, among the foreigners then in Greece, to have selected a person so utterly incompetent to furnish Prince Leopold either with information or counsel. Jealousy and duplicity, as usual, were too strong in the breast of Capodistrias to admit of his concealing them.

Prince Leopold, after wearying the Allies and tormenting the English ministers with his negotiations, resigned the sovereignty of Greece on the 17th May 1830. Whether he would have gained in Greece the honour he has won as a wise ruler on the throne of Belgium, cannot be known; but when we reflect how many years of anarchy he would have saved the Greeks, it must be owned that he would have served humanity well by estimating more accurately than he did estimate it the responsibilities he incurred when he accepted the sovereignty of Greece.

The position of Capodistrias had been changed, and his power was shaken, by the nomination of Prince Leopold, nor did he recover his equanimity on the prince's resignation. As often happens to successful intriguers, he found himself now embarrassed by his false pretences and provisional measures. He had told the Greeks that it was necessary to put an end to the Revolution. They re-echoed his own phrases, and clamoured for the establishment of permanent institutions, and, above all, for legal tribunals. Capodistrias was puzzled to find that the people to whom he looked for support, were thwarting his measures when they believed they were assisting him to gain popularity. The president's firmness was further shaken by the French Revolution of July 1830, which placed Louis Philippe on the throne of France. This event encouraged the members of the constitutional opposition in Greece to commence an open and systematic hostility to his arbitrary measures. Shortly after this, he was still further alarmed by the insurrection in Poland, which he feared would prevent Russia from supporting the principles of the Holy Alliance against England and France. He was now compelled to hear his conduct arraigned. He was reproached with perpetuating anarchy in Greece, and with calumniating the Greeks as enemies of order. His administrative capacity was called in question, and his misgovernment was pointed out. But the mass of the nation wished reform, not change of government; and even his illegal proceedings were submitted to with patience. Viaro, it is true, became every day more hateful on account of his insolence; Agostino every day more ridiculous on account of his vanity.

Henceforward the government of the president became rapidly more tyrannical. Arrests were made A.D. 1830. without legal warrants. Spies were generally employed by men in office. Viaro, Mustoxidi, and Gennatas, collected round them a herd of Ionian satellites, who made a parade of the influence they exerted in the public administration. The partisans of Capodistrias began to believe that he would succeed in obtaining the presidency for life. Agostino, his younger brother, pretended to be his political heir. He acted the generalissimo of Greece, and formed a body-guard of personal dependants, who were better clothed and paid than the rest of the army. This conduct excited indignation among the veteran armatoli, who conceived a deep-rooted resentment against the whole Capodistrian family.

The Revolution established the liberty of the press, of which the Greeks had made a moderate and intelligent use. As early as 1824, political newspapers of different parties were published simultaneously at Mesolonghi, Athens, and Hydra. In 1825 the government found it necessary to establish an official gazette (Γενική 'Εφημερίς) at Nauplia. Capodistrias silenced the press, and the Greeks, unable to discuss their grievances, resorted to force as the only means of removing them.

Polyzoides, a man of moderate opinions, a lawyer, and a Liberal, deemed the time favourable for the establishment of a political and literary newspaper of a higher character than any which had survived the hostility of the president's government. There is no doubt that he contemplated strengthening the Liberal party, and gaining proselytes to the constitution. His conduct was strictly legal. By the law of Greece the press was free; but to comply with the police exigencies of a suspicious government, copies of the prospectus of the new paper, which was called the *Apollo*, were sent to the minister of public instruction, and to the president. Viaro, who acted as minister of justice, sent to inform the editor, that as no law existed regulating the publication of newspapers, the power of licensing their publication belonged to the government. The pretension was very Venetian, and in direct opposition to the law declaring the press to be free. Polyzoides resolved to obey the law; Viaro was determined to enforce his authority.

Early on the morning fixed for the publication of the *Apollo*, the chief of the police of Nauplia, followed by a strong guard, entered the printing-office and seized the press, then at work, without presenting any warrant. The editor sought redress from Viaro, and presented a petition to the senate, but his demands were neglected. It was evident that the will of Count Capodistrias was more powerful than the law of Greece. The president had himself inaugurated a new period of revolution. Men's minds were excited, and the Liberal party was irritated. The state of public affairs, both in Greece and on the continent of Europe, caused information to be eagerly sought after from other sources than the government papers, and the Greeks waited anxiously for the result of the contest between Capodistrias and the *Apollo*. A law circumscribing the liberty of the press was passed hurriedly through the senate. But while Viaro was pluming himself on his victory, the *Apollo* made its appearance at Hydra on the 31st March 1831, and its publication was continued under the protection of the Albanian municipality of that island until the assassination of Capodistrias.[1]

Maina had already resisted the president's authority. Hydra now called the legality of his proceedings in question. The president attempted to apologise for

---

[1] The *Apollo* was published twice a-week. While revising these pages, I have turned over the numbers of this paper, and I am surprised to find so much moderation and good sense in political articles written amidst the storm of party passions that then prevailed.

his arbitrary acts, by pleading the provisional nature of his government. His greatest fear was publicity. He felt that his motives would not bear investigation better than his deeds. He had succeeded in silencing the press abroad, and it now braved him at home. The *Courier* of Smyrna had criticised his measures with freedom, and published his edicts with severe comments. By the intervention of the Russian minister at Constantinople, he obtained from the Othoman government an order to the editor to abstain from criticising the conduct of the president of Greece.[1]

Capodistrias advanced in the path of tyranny; the Greeks prepared for open insurrection. Many persons were arrested on suspicion, and remained in prison without being accused of any offence or brought to trial.[2] Some just and more unjust accusations were made against men who disapproved of the president's conduct. Actions before provisional courts of judicature were commenced for official acts performed during the Revolution; yet no private individual was allowed to seek redress in the same courts for recent acts committed in violation of the president's own laws by the president's officials. Lazaros Konduriottes of Hydra, one of the most patriotic men in Greece, and one of the few whose public and private character was alike irreproachable, was accused of complicity with pirates. Several eminent men were exiled, and others only escaped the vexations of the police by seeking a voluntary banishment.[3] Judges were dismissed from office because they refused to transcribe and pronounce illegal sentences at the suggestion of

[1] *Courier de Smyrne*, 28th November 1830.
[2] Compare the picture of Greece drawn by Sir Stratford Canning in a Memorandum dated 28th December 1831, Annex A to Protocol of 7th March 1832.
[3] Men of different parties and discordant opinions were united in opposition to Capodistrias at this time: Hypsilantes, Mavrocordatos, Miaoulis, Konduriottes, Tombazes, Tricoupi, Klonares, Zographos, Pharmakides, Church, and Gordon.

Viaro. Klonares, a man of some legal knowledge, and of an independent character, was dismissed for signing one of the addresses to Prince Leopold which had not been submitted to the president's revision. Another judge publicly declared that he was driven from the bench because he refused to give an unjust decision in conformity with the desire of the Corfiot minister of justice. Sessines of Gastuni, the president of the senate, who had been raised to his high office on account of his servility, at last hesitated to support the tyranny of the president, and was instantly dismissed.

Extraordinary tribunals, which acted without fixed rules of procedure, whose members were destitute of legal knowledge, and removable at pleasure, and from whose judgments there was no appeal, were multiplied.

Insurrections followed. The president was particularly irritated by prolonged disturbances on the part of the students of Egina, because these disorders drew attention to his vicious system of public education, and demonstrated the falsehood of the reports he had caused to be circulated in Western Europe.

His difficulties were increased by the disorder in his financial administration. Many of his partisans in the Morea were alienated by his allowing Kolokotrones to enrol an armed band of personal followers, as in the worst times of the Revolution, and collect the cattle-tax. Kolokotrones, as might have been foreseen, acted the part of a military tyrant. He not only persecuted his own personal enemies, but allowed a similar licence to the brigands who followed his banner. Greece was relapsing into a state of anarchy, and several provinces were at last in open revolt.

Maina paid no taxes, and the Maniats were only prevented from plundering Messenia by the presence of the French troops. Hydra had constituted itself an

independent state, governed by its municipal magis- A.D. 1831.
trates. It collected the national revenues in several
islands of the Archipelago, and maintained a part of
the Greek fleet which espoused its cause. Syra, the
centre of Greek commerce, made common cause with
Hydra. Capodistrias had driven its merchants into
open opposition, by attempting to fetter their trade
with the restrictions of the Russian commercial system.
A general cry was raised for the convocation of a national assembly, and the president perceived that he
must either make concessions to regain his popularity,
lay down his authority, or employ force to keep possession of his power. He chose the last, and instead of
assembling the deputies of the nation, he commenced
a civil war, trusting to the assistance of Russia for the
means of crushing Hydra.

Some management was necessary to prevent the
diplomatic agents of England and France in Greece
from protesting against any employment of force. The
president expected to succeed in re-establishing his
authority in Syra without a contest, and the loss of
Syra would undermine the power of Hydra; for the
revenues of the customs were the principal resource of
the opposition for the payment of their fleet. The
best ships of Greece lay disarmed in the port of Poros,
but Capodistrias had still a few ships at sea, and these
might serve as a cover for obtaining succour to the
Greek flag from the Russian admiral. The plan of
making an attack, apparently with Greek ships, but in
reality with Russian forces, was well devised, but it
was betrayed to the Hydriots by one of the president's
confidants. The Hydriots determined to anticipate the
attack.

Kanaris, who was a devoted partisan of the president, commanded the corvette Spetzas, which was
fully manned, and lay at anchor in the port of Poros.

The municipal government of Hydra ordered Miaoulis with two hundred sailors to hasten to Poros, and take possession of the ships and arsenal. The brave old admiral departed immediately with only about fifty men, accompanied by Antonios Kriezes as his flag-captain, and by Mavrocordatos as his political counsellor. On the night of the 27th July 1831 he seized the arsenal and the disarmed ships, and, hoisting his flag in the Hellas, summoned Kanaris on board. That officer, refusing to surrender the corvette to an order of the municipality of Hydra, was put under arrest, and a party of Hydriots took possession of his ship.

The character of Capodistrias seemed to undergo a revolution when he heard that he had lost his fleet and arsenal. He no longer talked of the blessings of peace, of his own philanthropic feelings, and of the duties of humanity. He declared that he would wash out the stain of rebellion in the blood of his enemies. He called the Hydriots a band of barbarians and pirates, who assailed his authority because it had arrested them in a career of crime and pillage. He now spoke of law, to implore its vengeance, and of justice, to assert that the leaders of the opposition ought all to die the death of traitors. His expressions and his manner breathed a fierce desire to gratify his personal revenge.

The news of Miaoulis's success reached Nauplia while the ministers of France and England, and the commanders of their naval forces, were absent. The Russian admiral, Ricord, who was at anchor in the port, was induced by Capodistrias to sail immediately to Poros with the ships under his command. At the same time, the president sent a battalion of infantry, two hundred regular cavalry, and a strong body of irregulars, by land, to assist in regaining possession of the town.

Admiral Ricord arrived and summoned Miaoulis A.D. 1831. to surrender the arsenal and the ships in the port to the Greek government; but Miaoulis replied that the municipality of Hydra was the only legally constituted authority to which he owed obedience until the meeting of the national assembly. He therefore referred the Russian admiral to the authorities at Hydra, adding that he was resolved to retain possession of the fleet and arsenal as long as the municipality of Hydra left him in command. Ricord threatened to use force; Miaoulis retorted that he knew his duty as well as the Russian admiral.

Affairs remained in this position for several days, when the commanders of the French and English naval forces entered the port accidentally before returning to Nauplia.[1] They were consequently ignorant of the resolutions which might have been adopted by the residents of the Allied powers at Nauplia, and to prevent bloodshed they arranged with Ricord and Miaoulis that matters should remain in their actual condition until they should visit Nauplia and return with the decision of the Allies. It seemed at the time a strange proceeding, that both commanders should go to search for this decision, when the presence of one at least was required at Poros to watch the Russian admiral, who was guarding both the entrances into the port with a superior force, and could close them at any moment.

In the mean time, the residents of England and France, having returned to Nauplia, gave the president written assurances of the desire of their courts to maintain tranquillity in Greece under the existing government. But they excited the president's distrust by speaking of conciliation, by recommending the con-

[1] The French officer was Captain, afterwards Admiral, Lalande; the English Captain, afterwards Admiral, Lord Lyons.

vocation of a national assembly, and by refusing to order their naval forces to co-operate with Admiral Ricord in attacking the Hydriots.

The Russian admiral did not wait the return of the French and English commanders to commence hostilities. On the 6th of August a boat of the Russian brig Telemachus, which was guarding the smaller entrance, prevented a vessel bringing provisions from Hydra from entering the port. An engagement took place, in which both parties lost a few men, but the Russians succeeded in compelling the vessel to return to Hydra.

As soon as Capodistrias found that the English and French residents declined countenancing his schemes of vengeance, he sent off pressing solicitations to the Russian admiral to lose no time in recovering possession of the Greek fleet; and to the officers of the troops on shore to occupy Poros at every risk. He then pretended to listen to the counsels of the residents, and promised to convoke a national assembly. Some days later a proclamation was issued, dated 1st (13th) August, convoking the assembly on the 8th (20th) September.[1]

The message of Capodistrias was received by Admiral Ricord as an order to attack Miaoulis, and his operations, in a military point of view, were extremely judicious. He formed a battery to command the town and the smaller entrance; and having by this cut off the communications of Miaoulis with a part of the Greek fleet, he ordered the Russians to take possession of the corvette Spetzas and a brig, which were anchored in Monastery Bay. At the same time the Greek troops attacked Fort Heideck, which was occu-

---

[1] The existence of this proclamation, however, was not known even at Nauplia until after the events of Poros. A translation will be found in *Lettres et Documents Officiels relatifs au Derniers Evénements de la Grèce*, 123. This work was distributed in Paris by order of Mr Eynard of Geneva.

pied by Hydriots. The Russians and the president's troops were completely victorious. The corvette Spetzas was blown up, the brig was taken, and Fort Heideck was deserted by its garrison.

Miaoulis had now only thirty men on board the Hellas, and the other vessels under his orders were as ill manned.

On the day after the victory of the Russians, the inhabitants of Poros offered to capitulate, and it was arranged with Admiral Ricord that a hundred and fifty Greek regular troops should occupy the town, in order to save it from being plundered by the irregulars. During the night several vessels filled with the families of those who feared the vengeance of Capodistrias were allowed to pass the Russian squadron unmolested. On the 13th of August a hundred and fifty Greek regulars entered the town of Poros.

Admiral Ricord had promised to wait the return of Captains Lalande and Lyons. The Allied powers were bound by protocol to take every step relating to the pacification of Greece in concert. Miaoulis reposed perfect confidence in this arrangement until he was awakened from his security by the operations in Monastery Bay. And on the morning of the 13th August he observed that the Russian ships removed to stations which placed his ships under their guns. He sent an officer on board the Russian flag-ship to request Admiral Ricord to retain his previous position until the return of the French and English naval commanders, according to his promise; and he instructed the officer, in case the Russian admiral persisted in taking up a hostile position, to add that Miaoulis, though his crews were insufficient for defence, would destroy his ships rather than surrender them. Captain Phalangas was ordered to make a similar communication to Captain Levaillant of a French brig-of-war which had just entered the port. Levaillant urged the Russian admiral to wait the return of Lalande and Lyons, but without success. Miaoulis inferred that something extraordinary, and not favourable to the views of Capodistrias, must have occurred to induce Ricord to violate his promise. He knew that the president's object in getting possession of the Greek fleet was to enable the Russians to re-establish his power at Syra and Hydra under cover of the Greek flag. To save his country, he resolved to destroy the ships which might serve as cover for attacking it. At half-past ten, just as the Russian admiral had taken up his new position, a terrific explosion was heard, which was almost instantaneously followed by a second. Thick columns of smoke covered the Greek ships, and when they cleared away, the magnificent frigate Hellas, and her prize, the corvette Hydra, were seen floating as wrecks on the water.[1] Miaoulis and their crews escaped in their boats to Hydra.

The troops of Capodistrias rushed into the town of Poros in defiance of the capitulation, and immediately took possession of the arsenal. They then commenced plundering the houses, as if the place had been a hostile city taken by assault after the most obstinate resistance. The inhabitants most hostile to the government of the president having carried off their movables to Hydra, only the innocent who trusted to Admiral Ricord's assurance of protection remained. They were pillaged of all they possessed, and treated with inhuman cruelty. On this occasion, both officers and men behaved in the most disgraceful manner; and the sack of Poros is an indelible stain on the conduct of the Greek army, on

---

[1] The letter of Capodistrias, printed in Mr Eynard's *Lettres et Documents*, p. 125, gives a correct account of the events at Poros, until he cuts short the narrative, on arriving at the catastrophe, by inserting a letter of Kanaris. This is one of the president's usual artifices of composition. He thus communicates the catastrophe without the necessity of alluding to the cause of the conduct of Miaoulis.

the character of Capodistrias, and on the honour of Admiral Ricord. The Russian admiral might easily have put a stop to the cruelties which were perpetrated under his eyes, yet for twenty-four hours he permitted every crime to be committed with impunity. Justice was powerless, unless when some Poriot slew a soldier to defend the honour of his family. The historian is not required to sully his pages with a record of the deeds of lust and rapine which were committed by the Greek troops, but his verdict must be pronounced, as a warning to evil-doers. There is no scene more disgraceful to the Greek character in the history of the Revolution; and horrible tales of pillage, rape, and murder, then perpetrated, long circulated among the people. Anecdotes of cruel extortion and base avidity were told of several officers. When all was over, the troops returned to Nauplia and Argos with horses stolen from the peasants of Damala, which were heavily laden with the plunder of Poros.

The sack of Poros sowed the seeds of disorder in the Greek regular corps, and ruined the reputation of Capodistrias. General Gerard endeavoured in vain to bring back the army to a sense of duty, by blaming the conduct of the troops at Poros with great severity. Rhodios, the minister of war, who was a creature of Capodistrias, protected the worst criminals, and deprived the reproaches of the French general of their influence. This conduct increased the insubordination which the licence at Poros had created.[1]

Capodistrias was soon alarmed to find that even his own partisans spoke with indignation of the conduct of the Russian admiral and of the Greek troops. His enemies proclaimed that, in his eagerness to revenge himself on Miaoulis, he had given up the innocent inhabitants of a Greek town to pillage and slaughter

[1] Pellion, 211.

To withdraw public attention from the sack of Poros, he was now anxious to talk of a national assembly. The meeting of that assembly was inevitable, but the elections were not likely to be effected without some fierce contests. The president openly acted as the unscrupulous chief of an unprincipled party; but an avenging fate was at hand. He had indulged his appetite for a bloody vengeance; he was now sacrificed as a victim to private revenge.

The distinguished part which several members of the family of Mavromichales acted at the commencement of the Revolution, has been recorded in the earlier pages of this work. The best men of the house fell in battle. Kyriakoules and Elias are names which Greece will always honour. Petrobey, the chief of the family, though a man of no political capacity, was viewed by Capodistrias with ignoble jealousy. He enjoyed considerable influence in Maina, and Maina possessed a considerable degree of political independence. Capodistrias believed that centralisation was the direct path to order, and it was certainly the quickest way of increasing his personal authority. The influence of the family of Mavromichales appeared to be the principal obstacle to the success of his plans in Maina, and he removed its members from every official position which they occupied at his arrival in Greece. His persecutions constituted them the natural champions of the provincial franchises and fiscal immunities of the Maniats.

The lawless liberty that reigned in Maina was extremely offensive to the despotic principles of Capodistrias. He found both bad habits and criminal practices more powerful than either the local or the national government. Murder was legalised by written contracts. Bonds signed by living individuals were shown to the president, in which the penalty, in case of non-fulfil-ment, was a clause authorising the holder to murder the obligant, or two of his nearest relations. Capodistrias considered it to be his duty to put an end to a state of society so disgraceful to orthodox Christians in the nineteenth century. He imagined that the people of Maina would aid him in his honourable enterprise, not reflecting that the deeds of vengeance which excited his indignation were considered by the native population as a necessary restraint on a ferocious and faithless race, in a region and among a class where the law was powerless. Murder in Maina answered the same purpose as duelling in other countries where the state of society was less barbarous, and assassination was a privilege of Maniat gentility.

Personal jealousy made Capodistrias select the family of Petrobey as the scapegoats for the sins of Maina. The acts of rapine on shore and of piracy at sea which other Maniats committed were overlooked, and all the strength of the Greek government was employed to crush the detested house of Mavromichales.

During the celebration of Easter 1830, Janni, the brother of Petrobey, commonly termed the King of Maina, in company with one of the bey's sons, excited the people of Tzimova to revolt against the president's government. Many complaints had been laid before the Greek government against the acts of violence and extortion committed by this king of misrule, which he found it no easy matter to explain. He therefore declared himself the champion of the privileges of Maina, in order to evade answering for his own misdeeds. The people were in this way induced to make his cause their own. Janni Mavromichales seized the customhouse, and collected the public revenues in order to pay the men who took up arms. But this revolt was soon suppressed by the president, who persuaded George Mavromichales, the second son of

Petrobey, to hasten from Argos to Maina, with the assurance that all the disputes between the Greek government and the family of Mavromichales should be promptly and satisfactorily arranged if Janni would come in person to Nauplia. George believed Capodistrias; Janni believed George, and accompanied his nephew to the seat of government. The president soon violated his word. He put Janni under arrest, and ordered prosecutions to be commenced against both him and his son Katzakos, who had attempted to assassinate his own cousin Pierakos.

In the month of January 1831, Katzakos escaped from Argos, and about the same time Petrobey left Nauplia to return to Maina in General Gordon's yacht, which happened to sail for Zante. An insurrection had already broken out under the leading of Constantine, one of the boy's brothers. The yacht, not being able to touch at Maina, landed the boy at Katakolo, where he was immediately arrested, and sent back to Nauplia as a state prisoner. He was now detained on a charge of treason, and a committee of the senate, with Viaro for chairman, prosecuted the action against him. He was accused of inciting a rebellion in Maina, and of deserting his duty as a senator.[1] An extraordinary tribunal, with his prosecutor Viaro as president, was created to try him, and he was imprisoned as a criminal in Itch-kalé. About the same time Constantine Mavromichales was decoyed on board ship by Kanaris and carried to Nauplia, where he and George were placed under arrest.

Public sympathy was now strongly awakened in favour of the Mavromichales family. It was thought that Petrobey was severely treated, Constantine unfairly entrapped, and George unjustly detained. Con-

---

[1] The report of the committee is given in Eynard's *Lettres et Documents*, 127. It forms a general act of impeachment against the whole family.

stantine and George were allowed to walk about freely within the fortress of Nauplia, attended by two guards during the day. They were loud in their complaints. The mother of Petrobey, an old lady approaching her ninetieth year, petitioned the president to release the bey, who remained in prison untried. No proof could be found of his complicity in his brother's insurrection, and it was not a crime for a senator to quit Nauplia without a passport. It was reported that both the Russian minister Baron Rückmann and Admiral Ricord advised the president to release Petrobey. It is certain that Capodistrias consented to allow the prisoner to dine on board the Russian flag-ship at Admiral Ricord's invitation. It was generally supposed that this permission implied a pardon for past offences; and when Petrobey, on quitting Admiral Ricord's table, was conducted back to prison, even the partisans of the president were astonished at his conduct. It seems that Admiral Ricord had assured several persons that he would persuade the president to release the bey, and that his interference irritated Capodistrias, who became frequently peevish and changeable after the affair of Poros. Constantine and George were exasperated and alarmed by what they supposed to be a sudden and unfavourable change in the president's views.

Three days after Petrobey's visit to Admiral Ricord, at early dawn on the 9th October 1831, Capodistrias walked as usual to hear mass in the church of St Spyridion. As he approached the low door of the small church, he saw Constantine Mavromichales standing on one side and George on the other. He hesitated for a moment, as if he suspected that they wished to address him, and would willingly have avoided the meeting. But after a momentary pause, he moved on to enter the church. Before he reached the door he fell on the pavement mortally wounded by a pistol-ball in the back of the head. In the act of falling he received the stab of a yataghan through the lungs, and he expired without uttering a word.

Two guards were in attendance on the Mavromichales, and two orderlies accompanied the president. The assassins attempted to save themselves by flight. The pistol of one of the orderlies wounded Constantine, who was overtaken and slain. His body was carried to the square, where it remained exposed naked to the insults of the populace for several hours. It was then dragged through the streets and thrown into the sea.

The whole town was alarmed by the report of the pistols; the news of the president's assassination spread instantaneously, and the whole population poured into the streets. Yet George Mavromichales succeeded in escaping into the house of the French resident, though at a considerable distance from the scene of the murder. A furious mob followed close at his heels, and demanded that he should be delivered up. His pursuers proclaimed themselves the avengers of blood, and threatened to force open the doors of the French residency and tear the assassin to pieces. Baron Rouen informed them that France must protect the refugee until a formal demand was made for his surrender to justice by the lawful authorities. In a few hours the demand was made; but to save the criminal from the vengeance of the people, it was found necessary to convey him to the insular fort of Burdjee. His guilt was unquestionable, the proof was incontestable. He was condemned by a council of war, and executed on the 22d of October.

Greece had been depraved by the tyranny of Capodistrias; she was utterly demoralised by his assassination. She exchanged the sufferings of illegality for the tortures of anarchy. A.D. 1831.

The name of Capodistrias remained for some time a party spell, but time has proved the avenger of truth. His talents, his eloquent state papers, and his private virtues, receive their merited praise; but with all his sophistry, his cunning insinuations, and false pretences, they proved insufficient to conceal the wrongs which his vicious system of administration inflicted on Greece.

CHAPTER III.

ANARCHY. 9TH OCTOBER 1831 TO 1ST FEBRUARY 1833.

> "In rank oppression, in its rudest shape,
> The faction chief is but the sultan's brother,
> And the worst despot's far less human ape."
> *Prophecy of Dante.*

GOVERNING COMMISSION REFUSES TO GRANT A GENERAL AMNESTY — SECOND NATIONAL ASSEMBLY AT ARGOS — ROMELIOT MILITARY OPPOSITION — AGOSTINO PRESIDENT OF GREECE — ROMELIOTS EXPELLED FROM ARGOS — SIR STRATFORD CANNING'S MEMORANDUM — ROMELIOTS INVADE THE MOREA — CONDUCT OF THE RESIDENTS — AGOSTINO EJECTED FROM THE PRESIDENCY — GOVERNING COMMISSION — STATE OF GREECE — ANARCHY — FRENCH TROOPS GARRISON NAUPLIA — DJAVELLAS OCCUPIES PATRAS — KOLOKOTRONES RALLIES THE CAPODISTRIANS — NATIONAL ASSEMBLY AT PRONIA — CONSTITUTIONAL LIBERTY IN ABEYANCE — INTRIGUES OF THE SENATE — MUNICIPAL INSTITUTIONS ARREST THE PROGRESS OF ANARCHY IN THE MOREA — CONDITION OF MESSENIA — POSITION OF KOLOKOTRONES AND KOLETTES — TRUE NATURE OF THE MUNICIPAL INSTITUTIONS IN GREECE NOT GENERALLY UNDERSTOOD — ATTACK ON THE FRENCH TROOPS AT ARGOS — ESTABLISHMENT OF THE BAVARIAN DYNASTY.

The assassination of Capodistrias destroyed the whole edifice of his government, which for some time had derived an appearance of stability from nothing but his talents and personal influence. The persons whom he had selected to act as his ministers and official instruments employed his name as their ægis, and rallied round his brother Agostino, who had been treated as the president's heir, from motives of flattery, at a time when no one contemplated the possibility of his ever succeeding to power.

The senate was filled with the most daring and

unprincipled partisans of the Capodistrian policy. A few hours after the president's murder it appointed a governing commission to exercise the executive power until the meeting of the national assembly. This commission consisted of three members—Count Agostino Capodistrias, Kolokotrones, and Kolettes. Agostino was named president. His incapacity, joined to the irreconcilable hostility between the other two members, induced the senate to believe that it could retain the powers of government in its own hands. The people judged more correctly, and prognosticated an approaching civil war. A general amnesty for political offences was instinctively felt to be the only means of preserving any degree of order. A few political leaders and military chieftains, who desired to fish in troubled waters, determined to frustrate all attempts at pacification. A large body of well-paid Moreot troops looked to Kolokotrones as their leader; a still larger number of the veteran soldiers of continental Greece, whose pay was in arrear, considered Kolettes as their political advocate.

The municipality of Syra made a vain endeavour to consign past contentions to oblivion by acknowledging the authority of the governing commission. The constitutionalists at Hydra made conciliatory proposals to the new executive. They asked for a general amnesty for all political offences except the assassination of the president, and they required that the governing commission should be increased to five members by the aggregation of two persons chosen from among the constitutionalists. These proposals were rejected with disdain. Count Agostino pretended that a national assembly could alone grant a general amnesty, and the members of the commission, in order to avoid receiving two colleagues, declared that they had no power to enlarge the executive body. The reply was evasive, and felt to be insulting. The exiles only wished a guarantee against governmental prosecutions until the meeting of the national assembly, and they knew that the senate had the power to add to the body it had created.

The contest for absolute power by the Capodistrians, and for life and property as well as liberty by the constitutionalists, was now resumed with embittered animosity. Both parties saw that their safety could only be secured by the command of a devoted majority in the national assembly, and both prepared to secure success in the coming elections by force of arms. Hydra was kept closely blockaded by the Russian fleet.

The influence of the Capodistrians in the Morea gave them a considerable majority in the second national assembly at Argos; but they derived much of their authority as a party from the open support of the Russian admiral, Ricord. In some places, the Capodistrians, though they formed a minority, obtained the assistance of a military force, and held a meeting, in which they elected a deputy, in violation of every legal and constitutional form. Yet these deputies were received into the assembly, and their elections were declared valid. Both parties circulated atrocious calumnies against their opponents. The Capodistrians accused the French and English of being privy to the assassination of the president. Agostino boasted of his hatred to the French. He dismissed General Gerard from his command in the Greek army, and he intimated to General Guehencuc, who commanded the French army of occupation in the Morea, that the financial condition of the country imposed on the Greek government the obligation of observing the strictest economy in paying foreigners. On receiving this intimation, the French general immediately recalled all the French officers in the Greek service, in order to prevent their being dismissed in the same manner as General Gerard. The constitutionalists at Hydra spread a report that the murdered president had bribed six Hydriot traitors to assassinate the leaders of the opposition; and it was generally believed that Agostino and Admiral Ricord had sworn to send Miaoulis, and all the sailors who had taken part in the affair of Poros, to Siberia.

The proximity of Argos to the garrison of Nauplia and to the Russian fleet gave the Capodistrians the command of the town. The deputies of Hydra were not even allowed to land at Lerna, for it was considered to be the safest way to exclude opposition. Those of Maina were stopped at Astros. To prevent even a murmur of dissatisfaction with the actual government from being heard in the assembly, the senate named a commission, which was ordered to verify the election of each deputy before he was allowed to take his seat in the assembly. This unconstitutional proceeding was supposed to have been counselled by Russia, and awakened very general dissatisfaction even in the Capodistrian party.

The military chiefs of continental Greece came to the assembly as deputies from the districts in which they possessed local influence, or to which the majority of their followers belonged. They cared little for constitutional liberty, but they were now ready to join any opposition, unless they were allowed to receive the high pay and ample rations which were enjoyed by the followers of Kolokotrones and the other Capodistrian chiefs. Kolettes was in a position to assist them in their object, and they had not forgotten the liberality with which he had poured the proceeds of the English loans into their hands. Kolettes was not a babbler, like most Greek statesmen. The astute Vallachian could assume an oracular look and remain silent when he wished to conceal his thoughts. In the present case, his prudence led Agostino and his counsellors to suppose that he was intent on retaining his place in the executive body. But it was evident that a number of the continental chiefs would openly oppose the election of Agostino to the presidency of Greece, even though Kolettes might remain neutral. It was resolved to crush this opposition before it could make common cause with the constitutionalists. Several Romeliot captains belonged to the Capodistrian party; of these the most influential were the Suliot chief Kitzos Djavellas, and Rhangos, a captain of armatoli, who on one occasion, as has been already mentioned, joined the Turks.

The Romeliot chiefs came to Argos attended by bands of followers, who, according to the established usage of Greece, were supplied with rations by the government. In this way the partisans of Kolettes assembled about five hundred good soldiers at Argos. All these men had claims for arrears of pay, and most of them had individual grievances, which Capodistrias had neglected to redress. Kolettes warmly supported their claims, and assured them that he would do everything in his power to obtain justice. He was aware that he must unite his cause with theirs, for without their support his political influence would be annihilated. He was distrusted by Agostino, disliked by Admiral Ricord, and hated by Kolokotrones.

For some days before the opening of the assembly, the different factions employed their time in arranging their plans. Some individuals doubtless acted from patriotic motives, but the conduct of the majority of the Romeliots, as well as of the Capodistrians, was guided by self-interest and personal ambition.

The Romeliot chiefs, finding themselves in a

minority, demanded that the constitutional deputies who had met at Hydra should be allowed to take their seats in the assembly. This demand was rejected, on the ground that new deputies had been elected, and that these new elections had received the sanction of the commission named by the senate. The Romeliots then drew up a protest containing a declaration of their principles.[1] They characterised the nomination of the governing commission by the senate as an illegal act; they objected to the appointment of the commission to verify the elections of deputies by the senate as an unconstitutional infringement of the right of the national assembly; and they proclaimed their adhesion to the following principles and resolutions: That national union ought to precede the meeting of a national assembly; that the national assembly ought to verify the elections of its members, and appoint its own guard, as on former occasions. The order in which the constitutional rights of the nation were to be discussed was also fixed, and resolutions were proposed, relative to the choice of a sovereign and to the nature of the provisional government which was to act until his arrival. The attempt to interfere with the proceedings of the Allied cabinets displeased their diplomatic agents at Nauplia, and inclined them to favour Agostino and the Capodistrians.

The rival parties trusted more to force than to right. Each assumed that it was the national party, and two hostile assemblies were opened on the same day.

The deputies of the Capodistrian party, to the number of a hundred and fifty, met on the 17th of December 1831 in the church of the Panaghia, and, after taking the prescribed oath, walked in procession to the schoolhouse, which had been fitted up as the place

[1] Dated 18th (30th) November 1831.

of meeting for the national assembly. A strong guard, under the command of Kitzos Djavellas, and an escort of cavalry, under Kalergy, secured a public triumph to the Capodistrians. They met in security, elected their president, issued a proclamation, and proceeded to business.

The Romeliots were not strong enough to make any public display; but they also held their meeting, elected their president, and issued their proclamation. They called upon the residents of the Allied powers, as protectors of Greece, to enforce a general amnesty, and they invited the French troops in the Morea to occupy Argos to preserve order. The residents, knowing that neither party was disposed to obey the law or listen to the dictates of justice, allowed things to take their course.

On the 20th December, Agostino Capodistrias was elected president of Greece, and invested with all the authority which had been conferred on his murdered brother. He and Kolokotrones had already resigned their power as members of the governing commission named by the senate, into the hands of the national assembly. Kolettes, not recognising the Capodistrian assembly, and not having resigned his power, pretended to be the only man now entitled to conduct the executive government.

The Capodistrians feared that, if the Romeliots were allowed time to summon the deputies from Hydra and Maina to their aid, they might be strong enough to overthrow the government. To prevent this they resolved to expel the Romeliot chiefs from Argos before additional troops could arrive to reinforce Kolettes's partisans. Agostino Capodistrias, Admiral Ricord, Kolokotrones, Metaxas, and Djavellas all agreed that an immediate attack was necessary to insure victory. Once driven beyond the Isthmus of

Corinth, the Romeliots might be treated as lawless bands of brigands intent on plunder.

A Russian lieutenant named Raikoff, who had been promoted by Capodistrias to the rank of colonel, was summoned from Nauplia, with four guns and a company of artillerymen, to assist the government troops already in Argos. Raikoff was a warm partisan, and pretended to be a confidential agent of Russian policy. Strengthened by this reinforcement, the troops of Agostino attacked the Romeliots. A fierce civil war was carried on in the streets of Argos for two days, before the Romeliots, though inferior in number and ill supplied with ammunition and provisions, were expelled from the town and compelled to retreat to Corinth.

Sir Stratford Canning arrived at Nauplia to be a witness to these proceedings. The three powers had at last come to an agreement on Greek affairs, and selected a Bavarian prince to be king. Sir Stratford was on his way to Constantinople as English ambassador to obtain the sultan's recognition of the Greek kingdom, and he visited Nauplia to announce to the Greeks the arrangements which had been adopted by the Allies, and to prepare them to receive their king with order and unanimity. Sir Stratford found that Agostino was a fool utterly incapable of appreciating his position, and he counselled conciliatory measures, and urged the necessity of moderation, in vain. The empty head of the Corfiot was inflated with presumption. Before quitting Greece, Sir Stratford communicated to Agostino a memorandum on the state of the country, urging him in strong terms to terminate the civil war he had commenced.[1] Though the observations in this document produced no effect on the Greek government, and very little on the ulterior conduct of

[1] *Parliamentary Papers*, Annex A to the Protocol of 7th March 1832. The memorandum is dated 28th December 1831.

Mr Dawkins, Baron Ronen, and Baron de Rückmann, the residents of the three Allied powers at Nauplia, yet they were so judicious that they made a deep impression on the ministers in conference at London. The anarchy in Greece threatened to render Sir Stratford's mission to the sultan useless; and he warned Agostino that, by destroying the houses of the peaceful inhabitants of Argos, and plundering their shops, as a prelude to a bloody intestine war, Greece proclaimed herself in the face of Europe to be unworthy of the independent position as a nation to which the Allied powers were endeavouring to elevate her. This memorandum was supported by formal notes of the residents, recommending Agostino to publish a general amnesty and convoke a free national assembly. But shortly after the departure of Sir Stratford from Greece, the residents ceased to insist on the measures they had advised; and Admiral Ricord, who had never moderated the violence of his language, continued to encourage the Capodistrians to push their attacks on the constitutionalists with vigour. He gave them hopes of being able to expel the French army of occupation from the Morea, and he pointed out to them the necessity of perpetuating their authority by forcing themselves on the new sovereign as ministers and senators. The position of the French troops who were protecting Messenia from being plundered by the Maniats was rendered so confined that they were obliged to drive the Capodistrian troops out of the town of Nisi, in order to keep open their communication with their headquarters at Modon, and secure a safe passage to the peasantry who brought provisions to their camp.

The political atmosphere of Europe was too troubled during the year 1831 to enable the Allies to give more than a casual glance at the affairs of Greece, whose unsettled condition was gradually destroying the importance of the country in the solution of what statesmen called the Eastern question. The attention of Great Britain and France had been absorbed by the creation of the kingdom of Belgium ; Russia had been occupied with the insurrection of Poland. But during the winter the condition of Europe became more tranquil, and the fate of Greece was again taken into consideration. On the 7th January 1832 a protocol was signed, authorising the residents at Nauplia to recognise the provisional government named by the national assembly, which, it was supposed, was a free meeting. On receiving this protocol, the residents, who knew that Sir Stratford Canning's memorandum was on its way to London, thought fit to recognise Agostino Capodistrias as president of Greece. On the 13th of February another protocol was signed, offering the throne of Greece to Prince Otho, a boy seventeen years old, the second son of the King of Bavaria.[1]

In the mean time the Romeliots were preparing to avenge their defeat at Argos. Their preparation went on slowly, until they heard that the Allies had chosen a king for Greece. They saw immediately that it was necessary to overthrow the government of Agostino, in order to have a share in welcoming the new monarch, and a claim to participate in the distribution of wealth and honours which would take place on the king's arrival.

After their retreat from Argos, the Romeliots formed a camp at Megara. The meeting, which arrogated to itself the title of a national assembly, met at Perachora, where it was strengthened by the arrival of the deputies from Hydra and Maina. Kolettes was supported by most of the eminent men in Greece. Konduriottes,

[1] Everything that can be urged in favour of this unfortunate choice will be found in Thiersch, *De l'État Actuel de la Grèce*, i. 306-314. Before the election, Thiersch, who was one of the prince's teachers, considered that it would be absolutely necessary for King Otho to join the Greek Church, i. 313.

Misoulis, Mavromichales, and Mavrocordatos, and a respectable body of constitutional deputies, sanctioned his proceedings. But the Romeliots looked to arms and not to justice for victory. Constitutional liberty was a good war-cry, but military force could alone open the road to power. The numbers of armed men collected at Megara at last rendered an advance on Nauplia necessary to procure subsistence. Every effort that revenge, party zeal, and sincere patriotism could suggest, was employed to urge on the soldiers. Commissions were distributed with a lavish hand among the bravest veterans. Civilians were suddenly made captains. Kolettes and the military chieftains cared nothing for moral and political responsibility; their sole object was to conquer power, and about the means they were quite indifferent. Mavrocordatos and the constitutionalists felt that the recognition of Agostino's government by the residents cut off all hope of a general amnesty, a free national assembly, or a legal administration, without a decided victory of the Romeliots. It was thought that the residents would not venture to employ the forces of the Allies to support a government which had rejected their own advice as well as the warnings of Sir Stratford Canning. The Greek leaders knew that none of the residents possessed the firm character, any more than the enlightened views, of Sir Stratford, and it was inferred with diplomatic sagacity that the instructions received with the protocols of the 13th and 14th February 1832 would place the residents in a false position with their cabinets.[1] Their recognition of a government illegally constituted had rendered the pacification of Greece impossible without further violence. Agostino, less sagacious than the constitutionalists, believed that his

[1] Thiersch has published a letter in which Mavrocordatos examines the state of public affairs in Greece at this time with ability and moderation.—Vol. I. p. 327.

recognition by the residents was equivalent to a guarantee on the part of the Allied powers; and he expected to see the troops of France support him at the Isthmus of Corinth as decidedly as the fleet of Russia had supported his brother at Poros.

At this late hour the residents made a feeble attempt to avert a civil war. They invited the general commanding the French army of occupation to occupy the Isthmus of Corinth, and authorised Professor Thiersch, who had visited Greece as an unrecognised agent of the Bavarian court, to negotiate with the deputies and military chiefs at Perachora and Megara. Thiersch favoured the constitutional party. He had been long in communication with the Philhellenic committees on the Continent. In the year 1829 he had advocated the election of Prince Otho to the sovereignty of Greece, and he had communicated with the Bavarian court on the subject. The object of his present tour was understood to be, to prepare the minds of the Greeks for the choice of a Bavarian prince; and now, when Otho was elected king, he stepped forward as a diplomatic agent of Bavaria, and was treated as such both by the residents and by the leaders of all parties among the Greeks.

The prudence of the constitutionalists, and the passions of the military chiefs, rejected every arrangement based on the continuance of the presidency of Agostino and the ratification of the acts of the assembly by which he had been elected. The mission of Thiersch failed, and its failure rendered the position of Agostino untenable. Those who had hitherto supported him perceived that they had ruined their cause by placing too much power in his hands, and by attempting to prolong his authority beyond the legal majority of the king chosen by the protecting powers. Agostino determined to cling to power, but the rapid advance of the Romeliots soon dispelled his hopes of Russian support and his visions of future greatness.

On the 6th of April the government troops stationed at the Isthmus of Corinth fled before the constitutionalists without offering any resistance. The heroes of the sack of Poros, the cavalry of Kalergy, and the generalship of Kolokotrones, the veteran commander-in-chief of the Peloponnesian army, were unable to retard the advance of the invaders, who marched straight to Argos. The residents were now in an awkward and not very honourable position. By an extraordinary piece of good-luck, they were relieved from the foolish part they were acting. On the very day the Romeliot troops entered Argos, the protocol of the 7th March 1832 arrived at Nauplia, and they were instructed to carry out the principles of Sir Stratford Canning's memorandum. It was easy for them to treat their recognition of Agostino's presidency as a temporary expedient, adopted to avoid a civil war, until they received the definitive instructions now placed in their hands. The memorandum declared "that the interests of the Greeks, and the honour of the Allies, required a system of provisional government calculated to preserve the country from anarchy." This could, in the present crisis of affairs, only be attained by ejecting Agostino from the presidency.

On the 8th of April they addressed a vague diplomatic note to the president they had recognised, inviting him to contribute to the execution of the protocol of the 7th of March. Agostino, trusting to the secret aid of Admiral Ricord, replied with a request for a copy of the document to which they alluded, and which had not yet been officially communicated to the Greek government. The residents were alarmed at his endeavour to gain time, and, their own interests being at stake, they proceeded with great promptitude to eject him from office. His incapacity secured them an A.D. 1832. easy victory in a personal interview. Without wasting their time in composing diplomatic notes, they walked to the government-house, while Agostino was still chuckling at his supposed victory over the diplomatists, entered his presence, and informed him without ceremony that he must immediately send his resignation to the senate. So far their conduct was extremely judicious, but they had not the clear heads which enable men to stop short in action at the precise limit of justice and prudence. In the spirit of diplomatic meddling, which involves nations in as much embarrassment as military ambition, they made the ejected president add a recommendation to the senate to appoint a commission of five persons to govern Greece until the king's arrival. Agostino was rendered amenable to their orders by a hint that any delay would produce a decree of the senate deposing him from the presidency. Convinced that his cause was hopeless, he wrote his resignation, and shortly after quitted Greece, with the body of his murdered brother, in a Russian ship.

The expedient of establishing peace by a diplomatic compromise, after allowing every passion which civil war excites to rage for three months, was a violation of common sense that could not prove successful. The same diplomatists had refused to prevent a civil war by enforcing a compromise before the opening of the assembly at Argos; yet they now imagined that their interference would avert anarchy. The Romeliot troops paid very little attention to these manoeuvres. They were resolved to reap the fruits of their victory, and it was not by naming a commission in which a hostile senate would be able to secure a majority that this end could be attained. Foreign interference rarely saves a nation from the direct consequences of its own vices, and anarchy was the natural result of the repeated illegalities which every party in Greece had committed.

The conduct of the residents deserves reprehension. They evidently thought more of concealing their own incapacity and inconsistency than of serving the cause of the Greeks, in the measures they adopted for carrying the protocol of the 7th of March into execution. They established a phantom of government, which they knew would be unable to pacify the country, because it appeared to them to offer the political combination least at variance with their own proceedings. Had they endeavoured to act in accordance with the laws and institutions of Greece, it is possible that they might have failed in preventing the Greeks from falling into a state of anarchy, but they would have saved themselves from all reproach. When the senate first assumed illegal powers, it was the duty of the residents to refuse to recognise its illegal acts. In the present crisis, had they paid any attention to the constitution of Greece, even as established by Capodistrias, they would have recommended the representation of both parties in the senate, and avoided the incongruity of composing an executive government of two hostile factions. The Russian resident wished the senate to remain unaltered, as it consisted entirely of Russian partisans, and was completely under the guidance of Admiral Ricord. But the English and French residents knew that its composition rendered the pacification of Greece impossible. The English resident, however, moved partly by jealousy of French influence, and partly by distrust of Kolettes's character, adopted the Russian policy concerning the immutability of the senate.

In conformity with the suggestion conveyed in the resignation of the presidency by Agostino, the senate named five persons whom the residents indicated as a A.D. 1832. governing commission. When the Romeliots heard the names that were pleasing to the diplomatists, they treated the election with contempt, and marched forward to attack Nauplia. The fortress was impregnable, but they had many stanch partisans within its walls, and expected to enter without much difficulty. The senate was terrified; the residents had again thrust themselves into a false position. It was necessary to effect a new diplomatic compromise, and for this purpose Kolettes was invited to confer with the diplomatists at the house of the French resident.

On the 10th of April, Kolettes rode into Nauplia in triumph. He had now the nation, the army, the senate, and the three protecting powers at his feet. Unfortunately for the Greeks, with all his talents as an intriguer, he had neither the views of a statesman nor the principles of a patriot. He had climbed to the elevation of a Cromwell or a Washington, and he stood in his high position utterly incompetent to act with decision, and prevented by his own absolute incapacity from serving either the constitutional cause or the interests of the Romeliot troops who had raised him to power.

Fourteen days were consumed in diplomatic shuffling and personal intrigues before the names of a new governing commission were finally settled. It was then composed of seven members, and not of five, as recommended by the residents. The constitution of Greece was grossly violated by this election; for the senate, at the instigation of the diplomatists, persisted in investing the governing commission with the executive power until the king's arrival, though both by law and invariable practice that power could only be conferred until the meeting of a national assembly, when it required to be ratified or reconstituted by a decree of the representatives of the nation. The object of the Capodistrians was to prevent the national assembly electing a president of the constitutional party. They even succeeded in paralysing the action of the constitutionalists in the governing commission, by enacting that the presence of five members was necessary to give validity to its decisions. Now, as there were two stanch Capodistrians in the commission, and one constitutional member, who was too ill to attend, it was evident that the two Capodistrians could arrest the action of the executive authority at any crisis by preventing a decision. Three members of the commission, Kolettes, Konduriottes, and Zaimes, were supposed to represent the constitutional opposition to the Capodistrian system; but the residents and the leading Capodistrians were aware that Zaimes was already a renegade. Two members were recognised to be the representatives of the Romeliot troops—Prince Demetrius Hypsilantes and Kosta Botzares.[1] Two members, as has been said, were stanch Capodistrians—Metaxas and Koliopulos or Plapoutas. This executive commission had a cabinet composed of seven ministers, who were all constitutionalists; but with the exception of Mavrocordatos, they were men without administrative knowledge, mere rhetoricians, who could clothe commonplace thoughts in official Greek. Even Mavrocordatos was misplaced as minister of finance. These ministers were severely blamed for accepting office without fixing a day for the meeting of the national assembly, and without insisting that the power of

[1] Hypsilantes expressed his repugnance to become a member of this commission in strong terms, and his observations exhibit good sense and patriotism, but he was persuaded by his friends to withdraw his objections. He was already suffering from the disease which soon after terminated his life. His letter is given by Thiersch, i. 369. In mentioning the nomination of Kosta Botzares, Thiersch observes that the Romeliot Greeks still regarded the Albanian tribe of Suliots with jealousy.—Vol. I. p. 381.

the governing commission should terminate when the assembly met. Their friends excused their neglect of constitutional principles by pleading the power of the residents; but those who scanned their political lives with attention, observed that they frequently contrived to advance their own interests by sacrificing the cause they adopted.[1]

Public opinion demanded the immediate convocation of a national assembly. To save the country from anarchy it was necessary to reconstitute the senate, according to the principles of conciliation laid down in Sir Stratford Canning's memorandum, and it might have been found necessary to throw the responsibility of maintaining order on Kolettes by creating him dictator. But the residents, the Russian admiral, the senate, and the ministers in office, were all opposed to the meeting of a national assembly.

The Capodistrian party soon recovered from its defeat. It succeeded in retaining possession of a considerable portion of the revenues of the Morea, and received active support from Admiral Ricord. The Romeliots, after overthrowing Agostino's government, daily lost ground. The commission of seven was either unable or unwilling to reward their services. The soldiers soon determined to reward themselves. They treated the election of the commission as a temporary compromise, not as a definitive treaty of peace, and they marched into different districts in the Morea, to take possession of the national revenues as a security for their pay and rations. Wherever they established themselves, they lived at free quarters in the houses of the inhabitants.

The financial administration of Mavrocordatos was

[1] Christides was Minister of the Interior, and General Secretary of State; Mavrocordatos, of Finance; Tricoupi, of Foreign Affairs; Zographos, of War; Balgares, of the Marine; Klonaris, of Justice; and Rizos Neroulos, of Ecclesiastical Affairs and Public Instruction.

not calculated to moderate the rapacity of the troops. The governing commission raised money by private bargains for the sale of the tenths, and the proceeds of these anticipated and frequently illegal sales were employed to reward personal partisans, and not to discharge the just debts due to the soldiers for arrears of pay. A small sum judiciously expended would have sent many of the Romeliot troops to their native mountains, where, as peace was now restored, they would have willingly returned, had they been able to procure the means of cultivating their property. The troops were neglected, while favoured chieftains were allowed to become farmers of taxes, or were authorised to collect arrears due by preceding farmers. These proceedings gave rise to intolerable exactions. The chieftains often paid their followers by allowing them to extort a number of rations from the peasantry, and defrauded them of their pay. Some drew pay and rations for a hundred men without having twenty under arms. Numbers of soldiers were disbanded, and roved backwards and forwards, plundering the villages, and devouring the sheep and oxen of the peasants. Professor Thiersch informs us that the bands of Theodore Grivas on the side of the constitutionalists, and of Thanasapulos on the side of the Capodistrians, spread terror wherever they appeared by their exactions and cruelty.[1] Eight thousand Romeliots were at this time living at free quarters in the Morea, and it was said that they levied daily from the population upwards of twenty thousand rations. The governing

---

[1] Grivas had taken into his pay a body of Mussulman Albanians. Compare Thiersch, i. 71, 121, 123, 152. "Les capitaines presque sans exception gardaient l'argent pour eux, et les troupes restèrent dans l'ancien état d'exinanition," p. 123. "Les plus grands désordres apparurent à la vente des dimes, où il y eût un commérage de capitaines, de primats, de haut employés, et pour ainsi dire des compagnies organisées qui pénétrèrent même dans quelques ministères et jusqu'au milieu du gouvernement," p. 152. It must be remembered that Professor Thiersch is the panegyrist of Kolettes and a partisan of the Romeliots.

commission solicited pecuniary advances from the three protecting powers, pretending that they would employ them for alleviating the misery of the people; but the Allies wisely refused to advance money, which they saw, by the misconduct of the government, would have been wasted in maintaining lawless bands of personal followers in utter idleness.

The position of the two hostile parties soon became clearly defined. The greater part of the Morea adhered to the Capodistrian party, as the surest means of obtaining defence against the exactions of the Romeliot soldiery. Several Moreot primates and deputies, who had hitherto acted with the constitutionalists, now abandoned the cause of the governing commission. Even in Romelia the Capodistrians possessed a rallying-point at Salona, where Mamoures maintained himself with a strong garrison. In the Archipelago, Tinos continued faithful to the Capodistrians, and served as a refuge for the officials of the party who were expelled from the other islands. Spetzas and Egina were also prevented from acknowledging the authority of the governing commission by ships of war commanded by Andrutzos and Kanaris.

All liberated Greece was now desolated by anarchy. Long periods of maladministration on the part of the government, and a cynical contempt for justice and good faith on the part of the civil and military leaders, had paralysed the nation. The Revolution, to all appearance, had been crowned with success. The Turks were expelled from the country, and Greece formed an independent state. Yet Greece was certainly not free, for the people were groaning under the most cruel oppression. The whole substance of the land was devoured by hosts of soldiers, sailors, captains, generals, policemen, government officials, tax-gatherers, secretaries, and political adventurers, all living idly at the public expense, while the agricultural population was perishing from starvation.

Evil habits, and the difficulty of procuring the means of subsistence, may form some excuse for the rapine of the soldiery, but no apology can be offered for the conduct of the members of the governing commission and of the ministry, who increased the miseries of the people by their malversations, or countenanced the dishonesty of their colleagues by retaining office. Honour as well as patriotism commanded every man who had a sense of duty, either to put a stop to the devastation of the country or resign his place as a ruler or a minister. The tenacity with which those who called themselves constitutionalists clung to office has fixed an indelible stain on their own political character, and destroyed the confidence of the Greek people in the honesty of public men. When Mavrocordatos, Tricoupi, Klonares, and Zographos, abandoned the cause of civil liberty, they destroyed all trust in the good faith of the statesmen of the Greek Revolution. The immediate effect of their misconduct was to constitute Theodore Kolokotrones, the veteran klepht, the champion of the people's rights.[1]

Before the constitutional ministers had been a month in office, their weakness had increased the insubordination of the military classes, and their misconduct had

---

[1] Alexander Soutzos echoes the popular feeling in a poem written in August 1832:—

Βεμούε εἰς τὴν Μακεδονίαν ὅτα πάθη τῶν ὑψοντων
Καὶ τοὺς δεσπότας τῶν μ' αἰσχροὺς μυρίας δικαιότητῶν.
Στὴν δεξιὰν της φέρουσα σύνταγμα καὶ νόμους
Ἡ 'Αναρχία μὲ κραυγὰς περίπατεῖ στοὺς δρόμους,
Πολιτικαὶ, Πολεμικοὶ μ' ἀπαίδεκες μεγάλης,
Ποῖοι οἱ λύσσι χαίρονται εἰς τὴν ἀνεμοζάλην,
'Αρπάζουν τὰς προσόδους μας, γυμνώνουν τὸν λαόν μας.
Καὶ ἀπειθὲς καὶ ἄτακτον τὸ στρατιωτικόν μας
Σὰν ὠρισμένο ἄλογον τοῦ Βασταγμὸν δὲν ἔχει, &c.

He also satirises the high officials for their desertion of the cause of constitutional liberty. One of them speaks thus:—

Τὸ σύνταγμά μας κύριε,—τὸ σύνταγμα ἐν χωρίῳ
Μήπως τὸ παιδρευθήκαμε; εἰς τί μᾶς χρησιμεύει

alienated their own partisans to such a degree, that they found it necessary to invite the French troops to occupy Nauplia and Patras, as the only means of securing their personal safety and the prolongation of their power.

On the 19th of May 1832 General Corbet entered Nauplia; but at Patras the governing commission was not so fortunate as to obtain French assistance, and that place fell into the hands of the Capodistrians.

The loss of Patras was caused by gross negligence on the part of Zographos, the minister of war. Ignorant of official business, and absorbed in personal intrigues, he left the Greek troops without instructions concerning their future conduct. The regular troops in garrison at Patras had supported the Capodistrians while in power, but they were disposed to obey the government, and not to follow the personal fortunes of any president. The hostility of Kolettes to the regular corps was notorious, and, through the neglect of Zographos, both the officers and men at Patras were easily persuaded by the partisans of Russian influence that it was the intention of the governing commission to disband the regular troops. While brooding over this report, which threatened them with the loss of a large amount of arrears of pay, they heard that French troops were invited to garrison Patras. They concluded that they were cheated by the minister of war, and betrayed by the governing commission. As long as they remained in garrison at Patras they were sure of being regularly supplied with rations and clothing, and of obtaining from time to time advances of pay; but once expelled from the town, they believed that they would be allowed to starve. The Capodistrians formed a strong party in the town, and they availed themselves of the excited feelings of the soldiers to declare, that regular troops who delivered a fortress like Patras to foreigners would render themselves guilty of treason. The constitutionalists had accused Capodistrias of selling Greece to the Russians; the Capodistrians now accused the constitutionalists of selling Nauplia and Patras to the French. The regular troops mutinied, deposed their commanding officer, who refused to sign a manifesto justifying their revolt, and invited Kitzos Djavellas, who was then at Vostitza, to assume the chief command at Patras.

Djavellas, who had retreated from the Romeliots, was at the head of about five hundred irregulars, and he was looking out for a position in which he could maintain his followers, and defend himself against the attacks of the Kolettists. He hastened to Patras, and entered it before the arrival of the French. When they made their appearance, Djavellas transmitted to their commanding officer a formal protest against the authority of the governing commission, and he refused to obey the order to admit the French troops into the fortress. The French commander, considering that it was the object of the Allies to maintain order and not to enforce the authority of any party, immediately retired, and the residents, who wished to avoid bloodshed, left Djavellas in peaceable possession of Patras.[1] Thus, by the incapacity of Zographos and the decision of Djavellas, the Capodistrians remained in possession of the commercial town of Patras, and of the fortresses of Rhion and Antirhion, with the command of the entrance into the Gulf of Corinth, until the arrival of King Otho.

This success emboldened the enemies of Kolettes. A great part of the Morea, and several districts of con-

[1] Thiersch has printed the correspondence of Djavellas. It must not be supposed that the letters were really written by the Suliot chief, who could hardly write a common note. Like most of the military documents of the Revolution, they were composed by a secretary. Nothing has falsified the history of the Greek Revolution more than the ambitious eloquence of pedantic secretaries.

tinental Greece, refused to admit the officials named by the governing commission. The demogeronts, wherever they were supported by the people, assumed the management of public as well as local business. They had been appointed by Capodistrias. They feared anarchy more than despotism, and they naturally sought protection from the military leaders of the Capodistrian party. The greater part of Arcadia and Achaia resisted the authority of the governing commission, while Argolis, Corinthia, and Laconia, generally acknowledged its power. Messenia and Elis were the scenes of frequent civil broils. In Phocis the Capodistrians maintained their ascendancy.

Kolokotrones, who held the rank of commander-in-chief of the Peloponnesian militia, stepped forward as the defender of the local authorities against the central government. His personal interest, his party-connections, and his hatred of Kolettes, determined his conduct. Had he acted from patriotic motives, he would have caught inspiration from the high national position into which accident had thrust him. The agricultural population was alarmed, and the astute old klepht seized the favourable moment for uniting his cause with the cause of the people, but his confined views and innate selfishness prevented his employing the power thus placed at his disposal for the general good.

Kolokotrones called the Peloponnesians to arms, and pronounced the proceedings of the governing commission to be illegal, in a proclamation dated the 22d June 1832.[1] Metaxas and Plapoutas had informed him that they had secured the co-operation of Zaimes in paralysing the action of the executive government. The Russian admiral had prompted him to proclaim

[1] The original proclamation is printed by Gennaios Kolokotrones, in a work entitled Διάφορα ἔγγραφα καὶ ἐπιστολαὶ ἀφορῶντα τὰς κατὰ τὸ 1832 συμβάντα κατὰ τὴν 'Ελλάδα ἀνωμαλίας καὶ ἀνοχίας, p. 214. Thiersch gives a translation, i. 395.

that the senate was the only legitimate authority in existence. The residents remained silent. Griva, the most lawless of the Romeliot chiefs, advanced without orders from the governing commission, and occupied Tripolitza at the head of a thousand men. The Capodistrians were already prepared to encounter the invaders of the Morea, and Gennaios Kolokotrones, who had more military courage, though less political sagacity than his father, had already formed a camp at Valtetzi.

The tide of success now flowed in favour of the Capodistrians. The advance of Griva was stopped. Elias Mavromichales was repulsed in his attempts to gain a footing in the rich plain of Messenia. The Capodistrians under Kalergy made a bold attempt to seize the mills at Lerna, but the attempt was defeated, though it was openly favoured by the Russian admiral. Civil war recommenced in many districts, and bands of troops, who recognised no government, plundered wherever they could penetrate.

The prudence of Kolokotrones, whom age had rendered more of a politician than a warrior, might have led him to avoid engaging in open hostilities against a government acknowledged by the protecting powers, on the eve of the king's arrival, had he been allowed to remain in undisturbed possession of the profits which he drew from his office as commander-in-chief in the Peloponnesus. But the members of the governing commission forced him into resisting their authority by appointing Theodore Griva to the chief command in the districts of Leondari and Phanari. The occupation of these places by the Kolettists would have rendered Kolokotrones little better than a prisoner in Karitena.

Amidst these scenes of anarchy a national assembly met at Pronia. The members of the governing commission, the ministers in office, the senators, the residents of the Allied powers, and the Russian admiral, were all hostile to the meeting. But a general amnesty before the king's arrival was necessary for pacifying the country, and a general amnesty could not be proclaimed without the sanction of a national assembly. It was also indispensable to obtain the assent of the nation to the election of the king chosen by the Allies. A national assembly could not therefore be entirely dispensed with, though it was feared that a national assembly would abolish the senate and choose a new executive government. Had a national assembly met immediately after the nomination of the governing commission, a civil war might have been avoided by the election of a senate, in which both the constitutionalists and Capodistrians, the Romeliots and the Moreots, the Hydriots, the Spetziots, and the Psarians, might have been duly represented, and in which local interests might have moderated factious passions. But the intrigues of Greek politicians and foreign diplomatists delayed the meeting for three months, and when it took place, old passions had been rekindled with fiercer animosity by fresh injuries. The violence of faction now exposed the corruption of political society in Greece, without a veil, to the examination of strangers. All ties were torn asunder in the struggle to gratify individual selfishness. The Suliots, Djavellas and Botzares, fought on different sides. Hydriot primates were found who deserted the cause of Hydra. The only great political body into which patriotism was likely to find an entrance, was the national assembly, and even there its voice was in great danger of being overpowered by party zeal. The illegal position and arrogant assumptions of the senate caused much animosity; the residents of the three powers were distrusted, because they appeared in league to support the illegal powers of the senate.

As soon as the assembly of Pronia met, a majority determined to abolish the senate, though it was openly supported by the residents. Many members believed that, as the residents had tamely submitted to the armed opposition of Djavellas at Patras, and had regarded with indifference the renewal of the civil war by Griva, Kolokotrones, and Kalergy, they would offer no opposition to the abolition of the senate. The diplomatists, however, regarded the senate with peculiar favour. They had made use of it to eject Agostino from the presidency, and to create a new government. Its very illegality made it a useful instrument, should it be necessary to employ force to establish King Otho's authority, for its abolition would always be a popular measure, and might serve as a pretext for the assumption of absolute power. On the other hand, the national assembly was considered to be doubly dangerous, because it was legally invested with great power, and not likely to be guided by the suggestions of foreign diplomatists in making use of that power.

Such was the state of Greece and the condition of parties when the national assembly of Pronia commenced its sittings. Nothing presaged that it would be able to establish order in the country.[1]

---

[1] Professor Thiersch asserts that he could have restored order had he been furnished with 100,000 dollars. The assertion only proves that he knew very little of arithmetic. It would not have sufficed to obtain the evacuation of the Morea by one-half of the Romeliot irregulars who were plundering the peasantry. He says, "Il y avait bien un moyen de sortir encore d'embarras. Je devais me mettre à la tête des affaires, et commencer le gouvernement du roi," vol. i. 107. Had the worthy professor done so, in all probability he would have prevented King Otho from coming to Greece. He is a perfect Wagner the *formulas* in politics.

"Wie nur dem Kopf nicht alle Hofnung schwindet
Der immerfort an schalem zeuge klebt,
Mit gier'ger hand nach Schätzen gräbt
Und froh ist wenn er Regenwürmer findet."

The assembly commenced its sittings on the 26th of July 1832. On the 1st of August it passed a decree proclaiming a general amnesty, and on the 8th it ratified the election of King Otho; but on the same day it abolished the senate. Of the legality of this measure there was no doubt, and had it occurred immediately after the expulsion of Agostino, it might have tranquillised Greece. Prudence now suggested that its abolition had become impolitic, since the residents had become its advocates; and the majority of the assembly would have acted judiciously, had it only reformed the existing senate on the principle of Sir Stratford Canning's memorandum. The constitutionalists formed a large majority in the assembly, and they were irritated by the conduct of the Greek ministers who had deserted the constitutional cause. The senate was composed of Capodistrians, and it was adopting active measures to increase the violence of the civil war which was desolating the country. The governing commission and the Greek ministers took part with the senate against the representatives of the nation; and the residents, taking advantage of this conduct on the part of the executive, protested against the decree of the national assembly, asserting that it was a violation of the principles of the pacification they pretended to have established.

Large bodies of Romeliot troops were quartered in the village of Aria, at a short distance beyond Pronia. The soldiers beset the gates of Nauplia and the doors of the assembly every morning clamouring for pay. The governing commission promised to pay their arrears; but it failed to keep its promise. The ministers were accused of this violation of the public faith in order to produce the catastrophe which ensued, and their friends and the senators incited the soldiers to demand payment from the national assembly. On the

26th August the soldiers of Grigiottes burst into the hall of the assembly, dragged the president from his seat, insulted and ill-treated many deputies, and carried off the president and several deputies, as hostages for the payment of their arrears, to their quarters at Aria. This disgraceful riot put an end to the last national assembly in revolutionary Greece.[1]

This scene of military violence forms an important event in the history of Greece. It prolonged the revolutionary state of the country for eleven years, by placing constitutional liberty in abeyance. It threw the people into an unquiet and dangerous temper, by sweeping away those free institutions which had infused energy into the nation during its struggle for independence. The executive power was made the prize of a successful faction. The central government was not established on a legal basis, and the military chiefs ceased to acknowledge its control. Eleven years of Bavarian domination was the expiation of the violence committed at Pronia.

Prince Demetrius Hypsilantes died in the month of August. About the same time, a deputation, consist-

[1] Papadopulos Vretos, an Ionian, was then Baron de Rückmann's doctor. He tells us that he dined with the Russian resident the day after the dissolution of the assembly. After dinner, the English resident, Mr Dawkins, called and narrated the following occurrence, which makes the Ionian infer that the British cabinet destroyed the liberty of Greece. He makes the English resident say, "As I was riding out yesterday with Griffith" (his secretary, who spoke Greek well), "we were surrounded by a crowd of filthy palikaria, shouting and gesticulating like demons. All spoke at the same time, and all appeared to be delivering set speeches, so that the road was an oratorical pandemonium. When I could find an opportunity to make myself heard, I asked Griffith what was the play they were acting for our private edification. After many vain efforts he obtained a partial hearing. The soldiers declared they had no bread, no clothes, and no money. It would have been superfluous for them to have told any one who looked at them that they were without credit. I saw that instantly. They wished my Excellency to take their case into consideration and provide for their wants. I stated to them that my functions did not allow me to become their commissary; but, pointing with my whip to the hall of the national assembly, I said, that I believed there were many persons in that building who possessed great experience as commissaries and paymasters. They seized my hint with wonderful alacrity, and set off running and whooping like wild Indians. Griffith and I took a long ride, and when we returned in the evening we heard of the great event of the day."—*Mélanges Politiques*, p. 23.

ing of three members, two of whom were members of the governing commission, was sent to Munich with addresses of congratulation to the kings of Greece and Bavaria.[1] The commission was thus left incomplete, for the presence of five members was required to give validity to its acts. Yet on this occasion the residents did not protest against the virtual dissolution of the executive government of Greece. Greece surely stood in greater want of a legal executive than of an illegal senate; but the diplomatists looked on with indifference, while the governing commission committed suicide.

Greece was now without any legal central authority. The senate had been abolished by the national assembly, and the national assembly had been dissolved by the soldiery. The senate made the protest of the foreign diplomatists a ground for prolonging its existence. Three places in the governing commission were vacant; two had been occupied by constitutionalists, one by a Capodistrian. The senate attempted to violate the terms of the pacification sanctioned by the residents, and named three Capodistrians. George Konduriottes, the president, resisted this pretension, but, possessing neither the talents nor the energy necessary for carrying on a contest with the senate, he withdrew to Hydra. Only three members of the government now remained at Nauplia—Kolettes, Zaimes, and Metaxas—and they claimed the whole executive power. It was generally felt that chance had made as good a selection as it was possible to make under the circumstances. The senate yielded at last to public opinion, and passed a decree investing these three men with the whole executive power.

But the intrigues of Admiral Ricord soon determined a majority of the senators to repudiate this

[1] Kosta Botzares, Plapoutas, and Admiral Miaoulis.

decree, and all Greece was astonished by the strange intelligence that seven senators had secretly quitted Nauplia. On the 21st November these seceders were joined at Astros by the president, Tsamados, and two additional members, and met by Kolokotrones with a body of Moreot troops. Ten of the thirteen senators who had signed the address to the King of Bavaria were now present. They had carried with them the government printing-press, and they issued proclamations annulling the decree which had invested Kolettes, Zaimes, and Metaxas with the executive power until the king's arrival. Trusting to the military force of the Capodistrian party under Kolokotrones, and to the support of the Russian admiral, the seceders assumed the executive authority.

On this occasion, Kolettes, Zaimes, and Metaxas acted with sense and courage. They took prompt measures to secure order and maintain their authority within the walls of Nauplia. Beyond the fortress they were powerless. The residents recognised them as the legal government, and the French garrison placed their persons in security.

The senate, having failed to produce a revolution, sought revenge by increasing the existing anarchy. It appointed a military commission to govern Greece, consisting of several powerful chiefs. Kolokotrones, Grigiottes, Djavellas, and Hadgi Christos, Moreots and Romeliots, Albanians and Bulgarians, formed an alliance, and leagued together. Anarchy reached such a pitch, that the minister of war, Zographos, informed the minister of finance, Mavrocordatos, that it was impossible to obtain an exact account of the numbers of the soldiers who were drawing pay and rations. Of the number of men actually under arms he had no idea.[1]

[1] *Rapport des Ministres*, 28th November 1832; Thiersch, i. 148.

At first sight the conduct of the seceding senators A.D. 1832. looks like the proceedings of maniacs; but the Capodistrians had never abandoned the scheme of Agostino, and they still hoped, by seizing the forcible direction of the administration in the greater part of the Morea, to compel the regency which would govern Greece during the king's minority, to purchase their support by appointing them senators for life. The Russian admiral supported them in their desperate schemes, while the Russian resident, remaining passive, was at liberty to disavow their proceedings in case of failure. It is needless to follow these abortive intrigues further. The senators, finding that they had no chance of obtaining effectual support from the Greeks, adopted the extraordinary expedient of endeavouring to procure assistance from Russia, by naming Admiral Ricord president of Greece. This act of treason and folly proves the justice with which Capodistrias had been reproached for selecting his senators from the most ignorant and unprincipled political adventurers. Some persons have supposed that there was malice as well as folly in the conduct of the senators; and that, though they were eager to proclaim that they preferred Russian protection to Greek independence, they also intended to hint to Admiral Ricord that it was his interest and the interest of other Russian agents to purchase her silence in order to throw a veil over many intrigues.

Amidst the general anarchy, the commission of seven generals was unable to place any restraint on the soldiery. The men under arms no longer obeyed their officers, but formed bands like wolves, hunting for their prey under the boldest plunderer. A veil may be dropped on their proceedings. But it is of some importance to explain in what manner a part of the Morea escaped their ravages.

The revival of the municipal institutions of the

Morea at this period has been already mentioned. The weakness of the government relieved the local authorities from the incubus of a tyrannical central administration, which had been imposed on them by Capodistrias. The exigencies of the time forced them to act without waiting for the initiative of ministers and the orders of prefects. The condition of the country and the agitation of the people again made the municipal authorities feel that they were responsible to their fellow-citizens, by whom they were supposed to be elected. They were often called upon to make arrangements for quartering and feeding troops, who came to defend or plunder the country, as circumstances might determine. They were compelled to collect the public revenues to meet these demands; to arm strong bodies of peasantry, and to form alliances with neighbouring municipalities, in order to check the rapacity of the soldiery. Their difficulties induced them to look to Kolokotrones for assistance, whose military force was so far inferior to that of the Romeliots as to render it imperative on him to form an alliance with the people. His office as commander-in-chief in the Morea, and his personal relations with most of the local magistrates chosen during the administration of Capodistrias, pointed him out as the natural defender of the agricultural population. The difficulty was to make the old klepht feel that it was his interest to protect and not to plunder; that his robberies must be confined to the central administration; and that he must aid and not command the local authorities. The end was partially attained, and in many districts the demogeronts acquired sufficient power to protect their municipalities against the military chiefs of the Capodistrian faction, and to repulse the attacks of the Romeliot troops.

The governing commission and the constitutional

ministers forfeited their claim to the allegiance of the Greeks, by their neglect to restrain the exactions of the Romeliots, who had raised them to power. Strangers had a better opportunity of observing the evil effects of their misconduct in Messenia than in other parts of the country, as the presence of the French army of occupation enforced neutrality within certain limits, and yet left free action to the rival factions in its immediate vicinity.

Great part of the rich plain which extends from Taygetus to Ithome was national property. Statesmen and chieftains, Romeliots and Moreots, were eager to become the farmers of the public revenues. The bey of Maina and the whole of his ambitious and needy family aspired to quarter themselves, with all their Maniat adherents, in this rich province. The native peasantry and the opponents of the Mavromichales were alike hostile to the pretensions of the Maniats. Party intrigues were carried on in every village, and no province was more tormented by the incessant strife which makes the municipal administration of the Greeks a field for the exhibition of strange paroxysms of selfishness. Some of the demogeronts allied themselves with Kolokotrones; some discontented citizens formed connections with the family of Mavromichales.

The presence of a French garrison at Kalamata complicated the politics of the municipal authorities in Messenia. Their local interests and personal feelings favoured the French, who had protected them from being plundered by the Maniats, and who afforded them a profitable market for their produce. But the Capodistrian faction, excited by Kolokotrones and Admiral Ricord, were indefatigable in calumniating and intriguing against the French. The officers commanding the Kalamata sought to tranquillise the people, by inviting the peasantry to pursue their labours, and by assuring the demogeronts of their readiness to assist in maintaining order in the neighbourhood of their encampment. But the partisans of Kolokotrones pointed to the neutrality proclaimed by the residents at Nauplia, and to the retreat of the French troops from Patras, as proofs that the French could not interfere in the internal administration of Messenia. The French were accused of being constitutionalists like the Maniats, and the agricultural population feared the lawless conduct of the adherents of the family of Mavromichales. Kolokotrones had already convinced many that he was acting sincerely as the protector of the people. To him, therefore, the demogeronts of most of the villages in Messenia turned for support.

Niketas came with a small body of chosen troops to protect the agricultural population from an invasion of the Maniats. The Mavromichales were not deterred by these preparations for defence. They had claims on the governing commission for their long opposition to Capodistrias, which they did not think were entirely cancelled by the assassination of the president. They pretended that they were entitled to be the tax-gatherers of Messenia, and their followers were eager to exchange the black bread of the lupin-meal, which formed their hard fare in Kakovouli, for the wheaten cakes and roast lambs.[1]

Elias Mavromichales, called Katzakos, invaded the district between the lower ridges of Taygetus and the Pamisus more than once at the head of three or four hundred men. But his progress was always arrested by Niketas, who was a better soldier, and who, in addition to his superior skill in partisan warfare, was sup-

---

[1] Kakovouli, or the land of evil counsel. The lupins are ground after the pulse has been long steeped in water to extract some injurious matter. The bread is black, hard, and bitter.

ported by the whole of the population in the plain capable of bearing arms. The approach of the Maniats caused excessive terror, and the alarm was justified by their conduct. The French troops at Kalamata saw more than one Greek village suddenly attacked and plundered by the modern Spartiates, as the Maniats termed themselves. The armed men descended from their mountains attended by numbers of women, whose duty it was to carry off the booty. These women were seen by the French returning, carrying on their back bundles of linen, bedding, and household utensils, and driving before them asses laden with doors, windows, and small rafters.[1] Niketas, however, invariably succeeded in driving Elias and his Maniats back into the mountains.

Arrangements were ultimately adopted which put an end to these devastating forays of the Maniats. Niketas placed himself at the head of a band of veterans, and moved about from village to village watching the slopes of Taygetus, and taking care that the armed peasantry should always be informed where they were to join him in case of any attack. The demogeronts were in this way enabled to provide the supplies of money and provisions necessary for the defence of the district, and the agricultural population was not prevented from cultivating the land.

Kolokotrones and Kolettes were the two great party leaders at this time, but neither possessed the talents necessary to frame, nor the character necessary to pursue, a fixed line of policy. Accident alone determined their political position, and made the first, though a partisan of despotic power, the defender of liberal institutions, and the second, though calling himself a constitutionalist, a tyrant, and the enemy of a national assembly. Like their partisans, they had no honest

[1] Peillou, 316.

convictions, and they drifted up and down with the current of faction without an effort to steer their course according to the interest of Greece. Kolettes came into the Morea to establish constitutional liberty. His followers plundered the country, and dispersed the national assembly. Kolokotrones was the instrument of the Capodistrians and the Russians to perpetuate despotic power. His position compelled him to become the champion of order and liberty.

There is no doubt that though many arbitrary and unjust acts could be cited against Kolokotrones and Djavellas, yet greater security for life and property existed in the provinces over which their authority extended, than in the provinces which submitted to the governing commission. But it is certain that this result was obtained by the accidental revival of national institutions, and not by the patriotism or the wisdom of the leaders of the Capodistrians. The military chiefs on both sides were equally rapacious; the political leaders equally ignorant, selfish, and corrupt. Honest men of both parties kept aloof from the public administration.

Both Greeks and foreigners had praised the municipal organisation of Greece which existed under the Turkish domination; and it undoubtedly tended to check in some degree the evils which resulted from the excessive fiscal rapacity of the Othoman government. Yet it could do but little to protect the people from injustice; for the municipal magistrates were responsible to their Othoman rulers, not to those who elected them, or to the law of the land, for the exercise of their authority. It made Greeks the instruments of Othoman oppression, and in this way it introduced a degree of demoralisation into the local administrations, which the Revolution failed to eradicate. It may be truly said that this vaunted institution never protected the liberties of the people except by accident. The law had no power to restrain the selfishness of the local magistrates. The primates employed the municipalities, like the Turks, as fiscal engines for their own convenience. The military chiefs were the enemies of every species of order and organisation. The torpid ministers, the literary enthusiasts, and the intriguing politicians, who acted an important part during the Revolution, allowed the local institutions to be destroyed, and they had not the capacity necessary for organising an efficient central administration.

At the end of the year 1832 Greece was in a state of almost universal anarchy. The government acknowledged by the three powers exercised little authority beyond the walls of Nauplia. The senate was in open rebellion. The Capodistrians under Kolokotrones and Djavellas had never recognised the governing commission. A confederation of military chiefs attempted to rule the country, and blockaded the existing government.

The commission of three members, which exercised the executive power, alarmed at the prospect of being excluded from power before the king's arrival, implored the residents to invite the French troops to garrison Argos. Four companies of infantry and a detachment of artillery were sent from Messenia by General Gueheneuc to effect this object. In the mean time, General Corbet, who commanded at Nauplia, detached two companies and two mountain-guns to take possession of the cavalry barracks at Argos, in order to secure quarters for the troops from Messenia. The town was filled with irregular Greek soldiery, under the nominal command of Grigiottes and Tzokres. Those men boasted that they would drive the French back to Nauplia, and that Kolokotrones would exterminate those who were advancing from Messenia. The prudent precautions of the French officers prevented the troops being attacked on their march, and the whole force united at Argos on the 15th of January 1833.

On the following day the French were suddenly attacked. The Greeks commenced their hostilities so unexpectedly, that the colonel of the troops, who had arrived on the preceding evening, was on his way to Nauplia to make his report to General Corbet when the attack commenced. The French soldiers who went to market unarmed were driven back into the barracks, and a few were killed and wounded. But the hostile conduct of the Greek soldiery had prepared the French for any sudden outbreak, and a few minutes sufficed to put their whole force under arms in the square before their quarters. The Greek troops, trusting to their numbers, attempted to occupy the houses which commanded this square. They were promptly driven back, and the streets were cleared by grape-shot from the French guns. The Greeks then intrenched themselves in several houses, and fired from the windows of the upper stories on the French who advanced to dislodge them. This species of warfare could not long arrest the progress of regular troops. The French succeeded in approaching every house in succession with little loss. They then burst open the doors and windows of the lower story, and, rushing up-stairs, forced the armatoli and klephts to jump out of the windows, or finished their career with the bayonet. In less than three hours every house was taken, and the fugitives who had sought a refuge in the ruined citadel of Larissa were pursued and driven even from that stronghold.

Never was victory more complete. The French lost only forty killed and wounded, while the Greeks, who fought chiefly under cover, had a hundred and sixty killed, and in all probability a much greater number wounded. Grigiottes was taken prisoner, but was soon released. A Greek officer and a soldier accused of an attempt at an assassination were tried, condemned, and shot.[1]

While the Greek troops were plundering their countrymen and murdering their allies, the three protecting powers were labouring to secure to Greece every advantage of political independence and external peace.

A treaty was signed at Constantinople on the 21st July 1832, by which the sultan recognised the kingdom of Greece, and ceded to it the districts within its limits still occupied by his troops, on receiving an indemnity of forty millions of piastres, a sum then equal to £462,480.[2] The Allied powers also furnished the king's government with ample funds, by guaranteeing a loan of sixty millions of francs. The indemnity to Turkey was paid out of this loan.[3]

The Allied powers also secured for the Greek monarchy an official admission among the sovereigns of Europe, by inviting the Germanic Confederation to recognise Prince Otho of Bavaria king of Greece, which took place on the 4th October 1832.[4] The protectors of Greece have often been reproached for the slowness of their proceedings in establishing the independence of Greece; yet when we reflect on the anarchy that prevailed among the Greeks, the difficulties thrown in their way by Capodistrias, the desertion of Prince Leopold, and the small assistance they received from Bavaria, we ought rather to feel surprise that they succeeded at last in establishing the Greek kingdom.

---

[1] Compare Pellion, 363; Lacour, *Excursions en Grèce*, 260. Both had access to official accounts, and yet they differ in their statements of the French loss.
[2] *Parliamentary Papers*, Annex A to Protocol of 30th August 1833.
[3] Each of the three powers guaranteed a separate series of bonds for twenty millions of francs, or £781,273, 6s. 8d. sterling. The contract between the Greek government and the house of Rothschild was signed 12th January 1833. The loan was effected at 94, interest at 5 per cent
[4] *Klübers Quellensammlung zu dem öffentlichen Rechts des Teutschen Bundes. Fortsetzung*, 1832, p. 75.

288   ESTABLISHMENT OF THE BAVARIAN DYNASTY.

BOOK V.
CHAP. III.

The King of Bavaria concluded a treaty of alliance between Bavaria and Greece on the 1st November 1832. He engaged to send 3500 Bavarian troops to support his son's throne, and relieve the French army of occupation. This subsidiary force was paid from the proceeds of the Allied loan; for Bavaria had neither the resources, nor, to speak the truth, the generosity, of France.[1] A convention was signed at the same time, authorising Greece to recruit volunteers in Bavaria, in order that the subsidiary force might be replaced by German mercenaries in King Otho's service.[2]

On the 16th January 1833, the veterans of the Greek Revolution fled before a few companies of French troops; on the 1st of February King Otho arrived at Nauplia, accompanied by a small army of Bavarians, composed of a due proportion of infantry, cavalry, artillery, and engineers.[3] As experience had proved that there were no statesmen in Greece capable of governing the country, it was absolutely necessary to send a regency composed of foreigners to administer the government during King Otho's minority. The persons chosen were Count Armansperg, M. de Maurer, and General Heideck.

The Bavarian troops landed before the king. Their tall persons, bright uniforms, and fine music, contrasted greatly to their advantage with the small figures and well-worn clothing of the French. The numerous

---

[1] The French government was desirous of obtaining the joint guarantee of King Louis of Bavaria to the loan, in order to facilitate the progress of the measure through the French Chambers. But King Louis refused, alleging that neither the state of his finances nor the interests of Bavaria allowed him to aid his son in raising money for Greece. Yet he took care that his son should expend large sums of Greek money in Bavaria without any advantage to Greece.—*Klübers Pragmatische Geschichte der Nationalen und Politischen Wiedergeburts Griechenlands,* p. 509.

[2] The treaty is printed in the Greek Government Gazette, 'Ἐφημερὶς τῆς Κυβερνήσεως, No. 18; the convention in No. 20, 1833.

[3] King Otho embarked at Brindisi on board the English frigate Madagascar, commanded by Captain (Lord) Lyons, on the 15th January 1833, and was joined at Corfu by a fleet of transports bringing the Bavarian troops from Trieste.

mounted officers, the splendid plumes, the prancing horses, and the numerous decorations, crosses, and ornaments of the new-comers, produced a powerful effect on the minds of the Greeks, taught by the castigation they had received at Argos to appreciate the value of military discipline.

The people welcomed the king as their saviour from anarchy. Even the members of the government, the military chiefs, and the high officials, who had been devouring the resources of the country, hailed the king's arrival with pleasure; for they felt that they could no longer extort any profit from the starving population. The title, however, which the Bavarian prince assumed—Otho, by the grace of God, King of Greece—excited a few sneers even among those who were not republicans; for it seemed a claim to divine right in the throne on the part of the house of Wittelspach. But every objection passed unheeded; and it may be safely asserted that few kings have mounted their thrones amidst more general satisfaction than King Otho.

CHAPTER IV.

BAVARIAN DESPOTISM AND CONSTITUTIONAL REVOLUTION. FEBRUARY 1833 TO SEPTEMBER 1843.

> "What! shall reviving thraldom again be
> The patched-up idol of enlightened days?
> Shall we who struck the lion down—shall we
> Pay the wolf homage?"

LANDING OF KING OTHO—THE REGENCY, ITS MEMBERS AND DUTIES—ROYAL PROCLAMATION — ADMINISTRATIVE MEASURES — MILITARY ORGANISATION —CIVIL ADMINISTRATION—MUNICIPAL INSTITUTIONS—FINANCIAL ADMINISTRATION—MONETARY SYSTEM—JUDICIAL ORGANISATION—THE GREEK CHURCH, REFORMS INTRODUCED BY THE REGENCY—SYNODAL TOMOS—MONASTERIES—PUBLIC INSTRUCTION—RESTRICTIONS ON THE PRESS—ROADS—ORDER OF THE REDEEMER—QUARRELS IN THE REGENCY—KOLOKOTRONES'S PLOT—ARMANSPERG INTRIGUE—ARMANSPERG'S ADMINISTRATION—BAVARIAN INFLUENCE—DISPUTES WITH ENGLAND—ALARMING INCREASE OF BRIGANDAGE—INSURRECTIONS IN MAINA AND MESSENIA—BRIGANDAGE IN 1835—GENERAL GORDON'S EXPEDITION—INSURRECTION IN ACARNANIA—OPINIONS OF LORD LYONS AND GENERAL GORDON ON THE STATE OF GREECE—BRIGANDAGE CONTINUES—KING OTHO'S PERSONAL GOVERNMENT—ATTACKS ON KING OTHO IN THE ENGLISH NEWSPAPERS—CAUSES OF THE REVOLUTION OF 1843—REVOLUTION—OBSERVATIONS ON THE CONSTITUTION—CONCLUSION.

KING OTHO quitted the English frigate which conveyed him to Greece on the 6th February 1833. His entry into Nauplia was a spectacle well calculated to inspire the Greeks with enthusiasm.

The three most powerful governments in Europe combined to establish him on his throne. He arrived escorted by a numerous fleet, and he landed surrounded by a powerful army.[1] King Otho was then seventeen

---

[1] Twenty-five ships of war and forty-eight transports were anchored in the bay of Nauplia, and three thousand Bavarian troops had already landed.

years old.[1] Though not handsome, he was well grown, A.D. 1833. and of an engaging appearance. His countrymen spoke favourably of his disposition. His youthful grace, as he rode towards his residence in the midst of a brilliant retinue, called forth the blessings of a delighted population, and many sincere prayers were uttered for his long and happy reign. The day formed an era in the history of Greece, nor is it without some importance in the records of European civilisation. A new Christian kingdom was incorporated in the international system of the West at a critical period, for the maintenance of the balance of power in the East.

The scene itself formed a splendid picture. Anarchy and order shook hands. Greeks and Albanians, mountaineers and islanders, soldiers, sailors, and peasants, in their varied and picturesque dresses, hailed the young monarch as their deliverer from a state of society as intolerable as Turkish tyranny. Families in bright attire glided in boats over the calm sea amidst the gaily decorated frigates of the Allied squadrons. The music of many bands in the ships and on shore enlivened the scene, and the roar of artillery in every direction gave an imposing pomp to the ceremony. The uniforms of many armies and navies, and the sounds of many languages, testified that most civilised nations had sent deputies to inaugurate the festival of the regeneration of Greece.

Nature was in perfect harmony. The sun was warm, and the air balmy with the breath of spring, while a light breeze wafted freshness from the sea. The landscape was beautiful, and it recalled memories of a glorious past. The white buildings of the Turkish town of Nauplia clustered at the foot of the Venetian fortifications and cyclopean foundations that crown its

[1] King Otho was born on the 1st June 1815.

rocky promontory. The mountain citadel of Palamedes frowned over both, and the island fort of Burdjee, memorable in the history of the Revolution, stood like a sentinel in the harbour. The king landed and mounted his horse under the cyclopean walls of Tyrinthus, which were covered with spectators. The modern town of Argos looked smiling even in ruin, with the Pelasgic foundations and medieval battlements of the Larissa above. The Mycenæ of Homer was seen on one side, while on the other the blue tints and snowy tops of the Arcadian and Laconian mountains mingled in the distance with the bluer waters of the Egean.

Enthusiasts, who thought of the poetic glories of Homer's Greece, and the historic greatness of the Greece of Thucydides, might be pardoned if they then indulged a hope that a third Greece was emerging into life, which would again occupy a brilliant position in the world's annals. Political independence was secured : peace was guaranteed : domestic faction would be allayed by the equity of impartial foreigners, and all ranks would be taught, by the presence of a settled government, to efface the ravages of war, and cultivate the virtues which the nation had lost under Othoman domination. The task did not appear to be very difficult. The greater part of Greece was uninhabited. The progress of many British colonies, and of the United States of America, testify that land capable of cultivation forms the surest foundation for national prosperity. To insure a rapid increase of population where there is an abundant supply of waste land, nothing is required but domestic virtue and public order. And in a free country, the rapid increase of a population enjoying the privilege of self-government in local affairs, and of stern justice in the central administration, is the surest means of extending a nation's power. The dreamer, therefore, who allowed visions of the increase of the Greek race, and of its peaceful conquests over uncultivated lands far beyond the limits of the new kingdom, to pass through his mind as King Otho rode forward to mount his throne, might have seen what was soon to happen, had the members of the regency possessed a little common-sense. The rapid growth of population in the Greek kingdom would have solved the Eastern question. The example of a well-governed Christian population, the aspect of its moral improvement, material prosperity, and constant overflow into European Turkey, would have relieved European cabinets from many political embarrassments, by producing the euthanasia of the Othoman empire.

Prince Otho of Bavaria had been proposed as a candidate for the sovereignty of Greece before the election of Prince Leopold. It was then urged that, being young, he would become completely identified with his subjects in language and religion.[1] But the Allies rejected him, thinking that a man of experience was more likely to govern Greece well, than an inexperienced boy of the purest accent and the most unequivocal orthodoxy. Eloquent and orthodox Greeks had not distinguished themselves as statesmen; and though they might be excellent teachers of their language and ecclesiastical doctrines, they had given no proof of their being able to educate a good sovereign.

The resignation of Prince Leopold, and the refusal of other princes, at last opened the way for King Otho's election, and he became King of Greece under extremely favourable circumstances. King Louis of Bavaria was authorised to appoint a regency to govern the kingdom until his son's majority, which was fixed to be on the 1st June 1835, at the completion of his twentieth year.[2]

[1] Thiersch, i. 308-313. See note, vol. II. p. 257 of this work.
[2] Treaty of 7th May 1832, Art. ix. x.

294   THE REGENCY.

BOOK V.
CHAP. IV.

The regency was invested with unlimited power, partly through the misconduct of the Greeks, and partly in consequence of the despotic views of King Louis. The liberality of the three powers supplied the regents with an overflowing treasury. It has been already stated that the regency was composed of three members, Count Armansperg, M. de Maurer, and General Heideck. Count Armansperg was named president. Mr Abel, the secretary, was invested with a consultative voice, and appointed supplemental member, to fill any vacancy that might occur. Mr Greiner was joined to the regency as treasurer, and director of the finance department. Not one of these men, with the exception of General Heideck, had the slightest knowledge of the condition of Greece.

Count Armansperg enjoyed the reputation of being a very liberal man for a Bavarian nobleman at that time. He had been minister of finance, and he filled the office of minister of foreign affairs when the first attempt was made to obtain the sovereignty of Greece for King Otho. His ministerial experience and his rank rendered him well suited for the presidency of the regency, which gave him the direction of the foreign relations of the kingdom, and, what both he and the countess particularly enjoyed, the duty of holding public receptions and giving private entertainments. The count's own tact, aided by the presence of the countess and three accomplished daughters, rendered the house of the president the centre of polished society and of political intrigue at Nauplia. It was the only place where the young king could see something of the world, and meet his subjects and strangers without feeling the restraint of royalty, for M. de Maurer lived like a niggard, and General Heideck like a recluse.

M. de Maurer and Mr Abel were selected for their offices on account of their sharing the political opinions

Greeks in "envy, hatred, and malice, and all unchari- A.D. 1833.
tableness."

Count Armansperg galled the pride of Maurer by an air of superiority, which the jurist had not the tact to rebuke with polite contempt. Maurer was impatient to proclaim publicly that the title of president only conferred on the count the first place in processions and the upper seat at board meetings, and he could not conceal that these things were the objects of his jealousy. The count understood society better than his rival. When strangers, misled by the fine figure and expression of Maurer, addressed him as the chief of the regency, the lawyer had not the tact to transfer the compliments to their true destination, and win the flatterers by his manner in doing so, but he left time for the president to thrust forward his common-looking physiognomy with polished ease, vindicate his own rights, and extract from the abashed strangers some additional outpouring of adulation. The Countess of Armansperg increased the discord of the regents by her extreme haughtiness, which was seldom restrained by good sense, and sometimes not even by good manners. She was so imprudent as to offend Heideck and Abel as much as she irritated Maurer. It is necessary to notice this conduct of the lady, for she was her husband's evil genius in Greece. Her influence increased the animosity of the Bavarians, and prolonged the misfortunes of the Greeks.

The position of the regency was delicate, but not difficult to men of talent and resolution. A moderate share of sagacity sufficed to guide their conduct. Anarchy had prepared an open field of action. It was necessary to create an army, a navy, a civil and judicial administration, and to sweep away the rude fiscal system of the Turkish land-tax. We shall see how the Bavarian regency performed these duties.

The first step was to put an end to the provisional system of expedients by which Capodistrias and his successors had prolonged the state of revolution. It was necessary to make the Greeks feel that the royal authority gave personal security and protection for property, since their loyalty reposed on no national and religious traditions and sympathies. It required no philosopher in Greece, when King Otho arrived, to proclaim "that all the vast apparatus of government has ultimately no other object or purpose but the distribution of justice; and that kings and parliaments, fleets and armies, officers of the court and revenue, ambassadors, ministers, and privy councillors, were all subordinate in their end to this part of the administration."[1] The reign of anarchy coming after the despotism of Capodistrias, had enabled the people to feel instinctively that, in order to secure good government, it was indispensable that the laws and institutions of the kingdom should be more powerful than the will of the king and the action of government.

The second step was to prepare the way for national prosperity, by removing the obstacles which prevented the people from bettering its condition. There was no difficulty in effecting this, since uncultivated land was abundant, and the Allied loan supplied the regency with ample funds. The system of exacting a tenth of the agricultural produce of the country kept society beyond the walls of towns in a stationary condition. Its immediate abolition was the most certain method of eradicating the evils it produced. Relief from the oppression of the tax-collector, even more than from the burden of the tax, would enable the peasantry to cultivate additional land, and to pay wages to agricultural labourers. An immediate influx of labourers would arrive from Turkey, and the increase of the

[1] Hume's *Essay of the Origin of Government.*

population of Greece would be certain and rapid. One-tenth would every year be added to the national capital. The regency required to do nothing but make roads. The government of the country could have been carried on from the customs, and the rent of national property. The extraordinary expenses of organising the kingdom would have been paid for out of the loan. The regency did nothing of the kind; it retained the Turkish land-tax, neglected to make roads, spent the Allied loan in a manner that both weakened and corrupted the Greek nation, and left the great question of its increase in population and agricultural prosperity unsolved.

The members of the regency complained that the want of labour and capital impeded the success of their plans of improvement; yet they seemed to have overlooked the fact that if they had abolished the tenths, the people would easily have procured both labour and capital for themselves. Labour was then abundant and cheap in Turkey; capital in the hands of Greeks was abundant in every commercial mart in the Mediterranean. Yet the Bavarians talked of establishing agricultural colonies of Swiss or Germans, and of inviting foreign capitalists to found banks. It may be confidently asserted that the Greek monarchy would have realised the boast of Themistocles, and rapidly expanded from a petty kingdom to a great state, had the regency swept away the Turkish land-tax, and left the agricultural industry of Greece free to make its own career in the East.

On the day of the king's landing, a royal proclamation was issued, addressed to the Greek nation; the ministers in office were confirmed in their places, and the senate was allowed to expire, without notice, of the wounds it had inflicted both on itself and its country.

The royal proclamation was nothing more than a collection of empty phrases, and it disappointed public expectation by making no allusion to representative institutions nor to the constitution. It revealed clearly that the views of the Bavarian government were not in accordance with the sentiments of the Greeks. The silence of the regency on the subject of the Greek constitution was regarded as a claim on the part of King Otho to be an absolute monarch. The omission was generally blamed; but the acknowledged necessity of investing the regency with legislative power, in order to enable it to introduce organic changes in the administration, prevented any public complaint. It caused the Greeks, however, to scrutinise the measures of the Bavarians with severity, and to regard the members of the regency with distrust. The King of Bavaria had solemnly declared to the protecting powers that the individuals selected to govern Greece during his son's minority "ought to hold moderate and constitutional opinions;" the Greek people had therefore an undoubted right to receive from these foreign statesmen a distinct pledge that they did not intend to establish an arbitrary government.[1] The distrust of the Greeks was increased, because the omission in the royal proclamation was a deliberate violation of a pledge given by the Bavarian minister of foreign affairs, when the object of King Louis was to win over the Greeks to accept his son as their king. The Baron de Gise then declared that it would be one of the first cares of the regency to convoke a national assembly to assist in preparing a definitive constitution for the kingdom.[2] The royal word, thus pledged, was guaranteed by a proclamation of the three protecting powers,

---

[1] *Parliamentary Papers*, Annex A to Protocol of 26th April 1832.
[2] The letter of Baron de Gise, dated 31st July 1832, is printed in *Recueil des Traités, Actes, et Pièces concernans la Fondation de la Royauté en Grèce et le Tracé de ses Limites* (Nauplie, 1833), p. 62.

published at Nauplia, to announce the election of King Otho. In this document the Greeks were invited to aid their sovereign in giving their country a definitive constitution.[1] They answered the appeal of the Allies on the 15th of September 1843.

The oath of allegiance demanded from the Greeks was simple. They swore fidelity to King Otho, and obedience to the laws of their country.

The first measures of the regency had been prepared at Munich, under the eye of King Louis. In these measures too much deference was paid to the administrative arrangements introduced by Capodistrias, which he himself had always regarded as of a provisional nature; and the modifications made on the Capodistrian legislation were too exclusively based on German theories, without a practical adaptation to the state of Greece. The King of Bavaria had little knowledge of financial and economical questions, and he had no knowledge of the social and fiscal wants of the Greek people. He thought of nothing but the means of carrying on the central administration, and in that sphere he endeavoured honestly to introduce a well-organised and clearly defined system. The laws and ordinances which the regency brought from Bavaria would have required only a few modifications to have engrafted them advantageously on the existing institutions. Their great object was to establish order and give power to the executive government.

The armed bands of personal followers which had enabled the military chiefs to place themselves above the law, to defy the government, and plunder the people, were disbanded. A national army was created. The scenes of tumultuous violence and gross peculation which General Heideck had witnessed in the Greek armies, had made a deep impression on his mind.

[1] *Parliamentary Papers*, Annex D to Protocol of 20th April 1832.

Warned by his experience, the regency arrived with an army capable of enforcing order; and it fortunately found the Greek irregulars so cowed by the punishment they had received from the French at Argos, that they submitted to be disbanded without offering any resistance. It must not, however, be concealed, that the regency abused the power it acquired by its success. Bavarian officers, who possessed neither experience nor merit, were suddenly promoted to high military commands, many of whom made a short stay in Greece, and hardly one of whom bestowed a single thought on the future condition of the country.

The national army soon received a good organisation in print.[1] In numbers it was unnecessarily strong. Upwards of five thousand Bavarian volunteers were enrolled in the Greek service before the end of the year 1834, and almost as many Greek troops were kept under arms. This numerous force was never brought into a very efficient condition. Faction and jobbing soon vitiated its organisation. The regency was ashamed to publish an army-list. Promotion was conferred too lavishly on young Bavarians, while Greeks and Philhellenes of long service were left unemployed. It was a grievous error on the part of General Heideck to omit fixing the rank and verifying the position and service of the Greek officers who had served during the Revolution, by the publication of an official army-list while the personal identity of the actors in every engagement was well known.

The bold measure of disbanding the irregular army was a blow which required to be struck with promptitude and followed up with vigour in order to insure success. It is idle to accuse the regency of precipitancy and severity, for something like a thunderbolt could alone prevent an organised resistance, and a

---

[1] Ἐφημερὶς τῆς Κυβερνήσεως, 1833, Nos. 5, 6, and 7.

hurricane was necessary to dissipate opposition. The whole military power created by the revolutionary war, and all the fiscal interests cherished by factious administrations, were opposed to the formation of a regular army. Chieftains, primates, ministers, and farmers of the taxes were all deprived of their bands of armed retainers before they could combine to thwart the Bavarians as they had leagued to attack the French.

A.D. 1833.

The war had been terminated in the Morea by the arms of the French; in Romelia by the negotiations with the Porte: but the Greek soldiers, instead of resuming the occupations of citizens, insisted on being fed and paid by the people. When not engaged in civil war they lived in utter idleness. The whole revenues of Greece were insufficient to maintain these armed bands, and during the anarchy that preceded the king's arrival they had been rapidly consuming the capital of the agricultural population. In many villages they had devoured the labouring oxen and the seed-corn. Nevertheless, the wisest reform could not fail to cause great irritation in several powerful bodies of men. Unemployed Capodistrians, discontented constitutionalists, displaced Corfiots, and Russian partisans, all raised an angry cry of dissatisfaction. Sir Richard Church committed the political blunder of joining the cause of the anarchists. His past position misled him into the belief that the irregulars were an element of military strength. His own influence over the military depended entirely on personal combinations. His declared opposition to the military reforms of the regeny persuaded Count Armansperg that the difficulty of transforming the personal followers of chiefs into a national army was much greater than it was in reality. Count Armansperg had approved of disbanding the irregulars, when that measure was decided on at

Munich, and he concurred in the necessity of its immediate execution after the regency arrived at Nauplia. Yet, when he listened to the observations of Sir Richard Church, and counted the persons of influence opposed to reform, he became anxious to gain them to be his political partisans. He was sufficiently adroit as a party tactician to perceive that the Greeks were in that social and moral condition which leads men to make persons of more account than principles, and he saw that intriguers of all factions were looking out for a leader. His ambition led him to make his first false step in Greece on this occasion. He listened with affected approval to interested declamations against the military policy which put an end to the reign of anarchy. And, from his imprudent revival of the semi-irregular bands at a subsequent period, it seems probable that in his eagerness to gain partisans he gave promises at this time which he found himself obliged to fulfil when he was intrusted with the sole direction of the government. The opposition of Sir Richard Church to measures which were necessary in order to put an end to anarchy, and the selfish countenance given to this opposition by Count Armansperg, entailed many years of military disorder on Greece, and were a principal cause of perpetuating the fearful scourge of brigandage, which is its inevitable attendant.

The sluggishness of the Bavarian troops formed a marked contrast with the activity of the French during their stay in Greece. Though the French soldiers were in a foreign land, with which they had only an accidental and temporary connection, they laboured industriously at many public works for the benefit of the Greeks, without fee or the expectation of reward. At Modon they repaired the fortifications, and built large and commodious barracks. At Navarin they

reconstructed great part of the fortifications. They A.D. 1833.
formed a good carriage-road from Modon to Navarin,
and they built a bridge over the Pamisos to enable the
cultivators of the rich plain of Messenia to bring
their produce at every season to the markets of Kalamata, Coron, Modon, and Navarin.[1] The Bavarians
remained longer in Greece than the French; they
were in the Greek service, and well paid out of the
Greek treasury, but they left no similar claims on the
gratitude of the nation.

The civil organisation of the kingdom was based
on the principle of complete centralisation. Without
contesting the advantages of this system, it may be
remarked that in a country in which roads exist it is
impracticable. The decree establishing the ministry
of the interior embraced so wide a field of attributions,
some necessary and some useful, others superfluous
and others impracticable, that it looks like a summary
for an abridgment of the laws and ordinances of the
monarchy.[2] A royal ordinance, not unlike a table
of contents to a comprehensive treatise on political
economy, subsequently annexed a department of public
economy to this ministry.[3] These two decrees, when
read with a knowledge of their practical results, form
a keen satire on the skill of the Bavarians in the art of
government.

The kingdom was divided into ten provinces or
nomarchies, whose limits corresponded with ancient
or natural geographical boundaries. It is not neces-

---

[1] Maurer, *Das Griechische Volk in öffentlicher, kirchlicher und privatrecht-licher Beziehung*, B. 11. This work, written by the ablest member of the regency, is the best authority for the acts of the Greek government during 1833 and 1834, but it is full of personal prejudice and spite.
[2] *Government Gazette*, 1833, No. 14, dated 15th April 1833.
[3] *Government Gazette*, 1834, No. 18, dated 11th May 1834. Maurer gives us, very unnecessarily, the information that this ordinance was copied from the legislation of other countries. It speaks of introducing a system of canalisation in a country where wells are often wanting, and of rendering the rivers, which flow only "by the muses' skill," navigable.—*Das Griechische Volk*, II. 98.

sary to notice the details of this division, for, like most arrangements in Greece, it underwent several modifications.[1] Prefects, called nomarchies, and sub-prefects, called eparchs, had been already trained to the service by Capodistrias, and no difficulty was found in introducing the outward appearance of a regular and systematic action of the central government over the whole country.

With all their bureaucratic experience, the members of the regency were deficient in the sagacity necessary for carrying theory into practice where the social circumstances of the people required new administrative forms. Their invention was so limited that when they were unable to copy the laws of Bavaria or France they adopted the measures of Capodistrias. In no case were these measures more at variance with the political and social habits of the Greeks than in the modifications he made in their municipal system. This system, whatever might have been its imperfections, was a national institution. It had enabled the people to employ their whole strength against the Turks, and it contained within itself the germs of improvement and reform. Its vitality and its close connection with the actions and wants of the people had persuaded Capodistrias that it was a revolutionary institution. He struck a mortal blow at its existence, by thrusting it into the vortex of the central administration.

The regency virtually abolished the old popular municipal system, and replaced it by a communal organisation, which permitted the people only a small share in naming the lowest officials of government in the provinces. The people were deprived of the power of directly electing their chief magistrate or demarch.

---

[1] *Government Gazette*, 1833, No. 12. A new division was established by Count Armansperg, *Government Gazette*, 1836, No. 28; and this division was again changed by King Otho, *Government Gazette*, 1838, No. 24.

An oligarchical elective college was formed to name three candidates, and the king selected one of these to be demarch. The minister of the interior was invested with the power of suspending the demarchs from office, as an administrative punishment. In this way, the person who appeared to be a popular and municipal officer was in reality transformed into an organ of the central government. Demarchs were henceforth compelled to perform the duties of incompetent and corrupt prefects, and serve as scapegoats for their misdeeds. The system introduced by the regency may have its merits, but it is a misnomer to call it a municipal system.[1]

To render municipal institutions a truly national institution and a part of the active life of the people, it is not only necessary that the local chief magistrate should be directly elected by the men of the municipality; but also that the authority which he receives by this popular election should only be revoked or suspended by the decision of a court of law, and not by the order of a minister or king. To render the people's defender a dependent on the will of the central administration, is to destroy the essence of municipal institutions. The mayor or demarch must be respon-

---

[1] *Government Gazette*, 1834, No. 3. Maurer boasts that the object of the municipal law was to constitute the demarchies as moral beings. He ought to have foreseen that it would render the demarchs very immoral subjects, it. 117. In the *Parliamentary Papers* relative to Greece in 1836, there is a despatch of Sir Edmund Lyons claiming for Armansperg the authorship of the law, which is described as "founded on very liberal principles, and placing the administration of the affairs of the municipalities entirely in their own hands, and establishing the principle of election on the most liberal and extended scale." It is evident that Lyons was grossly deceived, and this despatch is valuable as illustrating the boldness and the falsehood of Armansperg's assertions. Abel was the principal author of the law, and Parish asserts that Armansperg opposed it as too republican. It deprived the people of the right of electing their chief magistrate. It rendered that chief magistrate dependent on the minister of the day, and not responsible for the due execution of his functions to the law alone. Compare *Additional Papers relative to the Third Instalment of the Greek Loan*, p. 37, and *Diplomatic History of the Monarchy of Greece*, by H. H. Parish, Esq., late Secretary of Legation to Greece, p. 314 and 326.

sible only to the law; and the control which the minister of the interior must exercise over his conduct must be confined to accusing him before the legal tribunals when he neglects his duty.

The decrees organising the ministry of the interior and the department of public economy, proved that the regency was theoretically acquainted with all the objects to which enlightened statesmen can be called upon to direct their attention; but its financial administration displayed great inability to employ this multifarious knowledge to any good practical purpose. The fiscal system of the Turks was allowed to remain the basis of internal taxation in the Greek kingdom. Indeed, as has been already observed, whenever the Bavarians entered on a field of administration, in which neither administrative manuals nor Capodistrias's practice served them as guides, they were unable to discover new paths. This administrative inaptitude, more than financial ignorance, must have been the cause of their not replacing the Turkish land-tax by some source of revenue less hostile to national progress. Where a bad financial system exists, reform is difficult, and its results doubtful. Entire abolition is the only way in which all the evils it has engendered in society can be completely eradicated. So many persons derive a profit from old abuses, that no partial reform can prevent bad practices from finding a new lodgment, and in new positions old evil-doers can generally continue to intimidate or cheat the people. To make sure of success in extensive financial changes, it is necessary to gain the active co-operation of the great body of the people, and this must be purchased by lightening the popular burdens. The greatest difficulty of statesmen is not in preparing good laws, but in creating the machinery necessary to carry any financial laws into execution without oppression.

It is always difficult to levy a large amount of direct taxation from the agricultural population without arresting improvement and turning capital away from the cultivation of the land. The decline of the agricultural population in the richest lands of the Othoman empire, and, indeed, in every country between the Adriatic and the Ganges, may be traced to the oppressive manner in which direct taxation is applied to cultivated land. The Roman empire, in spite of its admirable survey, and the constant endeavours of its legislators to protect agriculture, was impoverished and depopulated by the operation of a direct land-tax, and the oppressive fiscal laws it rendered necessary. The regency perhaps did not fully appreciate the evil effects on agriculture of the Turkish system; it was also too ignorant of the financial resources of Greece to find new taxes; and it was not disposed to purchase the future prosperity of the monarchy by a few years of strict economy.[1]

The fiscal measures of the regency which had any pretension to originality were impolitic and unjust. They were adopted at the suggestion of Mavrocordatos, who had the fiscal prejudices and the arbitrary principles of his phanariot education as a Turkish official.

Salt was declared a government monopoly; and in order to make this monopoly more profitable, several salt-works which had previously been farmed were now closed. This measure produced great inconvenience

---

[1] Without entering on the question of the comparative advantages of direct and indirect taxation, which often depend more on national circumstances than political science, it must be mentioned that the Greek peasantry and small proprietors were averse to commuting the tenths paid in kind for a fixed annual rate in money. They feared that they would be obliged to borrow money, and thus subject themselves to the evil of debt, and become serfs of the money lenders. The produce was always ready when it could be demanded; the money, they said, would always be demanded by the government officials when it was not ready, and then some ally of the official would appear to lend the sum demanded by the state at an exorbitant interest. Here we see how direct taxation in an agricultural community produces the evil of debts, which forms a political feature in ancient history.

in a country where the difficulties of transport presented an insuperable barrier to the formation of a sufficient number of depots in the mountains. The evils of the monopoly soon became intolerable,—sheep died of diseases caused by the want of salt, the shepherds turned brigands, and, at last, even the rapacious Bavarians were convinced that the monopoly required to be modified.[1]

The evils resulting from the salt monopoly were far exceeded by an attempt of the regency to seize all the pasture-lands belonging to private individuals as national property. In a ministerial circular, Mavrocordatos ordered the officials of the finance department to take possession of all pasture-lands in the kingdom, declaring "that every spot where wild herbage grows which is suitable for the pasturage of cattle is national property," and that the Greek government, like the Othoman, maintained the principle "that no property in the soil, except the exclusive right of cultivation, could be legally vested in a private individual." This attempt to found the Bavarian monarchy in Greece on the legislative theories of Asiatic barbarians, whom the Greeks had expelled from their country, could not succeed. But the property of so many persons was arbitrarily confiscated by this ministerial circular, that measures for resisting it were promptly taken. A widespread conspiracy was formed, and several military chiefs were incited to take advantage of the prevalent discontent, and plan a general insurrection. Government was warned of the danger, and saw the necessity of cancelling Mavrocordatos's circular. But many landed proprietors were deprived of the use of their pasture-lands by the farmers of the revenue for more than a year. The cultivation of several large

[1] Maurer, *Das Griechische Volk*, ii. 290.

estates were abandoned, and much capital was driven away from Greece.[1]

Though Mavrocordatos made an exhibition of extraordinary fiscal zeal at the expense of the people, he is accused by M. de Maurer of dissipating the national property, by granting titles to houses, buildings, shops, mills, and gardens, to his political allies and partisans, after the king's arrival, without any legal warrant from the regency, and without any purchase-money being paid into the Greek treasury. In short, with continuing the abuses which had disgraced the administration of the constitutionalists while they were in league with Kolettes, and acting under the governing commission.[2]

It would be a waste of time to enumerate the financial abuses which the regency overlooked or tolerated. They allowed the frauds to commence which have ended in robbing the nation of the most valuable portion of the national property, the English bondholders of the lands which were given them in security, and the greater part of those who fought for the independence of their country, of all reward. The regency showed itself as insensible to the value of national honesty as the Greek statesmen of the Revolution, and the progress of the country has been naturally arrested in this age of credit by the dishonesty of its rulers. By the repudiation of her just debts, Greece has been thrown entirely on her internal resources, and, after nearly thirty years of peace, she remains without roads, without manufactures, and without agricultural improvements.

[1] It is remarkable that Maurer, in his work on the administration of the regency, omits all mention of this important measure. The *suppressio veri* fixes a large share of its responsibility on him and his colleagues. There is no doubt that it created the aversion which has ever since been shown by wealthy Greeks in England, France, and Germany to making purchases of land in the Greek kingdom. Parish, *Diplomatic History*, p. 231; *The Hellenic Kingdom and the Greek Nation*, a pamphlet, 1836, p. 64.
[2] Maurer, *Das Griechische Volk*, ii. 286.

The monetary system of the Greek kingdom was a continuance of that introduced by Capodistrias, but the phœnix was now called a drachma. The radical defect of this plan has been already pointed out, and the value of the Spanish pillar dollar, on which it had been originally based, was daily increasing throughout the Levant. An accurate assay of these dollars at the Bavarian mint had proved that their metallic value exceeded the calculation of Capodistrias, and the drachma was consequently coined of somewhat more value than the phœnix, in order to render it equal to one-sixth of the dollar. The metal employed in the Greek coinage was of the same standard of purity as that employed in the French mint. It seems strange that the regency overlooked the innumerable advantages which would have resulted to Greece from making the coinage of the country correspond exactly with that of France, Sardinia, and Belgium, instead of creating a new monetary system.[1]

The highest duty the regency was called upon to fulfil was to introduce an effective administration of justice. M. de Maurer was a learned and laborious lawyer, and he devoted his attention with honourable zeal to framing the laws and organising the tribunals necessary to secure to all ranks an equitable administration of justice. Had he confined himself to organising the judicial business, and preparing a code of laws for Greece, he would have gained immortal honour.

The criminal code and the codes of civil and criminal procedure promulgated by the regency are excellent. In general, the measures adopted for carrying the judicial system into immediate execution ex-

---

[1] 1.1168 drachmas equal a franc, and 28.12 drachmas an English sovereign. The drachma is divided into 100 lepta; and the Greek coins are—two of gold, 40 and 20 drachmas; four of silver, 5, 1, ½, and ¼ drachma; and four of copper, 10, 5, 2, and 1 lepton. For observations on the system of Capodistrias, see vol. ii. p. 215.

hibited a thorough knowledge of legal administration. By Maurer's ability and energy the law was promptly invested with supreme authority in a country where arbitrary power had known no law for ages. His merit in this respect ought to cancel many of his political blunders, and obtain for him the gratitude of the Greeks.[1] It has been the melancholy task of this work to record the errors and the crimes of those who governed Greece much oftener than their merits or their virtues. It is gratifying to find an opportunity of uttering well-merited praise.

Some objections have been taken to the manner in which primary jurisdictions were adapted to the social requirements of a rural population living in a very rude condition, and thinly scattered over mountainous districts; but the examination of these objections belongs to the province of politics, and not of history.

It is necessary to point out one serious violation of the principles of equity in the judicial organisation introduced by the regency. In compliance with the spirit of administrative despotism prevalent in Europe, the sources of justice were vitiated whenever the fiscal interests of the government were concerned, by the creation of exceptional tribunals to decide questions between the state and private individuals; and these tribunals were exempted from the ordinary rules of judicial procedure. Thus the citizens were deprived of the protection of the law precisely in those cases where that protection was most wanted, and the officials of the government were raised above the law. The proceedings of these exceptional tribunals caused such general dissatisfaction, that they were abolished after

---

[1] For the criminal code, see *Government Gazette*, 1834, No. 3—It bears date the 30th December 1833;—for the organisation of the tribunals and notarial offices, No. 13; for the code of criminal procedure, No. 16; and for the code of civil procedure, No. 22. The German originals of these laws are printed in Maurer's work, *Das Griechische Volk*, iii. 304, 649.

the Revolution of 1843, and an article was inserted in the constitution of Greece prohibiting the establishment of such courts in future.[1]

The Greek Revolution broke off the relations of the clergy with the patriarch and synod of Constantinople. This was unavoidable, since the patriarch was in some degree a minister of the sultan for the civil as well as the ecclesiastical affairs of the orthodox. It was therefore impossible for a people at war with the sultan to recognise the patriarch's authority. The clergy in Greece ceased to mention the patriarch's name in public worship, and adopted the form of prayer for the whole orthodox Church used in those dioceses of the Eastern Church which are not comprised within the limits of the patriarchate of Constantinople.

When Capodistrias assumed the presidency, an attempt was made by the patriarch and synod of Constantinople to bring the clergy in Greece again under their immediate jurisdiction. Letters were addressed to the president and to the clergy, and a deputation of prelates was sent to renew the former ties of dependency. But Capodistrias was too sensible of the danger which would result to the civil power from allowing the clergy to become dependent on foreign patronage, to permit any ecclesiastical relations to exist with the patriarch. He replied to the demands of the Church of Constantinople by stating that the murder of the patriarch Gregorios, joined to other executions of bishops and laymen, having forced the Greeks to throw off the sultan's government in order to escape extermination, it was impossible for liberated Greece to recognise an ecclesiastical chief subject to the sultan's power.[2]

Capodistrias found the clergy of Greece in a deplor-

[1] Art. 101.
[2] *Correspondance du Comte Capodistrias, Président de la Grèce*, publiée par E. A. Bétant, l'un de ses Secrétaires. Genève, 1839. 4 vols. Vol. ii. 154.

able condition, and he did very little for their improvement. The lower ranks of the priesthood were extremely ignorant, the higher extremely venal. Money was sought with shameless rapacity; and Mustoxidi, who enjoyed the president's confidence, and who held an official situation in the department of ecclesiastical affairs and public instruction, asserts that simony was generally practised.[1] The bishops annulled marriages, made and cancelled wills, and gave judicial decisions in most civil causes. They leagued with the primates in opposing the establishment of courts of law during the Revolution; for they derived a considerable revenue by trading in judicial business; while the primates supported this jurisdiction, because the ecclesiastics were generally under their influence. Capodistrias, in spite of this opposition, deprived the bishops of their jurisdiction in civil causes, except in those cases relating to marriage and divorce, where it is conceded to them by the canons of the Greek Church. Against this reform the mitred judges raised indignant complaints, and endeavoured to persuade their flocks that the orthodox clergy was suffering a persecution equal to that inflicted on the chosen people in the old time by Pharaoh.

Capodistrias also endeavoured to obtain from the bishops and abbots, inventories of the movable and immovable property of the churches and monasteries under their control, but without success. Even his orders, that diocesan and parish registers should be kept of marriages, baptisms, and deaths, were disobeyed, though not openly resisted. Mustoxidi expressly declares that the opposition to these beneficial measures proceeded from the selfishness and corruption of the Greek clergy, who would not resign

---

[1] *Renseignemens sur la Grèce et sur l'administration du Comte Capodistrias, par un Grec témoin oculaire des faits qu'il rapporte.* Paris, 1833, p. 30.

the means of illicit gain. They knew that if regular registers of marriages, births, and deaths were established, the fabrication of certificates to meet contingencies would cease, and the delivery of such certificates was a very lucrative branch of ecclesiastical profits. Bigamy and the admission of minors into the priesthood would no longer be possible; and it was said that they were sources of great gain to venal bishops. Capodistrias failed to eradicate these abuses from the Church in Greece; for Mustoxidi declares, that if he had amputated the gangrened members of the priesthood, very little of the clerical body would have remained.[1]

The ecclesiastical forms of the regency were temperately conducted. An assembly of bishops was convoked at Nauplia to make a report on the ecclesiastical affairs of the kingdom. Its advice was in conformity with the wishes of those in power, rather than with the sentiments of a majority of the bishops; for political subserviency has been for ages a feature of the Eastern clergy. On the 4th August 1833, a decree proclaimed the National Church of Greece independent of the patriarch and synod of Constantinople, and established an ecclesiastical synod for the kingdom.[2] In doctrine, the Church of liberated Greece remained as closely united to the Church at Constantinople as the patriarchates of Jerusalem or Alexandria; but in temporal affairs it was subject to a Catholic king instead of a Mohammedan sultan. King Otho was invested with the power of appointing annually the members of the synod.[3] This synod was formed on

[1] *Renseignemens sur la Grèce et sur l'administration du Cte Capodistrias*, 35.
[2] *Government Gazette*, 1833, No. 23. Thirty-four bishops signed the Declaration of Independence.
[3] Maurer, with the candour which confers value on his vain-glorious volumes, tells us, that King Otho succeeded, in ecclesiastical affairs, as in all other authority, to the rights of the sultan. This information explains one of the causes of his arbitrary proceedings, and the oblivion of the Revolution.— *Das Griechische Volk*, ii. 160.

the model of that of Russia; but in accordance with A.D. 1833. the free institutions of the Greeks, it received more freedom of action.

When the important consequences which may result from the independence of a church in Greece filled with a learned and enlightened clergy are considered, the success of the regency in consummating this great work is really wonderful. The influences of Russia and the prejudices of a large body of the Greeks were hostile to reform; but the necessity of a great change in order to sweep away the existing ecclesiastical corruption was so strongly felt by the enlightened men in liberated Greece, that they were determined not to cavil at the quarter from which the reformation came, nor to criticise the details of a measure whose general scope they approved. Those, however, who had thwarted the moderate reforms of Capodistrias were not likely to submit in silence to the more extensive reforms of the Bavarians. An opposition was quickly formed. Several bishops were sent from Turkey into Greece as missionaries to support the claims of the patriarch to ecclesiastical supremacy. They were assisted by monks from Mount Athos, who wandered about as emissaries of superstition and bigotry. Russian diplomacy echoed the outcries of these zealots, and patronised the most intriguing of the discontented priests. Yet the Greek people remained passive amidst all the endeavours made to incite it to violence.

In the month of December 1833, the regency published an ordinance, declaring that the number of bishoprics in Greece was to be ultimately reduced to ten, making them correspond in extent with the nomarchies into which the kingdom was divided. This measure was adopted at the recommendation of the synod. In the mean time, forty bishops were named by royal authority to act in the old dioceses, and when these died the sees were to be gradually united, until ten only remained.[1] The synod was reproached with subserviency for proposing this law, which was generally disapproved.

A reaction in favour of renewing ecclesiastical relations with Constantinople soon manifested itself. Death diminished the number of the bishops, and the synod named by King Otho had not the power of consecrating an orthodox bishop, so that when the Revolution of 1843 occurred, many sees were vacant. The constitutional system did as little for some years to improve the Church as preceding governments. But the Greek people did not remain indifferent to the revival of religious feeling, which manifested itself in every Christian country about this period. Among the Greeks the ideas of nationality and Oriental orthodoxy are closely entwined. The revival of religious feeling strengthened the desire for national union, and a strong wish was felt to put an end to the kind of schism which separated the free Greeks from the flock of the patriarch of Constantinople.

Secret negotiations were opened, which, in the year 1850, led to the renewal of amicable relations. The patriarch and synod of Constantinople published a decretal of the Oriental Church, called a Synodal Tomos, which recognised the independence of the Greek Church, under certain restrictions and obligations, which it imposed on the clergy. Much objection was made to the form of this document, particularly to the assumption that the liberties of the National Church required the confirmation of a body of priests notoriously dependent on the Othoman government, and which might soon be filled with members aliens to the Greek race. Two years were allowed to pass before the Greek government accepted the terms of peace

[1] *Government Gazette*, 1833, No. 38.

offered by the Church of Constantinople. In 1852 a [A.D. 1853.] law was adopted by the Greek Chambers, enacting all the provisions of the Synodal Tomos, without, however, making any mention of that document. By this arrangement the independence of the Church of Greece was established on a national basis, and its orthodoxy fully recognised by the patriarch and synod of Constantinople.[1]

The re-establishment of monastic discipline, and the administration of the property belonging to ecclesiastical foundations, called for legislation. War had destroyed the buildings and dispersed the monks of four hundred monasteries. Many monks had served as soldiers against the infidels; but a much greater number lived on public charity, mixing with the world as mere beggars and idlers. The respect for monachism had declined. It was neither possible nor desirable to rebuild the greater part of the ruined monasteries; but it was necessary to compel the monks to retire from the world and return to a monastic life. It was also the duty of the government to prevent the large revenues of the ruined monasteries from being misappropriated. The regency suppressed all those monasteries of which there were less than six monks, or of which the buildings were completely destroyed, by a royal ordinance of the 7th October 1833.[2] The number thus dissolved

---

[1] A volume hostile to the *Synodal Tomos*, which contains much sound reasoning, with some unnecessary theological violence, was published by a learned ecclesiastic, the archimandrite Pharmakides. It is entitled, 'Ο Συνοδικὸς Τόμος ἢ περὶ ἀληθείας. For the *Tomos*, see p. 37.

[2] The ordinance of 1833 was framed on the report of the synod, and a catalogue of the 412 monasteries suppressed was annexed to the report, which is dated 19th (31st) August 1833. This document, which would be of great historical and topographical interest, has not been printed, and it is said not to exist in the archives of the ministry of ecclesiastical affairs. A work entitled Τὰ Μοναστηριακά, published in 1859 by Mr Mamoukas, under-secretary of state in the ecclesiastical department, and editor of the *Acts of the Greek National Assemblies*, contains the measures adopted with regard to the existing monasteries. There is a third class of monasteries, which possess considerable estates in Greece, concerning which it is difficult to procure information:—viz., those of Mount Athos, of the Holy Sepulchre, and of Mount Sinai.

amounted to four hundred and twelve, and the property which fell into the hands of the government was very great. One hundred and forty-eight monasteries were re-established, and two thousand monks were recalled to a regular monastic life. The surviving nuns were collected into four convents. The lands of the suppressed monasteries were farmed like other national property, and they were so much worse cultivated by the farmers of the revenue than they had been formerly by the monks, that the measure created much dissatisfaction. The ecclesiastical policy of the regency in this case received the blame due to its financial administration. As far as regards the treatment of the monasteries, no conduct of foreigners, however prudent, could have escaped censure.

Much has been done in Greece for public instruction since the arrival of King Otho. The regency, however, did little but copy German institutions, and so many changes have been subsequently made, that the subject does not fall within the limits of this work. The regeneration of Greek society, by a wiser system of family education than seems at present to be practised, will doubtless one day supply the materials for an interesting chapter to some future historian of Greek civilisation.

The regency did not establish an university, and King Otho never showed any love for learning. Much dissatisfaction was manifested at the delay; and in the year 1837 the Greeks took the business into their own hands, with a degree of zeal which it would be for their honour to display more frequently in other good causes. A public meeting was held, and all parties united to raise the funds necessary for building an university by public subscription. The court yielded slowly and sullenly to the force of public opinion. The royal assent was extorted rather than given to the measure, but after an interval the king himself became A.D. 1832. a subscriber, and sycophants called the university by his name.

In a country divided as Greece had long been by fierce party-quarrels, it was natural that every measure of the government should meet a body of men ready to oppose it. The liberty of the press could not fail to give a vent to much animosity, and the restoration of legal order by the regency resuscitated the liberty of the press, which Capodistrias had almost strangled. Four newspapers were established at Nauplia, and the measures of the regency were examined with a good deal of freedom. Many of the criticisms of the press might have been useful to the regency from their intelligence and moderation, and from the intimate knowledge they displayed concerning the internal condition of the country. Though the regency paid little attention to these articles, it allowed those in which ignorance and violence were exhibited to ruffle its equanimity. The liberty of the press was declared by the two liberals, Armansperg and Maurer, to be of little value to the Greeks, unless the press could be prevented from blaming the conduct and criticising the measures of their rulers. Most of the Bavarians were galled by frequent allusions to the magnitude of their pay, and the trifling nature of their service. They demanded that the press should be silenced. The wishes of the members of the regency coincided with these demands. The spirit of Viaro Capodistrias again animated the Greek government.[1]

The regency did not venture to establish a censor-

[1] The four newspapers published at Nauplia were *Athena*, *Helios*, *Chronos*, and *Triptolemos*. The Greek press did not then use more violent language concerning any member of the regency than Maurer afterwards used against his colleague, Armansperg. But "it is one of the conditions of bad governors to give heed to what they hear said of them, and to take ill that which, if it had been said, they had better not have heard," as Ferdinand the Catholic told other regents.—See Help's *The Spanish Conquest of America*, i. 182.

ship. It was, however, determined to suppress the newspapers most opposed to the government by indirect legislation. In the month of September 1833 several laws were promulgated regulating the press, and police regulations were introduced worthy of the Inquisition in the sixteenth century.¹ Printers, lithographers, and booksellers, were treated as men suspected of criminal designs against the state, and placed under numerous restrictions. The editors of newspapers and periodicals were compelled to deposit the sum of five thousand drachmas in the public treasury, to serve as a security in case they should be condemned to pay fines or damages in actions of libel. As the interest of money at Nauplia was then one and a half per cent per month, it was supposed that nobody would be found who would make the deposit. The end of the law was attained, and all the four political newspapers immediately ceased. By this law another liberal ministry in Greece became bankrupt in reputation. The want of public principle and conscientious opinions among Greek statesmen, is manifested by the names of the ministers which appear attached to these ordinances against the liberty of the press. They are Mavrocordatos, Kolettes, Tricoupes, Psyllas, and Praïdes.

To counteract the bad impression produced by the restraints put on the liberty of the press, the Greek government pretended to be seriously occupied in improving the material condition of the people. Starving the mind and stuffing the body is a favourite system with tyrants. The Bavarians, however, only stuffed the Greeks with printed paper. A royal proclamation was published announcing that the regency was about to construct a net-work of roads.² A plan was adopted

---

¹ *Government Gazette*, 1833, No. 29. 1, Concerning printers, lithographers, and booksellers. 2, Concerning the press. 3, Concerning criminal abuses of the press.
² *Government Gazette*, 1833, No. 29. More than a quarter of a century has

by which every part of the kingdom would have found ready access to the Ionian and Egean seas, and its execution was absolutely necessary to improve the country. The whole of the roads proposed might easily have been completed in about ten years, had the Bavarian volunteers and the Greek conscripts worked at road-making with as much industry as the French had done while they remained in Greece. King Louis of Bavaria declared that the Bavarians would confer benefits on Greece without being a burden on the country. The greatest benefit they could have conferred would have been to construct good roads and stone bridges. They neglected to do this, and, in direct violation of their king's engagement to the protecting powers, they rendered themselves an intolerable burden.[1]

Enough has been now said of the legislative and administrative measures of the regency.

On the 1st of June 1833 they decorated the monarchy with an order of knighthood, called the order of the Redeemer, in commemoration of the providential deliverance of Greece.[2] The order was divided into five classes. From an official list, published a few weeks before the termination of Count Armansperg's administration as arch-chancellor, it appears that the grand cross had been conferred on forty-nine persons, exclusive of kings and members of reigning families. Among these there were only three Greeks and one Philhellene. The names of Kanaris, Mavrocordatos, Gordon, and Fabvier, are not in the list, which it is

---

now elapsed, yet the roads from Athens to Chalcis and from Athens to Corinth are unfinished, and many roads are in a worse condition than they were under the Turks.

[1] *Parliamentary Papers*, Annex A to Protocol of 26th April 1832.

[2] *Government Gazette*, 1833, No. 29. The following number contains patterns for the embroidery of the uniforms of civil officials. Ministers and monarchs were forced to send to Munich and Paris for their coats, and when they first made their appearance in their new clothes, it was evident that they had sent very bad measures. Most of them looked as if they had starved since their coats were ordered.

impossible to read without a feeling of contempt for those who prepared it. The subsequent destiny of the order has not been more brilliant than its commencement. French ministers have obtained crosses in great numbers for unknown writers, and Bavarian courtiers and German apothecaries have been as lucky as French savants. While it was lavished on foreigners who had rendered Greece no service, it was not bestowed on several Greeks who had distinguished themselves in their country's service.[1]

Before recounting the quarrels of the regency, it is necessary to say a few words more concerning the characters of the men who composed it.

Count Armansperg came to Greece with the expectation of being able to act the viceroy. He aspired to hold a position similar to that of Capodistrias, but neither his feeble character nor his moderate abilities enabled him to master the position. He might have given up the idea had he not been pushed forward by the countess, who possessed more ambition and less wisdom than her husband.[2] Armansperg selected Maurer and Abel as his colleagues, knowing them to be able and hard-working men, and believing that he should find them grateful and docile. Armansperg never displayed much sagacity in selecting his subordinates, and he soon found to his dismay that Maurer and Abel were men so ambitious that he could neither lead nor drive them. Without losing time he set about undermining their authority.

The merits of Maurer are displayed in his legislative measures; his defects are exposed in his book on Greece. His natural disposition was sensitive and touchy; his sudden elevation to high rank turned his head. He

---

[1] The Greek Almanac of 1837 gives a list of 591 Knights of the Redeemer. Of these 374 are Bavarians and foreigners, 154 Greeks, and 24 Philhellenes. The rest are emperors, kings, princes, &c.
[2] Maurer, II. 56.

could never move in his new sphere without a feeling
of restraint that often amounted to awkwardness.
He wished to save money, and he did so; but he felt
that his penuriousness rendered him ridiculous. His
want of knowledge of the world was displayed by the
foolish manner in which he attempted to obtain the
recall of Mr Dawkins, the British resident in Greece,
because Mr Dawkins thought Count Armansperg the
better statesman. His ignorance of Greece is certified
by his informing the world that it produces dates,
sugar, and coffee.[1]

Mr Abel was an active and able man of business,
but of limited bureaucratic views; rude, bold, and
sincere.

The opinions of General Heideck were not considered
to be of much value, but his support was important, for
it was known that his conduct was regulated by what
he conceived to be the wish of the King of Bavaria.

The merits of the different members of the regency
may be correctly estimated by the condition in which
they placed the departments of the state under their
especial superintendence. Until the 31st of July 1834,
the departments of justice, military affairs, and civil
administration, were directed by Maurer, Heideck, and
Abel; and they laid the foundations of an organisation
which has outlived the Bavarian domination, and forms
a portion of the scaffolding of the constitutional monarchy of Greece, as established after the Revolution of
1843. The department of finance was intrusted to
Armansperg, and he retained his authority for four
years, yet he effected no radical improvements. He
found and left the department a source of political and
social corruption. It was not until the end of the year
1836, and then only when forced by the protecting
powers and the King of Bavaria, that he published any

[1] Maurer, ii. 310.

accounts of the revenue and expenditure of his government, and the accounts published were both imperfect and inaccurate.[1]

The policy of the regency did little to extinguish party spirit and personal animosity among the Greeks. Indeed, both the members of the regency and the foreign ministers at Nauplia did much to nourish the evil passions excited by the reign of anarchy. Armansperg was a partisan of English influence; Maurer and Abel, strong partisans of France. Russia, having no avowed partisan among the Bavarians, maintained her influence among the Greeks by countenancing the Capodistrian opposition, protecting the monks and clergy from Turkey, and the adventurers from the Ionian Islands, and flattering the ambition of Kolokotrones. The French minister protected Kolettes and the most rapacious of his friends, because they were supposed to be devoted to the interests of France. England made a pretence of supporting a constitutional party, but her friends were chiefly remarkable for their frequent desertion of the cause of the constitution.

The regency excluded Kolokotrones and the senators, who had attempted to welcome King Otho with a civil war, from all official employment. But the unpopularity of several measures enabled these excluded Capodistrians to raise a loud if not a dangerous opposition, and they availed themselves with considerable skill of the liberty of the press, as long as the regency allowed them to enjoy it. At the same time they formed a secret society called the Phœnix, to imitate the Philiké Hetairia, and pretended to be sure of Russian support.

---

[1] Maurer, who, it must be owned, is a prejudiced witness, says, that as long as Armansperg could make Greiner work at official details, he did nothing but loll on his sofa and read the chapter on the French Revolution in Rotteck's *Universal History*, or ride out and then take his siesta. His colleagues, who could not obtain from him a budget, reproached him at their board meetings with his inactivity.—*Das Griechische Volk*, ii. 319, 519; Turish, *Diplomatic History*, 296; *Government Gazette*, 1836, Nos. 61, 65, 88, 89, 90, 91, 92.

distrias when he heard that Miaoulis had seized the Greek fleet at Poros. The Greeks did not consider an abortive conspiracy a very serious offence. Violence had been so often resorted to by all parties, that it was regarded as a natural manner of acquiring and defending power. No political party had paid much respect either to law or justice, but very different conduct was expected from M. Maurer. The worst aspect of the conspiracy was the revival of brigandage, which was evidently systematic. But it was not easy to procure evidence of the complicity of the leading conspirators with the crimes of the brigands. Kolokotrones and Plapoutas were tried for treason, and, by a strained application of the law, and an unbecoming interference of the executive power with the course of justice, they were found guilty and condemned to death. The sentence was commuted to imprisonment for life; but a complete pardon was granted to both criminals on King Otho's majority.[1]

The quarrels in the regency now became the leading feature of the Greek question, not only in Greece, but at the courts of Munich, London, Paris, and St Petersburg.[2] The improvement of Greece was utterly forgotten. There can be no doubt that Armansperg's vanity persuaded him that Dr Franz, in the petitions circulated among the Greeks, had given the King of Bavaria excellent advice. He now saw the advantage which Maurer's violent persecution of Kolokotrones afforded him, and he profited by it. Maurer was as ambitious as Armansperg, but less prudent. In vain the Greek ministers, who respected his talents, endeavoured to moderate his vehemence. Several resigned rather than sanction the trial of Kolokotrones on evi-

---

[1] The act of accusation against Kolokotrones and Plapoutas is given by Parish, 270. It is more like a party statement than a legal document.
[2] See Maurer's notice of these quarrels, ii. 53, 56, 93.

330   QUARRELS IN THE REGENCY.

BOOK V.
CHAP. IV.

dence, which appeared to them insufficient. It may be mentioned, in order to convey some idea of the manner in which public business was carried on at this time, and the contempt with which the Greek ministers allowed themselves to be treated by the Bavarians, that the arrests, which took place on the 19th of September 1833, were made by order of the regency, without holding a cabinet council, and without the knowledge of the ministers of the interior and of justice. When Psyllas, the minister of the interior, remonstrated with Maurer on the arbitrary manner in which he was proceeding, Maurer became so indignant that he threatened the minister with a legal prosecution for neglecting his duty in not discovering a conspiracy known to so many Greeks. The ministry was modified by the infusion of additional servility. Mavrocordatos was removed to the foreign office, and a young Greek recently arrived from Germany, Theochares, was appointed minister of finance, in which office he was a mere cipher. Schinas, an able and intriguing sycophant of the phanariot race, became Maurer's minister of ecclesiastical affairs. Kolettes was now all-powerful in the ministry.[1]

Maurer, Heideck, Abel, and Gasser, the Bavarian minister at the Greek court, formed an alliance with M. Rouen, the French minister, and prepared for a direct attack on Armansperg, in which they felt sure of a signal victory. Armansperg, on the other hand, was vigorously supported by Mr Dawkins, and still more energetically by Captain (Lord) Lyons, who commanded H.M.S. Madagascar. The count had a not inconsiderable party among the Greeks and Bavarians. The Russian minister, Catacazy, and the whole body of the Capodistrians, assisted his cause by their hostility to Maurer and Kolettes. In general the

[1] *Government Gazette*, 1833, No. 31.

Greeks watched the proceedings of both parties with anxiety and aversion, fearing a renewal of civil war and anarchy.

Armansperg laid his statement of the nature of the dissensions in the regency before the King of Bavaria. Maurer wasted time in attacking Dawkins, who had roused his personal animosity as much by satirical observations as by thwarting the policy of the regency.[1] Dawkins was accused of representing the proceedings of Maurer and his friends as being too aristocratic, too revolutionary, and too Russian, all in a breath. People said that, though the accusation looked absurd, it might be true enough; and they expressed a wish to hear how Dawkins applied his epithets to the measures he criticised. An envoy was sent to persuade Lord Palmerston to recall Dawkins: a worse pedant, and a man less likely to succeed than Michael Schinas, could not have been selected. He soon found that he had travelled to London on a fool's errand.

The great attack on Count Armansperg was directed against what Maurer probably supposed was the most vulnerable part of a man's feelings. No disputes had occurred among the members of the regency while they were carving their salaries and allowances out of the Greek loan. No one then suggested that both political prudence and common honesty demanded the most rigid economy of money which Greece would be one day called upon to repay. On the 10th October 1832, Armansperg, Maurer, and Heideck, held a meeting at Munich, at which, among other shameful misappropriations of Greek funds, they added nearly £4500 to Count Armansperg's salary, in order to enable him to give dinners and balls to foreigners and phanariots.[2]

---

[1] Maurer supplies ample evidence of his own readiness to listen to spies and talebearers. The phrases, *es ging die Rede, es ging die Sage, eines Tages kam, wie ich aus sehr guter Quelle weiss*, and such eavesdropping, abound in his work.

[2] We must not forget that the Bavarians were dividing the spoil of Greece

ARMANSPERG'S ADMINISTRATION.

Nemesis followed close on their crime. The count's dinners and balls destroyed Maurer's peace of mind, and to regain it he sought to deprive the count of his table-money. At last, in the month of May 1834, the majority of the regency deprived the president of what was called the representation fund, and reduced his extra pay to a sum which, if it had been originally granted, would have been considered amply sufficient, but now the conduct of the majority was so evidently the result of personal vengeance, that its meanness created a strong feeling in Armansperg's favour.

Both parties awaited a decision from Munich. The state of Greece was assuming an alarming aspect; brigandage was reviving in continental Greece on an alarming scale; and the protecting powers felt the necessity of putting an end to the unseemly squabbling which threatened to produce serious disturbances. The British government advised the King of Bavaria to recall Maurer and Abel. The Russian cabinet gave the same advice. The King of Bavaria adopted their opinion, and resolved to leave Count Armansperg virtually sole regent. His decision arrived in Greece on the 31st July 1834, and it fell on Maurer and Abel like a thunderbolt. They were ordered to return instantly to Bavaria; and in case they showed any disposition to delay their departure, authority was given to Count Armansperg to ship them off in the same summary manner in which Dr Franz had been sent to Trieste. Maurer was replaced by M. Von Kobell, a mere nullity, whose name only requires to be mentioned, because it appears signed to many ordinances affecting the welfare of the Greeks.[1] Heideck was allowed to remain, but he was

before the loan contract was signed. The signature did not take place until 1st March 1833. Maurer's explanation of his conduct is given in his work, ii. 529.

[1] *Government Gazette*, 1834, No. 25. Maurer gives the following account of his successor: "Herr von Kobell nachdem er denn auf einmal wieder credit

ordered to sign every document presented to him by A.D. 1834. the president of the regency. During the remainder of his stay in Greece he occupied himself with nothing but painting. The Greeks saw Maurer and Abel depart with pleasure, for they feared their violence; but at a later period, when they discovered that Count Armansperg was neither as active an administrator nor as honest a statesman as they had expected, they became sensible of the merits of the men they had lost.[1]

Count Armansperg governed Greece with absolute power from August 1834 to February 1837. He held the title of president of the regency until King Otho's majority on the 1st June 1835, when it was changed to that of arch-chancellor, which he held until his dismissal from office.[2] His long administration was characterised by a pretence of feverish activity that was to produce a great result at a period always very near, but which never arrived. Like Capodistrias, he was jealous of men of business, and insisted on retaining the direction of departments about which he knew nothing, in his own hands. He wasted his time in manœuvres to conceal his ignorance, and in talking to foreign ministers concerning his financial schemes and his projects of improvement. On looking back at his administration, it presents a succession of temporary expedients carried into execution in a very imperfect manner. He had no permanent plan and no consistent policy. In one district the Capodistrians were allowed to persecute the constitutionalists, and in another the Kolettists domineered over the Capodistrians. Bri-

---

gefunden, seine bedeutenden Schulden bezahlt, eine Lotterie collecte für seine beide Töchter erhalten, einen seiner. . . . . . . Söhne im Cadetten corps untergebracht hatte, s. s. w., eilte nach Griechenland, nicht um dort zu arbeiten und dem Lande nutzlich zu seyn."—*Das Griechische Volk*, ii. 535. It may be doubted whether any of the Greek newspapers suppressed by Maurer ever equalled the ribaldry of this passage, deliberately penned and published.

[1] Maurer gives instances of Armansperg's political dishonesty, ii. 60, 61.
[2] *Government Gazette*, 1835, June, No. 1; 1837, No. 4.

gandage increased until it attained the magnitude of civil war, and the whole internal organisation of the kingdom, introduced by the early regency, was unsettled.

The nomarchies and eparchies were called governments and sub-governments (dioikeses). The army was disorganised, and the rights of property were disturbed and violated. Public buildings were constructed on land belonging to private individuals, without the formality of informing the owner that his land was required for the public service. Ground was seized for a royal palace and garden, and some of the proprietors were not offered any indemnification, until the British government exacted payment to a British subject in the year 1850. In order to prevent the members of the Greek cabinet from intriguing against his authority, like Maurer and Abel, the arch-chancellor took care that all the ministers should never be able to speak the same language; and he deprived the cabinet of all control over the finance department, by keeping the place of minister of finance vacant for a whole year.[1] His lavish expenditure at last filled all Greece with complaints, and alarmed the King of Bavaria.

Count Armansperg's inconsiderate proceedings forced him to solicit from the protecting powers the advance of the third series of the Allied loan. Russia and France demanded some explanation concerning the expenditure of that part of the first and second series which had been paid into the Greek treasury. The accounts presented by Count Armansperg were not considered satisfactory. The British government took a different view of the count's explanations. Lord Palmerston supported his administration warmly, and applied to Parliament, in 1836, for power to enable

---

[1] *The Hellenic Kingdom and the Greek Nation*, a pamphlet (London, 1836), p 76.

the British government to guarantee its proportion of the third instalment of the loan without the concurrence of the other powers.[1]

Sir Edmund (Lord) Lyons had succeeded Mr Dawkins as English minister at the Greek court. He supported Count Armansperg with great zeal and activity. But the Greek government was pursuing a course which every day rendered the count more unpopular.

In the month of May 1836, King Otho left Greece in search of a wife, and during his absence, which lasted until the beginning of the following year, Count Armansperg was viceroy with absolute power.[2] His authority was supported by an army of 11,500 men, of whom 4000 were Bavarians. Money had now become more abundant in Greece, and several editors of newspapers, having made the necessary deposit in the treasury, resumed the publication of their journals. The opposition of the press again alarmed the Bavarians, and the count resolved to attempt to intimidate the editors by government prosecutions. The *Soter* was selected as the first victim, and very iniquitous preparations were made to insure its condemnation. Two judges were removed from the bench, in the tribunal before which the cause was brought, immediately before the trial. This tampering with the course of justice created vehement discontent, but it secured the condemnation of the editor. The punishment inflicted on the delinquent, however, was not likely to silence the patriotic, for it enabled them to gain the honours of martyrdom at a very cheap rate. The editor was fined two thousand drachmas, and

---

[1] *Parliamentary Papers* relating to the third instalment of the Greek loan, 1836; Parish, *Diplomatic History*, p. 301; *Parliamentary Debates*; and *Annual Register*.

[2] The ordinance investing Armansperg and his motley cabinet with power is dated 5th May.—*Government Gazette*, 1836, No. 18.

condemned to a year's imprisonment. The arch-chancellor's triumph was short. An appeal was made to the Areopagus, and the sentence of the criminal court was annulled.[1] As might have been expected, the attacks of the press became more violent and more personal.

Count Armansperg's recall was caused by the complete failure of his financial administration. The King of Bavaria selected the Chevalier Rudhart to replace him, still believing that the Greeks were not yet competent to manage their own affairs. On the 14th of February 1837, King Otho returned to Greece with Queen Amalia, the beautiful daughter of the Grand Duke Oldenburg.[2] M. Rudhart accompanied him as prime minister. The views of Rudhart were those of an honest Bavarian. He had studied European politics in the proceedings of the Germanic diet, and he contemplated emancipating King Otho from the tutelage of the three protecting powers by Austrian influence. Had the thing been feasible, he possessed neither the knowledge nor the talents required for so bold an enterprise. The Greeks and Bavarians were already ranged against one another in hostile parties. Sir Edmund Lyons seized the opportunity of avenging the slight put upon his mission, by keeping him in ignorance of Armansperg's recall. He connected the opposition of the British cabinet to the nomination of Rudhart, with the hostility of the Greeks to the Bavarians, and animated them to talk again of constitutional liberty. Rudhart claimed as a right the absolute power which Maurer and Armansperg had silently assumed. In one of his communications to

---

[1] For the sentence condemning the editor, see supplement to the *Courrier Grec*, 6th September 1836; and for the decision of the Areopagus, the 'Αθηνά, 10th October 1836.

[2] *Government Gazette*, 1837, No. 4. King Otho was married on the 22d November 1836.

the British minister, he declared that he exercised arbitrary power by the express order of King Otho, and that the King of Greece, in placing the royal authority above the law, exercised a right for which he was responsible to no one.[1] This assertion was so directly at variance with the promises of the King of Bavaria, and the assurances which the three protecting powers had given to the Greeks, that Sir Edmund Lyons was furnished with good ground for attacking the policy of the Bavarians. He pushed his attacks to the utmost verge of diplomatic license; and Rudhart, who defended a bad cause without vigour and promptitude, soon found it necessary to resign.[2] He held office for ten months, and was succeeded by Zographos, who was then Greek minister at Constantinople.

From this time the nominal prime minister was always a Greek; the war department was the only ministry henceforth occupied by a Bavarian; but Bavarian influence continued to direct the whole administration until the revolution in 1843. From 1833 to 1838, during a period of five years, the Greeks had exercised no control over their government, which received its guiding impulse from Munich. Those who ruled Greece were responsible to the King of Bavaria alone for their conduct in office. It is not surprising, therefore, that Greece was ill-governed; yet something was done for the good of the country. The early period of the regency was marked by the introduction of a system of administration which put an end, as if by enchantment, to the most frightful anarchy that ever desolated any Christian country in modern times. Many wise laws were enacted, and some useful measures were carried into execution promptly and thoroughly. The

---

[1] Parish, *Diplomatic History*, 402.
[2] See a letter of Sir E. Lyons to Chevalier Rudhart; Parish, *Diplomatic History*, Appendix, 218; Lesur, *Annuaire Historique, Documens*. Rudhart resigned on the 20th December 1837.

errors committed were probably fewer, and the good results produced much greater, than could have been obtained by any cabinet composed solely of Greeks. Deficient as Maurer, Armansperg. and Rudhart might be in the qualities of statesmen, as administrators they were far superior to any Greeks who could have been placed in the position they held. It is certain that they erred greatly from ignorance of the institutions of Greece, and it must be acknowledged that they often sacrificed the interests of the Greeks to the interests of the Bavarians in Greece; but Kolokotrones, Mavrocordatos, Konduriottes, and Kolettes, had all proved themselves more unprincipled, and quite incapable of governing the country.

In considering what the Bavarians did, it is well to reflect on what they might have done. The three powers had guaranteed the inviolability of the Greek territory; there was therefore no need of any military force to defend the country against the Turks. Greece only required the troops necessary to repress brigandage and enforce order. The navy of Greece had almost entirely disappeared, and the only maritime force required was a few vessels to prevent piracy. On the other hand, a very great expenditure on roads, ports, packet-boats, and other means of facilitating and cheapening communications, was absolutely necessary to improve the condition of the agricultural population, and give strength to the new kingdom. The population was scanty, and the produce of agricultural labour was small, even when compared with the scanty population. At the same time the demand for agricultural labour was so partial and irregular, that at some short periods of the year it was extremely dear; and though good land was abundant, extensive districts remained uncultivated, because the expense of bringing the produce to market would have consumed all profit. Something would have been done for the improvement of the country by constructing the roads indicated by the government as necessary, when the regency destroyed the liberty of the press; but instead of carrying this wise plan into execution, the resources of Greece were consumed in equipping a regiment of lancers, in military and court pageantry, in building royal yachts and a monster palace. The consequence of neglecting roads and packets was that brigandage and piracy revived. The Allied loan was wasted in unnecessary expenditure. The whole surplus labour and revenue of Greece was consumed for many years in unproductive employments. A considerable army was maintained, merely because Greece was called a kingdom; and a navy was formed for no purpose apparently but that the ships might be allowed to rot.

The state of the Levant from 1833 to 1843 was extremely favourable to the progress of Greece. The affairs of the Othoman empire were in a very unsettled state, and the Christian population had not yet obtained the direct interference of the Western powers in their favour. Thousands of Greeks were ready to emigrate into the new kingdom, had they seen a hope of being able to employ their labour with profit, and invest their savings with security. The incapacity of the rulers of Greece, and the rude social condition of the agricultural population, perpetuated by retaining the Othoman system of taxing land, allowed this favourable opportunity for rapid improvement to escape.

The three protecting powers have been blamed for not appropriating the proceeds of the loan to special objects, and for not enforcing the construction of some works of public utility. But this was perhaps impossible. Neither King Louis of Bavaria nor the Emperor Nicholas would have consented to submit the public expenditure to the control of a representative assembly in Greece; and neither France nor England could have made special appropriation of funds for the benefit of the country, without requiring the existence of some constitutional control over the Bavarians on the part of the Greek people. It is, however, extremely probable that all parties, taking into consideration the manner in which the English loans had been expended, considered the members of the regency more competent and more inclined to check malversation than any Greeks who could have been found. Examples of activity, intelligence, eloquence, courage, and patriotism, were not wanting among the Greeks; but the Revolution produced no individual uniting calm judgment and profound sagacity with unwearied industry and administrative experience. It did not produce a single man deserving to be called a statesman.

After M. Rudhart's resignation the office of president of the council of ministers was filled by a Greek; but the president was only nominally prime minister, for King Otho really governed by means of a private cabinet. The Greek ministers were controlled by Bavarian secretaries attached to each department with the title of referendaries. Greeks were found servile enough to submit to this control, and to act the part of pageant ministers. The proceedings of the government grew every year more arbitrary. The king was a man of a weak mind, and not of a generous disposition. The flatterers who surrounded him appear to have persuaded him that the Greek kingdom was created for his personal use, and his political vision rarely extended beyond his capital. In the greater part of the kingdom the creatures of the court ruled despotically. The police kept men in prison without legal warrants; and torture was inflicted both on men and women merely because they were suspected of having furnished brigands with food. The press was prosecuted for complaining that Greece was deprived of her constitutional liberties.

The English minister, Sir Edmund Lyons, complained of injuries inflicted on British and Ionian subjects. His reclamations were left long unanswered, and remained for years unredressed. Attempts were made to obtain his recall; and when they failed, he was personally and publicly insulted at the Greek court in a manner that compelled him to exact ample satisfaction.

During a theatrical representation at the palace, the British minister was left, by an oversight of the master of the ceremonies, without a seat in the court circle, and allowed to stand during the whole performance in a position directly in view of the king and queen, who seemed rather to enjoy the sight as the most amusing scene in the court comedy. Such conduct could not be overlooked. The minister of foreign affairs was compelled to make a very humble apology by express order of the king, and the Bavarian baron who acted as master of the ceremonies was shipped off to Trieste in the same summary manner as Dr Franz and M. Maurer had been. This severe lesson prevented open acts of insult in future; but the animosity of the court to the person of Sir Edmund Lyons was shown in minor acts of impertinence. On one occasion his groom was carried off by the gendarmes from his residence, and kept all night in prison on a charge of squirting water on a passer-by. These miserable disputes gradually alienated England and Greece, and victory over the court of Athens in such contests certainly reflected little honour on the diplomacy of Great Britain. A tithe of the energy displayed by Sir Edmund Lyons and Lord Palmerston in humiliating King Otho, and in adjusting questions of etiquette, would have settled every pending demand for justice on the part of British and Ionian subjects. Years of wrangling between the two courts might have been spared.[1] Greece would not have been rendered contemptible by her determined denial of justice, and England would not have been rendered ridiculous by employing a powerful fleet to collect a small debt from the Greek nation, when it was only due by the Greek government.[2] France also would not have exhibited her jealousy of England, by advising the Greek government to resist demands which, when her protection was solicited, she compelled Greece not only to pay as just, but also to record the fact that she had for years resisted these just demands in a solemn convention.[3]

While the quarrels with the English minister kept the Greek court in a state of irritation, the nation was suffering from brigandage, and secret societies and orthodox plots were again attempting to excite the people to revolt.

The disbanding of the irregular troops, and the refusal of the regency to pay the armed followers of the chieftains who assembled round Nauplia at the king's arrival for the purpose of intimidating his government, suddenly deprived many soldiers of the means of subsistence. Great disorder naturally ensued. The transition from anarchy to order could not be effected in a day by human strength or human wisdom. Bands of irregulars, who had lived for several years at free quarters and in absolute idleness, were neither disposed to submit to any discipline nor to engage in any useful employment. Severe treatment was unavoidable, but prudence was necessary in enforcing mea-

---

[1] On the 11th May 1839, the Greek government delivered to all the foreign missions at Athens, except the British, a lithographed exposition in reply to the reclamations of the British government.
[2] The British fleet seized private ships and cargoes at sea without a declaration of war. This may be internationally legal, but is unquestionably unjust.
[3] M. Thouvenel counselled resistance in February. Baron Gros, in April 1850, recommended the Greek government to acknowledge its injustice.—*Parliamentary Papers respecting the Demands made upon the Greek Government—Further Correspondence*, p. 346.

sures of severity. During the latter years of the Re- A.D. 1833.
volution the armed bands had separated their cause
from that of the people. They pretended to have
rights more extensive than the rest of the nation, and
they exercised these rights by plundering their fellow-
citizens. During the anarchy that followed the assassination of Capodistrias, Mussulman Albanians had
been introduced into the Peloponnesus as allies of the
Romeliot armatoli, and many villages had been sacked
by these mercenaries.[1]

The early regency carried the disbanding of the
irregulars into effect with so much vigour that the
whole of these disorderly bands were expelled from
the Peloponnesus, and during the summer of 1833 the
greater part was driven to choose between entering
the regular army or crossing the frontier into Turkey.

The state of the Othoman empire was singularly
favourable to the project of relieving Greece from
her disorderly troops. The sultan's army had been
defeated at Koniah by the Egyptians under Ibrahim
Pasha on the 21st of December 1832, and a Russian
army arrived at Constantinople soon after to protect
Sultan Mahmud's throne. The Christians in European Turkey expected to witness the immediate dissolution of the Othoman empire. The Mussulman
population in Albania, Macedonia, and Bosnia was
extremely discontented with the fiscal arrangements
and measures of centralisation adopted by the sultan,
and several districts were in open rebellion. A large
portion of the irregular troops who quitted Greece

---

[1] Thiersch, L 71. Almost every traveller who ventured to make even the smallest excursion in Greece during the winter of 1832-3 was plundered. Professor Ross was robbed near Marathon, and Mr Wordsworth fell into the hands of brigands on Mount Parnes, was wounded, and only escaped being detained for ransom in consequence of a severe snow-storm. He says: "For several months the entrance into the Peloponnesus from continental Greece has been rendered impassable for travellers by the violence of the military banditta."—*Athens and Attica*, p. 251; compare pp. 22, 49, 227, 242, and 255, first edition.

found employment in consequence of the local disturbances in Turkey, and they laid waste a considerable part of Epirus and Thessaly, as they had previously ravaged a part of the Peloponnesus.

As early as the month of May 1833, a strong body of Greeks, having crossed the frontier, joined a number of unpaid Albanian soldiers in the pashalik of Joannina, and surprised the town of Arta, which had successfully resisted the attacks of the Greeks during the Revolution. For three days these lawless bands remained masters of the town, which they plundered without mercy. Neither age, sex, nor religion served to protect the inhabitants. Every act of cruelty and brutality of which man can be the perpetrator or the sufferer was inflicted on persons of both sexes and of every class. Torture, too sickening to describe, was employed to compel women and children to reveal where money and jewels were concealed. When gorged with booty, lust, and cruelty, these bandits quitted Arta, gained the mountains, and separated into small bands in order to evade pursuit and obtain the means of subsistence until they could plan some fresh exploit. The fame of the sack of Arta allured the greater part of the disbanded irregulars across the frontier, and relieved the Bavarians from a dangerous struggle.

The state of Albania became still more disturbed towards the end of the year 1834, and many of the Greek armatoli and irregulars formed alliances with the municipalities of Christian districts, which secured to them permanent employment. Had Count Armansperg employed the respite thus obtained with prudence, order might have been firmly established in Northern Greece; but his frequent changes of policy and indecisive measures produced a series of political insurrections, and revived brigandage as an element of society in Greece.

Piracy was suppressed at sea by the assistance of the Allies. In the spring of 1833 upwards of one hundred and fifty pirates were captured and brought to Nauplia for judgment. Many of these were irregular troops, who had seized large boats and commenced the trade of pirates.

In 1834 an insurrection occurred in Maina, which assumed the character of a civil war. It was caused by a rash and foolish measure of the regency. Ages of insecurity had compelled the landlords in the greater part of Greece to dwell in towers capable of defence against brigands. These towers were nothing more than stone houses without windows in the lower story, and to which the only access was by a stone stair detached from the building, and connected, by a movable wooden platform, with the door in the upper story. In Maina these towers were numerous. The members of the regency attributed the feuds and bloodshed prevalent in that rude district to the towers, instead of regarding the towers as a necessary consequence of the feuds. The members of the regency appear to have imagined that the destruction of all the towers in Greece would insure the establishment of order in the country. In the plains this was easily effected. Peaceful landlords were compelled to employ workmen to destroy their houses instead of employing workmen to repair them. The consequence was, that fear of the attacks of disbanded soldiers and avowed brigands drove most wealthy landlords into the nearest towns, and many abandoned the agricultural improvements they had commenced.

In Maina the orders of the regency were openly opposed. Every possessor of a tower, indeed, declared that he had no objections to its destruction, but he invited the government to destroy every tower in Maina at the same time, otherwise no man's life and property would be secure. Some chiefs affected to be very loyal, and very eager for the destruction of towers. Bavarian troops were marched into the country to assist these chiefs in destroying their own and their enemies' towers. The appearance of the Bavarians induced the majority of the Maniat chiefs to form a league, in order to resist the invaders. The people were told that the foreigners came into the mountains to destroy the monasteries, imprison the native monks in distant monasteries, and seize the ecclesiastical revenues for the king's government. Several skirmishes took place. A Bavarian officer, who advanced rashly into the defiles with part of a battalion, was surrounded, cut off from water, and compelled to surrender at discretion. The victorious Maniats stripped their prisoners of their clothing, and then compelled the Greek government to ransom them at a small sum per man. This defeat dissolved the belief in the invincibility of regular troops, which had been established by the daring conduct of the French at Argos.

The regency could not allow the war to terminate with such a defeat. Fresh troops were poured into Maina, strong positions were occupied, the hostile districts were cut off from communications with the sea, and money was employed to gain over a party among the chiefs. A few towers belonging to the chiefs most hostile to the government were destroyed by force, and some were destroyed with the consent of the proprietors, who were previously indemnified. Partly by concessions, partly by corruption, and partly by force, tranquillity was restored. But the submission of Maina to the regency was only secured by withdrawing the Bavarian troops, and forming a battalion of Maniats to preserve order in the country. Maurer asserts that the Maniats converted their towers into ordinary dwellings: anybody who visits Maina, even though a quarter of a century has elapsed, will see A.D. 1834. that his assertion is inaccurate.[1]

Other insurrections occurred in various parts of Greece; but those of Messenia and Arcadia in 1834, and of Acarnania in 1836, alone deserve to be mentioned on account of their political importance.

The insurrection in Messenia occurred immediately after the recall of Maurer and Abel, but would have broken out had they remained. Count Armansperg was so helpless as an administrator, in spite of his eagerness to govern Greece, that he was at a loss to know what measures he ought to adopt, and allowed himself to be persuaded by Kolettes to call in the services of bands of irregulars. Large bodies of men, who had just begun to acquire habits of industry, were allured to resume arms, with the hope that Kolettes would again be able to distribute commissions conferring high military rank, as in the civil wars under Konduriottes and against Agostino. Years of military disorganisation, and its concomitant—an increase of brigandage—were the immediate results of Count Armansperg's imprudence.

The leaders of the insurrection in Messenia and Arcadia were friends of Kolokotrones and Plapoutas, men who had been connected with the Russian plot, and who were in some degree encouraged to take up arms by the supposed favour with which Count Armansperg had viewed the intrigues of Dr Franz. Their project was to extort from the regency the instant release of Kolokotrones and Plapoutas, and to secure for themselves concessions similar to those accorded to the Maniats.

The commencement of the insurrection was in Arcadia. In the month of August 1834, considerable bodies of men assembled in arms at different places.

[1] *Das Griechische Volk*, ii. 509.

Kolias Plapoutas, a man without either influence or capacity, presuming on his relationship with the two imprisoned klephtic chiefs, assumed the title of director of the kingdom, and issued a proclamation demanding the convocation of a national assembly. Other leaders proclaimed the abolition of the regency and the majority of King Otho.

Kolias Plapoutas, at the head of four hundred men, attempted to arrest the eparch of Arcadia at Andritzena without success. Captain Gritzales, who had collected about three hundred men in the villages round Soulenia, was more successful at the commencement of his operations. He made prisoners both the nomarch of Messenia and the commandant of the gendarmerie in the town of Kyparissia.[1] A third body of insurgents, consisting of the mountaineers from the southern slopes of Mount Tetrazi, defeated a small body of regulars, and entered the plain of Stenyclerus as victors.

Kolettes, into whose hands Armansperg, in his panic, had thrust the conduct of government, because he held the ministry of the interior, even though he had been a stanch partisan of Maurer, resolved to use his power in such a way as to have little to fear from the count's enmity when the insurrection was suppressed. He determined, therefore, to restore some of his old political allies, the chiefs of the irregular bands of Northern Greece, again to power. Had he allowed the Bavarian troops and the Greek regulars to suppress the insurrection, which they could have effected without difficulty, he would have strengthened the arbitrary authority of Armansperg, whom he well knew was at heart his implacable enemy. Kolettes was himself under the dominion of many rude prejudices. To his dying

---

[1] Kyparissia is called by the modern Greeks Arkadia, but the ancient name has been revived in the official nomenclature of the kingdom to avoid confusion.

day he considered the military system of Ali of Joannina as the best adapted for maintaining order in Greece. On this occasion, therefore, he repeated, as far as lay in his power, the measures by which he had overpowered the Moreot primates and the Moreot klephts under Kolokotrones in 1824. Several Romeliot chiefs of his party were authorised to enrol bands of veterans, and with these personal followers, who required no preparation and no magazines, as they lived everywhere by the plunder which they extorted from the Greek peasantry, Kolettes expected to crush the insurrection before the regular troops could arrive. The irregulars were, however, as usual, too slow in their movements.

General Schmaltz, a gallant Bavarian colonel of cavalry, was appointed commander-in-chief of the royal army. He soon encompassed the insurgents with a force of two thousand regulars and about three thousand irregulars. The rebels, who never succeeded in assembling five hundred men at any one point, fought several well-contested skirmishes, but they were soon dispersed and their leaders taken prisoners.[1] Count Armansperg did not treat the rebels with severity. He knew that they were more likely to join his party than the Kolettists by whom they had been defeated. Perhaps he also feared that a close examination of their conduct might throw more light than was desirable on the connection that had grown up between the Capodistrian conspiracy and the Armansperg intrigue. In six weeks tranquillity was completely re-established. But for many months bands of irregular soldiery continued to live at free quarters in the plain of Messenia. Kolettes felt himself so strongly supported by the Romeliot chiefs, and by French in-

---

[1] The *Soter* newspaper, during the month of August 1834, O.S., notices the principal events of this insurrection.

fluence, that he conceived great hopes of being named prime minister on King Otho's majority; but he was defeated by the influence of Great Britain at the court of Bavaria. Armansperg, as has been already mentioned, was named arch-chancellor, and Kolettes was sent to Paris as Greek minister.

The insurrection of 1834 was no sooner suppressed than the Bavarians became alarmed at the power which Kolettes had acquired. The irregular bands which had been recalled into activity were slowly disbanded, and the chiefs saw that fear alone had compelled Count Armansperg to resort to their services. The policy of suddenly recalling men to a life of adventure and pillage, who were just beginning to acquire habits of order, could not fail to produce evil consequences. Hopes of promotion, perfect idleness, and liberal pay, were suddenly offered to them; and when they fancied that, by a little fighting and a few weeks marching, they had attained the object of their hopes, they found that they were again to be disbanded and sent back to learn the hard lessons of honest industry. Many of them determined that Greece should soon require their services. It was not possible to produce a popular insurrection at any moment, but there was no difficulty in organising a widespread system of brigandage. A project of the kind was quickly carried into execution.

During the winter of 1834 and the spring of 1835 brigandage assumed a very alarming aspect. Several Bavarians were waylaid and murdered.[1] Government money was captured, even when transmitted under strong escorts; and government magazines, in which the produce of the land-tax was stored, were plundered. In the month of April the intrigues of the military

---

[1] *Reise durch alle Theile des Königreiches Griechenland* in 1834-1835, von Dr Fiedler, vol. i. pp. 146, 159.

chiefs alarmed the agricultural population to such a degree that several districts in Western Greece petitioned the prefects to be allowed to enrol national guards, to whom they engaged to guarantee three months' pay from the municipal funds. By this means they expected to retain the irregulars in their native districts, and to insure their protection in case of attacks by strangers. To this anomalous and temporary expedient Count Armansperg gave his consent.

But as the summer of 1835 advanced, the disorders in continental Greece increased. Numerous bands of brigands, after laying a number of villages under contribution, from the mouth of the Sperchius to the banks of the Achelous, concentrated upwards of two hundred men in the district of Venetico, within six miles of Lepanto. A Bavarian officer of engineers was taken prisoner with the pioneer who accompanied him, and both were murdered in cold blood. The house of Captain Prapas, an active officer of irregular troops and a chief of the national guards in Artolina, was burned to the ground during his absence, and his flocks were carried off. In the month of May, the house of Captain Makryiannes, near Simau, was destroyed, and seven members of his family, including his wife and two girls, were cruelly murdered. An attack was shortly after made on the house of Captain Pharmaki, an officer of irregulars of distinguished ability and courage, who was living within a few hundred yards of the walls of Lepanto. Pharmaki was severely wounded, and one of his servants was killed; but he beat off the brigands, and prevented them from setting fire to his house. For six weeks every day brought news of some new outrage, but Count Armansperg turned a deaf ear to all complaints. He assured the foreign ministers that the accounts which reached them were greatly exaggerated, and that he had adopted effectual measures for restoring order. In reality, he neglected the commonest precautions, and left entirely to the nomarchs and commanders of troops in the disturbed districts the care of taking such measures as they might think necessary. The count was absorbed with the intrigues which ended in persuading King Otho, whose majority occurred on 1st June 1835, to prolong the absolute power which he had exercised as regent with the title of arch-chancellor.

The first step of the arch-chancellor was to send Kolettes to Paris as Greek minister. While Kolettes remained minister of the interior, it was thought that he encouraged, or at least tolerated, the extension of brigandage, and looked with secret satisfaction at the supineness of the regency. General Lesuire, the Bavarian minister of war, was also accused of regarding the disorders that prevailed with indifference, though from very different motives. Brigandage furnished Kolettes with arguments for reviving the system of chieftains with personal followers, and to Lesuire it supplied arguments against intrusting the Greeks with arms, and for increasing the number of Bavarian mercenaries in the king's service. The accounts which the Greek government received of the conduct of the irregulars enrolled by Kolettes's authority during the insurrection of Messenia, persuaded the minister of war that these troops differed from the brigands only in name. It is certain that he kept both the Greek and German regular battalions in high order; but he neglected the irregular corps in a way that afforded them some excuse for the exactions they committed. A battalion of irregulars, under Gardikiotes Grivas, was left without pay and clothing at a moment when it was disposed to take the field against the brigands, and might have prevented their incursion to the walls of Lepanto. The scanty pensions of the Suliots at Mesolonghi were allowed to fall into arrear. A number of veteran armatoli, to whom pensions had been assigned on condition of their residing at Lepanto and Vrachori, were completely neglected, and were so discontented with the conduct of the government, that when the house of Pharmaki was attacked, and the firing was heard in the whole town of Lepanto, not one would move from the walls to assist that gallant chief. The landed proprietors and the peasantry were almost as much irritated at the neglect shown by the government as the starving soldiers. Loud complaints were made that the population in the provinces was left without defence, while Armansperg was lavishing crosses of the Redeemer on diplomats, and pay and promotion on Bavarians whose service in Greece had been confined to marching from Nauplia to Athens, when the king removed his capital from the first of these cities to the second.

As soon as Armansperg's intrigues were crowned with success, he got rid of Lesuire as well as Kolettes, and General Schmaltz became minister of war. About the same time Mr Dawkins was recalled, and Sir Edmund Lyons was named British minister at King Otho's court. At the recommendation of Sir Edmund, Armansperg named General Gordon to the command of an expedition which was sent to clear Northern Greece of brigands. Gordon was not attached to any political party: he distrusted Kolettes, and had little confidence in Armansperg; but he knew the country, the people, and the irregular troops, as well as any man in Greece.

On the 11th of July he left Athens with his staff; and after visiting Chalcis, in order to make himself fully acquainted with the state of the troops of which he had assumed the command, he formed his plan of operations. His measures were judicious, and they were executed with energy. A body of regular troops was sent forward from Chalcis by Thebes, Livadea, and Salona, to Loidoriki, whither Gordon proceeded, following the shore of the channel of Euboea to the mouth of the Sperchius. He stopped a couple of days at Patradjik (Hypate) to post the troops necessary to guard the passes on the frontier, and then descended by the defiles of Oeta and Korax to Loidoriki, where he was joined by the regulars from Chalcis. By this rapid march he effectually cleared all Eastern Greece of brigands. They all moved westward, for they saw that if any of them remained in Phocis they would have been hunted down without a chance of escape.

At Loidoriki, Gordon divided the force under his orders into three divisions. It was much more difficult to drive the brigands westward from the Etolian mountains than it had been to clear the more open districts in Eastern Greece. One division of the army kept along the ridge of the mountains which bound the Gulf of Corinth to the north. The centre, with the general, marched into the heart of the country, through districts cut by nature into a labyrinth of deep ravines, and descended to Lepanto from the north-east, after passing by Lombotina and Simon. The right division moved up northward to Artolina, in order, if possible, to cut off the brigands from gaining the Turkish frontier.

The principal body of the brigands, consisting of one hundred and thirty, maintained its position in the immediate vicinity of Lepanto for six weeks, and it continued to levy contributions from the country round until the general arrived at Loidoriki. It then broke up into several small bands, and, picking up its outlying associates, gained the Turkish frontier by following secluded sheep-tracks over the Etolian mountains. The national guards, which the communities in the

provinces of Apokuro and Zygos had taken into their
pay, as soon as they were sure of effectual support from
the troops under Gordon, commenced dislodging the
brigands from their positions between the Phidari
(Evenus) and the Acheloua.

From Lepanto, Gordon marched to Mesolonghi and
Vrachori. The officers under his orders found no difficulty in clearing the plains of Acarnania, and when
this was effected, he followed the rugged valley of
Prousos to Karpenisi, where he arrived on the 11th of
August. The arrangements he had adopted for securing to the Suliots and the veterans at Lepanto and
Vrachori the regular payment of their pensions, and
the good conduct of the detachments of regulars which
he sent to support the local magistrates, insured active
co-operation on the part of the native population. The
spirit of order, which the neglect of the royal government had almost extinguished, again revived.

In one month after quitting Athens, tranquillity
was restored in the whole of continental Greece. But
as about three hundred brigands had assembled within
the Turkish territory, and marched along the frontier
with military music, it seemed that the difficulty of
protecting the country would be greater than that of
delivering it. The general's Oriental studies now proved
of as great value to Greece as his military activity and
geographical knowledge. He opened a correspondence
with the pasha at Larissa ; and the circumstance of
an Englishman commanding the Greek forces, and of
that Englishman not only speaking Turkish fluently,
but also writing it like a divan-effendi, contributed more
than a sense of sound policy, to secure the co-operation
of the Turkish authorities in dispersing the brigands.

In the month of October Gordon's mission was terminated, and he was ordered to resume his duties at
Argos, as commander-in-chief in the Peloponnesus.

The brigands in Turkey had dispersed, but it was known that many had retired to Agrapha, where they were protected by Tzatzos, the captain of armatoli, and it was supposed that Tzatzos had not taken this step without the connivance of the derven-pasha. Gordon warned the Greek government that brigandage would soon recommence, unless very different measures were adopted from those which Count Armansperg had hitherto pursued, both in his civil and financial administration. And he completely lost the count's favour by the truths which he told in a memoir he drew up on the means of suppressing the brigandage, and maintaining tranquillity on the frontier.

The insecurity which prevailed near the Turkish frontier, even though brigandage had for a moment ceased, is strongly illustrated by the closing scene of Gordon's sojourn in the vicinity. Before quitting Northern Greece he wished to enjoy a day's shooting. On the 5th October he went with a party of friends to Aghia Marina. The brigands, who lay concealed on both sides of the frontier, had official friends, and were well informed of all that happened at Lamia. They were soon aware of Gordon's project. A band lay concealed in the thick brushwood that covered the plain, but did not find an opportunity of attacking him on the road. Soon after sunset the house he occupied was surrounded while the party was at dinner, but the alarm was given in time to allow the sportsmen to throw down their knives and forks, seize their fowling-pieces, and run to the garden-wall in front of the building. By this they prevented the brigands from approaching near enough to set fire to the house. A skirmish ensued, in which the assailants displayed very little courage. The firing brought a party of royal troops from Stelida to the general's assistance, but the obscurity of the night favoured the escape of the brigands, and on the following morning all traces of them had disappeared.[1]

The lavish expenditure of Count Armansperg brought on financial difficulties at the end of 1835, and both Russia and France considered his accounts and his explanations so unsatisfactory, that they refused to intrust him with the expenditure of the third series of the loan.[2] The state of Greece was represented in a very different manner by the foreign ministers at the court of Athens. The King of Bavaria, hoping to learn the truth by personal observation, paid his son a visit. He little knew the difficulty which exists in Greece of acquiring accurate information, or of forming correct conclusions, from the partial information which it is in the power of a passing visitor to obtain, even when that visitor is a king. Truth is always rare in the East, and Greece was divided into several hostile factions, who were the irreconcilable enemies of truth. On the 7th of December 1835, the King of Bavaria arrived at Athens, where he was welcomed by the council of state with the assurance that his son's dominions were in a state of profound tranquillity, and extremely prosperous. His majesty was not long in Greece before he perceived that the councillors of state were not in the habit of speaking the truth.

In the month of January 1836, the brigands, who had remained quiet for a short time, reappeared from their places of concealment, and those who had found an asylum in Turkey began to cross the frontier in small bands. Not a week passed without their plundering some village. Accounts reached Athens of the

---

[1] General Gordon gave the following account of this affair in a private letter:—"Drosos Mansolas" (afterwards minister of the interior) "showed a degree of courage and coolness very uncommon in a Greek logiotatos. He behaved much better than his gun, which burst at the first discharge."

[2] Compare Parish, *Diplomatic History of the Monarchy of Greece*, p. 296, and *Annuaire Historique Universelle pour 1835*, p. 480.

unheard-of cruelties they were daily committing to extort money, or to avenge the defeats they suffered during the preceding year. Party spirit and official avidity had at this time so benumbed public spirit in the capital of Greece, that even the Liberal press paid little attention to the miseries of the agricultural population. The peasantry were neglected, for they had no influence in the distribution of places, honours, or profits. In the month of February, however, the evil increased so rapidly, and reached such an alarming extent, that it could no longer be overlooked even by Count Armansperg. Six hundred brigands established themselves within the Greek kingdom, ravaging the whole valley of the Spercbius with fire and sword.[1]

An insurrection broke out at this time in Acarnania, which had its sources in the same political and social evils as brigandage. It is peculiarly interesting, however, from affording some insight into the political history of Great Britain as well as Greece. Lord Palmerston persuaded the British government that it was for the interest of Great Britain to support the administration of Count Armansperg. This could only be done effectually by furnishing him with money; and to induce Parliament to authorise the issue of the third instalment of the loan, papers were presented to both Houses, proving that the Greek government was in great need of money. But when the want of money was clearly proved, it was objected that the want complained of was caused by lavish expenditure and gross corruption; and it was even said that Count Armansperg's maladministration was plunging Greece back into the state of anarchy from which the early regency had delivered the country. Additional papers were then presented to Parliament by the Foreign Secretary (which had been all along in his hands), to

[1] 'Αθηνά, (Greek newspaper), 4-16 February 1836.

prove that Greece was in a most flourishing condition, A. D. 1836. and that the prosperity she was enjoying was the direct result of the Count's administration.[1] The history of the insurrection is the best comment on these adverse statements.

The leaders of the insurrection in Acarnania were officers of the irregular troops who had distinguished themselves in the revolutionary war. Demo Tzelios, who commanded one body of insurgents, proclaimed that the people took up arms against Count Armansperg and the Bavarians, not against the king and the government. Nicolas Zervas, another leader, demanded the convocation of a national assembly. A third party displayed the phœnix on its standard, and talked of orthodoxy as being the surest way to collect the Capodistrians and Ionians in arms against the government at Athens. All united in proclaiming the constitution, and demanding the expulsion of the Bavarians. The people took no part in the movement.

Demo Tzelios entered Mytika without opposition, but was defeated at Dragomestra. Mesolonghi had been left almost without a garrison. The folly of the government was so flagrant, in the actual condition of the country, that the proceeding looked like treachery. The insurgents made a bold attempt to gain possession of that important fortress by surprise, but they were bravely repulsed by the few troops who remained in the place, and by the inhabitants, who regarded the insurgents as mere brigands. The rebels, though repulsed from the walls of Mesolonghi, were nevertheless strong enough to remain encamped before the place, and to ravage the plain for several days.[2]

[1] Papers relating to the third Instalment of the Greek loan, 1836; and Additional Papers relating to the third instalment of the Greek loan, presented to both Houses, August 1836.
[2] 'Αθηνᾶ, 12th (24th) February 1836. See also an account of this attack on Mesolonghi in Dr Fiedler's Reise durch alle theile des Königreiches Griechenland, I. 150.

These events produced a panic at Athens. Men spoke of the pillage of the Morea in 1824, when Konduriottes was president, of the sack of Poros by the troops of Capodistrias, and of the anarchy caused by Kolettes and the constitutionalists in 1832. Fortunately for Greece, the presence of the King of Bavaria prevented a renewal of these calamities. His majesty enabled the Greek government to procure money. Count Armansperg having rejected the plans proposed by General Gordon for averting a renewal of brigandage, was in this emergency again induced to practise the lessons he had learned from Kolettes in suppressing the insurrection of Messenia. Chieftains were allowed to enrol irregular troops, and reconstitute bands of personal followers. Kitzos Djavellas, Theodore Griva, Vassos, Mamoures, and Zongas were empowered to raise two thousand men, and to march against the insurgents. These bands of irregulars were followed by large bodies of regular troops. With these forces the country was cleared of insurgents and brigands without difficulty. Gordon had pointed out the operations by which Northern Greece can always be swept of enemies by a superior force in about a month. Before the end of May the last remains of the insurrection were trodden out in Acarnania, and all the large bands of brigands were again driven into Turkey. Sir Richard Church then made a tour of military inspection, to establish order, redress grievances, and pacify the people. On the 30th May Sir Edmund Lyons wrote from Athens to Lord Palmerston: "No inroads have been made on the frontier since the end of April, and tranquillity has prevailed throughout the country. General Church is still in Western Greece, and his reports of the loyal feelings of the inhabitants are extremely satisfactory."

Others, however, took a very different view of the

state of the country. The accounts given of the condition of Greece were so discordant, and the reports published in Western Europe were so variously coloured by personal feelings and party spirit, that some notice of this discordance is necessary, in order to show the reader how the streams of politics meander into the river of history.

The late Lord Lyons was a warm supporter of Count Armansperg, and appears to have received all the statements of the count with implicit confidence. On the 24th February 1836, Lyons wrote to Lord Palmerston that " the communes in Greece have the entire direction of their own affairs ; the press is unshackled ; the tribunals are completely independent ; private property is scrupulously respected ; the personal and religious liberty of the subject is inviolable."[1] Yet not one of these assertions was true.[2] While Sir E. Lyons was writing this despatch, the people of Athens were reading in the Greek newspaper of the morning an account of the attack on Mesolonghi, and an announcement that the insurgents remained unmolested in their camps in Western Greece, while on the frontier brigandage was making gigantic progress.[3] In the month of May, General Gordon, who took a view of the state of Greece totally different from that taken by Lord Lyons, resigned his command in the Peloponnesus, and before returning to England wrote to a friend at Athens: " From what I know of the state of the Peloponnesus, and the rapid and alarming increase of organised brigandage, I fear this will be but a melancholy summer. I am assured, and believe, that lately several captive robbers have bought themselves off. Faction is extremely busy, and crime enjoys impunity. Add

[1] *Parliamentary Papers*—Additional Papers, 1836, p. 32.
[2] Compare pp. 832, 849, 865, 873 of this volume.
[3] 'Αθηνά, 12th (24th) February 1836. Ἡ κυρτεία αιλίσει μὴ γιγαντιαῖα βήματα.

to this Church and his heroes (*hoc est oleum adde camino*), and we have a pretty picture. The bandits are now plundering in Romelia with crowns in their caps."[1] Many brigands were enrolled in the bands which the irregular chieftains were authorised to form in the spring of 1836; and after the dismissal of Count Armansperg, Lord Lyons himself complained that one of these amnestied robbers had been seen at a ball, given by a foreign minister at Athens to the King and Queen of Greece.[2]

The disturbed state of Greece can be proved by better evidence than that of a British minister at King Otho's court, or of a British officer in his service. It can be proved by facts which no party prejudices can distort. From the year 1833 to the year 1838, military tribunals were constantly sitting to deal out punishment to insurgents or brigands. To strangers who visited Greece, and who examined the events that occurred, instead of trusting to the reports they heard, it seemed that martial law was the only law by which King Otho was able to dispense even a modicum of justice to a great number of his unfortunate subjects.[3]

During the interval between the dismissal of Count Armansperg and the final expulsion of the Bavarians

---

[1] This last observation alludes to Count Armansperg having granted an amnesty to several of the chiefs of brigands whom Gordon had driven out of Greece in 1835, and to one who had taken part in the attack made on the General at Aghia Marina.

[2] An example of the different aspect which Greece presented to the British minister, and to an observant British traveller, will be found by comparing the *Parliamentary Papers* of 1836 with Colonel Mure's *Journal of a Tour in Greece in 1838*. Lord Lyons writes in 1836—"I denied that the peasantry were impoverished, or that they wore sheep-skins." Yet Colonel Mure in 1838, even in the town of Livadea, remarks that the students "reclined, squatted, romped, and reposed upon their shaggy goat-skin cloaks or hairy capotes, which protected them from the storm by day, and formed their mattress and bedding by night."

[3] The following proclamations of martial law will be found in the *Government Gazette*, 1833, No. 28; 1834, No. 28; 1835, first series, No. 12; second series, No. 3; 1836, No. 6. This last military tribunal was established in February 1836, and sat until June 1837. Various amnesties were granted by Count Armansperg, which furnished a supply of criminals for tribunals of a more regular kind at a later period.

in 1843, several trifling insurrections broke out in the Peloponnesus; and continental Greece continued to be tormented by bands of brigands, who committed horrid atrocities. In a single year more than one hundred persons presented themselves to the public prosecutors, who had been tortured or mutilated by brigands and pirates. Men had lost their noses and ears; women and children had been tortured with indescribable cruelty, in order to force them to reveal where their husbands and their fathers were concealed.[1] No traveller passed through the country without seeing traces of their misdeeds. Colonel Mure found brigandage the subject of conversation at every khan he visited in 1838, and he fell in with victims of the brigands, with gendarmes pursuing brigands, or with brigands themselves, in every part of Greece.[2] Even Attica suffered severely from their ravages; shepherds were repeatedly murdered, and the landed proprietors feared to visit their estates.

Several chiefs of robbers maintained themselves in the vicinity of Athens for years, and it was naturally supposed that they had found the means of obtaining powerful political protection.[3] A singular scene, which occurred when two famous brigands were led out to be executed, confirmed the general belief in some official complicity.

On the 5th of August 1839, Bibisi and Trakadha, who had been tried and condemned to death, were ordered to be executed in the vicinity of Athens. The

A. D. 1839.

---

[1] Dr Fiedler says: "Die Landräuber sind schon keine menschen mehr, aber die Seeräuber sind noch viel teuflischer. Es würde zu empörend sein ihre Schandthaten zu beschreiben."—ii. 46.

[2] *Journal of a Tour in Greece*, by William Mure of Caldwell, vol. I. p. 241; vol. ii. 2, 137, 144, 147, 186, 209, 257, 259, 274, 286, and 291. Compare also *Reise durch alle theile des Königreiches Griechenland in den Jahren 1834 bis 1837*, vol. i. 146, 159, 165, 162, 192, 193, 198; ii. 45.

[3] The first of these local brigands who gained distinction in Attica was named Burduba. After committing several atrocious murders, he was pardoned and enrolled in the municipal guard, but he was soon slain by the relations of one of his victims.

executioner was assassinated at the Piræus a few days before, and a new executioner was engaged to decapitate the criminals. An immense crowd was assembled to witness the death of men who were as much admired for their daring as they were feared and hated for their cruelty. The two brigands were surrounded by a strong guard of soldiers. The executioner ascended the scaffold on which the guillotine was placed. After waiting long for orders, he slowly commenced his work, but after some further delay, he fainted, or pretended to faint, and his powers of action could not be sufficiently restored to enable him to stand. The prefect wished to find another executioner, but the municipal authorities would give him no assistance. The populace began to enjoy the comedy they witnessed, instead of the tragedy they had expected to see. A reprieve was called for, and from the foot of the gallows the prefect was persuaded to despatch a message to King Otho asking for a reprieve, which, under the circumstances, it was impossible for his majesty to refuse.[1] Bibisi was condemned to imprisonment for life. As usually happens in Greece, both he and Trakadha were soon allowed to escape. They recommenced their robberies in the neighbourhood of Athens. At last they ventured to rob within sight of the royal palace. The court and the Greek ministers were roused from their habitual lethargy. A price was put on Bibisi's head, and he was soon shot by a gendarme, who had himself been a brigand. Trakadha perished even sooner. But brigandage continued to exist in Attica, and to flourish in the greater part of Greece for many years; and pages might be filled with accounts of robberies, murders, torturing, mutilation, and worse atrocities committed in every part of Greece.[2]

[1] 'Αθηνᾶ, 26th July 1839.
[2] The recent work of Mr Senior gives some account of the extent to which brigandage continued in 1855.

The evils of brigandage fell chiefly on the agricultural population, and neither the court, the Bavarians, nor the Greek ministers, appear to have paid any attention to the condition and the sufferings of the agricultural classes. The want of roads confined intercourse and material improvement to the sea-coast and the neighbourhood of commercial towns. The greater part of Greece, cut off from all hope of bettering its condition, remained in a barbarous and stationary condition.

King Otho became his own prime minister after the resignation of Mr Rudhart. His majesty possessed neither ability, experience, energy, nor generosity; consequently he was neither respected, obeyed, feared, nor loved; and the government grew gradually weaker and more disorganised. Yet he pursued one of the phantoms by which abler despots are often deluded. He strove to concentrate all power in his own hands. It never occurred to him that it was more politic to perform the duty of a king well, than to perform the business of half-a-dozen government officials with mechanical exactitude. King Otho observed but a very small portion of the facts which were placed directly before him; he was slow at drawing inferences even from the few facts he observed, and he was utterly incapable of finding the means of reforming any abuse from his own administrative knowledge or the resources of his own mind.

The king counted on his sincere desire to be the monarch of a prosperous and powerful nation for being able to govern the Greeks, and he expected that his personal popularity and his king-craft would prevent insurrections and suppress brigandage. Unfortunately he took no measures to root out the social evils that caused the one, or the political evils that produced the other. The king could form no firm resolutions himself, and he reposed no confidence in his ministers.

They were indeed not worthy of much, for both Bavarians and Greeks displayed far more eagerness to obtain ministerial portfolios, than zeal in performing the duties of the offices with which they were intrusted. King Otho observed the meanness of their intrigues and the selfishness of their conduct. He distrusted the Bavarians, because he perceived that they looked to Munich for their ultimate reward; and he despised the Greeks, because they were always ready to abandon the principles they avowed when he offered them either place or profit. With these feelings he attempted to govern without the advice of his ministers; and he only assembled cabinet councils in order to obtain the formal ratification of measures already prepared in his own closet. Even his majesty's commands were often communicated to his ministers by private secretaries. To insure complete subserviency, no minister was allowed to remain very long in office, and men were usually selected without influence or ability, and frequently without education.[1]

During the personal government of King Otho, a singular event envenomed the disputes which had arisen between Lord Lyons and the Greek court during Mr Rudhart's administration. The affair has always remained enveloped in mystery, but its effects were so important that the fact requires notice, though it eludes explanation. It placed the British minister in direct personal hostility to the sovereign at whose court he was accredited, and it was the principal cause of the

---

[1] Count Armansperg taught King Otho to form cabinets of ministers who could not communicate in a common language. He had often two ministers who could only speak Greek, and one who could speak nothing but German. But King Otho carried many things farther in the wrong direction than his arch-chancellor. The following is the copy of a letter written by a minister of foreign affairs, who held office during delicate negotiations with Lord Palmerston. It may be said to consist of eighteen words, twelve of which are strangely mis-spelt:—

Κυριε, σας εδοτιο ταυτα οφιλιν ἐπιταγυ της Α. Μ τις Βασιλισις στοι εθριος τρίτυν εις τας 7½ μ. μ. θιλει σας διχθει η Α. Μ ἡ Βασίλισσα.

bitter animosity that King Otho has ever since shown to England.

A Greek newspaper which King Otho was said to read with particular pleasure, thought fit, in an unlucky hour, to insert extracts from an English pamphlet, ridiculing the condition of a nation that was governed by a young queen. A reply appeared in the *Morning Chronicle*, observing that it was fortunate for Great Britain that the only reproach which could be made to the sovereign was that she was young. Time would too soon remove the reproach, but the article in the Greek newspaper was in very bad taste in a country where the sovereign was reproached with being incompetent to govern. The *Morning Chronicle* then asserted that a certificate had been signed by several Bavarians, then members of King Otho's household, declaring that his majesty was incapable of governing his little kingdom. The Bavarian consul at Athens was an Englishman, and he considered it his duty to step forward and contradict the correspondent of the *Morning Chronicle*. The anonymous writer defended his veracity, reiterated his assertion, and added that the document was dated in the year 1835, and was signed by Dr Wibmer, King Otho's physician, Count Saporta, the marshal of the royal household, Baron Stengel and Mr Lehmaier, private secretaries to the king, and members of his private council or camarilla. This rejoinder was widely circulated, and caused a loud outcry at Athens. The Greek newspapers declared that their king had been grossly insulted and calumniated, either by the English or the Bavarians, or by both. In order to tranquillise the public, and throw the whole odium on the English, Dr Wibmer, Baron Stengel, and Mr Lehmaier, published a declaration, asserting that they had never signed any such certificate.[1] But in

[1] 'Αθηνά, 1839, No. 632. The declaration is dated 23d July 1839.

the mean time it was reported that an indirect communication had been made to the courts of Greece and Bavaria that, in case of further discussion, the document would be published in the *Morning Chronicle*. It is certain that a short time after publishing their declaration, Wibmer, Stengel, and Lehmaier, suddenly resigned their offices, and returned to Bavaria. The precise nature of the mysterious certificate remained a secret.

But whatever the document might be, since it was signed in 1835, during Count Armansperg's administration, it was inferred that it could only have become known to foreigners by having been treacherously communicated to the count's friend, Lord Lyons, and having, through the imprudence of Lord Lyons, fallen into the hands of some person who made use of it to gratify a private spite. The wound given was severe, and the press never allowed it to heal. Even English diplomatists and officials were so imprudent as to be constantly harping on the question of the mysterious certificate.

As years rolled on, the misgovernment of King Otho became more intolerable. The agricultural population remained in a stationary condition. They were plundered by brigands, pillaged by gendarmes, and robbed by tax-collectors. They had to bear the whole burden of the conscription, and pay heavy municipal taxes; yet their property was insecure, and no roads were made. The Bavarians reproached Capodistrias with having neglected to improve the Turkish system of levying the land-tax, to construct roads and bridges, and to establish security for persons and property.[1] The Greeks now reproached the Bavarians with similar neglect. A remedy was required, and the people, having long patiently submitted to the despotic authority of the

[1] Thiersch, i. 57.

Bavarians, now began to clamour for a constitutional government. The first step to a free government was the expulsion of the Bavarians, and all parties in Greece agreed to unite their strength for this object. The administrative incapacity of King Otho's councillors disgusted the three protecting powers as much as their arbitrary conduct irritated the Greeks.

England and Russia supported the parties who demanded constitutional government. Nationality was so interwoven with orthodoxy, and orthodoxy appeared to be so completely under Russian control, that the establishment of a constitutional and national government was supposed by the cabinet of St Petersburg to be the surest means of rendering Greece subservient to the schemes of the Emperor Nicholas in the East. The Capodistrians carried their designs further than the Russian cabinet, for they proposed dethroning King Otho. For several years great exertions had been made to arouse the orthodox prejudices of the Greeks, and hopes were entertained that a revolution would afford an opportunity of placing the crown of Greece on the head of an orthodox prince. But when the time came, no orthodox prince fitter to govern Greece than King Otho could be found.

The English party acted under the guidance of Lord Lyons, who for several years had been the firm advocate of liberal measures, and a return to a constitutional system.

France still proposed what Louis Philippe and his ministers called a policy of moderation. The French minister in Greece was instructed to recommend the Greek government to improve the provincial councils and the municipal administration. The evils against which the people complained were defects in the central administration, consequently the advice of France was futile.

The destruction of the representative system, the annihilation of independent action in the municipal authorities, the low state of political civilisation, the still lower state of political morality, and the general lassitude which follows after a great national exertion, would in all probability have enabled King Otho and the Bavarians to rule Greece despotically for some years more, had not Great Britain and Russia publicly called upon the king's government to remedy the financial embarrassments in which it was involved. The Russian minister warned King Otho that he must prepare to pay the interest of the Allied loan. The king determined to augment his revenues in order to meet the demands of the Allies, and in the year 1842 he made some administrative changes which rendered his government more oppressive. A law regulating the custom duties was adopted, which caused so much discontent among the mercantile classes, and so many complaints, that the government was compelled to modify it by a new law before it had been many months in operation.[1]

The Russian cabinet expected that King Otho, when threatened with a constitution, would have thrown himself on its support; but finding that its counsels were neglected, the emperor made a peremptory demand for immediate payment of the interest due on the Allied loan.[2] The menacing tone of this demand was interpreted by the orthodox party to authorise the friends of Russia to adopt revolutionary measures. But to insure the approbation of the Emperor Nicholas, the partisans of Russian influence considered it necessary to give the movement as much as possible a religious character, and they made it their object to replace

[1] This law is translated in Lesur, *Annuaire Historique*, 1842. The modification took place in 1843.
[2] An extract from the Russian note is given in Lesur, *Annuaire Historique*, 1843. It was dated 23d February (7th March) 1843. See *Documents*.

the catholic Otho by an orthodox prince. As orthodoxy was in no danger, and no orthodox king was forthcoming, the direction of the revolution passed into the hands of the constitutionalists, who demanded a definite political object, the convocation of a national assembly.

The union of the orthodox and constitutional factions was absolutely necessary, in order to give a popular movement any chance of success. This was easily effected, for both desired the immediate expulsion of the Bavarians: the orthodox party was not unfavourable to the convocation of a national assembly, and the constitutional party felt no disposition to defend King Otho, had a better sovereign been proposed as his successor. It may be observed that both parties were destitute of leaders possessing any political talent.

The British government had long advocated liberal institutions, but Lord Palmerston was no longer in office, and some doubt was entertained whether the Tories would not openly oppose a revolutionary movement. The friends of constitutional liberty brought on a discussion in the House of Commons on the 15th August 1843, which proved that all parties in England considered the Greeks entitled to representative institutions. Lord Palmerston said: "I hope that her Majesty's ministers will urge strongly upon the King of Greece the necessity of his giving a constitution to his people in redemption of the pledge given by the three powers in 1832, and repeated by Baron Gise, his father's counsellor." And Sir Robert Peel, then Prime Minister, after alluding to the financial condition of Greece, continued: "Russia, France, and England have made strong representations likewise on other matters, connected with the necessity of giving satisfaction to the just wishes of the people. I must abstain at present from any more direct allusion on this subject, but I can assure the house that many points alluded to by the noble lord have not been overlooked." These were solemn warnings given in the face of all Europe; but King Otho refused to listen to the voice of nations, and remained loitering with fatuity on the brink of a precipice.[1]

A revolution being inevitable, all parties agreed that it ought to commence at Athens, and that King Otho should be compelled to dismiss all the Bavarians in the Greek service, to acknowledge the constitution, and to convoke a national assembly for its revision. The orthodox party consented that these points should be those mooted at the commencement of the revolution, being convinced that the king's pride would induce him to reject the first. But, at all events, they felt so sure of commanding a majority in a national assembly, that they believed it would be in their power to declare the throne vacant, and to proceed to elect a new king the moment they could find a suitable orthodox candidate.

On the day preceding the revolution, the court obtained authentic information of the conspiracy. Orders were given to arrest General Makryiannes and many of the leaders; but it was already too late. The gendarmes who surrounded Makryiannes's house did not invest it until after dark, and they did not attempt to make the arrest until midnight, hoping to surprise several leaders at the same time. Their movements had been watched, and a strong body of conspirators had introduced themselves unobserved

---

[1] That a revolution was considered inevitable both in England and Greece is proved by an article in *Blackwood's Magazine* for September 1843, "The Bankruptcy of Greece;" and a letter from Athens, dated 5th September, and published in the *Morning Post* of the 23d, announces the approaching revolution in terms which indicate that its information was derived from the Russian party. It says, that "the Greeks have so fully made up their minds to put an end to the Bavarian dynasty as to be resolved not even to accept a constitution at the hands of King Otho."

which fortune had intruded them. They met, at the requisition of the conspirators, when Kalergy marched to the palace. The phanariots and courtiers in the body endeavoured to gain time, and tried to raise a long discussion. They knew that the constitution would send them back to their former nullity. The murmurs of the constitutionalists assembled outside the place of meeting at last put an end to all discussion, and the council of state pledged itself to support the constitution. Andreas Londos, Rhigas Palamedes, and Andreas Metaxas, were deputed to wait on the king and advise his majesty to dismiss the Bavarians, appoint a new ministry, and convoke a national assembly.

Morning dawned before this deputation reached the palace. King Otho was in no hurry to receive the men who composed it. He still counted on effectual support from the German ministers at his court, and his immediate object was to afford them time to take some step in his favour. The deputation was at last received, but while the king was treating with its members, he was endeavouring to open a communication with his own creatures in the council of state, who, he thought, might now be sufficiently numerous to pass a new resolution in his favour.

His majesty's delay was beginning to exhaust the patience of the constitutionalists, and those most hostile to his person began to display their feelings. The greater part of the population of Athens was assembled in the extensive square before the palace. The troops occupied only a small space near the building. Children were playing, boys were shouting, and apprentices were exclaiming that the king was acting with Bavarian precipitancy, which had long been a byword with the Greeks for doing nothing. Men were exhibiting signs of dissatisfaction, and talking of the departure of Agostino from Nauplia under circumstances not very dissimilar.

Suddenly a few carriages arrived in quick succession: they contained the foreign ministers.[1] A faint cheer was raised as the Russian and English ministers appeared; but in general the people displayed alarm, remained silent, or formed small groups of whisperers. At this moment it was fortunate for Greece that Kalergy was at the head of the troops. On that important day he was the only leading man of the movement who was in his right place. He had the good sense to declare to the foreign ministers that they could not enter the palace until the deputation of the council of state had terminated its interview, and received a final answer from his majesty. The representatives of the three Allied powers being made acquainted with the demands of the deputation, acquiesced in this arrangement on receiving from Kalergy the assurance that his majesty's person should be treated with the greatest respect. The ministers of Russia, England, and France departed, deeming that their presence might tend to prolong the crisis and increase the king's personal danger. The Austrian and Prussian ministers thought the field was clear for action on their part, and they resolved to act energetically. They insisted on seeing the king. They used strong language, and made an attempt to bully Kalergy, who listened with coolness, and then quaintly observed that he believed diplomatic etiquette required them to follow the example of their *doyen*, the Russian envoy, and that common sense suggested to him that it would be prudent for them to act like the representatives of the three protecting powers.

When King Otho learned that the German diplo-

---

[1] The *doyen* of the *corps diplomatique* was M. Catacazi, the Russian envoy; Lord Lyons (then Sir Edmund) was English minister, M. Piscatory was French minister, Baron Prokesch d'Osten was Austrian minister, and Count Brassier de St Simon was Prussian minister.

matists had been unable to penetrate into his palace, he saw that it was necessary to abandon absolute power in order to preserve the crown. Without any further observation he signed all the ordinances presented to him; and on the 15th of September 1843, Greece became a constitutional monarchy. The Bavarians were dismissed from his service; a new ministry was appointed, and a national assembly was convoked.

That national assembly met on the 20th of November 1843, and terminated its work on the 30th of March 1844, when King Otho swore obedience to the constitution which it had prepared.

It is not the business of the historian of Greece under foreign domination to judge this constitution. It is only necessary for him to record the fact that it put an end to the government of alien rulers, under which the Greeks had lived for two thousand years. Its merits and defects belong to the history of Greece as a constitutional state; and perhaps more than one generation must be allowed to elapse before they can be examined with the light of experience. Still, before closing this record of the deeds by which the Greeks established their national independence, it is necessary to notice some shortcomings in this charter of their political liberty.

The constitution of 1844 is a compilation from foreign sources, and not the production of the national mind. Greece had no Lycurgus to make laws for the attainment of theoretic excellence, nor any Solon to devise remedies for existing social evils. National wants and national institutions were alike overlooked. The municipal system which Capodistrias had defaced, and which Maurer had converted into an engine for riveting the fetters of centralisation on the local magistrates, was neither revived as a defence for the people's rights, nor adapted to aid the progress of Greek society.

The section of the constitution which determines the public rights of the Greek citizen, omits all reference to those rights in his position as an inhabitant of a parish, and as a member of a municipality and provincial district. Indeed, the interests of the citizen, in so far as they were directly connected with his locality and his property, were completely neglected, and only his relations with the legislature and the central government were determined.

The spirit of imitation also introduced some contradictions into the constitution of Greece extremely injurious to the cause of liberty. Universal suffrage was adopted for choosing members of the legislature, while the chief magistrates in the municipalities were selected by the king from three candidates chosen by an oligarchical elective body. As far as the rights of the citizens in municipalities were concerned, all the evils of the Capodistrian and Bavarian systems were left without reform. The municipalities remained in servile dependence on the king, the ministers of the day, and the prefects of the hour. The demarch was not directly elected by the people, and the minister of the crown exercised a direct control over the budget of the demarchy. Yet the people, though not allowed to elect their own local chief, were nevertheless intrusted with the election of deputies to the lower legislative chamber. And this introduction of universal suffrage in the institutions of Greece was completely exceptional, for a property qualification was retained for the electors who appointed provincial councillors. A system tending more directly to perpetuate maladministration in the municipalities, nullity in the provincial councils, and corruption in the chamber of deputies, could not have been devised. Individual responsibility was destroyed, the influence of the court was extended, and the power of faction increased.

The constitution of Greece opens the section of the public rights of citizens with an article which figures in most modern constitutions since the French constitution of 1793.[1] It declares that all Greeks are equal in the eye of the law. In many of the constitutions in which a similar article appears, it is a direct falsehood: in the constitution of Greece it is not strictly true. The Greeks who framed the constitution knew that the phrase was introduced in France originally to enable the people to boast of an equality which the French, at least, have never enjoyed. To render all the citizens equal before the law, something more is necessary than to say that they are so. The legislation which would insure equality must render every individual, whatever be his rank or official station, responsible for all his acts to the persons whom those acts affect. The law must be equal for all, and superior to all. Neither a minister of police, a general, nor an admiral, any more than a prefect, must be permitted to plead official duty for any act as an excuse for not answering before the ordinary tribunals of the country. No officer of government must be allowed to escape personal responsibility by the plea of superior orders. The sovereign alone can do no wrong. There can be no true liberty in any country where administrative privileges exempt officials from the direct operation of the law, as it affects every other citizen of the state, and as it is administered by the ordinary tribunals of the country. The Greeks did not lay down this principle in their consitution; they preferred the nominal equality of France to the legal equality of English law.

The two most influential leaders in the national

---

[1] A translation of the Greek constitution is given in *Parliamentary Papers*, 1844—"Correspondence relative to recent events in Greece."

assembly were Mavrocordatos and Kolettes. Both endeavoured to preserve every official privilege introduced by Capodistrias and the Bavarians, for the purpose of placing the agents of the government above the law of the land. It was only through the support which Lord Lyons gave to a small party of deputies, that Mavrocordatos was induced to insert an article in the constitution expressly forbidding the re-establishment of the exceptional tribunals which Capodistrias, the regency, and King Otho, had used as instruments of fiscal extortion and illegal oppression. The abolition of the exceptional tribunals then in existence was declared in another article of the constitution.[1] The opposition which the leading statesmen of Greece made even to this tame protest against the illegal and unconstitutional proceedings of past governments, presaged that they were not likely to prove either active or intelligent artificers of the institutions still required in order to establish the civil and political liberties of the Greeks on a firm foundation. But the living generation had accomplished a great achievement. The future destinies of the Greek race were now in the hands of the citizens of liberated Greece.

Before finally releasing the reader who has followed the author through the preceding pages, it may not be altogether unnecessary to look back at the origin of the Greek Revolution, and examine how far it has been crowned with success, or in what it has failed to fulfil the expectations of reflecting men. A generation has already passed away; most of the actors in the drama are dead; the political position of Greece itself has changed; so that a cotemporary may now view the events without passion, and weigh their consequences with impartiality.

[1] Compare Articles 89 and 101.

The Greek Revolution was not an insurrectional movement, originating solely in Turkish oppression. The first aspirations for the delivery of the orthodox church from the sultan's yoke were inspired by Russia; the projects for national independence by the French Revolution. The Greeks, it is true, were prepared to receive these ideas by a wave in the element of human progress that had previously spread civilisation among the inhabitants of the Othoman empire, whether Mussulman or Christian.

The origin of the ideas that produced the Greek Revolution explain why it was pre-eminently the movement of the people; and that its success was owing to their perseverance, is proved by its whole history. To live or die free was the firm resolve of the native peasantry of Greece when they took up arms; and no sufferings ever shook that resolution. They never had the good fortune to find a leader worthy of their cause. No eminent man stands forward as a type of the nation's virtues; too many are famous as representatives of the nation's vices. From this circumstance, the records of the Greek Revolution are destitute of one of history's most attractive characteristics: it loses the charm of a hero's biography. But it possesses its own distinction. Never in the records of states did a nation's success depend more entirely on the conduct of the mass of the population; never was there a more clear manifestation of God's providence in the progress of human society. No one can regard its success as the result of the military and naval exploits of the insurgents; and even the Allied powers, in creating a Greek kingdom, only modified the political results of a revolution which had irrevocably separated the present from the past.

Let us now examine how far the Greek Revolution has succeeded. It has established the independence of

Greece on a firm basis, and created a free government in regions where civil liberty was unknown for two thousand years. It has secured popular institutions to a considerable portion of the Greek nation, and given to the people the power of infusing national life and national feelings into the administration of King Otho's kingdom. These may be justly considered by the Greeks as glorious achievements for one generation.

But yet it must be confessed that in many things the Greek Revolution has failed. It has not created a growing population and an expanding nation. Diplomacy has formed a diminutive kingdom, and no Themistocles has known how to form a great state out of so small a community. Yet the task was not difficult: the lesson was taught in the United States of America and in the colonial empire of Great Britain. But in the Greek kingdom, with every element of social and political improvement at hand, the agricultural population and the native industry of the country have remained almost stationary. The towns, it is true, are increasing, and merchants are gaining money; but the brave peasantry who formed the nation's strength grows neither richer nor more numerous; the produce of their labour is of the rudest kind; whole districts remain uncultivated; the wealthy Greeks who pick up money in foreign traffic do not invest the capital they accumulate in the land which they pretend to call their country; and no stream of Greek emigrants flows from the millions who live enslaved in Turkey, to enjoy liberty by settling in liberated Greece.

There can be no doubt that the inhabitants of Greece may, even in spite of past failures, look with hope to the future. When a few years of liberty have purged society from the traditional corruption of servitude, wise counsels may enable them to resume their progress.

But the friends of Greece, who believed that the

Revolution would be immediately followed by the multiplication of the Greek race, and by the transfusion of Christian civilisation and political liberty throughout all the regions that surround the Egean Sea, cannot help regretting that a generation has been allowed to pass away unprofitably. The political position of the Othoman empire in the international system of Europe is already changed, and the condition of the Christian population in Turkey is even more changed than the position of the empire. The kingdom of Greece has lost the opportunity of alluring emigrants by good government. Feelings of nationality are awakened in other Oriental Christians under Othoman domination. The Greeks can henceforth only repose their hopes of power on an admission of their intellectual and moral superiority. The Albanians are more warlike; the Sclavonians are more laborious; the Roumans dwell in a more fertile land; and the Turks may become again a powerful nation, by being delivered from the lethargic influence of the Othoman sultans.

The Othoman empire may soon be dismembered, or it may long drag on a contemptible existence, like the Greek empire of Constantinople under the Paleologues. Its military resources, however, render its condition not dissimilar to that of the Roman empire in the time of Gallienus, and there may be a possibility of finding a Diocletian to reorganise the administration, and a Constantine to reform the religion. But should it be dismembered to-morrow, it may be asked, what measures the free Greeks have adopted to govern any portion better than the officers of the sultan? On the other hand, several powerful states and more populous nations are well prepared to seize the fragments of the disjointed empire. They will easily find legitimate pretexts for their intervention, and they will certainly obtain a tacit recognition of the justice of their proceedings from the public opinion of civilised Europe, if they succeed in saving Turkey from anarchy, and in averting such scenes of slaughter as Greece witnessed during her Revolution, or as have recently occurred in Syria.

It is never too late, however, to commence the task of improvement. The inheritance may not be open for many years, and the heirs may be called to the succession by their merit. What, then, are the merits which give a nation the best claim to greatness? Personal dignity, domestic virtue, truth in the intercourse of society, and respect for justice, make nations powerful as surely as they make men honoured. But I wander too far from my subject; so, instead of moralising further, I shall conclude with the words of the old English song—

> "Only the actions of the just
> Smell sweet and blossom in the dust."

APPENDIX.

[THE two papers which follow have been added to show the manner in which able officers urged the Greeks to avail themselves of naval and military science. Captain Hastings, the author of the first paper, never obtained any important command; and though he introduced great practical changes in naval warfare, and fell, " dying in Greece and in a cause so glorious," he has missed gaining a name.

Sir Charles Napier, who gave the second paper to the writer of this work, has won imperishable fame on a wider and more glorious field than the Greek Revolution. The name of Hastings hardly finds a place in the history of Greece; that of Napier will live for ever in the history of England.]

I.

MEMORANDUM by FRANK ABNEY HASTINGS, ESQ., on the use of Steamers armed with heavy guns against the Turkish Fleet. Communicated to Lord Byron in 1823, and laid before the Greek Government, with some modification, in 1824.

Firstly, I lay down as an axiom that Greece cannot obtain any decisive advantage over the Turks without a decided maritime superiority; for it is necessary to prevent them from relieving their fortresses and supplying their armies by sea.

To prove this it is only necessary to view the state of the Greek armies, and that of their finances.

They are destitute of a corps of artillery, of a park of artillery, of a corps of engineers, and of a regular army. With all these wants, I ask, how is it possible to take a fortress but by famine? This, however, is difficult, even if the sea was shut against the Turks; for, from the state of the Greek finances, and the formation of the army, troops can scarcely remain long enough before a place furnished with a formidable garrison, and tolerably supplied with provisions, to reduce it. However, famine is the only resource, and it is by that alone that the fortresses now in the hands of the Greeks have been reduced.

The localities of the country are also such, and the difficulty of moving troops so great, that, without the aid of a fleet, all the efforts of an invading army would prove fruitless. But on the contrary, were an invading army followed by a fleet, I fear that all the efforts of the Greeks to oppose it would be ineffectual. The question stands thus, Has the Greek fleet hitherto prevented the Turks from supplying their fortresses, and is it likely to succeed in preventing them? I reply, that Patras, Negropont, Modon, and Coron have been regularly supplied, and Mesolonghi twice blockaded.

Is it likely that the Greek marine will improve, or that the Turkish will retrograde? The contrary is to be feared. We have seen the Greek fleet diminish in numbers every year since the commencement of the war, while that of the Turks has undeniably improved, from the experience they have gained in each campaign. Witness the unsuccessful attempts with fire-ships this year (1823). The Turks begin to find fire-ships only formidable to those unprepared to receive them.

Is the Greek fleet likely to become more formidable? On the contrary, the sails, rigging, and hulls are all getting out of repair; and in two years' time thirty sail could hardly be sent to sea without an expense which the Greeks would not probably incur.[1]

We now come to the question, How can the Greeks obtain a decisive superiority over the Turks at sea? I reply, By a steam-vessel, armed as I shall describe. But how is Greece to obtain such a vessel? The means of Greece are much more than amply sufficient to meet this expenditure. However, there are various reasons which it is not necessary to detail, but which would probably prevent the Greek government from adopting the plan. It therefore becomes necessary to ascertain how such a vessel might be equipped without calling on the Greek government to contribute directly. If proper statements were made to the Greek committee in England, I think it might be induced to bear some part of the expense. I will contribute £1000 on the condition that I have the command, and that the vessel is armed in the manner I propose. If this does not form a sufficient fund, I think that the deficiency may be made up by a loan; a guarantee being given that a certain portion—say one-half of all prizes

[1] The English loan had not yet been obtained.

—shall be applied to the payment of the interest and the extinction of the debt. The same proportion would be set apart to meet the expenses of the vessel, so that the Greek government might be called upon to bear no other expenses but the wages of the crew.

I shall now explain the details of the proposed armament, and the advantages which I think would result from it. It would be necessary to build or purchase the vessel in England, and send her out complete. She should be from 150 to 200 tons burden, of a construction sufficiently strong to bear two long 32-pounders, one forward and one aft, and two 68-pounder guns of seven inches bore, one on each side. The weight of shot appears to me of the greatest importance, for I think I can prove that half a dozen shot or shells of these calibres, and employed as I propose, would more than suffice to destroy the largest ship. In this case it is not the number of projectiles, but their nature and proper application that is required.

In order that the vessel should present less surface to the wind and less mark to the enemy, combined with a greater range of pointing and more facility for the use of red-hot shot, the bulwark should be sufficiently low to admit of the guns being fired over it. From the long 32-pounders I propose launching red-hot shot, because, though perhaps not more destructive than shells, they give a longer range; and the fuel required to impel the vessel could easily be made to heat the shot. The idea being rather novel, startles people at first, because, as it has never been put in practice, they imagine there must be some extraordinary danger to which it subjects your own vessel. But this is not the case. The real reason why it has never been adopted hitherto is, that on board a ship you cannot lay your guns before you introduce your red-hot shot, as on shore. This arises, of course, from the motion of the vessel. In other words, the danger arises from the possibility of fire communicating to the cartridge during the operation of running-out and pointing the gun. If, however, it be proved by experience that, with proper precautions, the shot may be allowed to remain any length of time in the gun without setting fire to the cartridge, this difficulty (and it is the only difficulty) vanishes. In fact, during the siege of Gibraltar the guns were pointed against the block-ships after being loaded, it being found that one wet wad alone was sufficient security, and that with it the shot might absolutely be left to get cold in the gun. It may, however, be thought necessary to cast iron bottoms for the hot shot, of the same form as those of wood which I propose to make use of in loading the guns with shells. These may be placed over the wad, and then the gun may be well sponged, to drown any particles of powder that might by accident escape from the cartridge. With this precaution the shot might be left to cool in the gun, and there could therefore be no want of time to run out and point it. But this would be unnecessary if the gun worked over the bulwark, for it could then be loaded with its muzzle just outside the vessel, having been previously laid to its elevation, the direction being obtained by a slight movement of the helm. Thus there would be no necessity for touching the gun after the shot was once introduced. Perhaps the precautions I propose are in part superfluous, as hot shot are fired on shore without observing them.

Of the destructive effect of hot shot on an enemy's ship it is scarcely necessary for me to speak. The destruction of the Spanish fleet before Gibraltar is well known. But if I may be permitted to relate an example which came under my proper observation, it will perhaps tend to corroborate others. At New Orleans the Americans had a ship and schooner in the Mississippi that flanked our lines. In the commencement we had no cannon. However, after a couple of days, two field-pieces of 4 or 6 lb. and a howitzer were erected in battery. In ten minutes the schooner was on fire, and her comrade, seeing the effect of the hot shot, cut her cable, and escaped under favour of a light wind. If such was the result of light shot imperfectly heated—for we had no forge—what would be the effect of such a volume as a 32-pounder? A single shot would set a ship in flames.

Having treated the subject of hot shot, I shall now pass to the use of shells. It has long been well known that ships are more alarmed at shells than at other projectiles. However, they rarely do the mischief apprehended from them, in consequence of the difficulty of hitting so small an object as a ship with a projectile thrown vertically. This uncertainty prevents bomb-vessels being employed against ships. If, however, shells be thrown horizontally, their effect would be equally great, and the chance of hitting the object aimed at reduced to the same certainty as if shot were used within a certain range. If the shell passed inside the vessel and exploded, the result would be the same as if it had been thrown vertically. My object, however, would be, to arrange it so as to make the shell stick in the ship's side and explode there. The result in this case would be much more decisive, and it would tear away a part of her side, and might send her instantly to the bottom. In both cases it would probably destroy a number of the crew and set fire to the ship.

It remains, therefore, to ascertain whether shells can be thrown to a sufficient distance with precision from guns and carronades, and without any danger to your own vessel. The danger of transporting shells is considerably less than the danger of passing powder. It is, therefore, only necessary to prove how they may be fired without danger. The danger of firing a shell from a gun longer than a howitzer or a carronade is, that it might, by rolling in the bore, destroy the fusee and explode in the gun; also, that the fusee might break from the successive blows it would receive before it quitted the muzzle. Now, both these objections are obviated by attaching the shell to a wooden bottom, hollowed out to receive its convexity. Each shell would be kept in a separate box.

We now come to the plan of attack. In executing this, I should go directly for the vessel most detached from the enemy's fleet, and when at the distance of one mile, open with red-hot shot from the 32-pounder forward. The gun laid at point blank, with a reduced charge, would carry on board *en ricochetant*. I would then wheel round and give the enemy one of the 68-pounders with shell laid at the line of metal, which would also ricochet on board him. Then the stern 32-pounder with a hot shot, and again the 68-pounder of the other side with a shell. By this time the bow-gun would be again loaded, and a succession of fire might be kept up as brisk as from a vessel having four guns on a side. Here the importance of steam is evident.

With good locks, tubes, Congreve's sights, and other improvements in artillery, I really see almost as much difficulty in missing a ship of any size in tolerably smooth water as in hitting her. In firing from a ship, the great difficulty is in the elevation; but when my guns were laid at point blank, or two degrees of elevation, neither shot nor shells would ricochet over the enemy.

With regard to any risk of the steam machinery being destroyed by the enemy's fire, there is of course some risk, as there always must be in military operations of the simplest kind; but when we consider the small object a low steamer would present coming head on, and the manner in which the Turks have hitherto used their guns at sea, this risk really appears very trifling. The surprise caused by seeing a vessel moving in a calm, offering only a breadth of about eighteen feet, and opening a fire with heavy guns at a considerable distance, may also be taken into account. I am persuaded, from what I have seen, that in many cases the Turks would run their ships ashore and abandon them, perhaps without having the presence of mind to set fire to them.

It would be necessary to have a Greek brig always in company to carry coals and to tow the steamer, for the steam would only be used in action.[1]

---

[1] The remainder of the memorandum is occupied with financial calculations, and with accounts relating to the numbers and pay of the crew. The manner in

II.

MEMORANDUM by SIR CHARLES NAPIER, G.C.B., on Military Operations in the Morea against IBRAHIM PASHA in 1826.

If my judgment is correct, the following would be the outline of operations for a regular military force, and explains why I think Napoli di Malvasia (Monomvasia) so important:—

1. At Napoli di Malvasia I would establish my magazines and form the army. I would provision and garrison Napoli di Romania (Nauplia) the best way I could, and leave in it the best of the irregular troops under the command of the most deserving Greek chief. Having done so, I would leave them and the government (with the example of Mesolonghi) to make their defence, and, having cleared myself of all intrigues, take post at Malvasia.

2. When the preparations for the campaign were sufficiently advanced to enable me to act, I would advance with my whole force, *regular* and *irregular*, to Sparta, or near it, according to circumstances of the ground and roads. Then I would prepare a position with fieldworks, to cover the fortress of Napoli di Malvasia against a force coming from Kalamata, or Tripolitza, or Leondari.

3. This done, if the enemy had his headquarters at Tripolitza, with the mass of his force in that town, I would endeavour to cut off his communications with Navarin, Modon, and Coron, by occupying the position of Leondari, sending one-half of my irregulars into the defiles of Mount Chelmos, and the other half to my rear, towards the fortresses of Navarin, Modon, and Coron. I would concentrate my whole regular force at Leondari, except a small portion left in position at Sparta to secure my communications with Napoli di Malvasia. In fact, Sparta would be the pivot on which all operations would turn, according to the point on which the enemy had assembled his force.

4. In this state I would remain, strengthening Leondari by fieldworks; and the enemy, no longer able to pass his convoys of provisions from the coast, must attack me in my strong position (and such positions cannot fail to be found in such a country at every turn). If he defeats me, I retire, and my troops rally on Sparta in

---

which the plan was eventually carried into execution, and some of its results, were narrated by Captain Hastings in a pamphlet written a short time before his death—*Memoir on the use of Shells, Hot Shot, and Carcass-Shells from Ship-Artillery.* By FRANK ABNEY HASTINGS, Captain of the Greek steam-vessel of war Kartaria. London, 1828. Published by Ridgway.

the prepared position, where another battle may be fought. If again defeated, the remains of my beaten force retire into Napoli di Malvasia, and await a siege.

5. Suppose that the enemy has begun the siege of Napoli di Romania. Then, instead of marching upon Leondari, I would march upon the rear of the besieging army, and post my force so as to cut off his supplies from Tripolitza; and I would send all my irregulars round that town and along the road to Navarin as far as Leondari and Kalamata. I would strengthen my position as before, and the enemy must again come and attack me or *starve*. If he beat me, I would (as before) retire to Sparta, and if again beaten, enter Malvasia and await a siege.

6. Suppose neither of the above operations could be effected in consequence of the enemy's force being too great, or from some other cause. Then I would remain at Sparta with my irregulars pushed into the defiles along my front, so as to guard the road from Leondari into Messenia; and I would closely observe him, that I might be ready to take advantage of any error he might commit, or fall with my whole force upon any convoy by a rapid march from Sparta, and retire with equal celerity to my position.

7. It is pretty clear, by such a plan, the enemy could not besiege Napoli di Romania, unless he had so large a force that he could form two armies—one to besiege the town, and another to cover the siege by marching against Sparta; and, besides, he would require a force to protect all his convoys from my irregular troops. This, we know, he has not. The real defence of Napoli di Romania depends on Napoli di Malvasia.

8. I have said, that if beaten at Sparta I would go to Malvasia and abide a siege. Suppose, then, the enemy attempted this operation, he would find it very difficult, as I would leave all the irregular troops under an active partisan in the mountains. These would terribly infest his supplies. The place itself is, I am told, of great strength, and, however closely blockaded by the sea, could be supplied by boats at night, and under certain circumstances of weather. If not blockaded by sea very closely, the greatest part of the army would be transported to Napoli di Romania, from whence the same game would be played in favour of Malvasia that she played in favour of Romania, supposing the latter besieged.

Thus, in this sketch, I have endeavoured to show that you may always oblige the enemy to attack you in your own position with your back to a fortress, thus uniting offensive war with defensive positions, which is the secret of mountain warfare—a warfare that requires more science and better drilled troops than any other.

Peasants may maintain a long war in their mountains without science, but *no results are produced.*

It will be seen in the plan I propose that a single defeat to the enemy would be followed by his total destruction, because, as he would be driven to fight for want of provisions, his army must starve after a defeat, for the victorious army would remain between him and Navarin, from whence he received his supplies. It is true that, if his defeat took place at Sparta, he might escape by Kalamata, though to retreat through a country of defiles exposed to a hostile peasantry is very difficult. But let us suppose he accomplished his object and reached Navarin. Still great results are produced to the Greeks, who would at once besiege him, and the whole country would be recovered, and Tripolitza and Leondari fortified. It is much to be doubted if the Turks could long resist in Navarin when besieged in a scientific manner. I think it certain that ten days or a fortnight would oblige Navarin to surrender.

With the force now under Ibrahim Pasha, I think he could not resist five thousand disciplined troops supported by *one thousand veteran Europeans.* With such a force, and twenty pieces of light artillery, the Morea might be liberated in a month, and great things undertaken.

It is evident that my plan is but an outline, which admits of modifications in filling up the details of execution according to accidents of roads, mountains, supplies, the enemy's strength, positions, movements, &c. In the various operations of the foregoing plan, the garrison of Corinth would come out and take post in the passes commanding the entrance into the plain of Tripolitza from the north-east.

A great advantage of this plan is, that young Greek regulars are not required to attack, but to defend positions. Every old soldier knows how to estimate this advantage. My own opinion is, that neither Greeks nor Turks would succeed in attacking a well-chosen position. The first round of cannon-shot would defeat their column, and make them refuse to advance.

C. N.

INDEX.

ABBAS PASHA, operations under, ii. 94, 95.
Abbas, Tahir, an Albanian leader, i. 100, 106, 112—his mission to the Greeks, 113 et seq.
Abel, Mr, secretary to the Regency, ii. 294—dismissed from office, &c., 332.
Aberdeen Lord, his negotiations, &c., regarding Greece, ii. 222.
Aboulabad, suppresses the revolt in the Chalcidice, i. 252 — operations on Mount Athos, &c., 254—sack of Niausta, &c., 255.
Acarnania, affairs of, 1822, i. 331—movements of the Greeks into, ii. 185—insurrection in, 357 et seq.
Achmet I., privilege granted to Athens by, i. 4.
Achmet Bey, defeated at Valtetsi, i. 252—his escape from Tripolitza, 269—his death at Splanga, 333.
Acrocorinth, the, taken by the Greeks, i. 277—by the Turks, 351—recaptured by the Greeks, ii. 21.
Acropolis, besieged by Reshid, ii. 117—its capitulation, 132.
Adam, Sir F., attempts to mediate at Mesolonghi, ii. 102.
Adrianople, massacres of Greeks at, i. 234.
Aghias Mynas, massacre at monastery of, i. 318.
Aghionoros, the, see Athos.
Agoyiates or muleteers, the, i. 23.
Agrapha, privileges of, i. 22—sketch of its history, and proceedings of Ali Pasha against it, 26 — insurrection in, and its suppression, 242 et seq.
Agricultural population, the, in Greece, i. 15—state of, in the Principalities, 140 et seq.
Agridha, first revolutionary outbreak at, i. 180.

Akrata, first insurrectionary movement at, i. 160.
Albania, southern, the pashalik of Joannina, i. 4—condition, &c., of the population, their origin, language, &c., 41 et seq.—the Guegks and Turks, 42—their adoption of Mohammedanism, 43—character of the country, social state, &c., 44 et seq.—population on the decrease, 45—administrative divisions under the Turks, 46—the Musulmans and Christians in, 43.
Albanian language, the, i. 41.
Albanians, distribution, numbers, &c., of the, in Greece, i. 34 et seq.—those of Lalla and Bardunia, 36—of Hydra, Spetzas, &c., 37—their military influence in Turkey, 47—employed as mercenaries in Greece, 49—desertion of Ibrahim by, ii. 191.
Alexander, the emperor, expectations of the Hetairists from, i. 138, 139—disavows the attempt in the Principalities, 156—his views on the Greek insurrection, and rupture with Turkey, 238 et seq.—the expectations of the Greeks from him, ii. 160—his death, 171.
Ali Kumurgee contrasted with Dramali, i. 351.
Ali Pasha of Argos, plans proposed to Dramali by, i. 352, 353—occupies Nauplia, 354—refuses to sign the capitulation of Nauplia, 360.
Ali Pasha of Joannina, i. 4—overthrow of the power of the armatoli by, 28—his proceedings towards the klephts, 29—becomes Dervendji, and his policy, 49—his objects, and means of working them out, 50 et seq.—his policy and measures against the Bulotes, 55—his second attack on them, 57 et seq.—his treacheries and cruelties

toward them, 62—his character, 70—
his parentage and early career, ib. et
seq.—his court, and encouragement
of literature, 72—his cruelty, 73—the
fate of Euphrosyne, 74 et seq.—anecdotes of him, 78—policy pursued by
him, 79—the destruction of Khor-
moro, 80—and of Gardhiki, 82—first
measures of the sultan against him,
85—attempts on Ismael Pacho, 86—
declared a rebel, 87—his defensive
preparations, 88 et seq.—his appeal to
the Greeks, and its failure, 92 et seq.—
Joannina besieged, 96 et seq.—his surrender, 115—his death, 116.
America, supplies to Greece from, in
1827, ii. 159.
Amnesty, the proposed, refused by the
governing commission, ii. 249.
Amphissa, see Salona.
Anagnostaras, a klepht, i. 162, 183—
at the outbreak of the Revolution, 184
—peculations of, ii. 43—his death at
Sphakteria, 68.
Anarchy, general, after the fall of Tri-
politza, i. 270.
Anatolikon, besieged by the Turks, ii. 13
—taken, 101—death of Hastings at,
139—evacuated by the Turks, 207.
Andreas, Paul, a Moldavian banker, i. 142.
Anhmet, a Danish volunteer at Nauplis,
i. 394.
Antiparos, islet of, ii. 42.
Apollo newspaper, suppressed by Capodistrias, ii. 292.
Apostoles, fire-ships proposed by, i. 218.
Aracbova, Turks defeated at, ii. 122.
Arcadia, insurrection of 1834 in, ii. 317.
Areopagus of Eastern Greece, the, i. 341
—quarrel with Odysseus, 343.
Argos, the national assembly at first
meets at, i. 293—flight of the government from, 355 et seq.—disorders of
the troops, 356—national assembly of,
ii. 229—the second national assembly,
250 et seq.—attack on the French at,
285 et seq.
Armauspreg, Count, his character, ii. 204
et seq.—his intrigue against Maurer,
&c., 317 et seq.—his administration,
333 et seq.—his recall, 336.
Armatoli, the, i. 24 et seq.—measures of
Ali Pasha against, 74 et seq.—their
atrocities, ii. 7.
Armatolixa, number of the, i. 25.
Army, abuses regarding its pay, rations,
&c., ii. 42—measures of Capodistrias
for organising it, 209 et seq.—organisation of it by the Regency, 302.
Arusaut-oghou, voevode of Kalavryta,
i. 161, 182.

Arsenal, the Turkish, destroyed by fire,
ii. 5.
Arta, sacked by brigands, ii. 344—gulf
of, its command obtained by the
Greeks, ii. 206—valley of, revolt in,
and its suppression, i. 243.
Asemaki, a Hetairist, treason of, i. 124.
Asia Minor, ravages of the Psarians, &c.,
in, ii. 14—revolt in, 15.
Aslan Bey, his advance to Athens, and
retreat, ii. 205.
Aspropotamos, valley of, revolt in, and
its suppression, i. 244.
Athens, state of, under the Turks, i. 4—
its state at the outbreak of the Revolution, 199—massacres of Turks, and
blockade of the Acropolis, 200—capitulation of, 347 et seq.—its violation
by the Greeks, 348—state of, in 1822,
373—Odysseus governor, 374—commencement of siege, ii. 116—attempts
to raise it, 120—further attempts to
relieve, 130 et seq.—operations before,
143—the fall of, 152.
Athos, Mount, or Aghionoros, i. 248,
249—suppression of revolt in, 253—
naval skirmish off, ii. 14.
Attica, Gouras' exactions in, ii. 115—
brigandage in, 363.
Austrian government, treatment of Hypsilantes by, i. 165.

Bairam, Ibrahim's celebration of the, at
Makry, ii. 51.
Balestra, Colonel, i. 323 note.
Bardunia, the Albanians of, i. 36—flight
of the Albanians and Turks of, 185,
186.
Bavarian administration, general review
of it, ii. 327 et seq.
Bavarians, their overthrow in 1843, ii.
377.
Benderli, Ali, grand vizier, i. 230—dis-
placed, 233.
Berat, pashalik of, i. 46.
Berats and Beratlees, the system of, i.
131.
Bibisi, a brigand, ii. 363, 364.
Boboliua, a Spetziot heroine, i. 266.
Boscola, ravaged by the Turks, ii. 2.
Botases, a Spetziot captain, i. 263—
named vice-president, ii. 20.
Botzares, Constantine, ii. 65.
Botzares, George, joins Ali Pasha, i. 57
—his defeat and death, 58—Ali's
treachery to him, 62.
Botzares, Kosta, a member of the gov-
erning commission, ii. 264.
Botzares, Marco, i. 323—at Petta, 327-
329—his victory and death at Kar-
penisi, ii. 10 et seq.

INDEX. 395

Botsares, Nothi, ii. 81—his conduct during siege of Mesolonghi, 101 *note*—heads the final sortie, 107.

Bowring, Sir John, and the Greek loan, ii. 155, 156.

Brigandage, its prevalence under the Bavarians, ii. 342 *et seq.*—its increase, 350 *et seq.*—suppressed by Gordon, 353 *et seq.*—again breaks out, 362.

Brigands or klephts, rise of the, i. 27—their proceedings, cruelties, &c., 28 and *note*.

Broughton, Lord, *see* Hobhouse.

Bucharest, the peace of, i. 138—the Revolution at, 152—recaptured by the Turks, 152.

Budrun, the naval battles of, ii. 56.

Buduros, Vasili, i. 210.

Bulgares, George, governor of Hydra, i. 210.

Bulgari, Count, confidant of Capodistrias, ii. 192.

Bulgaris, first Turkish governor of Hydra, i. 40.

Bulwer, Sir Henry Lytton, on the expenditure of the Greek loan, ii. 27.

Burbaki, Colonel, attempts to relieve Athens, ii. 131—his defeat and death, 132.

Burdett, Sir F., and the Greek committee, ii. 155.

Burdjev fort, defended by Hastings, &c., i. 364—abandoned, 367.

Burduba, a brigand, ii. 363 *note*.

Byron, Lord, declines to make advances for the fleet, ii. 21—his arrival in Greece, 22—his character, *ib.*—his opinion of the Greeks, 23 *et seq.*—his views of the contest, 25—an evening with London, 38 *note*.

Canning, the recognition of the Spanish revolted colonies by, ii. 165—his reply to Greek memorial, 167—advocates the establishment of Greece, 170—his death, and change of policy, 182.

Canning, Sir Stratford, ambassador to Turkey, ii. 171—plan for settlement of Greece proposed by him, 222—his memorandum on Greece, 255.

Cantacuzenos, Prince George, i. 166—his flight, 167.

Cantacuzenos, Gregorios, i. 261.

Capitan-pasha, position, &c., of the, i. 3.

Capitation-tax or haratch, the, i. 22.

Capitulations, violations of, by the Greeks, i. 261, 263, 277, 318.

Capodistrians, the party of, and their struggles, ii. 249, 250—their proceedings in the assembly, 251—new intrigues, &c., 264, 265.

Capodistrias, Agostino, appointed general, and his character, ii. 207—a member of the governing commission, 249—chosen president, 254—ejected from office, 260.

Capodistrias, Count John, refuses the direction of the Hetairia, i. 135—appointed president, ii. 138, 139—convention with Albanians in Ibrahim's service, 191—his election as president, previous life, and character, 195 *et seq.*—his first administrative measures, 198—his views and policy, 199—his organisation of the army, 200 *et seq.*—military operations during 1828, 205 *et seq.*—his civil administration, 208 *et seq.*—appointment of his brother Viaro, 210—financial administration, 213 *et seq.*—judicial, 216—education, &c., 218—his arbitrary proceedings, 219—the national assembly of Argos, 220—his intrigues against Leopold, 224 *et seq.*—his increasing tyranny after Prince Leopold's resignation, 230 *et seq.*—insurrections against him, 234—affair of Poros, 235 *et seq.*—efforts of sack of Poros on his reputation, &c., 241—his proceedings in Maina and against Mavromichales, 242 *et seq.*—his assassination, 244 *et seq.*

Capodistrias, Viaro, his character and tyrannies, ii. 210 *et seq.*, 232.

Caradja, Prince Constantine, i. 297.

Central government, opposition to formation of, in Greece, i. 272.

Centralisation, progress of, under Mahmud, i. 35.

Cerigo, massacre of Turks at, i. 216.

Chalcidicé, the free villages of the, i. 248—the Revolution in, 251—its suppression, 252.

Charalambes, an opponent of Hypsilantes, i. 289.

Chios, state of, at the outbreak of the Revolution, i. 306—invaded by the Greeks, and precautionary measures of Mahmud, 307—defeat of the Greeks, 311—massacres of the population, 312 *et seq.*—further devastations, and numbers massacred, 319—indignation excited by the massacre, 320—atrocities of the Greek sailors at, ii. 15—attempt of Fabvier at, 187.

Christians, position and treatment of, under Turkey, i. 5.

Christos, Hadji, a leader of irregular cavalry, ii. 66.

Church, Sir Richard, his arrival in Greece, and character, ii. 135—ap-

INDEX.

pointed arch-general, 138—operations before Athens, 143—his indecision, &c., 146—his neglect during the massacre at St Spiridion, ib. et seq.—new plans, 149—defeat, 150 et seq.—orders the surrender of the Acropolis, 152—his position after the battle of the Phalerum, 174—movements and operations in Acarnania, 185—disorganisation among his troops, 187—left in command by Capodistrias, 201—forces under him, and their state in 1828, 206.

Civil war, the first, ii. 28—the second, or of the Primates, 34 et seq.—evils caused by them, 37.

Clergy, the Greek, their position and views, i. 12—character of, under Capodistrias, ii. 213.

Cobbett, his attacks on the Greek committee, &c., ii. 158.

Cochrane, Lord, his arrival in Greece, and character, ii. 137—appointed arch-admiral, 138—operations near Athens, 144—success at the Piraeus, ib.—at the surrender of St Spiridion, 146—at the battle of the Phalerum, 151—price paid for his services, 155—first naval review, 157—naval operations in 1827, 176.

Codrington, Sir Edward, ii. 178—battle of Navarin, 179 et seq.—blamed for allowing deportation of Greeks to Egypt, 183—convention concluded for evacuation of Morea, 188.

Commercial navy, the Greek, its rise, &c., i. 205.

Commissariat, its inefficient condition, i. 282—abuses in it, ii. 42.

Communal system, origin, &c., of the, in Greece, i. 16 et seq.—its influence at the opening of the Revolution, 283.

Congress of Verona, views of the powers at, on Greece, ii. 102.

Constantinople, the Greek population of, i. 10—precautionary measures at, 227—executions of Greeks; the patriarch, &c., 228 et seq.—anarchy and murders in, 232—fire at, and destruction of arsenal, &c., ii. 5.

Constitution of Epidaurus, cause of its failure, i. 295, 296—its proclamation, 298.

Corfu, emigration of Sulliots to, i. 58.

Corinth capitulates to the Greeks, and violation of the capitulation, i. 277—captured by the Turks, 351.

Coron relieved by the Turkish fleet, ii. 14—occupied by the French, 192.

Cos, massacres of Greeks at, i. 234.

Crete, island and pashalik of, i. 5—massacres of Greeks in, 235—repulse of the Egyptian fleet from, ii. 61.

Currency, debasement of, in Turkey, ii. 8.

Customs, administration of, under Capodistrias, ii. 213.

Cyprus, massacres of Greeks in, i. 235.

Cyril, a deposed patriarch, murdered, i. 231.

Danis, Colonel, at Patra, i. 328.

Dawkins, Mr, anecdote of, ii. 225 note—attacks of Maurer on, 331—succeeded by Sir E. Lyons, 335.

Dellyannes, an opponent of Hypsilantes, i. 282—joins the war of the primates, ii. 36—imprisoned, 37.

Demogeronts, the, in the Morea, i. 21.

Dervenaki pass, the, i. 352—defeat of Dramali at, 361.

Dervendji-pasha, the, his duties, &c., i. 24.

Dervenochoria, the, i. 4—its privileges under the Turks, 27—the Revolution in, 195.

Diakos, Athanasios, a leader of the Greeks, and his character, i. 193.

Diamantes, Captain, i. 252.

Dikaios, Gregorios (Pappa Phlessa), his character, &c., i. 175, 176—operations against Dramali, 360, 361, 362—defeat and death of, ii. 74 et seq.

Djavellas, Kitso, defence of Klissova by, ii. 102—heads the final sortie, 107—occupies Patras, 278—arrested, 328.

Djavellas, Photo, a Suliot, joins Ali Pasha, i. 57, 62—defeated near Navarin, ii. 65—saves Mesolonghi, 95.

Djeladeddin Bey, attack by Botsares on, ii. 10 et seq.

Dost, Demir, i. 82—his murder by Ali Pasha, 83.

Dragashan, battle of, i. 162 et seq.

Dragomestre, movement of Church to, ii. 142.

Drakos, a Suliot leader, i. 111.

Dramali, Mohammed, named dervendji, and operations against Ali, i. 95—suppression of the revolt on Mount Pelion by, 247—operations assigned to, in 1822, 342—the expedition of, 342 et seq.—takes Corinth, 351—his plans, 352—want of supplies, and his position, 355—at Argos, 357—retreats, 360—his defeat, 361 et seq.—his death, 364.

Dyovuniotes, submission of, to Reshid, ii. 118.

Dystomo, the Greek camp at, ii. 95—Turks defeated at, 128.

Economos, Antonios, Insurrection of, at Hydra, i. 210 et seq.—his fall, 215 et seq.—his death, 217.

Education, state of, in Greece before the Revolution, i. 18 et seq.—spread of, among the Greeks, as a cause of the Revolution, 119—measures of Capodistrias for, ii. 218—and of the regency, 320.

Egina, the orphan asylum at, ii. 218.

Egribos, the pashalik of, i. 4.

Egyptian troops, discipline maintained by the, ii. 59—contrasted with the Greek, 61.

Eles Aga, voevode in Chios, i. 311.

Ellice, Edward, his connection with the Greek loan, &c., ii. 155.

Elmas Bey, leader of the Albanians in Tripolitza, i. 266, 267—defeated at Arachova, ii. 122.

England, protocol regarding Greece signed, ii. 172—her Continental relations in 1826, ib.—treaty of 6th July 1827, 174—hatred of Capodistrias to, 196—disputes with, 310.

English government, their indignation at the violation of Ionian neutrality, ii. 12.

Epidaurus, the assembly of, i. 293—the constitution of, 293 et seq.—cause of its failure, 295, 296.

Erisso, Turkish ship burned at, i. 219 et seq.

Euboea, operations in, 1822, i. 302 et seq.—campaign in, 1823, ii. 3.

Eugenios succeeds Gregorios as patriarch, i. 222.

Euphrosyne, the history of, i. 74 et seq.

Europe, state of public opinion on Greece in, ii. 3.

European powers, history of their negotiations, &c., regarding Greece, ii. 161 et seq.

Evrenos or Ghazi Gavrinos, privilege held by descendants of, i. 5.

Fabvier, Colonel, attempt on Tripolitza, ii. 61—defeated at Khaidari, 117—attempts to relieve Athens, 118, 121—succours Athens and enters the Acropolis, 124—surrenders the Acropolis, 152—failure at Chios, 187—neglect of, by Capodistrias, 201—his resignation, 205.

Fauvel, M., efforts of, to save the Turks at Athens, i. 342.

Fellows, Sir Thomas, ii. 182.

Finances, the Turkish, their disordered state, i. 130—in 1823, ii. 6—their organisation by Capodistrias, 213—their maladministration, 266—under the regency, 308.

Fire-ships, first employment of, by the Greeks, i. 218 et seq.—useless expenditure on, ii. 13—failures of, at Budrun, 56—and at Mytilene, &c., 61.

Fleets, operations of the, in 1822, i. 365, 366—comparison between them, 372—the Turkish, 1823, ii. 14—the Greek, 15—operations of the, during siege of Messolonghi, 97.

France, her invasion of Spain in 1822, ii. 163—a party to the treaty of 6th July 1827, 174—joins England against Russia on the Greek question, 223.

Franz, Dr, ii. 327 et seq.

French, the, intrigues of Ali with, i. 57—occupy the Morea, ii. 192—public works, &c., by the troops, 193—garrison Nauplia, 269—attack on them at Argos, 285 et seq.

Fustinello, the, the costume of the Tosks, i. 48.

Galata, massacre of Turkish merchants, &c., at, i. 146.

Galaxidhi, a commercial town, i. 205, and note—the destruction of, by the Turks, 272.

Galloway, Mr, the contractor for the Greek steamers, ii. 156.

Gardhiki, alliance between, and Khormovo, i. 51—its destruction by Ali Pasha, 52.

Gatsos, a leader of the revolt at Niausta, i. 254, 255—apostacy of his wife, 256.

Gazes, Anthimos, heads the revolt on Mount Pelion, i. 245, 246.

Gennadios, Professor, anecdote of, ii. 100 note.

Gennatas, a favourite of Capodistrias, ii. 213, 218.

Georgaki, a Vallachian leader, and his character, i. 150—troops under him, 155—notices of him, 157—arrests Vladimiresko, 160—his conduct at Dragashan, 162, 163—his continued resistance and death, 168 et seq.

Gerard, Colonel, ii. 203—on the sack of Poros, 241—dismissed, 250.

Germanos, bishop of Patras, a leader of the Morcot Hetairists, i. 174, 178—forgery of letter by him, 179—heads the insurgents, 186—intrigues against Kolokotrones, 276—opposes Hypsilantes, 289—his pretensions, 292.

Ghiones, Ghika, a Hydriot, i. 210.

Glarakes, sent to command in Chios, i. 310.

Gogos, an Albanian chief, i. 324—his treachery, 325 et seq.—betrays Botsarus, 327—his conduct at Petta, 328 et seq.—openly joins the Turks, 331.

Gordon, General, on the Hetairia, i. 125—his account of the movement in the Priachalities, 147 note—his opinion of Panourias, 190—on the cruelties of the Greeks, 237—on the massacre of Tripolitza, 269—character of Hastings by, 319 note—on the Chios massacre, ib.—on the abuse of the Greek loan, ii. 27—on the conduct of the leaders during the siege of Mesolonghi, 101 note—his character and influence, 129—operations for relief of Athens, 131—repulse of Reshid, 132—resigns in consequence of the massacre of St Spiridion, 147—his expedition against the brigands, 353 et seq.—his danger during it, 356—on the state of the country, 361.

Goss, Dr, of Geneva, ii. 128.

Gouras, peculations of, ii. 43—Odysseus surrenders to, 82 et seq.—murders him, 94—commands at Dystomo, 95—his exactions, &c., in Attica, 115—besieged in Athens, 116—his death, 118—death of his widow, ib. note.

Gouzi, Pylio, a Suliot chief, treason of, i. 81.

Governing commission, the first, its proceedings, ii. 219—new, 261, 263.

Grain, compulsory supplies of, to Constantinople, i. 140.

Gravia, Odysseus defeated at, i. 372.

Great Britain, conduct of the government toward Greece, ii. 161—recognises the revolted Spanish colonies, 163—negotiations at Constantinople, ib.—reply to Greek memorial, 167—complaints by Turkey of her conduct, 168—wavering policy after Canning's death, 189—views and policy, 1829, 222 et seq.

Greece, interest of, i. 1—its population, Othoman divisions of, 3 et seq.—distribution, numbers, &c., of the Albanian race in, 34 et seq.—causes of the Revolution, 118 et seq.—see Greek Revolution—benefits conferred by Roman law, 129—Turkish population on the outbreak of the Revolution, 171—want of preparation on both sides, ib. et seq.—attempt to defer the outbreak, 177—first rising, 180—spread of the Revolution to continental, 195—the islands, and outbreak of the Revolution in them, 204 et seq.—continental organisation of, in 1821, 283 et seq.—demand for a central government, 292—national assembly convoked, 293—expedition of Marcocordatos to Western, 321—his operations there, 322 et seq.—successes of 1822, and their result, ii. 1, 2—views in Europe on the struggle, 2 et seq.—negligence of government, 1823, 7—the first civil war, 23 et seq.—preparations in Egypt against, 28—the government in 1824, 29—its members, &c., 30—general anarchy in 1826, 126—suffering in 1827, 158—relief from America, 159—views of the powers at the Congress of Verona, 162 et seq.—places herself under protection of England, 170—the Russian memoir of 1823, 161 et seq.—treaty between the three powers, 174—state in 1827, ib. et seq.—termination of hostilities, 207—nomination of Prince Leopold as king, and his subsequent resignation, 221, 224 et seq.—presidency of Capodistrias, 185 et seq.—assassination of Capodistrias, and its effect, 248—the governing commission, 249 et seq.—Agostino Capodistrias president, 254 et seq.—Sir S. Canning's memorandum, 256—Agostino ejected, and new governing commission, 261 et seq.—state of the country, 262—general anarchy, 266 et seq.—civil war renewed, 272—national assembly of Pronis, 274 et seq.—its dissolution, 276—intrigues of the senate, 279 et seq.—increasing anarchy in 1832, 285—treaty recognising its independence, 287—Otho recognised as king, ib.—treaty with Bavaria, 288—landing of Otho, ib. 290—the Bavarian regency, 294—first administrative measures, 301—military organisation, 302—civil administration, 305—municipal institutions, 306—finances, 308—monetary system, 312—judicial organisation, ib.—the church, 314—monasteries, 319—public instruction, 320—state, &c., of the press, 321—neglect of roads, 322—Order of the Redeemer, 323—quarrels in the regency, 324 et seq.—Kolokotrones's plot, 326—the Armansperg intrigue, 327—administration of Armansperg, 332 et seq.—general review of the Bavarian administration, 337 et seq.—disputes with England, 340 et seq.—brigandage, 342 et seq., 350 et seq.—insurrection in Maina, 345—in Messenia, 347—brigandage suppressed by Gordon, 353 et seq.—it again breaks out, 362—personal government of Otho, 365—the Revolution of 1843, and its causes, 368 et seq.—the constitution, and ob-

INDEX.

servations on it, 317 et seq.—general review, 320 et seq.
Greek army, contrasted with the Egyptian, ii. 64.
Greek bishops, executions of, at Constantinople, i. 233.
Greek chiefs, submission of, to Reshid, ii. 115.
Greek church, the, its condition, &c., i. 8 et seq.—its head, 9—under the regency, ii. 814.
Greek committees at London, &c., conduct of, ii. 154 et seq.
Greek fleet, the, its first cruise, i. 213—cruise of 1822, 315—its insubordination, &c., 1823, ii. 15—its operations before Mesolonghi, 88.
Greek government, their neglect of preparations on Ibrahim's invasion, ii. 63—their lethargy during siege of Mesolonghi, 92.
Greek Islands, population of, before the Revolution, i. 3.
Greek loans, the, and their misappropriation, ii. 26 et seq.—way in which expended, 33.
Greek orthodoxy and nationality, distinction between, i. 8.
Greek Revolution, the, its causes, i. 118 et seq.—the Turkish system of law, 119—spread of education, ib.—secret societies, 120—the Philiké Hetairia, ib. et seq.—its general causes, 126—aided by the decline of the Turks, 127.
Greek troops, their rapacity, i. 245.
Greeks, numbers of, before the Revolution, i. 2—their position and treatment under the Turkish government, 5 et seq.—effect of the treaty of Kainardji on their condition, 6—their state just before the Revolution, 7—their divided state at the opening of the Revolution, 10—the clergy, 12—the primates, 13—the urban population, 14—the rural, 15—their municipal institutions, 16—education among them, 18—general review of their condition on the eve of the Revolution, 20—the Moreots, 29 et seq.—the Maniots and Tzakonians, 32—the Islanders, 33—decline to support Ali Pasha, 92 et seq.—appeal of the Turks to them, 94—their influence in Turkey, 128—effects of treaty of Kainardji on them, 130—the system of Rorais, 131—its results, and increased hatred between them and the Turks, 132—their representations of Sultan Mahmud, 226—massacres of, 233, 234, 312 et seq.—examples of their cruelty, 236, 237—violations of capitulations, 261, 263—fraudulent division of booty at Navarin, 263—their position after the campaign of 1821, 276—contrast between the peasantry and the troops, 279—opposition to formation of central government, ib.—the primates and military chiefs, 280—revolutionary organisation, 281—broils and disorders among them, 1822, 335—supply the Turks with provisions, ii. 142.

Gregorios, the patriarch, his execution, i. 229—his burial and character, 230 et seq.
Grevens, the bishop of, and Ali Pasha, i. 78.
Grigiottes enters the Acropolis, ii. 119, 124—taken by the French at Argos, 287.
Grivas, Gardikiotes, a leader of irregulars, ii. 352.
Grivas, Theodore, cruelties, &c, of, ii. 264—driven back, 272.
Gropius, M., efforts of, to save the Turks at Athens, i. 348—Austrian consul at Athens, ii. 130.
Guegha, the, a branch of the Albanians, i. 12.
Guehenoue, General, ii. 250.

Halet Effendi, Turkish minister, i. 126—his first measures against the Hetairists, 227—dismissed, 233.
Hamilton, Captain, compels observance of the capitulation of Nauplia, i. 369—at Nauplia, ii. 79—his influence, 138, 139.
Hane, an English volunteer at Nauplia, i. 364, 367.
Harauch, or capitation-tax, the, i. 22.
Harrington, the Earl of, see Stanhope.
Hassan Ghazi, defeat of Albanian brigades by, i. 42.
Hastings, Frank Abney, first notice of, i. 319 and note—defends the Burijee fort, 364, 365—his memoir to the government, ii. 30—his character, 129—succours Gordon at Munychia, 132—success at Oropos, 133—expedition to Gulf of Volo, 139 et seq.—victory of, at Salona, 176—conducts the movement into Acarnania, 185—takes Vasiladi, 186—his death, 188—extracts from his letters, ib. note—his memorandum on the use of steamers, &c., 385.
Heidech, Colonel, ii. 128—expedition to Oropos, and its failure, 133—administration of the customs under, 215—his character, 204 et seq.
Hellas frigate, the, ii. 144, 145—her cost, &c., 157—destroyed at Poros, 210.

INDEX.

Hetairia and Hetairists, see Philiké Hetairia.

Heyden, Count, ii. 182.

Hobhouse, Mr, his connection with the Greek loan, &c., ii. 155.

Holy Alliance, the, their declaration against Greece, ii. 3.

Howe, Dr, on the peculations of the Philhellenes, &c., ii. 154 *note*—his management of the American supplies, 154.

Hospodars, the, their government in Wallachia and Moldavia, i. 132.

Hume, Joseph, and the Greek loan, ii. 155, 156.

Hussein Bey Djeritles, force under, for attack of Kasos, ii. 47—its destruction, 46—at the siege of Navarin, 66—captures Sphakteria, 68—killed at assault of Klissova, 103.

Hydra, the Albanian population of, i. 37—the town, &c., *ib.*—character of the population, 38—the government, &c., *ib.*—under the Turks, taxation, &c., 40—social state, population, &c., 204, 205, 206—the primates resist the Revolution, 209—joins the Revolution, 212—activity at, after the fall of Psara, ii. 52—massacre of Turkish prisoners at, 58, and *note*—resistance of, to Capodistrias, 232, 234—the deputies from, prevented reaching the assembly, 251—they arrive, 257.

Hydriot sailors, their mutinous conduct in 1823, ii. 17—their want of patriotism, 100.

Hydriots, their supremacy in 1821, ii. 30—their conduct in 1827, 157.

Hypatros, a Hetairist, murdered, i. 121, 254.

Hypsilantes, Alexander, becomes head of the Hetairia, his career and character, i. 135 *et seq.*—his expectations from Russia, 139—invades Moldavia, 142—his inefficiency, 143 *et seq.*—present at the massacres at Jassi, 148—tyrannical proceedings, *ib. et seq.*—at Bucharest, 152—his hopes from Russia, 152, 153—general distrust of him, and repudiated by Russia, 155 *et seq.*—his deceitful conduct, 158—arrest and death of Vladimiresko, 159 *et seq.*—battle of Dragashan, 161 *et seq.*—his last acts, and flight, 164—his after fate, 165, 166—distrust of him among the Greeks, 175.

Hypsilantes, Demetrius, his arrogance at Monemvasia, i. 260—at the surrender of Navarin, 262—retires from before Tripolitza, 264—returns after its surrender, 269—loss of his influence and authority, 270—his arrival in Greece, and character, 285—claims supreme authority, 286 *et seq.*—his weakness and errors, 287—intrigues of the Peloponnesian senate against him, 289—convokes a national assembly, 293—deserts the popular cause, 294—authorises invasion of Chios, 307—regiment of regulars formed by, 323 *note*—intrigue of Mavrocordatos against, 341—alliance with Odysseus, &c., *ib.*—patriotism of, during invasion of Dramali, 358—operations against Dramali, 361, 362—at Lerna, ii. 78—appointed to a command by Capodistrias, 201—his inactivity, 204—operations in 1828, 205—a member of governing commission, 264—his death, 274.

Hypsilantes, Nicolas, i. 162.

Hyakos, Andreas, a partisan of Ali's, i. 94.

Iatrakos of Mistra, ii. 71.

Ibrahim Pasha, named Pasha of the Morea, ii. 28—sets sail, 53, 54—junction with the Turkish fleet, 55—battles of Budrun, 56—order maintained by his troops, 59—engagement off Mytilene, 60—driven back from Crete, 61—lands in Greece, 62—defeats the Greeks, 65—captures Sphakteria, 67—and Pylos and Navarin, 70—his fleet defeated at Modon, 72—overruns the Morea, 73—victorious at Maniaki, 75—defeats Kolokotrones, 77—takes Tripolitza, and threatens Nauplia, *ib.*—defeated at Lerna, 78—again defeats Kolokotrones, 80 *et seq.*—further operations and successes, 81—ordered to aid in the siege of Mesolonghi, 82—co-operates in siege of Mesolonghi, 98—successes, 100, 101—repulse at Klissova, 103—capture of Mesolonghi, 108 *et seq.*—returns to the Morea, 112—operations during 1826, 113—devastates the country, and misery caused, *ib. et seq.*—repulsed from Maina, 114—measure of, against Hastings, 177—battle of Navarin, 178 *et seq.*—Greek slaves sent to Egypt by, 183—sufferings of his troops, and desertion of the Albanians, 191—evacuates the Morea, 192.

Ignatius, bishop of Arta, i. 177—circular against the Suliots by, 58—and Ali Pasha, 79.

Ionian Islands, murder of Turks in the, i. 237—violations of neutrality in, 275 *et seq.*, ii. 18—shelter given fugitive Greeks in, 19—proceedings of the government on violation of neutrality,

21—connection of Capodistrias with, 195.
Iskos, Andreas, joins the Turks, i. 335—and again the Greeks, 339—submits to the Turks, ii. 115.
Islanders, the Greek, and their character, &c., i. 32.
Islands, the, statistics, social state, &c., of, i. 201 et seq.—their organisation by Capodistrias, ii. 209—their administration by his brother, 211.
Ismael Gibraltar Pasha, destruction of Galaxidhi by, i. 272—force under, for attack of Kasos, ii. 47—its destruction, 48.
Ismael Pasho Bey, attempt of Ali Pasha against, i. 86—named his successor, 87—his movements against Ali, 91 et seq., 95—captures Previsa, 96—his operations against Joannina, 98 et seq.—his death, 99, 101.
Istira, the, i. 140.
Ithaca, violation of neutrality at, ii. 19.

Janissaries, the, their disaffection in 1823, ii. 5—their destruction, 173.
Joannina, the pashalik of, i. 4, 46—siege of, 96 et seq.—its surrender, 115 et seq.
John of Parga, fire-ships constructed by, i. 219, 220.
Jourdain, Colonel, at Nauplia, i. 364, 365.
Judicial system, the, under the regency, ii. 212.
Justice, Othoman system of, i. 119—administration of, among Greeks and Turks, 129 et seq.—failure of Capodistrias to organise its administration, ii. 218 et seq.

Kainardgi, treaty of, its effect on the condition of the Greeks, i. 5—its effects on Greek population in Turkey, 139.
Kakoubi, defeat of Ali Pasha at, i. 58—captured by him, 61.
Kalamata, capture of, and murder of the Turks, i. 184.
Kalamos, flight of the Acarnanians to, 1822, i. 334.
Kalarites, revolt at, i. 243.
Kalavryta, the insurrection at, and massacre of the Turks, i. 181, 182.
Kalergy, General, wounded and taken at the Phalerum, ii. 151—conducts the Revolution of 1843, 373 et seq.
Kalinkudi, defeat of the Greeks at pass of, ii. 19.
Kanaris, Constantine, destroys the capitan-pasha's ship, i. 316—again destroys a Turkish man-of-war, 370—a supporter of Capodistrias, ii. 235—arrested, 230.
Kara Ali, capitan-bey, cruise of, in 1821, i. 271, 273—return to Constantinople, and promoted, 275—expulsion of the Greeks from Chios, 311—massacres there, 313—efforts to arrest these, 314—destruction of his ship, and his death, 318.
Karaiskaki, feud with Rhangos, i. 335—defeated near Navarin, ii. 66—operations for relief of Messolonghi, 95—fails to co-operate in the sortie from Messolonghi, 108—defeated at Khaïdari, 117—attempts to relieve Athens, 119—victory at Arachova, 122—at the surrender of St Spiridion, 146—his death and character, 148.
Karatasos, a leader of the revolt at Niausta, i. 254, 255—his wife tortured, 255—defeat of, by the Egyptians, ii. 95.
Karavia, massacre of the Turks at Galatz by, i. 146—treachery of, at Dragashan, 162, 163.
Karaylanni, Athanasios, i. 359.
Karitena, repulse of Greeks at, i. 187, 194.
Karpenisi, victory and death of Marco Botzaros at, ii. 10—evacuated by the Turks, 202.
Karteria steamer, the, ii. 132, 133, 139 et seq.
Karystos, besieged by the Greeks, i. 301—check of Turks at, ii. 2.
Kasiotes, naval successes of the, in 1822, i. 372.
Kasos, discontent in, i. 204—population, &c., i. 205 note—its state and prosperity, ii. 46—description of it, 47—its destruction, 48.
Kassandra or Pallene, the peninsula of, i. 248.
Kastri, the Albanians of, i. 40.
Katz-Antoni, cruelty of Ali Pasha toward, i. 22.
Katzaro, captain of body-guard to Mavrocordatos, ii. 18.
Katsiko-Jani, murder of, by Ali Pasha, i. 20.
Khaïdari, defeat of the Greeks at, ii. 116.
Khasikakhoria of the Chalcidici, the, i. 248.
Khormovo, the destruction, &c., of, by Ali Pasha, i. 62.
Khosref Mehemet, capitan-pasha, instructions to, ii. 5—his character, and naval operations in 1823, 14—force under, for attack of Psara, 48, 49—destruction of Psara, 51—junction

with the Egyptian fleet, 55—his cowardice, and battles of Budrun, 58 et seq.—failure at Samos, 60—his cowardice before Mesolonghi, 89—brings supplies to Reshid Pasha, 97.

Khurshid, pasha of the Morea, i. 101 note—appointed to command against Ali Pasha, 101—siege of Joannina, 107 et seq.—outbreak of the Revolution, ib.—his difficulties, and course he followed, 108 et seq.—patriotic course followed by him, 110—captures Litharitza, 112—surrender of Ali Pasha, 115—and his death, 115—repulsed in attempts to penetrate into Acarnania, 203—precautionary measures of, and their effect, 241, 242—suppresses the revolt at Arta, 244—his moderation, ib.—his harem captured at Tripolitza, 269—preparations and plans in Western Greece, 1822, 322—operations assigned to, in 1822, 341—his jealousy of Dramali, 350—operations after the defeat of Dramali, 375—his execution, 377.

Kiamil Bey, murder of, i. 277, 278.
Kiapha captured by Ali Pasha, i. 63—fort built by him, 64.
Klutaybe, see Reshid Pasha.
Kleisura, the pass of, i. 52.
Klephts or brigands, see Brigands—undue laudations of them, ii. 42.
Klisova, repulse of the Turks at, ii. 102.
Klonares, arbitrary proceeding of Capodistrias toward, ii. 214.
Koering, Mr, ii. 128 and note.
Kokoville, Nicolas, i. 210.
Kolandrutzos, a Spetziot captain, i. 263.
Kolettes, John, i. 244—enmity between, and Odysseus, 305—minister-at-war, his character, &c., 345—cowardice and flight of, ii. 8—party formed by, 1824, 31—his position and character, 32—suppresses the war of the primates, 37—during Ibrahim's invasion, 73, 71—force under, for relief of Athens, and his defeat, 121—a member of the governing commission, 248—supports the Romeliots, 252 et seq.—the party of, 257—his influence and position in 1832, 263—a member of new governing commission, 264—party headed by, 263—sent as minister to Paris, 352.
Kolodemo, murder of Lazarus Konduriottes by, i. 32.
Kolokotrones, Gennaios, i. 323, ii. 272—his treachery, i. 328.
Kolokotrones, Panos, ii. 28.
Kolokotrones, Theodore, at the outbreak of the Revolution, i. 182, 183, 184—his exploits as a klepht, 32—sketch of his previous career, 183 et seq.—his conduct at Tripolitza, 265—the citadel surrendered to him, 268—loss of his influence from his conduct there, 270, 275—his failure at Patras, 276—disposed to support Hypsilantes, 268—operations against Dramali, 300 et seq., 363—his conduct at Nauplia, 368—his indifference to the disorders of the troops, ii. 21—the civil war of, 28—his rebellion crushed, 29—joins the war of the primates, 36—imprisoned, 37—made commander-in-chief, 79—defeated near Tripolitza, 77—forces assembled, 79—again defeated, 80 et seq.—his operations during 1826, and military inefficiency, 114—coalition with Konduriottes, 120, 127—proposes election of Capodistrias, 139—tyrannies, &c., of, under Capodistrias, 234—a member of the governing commission, 248—heads the Capodistrians, 271—civil war, ib.—party headed by, 262, 263—his plot against the regency, 326 et seq.—arrested, 328.

Kombotti, repulse of Turks at, i. 325.
Konduriottes, George, named president, ii. 30—his cruelties after the war of the primates, 37—his inefficiency shown on Ibrahim's invasion, 63, 64—his timidity, &c., 73—coalition with Kolokotrones, 120, 127—supports Kolettes, 257—a member of new governing commission, 264.
Konduriottes, Lazarus, a Hydriot, i. 210, ii. 233.
Konduriottes, the family of, and murder of Lazarus, i. 30.
Konlarides, the, a Turkish tribe, i. 213.
Konstantinus Economos, funeral oration on the patriarch by, i. 231 note.
Kontoyannes, submission of, to Reshid, ii. 115.
Koutsonika, a Suliot, treason of, i. 61.
Kranidi, the Albanians of, i. 10.
Kriezes, Admiral, ii. 207, 238.
Krommydi, defeat of the Greeks at, ii. 68.
Kughni, the defence of, by the Suliots, i. 61.
Kurd Pasha, proceedings of, as derwendji-pasha, i. 25.
Kutchuk Hussein, protection of the Hydriots by, i. 39.
Kydonies, the destruction of, ii. 221 et seq.
Kyriakoules, i. 303.

Lalande, Captain, ii. 237 and note.

INDEX. 403

Lalla, the Albanian Mussulmans of, i. 36.
Land-tax retained by Capodistrias, ii. 214.
Larissa, defence of castle of, i. 357, 358.
Laybach congress, the declaration of the sovereigns at, i. 238.
Leake, Colonel, his estimate of population of Greece, i. 8 note—poem on Ali Pasha published by, 78 note—anecdote of Ali by, 78.
Lehrmaier, M., ii. 367, 368.
Lokhonia, massacre of Turks at, i. 216.
Lekkas, Captain, instigates the massacre at Athens, i. 348—his fate, 349.
Leopold, Prince, nominated King of Greece, ii. 221, 224—addresses to him, and intrigues of Capodistrias against him, 225 et seq.—his conduct in first accepting and then resigning, 227 et seq.
Lerna, defeat of Ibrahim at, ii. 78.
Lesuire, General, ii. 352.
Literature, encouragement of, by Ali Pasha, i. 72.
Lithi, atrocities of the Greek sailors at, ii. 15.
Livadea captured by the insurgents, i. 197—massacre of the Turks, 199.
Loans, way in which expended, ii. 38.
London, conduct of Greek committee at, ii. 154 et seq.
Londos, Andreas, a leader of the primates, his character, ii. 35—retires to Acarnania, 37—released, 74—his failure at Tripolitza, 91.
Louis, King of Bavaria, ii. 293, 295.
Lyapides, the, a tribe of the Toaks, i. 44.
Lykourgos, attempt of, to excite revolt in Chios, i. 307 et seq.—his failure and flight, 311 et seq.
Lyons, Captain Sir E., ii. 237 and note—British resident, 335, 336—on the state of Greece in 1830, 360, 361—disputes with, 341.

Macedonia, suppression of the revolt in, i. 248.
Malenkhoria of the Chalcidice, the, i. 243.
Mahmud II., accession of, i. 65—his personal appearance and character, 66 et seq.—state of the empire, 68 et seq.—at first supports Ali Pasha's policy, 80—first measures of, against Ali Pasha, 85—declares him a rebel, 87—his means of attack, and plans, 90 et seq.—measures for the subjugation of Ali, 101—fall of Ali, 115—his preparations in the Principalities, 155—preparations in Greece ordered, 173—his policy with regard to the Revolution, 225—the representations of him by the Greek historians, &c., 226—suppressive measures, 227—executions ordered, 228—that of the patriarch, 229 et seq.—increased severities, and his motives, 232—change of ministry, 233—restores order and arrests the massacres, 235—rupture with Russia, 238—his difficulties, 240—his successes, 256—difficulties overcome by him, 257—precautionary measures at Chios, 307—measures for its recovery, 310 et seq.—preparations in 1822 for reconquest of Greece, 340—his plan, 341—his firmness, ii. 2, 3—his policy, 4—destruction of arsenals, &c., by fire, 5—his plan of campaign, 6—negotiations with Mohammed Ali for aid against the Greeks, 28—reforms in army and navy, 45—his plans and preparations, 46—convention of Akermann, and destruction of the janizaries, 173—the war with Russia in 1828-9, 190—the treaty of Adrianople, 222—recognises independence of Greece, 257.
Mahmud, grandson of Ali Pasha, executed, i. 117.
Maina, under the capitan-pasha, i. 4—Ibrahim repulsed from, ii. 114—resistance of, to Capodistrias, 232, 234—social state of, and proceedings of Capodistrias, 242—the deputies from, prevented reaching the assembly, 251—they arrive, 257—the insurrection of 1834 in, 345.
Maison, General, occupies the Morea, ii. 192.
Makriyannes, Captain, his gallantry at Lerna, ii. 78—during the sortie from Mesolonghi, 107, 108—conveys intelligence of the state of Athens, 124—outrage by brigands on, 351—during the Revolution of 1843, 372.
Makry, Ibrahim's celebration of the Bairam at, ii. 54 et seq.
Makrynoros, repulses of Khurshid at, i. 209.
Makrynoros, passes of, occupied by the Greeks, ii. 207.
Makrys, character of, ii. 41, 42.
Martin, W., defence of Anatolikon by, ii. 13.
Maurer, M. de, his character, ii. 294 et seq.—dismissed from office, 332.
Maniaki, defeat of the Greeks at, ii. 75.
Maniats, the, their character, &c., i. 32—ravage Messenia, &c., ii. 252.
Manioles, Drosos, i. 342.
Mavrocordatos, Alexander, his arrival, and appointed to direction in Western

Greece, i. 290—his measures for organising it, ib. et seq.—communications between the Suliots and, 112, 113 et seq.—military failure of, at Patras, 297—constitution of Epidaurus, 298—president of Greece, 299—his character and position, 300 et seq.—his failure to aid the Chiots, 315—expedition to Western Greece, 321 et seq.—defeat of Petta, 322 et seq.—enters Mesolonghi, 336—his measures for defence, 337—intrigues against Hypsilantes, &c., 314, 315—displaced, ii. 7—his inefficiency, 9—efforts of, to secure just distribution of prize-money, 20—his intercourse with Lord Byron, 24, 25—his position and conduct after Byron's death, 31, 32—his henchmen, 41—during Ibrahim's invasion, 64—measures for defence of Navarin, 67—his escape, 70—his declining influence, 130—supports Kolettes, 258—removed from ministry of finance, 261.

Mavromichales, account of family of, ii. 242 et seq.

Mavromichales, Constantine, arrested, ii. 244—one of the assassins of Capodistrias, 245—slain, 246.

Mavromichales, Elias, death of, i. 302 et seq.

Mavromichales, Elias, or Katzakos, ravages Messenia, ii. 282—arrest and escape of, 244—one of the assassins of Capodistrias, 245.

Mavromichales, George, at the defence of Navarin, ii. 70, 71—defence of Lerna by, 78, ii. 243, 244—his execution, 246.

Mavromichales, Janni, revolts against Capodistrias, ii. 243—arrested, 244.

Mavromichales, Kyriakoules, i. 312—his death, 333—Gordon's character of him, ib.

Mavromichales, Petros—see Petrobey.

Megara, privilege of, under the Turks, i. 37—the Revolution in, 195.

Megaspelaion, monastery of, threatened by Ibrahim, ii. 113 and note.

Mehmet Pasha, cowardice of, in command of the fleet, i. 370—defeated by Kanaris, 371—operations under, 376.

Mehmet Salik, Khurshid's kaimakam in the Morea, i. 173—measures against the Revolution, 178—saves the Greeks of Tripolitza from massacre, 161.

Meletl, Hadji, primate of the Dervenokhoria, i. 194.

Mesolonghi, outbreak of the Revolution at, and massacre of the Turks, i. 201—first siege of, i. 336 et seq.—the assault, and its defeat, 338—the second siege, ii. 83 et seq.—its state and defences, 85—the siege, 86 et seq.—Vasiladi and Anatolikon taken, 101—failure of the fleet, 101—failure of provisions, 105—final sortie, 106—fall of the place, 110 et seq.—numbers who perished, and heroism of the defence, ib.—evacuated by the Turks, 207.

Messenia, state of, in 1832, ii. 281—insurrection of 1834 in, 347.

Metaxas, a member of the governing commission, ii. 261, 271.

Metzovo, the pass of, i. 60.

Miaoulis, Andreas, cruise of fleet under, i. 217, 224—cruise of, in 1821, 273—engages the Turkish fleet, 275—placed at head of fleet, 1823, and his cruise, 315—attempts to control the armatoli in Skiathos, ii. 8—cruise of, 1823, and conduct of the fleet, 15—his danger, 16—declines the command, 18—cruise of, after destruction of Psara, 52—battles of Budrun, 55 et seq.—arrests the Turkish attempt on Samos, 60—success of, at Modon, 72—co-operates in defence of Mesolonghi, 88—throws supplies into it, &c., 97—failure to relieve it, 104—proceedings of, at Poros, 229 et seq.—supports Kolettes, 258.

Military system, the, in the Morea, i. 188.

Miller, Colonel, ii. 169 note.

Mirdite, the, an Albanian tribe, i. 43, ii. 2.

Mistra, flight and massacre of Turks of, i. 186.

Modon, relieved by the Turkish fleet, ii. 14—naval success of the Greeks at, 72—occupied by the French, 192.

Mohammed II., charter to Agrapha from, i. 26.

Mohammed Ali, negotiations with, for aid against the Greeks, ii. 26—plans concerted with, 46—force for attack of Kasos, 47—his preparations, and force sent, 53—unwilling to continue the war in 1826, 114—convention for evacuation of Morea, 188.

Mohammed Pasha, assassination of Ali Pasha by, i. 110.

Moharrem Bey at the battle of Navarin, ii. 182.

Moldavia, position, &c., of the Greeks in, i. 11—oppressive government of the hospodars of, 130—see Principalities—invaded by Hypsilantes, 142—military operations in, 166.

Monasteries and monks of Mount Athos, the, i. 240—reorganised under the regency, ii. 319.

Monemvasia, surrender of, to the Greeks, i. 260—the capitulation violated, 261.
Monetary system, the regency's, ii. 312.
Morea, the pashalik of the, i. 3—and the Moreots, social condition of, before the Revolution, 29 et seq.—precautions of the Turks in, 173—the Hetairists there, 174—attempts to defer the outbreak, 177—the insurrection general, 182—the military system in, 188—successes of the Greeks, 195—the primates of, their party in 1824, ii. 30, 31—progress of Ibrahim Pasha, 73—devastated by Ibrahim, 113—convention for its evacuation, 188—its organisation by Capodistrias, 209—invaded by the Romeliots, 258.
Morning Chronicle, its attack on King Otho, ii. 367.
Muhurdar Besiari, an Albanian leader, i. 100, 106, 111.
Mukhtar Bey, grandfather of Ali Pasha i. 71.
Mukhtar Pasha, his intrigue with Euphrosyne, and its results, i. 71 et seq., 77 note—pasha of Berat, 89—deserts his father, 97—execution of, 117.
Muleteers, importance of the, in Greece, i. 23.
Municipal institutions of Greece, the, i. 16 et seq.—revived in the Morea, ii. 230 et seq.—not understood, 284—organisation of, under the regency, 308.
Municipal system, enmity of Capodistrias to, ii. 209.
Munychia, repulse of the Turks at, ii. 132.
Murusi, dragoman of the Porte, executed, i. 228.
Murzinos, an insurgent chief, i. 184.
Mustai Pasha of Skodra, i. 88—measures of, against Ali Pasha, 89—operations assigned to, 1823, ii. 5—operations under, 9—check at Karpenisi, 10 et seq.—his continued advance, 12—joins Omer Vrioni, 13—siege of Anatolikon, 13.
Mustapha IV., death of, i. 66.
Mustaphe Bey, defeated at Arachova, ii. 122.
Mustapha, bey of Patras, treacherous murder of, i. 271.
Mustoxidi, a favourite of Capodistrias, ii. 213.
Mytilene, naval action off, ii. 60.

Napier, Sir Charles, memorandum by, on military operations in the Morea, ii. 390.
National assembly, convocation of, i. 293

—of Argos, ii. 220—the second, at Argos, 250 et seq.—of Trœzene, proceedings of, 153—Capodistrias elected by it, 195—of Pronia, its meeting and proceedings, 271 et seq.—rising of the military against it, 276.
Naupaktos capitulates to the Greeks, ii. 207.
Nauplia, capitulation of, to the Greeks, i. 353—their conduct, 354—continued operations against, 304—naval engagement off, 365—its surrender, 368—aspect of, in 1824, ii. 39—threatened by Ibrahim, 77—garrisoned by the French, 269—landing of Otho at, 280 et seq.
Navarin, surrender of, to the Greeks, and violation of the capitulation, i. 262—the Greeks defeated in attempting to relieve it, ii. 65—besieged by Ibrahim, 67—capitulates, 70—battle of, 178 et seq.—occupied by the French, 192.
Navy, abuses and peculations in connection with it, ii. 138.
Naxos, massacre of Turks at, i. 236.
Nea-Mone, storming, &c., of monastery of, i. 313.
Negris, Theodore, organisation of Eastern Greece, i. 290, 291, 292—his share in constitution of Epidaurus, 298—as minister, 345—plunder and fate of his library, 356.
Neroulos, Rhizos, i. 143, 144 note.
New York, conduct of the Philhellenes at, ii. 158.
Niausta, massacre of Turks at, i. 254—sacked by the Turks, 255.
Nicholas, the czar, his accession and policy, ii. 171—his views, and declares war with Turkey, 182.
Niketas, at the outbreak of the Revolution, i. 182, 181—forces under, 1822, 342—operations of, 343—operations against Dramali, 360, 361, 362—enforces observance of the capitulation of the Acrocorinth, ii. 21—retires to Acarnania, 37—defence of Messenia by, 282, 283.
Nivitsa, capture of, by Ali Pasha, i. 57.
Normann, General, i. 325—defeated at Peita, 326 et seq.
Notaras, Panayotaki, joins the war of the primates, ii. 36—his cowardice, 131, 132.
Nourka, treachery of, at Vrachori, i. 202.
Noutzas, Alexander, murdered by Odysseus, i. 340.

Odysseus, a partisan of Ali's, i. 91, 95—conduct of, in Eubœa, 304—his trea-

amiable conduct and character, 305—
forces under, 1842, 342—quarrel with
the Areopagus, 343—murder of Noutzas and Palaskas, 346—becomes governor of Athens, 374—cruelties, 375
—treacherous negotiations, 376—victory of, at Karystos, ii. 9—the treason
of, 22 *et seq.*—murdered, 24.
Omer Vrioni, a partisan of Ali's, i. 89—
deserts him, 96—defeat of the Greeks
at Stura by, 303 *et seq.*—army under,
1822, 322—victory of, at Splanga,
335—terms granted the Suliots, *ib.*—
submission of various leaders to, 335
—joins Reshid Pasha, 336—at the
siege of Mesolonghi, 357—defeat of
the assault, and his retreat, 358—
operations assigned to, in 1822, 347—
operations assigned to, 1823, ii. 8—
joined by Mustai Pasha, 13.
Oropos, failure of Hebleck at, ii. 133.
Orphan asylum, an, built by Capodistrias,
ii. 218.
Otho, King, his election ratified by assembly of Pronia, ii. 275—his landing,
283 *et seq.*, 290 *et seq.*—the regency,
294 *et seq.*—his marriage, 335, 358—
his system of government, 340—his
personal government, 363—the affair
of the certificate, and dispute with
Lyons, 366—his misgovernment, 368
—the Revolution of 1843, 372 *et seq.*
Ottoman empire, state of the, in 1820,
and the policy of Sultan Mahmud, i.
65 *et seq.*—the system of administration, 68—its apparent approaching
fall, 69—disorder in its finances, 130.
Ottoman government, administration of
justice under, i. 112.

Palamedes fort at Nauplia, the, i. 362.
Palaska, a Suliot, i. 63.
Palaskas, Christos, murdered by Odys-
seus, i. 346.
Palmerston, Lord, supports Armansperg,
ii. 334.
Panourias heads the Revolution at Sa-
lona, i. 196.
Papadiamantopulos, heroic death of, ii.
111.
Papas, Emmanuel, leader of the revolt
of the Chalcidice, i. 252.
Pappanikolo, Turkish ship burned by, i.
210.
Pasano appointed to succeed Hastings,
and his cowardice, ii. 208.
Pasture lands, attempted seizure of,
under the regency, ii. 310.
Patradjik, repulse of Greeks at, i. 312.
Patras, outbreak at, i. 186—repulse of
the Greeks at, 187—failure of the
Greeks at, 276—failure of Mavrocordatos at, 297—captured by the Capodistrians, ii. 269.
Patriarch of Constantinople, position
and power of the, i. 9—his official
influence, 128—anathema of Hypsilantes by, 156, 227—his execution,
229.
Peasantry of Albania, the, i. 45.
Peculation, examples of, in army and
navy, ii. 42 *et seq.*
Pehlavan Baba, operations of, against
Ali, i. 95—degraded and executed,
101.
Pelion, Mount, revolt in, and its suppression, i. 245 *et seq.*
Peloponnesian senate, the, its formation,
&c., i. 255—intrigues against Hypsilantes, 283—reconstituted, and its
proceedings, 294 *et seq.*
Pentapegadhia, contests at the pass of,
i. 111.
Pentornea, the Greeks defeated at, ii.
24.
Pergamus, massacres of Greeks at, ii. 16.
Pestilence, ravages of, after the fall of
Tripolitza, i. 270.
Petra, capitulation of the Turks at, ii.
203.
Petrobey of Maina (Petros Mavromichales), a leader of the insurrection,
i. 182—his character, &c., 183—his
proceedings, 184—commands before
Tripolitza, 265—disposed to support
Hypsilantes, 288—during the invasion
of Dramali, 358—Capodistrias jealous
of him, and measures against him, ii.
242 *et seq.*—arrested, 244.
Petta, the Greek position at, i. 325—
their defeat there, 326 *et seq.*—its
effects, 331.
Pauloickas assumes government of
Moldavia, i. 166.
Phalerum, battle of the, ii. 159 *et seq.*
Phanariots, the, use made of, by the
Turkish government, i. 126.
Pharmaki, an associate of Georgaki's, i.
168—his death, 169.
Pharmaki, Ali, and Kolokotrones, i. 101.
Pharmaki, Captain, attacked by brigands,
ii. 351.
Philhellenes, the corps of, i. 323—at
Petta, 328 *et seq.*—destroyed there,
331—conduct of the, ii. 164.
Philhellenic committees, their activity
in 1826, ii. 128.
Philiké Hetairia, the, its failure in Epirus,
i. 97—its objects, 120—first members,
and organisation, 121—its schemes,
&c., 122—treacheries of members, 124
—distrusted by the Greeks, 134—

INDEX. 407

Alexander Hypsilantes named its head, 135—history of the attempt in the principalities, 143 et seq.—its progress in the Morea, 173, 174—proceedings, &c., of its agents there, 176—urge the massacre of the Turks, 188—executions of members at Constantinople, 228.
Philip of Macedon, parallel between, and Khurshid, i. 109.
Philomuse society, the, i. 120.
Philemus, Pappa, see Dikaios.
Phocis, ravaged by the Turks, ii. 8.
Phonia, murders of Turks at, i. 180.
Phrantzes, account of the massacre at Navarin by, i. 203—account of an alleged miracle by, ii. 113 note.
Piada, removal of the national assembly to, i. 283.
Pinotzi, a Hydriot captain, i. 214—cruise of fleet under, ii. 18.
Piræus, exploit of Cochrane at, ii. 144.
Plaputza, Kolias, ii. 348—a member of the governing commission, 264, 271—arrested, 328.
Poliani, the Greeks defeated at, ii. 77.
Polyzheros, revolt at, i. 251.
Polyzoides, establishment of the *Apollo* by, ii. 211.
Pontropoulos, Nikolas, at the surrender and massacre of Navarin, i. 202.
Popoff, Aristides, a Hetairist, executed, i. 124.
Population, decrease of, in Albania, i. 45—its decline in European Turkey, 48.
Poros, the Albanians of, i. 40—the affair of, ii. 285—destruction of the fleet at, 286—sack of the town, 240 et seq.
Porro, Count, ii. 128.
Portaia or Trikkala, the pass of, i. 90.
Portugal, the interference of England in, ii. 172.
Prapas, Captain, outrage by brigands on, ii. 351.
Premeti, Ibrahim, i. 243, 244.
Press, the, tyranny of Capodistrias toward, ii. 231—measures of the regency regarding, 322.
Primates of Greece, the, i. 19—of the Morea, the, 29—their selfish conduct in 1821, 250, 284—the war of, and its suppression, ii. 31.
Principalities, the, their government and state before the Revolution, i. 139 et seq.—the native race, 141 et seq.
Prize money, fraudulent appropriations of, i. 214, ii. 20.
Proesti, the, in the Morea, i. 20, 31.
Psara, discontent in, i. 204—population, &c., 205 note, 206—joins the Revolu-

tion, 209—description of it, and character of the population, ii. 10—attack on Samos, and want of preparations, 50—its destruction, 51 et seq.
Psarian sailors, adventures and escape of, ii. 10.
Psariana, naval operations of the, 1822, i. 372—their naval successes in 1823, ii. 14.
Pylos, besieged by Ibrahim, ii. 65—its surrender, 70.

Raikoff, Lieutenant, expels the Romeliots from Argos, ii. 255.
Ralli, attempt of, to excite revolt in Chios, i. 207.
Raybaud, Colonel, account of the massacres at Tripolitza by, i. 268.
Redeemer, Order of the, ii. 323.
Redoruni, defeat of George Botsares at, i. 58.
Regency, the Bavarian, its members and history, ii. 294—its duties, 298—proclamation, 299, 300—administrative measures, 301—military organisation, 302—civil administration, 305—municipal institutions, 306—finances, 308—monetary system, 312—judicial organisation, 313—the church, 314—monasteries, 319—education, 320—measures regarding the press, 321—neglect of roads, 322—Order of the Redeemer, 323—quarrels in, 324 et seq.—Kolokotrones's plot, 326—the Armansperg intrigue, 327—broken up, 332—general review of its administration, 337 et seq.
Rendina, the Agraphiots defeated at, i. 243.
Reshid Pasha (Kiutayhe), victory of, at Petta, i. 329 et seq.—subsequent movements, 334—joined by Omer Vrioni, and first siege of Mesolonghi, 335 et seq.—suppression of the revolt on Mount Pelion, ii. 7—his invasion of Western Greece, 84—the siege of Mesoloughi, 85 et seq.—his forces, ib.—arrival of fleet, and assaults, 87—his difficulties, 89—construction of the mound, 90—its destruction, 91—fortifies his camp, 96—receives supplies from the fleet, 97—Ibrahim co-operates with him, 98—cruelties, 99—capture of Mesolonghi, 108 et seq.—his operations during 1826, 114 et seq.—victory at Khaidari, 116—siege of Athens, 117—successes, 118—repulse at Munychia, 132—on the massacre of St Spiridion, 147—victory at the Phalerum, 150—capitulation of the Acropolis, 152—his honourable conduct,

and further successes, 153—operations against him in 1828, 205—made grand vizier, 207.

Residents, the, their feeble conduct, ii. 239—compel Agostino's resignation, 240.

Rhangos, a leader of armatoli, i. 241—deserts to the Turks, 335—and again to the Greeks, 339—submission of, to Itembid, ii. 115.

Rhion, captured by the French, ii. 192.

Rhodes, massacres of Greeks at, i. 234.

Rhodios, secretary of state, made colonel of the regulars, ii. 39, 40—during Ibrahim's invasion, 73, 74—minister at war, 241.

Ricardo, Messrs, contractors for the second Greek loan, ii. 155.

Ricord, Admiral, proceedings of, at Poros, ii. 238 et seq.—his conduct during the sack, 241—urges the release of Petrobey, 245—supports the Capodistrians, 250, 254—intrigues of, 277.

Roads, neglect of, under the Bavarians, ii. 323.

Roman law, benefits conferred on Greece by, i. 129.

Romeliot armatoli, their party in 1824, ii. 31—at Psara, 49, 51.

Romeliots, the, their condition, i. 22 et seq.—oppose the Capodistrians, ii. 252 et seq.—expelled from Argos, 255—they invade the Morea, 257—their exactions in the Morea, 266—outrage on the national assembly by them, 275.

Romey, Colonel, ii. 67.

Rouen, Baron, French resident, ii. 246, 256.

Rouman race, the, in the Principalities, i. 141—their hatred of the Greeks, 142.

Routsos, a Mesolonghian, treachery of, ii. 86—beheaded, 87.

Rückmann, Baron, ii. 245, 256.

Rudhart, M., his administration, ii. 336—his character, &c., ib.—dismissed, 337.

Rural population, the, in Greece, i. 15.

Ross, Dr, ii. 159 note.

Russia, complicity of, in the schemes of the Hetairists, i. 123—hostile position of, and Turkey before the Revolution, 137 et seq.—rupture between Turkey and, 237 et seq.—the expectations of the Greeks from, ii. 160—her conduct, 161—protocol regarding Greece signed, 172—treaty of 6th July 1827, 174—connection of Capodistrias with, 195, 196, 197—views and policy, 1829, 229 et seq.

Russian memoir of 1828 on the Greek question, ii. 161 et seq.—its effect 166.

Sacred battalion, the, in Vallachia, i. 153 —destroyed at Dragashan, 162, 163.

Sachturi, a Hydriot captain, i. 214—governor of Navarin during the siege, ii. 67—deserts his duty, 70.

Salih, son of Ali of Joannina, executed, i. 117.

Salih Pasha becomes grand vizier, i. 233.

Salona, the Revolution in, i. 195—massacre of the Turks, 197—occupied by the Turks, ii. 94—victory of Hastings at, 176—capitulates to the Greeks, 205.

Saloniki, massacres of Greeks, i. 234.

Salt, a government monopoly under the regency, ii. 303.

Samos joins the Revolution, i. 217—administration of Lykourgos in, 312—attack by the Psarians on it, ii. 50—intended attack by the Turks on, 53 —failure of the Turkish attempt on, 60.

Samothrace, massacre by the Turks at, i. 236.

Samuel, the leader of the Suliots, i. 60 —his defence against Ali, 61—his death, 62.

Santa Rosa, Count, his career and death, ii. 62.

Saphaka, a Greek leader, defeated, ii. 64.

Savas, a Vallachian leader, i. 150—his character, 151—troops under him, 153 —intrigues, 154, 155, 156 et seq.—joins the Turks, 161—beheaded by the Turks, 166.

Schmats, General, suppresses insurrection in Messenia, ii. 349.

Sclavonian races under Turkish rule, numbers of, i. 8.

Secret societies, influence of, in Greece, i. 120.

Seid Ali, attempt to murder, i. 181.

Seko, monastery of, its siege and capture, i. 168 et seq.

Selanik or Thessalonica, the pashalik of, i. 8.

Seliktar Poda, an Albanian leader, i. 100.

Selim III., the attempted reform and fall of, i. 65.

Selim Pasha refuses to sign the capitulation of Nauplia, i. 362.

Senate, its formation, powers, &c., ii. 220.

Sessini of Gastouni, a leading primate, ii. 35—anecdote of him, 36 note—imprisoned, 37—dismissed from office, 234.

Sheik-ól-Islam, murder of the, i. 214.
Shkipetar, the, the native name of the Albanians, i. 41.
Siphekas, submission of, to Reshid, ii. 115.
Skaltzodemos, a klepht, i. 128.
Skiathos, atrocities of the armatoli in, ii. 7.
Skodra, pashalik of, i. 46.
Skopelos, atrocities of the armatoli in, ii. 7.
Skourta, Turkish convoy taken at, ii. 117.
Skourti appointed lieutenant-general of the Greeks, ii. 64—defeated, 65.
Skuleni, the affair of, i. 167.
Smyrna, disorders at, and massacres of Greeks, i. 234—naval engagement off, 216.
Soliotes, an insurgent leader, i. 180.
Soutzos, Alexander, hospodar of Vallachia, his death, i. 115 and note.
Soutzos, John, eparch of Venetico, ii. 31.
Soutzos, Michael, hospodar of Moldavia, i. 143, 144—his weakness, &c., 147—deposed, and flies to Russia, 168.
Spain, the suppression of constitutionalism in, ii. 143.
Speliades on the state of Greece in 1822, i. 344.
Spezzas, the Albanian population of, &c., i. 40—state of, 204—population, &c., 205 note—the Revolution proclaimed at, 208—activity at, after the fall of Psara, ii. 52.
Spezziots, conduct of the, 1823, ii. 17.
Sphakia, the district of, in Crete, i. 5.
Sphakteria captured by the Egyptians, ii. 67 et seq.
Spiridion, the monastery of, defended by the Turks, ii. 115—its capitulation, and massacre of the garrison, 147.
Splangs, defeat of the Greeks at, i. 333.
Stalkos, broil between, and Vlachopulos, i. 335, ii. 31.
Stamatopoulos, Nikolas, i. 357.
Stamati Gatzu, captain of armatoli, i. 213.
Stanhope, Colonel Leicester (the Earl of Harrington), ii. 25, 26—ordered home, 168, 169.
Stemmers, Captain Hastings's memorandum on the use of, ii. 335.
Stelida, repulse of Greeks at, i. 342.
Stengel, Baron, ii. 367, 368.
Stournari, a partisan of Ali's, i. 91.
Strogonoff, the Baron, Russian ambassador to Turkey, i. 238.
Stura, defeat of the Greeks at, i. 303.
Sturnari, Nicolas, heads the revolt in the valley of the Aspropotamos, i. 244.
Stuyvesant, Mr, ii. 159 note.
Suleiman Pasha of Larissa, named dervendji in room of Ali, i. 93—degraded and executed, 94—proceedings of, as dervendji-pasha, 25.
Suliots, the, their origin and country, i. 51—acquire the right of bearing arms, 53—social state, &c., of the country, 54—Ali Pasha's operations against them, 55 et seq.—his second attack on them, and treachery of the chiefs, 57 et seq.—their conquest and fate, 62 et seq.—serve against Ali on his rebellion, 98—they join him, 100—their military system, &c., 102 et seq.—they join the Greeks, 110, 111—measures of the Greeks for aiding them, 1822, 322 et seq.—their capitulation to Omer Vrioni, 333—their removal to the Ionian Islands, 334.
Sulu Proshova, a Mussulman klepht, i. 28.
Synodal Tomos of 1850, the, ii. 318.
Syra joins Hydra against Capodistrias, ii. 235.
Syrako, revolt at, i. 243.

Tahir, capitan-pasha, at the battle of Navarin, ii. 182.
Talanti, massacre of Turks at, i. 199—Greeks defeated at, ii. 121.
Tarella, Colonel, i. 322—slain at Peita, 331 and note.
Taxation, the Turkish system of, in Greece, i. 14.
Tchamides, the, a Toak tribe, i. 43.
Tchanderlik destroyed by the Psarians, ii. 14.
Tebellu, the birthplace of Ali Pasha, i. 70.
Te Deum, the first Greek, i. 181.
Tennant, Sir J. E., account of massacre of Turkish prisoners, by, ii. 58 note.
Targovisht, skirmish at, i. 161.
Thanasopulos, cruelties of bands of, ii. 266.
Theodorides, Achilles, abandonment of the Acrocorinth by, i. 351.
Thessalo-Magnesian senate, the, i. 246.
Thessalonica or Selanik, the pashalik of, i. 5.
Thiersch, Professor, ii. 271 note—his character, &c., 259.
Thomas, Captain, ii. 176, 177.
Three powers, treaty between the, regarding Greece, ii. 174—their discordant views, 189—proceedings, protocols, &c., in 1829, 221 et seq.
Tombasse, Jakomaki, commands the

Greek fleet, and his character, L 212
—second cruise, 217—Turkish ship
burned, 218 et seq.—his inefficiency,
220—Mydonians saved by him, 223—
attempts to excite insurrection at
Chios, 306.
Tophana, destruction of the Turkish
arsenals at, ii. 5.
Toshides, the, a tribe of the Tosks,
i. 43.
Tosks, the, a branch of the Albanians,
L 43—their costume, 48.
Trakedha, a brigand, ii. 363, 384.
Treason, examples of, among the Greek
chiefs, ii. 93.
Trichari, a commercial town, L 205
and note—suppression of the revolt
in, 217—subdued by the Turks, ii. 7.
Tricoupi on the Hetairia, L 125—correction of his history, 180—on the numbers massacred at Chios, 319 note—
neglect of Santa Rosa by, ii. 69
note—his character and influence, 130.
Trikkala or Portaia, the pass of, i. 90.
Trikorphas, Greeks defeated at, ii. 80—
surprise it, but again driven out, 81.
Tripolitza, blockaded by the Greeks, L
259, 260—conduct of the Greek
leaders before, and its surrender, 264
et seq.—general massacre, 267—epidemic in, 293—taken by Ibrahim, ii.
77—attempt of Fabvier on, 81.
Trœzene, meeting of national assembly
of, ii. 138—organisation and review
of the army at, 202 et seq.
Tsamadou, Demetrios, i. 210—aids in
defence of Navarin, ii. 67—his death
and character, 68.
Turkey, decline of population in, L 68—
effects of treaty of Kainardgi on
Greek population in, 130—relations
between, and Russia before the Revolution, 137 et seq.—rupture with Russia, 237 et seq.—complaints against
England, ii. 148 et seq.—the war of
1828 with Russia, 180.
Turkish fleet, the, its first cruise, 217
et seq.—line-of-battle ship burned,
220—cruises of, in 1821, 271—Galaxidhi destroyed, 272—defeated near
Smyrna, 319—its arrival at Mesolonghi, ii. 87—retreats, 88.
Turkish government, sketch of the position of the Greeks under the, L 5.
Turkish prisoners, massacre of, at Hydra,
ii. 58 note.
Turks, moral and physical decline of
the, L 127—their depressed state,
128—administration of justice among,
130—hatred between them and the
Greeks, 132—number of, in Greece

before the Revolution, 172—their
want of preparation, ib. 173—first
murders, 180—examples of their
cruelty, 236—massacre of, at Galata,
146—at Yassi, 147—massacres of, 180,
181, 182, 184, 186, 187, 197, 199, 200,
201, 203, 214, 240, 251, 254, 261, 263,
267, 269, 277, 313.
Tzakonians, the, their character, &c.,
L 32.
Tzellos, Demo, ii. 352.
Tzonga, a leader of armatoli, L 202, 203.

Urban population, the, in Greece, L 14.
Urquhart, Lieut., Hydriot corps under,
ii. 144.

Vaïsa, Anastasios, massacre of the Gardhikiots by, L 83.
Valiare, massacre of the Gardhikiots at,
L 82—inscription commemorating it,
84.
Vallachia, position, &c., of the Greeks
in, L 11—oppressive government of
the hospodars of, 139—see Principalities—progress of the movement in,
155.
Vallachian or Roman race, numbers of
the, i. 3.
Valtetzi, victory of the Greeks at, L 252.
Valtinos, George, joins the Turks, i.
335—and again the Greeks, 132.
Vamhas, Neophytos, his character, L
213.
Variadhes, how recovered by the Suliots,
L 105.
Varnakiotes, a partisan of Ali's, L 94—
a leader of armatoli, 202, 203—a
leader at Petta, 327—deserts to the
Turks, 335—flies to Kalamo, 330.
Vasiladi, fort, taken by the Turks, ii.
101—captured by Hastings, 126.
Vasiliké, an Athenian slave, L 4.
Vasos, a Montenegrin leader, L 302.
Vamos, cowardice of, before Athens, ii.
131, 132.
Vehid Pasha, defensive measures at
Chios, L 308 et seq.
Veli, father of Ali Pasha, L 71.
Veli Pasha, son of Ali, L 62—removed
from the Morea to Larissa, 85—and
thence to Lepanto, 86—defence of
Previsa intrusted to, 90—flight of,
from Lepanto, 95—gives up Previsa,
96—his death, ib., 117.
Vlachopulos, broil between, and Stailas,
L 335, ii. 33—excess of rations
drawn by, 43—during the Revolution of 1813, 373.
Vladimiresko, Theodore, L 150—his
character, 151—troops under him,

154—intrigues, ib., 156—his views, 158—his murder, 159 et seq.
Volo, blockaded by the Greeks, and relieved, i. 247—expedition of Hastings to, ii. 110.
Vonitza, captured by the Greeks, ii. 202.
Vostitza, meeting of Hetairists at, i. 176.
Vrachori, attacked and taken by the Greeks, i. 201 et seq.

Washington, contrast between, and Hypsilantes, i. 289.
Wibmer, Dr, ii. 307, 308.
Wrede, Prince, envoy to Prince Leopold, ii. 229.

Yanko, Nicholas, treachery of Ali Pasha to, i. 75.
Yasi, massacre of Turks at, i. 117.
Yusuf, Mutm, great-grandfather of Ali Pasha, i. 71.
Yusuf Berkoftzales, operations assigned to, ii. 6—ravages Phocis, &c., 7, 8.

Yusuf Bey, measures of, to suppress the revolt in the Chalcidice, i. 251—superseded, 252—plan proposed to Dramali by, 352.

Zacharias, a Morrot klepht, i. 32.
Zagora, revolt in, i. 216 et seq.
Zaimes, Andreas, intrigues of, against Kolokotrones, i. 276—heads the war of the primates, and his character, ii. 34—flies, 37—released, 74—a member of new governing commission, 201.
Zaimes, Asimaki, i. 181.
Zante, violation of neutrality at, i. 272.
Zapandir, massacre of Turks of, i. 203.
Zaphiraki, primate of Niausta, i. 254—his death, 255—death of his wife, ib., 256.
Zeituni, attempt of the Greeks on, and their defeat, i. 341, 342.
Zervas, Nicolas, ii. 352.
Zographos succeeds Rudhart as premier, ii. 337.
Zongas, an adherent of Ali's, i. 84.

THE END.

www.ingramcontent.com/pod-product-compliance
Lightning Source LLC
Chambersburg PA
CBHW050848300426
44111CB00010B/1180

TO THE MEMORY OF

MARIA MITCHELL,

THIS BOOK IS DEDICATED

BY HER NEPHEW

THE AUTHOR.

CONTENTS.

CHAPTER I.—**Physics:**—Mass, molecule, atom, molecular motion, atomic motion, properties of matter chemical and physical, impenetrability, magnitude, divisibility, porosity, compressibility, expansibility, elasticity, mobility, cohesion, adhesion, hardness, brittleness, tenacity, malleability, ductility. States of matter—solid, liquid, gaseous, radiant; machines, levers, planes, wedge, screw, friction, capillarity, specific gravity, density, heat, distillation, solution, solubility, crystallization, crystals, light, electricity, electrolysis, electricity in the mouth, weights and measures, metric system, percentage solutions, conversion of volume to weight, thermometry...................Pages 1 to 31.

CHAPTER II.—**Chemical Philosophy:**—Molecule, atom, element, compound, symbols, table of constants of the elements, writing symbols, atomic weight, positive and negative elements, quantivalence, artiads and perissads, compound molecules, law of definite and multiple proportions, binary compounds, radicals, ternary compounds, acids, bases, salts, how to read formulæ, ammonium compounds, nomenclature—old and new, chemical change, reactions, *laws of double decomposition*, insoluble substances, volatile compounds, chemical equations, chemical arithmetic, *circumstances influencing chemical attraction:* Mendeleef's tables of the elements, Lothar Meyer's classification, general properties of the metallic elements, general properties of alloys of metallic elements..............Pages 32 to 91.

CHAPTER III.—**Inorganic Chemistry. Monads:**—Potassium, sodium, [ammonium], lithium, *silver*, hydrogen, iodine, bromine, chlorine, fluorine, and their compounds.
Dyads:—Barium, calcium, magnesium, zinc, cadmium, lead, uranium, copper, *mercury*, tellurium, sulphur, oxygen, and their compounds. *Amalgams:* Rollins's copper amalgam, Chandler's, Weagant's processes, Bogue's process, Ames's process; *dental amalgam alloys.* Compounds of mercury; corrosive sublimate, calomel, vermilion; *compounds of sulphur;* action of sulphuretted hydrogen on metals.

Triads:—Bismuth, gold, antimony, boron, arsenicum, phosphorus, nitrogen, and their compounds. *Gold:* occurrence, preparation, properties. Refined gold, chemically pure gold, agents used for precipitating gold, crystal gold, beating gold, cohesive gold, corrugated gold, effect on gold of alloying, appearance of gold alloys, gold base plate, compounds of gold, purple of Cassius. Phosphoric acid, common and glacial. Nitrogen monoxide or *laughing gas,* nitric acid.

Tetrads:—*Aluminium,* cerium, *tin,* palladium, *platinum,* iridium, silicon, titanium, carbon, and their compounds. Alums, *artificial teeth,* enamels, platinum, *colors for enamels,* silex, rutile.

Hexads:—Manganese, iron, nickel, cobalt, chromium, and their compounds. Cobalt blues. Chromic oxide, anhydride or "acid".............................Pages 92 to 213.

CHAPTER IV.—**Organic Chemistry** — *Theory:* radicals, chains, homologous series, types, substitution, derivatives, isomerism, decomposition, combustion and decay, fermentation, putrefaction. Hydrocarbons: paraffines, mineral oil, vaselene, oil of turpentine, terpenes, essential oils; oil of cloves, eugenol; India-rubber, dental rubber, gutta-percha, camphor, resins, myrrh, gums, naphthalene, naphthols. Ethyl series of radicals, alcohols, alcohol. Glycerine, glycerites, boroglyceride, glyceroborates. *Creasote. Carbolic acid.* Phenol compounds, resorcin, eucalyptol. Carbohydrates: sugars, honey, gums, collodion, celluloid. Ethers: chloroform, iodoform, iodol; aldehydes: paraldehyde, chloral hydrate; Ketones. Organic acids: acetic, trichloracetic, benzoic, eugenic, hydrocyanic, oleic, oxalic, lactic, salicylic, [salol, betol] sozolic, tartaric, [tartar emetic]. Alkaloids: aconitine, atropine, chinoline, cannabine, cocaine, morphine, quinine, strychnine, veratrine, "antipyrine", "antifebrine", alstonine, apomorphine, caffeine, cytisine, ditaine, erythrophleine, ethyl-oxy-caffeine, hyoscyamine, isatropyl cocaine, jerubebine, lamine, oxy-propylene-di-iso-amylamine, ulexine. Proteids: albumins, globulin, etc. Fermentation. Ferments. Putrefactive fermentation in the mouth. Fungi. Bacteria. Microbe of dental caries. Pus and suppuration. Disinfection: antiseptics, germicides, disinfectants. *Miller's mouth washes.* Deodorizers. Antiseptics: alantol, betol, bismuth oxyiodide, creolin, cresylic acid, iodine trichloride, mercuric albuminate, mercuric oxy-cyanide, oxy-naphthoic acid, tribrom-phenol, sodium silico-fluoride....Pages 214 to 308.

CHAPTER V.—**The Teeth and the Saliva:**—Tooth structure, chemical constitution of the teeth. Enamel, dentine, cement. Table of analyses. Action of various substances on the teeth. Chemistry of caries; chemical theory, vital theory, germ theory. The saliva: physical characters, chemical composition, functions, changes; parotid saliva, submaxillary, sublingual; buccal mucus. Tartar. Salivary calculi.......Pages 309 to 329.

CHAPTER VI.—**Practical Work in Dental Chemistry progressively arranged:**—I. Short course of a score of experiments illustrating principles of general chemistry.

II. Professor J. H. Salisbury's course of sixty experiments illustrating the practical application of chemistry to dentistry..Pages 330 to 342.

CHAPTER VII.—**Practical Work in Dental Chemistry**—*Continued.*
III. Short course in blowpipe analysis.

IV. Reactions of the more important metals in the wet way: silver, lead, mercury, copper, gold, platinum, zinc, tin, aluminium.

V. Short scheme for qualitative analysis of ordinary metals................................Pages 343 to 361.

CHAPTER VIII.—**Chemical Work in the Dental Laboratory:**—Refining gold, testing amalgams, manipulating vulcanite, compounding rubber. Short method of qualitative and quantitative analysis of dental amalgam alloys. Analysis of cements. Testing rubbers................................Pages 362 to 377.

CHAPTER IX.—**Complete Course in Salivary Analysis:**—Analysis of teeth, tartar, and of urine................Pages 378 to 393.

Glossary....................................... Pages 394 to 399.
Index....................................... Pages 400 to 411.

THE
Dentist's Manual of Special Chemistry.

Second Edition.

CHAPTER I.
PHYSICS.

1. **Matter.**— Anything which possesses weight or occupies space.
2. **Divisions of Matter.**—Mass, molecule, atom. (See also page 33).
3. **Mass.**—Quantity of matter made up of molecules.
4. **Molecule.**—Smallest subdivision of matter which can exist by itself.
5. **Atom.**—Smallest quantity of matter that can by combining form the molecule.
6. **Attraction of Mass,** or molar attraction: same as attraction of gravitation or tendency of bodies to approach one another.
7. **Molecular Attraction.**—Cohesion or adhesion.
8. **Atomic Attraction.**—Chemism or chemical affinity.
9. **Molar Motion.**—The ordinary, visible, mechanical motion, as that of a machine or its parts.

10. **Molecular Motion.**—Heat, light, magnetism, electricity.

11. **Atomic Motion.**—A constant revolution or swinging of the atom within a limited space.

12. **Properties of Matter.**—Qualities characteristic of matter. Two kinds, chemical and physical.

13. **Chemical Properties.**—Those resulting from the composition of the molecule with reference to its atoms and shown only by change of identity of the molecule: as combustibility, explosibility, etc.

14. **Physical Properties of Matter.**—The different ways in which matter presents itself to our senses. Two kinds, general and specific, or universal and characteristic. *General* properties are those common to all matter, as impenetrability, extension, porosity, etc. *Specific* properties are those observed in certain bodies only, or in certain states of those bodies, as solidity, color, tenacity, etc. Physical properties may be shown without change in the identity of the molecule.

15. **Physical Properties: Impenetrability.**—Property of matter in virtue of which two bodies cannot occupy the same space at the same time. Example: nail driven into wood, particles of wood make way for the nail.

16. **Extension or Magnitude.**—Property in virtue of which every body occupies a limited portion of space.

17. **Divisibility.**—Property of matter by virtue of which a body may be separated into distinct parts. Di-

visibility of matter practically limited *before* molecule is reached; theoretically should be limited by the atom.

18. **Porosity.**—Quality in virtue of which spaces or *pores* exist between the molecules of a body. Example: lead, if hammered, is made smaller because the size of the *pores* is reduced, the molecules being forced nearer together.

19. **Compressibility.**—Property in virtue of which a body may be reduced in size; it is a consequence and proof of porosity.

20. **Expansibility.**—Property in virtue of which a body may be increased in size. Opposite of compressibility. Example: iron when heated becomes larger or expands because its molecules are pushed further apart.

21. **Elasticity.**—Property in virtue of which bodies resume their original form or volume (size) when that form or volume has been changed by external force. Example: a piece of ordinary rubber after being stretched out resumes its original size when the force stretching it ceases to act.

22. **Mobility.**—Property in virtue of which the position of a body may be changed. **Inertia** is the incapability of matter to change its own state of motion or rest. Example: a book on a table cannot move itself and is said to have *inertia*; it can move, however, when sufficient force is applied to it and is said to have *mobility*.

23. **Cohesion.**—Force which unites molecules of the same kind as two molecules of water or two molecules of iron. Cohesion holds substances together and gives them form.

24. **Adhesion.**—Force which unites molecules of different kinds. Example: dip a glass rod into water and, on withdrawing it, a drop

will be found at its lower extremity, which remains suspended or *adheres* to it.

25. **Hardness.**—Property in virtue of which some bodies resist attempts to force passage between their particles. Example: a tooth possesses hardness.

26. **Brittleness.**— Property in virtue of which some bodies may easily be broken. Example: glass is not only hard, but is also easily broken or *brittle*.

27. **Tenacity.**—Property in virtue of which some bodies resist attempts to pull their particles asunder. Example: an iron wire is difficult to pull apart and is said to be tenacious.

Tenacity is proportional to sectional area: a rod of one square inch sectional area* will carry twice the load that a rod of the same material with sectional area of half a square inch will carry.

28. **Malleability.**— Property in virtue of which some bodies may be hammered or rolled into sheets. Example: gold can be beaten into sheets so thin that nearly 300,000 are necessary to measure an inch in height when they are placed one on another.

29. **Ductility.**—Property in virtue of which some bodies may be drawn into wire. Example: iron when heated may be drawn into a wire, hence is said to be ductile.

---

*The sectional area of a substance as, for example, a rod, is that of the surface of its cross section,

30. **States of Matter.**— Solid, liquid, gasous, and radiant. In the first, the attraction of the molecules is greater than their repulsion. In the second, their attraction and repulsion are equal. In the third, repulsion is greater than attraction. In the fourth, so few molecules are in the given space that they rarely strike each other in their paths of motion.

Fluid is a term applied to any thing which will adapt itself to the sides of the vessel containing it, hence includes both liquids and gases.

Vapors are gases produced by heat from substances usually solid or liquid at ordinary temperatures.

Examples: *solids:* wood, metals; *fluids:* air, water; *liquids:* water, oil, alcohol; *gases:* air, oxygen, hydrogen; *vapor:* steam.

31. **Force.**—Cause tending to produce, change, or destroy motion. Example: gravity, friction, electrical or magnetic attraction, etc.

32. **Work.**—Overcoming of resistance.

33. **Energy.**—Power of doing work.

34. **Foot-pound.**—Amount of work required to raise one pound one foot high.*

35. **Horse-power.**—Ability to perform 33,000 foot-pounds in a minute.

36. **Machine.**—Contrivance for utilizing energy by

---

*The work required to raise one kilogram through one meter, against the force of gravity, is called a kilogram-meter.

which power can be applied more advantageously to resistance and, in general, intensity of energy be transformed.

37. **Laws of Machines.**—1. Gain in intensity of power =loss in time, velocity, or distance and *vice versa*.
2. Power × distance=weight × distance.
3. Power × velocity=weight × velocity.

38. **Lever.**—Any inflexible bar, straight or curved, resting on a fixed point or edge called the *fulcrum*. Every lever has two arms, the power-arm and the weight-arm. The power-arm is the perpendicular distance from the fulcrum to the line in which the power acts; the weight-arm is the perpendicular distance from the fulcrum to the line in which the weight acts.

When the lever is not a straight bar, or when power and weight do not act parallel to each other, the lever is called a bent lever.

39. **Kinds of Levers.**—(1)Fulcrum between power and resistance (weight) as in crowbar, (2)weight between power and fulcrum as in wheelbarrow, (3) power between weight and fulcrum as in human forearm.

40. **Laws of the Lever.**—
Power × power-arm=weight × weight-arm.

A given power will support a weight as many times as great as itself, as the power-arm is times as long as the weight-arm.

The continued product of the power and lengths of the alternate arms beginning with the power-arm=the continued product of the weight and lengths of the alternate arms beginning with the weight-arm.

41. **Law of Wheel and Axle.**—The power multiplied by the radius, diameter, or circumference of the wheel= the weight × the corresponding dimension of the axle.

42. **Pulley.**—A wheel, turning on an axis, provided with a cord, which passes over the grooved circumference of the wheel. The axis is supported by a frame called the *block*.

43. **Inclined Plane.**—Hard, smooth, inflexible surface used in most cases to aid in the performance of work against the force of gravity. It is inclined so as to make an oblique angle with the direction of the force to be overcome, and in most cases is inclined to the horizon at an acute angle.

44. **Wedge.**—Movable inclined plane in which power usually acts in a direction parallel to base. It is used for moving great weights short distances. More commonly a wedge is *two inclined planes* united at their base. With given thickness, the longer the wedge the greater the gain in intensity of power.

45. **Screw.**—Cylinder with spiral groove or ridge, called the *thread*, winding about its circumference. By aid of the screw a given power will support a weight as many times greater than itself as the circumference described by the power is times as great as the distance between two adjoining turns of the thread.

46. **Friction.**—Resistance encountered by a moving body from the surface on which it moves. Is greatest at beginning of motion, increases with roughness of surfaces, greater between soft bodies than hard ones, is nearly proportional to pressure, is not affected by extent of surface within ordinary limits, is greater between surfaces of the same material than between those of different kinds; rolling friction less than sliding friction; friction diminished by polishing or lubricating the surfaces.

47. **Capillarity.**—When a glass rod is placed vertically in water the latter rises above its level at the sides of the glass. The finer the rod the greater the capillary ascent. If the rod be dipped into a liquid *which does not wet* it, as mercury, the liquid will be depressed instead of raised.

48. **Displacement.**—A body which sinks in water dis-

places exactly its own bulk of water and loses in weight an amount just equal to the weight of water displaced.

49. **Specific Gravity.**—Relative weights of equal bulks of bodies referred to an assumed standard; for liquids and solids, the standard is distilled water at a temperature of 4° C. or 39.2° F. For gases, the standard is air or hydrogen. If a substance weighs four times as much as the same bulk of water, it is said to have a sp. gr. of 4.

50. **Calculation of Specific Gravity of Solids and Liquids.**—(*a*) For solids use the following formula:

$$\text{Sp. gr.} = \frac{W}{W-W^1}$$

in which $W =$ weight of body in air, W^1 its weight in water (suspended by a light thread from the scale pan). Example: weight of a body in air, *i. e.*, ordinary weight, is 50 ounces; its weight in water is 42 ounces. $W=50$, $W^1=42$, $W-W^1=50-42$ or 8; $\frac{W}{W-W^1} = \frac{50}{8} = 6.25$, sp. gr. In other words the weight of the body divided by the weight of an equal volume (bulk) of water is the specific gravity of the body.

(*b*) If the body is lighter than water, fasten a heavy body to it and weigh in water. Weigh the heavy body in water. Weigh the light body in air. Then subtract the water weight of the combined mass from the water weight of the heavy body, and add to the difference the air weight of the light body. Then divide air weight of cork by the sum. Example: required to find the specific gravity of a piece of cork. Attach to it a piece of iron:

1. Weight of combined mass in water - 51.5 grains.
2. Weight of iron in water - - - 66.9 grains.
3. Weight of cork in air - - - 4.6 grains.
4. 66.9−51.5=15.4.
5. 15.4+4.6=20.
6. $\dfrac{4.6}{20}$ =0.23, sp. gr. of cork.

(c) To find the sp. gr. of solids which dissolve in water, weigh them in some liquid in which they are insoluble, and find the specific gravity as before. Multiply result by specific gravity of liquid used and the product will be the true specific gravity. Example: to find specific gravity of sugar. Suppose it weighs 10 grains in air and 4.56 grains in oil of turpentine. 10—4.56=5.44 grains. 10÷5.43=1.84 or sp. gr. referred to turpentine. Ascertain from tables the sp. gr. of turpentine(=0.86), multiply 1.84 by 0.86, and the product, 1.58, is the true sp. gr. of the sugar.

(d) To find the specific gravity of a powder insoluble in water, weigh a flask empty; weigh the flask full of water; weigh the flask partly full of the powder; fill the flask now containing powder full of water and weigh again. Subtract weight of flask filled with water from weight of flask filled with powder and water mixed. *The difference will be the loss of weight of the powder.* Divide the weight of the powder in air by the loss of weight in water, and the quotient will be the specific gravity of the powder.

(*e*) To find the sp. gr. of liquids a special flask, called a picnometer or sp. gr. flask, is used which contains a certain weight of water when filled. This weight is marked on the flask. To ascertain the sp. gr. of a liquid by means of its use, weigh it, fill it with the liquid and weigh it, subtract weight of flask, and divide difference by number marked on the flask. The quotient will be the sp. gr. of the liquid. The temperature of the liquid should be that marked on the flask.

Instruments called *hydrometers*[*] are also used for finding the sp. gr. of liquids, and are long, narrow, glass or metal tubes provided with a bulb near the bottom filled with air, and a smaller one below it filled with mercury. To find the sp. gr. it is merely necessary to drop the hydrometer into the liquid and read off the number on the scale at the surface of the liquid.

---

[*]Hydrometers should be those carefully standardized to a certain temperature, as 77° F., and used in liquids warmed or cooled to that temperature.

51. **Density.**—In chemistry, the term density should mean the weight of a gas referred to *hydrogen* as a unit. [Specific gravity of gases means their weight referred to *air* as a unit. Thus the density of chlorine is said to be 35.5, but its specific gravity 2.47. This means that chlorine is 35.5 times as heavy as hydrogen, but 2.47 times as heavy as air. In this book the term density will be used only in the case of gases. In some books the term density is used to mean specific gravity and is applied to solids].

52. **Law of Avogadro.**—Equal volumes of all bodies in the state of gas, and at the same temperature and pressure, contain the same number of molecules. Hence (*a*) the specific gravities of any two gases are to each other as the weights of their molecules, and (*b*) their molecules are all of the same size.*

53. **Law of Mariotte.**—Volume of a confined gas is inversely proportional to the pressure. That is, the greater the pressure the less the volume and *vice versa*. The standard pressure is 760 millimetres or 30 inches of the barometric pressure.

54. **Law of Charles.**—Volume of a gas varies directly with the absolute temperature†. That is, the cooler the gas the smaller its volume, and *vice versa*. A gas expands $\frac{1}{273}$ its volume in passing from 0° to 1° C. or $\frac{1}{460}$ its volume for one degree Fahrenheit.

---

*Avogadro's law finds application in the determination of molecular weights.

†The temperature of −273° C. is called the *absolute zero* of temperature. Absolute temperatures are obtained by adding 273 to the reading on the Centigrade thermometer.

55. **Standard Temperature and Pressure.**— 0° C. and 760 m. m. pressure. (See page)

56. **Effects of Heat.**—In general, heat in the first place expands bodies, then overcomes cohesion to such extent that the body melts and becomes liquid, then finally overcomes cohesion entirely and the liquid boils and passes into the gaseous state.

57. **Laws of Fusion.**—(1) Every solid begins to melt at a certain temperature, which is invariable for the given substance if the pressure be constant. When cooling, the substance will solidify at the temperature of fusion. (2). The temperature of the solid, or liquid, remains at the melting point from the moment that fusion or solidification begins until it is complete.

58. **Thermal Unit.**—Amount of heat necessary to raise one pound of water from 0° C. to 1° C., or 1390 foot pounds. Sometimes applied to amount of heat necessary to raise one pound of water from 32° to 33° F., or 772 foot pounds.

59. **Specific Heat.**—When equal weights of different bodies are raised through the same number of degrees of temperature, they take up different amounts of heat; that is, different bodies possess different capacities for heat. Thus the amount of heat needed to raise a kilogram of water through 100° C. is 31 times as great as that needed to raise the same weight of platinum through the same interval of temperature. Water then being taken as a unit, the specific heat of platinum is $\frac{1}{31}$ or 0.032.

60. **Boiling Point.**—Temperature at which a liquid gives off vapor rapidly from the whole liquid; at sea level boiling point of water is 100° C. or 212° F. **Superheated** steam is the result of applying considerable pressure to a boiling liquid, when its temperature will rise until the tension of the steam will overcome the pressure.

61. Evaporation.—Quiet formation of vapor at the surface of a liquid.

62. Distillation.—Conversion of a liquid into gas and recondensation of the gas into liquid. Operation performed in a still, consisting of a retort in which the liquid is boiled and a condenser for changing the vapor back to liquid.

63. Fractional Distillation.— Different substances boil at different temperatures. Raising the temperature of a mixture of two liquids to a point above the boiling point of one, but below that of the other, will vaporize the one but not the other.

64. Destructive Distillation.—Distillation of dry substances so as to destroy them and obtain liquids or gases. Example: coal for illuminating gas.

65. Sublimation.—Such solids as do not melt when heated, but pass directly into vapor, are said to sublime. Example: camphor.

66. Solution.—May be either *physical* or *chemical*. Physical, either (*a*) result of adhesion of liquid to solid overcoming cohesion of molecules of the solid, or (*b*) feeble combination of the solid with water and diffusion of this compound through remaining water. Example of (*a*): sugar dissolved in water; on boiling away the water the sugar may be recovered entirely unchanged. Example of (*b*): dried alum when dissolved in water separates again in crystals in which water is found.

Chemical when, by chemical action between two substances, a soluble compound is formed, which dissolves in the water present. Example: silver forms with nitric acid by chemical action a soluble compound, silver nitrate, which then dissolves in water that may be present. Similarly an acid, attacking tooth structure, forms more or less soluble compounds with the lime and magnesia of the tooth.

67. **Solvents.**—All liquids are solvents.

Water is the best general solvent especially for metallic salts. Alcohol is the best solvent for resins. Mercury dissolves many metals. Gases may be dissolved in liquids. Some liquids dissolve in liquids, as essential oils in alchohol, and the process is called *liquid diffusion*.

68. **Saturated Solution.**—When a liquid has dissolved all of a solid that it can at a given temperature, the solution is called a *saturated* one.

69. **Solubility.**—The solubility of a substance is denoted by the amount of it, *by weight,* which a given amount of a solvent, as water or alcohol, will take up at a given temperature. Thus one part of alum is soluble in 10.5 parts of water at 59° F.

70. **Deliquescence.**—Bodies, which absorb water from the air and become liquid, are said to *deliquesce.* Example: zinc chloride. Such substances are said to be *hygroscopic*.

71. **Efflorescence.**—Substances, which on exposure to air lose water from their crystals,

are said to effloresce. Example: ferrous sulphate (ordinary green vitriol.)

72. **Dialysis.**—Liquid diffusion, when liquids are separated by some porous diaphragm as bladder or parchment paper. Passage of liquid through the diaphragm is called *Osmosis*.

73. **Dialyzer.**—Glass cylinder open at one end and closed at the other by the membrane used as a separating medium.

74. **Colloids and Crystalloids.**—Easily crystallizable bodies pass through the membranes readily. Those which do not crystallize pass through with difficulty and are called *colloids*. Examples: crystalloid, alum; colloid, gelatine.

75. **Dialysate.**—Term applied to a substance which has been dialyzed, *i. e.* has passed through the membrane of the dialyzer.

76. **Crystals.**—Solid substances bounded by plane surfaces symmetrically arranged according to fixed laws. (See Section 80).

77. **Crystallization.**—Change of substances from melted state or solution to solid state, with assumption of geometrical form. Essential condition, possibility of free motion of smallest particles.

78. **Amorphous—Polymorphous.**—A body never obtained in crystalline state is said to be *amorphous, i. e.*, without definite form or shape; a body having two or more different crystalline forms is called *polymorphous*. The same body always assumes the same crystalline form under the same conditions, but under

different conditions may assume different crystalline shapes. A substance is said to be *isomorphous* with another when it crystallizes in exactly the same form. Example: glue is amorphous, sulphur is polymorphous, sulphate of magnesium is isomorphous with sulphate of zinc.

79. **Water of Crystallization.**—Water taken by substances separating from solutions as a necessary part of their crystals. Amount invariable for same substance at same temperature. Example: each crystal of alum has 24 molecules of water to one of alum itself, and the formula of the crystal is $K_2Al_2(SO_4)_4.24H_2O$.

80. **Systems of Crystals.**—Based on imaginary lines called *axes* passing through the centre of the crystal and connecting opposite angles or opposite parallel sides. For convenience, six systems of crystals may be considered.

First system: axes three, at right angles, equal lengths. *Isometric system.* Forms: cube, octahedron.

Examples of the first system of crystals: native silver, chloride of silver, calcium fluoride, native copper, native gold.

Second system: axes three, right angles, one longer or shorter than other two. *Tetragonal* or *Dimetric system.* Form: right square prism.

Example of the second system: copper pyrites.

Third system: axes three, right angles, unequal lengths. *Trimetric* or *Orthorhombic system*. Forms: right rhombic prism and rhombic octahedron. Examples of third system crystals: sulphates of lead, zinc, barium, magnesium.

Fourth system: axes three, unequal, only one at right angles to plane of other two. Simplest form: oblique rhombic prism. Examples: borax, green vitriol. *Monoclinic system*.

Fifth system: axes three, all unequal, and all inclined to each other. Crystals complicated and apparently irregular: rhomboidal prism, acute and obtuse rhombohedrons. Examples: blue vitriol, boracic acid. *Triclinic system*.

Sixth system: four axes, three in one plane at angle of 60° to one another, fourth longer or shorter than other three and at right angles to their plane. Example: quartz. *Hexagonal system*.

81. **Chemical Effects of Light.**—Many chemicals are affected by exposure to light. Solutions of several metals, among them silver and gold, throw down a part of the metal on exposure to sunlight; the latter has certain rays capable of producing chemical changes and known as actinic rays.

82. **Electricity due to Chemical Action.**—

All chemical change produces electricity. This kind of electricity is called voltaic or galvanic, and is most often developed by chemical action between liquids and metals. Example: when a strip of copper and a strip of zinc are placed in dilute sulphuric acid, a current of electricity will be found to flow in a wire connecting the two strips of metal above the acid. The apparatus is called a *galvanic element* or *cell*.

83. **Current of Electricity.**—In every galvanic cell, the plates and connecting wires must be conductors of electricity and the liquid used must be one which will act with greater vigor on one of the metals than on the other. The metal most actively attacked by the liquid forms the *positive* or generating plate; the other, the collecting or *negative* plate. *The current runs in the liquid from the positive plate to the negative; in the wire connecting the plates the current runs from the negative plate to the positive.*

84. **Closed Circuit.**—When wires from the two plates are in contact. When not, the circuit is *broken.*,

85. **Electrodes.**—Ends of the wires. Also called *poles*. The negative pole is attached to the positive plate and vice versa. Platinum strips are often fastened to the ends of wires and constitute the electrodes, and the wires are called *rheophores*.

86. **Galvanic Battery.**—A number of galvanic elements so connected that the current has the same direc-

tion in all. Usually they are connected "in series", that is, positive plate of one element with negative of the next.

87. **Forms of Cells.**—Hydrogen gas is generated by the action of an acid on a metal, and the various kinds of cells indicate the means used by their inventors to prevent the hydrogen from accumulating on the negative plate.

Potassium bichromate battery: two zinc plates having between them a carbon plate, all hung in a solution of potassium bichromate in dilute sulphuric acid. To make the latter, pour 167 C.c. of sulphuric acid into 500 C.c. of water and let the mixture cool. Dissolve 115 grams of potassium bichromate in 335 C.c. of boiling water and pour while hot into the dilute acid. Let the whole cool before using. [1 gram = 15½ grains Troy; 30 C. c. = 1 fluid ounce]. Chromic acid is formed, which destroys the hydrogen. Zinc plates should be removed from battery, when the latter is not in use. The zincs should be *amalgamated* by washing in dilute sulphuric acid, then pouring mercury on them while still wet with the acid. Rub in the mercury well and keep a little of it in the bottom of each cell.

The *gravity battery* is one in which the two solutions, zinc sulphate and copper sulphate, are separated, owing to the difference in their respective weights, the saturated solution of copper sulphate being heavier than that of the zinc sulphate, when the latter is in its proper condition.

88. **Storage Batteries.**—Are of many forms. They may be made from any pair of chemical compounds unstable in presence of each other. They are called also *secondary* batteries. They have no electro-motive force of their own, but are capable of being acted on by an external source of electricity, in such a way as to acquire the

power to give out an electric current, opposite in direction to that of the external source by which they are treated.

In some storage batteries the cell contains two or more large plates of sheet lead, and the liquid used is dilute sulphuric acid. A current is passed through the battery, and hydrogen gas accumulates on one plate and oxygen on the other. Disconnect the charging battery and a current in the opposite direction may now be obtained from the polarized cell*. Storage batteries are used by dentists to furnish motive power for the engine.

89. **Induced Current.**—Name given to instantaneous current produced in a conductor by the influence of a neighboring current or magnet.

90. **Faradic Battery.**—The current induced in a conductor by the influence of a neighboring current is known also as a secondary, interrupted, or Faradic current. In producing it an *induction coil* is used, which is a *double* coil of wire wound around a hollow cylinder of wood. The first or *primary* coil is made of large, thick, copper wire covered with silk or insulated. Upon this coil, and carefully insulated from it, is wound the *secondary* coil of longer and thinner wire. A bundle of soft iron wire is inside the inner coil to act as a magnet whenever a current from a battery shall be sent through the coil. Before the end of the bundle of wires there vibrates a piece of soft iron fastened to a spring. The latter rests against a screw which connects the inner coil by a wire with a galvanic battery. When a current is sent through the inner coil, an induced current is produced in the outer coil in the

---

*The polarization of the plates is caused by the accumulation of oxygen (negative) on the zinc (positive) plate, and of hydrogen (positive) on the carbon (negative) plate. Owing to the layers of gas on each plate a new or secondary current is developed.

opposite direction and the bundle of soft iron wires is magnetized at the same time. In consequence of the latter the hammer or soft iron in the spring is drawn toward the bundle and the current is thus broken. The bundle then becomes demagnetized and the hammer is brought back to the screw by the spring, the induced current now taking the opposite direction to what it did when the hammer was in contact with the bundle, and so on. The process is repeated as long as the current from the battery is sent through the primary coil. The induced current is therefore a *to and fro* current, or a *make* and *break* current, the make current being in opposite direction to the break. The *break* currents are the most powerful and are reinforced by the sudden demagnetization of the bundle or core of iron wires.

91. **Electrolysis.**— Many chemical compounds in solution may be decomposed by a strong galvanic current. This process is called electrolysis. Example: if a strong galvanic current is passed through water containing a little sulphuric acid, the water will be decomposed, that is, broken up into hydrogen and oxygen gases, the former being given off at the negative pole and the latter at the positive.

92. **Terms used in Electricity.**—*Circuit:* the entire path of the electrical current, including the battery itself, and the conducting medium, which unites the poles.

Dynamo: the dynamo-electric machine is one in which energy in the form of moving power is transformed into energy in the form of electricity.

Electricity.—Different kinds: galvanic electricity, also called *Voltaic*, is the term given to electricity evolved by chemical action, as in the bichromate battery. It is also called *dynamical*, or current-electricity.

Static electricity is that developed by friction.

Thermo-Electricity is that produced by the agency of heat. All metals are capable of producing thermo-electric currents.

Magneto-Electricity is the name given to electric currents developed by the relative movements of magnets and wires.

Potential: term used to denote the degree to which a body is electrified. The electrical condition of the earth's surface is taken as the potential zero point, and all bodies positively electrified, are said to have a higher potential than the earth, and all bodies negatively electrified, to have a lower potential. When electricity moves or tends to move from one place to another, there is said to be a *difference of potential* between the two places.

Resistance: term given to the obstruction offered to the passage of a current by the substance of the circuit through which it passes. Silver offers the least resistance, gutta percha very great.

Electro-motive force: term used to indicate that property of any source of electricity by which it tends to do work by transferring electricity from one point to another. Ten cells have ten times the electro-motive force of one cell.

Quantity: as applied to current electricity, term used to mean the strength of the current, or the amount per second acting to produce heat, magnetism, etc. It is the margin of effective electricity produced by any battery after the resistance of the circuit has been overcome.

Standard units of electrical measurement: the unit of electro-motive force is called the *volt:* the Daniell cell is said to have the electro-motive force of *one volt*, that is, the electro-motive force required to produce a current of the strength of one *ampere* in a circuit having a total resistance of one *ohm*. An ohm is the unit of resistance, and is approximately equal in resistance to that of a wire of pure copper one-twentieth of an inch in diameter, and two hundred and fifty feet long, or that of one-sixteenth of a mile of No. 9 galvanized-iron wire of ordinary quality. An ampere is the unit of current strength and represents the strength of current passing in a circuit having a total resistance of one ohm, with an electro-motive force of one volt. The *coulomb* or *weber* denotes the amount of electricity which a current of the strength of one ampere can furnish per second of time. It is the unit of quantity. The *farad* is the unit of capacity and represents the capacity of a condenser which contains one coulomb of electricity when the difference of potential between its opposing plates is one volt. A microfarad is a millionth of a farad.

93. **Ohm's Law.**—The effective strength of current in any given circuit is equal to the electro-motive force divided by the total resistance.

94. **Galvanic Electricity in the Mouth.**—Unpleasant sensations, from a disagreeable taste up to a slight shock, are sometimes experienced by those having metal in the mouth either in form of fillings or in teeth-plates. This is due to the development of galvanic electricity by contact with some other metals, as when pins, needles, metallic tooth-picks, etc. are touched to the fillings, or when the clasps or plates of artificial dentures come into contact with fillings, under peculiar conditions of oral fluids.

The fillings themselves, especially if of different metals, are thought to be a source of electricity, taken in connection with the fluids of the mouth; effort has been made to explain the destruction of certain fillings, as due to the development of such electricity.

95. American Weights and Measures:

APOTHECARIES' FLUID MEASURE.

60 minims (m.) make 1 fluid drachm.............. f₃
8 fluidrachms make 1 fluid ounce................. f℥
16 fluid ounces make 1 pint....................... O.
8 pints make 1 gallon..........................Cong.

APOTHECARIES' WEIGHT.

20 grains (gr.) make 1 scruple................ sc. or ℈
3 scruples   make 1 drachm................ dr. or ʒ
8 drachms   make 1 ounce................. oz. or ℥
12 ounces   make 1 pound................. lb. or ℔

SCALE.

lb.		oz.		dr.		sc.		gr.
1	=	12	=	96	=	288	=	5760
		1	=	8	=	24	=	480
				1	=	3	=	60
						1	=	20

TROY WEIGHT.

24 grains (gr.) make 1 pennyweight.............. dwt.
20 pennyweights make 1 ounce.................... oz.
12 ounces   make 1 pound.................... lb.

SCALE.

lb.		oz.		dwt.		gr.
1	=	12	=	240	=	5760
		1	=	20	=	480
				1	=	.24

AVOIRDUPOIS WEIGHT.

16 drachms (dr.) make 1 ounce..................... oz.
16 ounces   make 1 pound..................... lb.
25 pounds   make 1 quarter................... qr.
4 quarters   make 1 hundredweight............. cwt.
20 hundredweight make 1 ton...................... T.

SCALE.

T.		cwt.		qr.		lb.		oz.		dr.
1	=	20	=	80	=	2000	=	32000	=	512000
		1	=	4	=	100	=	1600	=	25600
				1	=	25	=	400	=	6400
						1	=	16	=	256
								1	=	16

96. Metric System:

MEASURES OF LENGTH.

1 millimetre	=	0.001 of a metre.
1 centimetre	=	0.010 of a metre.
1 decimetre	=	0.100 of a metre.
1 metre	=	**1 metre.**
1 decametre	=	10 metres.
1 hectometre	=	100 metres.
1 kilometre	=	1,000 metres.
1 myriametre	=	10,000 metres.

MEASURES OF SURFACE.

1 centiare	=	1 square metre.
1 Are	=	**100 square metres.**
1 hectare	=	10,000 square metres.

MEASURES OF VOLUME.

1 Cubic metre	=	1,000 Cubic decimetres.
	=	1,000 litres, or one kilolitre.
	=	1 stere.

MEASURES OF CAPACITY.

| **1 Litre** | = | { 1 Cubic decimetre, or 1000 Cubic centimetres. |

MEASURES OF WEIGHT.

1 milligramme	=	0.001 of a gramme.
1 centigramme	=	0.010 of a gramme.
1 decigramme	=	0.100 of a gramme.
1 gramme	=	**1 gramme**

MEASURES OF WEIGHT.—*Continued.*

1 decagramme	=	10 grammes.
1 hectogramme	=	100 grammes.
1 kilogramme (kilo)	=	1000 grammes.
1 tonneau	=	1000 kilogrammes.

Metric Equivalents.

WEIGHT

Unit of measurement.	Approximate equivalent.	Accurate equivalent.
1 gramme	15½ grains	15.432
1 grain	0.064 gramme	0.064
1 kilogramme (1000 grammes)	2⅕ pounds, avoirdupois	2.204
1 pound, avoirdupois	½ kilogramme	0.453
1 ounce, avoirdupois (437½ grains)	28⅓ grammes	28.349
1 ounce, troy or apothecary (480 gr.)	31 grammes	31.103

BULK.

1 Cubic centimetre	0.06 cubic inch	0.061
1 cubic inch	16⅓ Cubic centimetres	16.386
1 litre (1000 Cubic centimetres)	1 U. S. standard quart	0.946
1 United States quart	1 litre	1.057
1 fluidounce	29½ Cubic centimetres	29.570

LENGTH.

Unit of measurement.	Approximate equivalent.	Accurate equivalent.
1 inch	2½ centimetres	2.539
1 centimetre (1-100 metre)	0.4 inch	0.393
1 yard	1 metre	0.914
1 metre (39.37 inches)	1 yard	1.093
1 foot	30 centimetres	30.479
1 kilometre (1000 metres)	⅝ mile	0.621
1 mile	1½ kilometres	1.609

SURFACE.

1 hectare (10,000 square metres)	2½ acres	2.471
1 acre	⅔ hectare	0.404

Suppose we are directed to use 175 grammes of chloride of sodium, how much is it in ounces? We see by the table that one ounce equals 31 grammes; divide 175 by this, and we have 5.6, the required number of ounces. If we wish to measure 53 Cubic centimetres of any liquid, $53 \div 29.5$, the number of Cubic centimetres in one fluid ounce, $= 1.8$ fluid ounces, the required amount. Conversely, suppose we have a quantity of some chemical weighing three-quarters of a pound, and wish to find the metric equivalent. As one pound is equal to 0.453 kilogramme, three-quarters of a pound will be equal to three-quarters of that weight, or 0.33975 of a kilogramme; or, as one kilogramme equals 1000 grammes, three-quarters of a pound will equal 339.75 grammes.

1. To convert troy grains into centigrammes, multiply by 6.
2. To convert centigrammes into troy grains, divide by 6.
3. To convert troy grains into milligrammes, multiply by 60.
4. To convert milligrammes to troy grains, divide by 60.
5. To convert troy grains to grammes, or minims into fluidgrammes, divide by 15.
6. To convert grammes into grains, or fluidgrammes into minims, multiply by 15.
7. To convert drachms into grammes, or fluidrachms into fluidgrammes, multiply by 4.
8. To convert grammes into drachms, or fluidgrammes into fluidrachms, divide by 4. (All results approximate).

97. **Percentage Solutions.**—In order to make a percentage solution of a solid in a liquid *both* should be weighed. A five per cent solution by weight means a solution 100 parts of which contain 95 parts by weight of water to 5 parts by weight of the solid.*

*It is a common error to suppose that a five per cent solution is 5 grains of solid *to* 100 of water.

Ascertain the weight of a bottle, put into it the proper weight of solid then add liquid enough to make up the final weight.

For example, suppose it is required to make a 4 per cent. solution of cocaine hydrochlorate: weight of bottle, 400 grains; weight of bottle plus cocaine, 404 grains. It is evident that enough water must now be poured into the bottle, while in the scale-pan, to make the final weight 500 grains. Result, four grains of cocaine in ninety-six of water, or a four per cent solution.

Examples: supposing weight of bottle to be 400 grains how would a one per cent solution of corrosive sublimate be made? a one in 1000?† a 20 per cent solution of carbolic acid? Give total weights (bottle included) and the weights of the separate ingredients.

Answers: one grain of corrosive sublimate and ninety-nine of water. One grain of the solid and nine hundred and ninety-nine grains of water.

98. **Specific Volume.**—The relative bulks of equal weights of different bodies is their specific volume. Water being taken as a unit, the specific volume of any substance is the volume of a certain weight of it compared to that of an equal weight of water at 15° C. (59.6° F.).

To find specific volume, divide the volume of a given weight of the liquid by the volume of an equal weight of water, or divide the specific gravity of water (which is 1 or 1000) by the specific gravity of the liquid.

For example: what is the specific volume of glycerine? 100 grains of glycerine measure 84 minims; 100 grains of

---

†Carefully notice the difference between one *in* a thousand and one *to* a thousand.

water measure 105 minims; 84÷105=0.8; or 1000÷1,250 (the sp. gr. of glycerine)=0.800, sp. vol. of glycerine. That is, a given weight of glycerine will only measure eight-tenths as much as the same weight of water.

99. **To find the volume of a given weight of water in the American system.**— To change av. oz. of water to fl. oz. multiply by 0.96; tr. oz. of water to fl. oz. multiply by 1.05; grams of water to fl. oz. multiply by 0.0338.

Examples: how many fluidounces in 60 avoirdupois ounces of water? how many fluidounces in 10 troy ounces of water? how many fluidounces in 20 grams of water?

Answers: 60×0.96. 10×1.05. 20×0.0338.

100. **To find the volume of a given weight of any liquid.**—Multiply the volume of an equal weight of water by the specific volume of the liquid; or divide the volume of an equal weight of water by the sp. gr. of the liquid.

Examples: how many fluidounces in 200 troy ounces of nitric acid? 200 troy ounces of water are (200×1.05) fluidounces, or 210 fluidounces (see previous rule). 210 multiplied by the specific volume of nitric acid, 0.704, (found by dividing the specific gravity of the water by the specific gravity of the acid, 1.42) will give 147.8, which is number of fluidounces required.

101. **To find the weight of a given volume of water.**—Fluidounces to avoirdupois ounces, divide by 0.96; fluidounces to troyounces, divide by 1.05; fluidounces to grams, divide by 0.0338.

Examples: what is the weight of 13 fluidounces of

water? of a pint of water? of three pints? (Give answers in both avoirdupois and troy).

Answers: 13÷0.96. 13÷1.05. 16÷0.96. 16÷1.05. Three times the third and fourth answers.

102. **To find the weight of a given volume of any liquid.**—Divide the weight of an equal volume of water by the sp. vol. of the liquid, or multiply the weight of an equal volume of water by the sp. gr. of the liquid.

Example: find the weight (troy) of 200 fluidounces of nitric acid of sp. gr. 1.42. The weight troy of 200 fluidounces of water is 200÷1.05 or 190.4. Divide this by the specific volume of nitric acid, which is 0.704, and we have 270.4, which is the weight required in troy ounces.

103. **Thermometry.**—The Centigrade thermometer has its zero at the freezing point and its boiling point at 100°, the number of intervening degrees being 100. One degree Centigrade equals 1.8° of Fahrenheit. To convert Centigrade to Fahrenheit multiply by 1.8 and add 32. To convert Fahrenheit to Centigrade subtract 32 and multiply by $\frac{5}{9}$.

Examples: Convert 60° Centigrade to the corresponding Fahrenheit. 60 times 1.8 equals 108. The latter plus 32 equals 140. [Turning to the table on page 31, we find 60° C. equals 140° F]. Now find what degree Centigrade corresponds to 770° Fahrenheit. 770 less 32 equals 738. The latter multiplied by $\frac{5}{9}$ equals 410. [Consulting the table on page 31, we find 770° F equals 410° C.]

In general it is easier to consult the table if the latter is at hand when wanted, but as such is not always the case it is advisable to become familiar and ready with the rule.

PHYSICS. 31

Comparison of Centigrade and Fahrenheit Degrees.*

Cent.	Fahr.	Cent.	Fahr.	Cent.	Fahr.	Cent.	Fahr.
−40	−40.0	−5	+23.0	+30	+86.0	+65	+149.0
39	38.2	4	24.8	31	87.8	66	150.8
38	36.4	3	26.6	32	89.6	67	152.6
37	34.6	−2	28.4	33	91.4	68	154.4
36	32.8	−1	30.2	34	93.2	69	156.2
35	31.0	0	32.0	35	95.0	70	158.0
34	29.2	+1	33.8	36	96.8	71	159.8
33	27.4	2	35.6	37	98.6	72	161.6
32	25.6	3	37.4	38	100.4	73	163.4
31	23.8	4	39.2	39	102.2	74	165.2
30	22.0	5	41.0	40	104.0	75	167.0
29	20.2	6	42.8	41	105.8	76	168.8
28	18.4	7	44.6	42	107.6	77	170.6
27	16.6	8	46.4	43	109.4	78	172.4
26	14.8	9	48.2	44	111.2	79	174.2
25	13.0	10	50.0	45	113.0	80	176.0
24	11.2	11	51.8	46	114.8	81	177.8
23	9.4	12	53.6	47	116.6	82	179.6
22	7.6	13	55.4	48	118.4	83	181.4
21	5.8	14	57.2	49	120.2	84	183.2
20	4.0	15	59.0	50	122.0	85	185.0
19	2.2	16	60.8	51	123.8	86	186.8
18	−0.4	17	62.6	52	125.6	87	188.6
17	+1.4	18	64.4	53	127.4	88	190.4
16	3.2	19	66.2	54	129.2	89	192.2
15	5.0	20	68.0	55	131.0	90	194.0
14	6.8	21	69.8	56	132.8	91	195.8
13	8.6	22	71.6	57	134.6	92	197.6
12	10.4	23	73.4	58	136.4	93	199.4
11	12.2	24	75.2	59	138.2	94	201.2
10	14.0	25	77.0	60	140.0	95	203.0
9	15.8	26	78.8	61	141.8	96	204.8
8	17.6	27	80.6	62	143.6	97	206.6
7	19.4	28	82.4	−63	145.4	98	208.4
−6	+21.2	+29	+84.2	64	+147.2	+ 99	+210.2
						+ 100	212.0
110	+230	+210	+410	+310	+590	410	770
120	248	220	428	320	608	420	788
130	266	230	446	330	626	430	806
140	284	240	464	340	644	440	824
150	302	250	482	350	662	450	842
160	320	260	500	360	680	460	860
170	338	270	518	370	698	470	878
180	356	280	536	380	716	480	896
+190	374	290	554	390	734	490	+914
+200	+392	+300	+572	+400	752	+ 500	+932
+500	+932	+800	1472	+1100	+2012	+1400	2552
600	1112	+900	+1652	1200	2192	1500	2732
+700	+1292	+1000	+1832	+1300	+2372	+1600	+2912

*Barker.

CHAPTER II.

CHEMICAL PHILOSOPHY.

104. **Chemistry defined.**—Chemistry is the science which studies the properties, constitution, and laws of composition of bodies, whether crystalline, volatile, natural, or artificial.

105. **Field of chemistry.**—Chemistry studies such properties of matter as result from its atomic composition. *Chemical Philosophy* treats of the general facts of chemistry, the general laws deduced from these facts, and the operations which lead to a knowledge of the internal composition of matter. It comprises and classifies our knowledge of those phenomena which imply a change of substance.

Special Chemistry studies the character and properties of certain definite bodies, and shows in what manner they are governed by the laws of general chemistry, or chemical philosophy.

106. **Analysis and Synthesis.**—Chemical analysis is an operation by which the composition of matter is ascertained by splitting up a substance and separating its constituents from

one another. *Synthesis* is an operation by which simple bodies are combined to form compound ones, or compounds combined to form complex ones.

107. **Definitions---Molecule, Atom, Element, Compound.**---*Matter* or substance is the general term given to that which has length, breadth, and thickness. Any portion of matter which we perceive by the senses is called a *mass* of matter. Every mass of matter consists of molecules. A *Molecule* is the smallest particle into which any substance can be divided without losing its identity as that substance. The smallest particle into which common salt can be divided and still be salt and nothing but salt, is termed a molecule of salt. The smallest particle of iron which can exist free, that is, uncombined with anything else, is called a molecule of iron. Molecules are too small to be seen even with the aid of the most powerful microscope. Their existence, however, is now very generally admitted, as we are able to account for numerous phenomena if we assume that molecules exist. When a substance loses its identity, its molecules split up into small particles called *atoms*, which, however, have an attraction for one another and tend to form new molecules by coming together in groups. Thus, the molecule of mercuric oxide is composed of an atom of mercury combined with an atom of oxygen; when this substance is heated, its molecules break up, and the substance is no longer the oxide of mercury, but mercury and oxygen. When the molecules of oxide of mercury split up, the constituent atoms re-arrange themselves, those of the mercury forming molecules of mercury, and those of oxygen molecules of oxygen.

The molecule, then, is composed of atoms, held together by a certain attraction called by some *chemism*, by others *chemical affinity.* Each atom has an attractive power for other atoms, which is definite in quantity but neutralized when a sufficient number of other atoms approach it.

Definition 1. **A molecule** is the smallest particle of any substance which can exist by itself and remain free and uncombined. Molecules are destructible and divisible.

Definition 2. An **atom** is the still smaller particle entering into the composition of the molecule. Atoms cannot, in all probability, remain free and uncombined; they are indestructible and indivisible.

It follows from definition 2, that matter is indestructible.

Definition 3. **Element: a substance whose molecules are composed of the same kind of atoms,** as the molecules of gold; the molecules of any substance in Table 1 are composed of atoms of that substance, and of nothing else.

Definition 4. **Compound: a substance whose molecules are composed of different kinds of atoms.** The molecule of salt is not composed of atoms of sodium alone, nor of chlorine alone, but of an atom of sodium and an atom of chlorine.

Definition 5. **Mixture:** two or more substances form a *Mixture* when the particles of one are scattered throughout those of the other or others, without any change taking place in the chemical or specific properties of one or the other. Example: sand and sugar.

108. **Law of Avogadro.**—Equal volumes of all bodies in the state of gas and at the same temperature and pressure contain the same number of molecules. Therefore (*a*) the molecules of all bodies in the gaseous state are of the same size and (*b*) the weight of any molecule, as compared with that of hydrogen, is in proportion to the weight of any volume given, as compared with the same volume of hydrogen.

109. **How to determine the number of atoms in the hydrogen molecule.**—Suppose a given volume of hydrogen contains 10,000,000 molecules; by Avogadro's law the same volume of chlorine will contain 10,000,000 molecules. Combined, they form *two* volumes of hydrochloric acid gas which will necessarily contain 20,000,000 molecules. Analysis shows each molecule of hydrochloric acid gas to consist of two atoms, one of hydrogen and one of chlorine, that is, the 20,000,000 molecules of hydrochloric acid gas will contain 20,000,000 atoms of hydrogen and 20,000,000 of chlorine. Now there were but 10,000,000 molecules of hydrogen in the start, before combination, therefore each molecule of hydrogen must have contributed two atoms of hydrogen. So also with the chlorine.

From this it follows that there are two atoms in every molecule of hydrogen; and the weight of the atom (atomic weight) of hydrogen being taken as 1, the weight of its molecule (molecular weight) will be 2.

110. **Symbols.**—Chemists designate each element by an abbreviation called a *Symbol*,

which is often the first letter or first two letters of its Latin name.

Thus the symbol for potassium is K (Latin *Kalium*) that of gold Au (Latin *Aurum*).

A symbol not only designates an element but just one atom of that element having a definite weight (atomic weight).

Thus O not only signifies oxygen, but *one atom* of oxygen, or 16 parts by weight of oxygen.

The symbols of the elements with the atomic weights, specific gravity, specific heat, and melting point are now shown by Table 1.

The beginner should pay particular attention to those elements printed in large type. Note that the *metals*, as a rule, are positive to hydrogen, while the *non-metals** are negative to it. Observe that hydrates of elements at the positive end form bases, while hydrates of those at the negative end form acids.

Table 1 is that of Professor W. H. Seaman, M. D. The atomic weights are from the "Laboratory Yearbook" of Professor John Howard Appleton, as are also forty of the figures of specific gravity.†

---

*Antimony resembles metals in *physical* properties not chemical.

†The forty are those of Li, K, Na, Cl, Ca, Mg, P, S, Gl, C, Si, Al, Sr, Br, I, As, Te, Sb, Cr, Zn, Sn, Fe, Mn, Co, Ni, Cd, Mo, Cu, Bi, Ag, Rh, Pb, Pd, Hg, W, U, Au, Pt, Ir.

Those who intend to pursue the study of chemistry more in detail will do well to read Lothar Meyer's work on Theoretical Chemistry, or Remsen's book entitled "The Principles of Theoretical Chemistry." Among other works on chemistry of general value are those of Beilstein, Roscoe, and Schorlemmer, Jungfleisch. For an elementary work, Nichol's "Abridgment" of Eliot and Strer is satisfactory; the beginner will find the appendix valuable in its instructions about chemical manipulations.

Table I.
CONSTANTS OF THE ELEMENTS.
(Arranged by Prof. Seaman.)
ELECTRO-CHEMICAL SERIES.

Positive end: hydrates form bases. NAME.	SYMBOLS. Perissad Artiad.	Atomic weights.	Approx Atomic wghts.	Specific gravity (Water=1)	Specific Heat.	Melting Point. Centigrade
Cæsium	Cs	132.5830	132.6	1.88		26.5°
Rubidium	Rb	85.2510	85.3	1.52		37.0
POTASSIUM (Kalium)	K	39.0190	39.0	0.86	0.1695	62.5
SODIUM (Natron)	Na	22.9980	23.0	0.97	0.2934	97.0
LITHIUM	Li	7.0073	7.0	0.59	0.9408	180.0
BARIUM	Ba	136.7630	136.8	4.00		
STRONTIUM	Sr	87.3440	87.4	2.54		
CALCIUM	Ca	39.9900	40.0	1.58		
MAGNESIUM	Mg	23.9590	24.0	1.70 to 1.74	0.2499	
Glucinum (Beryllium, Be)	Gl	9.0850	9.1	2.10		
Yttrium	Y	89.8160	89.8	4.80		
Erbium	E	165.8910	165.9			
ALUMINIUM	Al	27.0090	27.0	2.50 to 2.67	0.2143	425.0
Zirconium	Zr	89.3670	89.4	4.10		
Thorium	Th	233.4140	233.4	7.90		
CERIUM	Ce	140.4240	140.4	6.62		
Didymium	D	144.5730	144.6	6.40		
Lanthanum	La	138.5260	138.5	6.10		
MANGANESIUM	Mn	53.9060	53.9	8.01 to 8.03	0.1217	
Gallium	Ga	68.8540	68.9	6.00		
ZINC	Zn	64.9045	64.9	7.10 to 7.20	0.0955	412.0
IRON (Ferrum)	Fe	55.9130	55.9	7.79 to 7.84	0.1138	2000.0
NICKEL	Ni	57.9280	57.9	8.60 to 8.82	0.1086	2000.0
COBALT	Co	58.8870	58.9	8.49 to 8.51	0.1069	1670.0
Thallium	Tl	203.7150	203.7	11.80	0.0338	294.0
CADMIUM	Cd	111.8350	111.8	8.45 to 8.69	0.0556	315.0
LEAD (Plumbum)	Pb	206.4710	206.5	11.33 to 11.39	0.0314	325.0
Indium	In	113.3980	113.4	7.40		
TIN (Stannum)	Sn	117.6980	117.7	7.30	0.0562	230.0
BISMUTH	Bi	207.5230	207.5	9.80	0.0308	264.0
Uranium	U	238.4820	238.5	18.40	0.0619	
COPPER (Cuprum)	Cu	63.1730	63.2	8.93 to 8.95	0.0951	1200.0
SILVER (Argentum)	Ag	107.6750	107.7	10.40 to 10.57	0.0570	1000.0
MERCURY (Hydrargyrum)	Hg	199.7120	199.7	13.60	0.0319	−40°.0
Palladium	Pd	105.7370	105.7	11.80	0.0592	High
Ruthenium	Ru	104.2170	104.2	11.40		
Rhodium	Rh	104.0550	104.1	11.00 to 11.20	0.0562	"
PLATINUM	Pt	194.4150	194.4	21.50	0.0324	3000
Iridium	Ir	192.6510	192.7	21.80	0.0325	1000
Osmium	Os	198.4940	198.5	22.40	0.0311	
GOLD (Aurum)	Au	196.1550	196.2	19.26 to 19.34	0.0324	1250
HYDROGEN	H	1.0000	1.0		3.4090	
SILICON	Si	28.1950	28.2	2.49	0.1774	
Titanium	Ti	47.9997	48.0			
Columbium (Niobium Nb)	Cb	93.8120	93.8	7.10		
Tantalum	Ta	182.1440	182.1	10.78		
Tellurium	Te	127.9600	128.0	6.18 to 6.24	0.0473	
ANTIMONY (Stibium)	Sb	119.9550	120.0	6.72	0.0557	450
CARBON	C	11.9736	12.0	2.27 to 3.52	0.1468 to 0.2415	nearly inf.
BORON	B	10.9410	10.9	2.63	0.2500	
Wolfram (Tungsten)	W	183.6100	183.6	17.20 to 18.30	0.0334	
Molybdenum	Mo	95.5270	95.5	8.62 to 8.64	0.0721	
Vanadium	V	51.2560	51.3	5.50		
CHROMIUM	Cr	52.0090	52.0	7.01		High
ARSENICUM	As	74.9180	74.9	5.63 to 5.67	0.0814	3000
PHOSPHORUS	P	30.9580	31.0	1.83 to 1.96	0.1887	
Selenium	Se	78.7970	78.8	4.28 to 4.80	0.0746	44
IODINE	I	126.5570	126.6	4.95	0.0541	100 to 217
BROMINE	Br	79.7680	79.8	2.99 to 3.19	0.0813	
CHLORINE	Cl	35.3700	35.4	1.33 (liquid)	0.1210	107
Fluorine	F	18.9810	19.0			
NITROGEN	N	14.0210	14.0		0.2438	
SULPHUR	S	31.9840	32.0	1.98 to 2.07	0.1776	
OXYGEN	O	15.9633	16.0		0.2175	

NEGATIVE END: hydrates form acids.

Such elements as neptunium, davyum, phillipium. decipium, etc., etc., are of no importance to the dentist. Moreover, Crookes, in his address to the Chemical Society of Great Britain, has questioned the elementary character of the so-called rare earths and proposes the term "meta-elements" for those substances which are neither compounds, mixtures, nor elements.

111. **Number of Atoms in Molecules of Elements.**—At ordinary temperatures most of the elements given in Table I contain two atoms in the molecule and are called, therefore, *Diatomic.* **Exceptions:** mercury, cadmium, zinc, barium are **Monatomic,** *i. e.*, have one atom in the molecule; ozone contains three atoms of oxygen; the molecule of phosphorus and of arsenic contains four atoms; that of sulphur, six, but at high temperatures, two.

Elemental Atoms and Molecules.—The symbols given in Table I should not be used to represent the elements in general; each symbol represents **one atom** of the element; thus, Zn does not represent zinc in general, but one atom of the element zinc with the properties of that atom, namely, definite unchanging weight and definite power of attraction for other atoms.

Rule 1.—To Denote a Number of Atoms of an Element, write the Symbol of the Element with the required number in Arabic Figures at the lower right hand corner of the Symbol.—Zn_2 means two atoms of zinc; H_3 means three atoms of hydrogen; O_4 means four atoms of oxygen. Where one atom of an element is to be represented, write the symbol only.

Rule 2.—To Denote a Molecule of an Element, write the Symbol of that Element with

the Figure 2 at its lower right hand corner.—Exceptions: write the symbols only of mercury, cadmium, zinc, and barium; write four after the symbols of phosphorus and arsenic, and six after sulphur. O_2 means one molecule of oxygen, composed of two atoms. Hg means one molecule of mercury, composed of one atom; P_4 means one molecule of phosphorus, composed of four atoms; S_6 means one molecule of sulphur, composed of six atoms. (See 111 for Atomicity).

Rule 3.—To Denote a Number of Molecules of an Element, write the required Number as a full sized Figure before the expression for one Molecule. $2O_2$ means two molecules of oxygen, each composed of two atoms. 2Zn means two molecules of zinc, each composed of one atom.

112. **Atomic weight.**—The atomic weight of an element denotes the weight of an atom of it referred to the weight of an atom of hydrogen as unity.

The *proportions* in which atoms combine also represent the weights of the atoms: thus, oxygen unites with other elements in proportions of 16, therefore 16 is the weight of the atom of oxygen.

113. **Determination of atomic weight.**—By quantitative analysis the weights of two elementary substances forming a compound is ascertained. The proportion of these weights, one to another, will be either the ratio of the atomic weights of the two elements, or else that

of some simple multiple, the latter being previously known from a comparison of the compounds of the element whose weight we are seeking. Thus, suppose it is desired to find the atomic weight of zinc. Suppose that on using a given weight of zinc and of hydrochloric acid a certain volume of hydrogen is evolved. Make a proportion:

Weight of hydrogen found: weight of zinc used $= 1 : x$. Now x will be either the atomic weight of zinc, or some multiple of it. From a comparison of the numerous zinc compounds we know the result obtained to be half the atomic weight. Double the value to find the accepted weight.

114. Quality of Combining Power of Atoms. Positive and Negative Elements.— When a current of electricity of sufficient strength is passed through a chemical compound in state of solution, *i. e.*, dissolved, the compound is broken up into its constituent elements. Of these elements some are found at the positive pole of the battery, others collect at the negative.

An element attracted to the *positive* pole is called a *negative* element; one attracted to the *negative* pole a *positive* element. Elements are not absolutely positive or negative but only relatively so, *i. e.*, with reference to one another. In Table 1 the list of elements is so arranged that each element is negative to the one below it and positive to the one above it. For example, suppose it be required to know which of the two elements, sulphur and oxygen, is positive to the other and which negative. Consulting Table 1, it will be found that oxygen is written *above* sulphur, therefore negative to it; sulphur is written *below* oxygen, therefore *positive* to oxygen.

115. **Quantity of combining power of Atoms.***—*One* atom of an element does not necessarily combine with, or take the place of, one atom of, another element. It may unite with 1, 3, or 5 atoms of another element, or with 2, 4, or 6 atoms of it. An atom of bromine for example may combine with one atom of hydrogen, but an atom of oxygen requires *two* of hydrogen, one of nitrogen requires *three* and so on.

The equivalence or quantivalence of an atom of an element, by which we mean the quantity of combining power which it has, is expressed as 1, 2, 3, 4, 5, 6, or 7, according as the atom will attach to itself, or be exchanged for, 1, 2, 3, 4, 5, 6, or 7 atoms of hydrogen, or the equivalent of those atoms.

If the atom combines with one atom of hydrogen, or exchanges for one atom of hydrogen, it is called a **Monad**, if with two a **Dyad**, if with three a **Triad**, if with four a **Tetrad**, if with five a **Pentad**, if with six a **Hexad**, if with seven a **Heptad**. Monads are equivalent to monads, dyads to dyads, etc. Dyads are equivalent to two monads, triads to three monads, etc. One monad and one dyad are together equivalent to one triad, etc.

The following table should now be carefully committed to memory:

TABLE 2. QUANTIVALENCE.†

MONADS.	DYADS.	TRIADS.
Potassium.	Barium.	Bismuth.
Sodium.	Calcium.	Gold.

*The terms quantivalence, equivalence, equivalency, and valence are all used to denote the quantity of the combining power of atoms.

†The elements are arranged in electro-chemical order, beginning with the positive and ending with the negative or least positive.

Table 2.—*Continued.*

Lithium.	Magnesium.	Antimony.
Silver.	Zinc.	Boron.
Hydrogen.	Lead.	Arsenic.
Iodine.	Copper.	Phosphorus.
Bromine.	Mercury.	Nitrogen.
Chlorine.	Sulphur.	
Fluorine.	Oxygen.	

Tetrads.
Aluminium.
Tin.
Platinum.
Silicon.
Carbon.

Hexads.
Manganese.
Iron.
Chromium.

Notice that those in-*ine* are all monads, that the gases hydrogen, oxygen, nitrogen are monad, dyad, and triad respectively.

Monads are said to be *univalent*.
Dyads   "   "   *bivalent*.
Triads   "   "   *trivalent*.
Tetrads "   "   *tetravalent*.
etc.,   etc.,   etc.

Rule 4. To express the Equivalence (Quantivalence) of an Atom, place a Roman Numeral above and to the right of the Symbol.

O^I means one atom of oxygen having 2 as its quantivalence, or *equivalence* as it is often called. N means one atom of nitrogen having 3 as its equivalence.

N. B.--Quantivalence is sometimes expressed by dashes,

thus: O", N'''; by some the points of attraction, or bonds, of an atom are expressed as follows:

Monad O—(one bond).
Dyad —O— (two bonds).
Triad —Ȯ— (three bonds).
Tetrad —Ȯ— (four bonds).
Pentad ⇃Ȯ↲ (etc.).
Hexad —Ȯ—
Heptad —Ȯ—

116. **Variations in Quantivalence.**—Unfortunately for the learner, the various elements do not always adhere to the quantivalence established in Table 2. Certain of the elements are not only of the quantivalence of Table 2, but of other quantivalence also.

This is the most difficult thing in chemical theory for the beginner to understand. It has been found by analysis that nitrogen, for example, is sometimes a monad, sometimes a triad, and sometimes a pentad. This is because one element may form several *different* compounds with another element.

Let the student now commit to memory the following table:

Table 3.—VARIATIONS IN QUANTIVALENCE.

List I.—Elements often either Monads, Triads, or Pentads.

Chlorine.................I, III, V.
Bromine................I, III, V.
Iodine...................I, III, V.
Nitrogen...............I, III, V.
Phosphorus............I, III, V.
Arsenic.................I, III, V.

List II.—Elements often either Triads or Pentads.

Antimony...............III, V.
Bismuth.................III, V.

List III.—Elements often either Dyads or Tetrads.

Carbon..................II, IV.

Silicon.................II, IV.
Tin......................II, IV.
Lead....................II, IV.
Platinum..............II, IV.

List IV.—Elements often either Dyads, Tetrads, or Hexads.
Sulphur..............II, IV, VI.
Selenium............II, IV, VI.

Other elements varying in quantivalence will be noticed whenever necessary. Table 3 includes the most important variations. It must be noticed that the equivalence of an atom always increases or diminishes by two; thus, chlorine may be either I, III, or V, but not I, II, or III.

117. **Artiads and Perissads.**—Atoms (or radicals)* which have an even number of free bonds, that is, dyads, tetrads, and hexads, are called *Artiads*. Those which have an uneven number of free bonds, that is, monads, triads, pentads, and heptads, are called *Perissads*.

118. **Theory of Variation in Quantivalence.**—The hypothesis is that an atom has but one equivalence, namely the highest it ever exhibits. If now two of its bonds mutually saturate one another, the quantity of combining power which the atom now has is less by two than its highest combining power; if two pairs of bonds mutually saturate each other, the atom has an equivalence now less by four than its highest, and so on. A heptad may thus become pentad, triad, and monad; a hexad may become tetrad and dyad.

COMPOUND MOLECULES.

119. **Relation of Molecular Weight to density of compound gases.**—All molecules have the same size (Avoga-

---

*For radicals see section 126

dro's law) therefore every molecular formula not only expresses the weight of the molecule, but also the volume it occupies. The volume occupied by the atom of hydrogen is assumed to be unity; the volume of its molecule will therefore be two, and of all molecules of all bodies, two also. Molecular weight, then, represents the weight of *two* volumes; density represents the weight of *one*.

Therefore *the density of any homogeneous substance in the state of gas is one-half its molecular weight.* Conversely, given the density of a substance in the state of gas and its *molecular weight is always equal to twice the density*.

120. **Law of definite and multiple proportions.**—A given compound always contains the same elements in the same proportions. Thus, a molecule of water is *always* composed of hydrogen atoms and oxygen atoms, and always of just so much hydrogen, two atoms, and of so much oxygen, one atom. Moreover, when two elements are capable of uniting in different proportions, the quantities of one which unite with a given quantity of another usually bear a simple relation to one another.

121. **Differences between Molecules.**— Molecules are of two classes, *elementary** (composed of like atoms) and *compound* (composed of unlike atoms).

122. **Formulæ.**—Compound molecules are represented by the symbols of the different elements forming the

---

*Elementary molecules have already been considered.

compound. This representation is termed a formula; thus, KCl is a formula representing one atom of potassium and one atom of chlorine, the two together combining to form a compound molecule.†

123. **Compound Molecules.** (*a*) **Binaries.** — Compound molecules are of two kinds: 1, Binary; 2, Ternary.

Binary Compounds are those whose molecule is composed of two atoms each one of a different element, as KCl.

Definition 6. **A Binary Compound is one formed by the direct union of two different elements or radicals, one of which must be positive to the other.**

Rule 5. **To name Binaries, put the name of the positive element first and the name of the negative element second. Then change the termination of the negative element to -ide.**

A compound of sulphur and potassium is named as follows:

(1). Consult Table 1, and find which is positive to the other.

(2). Put the name of the positive element first, that of the negative second: thus, potassium sulphur.

(3). Change the termination of the negative one, sulphur, to -ide, and we have potassium sulphide.

Example 1. Name compounds of the following: silver and chlorine, sodium and sulphur, iodine and potassi-

---

†The entire number of bonds in a molecule must be even.

um, hydrogen and oxygen, hydrogen and arsenic, phosphorus and zinc. Answers: silver chloride, sodium sulphide, potassium iodide, hydrogen oxide, hydrogen arsenide, zinc phosphide.

124. **Meaning of the terminations -ic,-ous, and hypo-ous.**—When the positive of two elements forming a compound is one of those which varies in equivalence (see Table 3) this variation is indicated by the use of the termination **-ic, -ous,** and **hypo-ous.**

Rule 6. **To name a binary compound whose positive element is one which varies in equivalence,** write the names of the elements precisely as in rule 5, but change the termination of the positive element to *-ic*, if this element exerts its highest equivalence (Table 3), to *-ous* if its next highest, and to *hypo-ous* if its lowest.

A compound of tetrad tin and chlorine would be called stann*ic* chloride; of dyad tin and chlorine, stann*ous* chloride; of monad chlorine and oxygen, *hypo*chlor*ous* oxide. (Notice in Table 1 that oxygen is negative to chlorine).

Example 2. What do triad chlorine and oxygen form? pentad antimony and chlorine?

Answers: Chloric oxide. Antimonous chloride.

Rule 7. **To write the formula for a binary compound,** write the symbol of the positive element first, then the symbol of the negative element. At upper right hand of symbol of positive element write the equivalence of that element; do the same to the negative. Transfer the Roman numerals indicating equivalence of positive element to lower right hand of negative element. Transfer the Roman numerals indicating equivalence of the negative element to the lower right hand of positive element. Write all transferred numerals in Arabic figures, changing them from Roman.*

To write the formula for stannic chloride:

(1) Symbol of positive element,   Sn;
(2) Symbol of negative element,   Cl;
(3) Arranged in order,   SnCl;
(4) Equivalence indicated, $\overset{IV}{Sn}\overset{I}{Cl}$;
(5) Numerals transferred, $SnCl_4$

N. B.—It is really never necessary to write the figure 1, as the symbol itself indicates one atom.

If **several molecules** of the binary compound are to be denoted, write the formula, inclose in brackets, and write the multiplier as a small-sized figure at lower right hand, or write a full-sized figure before the formula not inclosed in brackets.

Suppose it be required to denote 3 molecules of sodium iodide: the formula is NaI which denotes *one molecule* with all the properties of that molecule, namely, a certain unchangeable weight—the sum of the weights of the two atoms, called the molecular weight—or, in the case of

---

*Rule 7 has been deduced from the following: in all cases of chemical combination the chemical affinity of each atom must be satisfied. Atoms of the same valence, then, may mutually saturate one another, and unite in the ratio of one to one. Atoms of different valence cannot unite in the ratio of one to one; each one must furnish the same number of bonds, which number is in all cases the least common multiple of the two valences. Divide this l. c. m. by each valence to obtain the number of atoms of each constituent in the compound. Thus, triad nitrogen and dyad oxygen: $6 \div 3$ shows the number of nitrogen atoms; $6 \div 2 =$ the number of oxygen atoms.

gases, a certain volume always the same; to denote 3 molecules, write the figure 3 before the formula: thus, 3NaI; or bracket the formula (NaI) and write the figure 3 in small-sized type at the lower right hand: thus (NaI)$_3$.

Example 3. Denote five molecules of magnesium oxide, six of silver chloride, three of chlorous oxide.

Answers: 5MgO or (MgO)$_5$, 6AgCl or (AgCl)$_6$, 3Cl$_2$O$_3$ or (Cl$_2$O$_3$)$_3$.

Remark: In order to apply Rule 7 successfully, the following must be borne in mind: if a formula, obtained by Rule 7, shows after each symbol figures which contain common factors, these common factors must be removed from the figures; thus, the formula for stannic oxide, according to Rule 7, is Sn$_2$O$_4$; but 2 and 4 contain the common factor 2, therefore divide each by 2 and the result, SnO$_2$, is the proper formula. *

Example 4. Write the formulæ for platinic sulphide, hyposulphurous oxide, stannous sulphide:

Answers. PtS$_2$, SO, SnS.

125. **Variation in Equivalence of Certain Elements.**— Certain elements vary in equivalence in a puzzling manner, e. g. mercury, copper, iron, aluminium. As compounds of these metals are important, it is desirable that the variations in equivalence be thoroughly understood.

Mercury is a dyad; in some compounds, however, we find two atoms of mercury and two of a monad, as for example in calomel, the formula for which is Hg$_2$Cl$_2$. The formula Hg$_2$Cl$_2$ is explained graphically: Hg—Cl.
|
Hg—Cl.

Two atoms of dyad mercury would have four bonds (Rule 4, N. B.), and ought to take four atoms of monad chlorine, *but two of the bonds of the mercury satisfy*

---

*Sn$_2$O$_4$ is the same as 2SnO$_2$ or (SnO$_2$)$_2$, that is two molecules of Sn O$_2$.

each other instead of requiring two bonds of chlorine; the other two bonds of the mercury are satisfied by means of two chlorine bonds, hence Hg_2Cl_2, and not Cl_4 as might be expected. The same may be said of copper. Such compounds are called mercurous or cuprous compounds. Variation in equivalence may, in general, be explained by graphic formulæ.

Rule 8. **To write formulæ containing mercury or copper,** assign to *mercuric* atoms and *cupric* atoms an equivalence of *two* as in table 4; to *mercurous* and *cuprous* assign an equivalence of one. N. B. In the case of mercurous and cuprous note that two atoms of mercury or copper require two only of a univalent element.

Example 5. Write the formulæ for mercuric chloride, mercurous iodide, cupric oxide, mercurous chloride.

Answers. $HgCl_2$, HgI or Hg_2I_2, CuO, $HgCl$ or Hg_2Cl_2.

Compounds of **iron** are known to exist in which the molecule may consist of two atoms of iron and six of a monad, as for example, ferric chloride, Fe_2Cl_6; to such compounds the term *ferric* is applied.

Rule 9. **To write formulæ containing** *iron,* give two atoms of iron together, an equivalence of *six,* if the compound is called *ferric.* In *ferrous* compounds assign equivalence of *two* to iron.

N. B. While Hg_2Cl_2 is often written in the simpler form $HgCl$, it is not customary to write Fe_2Cl_6 in any simpler fashion; the formulæ of other compounds are usually simplified.

Example 6. Write the formulæ for ferric chloride, ferric oxide, ferrous sulphide, ferrous oxide, aluminic chloride.

Answers. Fe_2Cl_6, Fe_2O_3, [that is $(Fe_2)_2O_6$], FeS, FeO, Al_2Cl_6—like ferric.

Rule 10. **To read Binary Formulæ**, observe from figure at lower right hand of negative element what the equivalence of the positive element is. If the positive element is in its highest equivalence (Table 3) change its termination to -ic etc., as in Rule 6. Note that where sulphur is the positive element and the negative element oxygen, the figure 3 at the lower right hand of oxygen will denote sulphur as a hexad, hence sulphur*ic*: e. g., S_2O_6 or SO_3 is sulphur*ic* oxide.

In reading binary formulæ, the termination of the negative element is always changed to -ide.

Example 7. Read the formulæ of the following compounds used in dental medicine:

1, KBr. 2, KI. 3, HCl. 4, $SnCl_2$. 5, KCl. 6, K^2O. 7, H_2O. 8, Al_2Cl_6. 9, As_2O_3. 10 $AuCl_3$. 11, $HgCl_2$. 12, HgCl. 13, HgI. 14, ZnI_2. 15, ZnO. 16, MgO. 17, CaO.

Answers. 1, potassium bromide. 2, potassium iodide. 3, hydrogen chloride. 4, stannous chloride. 5, potassium chloride. 6, potassium oxide. 7, hydrogen oxide. 8, aluminic chloride. 9, arsenous oxide. 10, auric chloride. 11, mercuric chloride. 12, mercurous chloride (see Rule 8). 13, mercurous iodide. 14, zinc iodide. 15, zinc oxide. 16, magnesium oxide. 17, calcium oxide.

Example 8. Read the following formulæ (of use in studying ternaries): Cl_2O_5, N_2O_5, SO_3, SO, Cl_2O, Cl_2O_3, CO_2.

Answers. Chloric oxide, nitric oxide, sulphuric oxide,

hyposulphurous oxide, hypochlorous oxide, chlorous oxide, carbonic oxide.

126. **Radicals.**—A radical is an unsaturated group of atoms. It possesses free bonds, hence may enter into combination like single atoms.

Example: HO is an unsaturated group of atoms, for one bond of the oxygen is unprovided for, thus, H—O—. Hence HO is a radical.

127. **Nomenclature, and equivalence of radicals.**-The *names* of compound radicals end in -yl. Thus, HO is called hydroxyl.

The equivalence of compound radicals is always equal to the number of unsatisfied bonds, that is to the difference resulting from the subtraction of the equivalence of one of its constituents from that of the other:

Thus the equivalence of HO is *one* because it has one unsatisfied bond, that is, 2 (equivalence of oxygen) minus 1 (equivalence of hydrogen) equals 1 (equivalence of hydroxyl).

Radicals are therefore *perissad* and *artiad* like atoms. Perissad radicals can not exist free except by combining with one another.

128. **Ternary Compounds.**—

Definition 7. A ternary compound is one whose molecule is composed of three or more different kinds of atoms: thus, $KClO_3$ is a ternary because composed of K, Cl, and O. In every ternary formula there are at least three different symbols.

In ternaries the dissimilar atoms are linked together

by a third atom, and ternaries are of two classes, (*a*) those whose dissimilar atoms are linked by a bivalent atom, and (*b*) those whose dissimilar atoms are linked by a trivalent atom. The first class comprises many inorganic compounds, the second many organic.

In the first class the linking is usually performed by oxygen, sometimes by sulphur, sometimes by selenium and tellurium.

129. **Ternaries of the first class. Dissimilar atoms linked by oxygen or sulphur.**

There are three kinds: acids, bases, and salts.

Definition 8. **Acids** are corrosive substances having usually a sour taste, neutralizing alkalies, and changing blue vegetable colors to red. They give off hydrogen when brought into contact with a metal. Acids are either (hydracids), **ox-acids**, or **sulpho-acids**. [Hydracids are *binary* compounds of hydrogen, and are hydrochloric, HCl; hydrobromic, HBr; hydriodic, HI; hydrosulphuric, H_2S. They are also called· hydrogen (or hydric) chloride, hydrogen or hydric bromide, etc.].

Ox-acids are composed of hydrogen, some negative element, and oxygen: as HNO_3, nitric acid.

Sulpho-acids are composed of hydrogen, some negative element, and sulphur, as H_2CS_3, sulpho-carbonic acid.

Rule 11. To write the formulæ of many ox-acids and sulpho-acids:*

1. Write the formula of corresponding oxide or sulphide, simplifying if possible.
2. Add formula for a molecule of water, H_2O, in case of an ox-acid, or H_2S in case of a sulpho-acid.
3. Simplify if possible.

Suppose the formula for nitric acid be required: first write the formula for the corresponding oxide. By this we mean nitric† oxide and not nitrous or hyponitrous. Formula for nitric oxide is N_2O_5; add H_2O and we have $H_2N_2O_6$—the only thing to be added arithmetically being O to O_5 making O_6. Now simplify by taking out the common factor 2 and we have HNO_3. (See also Table 4 and note Rule 14, page 58).

---

*Rule 11 is deduced from the following: 1. An acid molecule is one consisting of one or more negative atoms united by oxygen to hydrogen.

· 2. Ternaries are formed by the direct union of the oxide of a more positive atom with the oxide of a less positive or negative atom. Whenever water is the positive oxide, the body produced is an acid: thus, of the two oxides, sulphuric and hydric, sulphuric oxide is the negative and hydric oxide (water) the positive, therefore the two on combining form an *acid*.

3. An acid, then, may be formed by the combination of a negative oxide with water.

Acids are also formed from water, H—O—H, by exchanging an atom of H for a negative monad. Thus, hypochlorous acid: exchange one atom of H for Cl and there is formed Cl—O—H.

†This rule gives always hydrated acids and is of service in obtaining formulæ of salts. The use of Table 4 is to be preferred.

Note. The formulæ for phosphoric, boric, arsenic, arsenous, and hypophosphorous acids are obtained by adding more than one molecule of water or (better) by Table 4, page 58.

Example 9. Write the formulæ for the following acids: sulpho-carbonic, sulphuric, sulphurous, hypochlorous, nitrous.

Answers: H_2CS_3, H_2SO_4, H_2SO_3, $HClO$, HNO_2.

N. B. The oxygen or sulphur of acids is said to have a linking function, uniting the hydrogen to the rest of the molecule; thus, the formula for nitric acid may be represented graphically as follows:

$H-O-N=O$ { the hydrogen atom being linked to the rest of the molecule by the oxygen atom.
$=O$

Definition 9. Bases are the opposite of acids. They neutralize acids, either partly or entirely, restore blue colors to vegetable colors turned red by acids, when concentrated decompose fats, forming soap, and act on the tissues as caustics.

Acids unite with metals to form salts, bases with acids to form salts, hydrogen being evolved in the one case, water formed in the other.

Inorganic bases are termed hydrates, by which term we shall hereafter call them. The molecule of a hydrate is composed of a positive atom or atoms, hydrogen, and oxygen: thus, R O H. R denoting any number of positive atoms.

The oxygen of bases is said to link the hydrogen to the positive element.

The formula for sodium hydrate may be represented graphically as follows: Na—O—H, in which the positive atom is linked by the atom of oxygen to the hydrogen.

Rule 12. **To write the formula for a hydrate**, first write the symbol of the positive element with its equivalence over it, then write OH in brackets with an equivalence of 1 over it. Next exchange figures representing equivalences, as in binaries.*

To write the formula for calcium hydrate:

1. Ca^{II}.
2. $(OH)^{I}$.
3. $Ca^{II}(OH)^{I}$.
4. $Ca(OH)_2$. Calcium hydrate.

Calcium hydrate represented graphically would be
$Ca\begin{smallmatrix}\diagup OH \\ \diagdown OH\end{smallmatrix}$

Example 10. Write the formulæ for barium hydrate, mercuric hydrate, arsenous hydrate, cuprous hydrate.

Answers. $Ba(OH)_2$, $Hg(OH)_2$, $As(OH)_3$, $CuOH$.

N. B. Where one molecule only of OH occurs it is not necessary to bracket. Instead of OH some authors write HO.

Definition 10. A **salt** resembles neither an

---

*Rule 12 is deduced from the following: a molecule of water consists of two atoms of hydrogen linked by oxygen. Exchange one of these hydrogen atoms for a positive univalent atom, and a base results. Thus, water is H—O—H: exchange H for K and we have K—O—H. But when it is necessary to form the hydrate of a bivalent atom it is necessary to take two molecules of water and one of the bivalent element. Thus, if calcium hydrate be required, take 2 H_2O, or H_4O_2. Substitute Ca for H_2 and we have CaH_2O_2 or $Ca(HO)_2$. The formulæ of bases may be obtained also by direct union of water with a positive oxide.

acid nor a base; its molecule consists of a positive atom united by oxygen to a negative atom; thus, KNO_3: K positive atom, N negative, O oxygen.

Exceptions. A salt may be formed from an acid and a metal, the latter replacing all the hydrogen of the acid; acids whose molecule contains two atoms of hydrogen may not always exchange both atoms for atoms of a metal, but one may be replaced and the other not: thus, $NaHSO_4$. Such a salt is called an *acid* salt. Those described in Definition 10 are called *normal* salts. *Double* salts are those whose molecules consist of two, different, positive atoms united by oxygen to the negative atom: thus, $KNaSO_4$, called potassium sodium sulphate, or the double sulphate of potassium and sodium.

Rule 13.* **To write the formula of a salt.**—First write the formula of the acid which, with the metal, forms the salt; bracket the non-hydrogen part of the acid formula, erase the H, and put in its place the symbol of the metal; write the equivalence of the metal after the bracket, and simplify if possible.

Note that *-ate* in a salt corresponds to *-ic* in an acid, *-ite* to *-ous*, hypo-ite to hypo-ous.

Examples: sodium sulph*ate* is formed from sulphur*ic* acid, sodium sulphite from sulphur*ous* acid, sodium hypochlorite from hypochlor*ous* acid.

Suppose the formula for mercuric nitrate be required. The termination *-ate* in a salt is used by chemists to sig-

---

*In writing the formulæ of a salt, as many molecules of the acid must be taken as is necessary to furnish a number of hydrogen atoms equal to the L. C. M. of the number of hydrogen atoms in the acid (*basicity*) and the valence of the replacing atom.

nify a higher equivalence of the negative element, just as –*ic* is used in the case of acids:

1. Write the formula for nitric acid: HNO_3.
2. Bracket the non-hydrogen part: $H(NO_3)$.
3. Erase the H and put into its place the symbol of the metal mercury: $HgNO_3$.
4. Write the equivalence of metal after bracket: $Hg(NO_3)_2$.
5. Simplify. (Not possible in this case).

The formulæ of salts may be written much more rapidly if the following table of compound **negative radicals** be committed to memory.

TABLE 4.

MONADS.

NO_3 (Nitrates).
NO_2 (Nitrites).
ClO_3 (Chlorates).
PH_2O_2 (Hypophosphites).
ClO (Hypochlorites).

DYADS.

SO_4 (Sulphates).
SO_3 (Sulphites).
CO_3 (Carbonates).
CrO_4 (Chromates).
Cr_2O_7 (Bichromates).

TRIADS.

PO_4 (Phosphates).
AsO_4 (Arsenates).
AsO_3 (Arsenites).
BO_3 (Borates).

TETRADS.

$FeCy_6$* (Ferrocyanides).
SiO_4 (Silicates).
P_2O_7 (Pyrophosphates).

HEXADS.

Fe_2Cy_{12}* (Ferricyanides)

Rule 14. **To write the formula of a salt by use of Table 4.** First write the symbol

---

*These will be explained under the head of theory of organic chemistry.

for the metal, with its equivalence indicated over it; next write the formula for the compound radical with its own equivalence over it; exchange equivalences; simplify if possible.

Suppose the formula of zinc hypophosphite be required:

1. $Zn^{ii}(PH_2O_2)^i$.
2. $Zn(PH_2O_2)_2$.

N. B. Acids being regarded by some as salts of hydrogen, their formulæ may be written from Table 4: thus, sulphuric acid may be written as hydrogen sulphate:

1. $H^i(SO_4)^{ii}$.
2. H_2SO_4.

Phosphoric acid and boric acid should be written from Table 4 altogether, as they are meta- and ortho-acids respectively, as regards their salts used in dental medicine.*

Example 11. Write the formulæ for the following salts used in dental medicine: cadmium sulphate, cupric sulphate, zinc sulphate, magnesium sulphate, magnesium hypochlorite, calcium sulphite, calcium hypophosphite (by Table 4), calcium carbonate, silver nitrate.

Answers: $CdSO_4$, $CuSO_4$, $ZnSO_4$, $MgSO_4$, $Mg(ClO)_2$, $CaSO_3$, $Ca(PH_2O_2)_2$, $CaCO_3$, $AgNO_3$.

---

*An ortho-acid is one whose molecule contains as much H as O: thus, ortho-phosphoric acid is H_5PO_5. The term "ortho-phosphoric" acid is, however, often given to H_3PO_4, which is really di-meta-phosphoric acid. A meta-acid is derived from an ortho-acid by subtraction of one or more molecules of water from the formula of the ortho-acid.

Example 12.† For practice write the formulæ of the following:

1. Cupric ferrocyanide,
2. Barium chromate,
3. Lead sulphate,
4. Ferric sulphate,
5. Ferric hypophosphite,
6. Aluminic hydrate,
7. Ferrous sulphate,
8. Sodium hypophosphite,
9. Potassium hypochlorite,
10. Calcium hypochlorite,
11. Potassium sodium sulphate,
12. Potassium sodium acid phosphate, or potassium sodium hydrogen phosphate,
13. Sodium hydrogen carbonate or sodium bicarbonate.

Answers:—

1. Cu_2FeCy_6,
2. $BaCrO_4$,
3. $PbSO_4$,
4. $Fe_2(SO_4)_3$,
5. $Fe_2(PH_2O_2)_6$,
6. $Al_2(HO)_6$,
7. $FeSO_4$,
8. $Na(PH_2O_2)$,
9. $KClO$,
10. $Ca(ClO)_2$,
11. $KNaSO_4$,
12. $KNaHPO_4$,
13. $NaHCO_3$.

TERNARIES OF THE SECOND CLASS. DISSIMILAR ATOMS LINKED BY TRIADS.

130. Ternaries of the second class are linked mostly by nitrogen. There are three kinds of those linked by nitrogen:—*amides*, in whose molecule *negative* atoms are linked to hydrogen by nitrogen,—*amines*, in whose molecule *positive* atoms are linked by nitrogen to hydrogen, and *alkalamides*, in whose molecule positive atoms are linked by nitrogen to negative ones. All may be derived by substitution from ammonia.

---

†This example may, at the discretion of the teacher, be omitted.

Rule 15. To read formulæ: commit to memory the following table:

TABLE 5.—USUAL TERMINATIONS IN VARIOUS BINARY AND TERNARY FORMULÆ.*

BINARIES.

Hydrochloric acid and all chlorides end in Cl_n.†

Hydrobromic acid and all bromides end in Br_n.

Hydriodic acid and all iodides end in I_n.

Hydrosulphuric acid and all sulphides end in S_n.

Hydrofluoric acid and all fluorides end in F_n or Fl_n.

All oxides end in O_n.

TERNARIES.

All hydrates end in $(OH)_n$.

Sulphuric acid and all sulphates end in $(SO_4)_n$.

Phosphoric acid and all phosphates end in $(PO_4)_n$.

Chromic acid and all chromates end in $(CrO_4)_n$.

Boric acid and all borates end in $(BO_3)_n$.

Nitric acid and all nitrates end in $(NO_3)_n$.

Chloric acid and all chlorates end in $(ClO_3)_n$.

Sulphurous acid and all sulphites end in $(SO_3)_n$.

---

*Graphic formulæ are not included in this table.

†n denoting any number.

Hypochlorous acid and all hypochlorites end in $(ClO)_n$.

Hypophosphorous acid and all hypophosphites end in $(PH_2O_2)_n$.

Suppose now that the formula to be read be HNO_3: it begins with H and contains no positive element, therefore is an acid; it ends in NO_3, therefore by Table 5 is ni*tric* acid. Suppose it be required to read the formula $Al_2(OH)_6$; it is not an acid because it does not begin with H, but is a hydrate, because it ends in OH; and it is alum*inic* hydrate by Rule 9. Suppose the formula be K_2CO_3. It is not an acid, nor a hydrate, but is a salt, because ending in oxygen preceded by a negative element. It is a carbonate by Table 5, hence is potassium carbonate. Suppose the formula be $Fe_2(CrO_4)_3$; it is a salt, and by Table 5 a *chromate*, and by Rule 9, *ferric* chromate.

Example 13. Read the formulæ given in the answers to example 12.

N. B. Consideration of formulæ of organic compounds is deferred to Chap. IV, but, as a sharp line of demarcation cannot always be drawn between many inorganic and organic compounds, the beginner will do well to note the following:

TABLE 6—ORGANIC COMPOUNDS.
BINARIES.

Hydrocyanic acid and all cyanides end in $(CN)_n$.

Hydroferrocyanic acid and all ferrocyanides end in $(FeCy_6)_n$.

Hydroferricyanic acid and all ferricyanides end in $(Fe_2Cy_{12})_n$.

Sulphocyanic acid and all sulphocyanates end in $(CNS)_n$.

TERNARIES.

Acetic acid and all acetates end in $(C_2H_3O_2)_n$.
Oxalic acid and all oxalates end in $(C_2O_4)_n$.
Tartaric acid and all tartrates end in $(C_4H_4O_6)_n$.
Salicylic acid and all salicylates end in $(C_7H_4O_3)_n$.

Example 14.* Read the following formulæ: $Pb(C_2H_3O_2)_2$, $K_2C_2O_4$, KCN, $K_4Fe(CN)_6$ or Cy_6, $KNaC_4H_4O_6$, $Na(CN)S$ or CyS, $Na_2C_7H_4O_3$.

Answers. Plumbic acetate, potassium oxalate, potassium cyanide, potassium ferrocyanide, potassium sodium tartrate, sodium sulphocyanate, sodium salicylate.

N. B. (*a*) **Ammonium Compounds** begin with (NH_4), a univalent positive radical: ammonium chloride is, therefore, $(N H_4)Cl$, ammonium sulphate $(NH_4)_2SO_4$, etc., etc.

Example 15. Read the following: NH_4NO_3, NH_4HO, NH_4MgPO_4.

Answers. Ammonium nitrate, ammonium hydrate, ammonium-magnesium phosphate.

(*b*) **Nomenclature — Old and New.**—The prefixes *proto-* and *per-* are used in older works instead of *-ic* and *-ate* on the one hand and *-ous* and *-ite* on the other; for example, instead of *mercurous iodide*, older writers speak of the *protiodide* of *mercury;* instead of *ferric sulphate* the *persulphate* of *iron* is the name given.

The term *acid* in some of the older books is given to what is now called *anhydride* or negative oxide; thus *arsenous acid* is used by some writers as the name for As_2O_3 which in this book is called arsenious anhydride or arsenous anhydride. The term *anhydrous acid* is also used by

---

*This example may be omitted until organic chemistry be taken up.

some writers instead of anhydride or oxide, and the term *hydrated acid* for what in this book is called simply *acid*. Oxides of sodium, potassium, magnesium, etc., are called *soda, potassa, magnesia, lime*, etc., by some authors.

Example 16. Give the new names for the following: baryta, perchloride of tin, protoxide of mercury, perchloride of iron, potash, alumina, protochloride of mercury, anhydrous phosphoric acid.

Answers. Barium oxide, stannic chloride, mercurous oxide, ferric chloride, potassium oxide, aluminum oxide, mercurous chloride, phosphoric anhydride or oxide.

N. B. Remember that in modern text books the term anhydride simply means an oxide which can combine with the elements of water to produce an acid, or in other words an acid minus water.

In many new text books, notably those by English authors, we find numeral prefixes, as di-, tri-, pent-, etc. Thus, CS_2 is called carbon disulphide, P_2O_5 phosphorus pentoxide, etc., etc. The old term for di- is bi-. Older writers use the prefix *sesqui-* in compounds where there are two atoms of one element and three of another; they also call hydrochloric acid *muriatic acid*, and term chlorides *muriates*. Sulphides are termed *sulphurets* by some.

Example 17. Give new names for the following: sesquioxide of iron, bisulphuret of carbon, sesquisulphide of iron, muriate of ammonia, bichloride of mercury, protosulphuret of iron, peroxide of hydrogen.

Answers. Ferric oxide (Fe_2O_3), carbonic disulphide, ferric sulphide (Fe_2S_3), ammonium chloride, mercuric chloride, ferrous sulphide, hydric dioxide.

Commercial terms.—For these, such as "salts of tartar," "sal volatile," etc., etc., see Glossary at the end of the book.

131. **Chemical change.**—In every chemical change one or more substances called *factors*

change into one or more substances called *products*.

Example: zinc and sulphuric acid change into zinc sulphate and hydrogen. Factors: zinc and sulphuric acid. Products: zinc sulphate and hydrogen.

132. **Fundamental laws of chemical change.**—I. The sum of the weights of the products of a chemical change are exactly equal to the sum of the weights of the factors. (Law of conservation of mass.—Lavoisier's Law).

Example: if phosphorus be burned in a closed jar, the latter will weigh as much after the combustion as before. That is, the weight of the products of the combustion is the same as that of the factors.

II. In any well-marked chemical change the relative weights of the several factors and products are definite and invariable.

(Law of Definite Proportions by Weight).

Suppose a given amount of sal-soda yields with hydrochloric acid a given amount of common salt. Five times the amount of sal-soda will yield five times the amount of salt.

III. In any well-marked chemical change the relative volumes of the aëriform factors or products, if measured under the same conditions, bear to each other a simple numerical ratio. (Law of Definite Proportions by Volume—Gay-Lussac's Law).

Example: oxygen combining with sulphur forms sulphurous oxide gas: the *volume* of the sulphurous oxide is the same as that of the oxygen; two volumes of hydrogen gas combine with one of oxygen to form two volumes of vapor of water.

133. Reactions—The chemical action between two substances on each other when brought together is called a **reaction**. The body, which when added to another causes the change, is called a **reagent**.

134. **Manner of Chemical Action.**—Chemical changes may take place as follows:

(*a*) By direct union of simpler molecules, forming a more complex one.

(*b*) By separation of a complex molecule into simpler ones.

(*c*) By substitution in a molecule of one atom or group of atoms for another or for several others.

(*d*) By mutual exchange of atoms between molecules.

(*e*) By re-arrangement of atoms within a single molecule, as shown by conversion of ammonium cyanate into urea.

Examples:

1. Chemical change of the first kind is represented by *synthetical* reactions; thus, hydrogen (one molecule) and chlorine (one molecule) form hydrochloric acid (two molecules).

2. Chemical change of the second kind is represented by analytical reactions: thus calcium carbonate (one molecule) yields one molecule of calcium oxide and one molecule of carbon dioxide.

3. Chemical change of the third kind is represented by the so-called substitution reactions, as for example when one atom of potassium replaces, *i. e.*, is substituted for, one atom of hydrogen in the molecule of water, forming potassium hydrate.

4. Chemical change of the fourth kind is represented

by the so-called metathetical reactions, as when ammonium sulphate and calcium carbonate exchange atoms mutually between their molecules, forming ammonium carbonate and calcium sulphate. This is sometimes called "double decomposition."*

135. Laws of Double Decomposition.— Berthollet's laws may be stated as follows:† (*a*). Whenever in a mixture of two or more substances it is possible by a rearrangement of the radicals to form a compound, volatile at the temperature of the experiment, such rearrangement will occur and the volatile compound will be formed. (*b*). Whenever on mixing two or more substances in solution, it is possible, by rearrangement of the radicals. to form an insoluble‡ compound, that rearrangement will occur and the insoluble compound will be formed as a precipitate.

In other words if solutions of two salts be mixed, and by double decomposition an insoluble salt can be formed, the double decomposition will take place and the insoluble salt will be formed. If the salt be only difficultly soluble, the double decomposition will take place be-

---

*Professor J. H. Salisbury explains double decomposition as follows: in many cases of substitution the element displaced combines with the element or radical with which the displacing element was previously combined and two new compounds are formed in which the radicals have changed places with each other. When compounds of two basylous radicals or metals are brought together in solution, a double decomposition occurs, consisting in change of place on part of the metals or basylous radicals with each other.

†Woody,

‡Insoluble in the menstruum present.

tween concentrated solutions, but not between dilute. If by double decomposition a volatile substance can be formed, the double decomposition will take place and the substance will be formed. If the volatile substance is soluble in water, the double decomposition may not take place until the solutions are concentrated, or until the substances are entirely deprived of water. For example, sodium nitrate and sulphuric acid may exist together in dilute solution, but upon concentration double decomposition takes place, the volatile nitric acid being given off.*

The insoluble compound formed by double decomposition separates from the solution as a *precipitate*.

In order that the student may become familiar with the principle of the laws, it is necessary that the principal insoluble and volatile compounds be known.

INORGANIC COMPOUNDS INSOLUBLE IN WATER.
1. Most compounds of the heavy metals.
2. Almost all oxides.
3. Nearly all carbonates and phosphates.

EXCEPTIONS.

1. Chlorides, sulphates, chlorates, and nitrates are soluble, but lead chloride, mercurous chloride, and silver chloride are insoluble; barium sulphate and strontium sulphate are insoluble; oxides, hydrates, sulphides, and iodides of the alkalies† and alkaline earths‡ are not insoluble.

136. **Important Volatile Compounds.** — Ammonia, carbonic acid, nitric acid, hydrochloric acid, sulphuretted hydrogen.

Example 18. How may lead sulphate be made by

---

*J. H. Salisbury.
†K, Na, NH$_4$.
‡Ca, Ba, Sr.

double decomposition? Calcic carbonate? Barium sulphate? Silver chloride?

Answers. From hydrogen sulphate, or a soluble sulphate, and lead nitrate or other soluble salt of lead. From sodium carbonate and calcium chloride. From barium ——— and ——— sulphate. From silver ——— and hydrogen ———.

137. **Modes of Decomposition.**—The separation of a compound body into its constituent elements may be produced in various ways:

1. By heat: when limestone is heated, it is decomposed into lime and carbonic acid. Chemically speaking, calcium carbonate is decomposed by heat into calcium oxide and carbon dioxide. When an amalgam is heated, it is separated into mercury, which is driven off, and some other metal or metals.

2. By electricity: electricity decomposes many substances, provided they are in a liquid or gaseous state. Hydrochloric acid gas may be decomposed by passing an electric *spark* through it; water, by passing an electric *current* through it. Solutions of the metals may be decomposed by electricity and the metals themselves deposited. (See Copper Amalgam).

4. By light: see Section 83.

138. **Chemical Equations.**—These represent what actually takes place in a reaction. The sum of the weights of the **factors** is always equal to the sum of the weights of the **products**.

Rule 16. **To write Chemical Equations.**—
1. Write formulæ of factors.
2. Connect formulæ of factors by plus sign.

3. Write formulæ of products, connected by sign of plus.

4. Between factors and products write the sign =.

Thus, silver nitrate and hydrogen chloride give silver chloride and hydrogen nitrate; to represent the reaction by an equation:

1. Formulæ of factors: $AgNO_3$, HCl.
2. Connected by plus sign: **$AgNO_3, + HCl$**.
3. Formulæ of products: $AgCl$, HNO_3.
4. Connected by plus sign: **$AgCl + HNO_3$**.
5. 2 and 4 placed equal to one another:
$AgNO_3 + HCl = AgCl + HNO_3$.

Rules for determining the changes which take place in chemical reactions.—To decide why, for example, silver nitrate and hydrogen chloride give silver chloride and hydrogen nitrate, certain rules should be committed to memory:

1. Find out which elements or radicals are positive and which negative. [In the above equation in the left hand member we find the metal, silver, (Table 1) positive, the radical, NO_3, negative, (Table 4). Hydrogen is positive and chlorine negative. (See Table 1). **Positives** combine with **negatives** and vice versa, hence on the right hand side in the products, Ag will be found with Cl, and not with H, and the latter with NO_3, and not with Ag].

2. Cause the positives to change places.

3. Pay due attention to quantivalence. [In the above equation, Ag being monad can take the place of H to form AgCl, and H being monad can take the place of Ag to form HNO_3].

4. Notice that compound radicals usually remain unchanged in products.

CHEMICAL PHILOSOPHY.   71

5. N. B. An acid and an alkali cannot exist free in the same solution, and the strongest acid usually selects the strongest base with which to combine.

Example 19. Complete the following equations:
1. $Zn + H_2SO_4 = ?$
2. $(NH_4)_2 SO_4 + CaCO_3 = ?$
3. $H_2 + Cl_2 = ?$
4. $(NaCl)_2 + H_2SO_4 = ?$
5. $(KClO_3)_2 = ?$
6. $FeS + H_2SO_4 = ?$
7. $S + O_2 = ?$
8. $P_2O_5 + (H_2O)_3 = ?$
9. $CaCO_3 = ?$

ANSWERS.
2. $CaSO_4 + \text{\textemdash}$.
5. $\text{\textemdash} + (O_2)_3$.
8. $H_6P_2O_8$ or $\text{\textemdash}$.
9. $CaO + \text{\textemdash}$.

Example 20. In example 18 give two equations illustrating each answer.

139. **Chemical Arithmetic.**—By use of equations we may calculate the weight of any substance required by any given process. The rule is, as the formula of the given substance is to the formula of the required substance so is the weight of the given substance to the weight of the required substance. Thus, how much sulphate of zinc can be made from 5 pounds of zinc?

Reaction: $Zn + H_2SO = ZnSO_4 + H_2$.
Proportion: $Zn : ZnSO_4 = 5 : x$.
Reduced to figures: $65 : 161 = 5 : x$.
Product of means put equal to that of extremes: $65 x = 161 \times 5$.
Algebraically: $x = \frac{161 \times 5}{65} = \frac{161}{13} = 12.3$ lbs.

Note: after the formulæ are written in the proper

proportion, the molecular weights are substituted for them.

140. **Relations of Chemical Change to Force.**—Chemical change is accompanied by heat, electricity, often by light, and bears a relation to vital force.

Solution is accompanied by heat, as when caustic soda is dissolved in water.

Neutralization is accompanied by heat, as when sodium hydrate is added to sulphuric acid.

Chemical action is accompanied by heat, as when sulphuric acid acts on zinc.

Precipitation is accompanied by heat, as when copper sulphate solution is precipitated by a strip of zinc.*

The heat evolved in any chemical process is a measure of its energy, and the tendency is toward those combinations and conditions which involve the greatest evolution of heat.

141. **Light.**—The luminous effects witnessed in many chemical combinations are due to the high temperature produced. Luminous flames are nothing more than gaseous matters containing solids heated to the point of incandescence.

142. **Electricity.**—All chemical reactions are accompanied by a disturbance of electrical equilibrium. Chemical reactions between metals and liquids are the most productive of electricity. When a liquid acts chemically on a metal, the liquid assumes the positive electrical condition and the metal the negative.

A galvanic current is produced whenever two metals are placed in metallic contact in a liquid which acts more powerfully on one than on the other.

---

*The heat is not always perceptible in all cases, and to measure it an instrument called a *calorimeter* should be used.

143. **Vital Force.**—An uninterrupted succession of chemical reactions goes on in the living body. New molecules are constantly arriving and old ones departing. Almost every vital act in the body may be said to be accomplished by oxidation, and therefore by a consumption of oxygen. Between the food and the absorbed oxygen an interplay of changes is essential to the maintenance of the vital functions, whether these consist in the production of heat, in muscular contraction, in mental activity, or in assimilation. The ultimate products of oxidation in the body are urea, carbonic acid, and water.

144. **Chemical Affinity.**—Bodies most opposed to each other in chemical properties evince the greatest tendency to combine together, and conversely. The metals and hydrogen have strong affinity for oxygen, chlorine, and iodine, but the attraction of metals for one another is more feeble by far, as is also the attraction of chlorine for iodine, etc., etc. Acids are drawn toward alkalies, and alkalies toward acids.

145. **Circumstances influencing Chemical Attraction.**—(*a*) Alteration of temperature: mercury absorbs oxygen at one temperature but gives it off at a higher one. (*b*) Solution: tendency toward formation of a substance *insoluble* in the medium of solution. (*c*) Heat: tendency toward formation of a *volatile* compound when substances are mixed and heated. (*d*) Nascent state: substances combine better in the *nascent state*, that is, when each is simultaneously liberated from some previous combination. (*e*) Influence of a base: as, for example, oxidation of platinum by fused po-

tassium hydrate. (*f*) Mere *presence* of certain bodies as ferments. (See Fermentation).

Porous bodies by their presence favor certain chemical change. Hydrogen and vapor of iodine mixed in a tube heated to redness do not combine, but immediately unite if spongy platinum be present with them. This change may be classified under *catalytic action* and further examples are not necessary.

Heat, light, and *electricity* are favorable to chemical change. Moreover, the *physical condition* of bodies, and *pressure* are to be reckoned as factors. Chemical change between substances in liquid or gaseous state, as a rule, is more easily brought about than when the substances are in the solid state. For example, tartaric acid and bicarbonate of sodium, if mixed dry, do not effervesce, but immediately do so when water is added.

Pressure arrests certain changes, notably, such as give rise to disengagement of gas. Thus, zinc is not attacked so well by acids in a closed tube as in an open one, owing to the pressure of the disengaged hydrogen. Pure zinc is not attacked by pure sulphuric acid, owing to condensation of gas on the surface of the metal. *Pressure facilitates* certain changes: under pressure chloride and nitrate of silver are decomposed by hydrogen; silver is displaced and hydrochloric acid or nitric acid formed. Under pressure of 20 atmospheres, an alcohol flame becomes as bright as that of a candle.

146. **Classification of the Elements.**—It is difficult to classify the elements in a manner which shall be entirely satisfactory.

There are a number of well-marked groups in which there is some connection between the atomic weights and the properties of the elements; as, for example, in one group chlorine, bromine, iodine; in another, sulphur, selenium, tellurium; in a third, lithium, sodium, potassium.

If in each of these groups the atomic weights of the first and last be added, and the sum divided by 2, there results very nearly the atomic weights of the middle members. Moreover, the chemical properties of an element in each group are much like those of others of the same group. Mendeleef has shown that, if all the light elements of atomic weights from 7 to 36 be arranged in the order of their atomic weights, the result is as follows:

I. $Li = 7; Be = 9; B = 11; C = 12; N = 14; O = 16; Fl = 19.$

II. $Na = 23; Mg = 24; Al = 27; Si = 28; P = 31; S = 32; Cl = 35.5.$

Proceeding from left to right, there is a gradual change in the properties of members of the series; basic properties grow weaker and acid properties stronger; the metals are at the left end, the non-metals at the right, and those classed sometimes with metals, sometimes with non-metals, in the middle, as, for example, silicon.

All the elements may be arranged in series like the above. The changes in the properties of the elements will be noticed to be *periodic*; that is, they change according to the increasing atomic weights, and are then repeated in a *new period*.

Corresponding members of the even periods or of uneven periods resemble one another more closely than the members of the even periods resemble those of the uneven periods; that is, for example, those of the 4th and 6th are more alike than they are to those of 5th and 7th, and those of 5th and 7th resemble each other closely.

For further consideration of the periodic law the reader is referred to "Remsen's Theoretical Chemistry." Other authorities are Meyer, Ostwald, Hortsmann, and M. M. Pattison Muir. The work of Muir on the Principles of Chemistry will be an aid to those who are not familiar with the German language.

DENTAL CHEMISTRY.

Table 7.—Mendeleef's Tables.*

No. I.

Series.	Group I. R_2O	Group II. RO	Group III. R_2O_3	Group IV. RH_4 RO_2	Group V. RH_3 R_2O_5	Group VI. RH_2 RO_3	Group VII. RH R_2O_7	Group VIII. RO_4
1	$H = 1$							
2	$Li = 7$	$Be = 9$	$B = 11$	$C = 12$	$N = 14$	$O = 16$	$F = 19$	
3	$Na = 23$	$Mg = 24$	$Al = 27$	$Si = 28$	$P = 31$	$S = 32$	$Cl = 35.5$	
4	$K = 39$	$Ca = 40$	$Sc = 44$	$Ti = 48$	$V = 51$	$Cr = 52$	$Mn = 55$	$Fe = 56, Co = 59, Ni = 59, Cu = 63$
5	$(Cu = 63)$	$Zn = 65$	$Ga = 70$	$Ge = 72$	$As = 75$	$Se = 79$	$Br = 80$	
6	$Rb = 85$	$Sr = 87$	$Y = 89$	$Zr = 90$	$Nb = 94$	$Mo = 96$	$= 100$	$Ru = 103, Rh = 104, Pd = 106; Ag = 108$
7	$(Ag = 108)$	$Cd = 112$	$In = 113$	$Sn = 118$	$Sb = 120$	$Te = 125$	$I = 127$	
8	$Cs = 133$	$Ba = 137$	$La = 139$	$Ce = 142$	$Di = 145$			
9	$(-)$							
10			$Yb = 173$		$Ta = 182$	$W = 184$		$Os = 195?, Ir = 193, Pt = 195, Au = 196$
11	$(Au = 196)$	$Hg = 200$	$Tl = 204$	$Pb = 207$	$Bi = 208$			
12				$Th = 231$		$U = 240$		

*None but approximate atomic weights are given.

Explanation of Table I.
R denotes the symbol of any element in the group. R_2O would mean that in uniting with oxygen, two atoms of any element in the group unite with one of oxygen. Each series is called a *small period*. Series 1 and 2 form the first *large period*; series 3 and 4 the second, and so on.

No. II.

			I.	II.	III.	IV.	V.	VI.
R_2O	I.		Li=7	K 39	Rb 85	Cs 133	— —	— —
RO	II.		Be=9	Ca 40	Sr 87	Ba 137	— —	— —
R_2O_3	III.		B 11	Sc 44	Y 89	La 139	Yb 173	— —
RO_2	IV.	(H_4C)	C 12	Ti 48	Zr 90	Ce 142	— —	Th 231
R_2O_5	V.	(H_3N)	N=14	V 51	Nb 94	Di 145	Ta 182	— —
RO_3	VI.	(H_2O)	O=16	Cr 52	Mo 96	— —	W 184	U 240
R_2O_7	VII.	(HF)	F=19	Mn 55	— —	— —	— —	— —
				Fe 56	Ru 103	— —	Os 195?	— —
RO_4	VIII.			Co 59	Rh 104	— —	Ir 193	— —
				Ni 59	Pd 106	— —	Pt 195	— —
R_2O	I.	H = 1	Na=23	Cu 63	Ag 108	— —	Au 197	— —
RO	II.		Mg 24	Zn 65	Cd 112	— —	Hg 200	— —
R_2O_3	III.		Al 27	Ga 70	In 113	— —	Tl 204	— —
RO_2	IV.	(H_4R)	Si 28	Ge 72	Sn 118	— —	Pb 207	— —
R_2O_5	V.	(H_3R)	P 31	As 75	Sb 120	— —	Bi 208	— —
RO_3	VI.	(H_2R)	S 32	Se 79	Te 125	— —	— —	— —
R_2O_7	VII.	(HR)	Cl 35.5	Br 80	I 127	— —	— —	— —

Explanation: in Table II the elements are in groups, but in such a way as to indicate the difference between the even and uneven periods. Thus at the top in line with, and to the right of R_2O, I, will be seen from left to right, the members of the even series: Li, K, Rb, etc., which belong to series 2, 4, 6, etc.

Then after those of the even series have been finished

those of the odd are taken up, beginning with H and going on to Na, Cu, etc., from left to right.

In other words corresponding members of even periods are given first, then corresponding members of odd periods.

147. **Meyer's Classification.**—Lothar Meyer arranges the periods somewhat differently, not in horizontal lines, but in lines so inclined that, if the table were pasted on a cylinder of the right size, the table would form a continuous spiral, beginning at the top with lithium, and ending at the bottom with uranium. Meyer has shown a very close connection to exist between the atomic weights and various properties of the elements.

The work of Mendeleef, and also of Meyer, has been of the greatest interest to chemists. The author has not thought it desirable to go further into details concerning the various classifications of the elements in a book like a Dental Chemistry, which is essentially practical in nature and limited in scope. But it is very desirable that those intending to teach chemistry should familiarize themselves as thoroughly as possible with the theoretical principles of the science. For this purpose the following books should be owned: J. P. Cooke's "Chemical Philosophy" and "New Chemistry"; Lothar Meyer's "Modern Theories of Chemistry", elsewhere referred to; M. M. Pattison Muir's "Treatise on the Principles of Chemistry." German text-books of value are Ostwald's "Lehrbuch der Allgemeinen Chemie", and A. Horstman's "Theoretische Chemie" to be found in Band I. 2. Graham-Otto's "Ausführliches Lehrbuch der Chemie." [Wöhler's "Outlines of Organic Chemistry" has been translated from the 8th German edition by Professor Remsen, and is useful in studying the Carbon Compounds]. Going into more special works of interest to the dentist, we find Krupp's "Die Legirungen", to be had in English with additions under the name of "The Metallic Alloys" by W. T. Brannt. There is also a work known as the "Techno-Chemical Receipt Book", which may prove handy for reference at times in regard to matters purely practical. But the subject of chemistry as a whole can not be intelligently comprehended until very diligent study has been given to theory.

TABLE 8.
Lothar Meyer's Arrangement of the Elements.

I.	II.	III.	IV.	V.	VI.	VII.	VIII.		
Li 7.01									
	Be 9.08	B 10.9	C 11.97	N 14.01					
Na 22.99					O 15.96	F 19.06			
	Mg 23.94	Al 27.04	Si 28	P 30.96					
K 39.03					S 31.98	Cl 35.37			
	Ca 39.91	Sc 43.97	Ti 48	V 51.1					
Cu 63.18					Cr 52.45	Mn 54.8	Fe 55.88	Co 58.6	Ni 58.6
	Zn 64.88	Ga 69.9	Ge 72.32	As 74.9					
Rb 85.2					Se 78.87	Br 79.76			
	Sr 87.3	?Y 89.6	Zr 90.4	Nb 93.7					
Ag 107.66					Mo 95.9	? 99	Ru 103.5	Rh 104.1	Pd 106.2
	Cd 111.7	In 113.4	Sn 117.35	Sb 119.6					
Cs 132.7					Te 126.3	I 126.54			
	Ba 136.86	La 138.5	Ce 141.2	Di? 145					
? 165					? 151	? 152			
	? 170	Yb 172.6	? 176	Ta 182					
Au 196.2					W 183.6	? 185	Os 195?	Ir 192.5	Pt 194.3
	Hg 199.8	Tl 203.7	Pb 206.39	Bi 207.5					
? 222					? 210	? 211			
	? 226	? 230	?Th 231.96	? 234	?U 239.8				

The spaces left blank are to be filled with elements yet to be discovered.*

---

*Mendeleef predicted the discovery of an element between calcium and titanium. Scandium was discovered and filled the place.

148. General Properties of the Metallic Elements.—Metals are, as has already been seen, elementary bodies, solids with exception of mercury, insoluble in water, and possessed of certain properties as lustre, fusibility, etc. Among the more important properties of metals we find

lustre,—power of reflecting light;

tenacity,—resistance to any attempt to pull asunder their particles;

malleability,—capability of being hammered or rolled into thin sheets;

ductility,—property of being drawn out into wire;

high specific gravity,—or weight relative to water;*

high conducting power,—for heat and electricity;

fusibility,—property of becoming liquid when heated;

capacity for heat, or specific heat;

expansibility,—property of expanding when heated;

crystalline structure,—shown by metals on cooling from fusion;

---

*Only seven have a sp. gr. below 6.72, but they vary from osmium, 22, to lithium, 0.59.

volatility,—property of being converted into vapor;
color;
odor and taste.

149. **The most lustrous metals** are gold, silver, platinum, palladium, steel, aluminium; zinc and lead are inferior in lustre; tin is naturally a brilliant metal, but not hard enough to be polished like steel.

150. **The specific heat of metals** is the amount of heat necessary to raise equal weights of different metals from the same given temperature to another given temperature. Water is assumed as the standard, and we find that the capacity for heat of the different metals is in the following order: iron, nickel, cobalt, zinc, copper, palladium, silver, cadmium, tin, antimony, gold, lead, platinum, bismuth. Suppose, now, a cubic inch of iron and a cubic inch of tin were both heated to the same temperature for the same time and placed each on a cake of paraffine, which would melt its cake the sooner? Iron, because its capacity for heat is greater than that of tin.

151. **All metals are somewhat volatile:** some are noticeably volatile, as mercury, arsenic; others to a limited extent, and a few with difficulty even at highest temperatures. Gold is somewhat volatile when alloyed with certain metals.

152. **The characteristic color of metals** ranges from pure white to bluish.* A few metals, as iron, copper, and zinc have an odor, especially when heated.

153. **The noble metals** are mercury, silver, gold, platinum, palladium, rhodium, ruthenium, osmium, iridium; they may be separated from their oxides by merely heating to redness.

---

*Lead is feebly tinted with blue, bismuth with pink, calcium with yellow.

154. **The decomposition of acids** by metals and replacement of hydrogen has already been alluded to.

155. **Metals are opaque**, except gold which if in thin leaves, transmits a greenish or purplish light.

156. Metals are nearly all **sectile**; that is, when cut with a knife they do not crumble. For example, gold is perfectly sectile, but pyrites and other minerals like it crumble under the knife.

Metals can be fused together and unite in all proportions forming alloys.

157. The metallic elements used in dentistry will be tabulated with reference to their symbols, Latin names, valence, specific gravity, etc., etc. Before studying them, certain definitions and explanations are necessary.

Fusing point: the temperature at which the various metals melt and become liquid. Lead melts at 617° Fahrenheit, hence its fusing point is said to be 617°.

Length of bar at 212° F., which measures 1 at 32° F. It is well known that heat expands metals: thus, a bar of aluminium, which at 32° F. is 1 foot long, at 212° F. will be $1\frac{22}{1000}$ foot. In the tabulated statements concerning length of bar in metals, fourteen, namely: aluminium, antimony, bismuth, cadmium, copper, gold, iron, lead, magnesium, palladium, platinum, silver, tin, and zinc are considered. Given any unit of measurement then, whether an inch, a foot, etc., etc., there will be at 212° F. a certain gain in length of the bar. It must, however, be remembered that, for the same kind of metal, the greater its specific gravity the greater its expansion for a given increase in temperature.

Tensile strength* is the resistance of the fibres or particles

---

*Under tensile strength the *absolute* tenacity of the metal is expressed in figures, while under tenacity it is expressed *relatively* as regards other metals.

of a body to separation, and the amount of weight or power required to tear asunder one square inch of a metal is given, in figures, in tons; thus, the tensile strength of iron (wrought) is said to be 29. This means that a weight of 29 tons, or a power equivalent to 29 tons, is necessary to tear asunder one square inch of the metal.

Tenacity: the metals are compared as regards tenacity with lead, which is the weakest; the tenacity of copper is said to be 18, which means that it is 18 times *more tenacious* than lead; copper is said to be in "3d rank," because of the ten metals, steel, iron, copper, platinum, silver, gold, palladium, zinc, tin, lead, there are only two which are more tenacious. Care should be taken to note that the "rank" of a metal is strictly relative, and, unless the metals with which it is compared be known, the idea conveyed by the term is wholly vague.

Malleability: the metals are compared with *gold*, which is the most malleable; *eight* metals in all are compared, namely: gold, silver, copper, tin, platinum, lead, zinc, iron. The malleability of zinc is said to be 7, which means that there are six metals more malleable; its rank, therefore, among the eight, is 7th.

Ductility: the standard is gold which is the most ductile. Ten metals are compared: gold, silver, platinum, iron, copper, palladium, aluminium, zinc, tin, iron. The ductility of zinc is said to be 8, which means that seven of the ten metals are more ductile. It is therefore 8th in rank. *It will be noticed that the comparison in regard to tenacity is made differently from either that in regard to malleability or to ductility.*

Conducting power with reference to heat: the metals are compared with silver, which is the best conductor, and *eleven* metals in all are considered; the conducting power of zinc is said to be 5, which means that four metals are better conductors; it is, therefore, 5th in rank.

Conducting power with reference to electricity: the metals are compared with silver, which is the best conductor of electricity. *Twelve* metals are considered, namely: silver, gold, copper, zinc, palladium, platinum, iron, nickel, tin, lead, antimony, bismuth. The conducting power of zinc for electricity is 290, silver being taken as 1,000 in conducting power. In other words, silver is $\frac{1000}{290}$, or 3.44, times a better conductor than zinc. But zinc is 4th in rank among the twelve, for only three are better conductors of electricity.

Resistance to air, etc: resistance to dry, pure air is one thing, but resistance to air containing moisture, carbonic acid, etc., is quite another. Under this head also, is mentioned the effect of sulphuretted hydrogen on the metal.

Solubility: under this head the best solvents for the metal are given, that is, substances having the power, like acids, to attack the metal and convert it into a liquid.

Direct combinations: under this heading is given a list of substances which unite directly with the metal, either in the cold or when heated, rubbed, or triturated with it, without the intervention of oxygen.

Structure: many of the metals have a crystalline structure, *i. e.*, when small particles of them are seen under the microscope, certain definite geometrical shapes are observed as cubes, rhombohedrons, etc. The form in which iron tends to crystallize is a regular octahedron: an eight-sided figure with equal axes at right angles to one another. Crystalline forms are classified into six systems. (See Chap. I). Many of the metals are to be found in the first or *isometric* system, in which there are three axes of equal length, and at right angles to each other, as in case of the cube and the octahedron. Copper crystals are examples of the isometric system.

Compounds: the metals form various compounds according to their equivalence, and Latin names are often used instead of English: for example, iron as a dyad, uniting with other elements, forms *ferrous* compounds; silver compounds are sometimes called *argentic*, as *argentic nitrate*, etc., etc.

TABLE NO. 9—NAMES AND PROPERTIES OF THE MORE IMPORTANT METALS.

Names.	Sp. gr.	Fusing Point; approximate Fahrenheit.	Weight of One Cubic Foot in Pounds.	Tensile Str'gth per sq. inch in tons.
*Aluminium	2.67	1292°	166.8	12.0
Antimony	6.72	1150°	419.5	0.5
Bismuth	9.80	507°	613.0	1.5
*Cadmium	8.69	442°	542.5	
*Cobalt	8.51	less than iron.	558.7	same as iron
*Copper	8.95	1996°	558.1	13 to 15
*Gold	19.34	2016°	1208.6	9.1
*Iron	7.84	3500°	489.4	29 (maximum)
Lead	11.36	617°	709.2	0.8 to 1.5
Magnesium	1.74	850°	108.6	
Manganese	8.01	less than iron	500.0	
Mercury	13.59	—39°	848.4	
*Nickel	8.67	less than iron	541.2	same as iron
*Palladium	11.8	same as iron	736.6	
*Platinum	21.53	greater than iron	1344.0	
Silver	10.53	1873°	657.3	18.2
Tin	7.30	442°	455.1	2 to 3.5
*Zinc	7.14	773°	445.7	3.3 to 8.3

N. B.—The star* refers to the wrought metal. Mercury, tin, cadmium, bismuth, lead, and zinc, are all fusible *below* red heat. Antimony, just below red heat. Silver, copper, gold, and aluminium, at bright red heat. Iron, cobalt, manganese, and palladium, at highest forge heat. Osmium, iridium, platinum, at heat of oxy-hydrogen blowpipe. Steel is to be melted in a furnace of special construction, called a wind furnace.

TABLE No. 10—TENACITY, RELATIVE MALLEABILITY, AND DUCTILITY OF THE MORE IMPORTANT METALS.

Name.	Tenacity.	Malleability.	Ductility.
Lead..................	1.00	6	10
Cadmium.............	1.20		
Tin....................	1.83	4	9
Zinc...................	2.00	7	8
Palladium.............	11.50	(10)	6
Gold..................	12.00	1	1
Silver.................	12.50	2	2
Platinum.............	15.00	5	3
Copper...............	18.00	3	5
Iron...................	27.50	8	4
Steel	42.00		
Aluminium............			7

Explanation: *tenacity*: if the weight required to pull asunder a wire of lead be taken as a standard and called 1, the weight required to pull asunder a wire of cadmium would be a little more, namely 1.2; that to pull asunder a wire of steel, for example, 42 times as much as the lead. *Malleability*: if the difficulty with which a mass of gold can be hammered or rolled into a thin sheet, without being torn, be represented by 1, iron will be found to be 8 times as difficult. *Ductility*: if the difficulty with which gold can be drawn into a wire be represented by 1, tin, for example, will be drawn with 9 times the difficulty.

TABLE No. 11—CONDUCTING POWERS OF METALS.

Name.	Heat.	Electricity.
Silver........................	1	1000, (standard).
Gold	2	779, (3d).
Copper.......................	3	999, (2d).
Aluminium...................	4	
Zinc.........................	5	290, (4th).
Iron	6	168, (7th).
Tin..........................	7	123, (9th).
Platinum.....................	8	180, (6th).
Lead........................	9	83, (10th).
Antimony....................	10	46, (11th).
Bismuth......................	11	12, (12th).
Palladium....................		184, (5th).
Nickel.......................		131, (8th).

Explanation: in the table under *heat*, the metals are arranged in the order of their conducting power, silver being the best conductor, gold next, etc., etc. In the table under *electricity*, silver is taken as the standard, as it is the best conductor of electricity, and the other metals are compared with it, in the pure state at 32° F. In some works gold is given 3d place in heat-conducting power, copper 2nd.

Properties of metals and uses: mercury is useful for *amalgamating* or dissolving other metals; antimony has the property of hardening lead and tin, when melted with them; bismuth and cadmium make tin capable of being melted at lower temperatures; nickel whitens copper, and is used in the manufacture of German silver. Gold, platinum, palladium, silver are limited in use by their high price, and the same is true to a certain extent of aluminium, although the price of this metal is lower now than formerly. Zinc has a comparatively high degree of expansibility; gold is the most malleable of metals as also the most ductile; silver is the best conductor of heat and electricity; the tenacity of metals is *usually* diminished by heating; malleability and ductility are developed in some metals by heating, but impaired by carrying heat too far; in alloys, heating impairs tenacity, malleability, and ductility; crystalline metals, as bismuth, lack malleability, etc.; metals may be obtained in crystalline form by electrolysis, either by introducing other metals in strips or rods into their solutions, as a rod of zinc into a solution of a lead salt, or by passage of a weak electric current through their solutions. Gold may be obtained in crystalline form by introduction of a stick of phosphorus into a solution of one of its salts.

158. General properties of alloys of the metallic elements.—Alloy is the name given to a combination obtained by fusing metals together. Alloys are, as a rule, chemical compounds dissolved in excess of one of the constituent metals, but many are merely mechanical mixtures, or *molecular mixtures,* as the term is. All alloys exhibit the metallic nature in their physical characteristics.

As regards **specific gravity**, an alloy of gold and silver is lighter than the theoretical mean of its constituents; brass, and an alloy of lead and tin, heavier; in other words, the gold and silver alloy is formed by expansion, the latter by contraction. In the formation of some alloys there is no change in volume. In **color**, alloys are usually **gray**, unless there is sufficient copper or gold to impart the characteristic color of those metals. Alloys are usually **harder** and **more brittle, less ductile** and **less tenacious,** than the constituent metal exhibiting these qualities in the highest degree; aluminium bronze is an exception, its tenacity being greater than that of either of the constituent metals.

The **fusibility** of an alloy is generally greater, *i. e.*, the alloy melts more readily than that of the least fusible constituent metal and sometimes than that of any constituent metal.* An alloy **heated gradually** to near its fusing point undergoes a change; its constituents reunite to form a mass now fusible; if the fluid be poured off, a solid alloy is obtained less fusible than the original. In this way copper is separated from silver. An alloy of zinc or of mercury is **decomposed** by heat, but at a higher temperature than the point of ebullition of the metal. As regards *temperature*, an alloy of 94 copper to 6 tin, if *slowly* cooled, becomes brittle, but, if cooled *rapidly* with cold

---

*Thus, tin unites with gold far below the melting point of gold.

water, malleable. Mercury, bismuth, tin, and cadmium give fusibility to alloys, tin hardness and tenacity, lead and iron hardness, antimony and arsenic brittleness. Metals are usually **fused** under a layer of charcoal to prevent oxidation; they are mixed by agitation and allowed to cool slowly.

Certain peculiarities of alloys as to **solubility** must be noticed: platinum is insoluble in nitric acid, but an alloy of platinum with silver or gold is soluble in the acid. Silver is readily soluble in nitric acid, but an alloy of silver with 25 per cent. gold is insoluble.

The **affinity** of an alloy for **oxygen** is greater than that of the separate metals, but the action of **air** is in general less on alloys than on the separate metals composing them, with some exceptions.

Some difficulty is occasionally experienced in obtaining **a perfectly uniform alloy,** on account of the different specific gravities of the metals composing it—each metal assuming the level due to its specific gravity. This result is not so likely to occur, when the metals employed are in small quantities, briskly stirred, and suddenly cooled. In alloying three or more metals differing greatly in fusibility, or that have but little affinity for one another, it is better to unite first those that most readily combine, and then this combination with the remaining metal or metals. If, for example, it is desired to unite a small quantity of lead with brass or bronze, some difficulty would be experienced in forming the alloy by direct incorporation of the metals, but union could be readily effected by first melting the lead with zinc or tin, and then adding the melted copper.

Alloys consisting of two metals, one readily oxidizable, the other possessing less affinity for oxygen, **may be readily decomposed** by the combined action of heat and air.

159. **Solders:** it is often necessary to unite several pieces of the same metal, or of different metals. For such work a kind of alloy called *solder* is used. Solders usually contain the metal on which they are to be used, together with some other metal or metals, which shall reduce the fusing point without affecting the color.

[A solder suitable for use in prosthetic dentistry should fuse at a much lower temperature than the plate upon which it is to be used. Its color should be as nearly as possible the same, and it should withstand the action of the fluids of the mouth nearly as well. These properties may be obtained by the addition of small amounts of silver, copper, or brass. (Essig.)].

Solders have been divided into two classes: (*a*) solders made by the fusion of the metal itself, without others, and (*b*) solders made on a metal with another metal; or by an alloy applied to the surfaces which are to be united. In the last case the metal or alloy must be more fusible than the metal to be soldered, and have a more powerful chemical affinity for it.

Hard solder is used for metals difficult to melt, *soft* solder for those not so difficult.

160. **General properties of the non-metallic elements.**—It is difficult to draw a sharp line between metals and metalloids, but as a general rule those that are not gaseous at ordinary temperatures have no metallic lustre, are of low specific gravity, neither malleable nor ductile, conduct heat and electricity very imperfectly. The nitrogen group, N, P, As, Sb, and Bi is remarkable for a change from non-metallic properties to metallic as the atomic weight increases, beginning with nitrogen, atomic weight 14 and gaseous, and ending with bismuth, 210,

which has well-marked metallic properties. Arsenic is a metalloid with strongly metallic characteristics, uniting with chlorine like a basic metal, but on the other hand uniting with oxygen to form anhydrides.

161. **Classification according to valence.**—Owing to the didactic character of this book those elements of importance to the dentist will be studied in such a way as to keep their *valence* and *electro-chemical* relations constantly in view.* Table 1 of Professor Seaman† will be taken as a basis for the classification.

---

*Those interested in the further study of theoretical chemistry should procure Lothar Meyer's "*Modern Theories of Chemistry,*" translated by Bedson and Williams.

†Professor Seaman divides, for didactic purposes, the elements as follows:
A. Gases: O, H, N, Cl, F.
B. Halogens: I, Br, Cl.
C. Metals: As, Sb, Fe, etc.
[Sub-classes of metals: metals of the alkalies, Na, K, Li; metals of the alkaline earths, Ba, Ca, Sr, Mg; metals proper, as Fe, Pb, Sn.].
D. Metalloids: as C, P, Si, S.

Witthaus's classification is excellent in many respects: Class I, typical elements: H and O. Class II, elements whose oxides plus water form acids, viz: Fl, Cl, Br, I, S, N, P, As, etc. Class III: elements whose oxides plus water in some form bases, in others acids: Au, Cr, Mn, Fe, Al, Pb, Bi, etc. Class IV, elements whose oxides plus water form bases only: Li, Na, K, Cu, Mg, Zn, etc.

CHAPTER III.

INORGANIC CHEMISTRY. THE ELEMENTS AND THEIR INORGANIC COMPOUNDS.

Monads.—The elements will be taken up in the order of their valence, monads first. Of monads those positive* to hydrogen will be treated first, then those negative to it.

TABLE 12. MONADS.

Potassium
Sodium
[Ammonium] } Monads positive to hydrogen.
Lithium
Silver

Hydrogen

Iodine
Bromine } Monads negative to hydrogen.
Chlorine
Fluorine.

Hydrogen forms *hydrides* with those elements positive to itself, as KH, potassium hydride. Combined with those negative to it iodides, bromides, chlorides, and

---

*See Table 1. The student will do well to study the properties of hydrogen (section 176) and of oxygen (section 241) before beginning this chapter.

fluorides are formed. Moreover, all in the list *above* hydrogen are positive to all in the list *below* hydrogen. The elements positive to hydrogen in this list are all metals, those negative, non-metals.

Potassium:—*Symbol:* K. *Latin name:* Kalium. *Equivalence:* I. *Specific gravity:* 0.86. *Atomic weight* (approx.): 39. *Revised atomic weight:* 39.0196. *Electrical state:* +. *Fusing point:* 144°F.

Brilliant, white metal, with high degree of lustre, soft, floats on water and takes fire spontaneously when thrown on it, yielding an alkaline solution.

162. Potassium compounds.

TABLE 13—SOME COMPOUNDS OF POTASSIUM.

Name.	Formulæ.	Uses, etc.
Chlorate	$KClO_3$	White, soluble in water (6 in 100). Used in mouth washes and gargles. In large doses is poisonous. Sparingly soluble in alcohol.
Bicarbonate	$KHCO_3$	Antacid, used in mouth washes. In large doses is corrosive poison. Soluble in water, insoluble in alcohol.
Bromide	KBr	White, soluble crystals. Given internally in convulsions, etc., and used locally to diminish sensibility before taking impressions.

TABLE 13.—*Continued*

Chloride	KCl	Transparent, colorless solid, soluble in water. Found in the body in fluids, blood corpuscles, and in muscle juice.
Iodide	KI	Made by dissolving iodine in potassium hydrate. Large, white translucent, cubical crystals of a saline taste. Readily soluble in water. Solutions dissolve iodine.

163. **Potassium hydrate.**—
Synonyms: Potassa U. S. P., Potassa Caustica (Br. P.), caustic potash.

Theoretical constitution: KHO or KOH, the hydrate (hydroxide) of potassium. Molecular weight, 56.

Preparation: by boiling potassium carbonate with slacked lime (calcium hydrate):

$K_2CO_3 + Ca(HO)_2 = CaCO_3 + 2KHO$.

Properties: the impure contains lime and is called potash by lime: purified by dissolving in alcohol and evaporating to dryness, remelted, and cast in sticks it is known as *potash by alcohol*. White, opaque sticks or lumps, alkaline, readily soluble in water, caustic, escharotic, and corrosive poison.

Potassa cum calce: equal parts KHO and CaO, grayish-white powder, milder, and less deliquescent; in a paste called *Vienna* paste, used in dentistry.

Robinson's remedy contains potassium hydrate and carbolic acid, equal parts.

Liquor potassæ is a 5 per cent solution of potassium hydrate in water.

Toxicology: potassium hydrate is a corrosive poison and its action on tissues is very violent and penetrating. Forty grains have caused death. In the treatment the stomach pump must *not* be used, dilute vinegar should at once be given, lemon juice, orange juice, olive oil, and milk freely. Stimulants are indicated if there is much pain. Solutions of potassium hydrate or carbonate have a soapy "feel" and are alkaline in reaction. Burns from the agent should be treated with dilute vinegar and then with oil.

164. **Potassium Nitrate.—**
Synonyms: nitre, saltpetre, Sal Prunella. Official name, Potassii Nitras.

Theoretical constitution: KNO_3, 1 atom of potassium, 1 of nitrogen, and 3 of oxygen to the molecule. Molecular weight, 101.

Preparation: made from crude sodium nitrate by double decomposition with potassium chloride.

Properties: colorless crystals, anhydrous, very soluble in hot water, readily soluble in cold, nearly insoluble in alcohol, permanent in dry air, neutral, odorless.

Uses in dentistry: locally and in mouth washes as an antiseptic and refrigerant. In refining gold, when it is used as an oxidizing agent for metals alloyed with gold. Roasting an alloy with nitre will often set the gold free.

Toxicology: potassium nitrate is poisonous, causing severe burning, abdominal pains, nausea, vomiting of blood, great prostration, tremors, collapse. One ounce has proved fatal. The treatment is to give an emetic, mucilaginous and demulcent drinks, and stimulants.

165. **Potassium Permanganate.**—

Synonyms: permanganate of potash. Official name, Potassii Permanganas.

Theoretical constitution: $K_2Mn_2O_8$ or $KMnO_4$, derived from permanganic acid. Permanganic acid, $H_2Mn_2O_8$, may be deemed to be derived from manganese heptoxide (Mn_2O_7) plus water (H_2O); potassium permanganate $K_2Mn_2O_8$, by exchanging the two atoms of hydrogen in the acid for two of potassium. Molecular weight, 313.8.

Properties and dental uses: potassium permanganate occurs in the form of dark purple crystals which impart a fine, deep, purple color to water even when in very minute proportions. It is a deodorizer, disinfectant, and, in concentrated solution, a caustic.

Condy's Fluid contains 32 grains of it to the pint of distilled water.

Liquor Potassii Permanganatis contains 64 grains to the pint of distilled water.

In dental practice the permanganate is used locally as a deodorizer, disinfectant, and antiseptic.

166. **Sodium**:—

Symbol: Na. *Latin name*: Natrium or Natron. *Equivalence*: I. *Specific Gravity*:—0.97. *Atomic weight* (approx.): 23. *Revised atomic weight*:—22.998. *Electrical* state: ×. *Fusing point:*— 206.°6 F. *Properties:*—Soft, white, readily oxidized metal.

167. Sodium Compounds.—
Sodium Hydro-Carbonate or Bicarbonate.

Synonyms: bicarbonate of sodium, bicarbonate of soda, sodium acid carbonate, sesquicarbonate of sodium, "baking soda."

Theoretical constitution: sodium hydrocarbonate, $NaHCO_3$, is what is called an **acid salt,** because *all* the hydrogen atoms of the acid from which it is derived have *not* been replaced by the positive atom. The term **acid salt** should not confuse the beginner as to the *reaction* of the substance to litmus paper, which has nothing to do with the theoretical name.

Sodium bicarbonate is composed of one atom of sodium, one of hydrogen, one of carbon, and three of oxygen. By weight 23 of sodium, 1 of hydrogen, 12 of carbon, 48 of oxygen; molecular weight, 84.

Preparation: made by passing carbon dioxide over sodium carbonate from which the larger portion of water of crystallization has been expelled:

$$\underset{\text{Sodium carbonate}}{Na_2CO_3} + \underset{\text{water}}{H_2O} + \underset{\text{carbon dioxide}}{CO_2} = \underset{\text{sodium bicarbonate.}}{2NaHCO_3}.$$

The *sodium carbonate* used is, as will thus readily be seen, an entirely different substance from the bicarbonate. The former is known in commerce as "sal soda," and familiarly known as "washing soda."

Properties: sodium bicarbonate is a white powder, having a mildly saline, cooling taste, a slightly alkaline reaction, is soluble in 12 parts of water, insoluble in alcohol; 8 parts of the bicarbonate are soluble in 100 of glycerine (by weight). Its solutions are nearly neutral to litmus paper.

Use in dentistry: sodium bicarbonate is in particular used as an antacid ingredient of dentifrices, and its uses, in general, in dental practice are in consequence of its antacid properties.

168. Various sodium compounds: all are soluble in water to a greater or less degree and most of them in solution turn red litmus blue. Many of them are white or colorless.

TABLE 14—SODIUM COMPOUNDS.

Name.	Formulæ.	Origin, Uses, etc.
Chloride	$NaCl$	Common salt is found in every fluid and organ of the body.
Sulphite	Na_2SO_3	Antiseptic, disinfectant, and deodorizer. Used in bleaching teeth with boracic acid.
Sulphate	Na_2SO_4	Glauber's salt.
Carbonate	$Na_2CO_3, 10H_2O$	Washing Soda.
Arseniate	$Na_2HAsO_4, 7H_2O$	Poisonous, colorless, efflorescent.
Hydrate	KHO	Caustic soda. Comes in form of sticks. Readily soluble.
Phosphates	Na_3PO_4	*Basic* phosphate, alkaline, and purgative.
	Na_2HPO_4	*Neutral* phosphate. Found in the tissues.
	NaH_2PO_4	Acid phosphate of sodium.

169. Sodium Borate or Borax.—

Synonyms: sodium biborate, sodium tetraborate, Sodii Boras (U.S.P), Sodæ Boras (B.P.).

Theoretical constitution: formula $Na_2B_4O_7$, explained by regarding it as $Na_2O.(B_2O_3)_2$ or $Na_2O.2B_2O_3$. Boric oxide (anhydride) B_2O_3, has the property of uniting directly with oxides of the positive elements sodium, potassium, etc. Borax is not, therefore, derived from boracic acid but formed by the direct combination of sodium oxide, Na_2O, with boric oxide or anhydride, B_2O_3. The molecule of sodium oxide combines with *two molecules* of boric oxide, forming $Na_2O.2B_2O_3$. Borax contains also ten molecules of water of crystallization, so that the full formula is $Na_2O.2B_2O_3 + 10H_2O$.

Properties and uses in dentistry: borax is a white, soluble, efflorescent substance which melts at a low heat, swells greatly, at a higher temperature becomes a clear liquid, then a vitreous substance (borax glass). It is useful in blow pipe analysis, as by the "borax bead" method; as a flux for melting metals; in soldering metals; in solution, for hardening plaster casts; as a local application, etc., etc.

170. Sodium Hypochlorite.—

Theoretical constitution: NaClO, one atom of sodium, one of chlorine and one of oxygen in its molecule. This substance is only indirectly of interest as one of the ingredients of the chlorinated soda solution.

Liquor Sodæ Chloratæ:

Synonyms: Labarraque's solution, solution of chloride of soda; chlorinated soda solution.

Preparation: made by decomposing a solution of chlorinated lime with one of sodium carbonate:

[Ca(ClO)$_2$ + CaCl$_2$] + 2NaCO$_3$ = [2NaClO + 2NaCl] + 2CaCO$_3$
Chlorinated lime.　　　　　　　　Chlorinated soda.　　Calcium carbonate.

Properties: clear, pale liquid, slightly greenish yellow in color, of faint chlorine odor, alkaline taste and reaction. Sp. gr., 1.044. Powerful disinfectant, deodorizer, antiseptic, bleaching agent.

Use in dentistry: used locally for its antiseptic properties and, in combination with powdered alum, as a bleaching agent for discolored teeth. It slowly decomposes on exposure to air and light, and should be kept in a dark place in a bottle provided with a glass stopper. It is advisable to keep soda and potash solutions in bottles whose glass stoppers have been dipped in paraffine.

Eau de Javelle contains *potassium* hypochlorite.

171. **Ammonium and its Compounds.—** Ammonium (NH$_4$) is what is known as a *radical.* (See Organic Chemistry). It is not positively known to exist nor is its oxide. There are reasonable grounds, however, for supposing that it does actually exist in certain compounds called the ammonium compounds, all of which contain NH$_4$ in their formulæ. Ammon*ium* is not ammon*ia;* the latter is a well-known gas, NH$_3$, while ammonium has never been isolated and has, therefore, only a hypothetical existence. Ammonium would

seem in the main to resemble sodium and potassium; there are, however, points of dissimilarity.

TABLE 15. COMPOUNDS OF AMMONIUM.

Names.	Formulæ.	Properties.
Hydrate, (Ammonia water).	H_4NHO or NH_4HO Sometimes written AmHO. May be deemed a hydrate of the radical ammonium.	Volatile, caustic liquid of powerful odor. Aqua Ammoniæ is a solution of ammonia gas in water, of sp. gr. 0.959. Aqua Ammoniæ Fortior contains 28 per cent. of the gas and is of sp. gr. 0.900; it is a powerfully corrosive poison.
Carbonate, Ammonii carbonas. Hartshorn salt. Sal Volatile.	$(NH_4HCO_3, NH_4NH_2CO_2)$ Really a mixture of the acid carbonate and the carbamate. Molecular wt., 157.	Has strong odor of ammonia and is freely soluble in water. Loses CO_2 and NH_3 on exposure to the air.
Chloride, or muriate. Sal ammoniac.	$NH_4Cl = 53.4$	White, crystalline powder; very easily soluble in water, but not hygroscopic. Used as flux in refining gold, etc., and locally.

Lithium:—
Symbol: Li. *Latin name:* Lithium. *Equivalence:* I. *Specific gravity:* 0.59. *Atomic wt.* (approx.): 7. *Atomic wt.* (revised): 7.0073. *Electrical State:* $+$. *Fusing point:* 356° F. *Properties:* White, oxidizable metal and the lightest metal known.

172. **Silver.—**
Symbol: Ag. *Latin name:* Argentum. *Equivalence:* I and III. *Specific gravity:* 10.40 to 10.57. *Atomic weight* 108. *Revised atomic weight:* 107.675. *Electrical state:* $+$. *Fusing point:* 1873°F. Expands on solidifying. *Length of bar* at 212 : 1.0021; (6th rank). *Wt. of cubic ft. in lbs.:* 657.3. *Tensile strength:* 18.2; (lead = 1). *Tenacity:* 12.5*; (5th rank). *Malleability:* 2; (2d rank). *Ductility:* 2; (2d rank). *Conducting power,* heat: 1; (1st rank). *Conducting power,* electricity: 1; (1st rank). *Resistance*

---
*Compared with lead.

to air, etc,; tarnished by sulphuretted hydrogen, but not affected by air. *Solubility:* in nitric acid, hot strong sulphuric, hydrochloric with difficulty; not attacked by caustic alkalies nor by melted nitre. It is dissolved by mercury. *Direct combinations:* with halogens, chlorine, bromine, etc., and with sulphur and phosphorus. *Color* white, brilliant. *Structure:* isometric crystals, when cooled slowly from fusion. *Consistence:* soft. Intermediate in hardness between gold and copper. *Compounds:* argentic, as argentic nitrate, etc. *Ordinary alloys:* silver coins, gold solders, silver solders, silver vessels, silver jewelry.

Occurrence: silver is found in combination with some of the halogens as chlorine, bromine, iodine, with various other non-metals as sulphur, arsenic, antimony, and with copper. It occurs in the Western states, in Mexico, Saxony, Hungary, Norway, South America and elsewhere. It is sometimes found *native**.

Preparation: the methods are various and elaborate. The Washoe process is to grind the ores with water, in iron pans heated by steam. Mercury is added, the sulphide of silver is decomposed by the iron, sulphide of iron formed and metallic silver set free, dissolved in mercury and the mercury separated by pressure and distillation.

---

*Native silver is that found not as a sulphide, etc., but uncombined. Native silver is found in crystals, threads, or amorphous masses, weighing often several pounds. It is associated, nearly always, with other metals in small quantities, and accompanied by its sulphide or chloride.

Pure silver may be prepared by reducing the chloride, by fusing it with dry sodium carbonate. Other methods are also used: one is to dissolve standard or other grades of silver in slightly diluted nitric acid, precipitate the solution by excess of common salt, place the well-washed chloride in water acidulated with hydrochloric acid, and add a few pieces of clean wrought iron: hydrogen is evolved which, uniting with the chlorine of silver chloride, leaves the silver as a spongy mass. After the removal of the iron and decantation of the liquid, the silver is well washed in hot water containing a little hydrochloric acid, dried and melted.

Uses in dentistry: silver is used in amalgam alloys and, according to Flagg, is the first, most important, and essential metal of a good amalgam alloy for filling teeth; it is the largest component of every truly good "submarine," "usual," or "contour" alloy in the market. Its presence in an amalgam is essential to proper setting; it notably maintains the bulk integrity of the filling; though discolored by sulphuretted hydrogen, the silver sulphide formed is highly conducive to the permanent saving of teeth largely decayed and predisposed to continued decay. Silver has also been used in dental plates.

173. **Silver alloys and alloys resembling silver.—**
Silver coinage: silver 90, copper 10. Silver vessels: silver 95, copper 5. Silver jewelry: silver 80, copper 20.

An alloy used in England **for temporary dentures** is silver 24 parts, platinum 3 to 10 parts.

German silver contains no silver, but is an alloy of copper, nickel, and zinc, in the proportions of 40.4 copper, 31.6 nickel, 25.4 zinc, and sometimes 2.6 iron.

174. *Silver solder* is 32.3 parts copper, 38.5 silver, 29.2 zinc. Others are as follows: (Richardson).

No. 1.	No. 2.	No. 3.
Silver, 66 parts.	Silver, 6 dwts.	Silver, 5½ dwts.
Copper, 30 parts.	Copper, 2 dwts.	Brass wire, 40 grains.
Zinc, 10 parts.	Brass, 1 dwt.	

When the plate to be united consists of pure silver alloyed with platinum, the solder may be formed of the standard metal (coin), with $\frac{1}{10th}$ to $\frac{1}{6th}$ its weight of zinc, according to the amount of platinum in the alloy.

175. **Compounds of silver.**
Silver Nitrate or Argentic Nitrate.—
Synonyms: lunar caustic, lapis infernalis. Official name, Argenti Nitras.

Theoretical constitution: $AgNO_3$, one atom of silver, one of nitrogen, three of oxygen; by weight, silver 107.7 parts, nitrogen 14, oxygen 48. Molecular weight, 169.7.

Properties and uses: on evaporating a solution of silver in nitric acid and water, nitrate of silver is obtained in the form of colorless, heavy, shining, rhombic plates. It is blackened by exposure to light, and by contact with organic matter. It is also prepared in stick form, by fusing and pouring into moulds. It is very soluble in water, and slightly in alcohol. It is used in dentistry as an astringent, styptic, and obtunding agent. It blackens tissues with which it comes in contact, and is a powerful escharotic. Should be kept in amber bottle with glass stopper.

Toxicology: silver nitrate is an irritant, corrosive poison. The antidote is common salt or sal-ammoniac. Emetics should be given, and white of egg administered freely.

Silver Sulphide.—Silver has a strong affinity for sulphur, the sulphide, Ag_2S, being formed in the mouth by action of sulphuretted hydrogen on an alloy containing silver. Silver can, therefore, not be used in connection with substances containing sulphur, as rubbers. Silver sulphide is soluble in nitric acid, is soft and malleable.

Silver Chloride, $AgCl$, is formed when either common salt or hydrochloric acid is added to a solution of silver nitrate.

Silver Oxide, Ag_2O, is obtained as a brown precipitate, when solution of silver nitrate is decomposed by potash. Take of silver nitrate 100 Gm., of distilled water 200 C.c., of solution of potassa (official) 600 C.c. Dissolve the silver nitrate in water and add solution of potassa as long as any precipitate is produced by it. Wash the precipitate with distilled water, until washings are nearly tasteless. Dry the product and keep it well protected from the light.

It parts with its oxygen easily and must not be heated nor brought into contact with ammonia. Should be kept in a well-closed bottle and in a cool place. It is used as a coloring matter for artificial teeth.

176. **Hydrogen.**—

Symbol: H. *Atoms in molecule*: H_2. *Atomic weight*: 1.

106 DENTAL CHEMISTRY.

Molecular weight: 2. *Density*: 1. *Specific gravity*: 0.0692. *Weight of one litre* of hydrogen gas: 0.0896 gramme. *How liquified*: by pressure of 650 atmospheres at—140° C.

Occurrence in Nature.—In volcanic gases and sun's atmosphere.

How made.—By decomposing an acid with a metal: thus, sulphuric acid with zinc: $H_2SO_4 + Zn = ZnSO_4 + H_2$.

Properties.—Has affinity for chlorine only; at higher temperatures for oxygen. Is a gas, colorless, tasteless, odorless, transparent, and but slightly soluble in water. Is the lightest known substance and burns with the hottest flame.

Use in dentistry.—Used in connection with oxygen in the *oxyhydrogen blow pipe* for fusing refractory substances. (See Oxygen). In combination with carbon alone forms *hydrocarbons*, among which are the volatile oils, as oil of cloves. (See Organic Chemistry).

177. **Compounds of hydrogen: hydrogen monoxide or water.—** Synonyms: Aqua; distilled water, *Aqua Destillata*. Theoretical constitution: H_2O, hydrogen monoxide, composed of two atoms of hydrogen and one of oxygen, by weight 8 parts of oxygen to 1 of hydrogen. Molecular weight, 18. Specific gravity, 1.

Origin: occurs in nature in lakes, rivers, etc., and in three states the solid as ice, the liquid, and the gaseous as steam or vapor. In the air it is in form of vapor. Seven-eighths of the human body is water. Is always formed when hydrogen or any substance containing hydrogen burns in the air.

The freezing point of water is 32° on the Fahrenheit scale of thermometers, but zero on the Centigrade; the boiling point is 212° on the Fahrenheit, but zero on the Centigrade. *Water is expanded by heat* and contracts on cooling, but after reaching 39° F. begins to expand again so that the volume of a given weight of water is less than the volume of ice formed from it. *Ice contracts, then, on melting.* On the other hand when water is converted into steam there is great expansion, one volume of water yielding 1700 volumes of steam. *The capacity of water for heat* is greater than that of all bodies except hydrogen. Adopting for the unit of measure that quantity of heat which will raise the temperature of one gram of water through one Centigrade degree those fractions of the unit of heat which will raise various substances, other than hydrogen, as iron, lead, or glass one degree are called the specific heats of the substances. (See Table 1). The specific heat of hydrogen is 3.4, that of iron 0.1138, that of lead 0.0314. (See Section 59.)

Water has a very general solvent power which, however, is limited and varies with temperature, some substances being much more soluble in hot water than in cold water. Among substances very soluble in water we find potassium carbonate and zinc chloride. (See Section 68).

Well waters on being evaporated yield a residue composed usually of compounds of calcium, magnesium, etc., which have previously been held in solution.

Water enters into the formation of crystals, readily shown by preparing a saturated solution of such salts as alum, potassium ferrocyanide, potassium nitrate, magnesium sulphate, and letting stand in a shallow dish until evaporation has taken place.

Water is the medium of chemical change. (See Section 141.)

Water combines with certain substances, forming *hydrates* with oxides of positive elements, and *anhydrides* with oxides of negative elements. Examples: quicklime and water form slaked lime; that is, calcium oxide and water form calcium hydrate; sulphurous oxide and water form sulphurous anhydride.

In general water is a limpid, colorless liquid, odorless, tasteless, neutral, poor conductor of heat and electricity, 773 times heavier than air, standard of specific gravity. The purest natural water is rain water. This, however, is somewhat contaminated with matters washed from the air. River and lake waters, especially those found in granitic regions, are the purest *potable* waters. *Mineral* waters are called alkaline, sulphurous, chalybeate, etc., according to prevailing constituents, and contain *usually* large amounts of solids in solution.

Use in dentistry: distilled water is used in the preparation of many dental formulæ. It is prepared by taking 80 pints of water, distilling two pints which are rejected, then distilling 64 pints. The term **aqua,** U. S. P., is used as a name for a solution of some gaseous or volatile body in water. Thus, **aqua chlori;** the term **liquor** is used when the substance dissolved is fixed or solid, as **Liquor Plumbi Subacetatis.**

178. **Hydrogen Dioxide.—**

Synonyms: hydrogen peroxide, hydric dioxide or peroxide, oxygenated water.

Theoretical constitution: H_2O_2, hydrogen dioxide, composed of two atoms of hydrogen and two of oxygen; by weight, 32 of oxygen to 2 of hydrogen, or 16 to 1. Molecular weight, 34.

Preparation: pass a stream of carbon dioxide through water containing barium dioxide in suspension:

$$BaO_2 + CO_2 + H_2O = BaCO_3 + H_2O_2.$$
Barium dioxide　carbonic dioxide　water　　barium carbonate　hydric dioxide.

Properties: in the purest form it is a syrupy colorless liquid, having an odor like chlorine or ozone, and a tingling, metallic taste. It is never used in the purest undiluted form in dental operations owing to the readiness with which it decomposes and gives off its oxygen. It is a powerful antiseptic, colorless, odorless, cleansing and stimulating, does not stain or corrode, and is not poisonous. It gives off its oxygen with effervescence in contact with many substances and notably with pus. Application to dentistry: is efferveses with pus, giving off nascent oxygen, which is a powerful bactericide; being one of the most cleansing of agents, it is used to clean cavities. Combined with weak alkali it bleaches. A "ten volume" solution of it is one which will give off ten parts by volume of oxygen; that is, one measure of it gives off ten measures of oxygen. A "two volume" solution contains 0.4 per cent. of the pure dioxide. A little acid is added to the solutions of the dioxide commonly used in dentistry as an aid to their stability.† Hydrogen dioxide should be kept in a cool place in a glass-stoppered bottle. Hydrogen dioxide is sometimes used in solution in glycerine instead of in water. It gives off its oxygen more slowly than when in aqueous solution.

179. **Iodine.**—*Symbol:* I. *Atoms in molecule:* I_2. *Atomic weight:* 127. *Molecular weight:* 254. *Density:* 127. *Specific gravity:* 4.95. *Weight of one litre of gas:* 11.37 grammes. *How liquefied:* at 225° F. *Solubility in water:* 7000 parts of water dissolve 1 of iodine. Freely soluble in alcohol and in aqueous solution of potassium iodide. *Occurrence in nature:* in combination, as iodides, etc, *How made:* from ashes of sea-weed. By action of chlorine

---

†Rollins has found that as ordinarily obtained it acts perceptibly on the teeth, and hence should be used with caution.

and heat on liquor obtained by leaching sea-weed ashes. *Properties:* solid, in brilliant scales, of gray metallic color. Gives off violet vapors. Imparts yellowish-brown stain to skin. Solutions when cold give blue color to boiled starch. Not so corrosive or poisonous as bromine, but yet poisonous in sufficient quantity. Antidote, starch.

Preparations used in dental pharmacy.—Tincture of iodine, *Tinctura Iodi*, is made of 80 grams of iodine in 920 grams of alcohol. Compound solution of iodine, *Liquor Iodi Compositus* is iodine 50 grams, potassium iodide 100 grams, distilled water 850 C. c. Decolorized tincture of iodine, *Tinctura Iodi Decolorata*, is iodine 40 grams, alcohol 400 C. c., stronger water of ammonia 90 C. c. Carbolized iodine solution, *Liquor Iodi Phenolatus*, is tincture of iodine 1 gram, phenol (carbolic acid) 12 centigrams, glycerine 8 grams, water 45 C. c.; it is a colorless liquid.

The antidote for iodine is starch.

Bromine.—*Symbol:* Br. *Atoms in molecule:* Br_2. *Atomic weight:* 80. *Molecular weight:* 160. *Density:* 80. *Specific gravity:* 3.187. *Weight of one litre of gas:* 7.15 grammes. *How liquefied:* at ordinary temperatures. *Solubility in water:* 33 parts water dissolve one of bromine.

Occurrence in nature: in combinations as bromides, etc. *How made:* action of sulphuric acid on bittern in presence of manganese dioxide. *Properties:* liquid, heavy, dark, brownish-red, less active than chlorine, bleaches, burns, is poisonous, colors starch yellow. Fumes violently. Is heavier than some metals, as aluminium.

180. **Chlorine.**—*Symbol:* Cl. *Atoms in molecule:* Cl_2.

Atomic weight: 35.4. *Molecular weight:* 71. *Density:* 35.4. *Specific gravity:* 2.47. *Weight of one litre of gas:* 3.17 grammes. *How liquefied:* 4 atmospheres or —40° F. *Solubility in water:* 1 part, by volume, of water dissolves nearly three volumes of chlorine gas. *Occurrence in nature:* always in combination, usual source common salt. *How made:* (*a*) action of H_2SO_4 on NaCl in presence of MnO_2; (*b*) action of air on moistened "chloride of lime." *Properties*: is a gas, greenish-yellow, of pungent taste and suffocating odor, wholly irrespirable, powerful bleaching agent and disinfectant. Combines with all elements except oxygen, nitrogen, and carbon.

Use in dentistry.—Chlorine gas has been used to bleach discolored teeth. It may be prepared as follows:

Place 20 parts, by weight, of commercial hydrochloric acid (sp. gr. about 1.16) in a flask, add 8 parts manganese dioxide, agitate, and after a time heat the flask on a sand bath (safety-tube may be used, which is a funnel-tube bent twice on itself). The equation is as follows:

$$4HCl + MnO_2 = MnCl_2 + 2H_2O + Cl_2.$$

The flask should be closed by a cork perforated by two holes, through one of which the safety-tube may be inserted, its lower end dipping below the surface of the acid; through the other hole a short glass tube bent at right angles should be inserted, its lower aperture being about an inch below the cork. The gas escapes through this second tube, called *deliv-*

ery tube, and may be collected in any way desired.

Chlorine water is used in dental practice as a local application. It is prepared by passing the gas into water in which it is readily soluble, one volume of water dissolving three volumes of chlorine gas. The solution *Aqua Chlori*, U. S. P., is a greenish-yellow liquid, slowly changing in the light to hydrochloric acid. It should not redden litmus but bleach it. It should be kept in a glass-stoppered bottle away from the light and in a cool place. It should contain 0.4 per cent of chlorine.

Toxicology.—Chlorine gas is an irritant poison, and is irrespirable, causing inflammation of the air passages. The treatment is instant removal to fresh air, inhalation of ammonia or very dilute sulphuretted hydrogen or ether-vapor. The inhalation of steam is said to be beneficial.

181. **Compounds of chlorine.—**
Hydrogen Chloride or Hydrochloric Acid.

Synonyms: muriatic acid, chlorhydric acid, Acidum Hydrochloricum.

Theoretical constitution: HCl, a hydracid, binary compound composed of one atom of hydrogen and one of chlorine; by weight 35.4 parts chlorine to 1 of hydrogen. Molecualr weight 36.4. Density of the gas, 18.25; sp. gr. 1.264. Absolute HCl contains 97.26 per cent. of chlorine and 2.74 per cent. of hydrogen.

Preparation: found free in small quantities

in gastric juice. Made from common salt and sulphuric acid:

$$H_2SO_4 + 2NaCl = 2HCl + Na_2SO_4$$
Sulphuric acid   sodium chloride   hydrochloric acid   sodium sulphate.

Properties: colorless, transparent gas of pungent odor, strongly acid reaction, very soluble in water, one volume of which dissolves 450 volumes of the gas forming the ordinary **muriatic acid.** Commercial muriatic acid is yellow, and the strongest contains 25 to 30 per cent. of the gas. *Acidum Muriaticum* or *Acidum Hydrochloricum*, U. S. P., is colorless, sp. gr. 1.16, contains 31.9 per cent of the gas. *Acidum Muriaticum Dilutum*, U. S. P.: strong acid 6 parts, distilled water 13 parts; sp. gr., 1.049.

Use in dentistry: it is used as a solvent for zinc, and sometimes as a local application. It dissolves iron and zinc readily and, when warmed, attacks tin.

Toxicology.—Hydrochloric acid is a corrosive poison, caustic and escharotic. It stains the skin at first white, then produces discoloration. The stain on black cloth is red, gradually disappearing in course of time. Burns by the acid should be treated first by washing the acid off well, then by application of sodium bicarbonate solution and oil. If the acid be taken internally, give at once magnesia or bicarbonate of sodium in milk at short intervals, then bland liquids as raw eggs, gruel, or oil.

182. **Fluorine.**—*Symbol*: F or Fl. *Atoms in molecule*: Fl_2. *Atomic weight*: 19. *Revised weight*: 18.9840. *Molecular weight*: 38. *Density*: 19. *Weight of one litre of gas*: 1.7

grammes. *Occurrence in nature*: in combination as in fluor-spar and cryolite which are fluorides. *How made*: cannot be readily isolated. *Properties*: colorless gas.

183. **Dyads.**—The dyads of importance will be studied in the same relative order as the monads.

TABLE 16. DYADS OF IMPORTANCE.

Barium
Calcium
Magnesium
Zinc
Cadmium   } Dyads positive
Lead   to hydrogen.
Uranium
Copper
Mercury

Tellurium
Sulphur   } Dyads negative to
Oxygen   hydrogen.

184. **Barium.**—*Symbol:* Ba; *Latin name:* Barium. *Equivalence:* II. *Specific gravity:* 4. *Atomic wt. (approx.):* 136.8. *Atomic wt. (revised):* 136.763. *Electrical state:* +. *Fusing point:* below red heat. *Properties:* malleable, decomposes water, gradually oxidizes.

Compounds of barium.—Barium chloride, $BaCl_2$, and barium nitrate, $Ba(NO_3)_2$, are both soluble in water and are used in laboratory work in testing for sulphuric acid and sulphates.

185. **Calcium.**—*Symbol:* Ca; *Latin name:* Calcium. *Equivalence:* II. *Specific gravity:* 1.58. *Atomic weight (approx.):* 40. *Atomic weight (revised):* 39.99. *Electrical state:* +. *Fusing point:* burns when heated. *Properties:* light yellow metal, about as hard as gold, very ductile, tarnishes slowly, decomposes water.

186. Calcium compounds. Calcium Sulphate.—

Synonyms: sulphate of calcium, sulphate of lime, plaster-of-Paris, calcic sulphate. Official name, Calcii Sulphas.

Theoretical constitution: $CaSO_4.2H_2O$, one atom of calcium, one of sulphur and four of oxygen; by weight 40 parts calcium, 32 parts sulphur, 64 parts oxygen. Molecular weight, 172.

Preparation: calcium sulphate occurs in nature as a mineral called gypsum. Gypsum, however, differs from the dried calcium sulphate of commerce in that it contains two molecules of water of crystallization; the full formula for gypsum is, therefore, $CaSO_4, 2H_2O$. Ground gypsum is called *terra alba*. Gypsum when heated to 392° F. loses its water of crystallization, becoming changed into a white, opaque mass having $CaSO_4$, without any H_2O, for its formula. This substance when ground is known as plaster-of-Paris and is anhydrous calcium sulphate; it readily recombines with water, becoming a hard mass on the addition of H_2O.

Properties and uses: the anhydrous sulphate, $CaSO_4$, plaster-of-Paris, is a hard, white, nearly insoluble substance. After taking up water it "sets" into a stone-like solid, and hence is useful in making moulds, casts, and immovable surgical dressings. If alum and gelatine be mixed with the plaster-of-Paris before addition of water, it forms a harder and less porous mass than the plaster alone, and presents a smooth surface which can be washed with water containing the various disinfecting agents.

187. **Calcium Carbonate.—**
Synonyms: calcic carbonate, Calcis Carbonas, carbonate of lime. Official name, Calcii Carbonas Præcipitatus.

Theoretical constitution: $CaCO_3$, one atom of calcium, one of carbon, three of oxygen; by weight 40 parts calcium, 12 carbon, 48 oxygen. Molecular weight, 100.

Origin and method of preparation: it occurs more or less pure in nature as chalk, limestone, marble, Iceland spar, coral, shell, etc. It is found in the bones, teeth, saliva, and in calculi and tartar.

It is obtained for dental uses (1) by precipitation, by mixing solutions of calcium chloride and sodium carbonate:

$$Na_2CO_3 + CaCl_2 = CaCO_3 + 2NaCl$$
Sodium carbonate + Calcium chloride = Calcium carbonate + Sodium chloride

(2) as prepared chalk (Creta Præparata) by grinding a native chalk in water, allowing the mixture to settle, decanting the upper portion, collecting and drying the finer particles.

Properties and uses: precipitated calcium carbonate is a neutral, white, tasteless, impalpable powder; it is insoluble in pure water and in alcohol, but soluble in water containing carbonic dioxide (carbonic acid). It is found as acid carbonate, dissolved in almost all natural waters, causing *hardness*, which may be removed by boiling, hence called "temporary" hardness.

It is used in dentistry as a polishing powder, as an ingredient of dentifrices, and as an antacid. It is useful as an antidote in cases of poisoning by acids.

188. **Calcium Oxide.—**
Synonyms: calcic oxide, lime, Calx, quicklime, burned lime. Official name, Calcii Oxidum.

Theoretical constitution: CaO, calcium oxide, one atom of calcium and one of oxygen in its molecule; by weight, 40 parts of calcium to 16 of oxygen. Molecular weight, 56.

Preparation: lime is obtained on a large scale by heating limestone or other calcium carbonate in a lime kiln:

$$CaCO_3 = CaO + CO_2$$
Calcium carbonate = Calcium oxide + Carbon dioxide.

For pharmaceutical purposes it is made by heating marble in a Hessian crucible.

Properties and uses: lime is a grayish-white amorphous solid, odorless, infusible, of alkaline taste and reaction. It becomes incandescent in the oxy-hydrogen flame, emitting a very intense white light. Made from marble it should be pure white.

189. **Calcium Hydrate.—**Slaked lime, Calcii Hydras. Formula, $Ca(HO)_2$. Molecular weight, 74. Prepared by adding 10 parts water to 16 of lime, letting cool, and straining. Dry, white, odorless, tasteless, alkaline pow-

der. None but recently prepared calcium hydrate should be used, as it soon becomes carbonate, absorbing carbonic dioxide from the air.

Mortar is a mixture of sand, water, and slaked lime: as the water evaporates mortar hardens, because part of the lime becomes a *carbonate*, absorbing carbon dioxide from the air, and part a *silicate* combining with the silicic acid of the sand.

Cement or hydraulic mortar is a mixture of powdered quartz, lime, and aluminium silicate; its hardening is due to the formation of calcium and aluminium silicates.

Lime Water or Liquor Calcis is a *clear* solution of calcium hydrate in water. Sugar increases the solubility of the calcium hydrate. Lime water is a colorless, nearly odorless liquid, of feebly caustic taste and alkaline reaction. It is a solution of about 15 parts calcium hydrate in 10,000 of water.

Milk of lime is lime water containing an excess of calcium hydrate, rendering it turbid.

Lime water is used in dentistry in form of gargle as an antacid, astringent, etc.

190. **Calcium Fluoride.—**

Synonyms: fluor-spar, fluoride of lime, Calcii Fluoridum.

Theoretical constitution: $CaFl_2$, one atom of calcium and two of fluorine, 40 parts by weight of calcium, and 38 of fluorine. Molecular weight, 78.

Preparation: calcium fluoride occurs in nature as fluor-spar; it is made artificially by treating a salt of calcium with potassium fluoride.

Properties: human bone contains about two per cent. of calcium fluoride; the enamel of teeth contains it also.

It is a very hard substance, insoluble in water, but decomposed by sulphuric acid, hydrofluoric acid being formed.

191. **Calcium Sulphite.**—Sulphite of lime, Calcii Sulphis. Formula $CaSO_3, 2H_2O$. Molecular weight, 156. Made by saturating milk of lime with sulphurous oxide, collecting, and drying the precipitate. It is a white powder, slightly soluble in water, soluble in sulphurous acid. It gradually becomes converted to sulphate. Used as an antiseptic.

192. **Chlorinated Lime.**—Official name, Calx Chlorata. Contains probably $Ca(ClO)_2$, calcium hypochlorite. It should yield 25 per cent. chlorine on addition of acid. It is prepared by the action of chlorine on calcium hydrate. It is a white or grayish-white, dry or but slightly damp powder or friable lumps, of feeble chlorine-like odor, and disagreeable, saline taste. It should be kept in well-closed vessels, in a cool, dry place. It is partially soluble in water and in alcohol. It is a disinfectant and a bleaching agent. It is used in dentistry as a deodorizer, disinfectant, antiseptic, and bleaching agent. It is poisonous in large doses.

193. **Calcium Phosphate.**—$Ca_3(PO_4)_2$, basic phosphate, tricalcic phosphate, bone phosphate: found in whole organism, constitutes two-thirds of the teeth, found in bones and in calculi; in the ash of albuminous substances; white, insoluble. Readily soluble in acid solutions.

194. **Calcium Hypophosphite.**—$Ca(H_2PO_2)_2 = 170$.
Prepared by dissolving phosphorus in milk of lime by aid of heat. Is a white salt, permanent in air, soluble in water, insoluble in alcohol.

195. **Magnesium.**—*Symbol*: Mg.; *Latin name*: Magnesium. *Equivalence*: II. *Specific gravity*: 1.70 to 1.74. *Atomic wt. (approx.)*: 24. *Atomic wt. (revised)*: 23.959. *Electrical state*: +. *Fusing point*: melts at red heat. *Properties*: magnesium is a brilliant, silver-white metal, lighter than silver or aluminium, tarnishing in damp air, burning easily and with a flame of dazzling brightness. It is soluble in dilute acids and unites directly with most of the negative elements.

TABLE 17.—COMPOUNDS OF MAGNESIUM.

Name.	Formula.	Properties, Uses, etc.
Chloride	$MgCl_2$	White, soluble, very bitter
Oxide	MgO	Known as magnesia or calcined magnesia. White, infusible, antacid, antidote to arsenic and caustic acids.
Sulphate	$MgSO_4$	"Epsom salts." White, soluble, very bitter.
Phosphate	$Mg_3(PO_4)_2$	Found in body along with calcium phosphate.
Ammonio-magnesium phosphate	$MgNH_4PO_4$	Called triple phosphate. Very soluble in acids, insoluble in alkalies.
Hypochlorite	$Mg(ClO)_2$	Used for bleaching purposes.

196. **Magnesium Carbonate.**—Synonyms: carbonate of magnesia, magnesia alba, salis amari. Official name, Magnesii Carbonas.
Formula, $4MgCO_3.Mg(HO)_2.H_2O$.

Two kinds are known to pharmacy, the "heavy" and the "light." Both are prepared by dissolving 25 parts of magnesium sulphate and 20 of sodium carbonate, each separately, in water, but the "light" carbonate is the result of mixing the solutions when cold, the "heavy" by dissolving in hot water and mixing while hot. There are certain other differences also in the methods of preparation, the light carbonate solution being much more dilute than the heavy. The light carbonate contains more carbonate and less hydrate, is about three times as bulky, and is partly crystalline. The heavy carbonate is wholly amorphous. Both form a light, white mass or powder, nearly insoluble in water, but readily soluble in dilute acids.

197. **Zinc.—**
Symbol: Zn.; *Latin name*: Zincum. *Equivalence*: II. *Specific gravity*: 7.10 to 7.20. *Atomic weight*: 65. *Revised atomic weight*: 64.904. *Electrical state*: +. *Fusing point*: 773° F. *Length of bar, etc.*: 1.0029; (2d in rank, cadmium = 1). *Wt. of cubic ft. in lbs.*: 445.7. *Tensile strength*: 3.3 to 8.3. *Tenacity*: 2; (8th rank). *Malleability*: 7; (7th rank). Brittle, until heated to between 248° and 302° F. *Ductility*: 8; (8th rank). *Conducting power* (*heat*): 5; (5th rank). *Conducting power* (*electricity*): 290 (silver = 1000); (4th rank). *Resistance to air, etc.*: tarnishes slowly; in moist air becomes coated with carbonate. *Solubility*: soluble in dilute acids, and in solutions of alkaline hydrates; slowly corroded by water, milk, and wine.

Direct combinations: oxygen, chlorine. With iron,

when heated to fusion. *Color and appearance*: bluish-white. *Structure*: crystalline; form of crystals, rhombohedral. *Consistence*: brittle. *Compounds*: zinc as zinc sulphide, zinc chloride, etc. *Alloys*: brass, bronze, bell metal, German silver, Aich's metal, arguzoid, Dutch metal, electrum, Muntz's metal, solders, sterro-metal, tutenag.

Occurrence: zinc is found usually either as sulphide, zinc-*blende*, ZnS. or as carbonate, *calamine*, $ZnCO_3$. It is also found as silicate and as oxide. Blende is found in Great Britain, Saxony, Aix-la-Chapelle, and in North America. Calamine occurs in Great Britain, Aix-la-Chapelle, Silesia, Spain, and in many other places. Red zinc ore or oxide is found chiefly in New Jersey.

Preparation: zinc is converted into vapor with comparative facility; it boils and distills at bright red heat. Hence, in order to extract zinc from its ores, the latter are first *calcined*, that is ignited in the air so as to burn off any oxidizable material, and the zinc obtained in form of oxide. The latter is then mixed with carbon and distilled, carbonic acid gas and zinc vapor being formed; the zinc vapor is condensed in suitable receivers.

Properties: under ordinary circumstances zinc is brittle, but when heated to about 300° F., it becomes malleable and ductile, and may be rolled into thin sheets. At about 400° F., it becomes brittle, melts at 775° and at 1842°

boils, volatilizes, and burns, if air be not excluded, with a fine greenish-white light, the oxide being formed.

Galvanized iron is iron covered with a coating of metallic zinc.

Dental uses: according to Flagg, zinc, in proportion of from 1 to 1½ parts in 100, if added to the usual 40 silver 60 tin alloys, seems to control shrinkage, imparts a "buttery" plasticity to the amalgam, adds to the whiteness of the filling, and assists in maintaining its color.

Zinc is used in making dies for swaging plates. It may be used, according to Essig, in making counter-dies.*

198. **Alloys of Zinc.—**

Zinc and tin alloy for casting dies for swaging plates is, according to Richardson, zinc 4, tin 1.

Zinc in Solders.—Solders made of the common commercial zinc are brittle, and are rolled with difficulty. They cause also a strong, brassy taste in the mouth, and should therefore be dissolved out of the finished work by pickling in nitric acid, the surface afterwards being burnished. *Pure* zinc in solders gives a plate that rolls easily,

---

*Dies for making artificial teeth. [Rollins in *Boston Medical and Surgical Journal*, 1884].

Metal plates are not as firm as rubber because they do not represent so perfect a reverse of the mouth. This is mostly due to the imperfect character and softness of the metal dies on which they are struck. A perfect die can be made by preparing the surface of the impression for electrotyping and then depositing copper on it which, if the die is to be used for striking, can be backed with a harder metal to the right firmness and form. Such a die is perfect and harder than any now in use.

makes a handsome solder and causes much less of the brassy taste, so little indeed that most people do not perceive it. (Chandler.)

199. Compounds of Zinc: Zinc Chloride.

Synonyms: butter of zinc, muriate of zinc. Official name, Zinci Chloridum.

Theoretical constitution: $ZnCl_2$, one atom of zinc and two of chlorine in the molecule; by weight, 64.9 parts of zinc to 70.8 of chlorine. Molecular weight, 135.7. It contains 47.83 per cent of zinc.

Preparation, properties, and uses: zinc chloride is made by heating zinc in a current of chlorine, or by the action of hydrochloric acid on granulated zinc or zinc carbonate, and evaporation of the solution to dryness.

It occurs in the form of hard, dirty-white masses, very deliquescent, and forming a clear solution with water.* Zinc chloride has a caustic, sharp taste, and is acid in reaction. It is soluble in alcohol and in ether. " Burnett's Disinfecting Fluid" contains zinc chloride, in proportion of from 205 to 230 grains to the ounce of water. The official solution of chloride of zinc, Liquor Zinci Chloridi, is an aqueous solution of zinc chloride containing 50 per cent. of the latter, or 23.92 per cent. of zinc.

It is made from 20 parts of granulated zinc, 1 part of nitric acid, 1 part of precipitated carbonate of zinc, and

---

*It is one of the most soluble substances known.

sufficient hydrochloric acid and distilled water. To the zinc, enough hydrochloric acid is added to dissolve it; the solution is filtered, nitric acid added, the whole evaporated to dryness, and the dry mass brought to fusion. After cooling, it is dissolved in 15 parts distilled water, the precipitated carbonate of zinc added, and the mixture agitated occasionally during the 24 hours. Finally it is filtered through washed asbestos free from iron, and enough distilled water added to it, through the filter, to make the product weigh 80 parts. The reaction is as follows:

$$\underset{\text{Zinc}}{Zn} + \underset{\text{hydrochloric acid}}{2HCl} = \underset{\text{zinc chloride}}{ZnCl_2} + \underset{\text{hydrogen}}{H_2}.$$

The solution is evaporated to dryness, and the dry mass fused in order to remove any excess of nitric acid. Zinc chloride solution cannot be filtered through paper; powdered washed glass or purified asbestos must be used.

The solution is a heavy, strongly caustic liquid, which should mix with alcohol without precipitation. Its sp. gr. is 1.555.†

If of a sp. gr. of 1.1275 at 68° F., it contains only 13.876 per cent of zinc chloride; if its sp. gr. is 1.2466 it contains 25.819 per cent; if 1.3869, 37.483 per cent.

Use in dentistry: zinc chloride is used in dental medicine for various purposes as an antiseptic, disinfectant, and deodorizer. A solution of it is used in connection with the oxide, to make a plastic filling (see zinc oxychloride).

Toxicology: chloride of zinc rapidly coagulates albumin. It is a caustic and irritant. Externally applied, it penetrates deeply into tissues and spreads, producing a white, thick, and hard eschar. In cases of poisoning from

---

†A solution of this strength is used in making the oxychloride cement.

internal administration, carbonate of sodium in milk, white of egg, or soap are the antidotes.

200. **Zinc Oxide.**—Official name, Zinci Oxidum. $ZnO = 80.9$. Made on a large scale by heating metallic zinc in a current of air. To make a pure white zinc oxide for pharmaceutical purposes, pure precipitated zinc carbonate should be heated at low red heat until the water and carbonic oxide are wholly expelled. This can be done below 500° F. The reaction is as follows:

$$2(ZnCO_3).3Zn(HO)_2 = 5ZnO + 2CO_2 + 3H_2O$$
Zinc carbonate   zinc oxide   carbonic acid   water

Too high heat will give the product a yellow color, and make it feel harsh. A small quantity should be used in heating. A good quality of zinc oxide should come in the form of a soft, flaky, impalpable powder of sp. gr. 5.6. It should turn yellow when heated in a test tube, and become white again on cooling.

It is insoluble in water but completely soluble in dilute acids. It is not darkened by sulphuretted hydrogen.

201. **Zinc Oxyphosphate.**—By the combination of zinc oxide with phosphoric acid a substance is obtained known familiarly as *oxyphosphate of zinc*. As known to dentists it comes in the form of a powder and a liquid. The powder is zinc oxide, and the liquid some variety of phosphoric acid. The two mixed, in propor-

tions, found by trial to be suitable for setting purposes, form the *oxyphosphate cement.*

When glacial phosphoric acid is used, the cement is termed oxy*meta*phosphate. The *pure* glacial phosphoric acid is preferred for use, as cements made from the commercial glacial acid have been found less durable.*

202. Zinc Oxychloride.—

Theoretical constitution: oxychlorides differ from chlorides, in that the former are *chlorides of the oxide of a metal,* while the latter are chlorides of the metal itself only.

There are various oxychlorides of zinc, whose formulæ are as follows:

(*a*) $ZnCl_2.6ZnO.6H_2O$;
(*b*) $ZnCl_2.3ZnO.4H_2O$;
(*c*) $ZnCl_2.9ZnO.3H_2O$.

It will be seen, therefore, that the general formula for the three is $ZnCl_2.nZnO.nH_2O$, n denoting any number.

Method of Preparation.—The oxychloride is prepared from a powder and a liquid, as in

---

*Rollins's process for making the oxymetaphosphate is as follows: Dissolve pure zinc in C. P. nitric acid to saturation, then evaporate to dryness, pack in a crucible, and heat till no more fumes are given off. Break up the crucible and, after separating the oxide of zinc, pulverize it to a very fine powder.

Take a pure solution of orthophosphoric acid (Section 266-1) which can easily be obtained of a strength of sixty per cent.; evaporate it in a platinum evaporating dish till white fumes come off. Then heat it to bright redness to be sure that it is all converted; cool, and make into a thick syrup. To make the filling, mix the powder and fluid in suitable proportions.

Slow-setting cements are less durable than those which set more rapidly. The powder should be worked into the acid gradually until the mass is stiff, the chief point being not to add too much powder at a time.

the case of the oxyphosphate. The powder is oxide of zinc, and the liquid a solution of zinc chloride in distilled water.*

Properties and uses: zinc oxychloride is a white substance, plastic when first mixed, but rapidly hardening with age.

It is used in dentistry for filling, "lining," and restoring color to discolored teeth.

203. **Zinc Oxysulphate.—**
Theoretical constitution: the mixture used in dentistry under this name is composed of a powder, consisting of one part of calcined zinc sulphate to two or three parts of calcined zinc oxide. Dissolved in a solution containing gum arabic and a little sulphite of lime, it forms a plastic mass soon setting and very dense when hard. (Flagg).

Uses in dentistry: zinc oxysulphate is used in dentistry as an adjunct to filling materials.

204. Other compounds of zinc.—

Zinc sulphate, $ZnSO_4$, $7H_2O$: white vitriol, white copperas, Zinci Sulphas. Occurs in small, colorless, transparent, efflorescent crystals, often mistaken for Epsom salt, astringent, emetic, irritant poison. Freely soluble in water, insoluble in alcohol. Disagreeable, metallic, styptic taste. Made by dissolving zinc in sulphuric acid: $Zn + H_2SO_4$ $ZnSO_4 + H_2$.

---

*Various methods of preparing the oxychloride have been suggested and as the zinc chloride is *very* soluble in water various strengths of solution have been used, such as 1 part to 2 of water, equal parts, etc., etc. According to Feichtinger (*Dingler's Pol. Journal*) a good method is to add 3 parts of zinc oxide and 1 part glass powder to 50 parts of a solution of zinc chloride of specific gravity, 1.5 to 1.6 to which is further added 1 part of borax dissolved in the smallest possible quantity of water.

Flagg heats oxide of zinc with borax, adds gradually more calcined oxide of zinc, and finally mixes with the zinc chloride solution.

Zinc iodide, $ZnI_2 = 318.1$. Official name, Zinci Iodidum. Made by digesting granulated zinc 30 Gm. (465 grains) iodine 100 Gm. (1550 grains) water 200 C. c. (6¼ fluid ounces) until colorless and free from odor of iodine, subsequently filtering through asbestos or powdered glass and evaporating filtrate rapidly to dryness at moderate heat. Zinc iodide is a white, granular substance, very readily soluble in alcohol and in water.

Zinc iodo-chloride has also been used in dentistry.

Toxicology of zinc compounds: the general antidotes are alkaline carbonates, as sodium carbonate; white of egg, soap and water, and mucilaginous drinks.

205. Cadmium.—

Symbol: Cd. Latin name: Cadmium. Equivalence: II. *Specific gravity:* 8.69. *Atomic weight:* 112. Molecule composed of one atom. *Revised atomic weight:* 111.835. *Electric state:* +. *Fusing point:* 442° F. *Length of bar,* etc.: 1.0031; (first in rank, most expansible). *Wt. of cubic ft. in lbs.:* 542.5. *Tenacity:* greater than tin. *Malleability, Ductility:* flexible, malleable, and ductile. *Conducting power* (electricity): somewhat lower than zinc. *Resistance to air:* gradually tarnishes in air; stained yellow by sulphuretted hydrogen. *Solubility:* soluble in nitric acid, in dilute hydrochloric, and sulphuric, but not in caustic alkalies. *Direct combinations:* oxygen, chlorine, sulphur. *Color and appearance:* like tin; white tinged with blue; lustrous. *Structure:* crystalizes in regular octahedrons on cooling. *Consistence:* harder than tin; not so hard as zinc; soft enough to mark paper. *Compounds:* cadmium, as cadmium sulphate. *Alloys:* fusible metal, amalgam alloys.

Occurrence: cadmium often accompanies zinc in its ores, and occurs as an impurity in commercial zinc. It is found in small quantities, not over 2 or 3 per cent., in ores of zinc. It occurs most abundantly as sulphide.

Preparation: the metal is obtained by converting the sulphide into oxide by heat, and then reducing this with coal or charcoal.

Uses in dentistry: cadmium is a constituent of easily fusible alloys. It resembles tin in color and appearance, and *creaks* like the latter when bent. It is unalterable in the air. It has been used in dental amalgam alloys.

206. Compounds of Cadmium.

Cadmium Sulphate: $3(CdSO_4)$. $8H_2O$. Obtained by dissolving metallic cadmium, its oxide, or carbonate in sulphuric acid; if metallic cadmium is used, a little nitric acid is added to hasten the reaction, and afterwards driven off by evaporation. Cadmium sulphate occurs in form of colorless, transparent crystals, resembling sulphate of zinc. In dentistry it has been used in various injections and lotions. It is poisonous. Percentage of cadmium, 43.74.

207. **Lead.**

Symbol: Pb. *Latin name*: Plumbum. *Equivalence*: II and IV. *Specific gravity*: 11.33 to 11.39. *Atomic weight*: 206.5. *Revised atomic weight*: 206.4710. *Electrical state*: +. *Fusing point*: 617° F. *Length of bar*, etc.: 1.0028 (3d rank, cadmium = 1, most expansible). *Wt. of cubic ft. in lbs.*: 709.2. *Tensile strength*: 0.8 to 1.5. *Relative tenacity*: 1 (lowest in rank). *Malleability*: 6; (6th rank). *Ductility*: 10; (10th rank). *Conducting power* (heat): 9; (9th rank). *Conducting power* (electricity): 83; (silver = 1000); (10th rank). *Resistance to air*, etc.: soon tarnishes; corroded by air in presence of carbonic acid. Discolored by sulphuretted hydrogen. *Solubility*: soluble in dilute nitric acid; attacked by hot sulphuric. *Direct combinations*: oxygen, chlorine, bromine, iodine, sulphur. Amalgamates readily. *Color and appearance*: bluish-white, brilliant. *Structure*: crystallizes in regular octahedrons, or in pyramids with four faces. *Consistence*: soft, leaves mark on paper. *Compounds*: mostly plumb*ic*, so-called, Pb''. *Alloys*: solder, type metal, pewter, fusible metal; has affinity for platinum and palladium.

Occurrence: lead occurs in nature chiefly as galena or galenite, which, like cinnabar, is a sulphide, PbS; 100 parts of the pure ore contain 86½ of lead. Another ore is *white-lead ore* or carbonate of lead. Galena is found in Great Britain, Spain, Saxony, and the United States. White lead ore is found in the valley of the Mississippi; in Australia, an ore called Anglesite, which is a sulphate of lead, is found. Other ores are crocoisite (a chromate), Wulfenite (a molybdate), and pyromasphite (a phosphate).

Preparation : galena is roasted, during which process two products, lead oxide and lead sulphate, are formed; the two products thus obtained are then strongly heated in a reverberatory furnace, metallic lead and sulphurous oxide being formed.

Dental uses: lead alloys with other metals, and is an ingredient of various solders: common solder is 50 parts lead and 50 parts tin. Lead is used in dentistry chiefly in making counter-dies. [Thin sheets of it are used for making patterns by which gold or silver plate is cut, so that bits of it may be found in the dentist's gold drawer; a very small amount of it will greatly impair the ductility of gold].

Compounds of lead: oxides of lead are used as coloring matters for artificial teeth. Plumbic peroxide (dioxide) PbO_2, is a chocolate-brown or puce-colored powder, which gives off its oxygen on being heated.

Litharge is plumbic oxide, PbO, prepared by heating melted lead in a current of air. It is pale yellow or orange yellow in color. By oxidizing litharge in a current of air and cooling slowly, a substance used in the arts as a pigment and called plumbic meta-plumbate, $Pb^{II}Pb^{IV}O_3$, or Pb_2O_3, is formed. The plumbic plumbates form the substances known as *red-leads*.

208. **Compounds of Uranium.—** An *oxide* of uranium is used by dentists as a coloring matter for artificial teeth.* Its formula is U_2O_3, uranic oxide, or uranyl oxide as it is sometimes called. Uranic nitrate heated in a glass tube till it decomposes yields pure uranic oxide in the form of a yellowish powder.

Another oxide of uranium is uranous oxide, UO, a brown powder.

209. **Copper.**
Symbol: Cu. *Latin name*: Cuprum. *Equivalence*: $(Cu_2)^{II}$ and II. *Specific gravity*: 8.914 to 8.952. *Atomic weight*: 63.2. *Revised atomic weight*: 63.173. *Electrical state*: +. *Fusing point*: 1996° F. *Length of bar*, etc.: 1.0017; (7th in rank). *Weight of cubic foot in lbs.*: 558.1.

---

*Rollins uses such oxides as contain the most oxygen, that is, uranic rather than uranous, plumbic dioxide rather than protoxide, etc., etc., because the coloring matters sometimes lose oxygen in firing.

Tensile strength: 13 to 15. *Tenacity*: 18, (Lead = 1); (3d rank). *Malleability:* 3; (3d rank). *Ductility:* 5; (5th rank). *Conducting power* (heat): 3; (3d rank). *Conducting power* (electricity): 999, (Silver = 1000); (2d rank). *Resistance to air*, etc.: in moist air becomes coated with green carbonate. Tarnished by sulphuretted hydrogen. *Solubility:* soluble in hot mineral acids, and attacked by vegetable acids in presence of air and moisture. Attacked by chlorine and nitric acid, and by sulphur when heated; slowly attacked by weak acids, alkalies, and saline solutions. *Direct combinations:* sulphur, chlorine, bromine, iodine, silicon, and various metals at red heat. *Color and appearance:* lustrous, flesh red. *Structure:* crystallizes in isometric forms. *Consistence:* somewhat softer than iron. *Compounds:* cuprous $(Cu_2)^{II}$ and cupric. *Alloys:* Aich's metal, aluminium bronze, arguzoid, bell-metal, brass, Britannia metal, bronze, Dutch-metal, electrum, German silver, gold coinage, gun-metal, Muntz's metal, pewter, silver coinage, some solders, speculum metal, sterro-metal, tutenag.

Occurrence: native copper exists near Lake Superior; in its ores it is found as oxide, sulphide, carbonate, and in combination with sulphide of iron, forming copper pyrites. The metal is found in England, Sweden, Saxony, Siberia, Australia, Chili, and in the United States.

Preparation: the ores are first roasted in air, then with silica fluxes and carbon, and finally a substance called copperstone is obtained, which contains both oxide and sulphide of copper. By repeating the roasting and heating, the oxide reacts on the sulphide, and metallic copper is obtained.

Pure Copper may be obtained by electrolysis. A solution of cupric sulphate is used, and the negative wire of a battery attached to a copper plate which is immersed in the solution. Pure copper is deposited on the plates, and may easily be stripped off.

Use in dentistry: copper is used as a constituent of some dental amalgam alloys.*

Alloys of Copper:

Babbitt Metal is an alloy of copper, 3 parts; antimony, 1 part; tin, 3 parts. The copper is fused and then antimony and tin are added to it. It melts at a moderately low heat; contracts but little; is brittle, but may be rendered less so by adding tin.

210. **Brass** is an alloy of copper and zinc. Common brass is made of 66.6 parts copper and 33.3 zinc; best brass, 71.4 copper to 28.6 zinc. Yellow brass is 60 copper to 40 zinc. Brass melts at 1869° F.

211. **Bell metal** is an alloy of 6 parts copper to 2 parts tin; some varieties are 78 copper to 22 tin. Cannon metal is 90 copper to 10 of tin.

212. **Bronze** is an alloy of copper and tin. **Aluminium bronze,** 900 parts copper to 100 of aluminium. The latter has been used for the under layer of teeth plates, and is said to be free from injurious oxidation and to be more easily manipulated than gold alloys or silver. It may be stamped and pressed, almost as easily as pure silver, while possessing the elasticity of steel. Its melting point is higher than that of pure gold, so that it may be made red hot without danger of melting, and can be manipulated

---

*See Copper Amalgam under Mercury.

with hard solder. Sauer solders it with from 14 to 16 carat red gold. Aluminium bronze is one-half lighter than 12 carat silver and almost half the weight of 14 carat gold. It oxidizes, superficially only, in the mouth; it is affected, superficially, by a 1 in 1,000 solution of corrosive sublimate, but not by carbolic acid.

213. **Gold aluminium bronze** oxidizes more readily, is softer, and not so elastic.

214. **Phosphor bronze** is copper, combined with from 3 to 15 per cent. of tin, and from ¼ to 2½ per cent. of phosphorus.

215. **Speculum metal** is an alloy of copper and tin; 66.6 copper and 33.3 tin.

216. **Compounds of Copper.—**
Cupric Sulphate: $CuSO_4, 5H_2O$. Known as sulphate of copper, blue vitriol, Roman vitriol, blue stone, blue copperas, vitriol of copper. Official name, Cupri Sulphas. Made on a large scale by dissolving copper in sulphuric acid, evaporating, and allowing to crystallize:

$$\underset{\text{Copper}}{Cu} + \underset{\text{sulphuric acid}}{2H_2SO_4} = \underset{\text{cupric sulphate}}{CuSO_4} + \underset{\text{water}}{2H_2O} + \underset{\text{sulphurous oxide}}{SO_2}.$$

It occurs in the form of blue, prismatic crystals, efflorescent, of astringent, metallic taste, soluble in 4 parts water, insoluble in alcohol. In dentistry it is used externally, dissolved in ammonia, as an astringent and styptic. It is poisonous; antidotes: milk, white of egg given freely.

217. **Mercury (quicksilver).**

Symbol: Hg. *Latin name:* Hydrargyrum. *Equivalence:* $(Hg_2)^{II}$ and II. *Specific gravity:* 13.596. *Atomic weight:* 199.7. Molecule composed of one atom. *Revised atomic weight:* 199.7120. *Electrical state:* +. *Fusing point:* liquid at ordinary temperatures. Boils at 660° F. *Length of bar* total expansion, 1.0180. Malleable at —40° F. *Resistance to air,* etc.: unaltered in air; does not leave streak on paper.

Solubility: soluble in dilute nitric acid and hot sulphuric; insoluble in hydrochloric acid. *Direct combinations:* dissolves all metals but iron combines directly with halogens and sulphur. *Color and appearance:* opaque, with metallic lustre; brilliant silver-white. *Structure:* octahedral crystals at —40° F. *Consistence:* liquid; slightly volatile. *Compounds:* mercurous (Hg_2)^{II} and mercuric. *Alloys:* amalgams. *Use in dental amalgam alloys:* mercury amalgamates readily with gold, zinc, tin, and silver; also with copper, platinum, palladium, and cadmium.

Occurrence and preparation: mercury is found in the form of **Cinnabar**, which is native mercuric sulphide. Large quantities of it are obtained in California; it is also found in Spain, Austria, Mexico, Peru, China, Japan, Borneo. Mercury is obtained from cinnabar, either by roasting the latter or by heating it with lime, which combines with the sulphur of the cinnabar, while the metal volatilizes and is condensed in suitable coolers.

The equation of the preparation of mercury is

$$HgS + 2O = Hg + SO_2$$
Mercuric sulphide. Oxygen. Mercury. Sulphurous oxide.

Dental uses: amalgams. Mercury readily alloys with other metals, forming combinations called *amalgams*.

This property of mercury may be readily shown by the following experiment: clean a copper cent with a little nitric acid, wash well with water, and on it place a globule of mercury; the latter soon covers the whole surface of the cent, giving it a white color. Heat the cent and its original color will be restored, the mercury volatilizing. Many of the alloys of mercury with other metals are soft when freshly formed, but harden with time, hence their value for fillings.

The combinations formed are, in the case of solid amalgams, definite compounds in which, however, there is but feeble chemical affinity between the constituents. Liquid amalgams are merely solutions of the various metals in mercury, and not, as a rule, definite chemical compounds. Many liquid amalgams become, however, after a time, white, solid, and crystalline. There is usually little or no contraction in volume, but in the case of silver and copper amalgams there is considerable, and in tin and lead slight, though perceptible. (Watts).

Amalgams are decomposed by heat.

218. The methods by which amalgamation may be made to take place are as follows:

1. Direct contact on part of the metal, either as a solid or in the finely divided state, with mercury, either at ordinary temperatures or at higher temperatures. Heat is evolved during the amalgamation.

2. Introduction of metallic mercury, or of sodium-amalgam, into a solution of a salt of a metal.

3. Introduction of a metal into a solution of a salt of mercury.

4. Contact of a metal with mercury and addition of a dilute acid.

In the last two cases a weak electric current is sometimes developed.

Electricity is often used to facilitate the union of mercury with a metal precipitated from a solution of one of its salts. (See *Copper Amalgam*).

219. **Antimony amalgam:** triturate 3 parts heated mercury with 1 part fused antimony; or triturate 2 parts antimony in a mortar, add a little hydrochloric acid, and gradually drop in 1 part of mercury. The amalgam is soft, decomposed by contact with air or water, and the antimony separates.

Amalgams containing antimony in notable quantity are fine grained, plastic, and do not shrink, but are excessively dirty to work. Used in small proportions in amalgams it is said to be of possible value in controlling shrinkage.*

220. **Cadmium amalgam:** cadmium amalgamates at ordinary temperatures. When complete saturation takes place, as through agency of sodium-amalgam in a solution of salt of cadmium, a compound of 78.26 Hg to 21.74 Cd is formed, having for its formula, therefore, Hg_2Cd, and being silver-white, granular, hard, brittle, heavier than mercury, and in octahedral crystals. (Watts).

Cadmium amalgamates easily, sets quickly, and resists sufficiently, but fillings containing it gradually soften and disintegrate, and, if there is a large proportion, the dentine becomes decalcified and stained bright orange-yellow from formation of cadmium sulphide.

. 221. **Copper amalgam:** there are various processes

---

*Dr. Chase's "alcohol tight" amalgam contains nearly five per cent. of antimony. (Weagant).

for making copper amalgam. Rollins, Ames, and others make it by *electrolysis*.

Rollins's method is as follows:*

Distilled water, five gallons; sulphate of copper, enough to saturate; sulphuric acid, one pound. Mix, filter, and pour into a wooden firkin with wooden hoops. All the chemicals should be absolutely pure. Place ten pounds of pure mercury in a glass jar and immerse in the copper solution. To the zinc plate of a galvanic battery attach a gutta-percha-covered wire, having one end bare for about an inch. This exposed end is to be immersed below the level of the surface of the mercury. Tie granulated pure copper in a bag and hang it in the copper solution, connecting with a wire to the carbon of the battery. The battery is to be kept in action till the mercury has absorbed enough copper to make a thick paste. Then remove and wash thoroughly in hot water till all of the sulphate solution has been removed. Squeeze out the softer amalgam and allow the remainder to harden. When it is hard, heat it, and renew the squeezing as before. This new method insures an amalgam of perfect purity, and is simpler than any of the old and faulty ways in use. Copper amalgam dissolves rapidly in mouths where the saliva is acid, and in this way serves as an indicator of the condition of the oral fluids. It stains teeth in a certain proportion of cases, particularly when teeth have lost their pulps, or when the dentine is of an open structure.

A battery answers for home manufacture, but on a larger scale a dynamo should be used.

Dr. T. H. Chandler, of Boston, has described to me the following processes for making copper amalgam, which he calls " No. 1 " and " No. 2." He thinks " No. 1 " an excellent filling:

---

*Boston *Medical and Surgical Journal*, February, 1886.

No. 1.—To a hot solution of sulphate of copper add a little hydrochloric acid, and a few sticks of zinc, and boil for about a minute. The copper will be precipitated in a spongy mass. Take out zinc, pour off liquor, and wash the copper thoroughly with hot water. Pour on the mass a little dilute nitrate of mercury, which will instantly cover every particle of the copper with a coating of the mercury. Add mercury two or three times the weight of the copper, triturate slightly in a mortar and finish by heating the mixture a few moments in a crucible.

No. 2.—Take finely divided copper (copper dust) obtained by shaking a solution of sulphate of copper with granulated tin. The solution becomes hot, and a fine brown powder is thrown down. Of this powder take 20, 30, or 36 parts by weight and mix in a mortar with sulphuric acid, 1.85 specific gravity, to a paste, and add 70 parts of mercury with constant stirring. When well mixed, wash out all traces of acid and cool off. When used, heat to 1300° F; it can be kneaded, like wax, in a mortar.

While in this plastic state, it is an excellent solder for metals, glass, etc., used by applying it to surfaces to be joined, pressing hard together and allowing it to set.

Weagant's process for making copper amalgam is as follows:

Nearly fill a vessel with a solution of copper sulphate, one part of a saturated solution to two or three parts water. Pour into it enough mercury to cover well the bottom of the glass, and stand a clean strip or plate of iron in the mercury, allowing the end to project above the glass. Pure precipitated copper in finely divided state will at once become deposited on the iron, and the mercury will gradually unite with the copper, creeping up the iron until the whole surface is covered with a film of amalgam. If the iron is placed for a moment in a weak solution of sulphuric acid just before being immersed in the copper bath, amalgamation takes place more rapidly.

It must be allowed to stand undisturbed until the change in the color of the solution shows that all the copper is precipitated. Then with a siphon draw off the liquid and renew the sulphate of copper. This proceeding may be repeated as long as the mercury takes up the copper. When all the mercury has become amalgamated, scrape off whatever amalgam adheres to the strip of iron, pour off the liquid, and turn the mass of amalgam into a mortar. Rub and wash it thoroughly, allowing a stream of water to fall upon it from a tap, cleaning out all the free metallic copper and scales of oxide of iron. As soon as it is as clean as it can be made, place it in a chamois skin and squeeze out the surplus mercury. Then the washing and grinding in the mortar must be repeated until the mass again becomes soft, when more mercury can be removed. The greatest care must be taken to remove all the little scales and grains of iron, or the amalgam will be dirty to work, and the best results from it cannot be obtained. When the amalgam has been well worked and all the mercury possible squeezed out, heat it gently in an iron vessel. The first time this must be done carefully, as steam from water which is retained in it becomes generated, and the mass will explode, flying in all directions. When the amalgam begins to get soft, rub in a mortar, and again squeeze out mercury. This heating, rubbing, and squeezing must be repeated again and again, until very little mercury can be removed and the amalgam is found to set instantly, and become very hard. It may then be made into little sticks or pellets, and laid away for use. To use it, place the quantity required in an iron spoon and heat it over a flame until mercury begins to show like sweat upon the surface. Then crush and grind the mass in a small mortar, and work together in the hand. If too soft, squeeze in a piece of chamois skin, using a pair of pliers if necessary. One soon learns how soft or dry to make it in order to get the best results. Do not throw away any of the scraps remaining, as they may be used over and over again an indefinite number of times, seeming to improve by age. Be careful not to heat too much, as some of the mercury volatilizes, leaving pure copper, which becomes oxidized by the heat and makes the amalgam dirty.

A weak solution of sulphate of copper is used instead of the saturated solution, as the precipitate is much finer and the amalgam requires less rubbing to bring it to shape.

Copper amalgam is composed of pure copper and pure mercury in variable proportions. The less mercury it contains the more quickly it sets and the harder it becomes. When properly made it is exceedingly pleasant to work, fine-grained and plastic, and sets either slowly or rapidly, as we desire it and are pleased to prepare it. It becomes very hard—harder in fact than any amalgam made from alloys. It is not known to shrink or expand in the least degree. It does not ball up nor change its shape in any way during the setting or afterwards, and finally, instead of having any injurious effect upon the teeth or surrounding tissues, it is decidedly beneficial to them, acting as an antiseptic or germ destroyer. But, although it does not cause discoloration of the teeth, the filling itself will quickly and emphatically become black —very black—upon the surface. It should always be carefully polished when hard, for, although polishing does not prevent its turning black, it is a polished black, and not so disagreeable and dirty looking as when left with a rough surface. (Weagant).

The sulphide of copper formed by the action of the sulphuretted hydrogen of the mouth on the copper of the amalgam is, according to Tomes, readily converted, on exposure to air and moisture, into copper sulphate, hence it is almost certain that the latter is formed on the exposed surface of the filling. Cupric sulphate is freely soluble, and hence is likely to permeate the dentine. Sulphides of the other metals are not so readily converted into soluble salts, hence will not permeate the dentine so thoroughly.*

222. **Gold amalgam:** gold, in leaf or filings, amalgamates readily with mercury at ordinary temperatures. For rapid amalgamation, heat should be used, and the gold be in the finely divided state.

Gold added to amalgams of tin and silver is valuable in that it controls shrinkage, balling, and discoloration, facilitates setting, and adds to edge-strength. Amalgams containing it are smoothly and easily worked. Some dentists use amalgams containing a very large proportion of gold.

223. **Palladium amalgam:—**

Palladium has been recently brought to notice as forming with three times its weight of mercury a desirable dental amalgam, especially useful in the sixth-year molars of young patients.†

Some care is necessary in the mixing, as palladium forms a true chemical compound with mercury, and the action is so intense that under certain circumstances an explosion may result. Palladium fillings become black, but do not discolor the tooth-substance.

The amalgam sets with such great rapidity that it is necessary to mix it quite soft in order to make a filling

---

*Copper sulphate has been successfully used abroad as a preservative for telegraph poles.

†Dr. E. A. Bogue has used palladium amalgam. In the proportion of seventy-five per cent. mercury to twenty-five per cent. of pure precipitated palladium the expense is greatly reduced.

before it is too hard to use.* It must be worked very quickly, and with heated instruments.

224. **Platinum amalgam:** metallic platinum does not unite readily with mercury. Spongy platinum unites with mercury, when triturated in a warm mortar with the latter, or in contact with acetic acid; or sodium-amalgam containing 1 per cent. sodium, if introduced into a solution of platinic chloride, will form an amalgam of silvery appearance. The amalgam containing 100 parts mercury, to 15.48 platinum, has a sp. gr. of 14.29, and has metallic lustre when rubbed; 100 mercury to 21.6 platinum is a dark gray solid; 100 mercury to 34.76 platinum is of 14.69 sp. gr., dark gray, but of no lustre; 100 mercury to 12 platinum is bright, but soft and greasy. The solid amalgam containing the most mercury is probably $PtHg_2$. Mercury exposed for some time to the action of platinic chloride forms a thick, pasty amalgam.

In general, it may be said that an amalgam of mercury and platinum alone does not harden well.†

Platinum, according to Essig, is of value only when combined with tin, silver, and gold, with the proper amount of mercury; under such circumstances, it seems to confer on the alloy the property of almost instantly setting, and of being much harder. According to Fletcher, the amalgam should be used immediately, before the platinum and mercury have time to set.

225. **Silver amalgam:** amalgamation takes place quickly, if the silver is in thin plates, or in powder, and dropped at red heat into heated mercury. The amalgam varies according to circumstances of formation, composition, etc., and is soft, or crystalline, or granular. The

---

*Dr. Chandler mixes gold in large proportion in order to render the palladium more tractable.

†Dr. Ames, of Chicago, has prepared platinum amalgam by electrolysis.

amalgam most readily formed has for its formula AgHg. [Amalgams of mercury and silver are said by Watts to *contract* considerably, but by others to expand. The *proportions* are undoubtedly of importance].

Amalgams composed of silver and mercury alone tend, when used as fillings, to change their shape. But silver used in connection with other metals is the most important element in a good amalgam for filling teeth.* Silver forms silver sulphide in contact with the sulphuretted hydrogen of the mouth, and both tooth and filling are blackened in consequence; but the tendency is toward preservation of the tooth.

226. **Tellurium** and mercury are said to unite directly, forming a tin-colored amalgam.

227. **Tin amalgam:** made readily and quickly by pouring mercury into melted tin, but readily enough by mixing the filings with mercury at ordinary temperatures. Tin amalgam has a white color, and, if there is not too much mercury, occurs in form of a brittle, granular mass of cubical crystals. In most cases there is *condensation*, but in the amalgam composed of 1 part tin to 2 mercury (melted and by volume) the condensation is scarcely perceptible.

Amalgams composed of mercury and tin alone do not harden sufficiently. In an alloy with other metals, tin is valuable in that it facilitates amalgamation, prevents discoloration, and diminishes conductivity.

228. **Zinc amalgam:** usually made by cooling melted zinc to as low a temperature as possible without letting it solidify, then pouring in mercury in a fine stream, and stirring constantly.

Amalgams of mercury and zinc alone are not common-

---

*Silver is the largest component of most of the reliable amalgam alloys on the market.

ly used. Added to alloys of tin and silver in as small proportion as one per cent., zinc controls shrinkage, adds to the whiteness of the filling, and tends to maintain color.*

229. **Dental amalgam alloys:** it will readily be perceived from a study of common **amalgams** that but few of them would be of service to the dentist. On the other hand combinations of metals, often first melted in tin, brought about through the agency of mercury—that is, amalgams of *several metals at once*,—alloy amalgams—have been found very useful, so that now large quantities are used. Amalgams for dental purposes are chiefly composed of tin and silver, in different proportions, of which Townsend's alloy of 60 tin to 40 silver may be taken as the type. Some dental amalgam alloys, as Hardman's and Lawrence's, contain copper in addition to tin and silver; some contain zinc, gold, etc. The list of metals used in the dental amalgam alloys comprises tin, silver, copper, zinc, gold, platinum, cadmium, antimony, palladium. The so-called "gold and platina alloys," according to Flagg, contain 50 per cent. of tin, more than 40 of silver, and from 2 to 7 of gold and platinum.

[In regard to the average proportions of tin and silver, Flagg finds 40 tin to 60 silver the best working formula, modified by additions of copper, gold, and zinc].

230. **Qualities desirable in dental amalgam alloys:** strength and sharpness of edge, freedom from admixture with any metal favorable to the formation of soluble salts of an injurious character in the mouth, capability of maintenance of color and shape, and non-liability to undue expansion. N. B.—Absolute freedom from discoloration can not often be obtained, nor is it always desirable, according to Flagg.

---

*Chandler's experiments with zinc lead him to prefer sifting in a small percentage of *pure* zinc dust at the "mix" rather than melting it with the other ingredients of an amalgam alloy.

231. **Discoloration of amalgam fillings:** the formation of sulphides, due to the sulphuretted hydrogen resulting from the decomposition of the food, is the main cause of the discoloration of amalgam fillings; black discoloration is found in fillings containing *silver* or *copper;* yellowish discoloration in those containing *cadmium*. According to Essig, it is not safe to suppose that a metal not of itself blackened by sulphuretted hydrogen—as gold or platinum—will secure the same immunity to alloys containing silver and mercury. It has been noticed that plugs, which apparently exclude the passage of a solution of indigo or ink, will show peripheral discoloration when exposed to the action of a sulphuretted hydrogen solution, though the surface directly exposed to the action of the sulphur was but slightly clouded.* (Essig).

Discoloration of gold fillings: Chandler takes the ground that the discoloration of gold in the mouth is due to oxidation of the steel worn from pluggers.

232. **Compounds of Mercury:—**
Mercuric chloride or **corrosive sublimate:** Synonyms: corrosive chloride, bichloride of mercury, "oxymuriate" of mercury, perchloride of mercury, deuto-chloride of mercury, Hydrargyri Perchloridum. Official name, Hydrargyri Chloridum Corrosivum.

Theoretical constitution: $HgCl_2$ or mercuric chloride. Mercury as a *dyad*. The molecule is composed of one atom of mercury to two of chlorine; by weight, mercury 200 parts, chlor-

---

*Chandler suggests that the discoloration and destruction of amalgam fillings may be due to galvanic action, the ingredients of fillings forming minute batteries, as it were, and destroying one another.

ine 70.8. Molecular weight, 270.8. Percentage of mercury, 73.85.

Preparation (pharmaceutical): made by taking 20 parts of mercuric sulphate and 16 of sodium chloride, reducing each to fine powder, mixing well, adding 1 part of black oxide of manganese in fine powder, triturating thoroughly in a mortar, and subliming:

$HgSO_4 + 2NaCl = HgCl_2 + Na_2SO_4$.
Mercuric sulphate. Sodium chloride. Mercuric chloride. Sodium sulphate.

The manganese oxide is added to oxidize any mercurous salt which may be present in the mercuric sulphate.

Properties: corrosive sublimate occurs as a white, heavy powder, or as heavy, colorless, rhombic crystals or crystalline masses. It has a metallic, acrid taste, an acid reaction, and is a violent poison. Specific gravity, 5.4. It is soluble in 16 parts of cold water, and 2 of boiling, in about 2 of alcohol, and 4 of ether. Its ready solubility in alcohol should be noted, as many compounds of the metals are insoluble in alcohol, or less soluble in it than in water. It is a powerful germicide, an aqueous solution of 1 in 20000 destroying the spores of bacilli in ten minutes. A solution of 1 in 5000 is used as a disinfectant. Aqueous solutions gradually decompose on exposure to light, or in contact with organic substances, such as sugar, gum, extracts, resin, etc. When mercuric chloride is being powdered, it should be kept moist with alcohol to prevent the poisonous dust from rising.

Dental uses: mercuric chloride in 1 in 20000 solution—half a grain in twenty-one fluid ounces of water (metric, 0.032 grammes in 620 C.c.) —is used as an antiseptic. As a germicide, 1 part in 2500 of water; 1 in 5000 as a disinfectant. It is used as a lotion, injection, or gargle.

Toxicology: corrosive sublimate is a powerful, irritant poison, and external application of it has been often attended by fatal results. In poisoning from internal administration, white of egg in milk, or else wheat flour mixed with milk, should be given; vomiting should be encouraged by emetics. White of egg in milk should be administered two or three times daily for some weeks. If salivation is troublesome, gargles of chlorate of potash and of alum should be used. In chronic poisoning, ptyalism is a prominent symptom.

In chronic mercurial poisoning the teeth are said to become brittle.

233. **Mercurous chloride or calomel:—**
Synonyms: mild chloride of mercury, subchloride of mercury, submuriate of mercury, Hydrargyri Subchloridum, protochloride of mercury. Official name, Hydrargyri Chloridum Mite.

Theoretical constitution: Hg_2Cl_2, two atoms of mercury (together bivalent) and two of chlorine; 400 parts by weight of mercury, and 70.8 by weight of chlorine. Molecular weight, 470.8. Its formula is sometimes written HgCl.

Preparation: either (1) by subliming mercuric sulphate 10 parts with sodium chloride 5 parts, 7 parts of metallic mercury having been previously triturated with the moistened mercuric sulphate.

$HgSO_4 + Hg = Hg_2SO_4$; then
$Hg_2SO_4 + 2NaCl = Hg_2Cl_2 + Na_2SO_4$.

Mercurous sulphate and sodium chloride yield mercurous chloride and sodium sulphate. Or (2) by precipitating by hydrochloric acid a solution of 300 grams of mercury in 270 C.c. of suitably diluted nitric acid.

Properties: sublimed calomel is a fine, white powder with very slight tinge of yellow. Tasteless, insoluble in both water and alcohol. Sp. gr., 6.56. Completely volatilized by heat. Precipitated calomel is bulkier than sublimated calomel. Exposed to sunlight, it acquires a grayish tinge becoming partially decomposed into metallic mercury and corrosive sublimate; boiled with water, the same change takes place slowly, and a mixture of it with sugar contains, after some time, an appreciable amount of the mercuric chloride. Mixed with water, it should give no white precipitate with ammonia. Given internally in sufficient quantity it produces salivation; cases are also on record where external application of it has produced salivation.

234. Mercuric Sulphide.—

Synonyms: sulphide of mercury, cinnabar, vermilion.

Theoretical constitution : HgS, mercur*ic* sulphide. Molecular weight, 231.7.

Preparation: it occurs as an ore and is then termed *cinnabar*. Made artificially, it is called *vermilion*.

The brilliancy of vermilion depends much on the manner in which it is prepared, and on the purity of the substances used in making it. One method of preparation is to heat to 122°F. the following mixture: mercury, 300 parts; sulphur, 114 parts; potassium hydrate, 75 parts; water, 450 parts. The presence of potassium hydrate facilitates the reaction. The mass, which is at first black, becomes red in the course of several hours; in order to cool it, it is poured into cold water, collected on a filter, washed, and dried. Several kinds of vermilion are found in commerce; the Chinese (made in the dry way by subliming a mixture of sulphur 1 part and mercury 7 parts in small lots) the German, and the French. Vermilion should sublime without residue, if pure.*

235. **Mercuric Iodide.—**

Synonyms: biniodide of mercury, red iodide of mercury, deut-iodide of mercury. Official name, Hydrargyri Iodidum Rubrum.

Theoretical constitution: HgI_2, mercuric iodide. Molecular weight, 453.2.

Preparation: formed when solution of potassium iodide is cautiously added to solution of mercuric chloride,

$$HgCl_2 + (KI)_2 = HgI_2 + 2KCl.$$
Mercuric chloride. Potassium iodide. Mercuric iodide. Potassium chloride.

Properties: occurs as a fine, heavy, crystalline, scarlet-red powder. Nearly insoluble in water, but soluble in hot alcohol, in solution of potassium iodide and of sodium chloride. Is a powerful irritant poison.

---

*Shown by heating *dry* in a tube called a *reduction tube*.

236. **Mercurous Iodide.—**
Synonyms: protiodide of mercury, yellow iodide, green iodide.
Theoretical constitution: Hg_2O_2 or HgI (like $HgCl$).
Preparation: made by triturating together with a little alcohol 127 parts of iodine and 200 of mercury.
$$Hg_2 + I_2 = Hg_2I_2$$
The trituration is continued until there is obtained a green mass, which, after washing in boiling alcohol, is dried.
Properties: mercurous iodide is a green-yellow powder, insoluble in water, alcohol, and ether. Exposed to the action of light, heat, alkaline chlorides or iodides, it is transformed into mercury and mercuric iodide.

237. **Tellurium.—**
Symbol: Te. *Latin name*: Tellurium. *Equivalence*: II, IV, VI. *Specific Gravity*: 6.18—6.24. *Atomic weight*: 128. *Revised atomic weight*: 127.960. *Electrical state*: — *Fusing point*: little below red heat. *Malleability, ductility*: brittle. *Conducting power* (heat): bad conductor. *Conducting power* (electricity): bad conductor. *Solubility*: soluble in hot sulphuric acid, in hot caustic alkali solutions; attacked by hot nitric acid. *Direct combinations*: hydrogen, oxygen, sulphur, bromine, chlorine, iodine. *Color and appearance*: silver white. *Structure*: crystallizes in rhombohedrons; like As and Sb. *Consistence*: hard and brittle. *Compounds*: tellurides; telluric, tellurous.

Properties and preparation: tellurium is in physical properties a metal, though chemically allied closely to sulphur and selenium. It is found native, though, in Hungary, and in combination with bismuth, lead, gold and silver. It melts at 500° C. When heated in the air it takes fire and burns with a blue flame tinged with green.

238. Sulphur.—

Symbol: S. *Atoms in molecule*: S_2 and S_6. *Atomic weight*: 32. *Molecular weight*: 64. *Density*: of vapor, 32. *Specific gravity*: 2.04. *Weight of one litre of vapor*: 2.86 grammes at 1000° C. *How liquefied*: melts at 114° C (237° F.) *Solubility*: insoluble in water. *Best solvent*: carbon disulphide. Nearly insoluble in alcohol.

Occurrence in nature: occurs free in earth of volcanic regions of Sicily.

How made: distill crude brimstone in retort; vapor conducted into large chamber condenses in form of powder known as *flowers of sulphur*. *Sulphur lotum* is flowers of sulphur which has been washed. Sulphur may be made by precipitation from sulphides by acids.

Properties: affinity for many of the metals, for oxygen, carbon, etc. Forms many compounds. Lemon yellow solid, melting at 234° F., and boiling at 824° F. Brittle, tasteless, odorless. Does not conduct electricity or heat. Precipitated sulphur is almost white in color.

Use in dentistry: flowers of sulphur is used in the manufacture of dental rubbers, as a vulcanizing material. Caoutchouc is heated till soft, then ground with 15 or 20 per cent. of sulphur and subjected to heat, pressure, and moisture.

Sulphurous acid: this substance, H_2SO_3, is made by dissolving sulphurous anhydride, SO_2, in water. [Sulphurous anhydride is made by burning sulphur and collecting the fumes]. Sulphurous acid is an unstable liquid of suffocating odor. Its compounds are *sulphites*. It is used for bleaching purposes, and should always be freshly prepared.

239. Hydrogen Sulphide or Sulphuretted Hydrogen.—

Synonyms: hydric sulphide, sulphydric acid, hydrosulphuric acid, Acidum Hydrosulphuricum.

Theoretical constitution: H_2S, two atoms of hydrogen to one of sulphur; by weight, 16 parts of sulphur to 1 of hydrogen; molecular weight, 34; density, 17.2 · sp. gr., 1.192. Weight of a litre, 1.540.

Origin and manufacture: it is found in volcanic gases, in some mineral springs, and as a result of the decomposition of organic matter containing sulphur, as in the intestines and in teeth. It is usually made by the action of a dilute acid on a sulphide, as for example:

$FeS + H_2SO_4 = FeSO_4 + H_2S$
Ferrous sulphide.   Sulphuric acid.   Ferrous sulphate.   Hydrogen sulphide

Properties: colorless, fetid gas, combustible, soluble in water, readily recognized by its odor, (that of rotten eggs) valuable as a re-agent, yields precipitates with salts of many metals. Blackens unsized paper saturated with solution of sugar of lead. Poisonous.

Application to dentistry: its odor, if recognized in the breath, indicates that decomposition is going on somewhere in the mouth.

Its action on the various metals and compounds used in dentistry is of the utmost importance. It forms *sulphides* with silver, mercury, lead, copper, bismuth; these sulphides are all dark in color, and the *blackening* observed in amalgam fillings is due to formation of them. It also forms sulphides with arsenic, antimony, cadmium, and tin, but these sulphides are not black; the sulphide of arsenic is yellow, that of antimony orange, cadmium yellow, tin yellow or brown. Sulphuretted hydrogen does not act on *metallic* gold, platinum, palladium, iridium, nor does it blacken iron, cobalt, nickel, manganese, zinc, chromium, or aluminium.

240 **Hydrogen Sulphate or Sulphuric Acid.—**
Synonyms: hydric sulphate, oil of vitriol, dihydric sulphate, vitriol, spirit or essence of vitriol.

Theoretical constitution: H_2SO_4, hydrogen sulphate, an oxacid composed of two atoms of hydrogen, one of sulphur, and four of oxygen; by weight two parts hydrogen, 32 of sulphur, 64 of oxygen. Molecular weight, 98. Its salts are *sulphates*; for example, zinc and sulphuric acid form zinc sulphate.

Preparation: the crude acid is prepared by the action of nitric acid on sulphurous oxide producing sulphuric oxide, which uniting with water forms sulphuric acid. The sulphurous oxide may be made by burning sulphur in air The acid is concentrated by evaporation until a sp. gr of 1.84 is obtained, when it contains about 96 per cent. of pure sulphuric acid.

Properties: colorless, odorless, heavy, oily liquid. Generates heat on addition of water Very caustic. Stains fabrics reddish, and chars organic matter. Stain removed by ammonia. Valuable for drying gases on account of its affinity for moisture. Sp. gr. (pure) 1.848; official, 1.843.

The charring of organic matter by sulphuric acid is due to the fact that it unites with the hydrogen and oxygen in them, leaving behind compounds so carbonaceous that the black color predominates. It corrodes animal tissues. Starch or cellulose boiled with dilute sulphuric acid is converted into glucose, cane sugar into levulose and glucose. Sulphuric acid dissolves most of the metals, but has little action on lead.

Acidum sulphuricum, U. S. P., called the C. P. acid, sp.gr. 1.84. Contains at least 96 per cent. of H_2SO_4.

Acidum sulphuricum dilutum, U. S. P., sp. gr., 1.067; 1 part of sulphuric acid by weight to 9 parts of distilled water.

Acidum sulphuricum aromaticum, about same strength as *dilutum*; contains alcohol, cinnamon oil, and tincture of ginger.

Application to dentistry: in the dental laboratory the acid is used for cleaning metallic plates previous to soldering and after soldering. Its action is more vigorous when it is diluted with water, say with about one-third of water, heat being generated. Its action on hemp paper is to reduce it to pyroxylin, hence it is used in the preparation of celluloid base.

In dental therapeutics, in dilute form, it is used as a local application in various affections of the mouth. It is caustic, and will dissolve thin, carious portions of bone.

Toxicology: the concentrated acid (or the dilute in large doses) is a corrosive poison. Its stain on cloth is usually a dirty brown or reddish brown, and the cloth becomes rotten and damp. It chars wood. Vomited matters will contain a brownish-colored, bloody liquid with free acid. The treatment is to give lime, magnesia, sodium carbonate, preferably in milk. The stomach pump should *not* be used in cases of poisoning from acids. *Burns* from the acid should be treated like those of hydrochloric acid.

241. Oxygen.—
Symbol: O. Atoms in molecule: O_2. Atomic weight: 16. Molecular weight: 32. Density: 16. Specific gravity: 1.10563, (air = 1). Weight of one litre of gas: 1.43 grammes. How liquefied: pressure of 300 atmospheres and temperature of $-140°$ C. Solubility: water dissolves 3 per cent. of its volume of oxygen gas.

Occurrence in nature: constitutes 20.93 per cent. by volume of atmospheric air. *Combined* with other elements constitutes two-thirds of the entire globe, eight-ninths of all water, one-half the weight of minerals, three-quarters of the weight of animals, and four-fifths of vegetables.

How made: by heating $KClO_3$ and MnO_2:

$$2KClO_3 = 2KCl + 3O_2.$$

Potassium chlorate.   Potassium chloride.   Oxygen.

Properties: has affinity for all elements save fluorine. Is a gas, colorless, odorless, tasteless, transparent. Supports combustion and hence life. *Oxidation* is the term for the combination of substances with oxygen. *Oxidizing agents* are those which part easily with their oxygen as HNO_3, KNO_3, $KClO_3$.

Use in dentistry: a body is called "combustible" when it unites readily with oxygen, heat and light being at the same time liberated. It is the oxygen in the air which supports combustion, and which affords us our artificial heat and light. Substances which burn with difficulty in the air, owing to the latter not being pure oxygen but a mixture of oxygen with nitrogen, will burn in pure oxygen with great readiness. Oxygen blowpipes are those in which the flame is blown with a jet of oxygen; oxyhydrogen blowpipes, those where the hydrogen burns in a stream of oxygen gas, producing a heat which fuses refractory substances such as flint, quartz, etc., and melts the various metals. Some metals, as platinum, which can not be fused in a furnace may be melted by the oxyhydrogen flame.

The Atmosphere.—Under the head of oxygen and nitrogen, air must be considered, which is not a *compound*, but when pure is a *mixture* of 20.93 parts of oxygen by volume to 79.07 of nitrogen. By weight, 23 parts of oxygen to 77 of nitrogen. In the air which we breathe are found small quantities of other substances such as watery vapor, carbon dioxide, ozone, ammonia, nitric and nitrous acids, hydrocarbons, solid particles of dust, sodium chloride, vegetable germs or spores, bacteria, etc., etc. Air in which animals are confined contains some of the organic exhalations from their bodies; in the neighborhood of large cities the air is contaminated by various substances like sulphuretted hydrogen poured forth from manufacturing establishments, furnaces, etc., etc. The air of cities contains more bacteria than that of the country. A cubic metre of Paris air was found to contain

3910 bacteria, as compared with 455 in a cubic metre of country air. Hospital air has been found to contain 40,000 to 79,000 microbes to the cubic metre.

TRIADS.

242. The following is a list of the most important triads:

TABLE 18. IMPORTANT TRIADS.

Bismuth } Triads positive to
Gold } hydrogen.

Antimony }
Boron }
Arsenicum } Triads negative to
Phosphorus } hydrogen.
Nitrogen. }

243. Bismuth.—

Symbol: Bi. *Latin name:* Bismuthum. *Equivalence:* III and V. *Specific gravity:* 9.78—9.80. *Atomic weight:* 207.5. *Revised atomic weight:* 207.5230. *Electrical state:* +. *Fusing point:* 507° F. *Length of bar:* 1.0014. *Weight of cubic ft. in lbs.:* 613.0. *Tensile strength:* 1.5. *Tenacity, malleability, ductility:* brittle. *Conducting power* (*heat*): 11; (11th rank). *Conducting power* (*electricity*): 12; (12th rank). *Resistance to air:* tarnishes in moist air. *Solubility:* soluble in nitric acid; in hot sulphuric acid; in aqua regia. *Direct combinations:* oxygen, chlorine, bromine, iodine, sulphur. *Color and appearance:* white with bronze tint; highly crystalline appearance. *Structure:* crystallizes in rhombohedrons. *Consistence:* hard, brittle. *Compounds:* bismuthous and bismuthic. *Alloys:* fusible metal, pewter, pewterer's solder.

Use in dentistry: for making readily fusible alloys.

Occurrence: this metal occurs native, disseminated

through rocks in veins. It is rather rare and is found associated with ores of nickel, cobalt, silver, and copper. Saxony and Bohemia are the chief sources, but it is also found in Transylvania, England, United States, Sweden, Norway, and Peru.

Preparation: to extract the metal the earthy matters containing it are heated and the melted bismuth is collected in suitable receivers.

244. Use in dentistry: the value of bismuth in alloys is due to its low melting point, and to the fact that it *expands* very considerably as it solidifies. Compressed bismuth is lighter than that which has not been so treated. It is more easily vaporized than many metals and boils at moderate white heat. It tends to crystallize from fusion in a remarkable manner, in rhombohedrons of great size and beauty, often mistaken for cubes.

An alloy of tin, lead, and bismuth, is employed for testing the finish of a die. Bismuth is used in the dental laboratory for making readily fusible alloys for dies and counter dies. It lowers the fusing point and imparts hardness when used in alloys.

245. **Compounds of bismuth.—**

Bismuth subnitrate: official name, Bismuthi Subnitras. Formula, $BiONO_3.H_2O$. Molecular weight, 303.5. It is, as will be seen from the formula, the nitrate of the oxide of bismuth. It is called bismu*thyl* nitrate by some authors, also bismuth trisnitrate and oxynitrate. Recent investigators deem it not a fixed and definite compound, but rather a mixture. The chemistry of its preparation is complicated; bismuth is first dissolved in nitric acid, forming the nitrate; next, bismuth subcarbonate is made from the nitrate, by the action of sodium carbonate; the bismuth subcarbonate is next redissolved in nitric acid, to form bismuth nitrate again; finally, the bismuth nitrate is converted into subnitrate by action of ammonia water. Good subnitrate of bismuth is soft, bulky, insoluble in water, soluble in nitric acid. It often contains arsenic as impurity. Treatment in poisoning, as for arsenic. Used in dentistry internally and topically.

246. **Alloys of bismuth.**—

Fusible alloys are of different compositions, but contain *bismuth*. One is bismuth 2 parts, lead 1 part, tin 1 part; melts at 200° F. Another is 50 bismuth, 12.5 cadmium, 25 lead, 12.5 tin.

Wood's metal, according to Essig, is bismuth 7, lead 6, and cadmium 1. Fuses at 180° F.

247. **Gold.**—

Symbol: Au. *Latin name*: Aurum. *Equivalence*: I, III. *Specific gravity*: 19.26 to 19.34. Precipitated gold, 19.49. *Atomic weight*: 196.2. *Revised atomic weight*: 196.155. *Electric state*: +. *Fusing point*: 2016° F. *Length of bar*: 1.0015; (8th rank). *Weight of cubic ft. in lbs.*: 1208.6. *Tensile strength*: 9.1. *Tenacity*: 12; (6th rank). *Malleability*: 1; (1st rank). *Ductility* 1; (1st rank). *Solubility*: soluble in aqua regia, free nascent chlorine or bromine, mercury; unaffected by action of single acids, alkalies, or sulphuretted hydrogen. *Direct combinations*: chlorine, bromine, phosphorus, antimony, arsenic, mercury. *Color and appearance*: orange yellow by reflected light, very brilliant, green by transmitted light. Lustre unaffected by high temperatures. *Consistence*: soft. *Compounds*: auric and aurous. *Alloys*: coinage, jewelry, etc., etc. *Structure*: isometric crystals.

248. Occurrence: gold occurs native, that is, uncombined with other metals. It is found almost everywhere, but in most regions in exceedingly small quantities. It occurs in England, Scotland, Ireland, Wales, Hungary, Transylvania, Sweden, Spain, Italy, Siberia, in the Ural Mountains, Japan, Ceylon, Borneo, Thibet, Africa, Brazil, Chili, Peru, Mexico, California, and Australia. The greatest quantities are now found in Africa, California, and Australia. Gold is either in form of *alluvial gold,* that is, washed down by rivers, or *gold-quartz,* the metal being disseminated in thin plates and branch-like fragments, through lumps of quartz-rock.

249. Preparation: *alluvial gold* is extracted by washing the alluvial deposits, the separation of earthy matters being readily effected owing to the high specific gravity of gold (19.3). In California and Australia a wooden trough, six feet long, resting on rockers and called a *cradle,* is used. At the head of it is a grating, on which the alluvial matter is thrown. A stream of water, entering the cradle, flows through and escapes at the lower end, leaving the gold in the trough, but carrying the earthy matters along with it. *Gold-quartz* must first be crushed, either by passing it through rollers or by use of stampers. After pulverization, the gold is dissolved out by mercury. The amal-

gam resulting is then subjected to pressure and excess of mercury thus squeezed out, the remainder being separated by distilling, leaving the gold.

250. **Refined gold** may be obtained in various ways. Chlorine gas has been used as a refining agent, when gold is to be separated from silver. Nitric acid or sulphuric acid may be used. Sulphuric acid converts silver or copper into sulphates, but does not attack gold.

American gold is liable to contain iridium, which may be separated from it by alloying the gold with silver, melting, and either pouring off the gold and silver alloy from the iridium or treating with nitric acid and then with aqua regia.

251. **Chemically pure gold** is obtained from refined gold in various ways: for example, refined gold may be dissolved in aqua regia, excess of acid driven off by heat, then alcohol and potassium chloride added to precipitate any platinum present. The filtered solution is then evaporated over the water bath, the residue dissolved in distilled water, until each gallon contains not more than half an ounce of the chloride, the solution allowed to settle, the supernatant liquid siphoned off, and the gold precipitated in the metallic state by one of the various precipitants, such as oxalic acid or sulphurous anhydride.

252. **Agents used for Precipitating Gold:** gold may be precipitated in the metallic state by various substances.

Oxalic acid precipitates gold from its chloride solution in several forms, spongy or crystalline. Gentle heat favors the process. The equation is:

$$2AuCl_3 + 3H_2C_2O_4 = 6HCl + 6CO_2 \quad 2Au.$$
Auric   Oxalic acid.   Hydrochloric   Carbon   Gold.
chloride.   acid.   dioxide.

Sulphurous acid precipitates gold in scales, " not sufficiently coherent or sponge-like for use as a filling material." (Essig).

Ferrous sulphate precipitates gold in form of a light-brown powder.

Phosphorus, when introduced into a heated solution of gold chloride, becomes coated with a film of metallic gold.*

Zinc and other base metals precipitate gold as a brown powder.

Metallic salts, besides ferrous sulphate, and *organic acids* besides oxalic, precipitate gold; the latter best from neutral solutions.

253. **Crystal gold** is obtained by reduction on a platinum pole by the electric current. Plates of pure gold are suspended in a solution of auric chloride. These are connected with a battery, so that, as the solution loses its gold by deposition of the metal, it is re-supplied by the suspended plates.

---
*Other non-metals become coated in the same way.

254. Pure gold may be beaten out so as to present a surface 650,000 times its original area.

Dentists' leaf-gold is usually beaten from fine gold; a very small quantity of any other metal materially injures its malleability. To prepare leaf gold, the metal is first melted in a crucible with a little borax, poured into a mold to form an ingot $\frac{3}{4}$ inch high, the ingot annealed and hammered with several annealings, until only $\frac{1}{6}$ inch high, passed between rollers until reduced to a thin ribbon, cut into pieces an inch square; 150 of these pieces are piled up, alternately, with pieces of tough paper or vellum 4 inches square rubbed over with a little fine plaster-of-Paris. Twenty vellums are then placed above, and twenty below the pile, which is firmly secured by passing two strong belts of parchment across it. The pile is placed on a heavy block of marble, and beaten with a hammer weighing about 16 pounds. After a time the middle leaves are shifted to the outside, and the beating continued, until the leaves are nearly the size of the vellums, when they are taken out and cut into 4 squares measuring an inch each way. They are then made into packets, with *gold beaters' skins* in alternate layers, and beaten with a ten-pound hammer. When they are 4 inches square they are cut into 4 equal squares, again made into packets with gold-beaters' skin, and hammered again with a seven-pound hammer to about $3\frac{1}{2}$ inches square. They are then lifted off the skin, cut down to one size, and packed between leaves of books. There are usually 25 leaves in a book, each of which is on an average $\frac{1}{282,000}$ of an inch thick. They are now usually beaten by mechanical power. These leaves show, when held up to the light, a fine green color. Rendered non-lustrous by heat, the color is ruby-red. Weak solution of potassium cyanide slowly dissolves them. *Fine gold*, *i. e.*, that which is perfectly free from impurities, is about as soft as lead. Its fineness is expressed by use of the term *carats*: gold coin containing 22 parts gold to 2 of alloy is said to be 22 carats fine; pure gold is 24 carats fine.

255. **Cohesive gold**, used for filling operations, may be obtained by heating foil to redness, by which the cohesiveness, which is greatly diminished by compression of the fibres in beating, is restored.

256. **Corrugated gold**, according to Essig, is prepared by placing the sheets of gold between leaves of a particular kind of unsized paper and tightly packing them in iron boxes, which are exposed to a temperature sufficiently high to carbonize the paper. On cooling, the gold is found to be exceedingly soft, non-cohesive, and to present a peculiarly corrugated condition of surface.

Use in dentistry: gold is used by dentists in fine powder, and in foil for filling purposes. It is an ingredient of some amalgam alloys, of alloys for bases for artificial dentures, and of solders. In minute division it is used as a coloring matter for artificial teeth.

Gold containing palladium or platinum is *lighter* in color; if it contains copper it is *redder* in color. Lead or antimony makes gold brittle, even if in minute proportion. Silver whitens the color of gold.

Table 19.—Effect on Gold of Alloying.

Malleability: impaired; seriously by As, Sn, Sb, Bi, Pb. *Ductility:* diminished. *Hardness:* increased. *Tenacity:* usually increased. *Specific gravity:* varies; with Zn, Sn, Bi, Sb, Co, sp. gr. greater than mean of components; with Ag, Fe, Pb, Cu, Ir, Ni, less than the mean. *Fusibility:* usually increased.

Gold and Copper have great affinity for one another and may be alloyed in all proportions. Copper diminishes the ductility of gold when it enters into the combination in a proportion over 10 to 12 per cent. *Pure* copper must be used for alloying. *Gold and Silver* readily mix but do not appear to form true combinations. One-twentieth of silver will modify color of gold. *Yellow Gold, Green Gold,* and *Pale Gold* are alloys of gold and silver. Alloys of gold, copper, silver and palladium are brownish-red in color, hard as iron, and never rust. *Nurnberg Gold* is an alloy of copper 90 parts, gold 2.5, add aluminium 7.5; it has the color of gold and remains unchanged.

The melting of metals constituting alloys is brought about by use of graphite crucibles, the gold being melted first. After it is entirely melted, it is heated as strongly as the furnace permits and the other metals added in as small pieces as practicable. The mixture is stirred with an iron rod sharpened on the point and previously heated to redness. When it is desired to toughen gold, use as a flux the following: one part charcoal to one sal-ammoniac adding to the gold *just before melting.*

Phosphor-iridium, as it is called, has some remarkable properties. It is prepared by Holland's process, in which iridium ore is heated in a Hessian crucible to a white heat, and, after phosphorous, has been added, the heating is continued for a few minutes. It has the power more than any other metal of retaining lubricants. It is slightly magnetic when alloyed with iron and is not attacked by acids or alkalies. The alloy with iron (50 per cent or less), is not affected by the best file.

[For further consideration of the subject of alloys the reader will find it useful to consult special works, among these may be mentioned Krupp's book which has lately been translated into English with additions by Brannt].

Table 20.—Specific Effects of Certain Metals on Gold When Alloyed With It.

Metal.	Effect.
Zinc:	forms hard, white, brittle alloy (when in equal proportions); does not unite so intimately as lead or tin.
Tin:	renders gold intractable to remarkable degree. The combination is attended by contraction(?).
Lead:	renders gold intractable.*
Antimony:	renders gold intractable. One part in 1920 too brittle for successful lamination.
Bismuth:	in almost inappreciable quantities renders gold intractable, as 1 in 1920.
Iron:	does not sensibly affect malleability, in the proportion of 1 to 11.
Mercury:	dissolves gold, and combines with it at all temperatures, but more readily when gold is in state of fine division and when heat is applied.
Arsenic:	malleability of gold affected, even by vapor of arsenic. The color of the gold may not be changed, even when it has become brittle.
Silver:	renders gold more fusible, increases hardness, does not materially affect malleability, makes color lighter.
Palladium:	equal parts: gray color, less ductile. 4 gold, 1 palladium: white, hard, ductile. Merest traces of palladium render gold brittle.
Copper:	hardens and toughens gold, gives deeper color, renders it capable of receiving rich polish, does not practically impair its malleability.
Platinum:	in small proportions hardens, and renders more elastic, without impairing malleability. Makes color pale and dull, if equal weights. Excess of platinum renders alloy infusible in blast furnace.

*A minute quantity of lead will color gold brownish, render it brittle, and reduce its tenacity from resistance to 18 tons per square inch to only 5 tons.

Table 21.—Appearance of Gold Alloys.

Alloy Metal	Color, etc.
Tin:	Light colored, very brittle.
Lead:	Dull colored, brittle.
Platinum:	Grayish or dull colored, malleable, tough, elastic.
Zinc:	Unequally malleable, brittle in spots.

257. **Gold Alloys and Alloys Resembling Gold:** gold coinage: gold 90, copper 10. Gold jewelry and plate: gold 75 to 92, copper 25 to 8.

Green gold: gold 75, silver 25.

Red gold: gold 75, copper 25.

Dutch gold is merely a species of brass, usually sold in very thin leaves or sheets. It is formed of 11 parts copper with 2 of zinc.

Fool's gold is iron pyrites, a sulphide of iron.

Oreide is a species of brass.

Pinchbeck gold is a kind of brass; *Mannheim gold* and *Similor* are also brass.

Talmi gold is 90 copper, to 10 aluminium, as is aluminium bronze.

Mosaic gold is a definite chemical compound, SnS_2, stannic sulphide, made by heating in a flask at low red heat, 12 parts tin, 6 mercury, 6 ammonium chloride, and 7 flowers of sulphur; everything sublimes except the stannic sulphide which remains in the bottom of the flask. [The name "Mosaic gold" is sometimes given to substances other than stannic sulphide].

Gold base plate: different formulas are in vogue, but the constituents are in the main gold, copper, and silver; some contain platinum as well. 18 carat gold plate is made by two formulas: No. 1 contains 18 dwts. pure gold, 4 fine copper, 2 fine silver; No. 2 is 20 dwts. gold coin, 2 fine copper, 2 fine silver. Gold plate, 22 carats fine, is 22 dwts. pure gold, 1 dwt. fine copper, 18 grains silver, 6 grains platinum.

Gold plate for clasps, wires, etc., etc.: gold used for this purpose should contain sufficient platinum to render it firmer and more elastic. A 20 carat alloy for such purposes is made by 2 formulas: No. 1 is 20 dwts pure gold, 2 fine copper, 1 fine silver, 1 platinum; No. 2 is 20 grains coin gold, 8 grains fine copper, 10 grains fine silver, 20 grains platinum.

Gold solder is 22.2 copper, 66.6 gold, 11.1 silver.

258. **Compounds of Gold.—**

Auric Chloride or the terchloride of gold, $AuCl_3$. Prepared by dissolving gold in aqua regia, using gentle heat. The solution evaporated to dryness, over the water bath, yields ruby-red, prismatic crystals, deliquescent, soluble in water, alcohol, ether, and of disagreeable, styptic taste; auric chloride stains the skin purple, but the stain is readily removed by potassium cyanide. It is an escharotic and disinfectant, and dissolved in ether is used in dentistry as an obtunding agent. Solutions should be kept in glass stoppered bottles, as the gold tends to deposit from solutions. It is a poison.

Auric Oxide, Au_2O_3, is prepared from the terchloride by digesting magnesia in it, by which magnesium aurate is formed. The latter is decomposed by nitric acid and the residue auric oxide, when dried, is a dark brown, easily decomposing powder.

Purple of Cassius is a compound of gold, tin, and oxygen.

It may be prepared by treating gold chloride with solution of stannous chloride, or by adding stannous chloride to a mixture of stannic chloride and auric chloride, as follows: 7 parts of gold are dissolved in aqua regia, and mixed with 2 parts of tin also dissolved in aqua regia; this solution is largely diluted with water, and a weak solution of 1 part tin in hydrochloric acid is added drop by drop, till a fine purple color is produced. The purple of Cassius remains suspended in water, but subsides gradually, especially if some saline substance be added. Purple of Cassius is a brown, reddish purple or black powder soluble in ammonia. It is used as a coloring for porcelain. Its composition is doubtful, probably $Au_2O.SnO_2.SnOSnO_2.4H_2O.$, that is a double stannate of aurous oxide and stannous oxide.

259. **Antimony.—**

Symbol: Sb. *Latin name:* Stibium. *Equivalence:* III and V. *Specific gravity:* 6.72. *Atomic weight:* 120. *Revised atomic weight:* 119.955. *Electrical state:* —. *Fusing point:* 842° F. *Length of bar:* 1.0011; (11th in rank). *Weight of cubic feet in lbs:* 419.5. *Tensile strength:* 0.5. *Tenacity, malleability, ductility:* brittle. *Conducting power (heat):* 10; (10th rank). *Conducting power (electricity):* 46; (silver = 1000); (11th rank). *Resistance to air, etc:* takes fire at red heat, but scarcely tarnishes in air. *Solubility:* in boiling hydrochloric acid to which a little nitric has been added: in fine powder, dissolved by solutions of higher sulphides of Na and K. *Direct combinations:* with chlorine, sulphur, oxygen, bromine, iodine. *Color and appearance:* brilliant bluish-white, like zinc. *Structure:* rhombohedral crystals like arsenic and red phosphorus; there is also an amorphous form. *Consistence:* hard, brittle. *Compounds:* antimonous (III) and antimonic (V). *Alloys:* Britannia metal, pewter, type metal, Babbitt's anti-friction metal.

Occurrence: antimony is found both native and combined. It occurs free in Germany. Gray antimony ore, the *sulphide*, Sb_2S_3, occurs in England, France, Hungary, and Borneo. An *oxide* is found in Algeria. *Red antimony*, which is a compound of the oxide and sulphide is found in Tuscany.

Antimony is also found in the United States and in Mexico.

Preparation: the principal ore (stibnite), which is a sulphide, yields regulus of antimony (metallic antimony) when melted with metallic iron. A purer article is obtained by roasting the crushed ore, converting it into an oxide; the latter is then fused with charcoal.

Properties: the metal is not attacked by hydrochloric acid. Nitric acid converts it into a white, insoluble oxide. Aqua regia dissolves it, forming a chloride called "butter of antimony"; water converts this chloride into an oxychloride.

$$SbCl_3 \;+\; H_2O \;=\; SbOCl \;+\; 2HCl.$$
Antimonous chloride.   Water.   Antimony oxychloride.   Hydrochloric acid.

This equation illustrates the formation of an oxychloride.

260. Uses in dentistry and the arts: antimony is valuable as a constituent of alloys: to give hardness to other

metals, and to cause them to expand and completely fill moulds on cooling.

It can be distinguished from other metals by its brittleness, crystalline structure, and hardness; it can easily be pulverized, and breaks from a slight tap of a hammer. It is not deemed a metal by some, being classed with arsenic and phosphorus, rather than with the metals. It burns at red heat, with odor of garlic and with white fumes, suggesting arsenic. The amalgam with mercury is soft and decomposed by contact with air or water, antimony separating. It has been used in dental amalgam alloys.

261. **Boron.—**
Symbol: B. *Latin name:* Boron. *Equivalence:* III. *Specific gravity:* 2.63. *Atomic wt. (approx.):* 10.9. *Atomic wt. (revised):* 10.941. *Electrical state:* —. *Properties:* amorphous, greenish powder, soluble in melted aluminium. Boron is not used in dentistry.

262. **Hydrogen Orthoborate or Boracic Acid.—**
Synonyms: boric acid, orthoboric acid, sedative salt of Homberg. Official name, Acidum Boricum.

Theoretical constitution: orthoboric acid, H_3BO_3, graphically, $B'''(HO)_3$. Composed of three atoms of hydrogen, one of boron, and three of oxygen. By weight, 3 parts of hydrogen, 11 of boron, and 48 of oxygen. Molecular weight, 62.

Preparation: boracic acid is made from borax by adding hydrochloric acid to a hot solution of the former, which causes a precipitate of boracic acid:

$Na_2B_4O_7$ + $2HCl$ + $5H_2O$ = $4H_3BO_3$ + $2NaCl$.
Borax.   Hydrochloric   Water.   Boric acid.   Common
         acid.   salt.

Properties: brilliant, white, shining, odorless, six-sided plates, greasy to the touch, slightly soluble in cold water 1 part in 25, soluble in 3 parts hot water, soluble in 6 parts alcohol, soluble in glycerine. Specific gravity, 1.517 at ordinary temperatures. Is a powerful antiseptic. Saturated with alcohol, burns with a green flame. Its solutions are but faintly acid; turmeric paper moistened with a solution of this acid becomes reddish-brown on drying. Heated with glycerine forms *boroglyceride*. (See Boroglyceride under head of Glycerine).

Use in dentistry: boracic acid is used for various antiseptic purposes. Combined with sodium sulphite it has been used as a bleaching agent for discolored teeth. (See Boroglyceride).

263. **Arsenic.—**
Metallic arsenic is not used in medicine or dentistry. One of its compounds, *arsenous oxide* or *anhydride*, is of importance, and the term **arsenic** is usually applied to this substance.

Arsenous Anhydride.—
Synonyms: arsenious acid, arsenious anhydride, white arsenic, ratsbane, white oxide of arsenic, Arseniosum Oxidum. Official name, Acidum Arsenosum.

Theoretical constitution: As_2O_3, arsenous oxide, two atoms of arsenic to three of oxygen, by weight 150 of arsenic to 48 of oxygen. Molecular weight, 198. Composed of 75.76 per cent. As and 24.24 per cent. O. [The molecule of vitreous arsenic is thought to be represented by the formula As_4O_6].

Preparation: arsenous oxide occurs in nature as arsenic "bloom," a term derived from the Saxon *bloma*, a lump. It is obtained by roasting ores of other metals containing it in a current of air. The arsenous oxide in the roasting process volatilizes and is condensed in suitable receiving chambers as a white powder.

Properties: it is found in the form of a fine, white, heavy powder or in glassy looking lumps. The powder is somewhat gritty, odorless, tasteless, permanent in air. Condensed from sublimation at 752° F., it is a transparent, vitreous mass, sp. gr., 3.738. When condensed at temperature slightly less, crystallizes in right rhombic prisms. Vitreous arsenic, on keeping, gradually becomes opaque and crystalline. When condensed at 392° F., it occurs in octahedral crystals, sp. gr., 3.69. This form is also obtained on evaporating a saturated aqueous solution. Vitreous arsenic is slightly more soluble than the opaque; 100 parts boiling water dissolve 12 parts of the vitreous; on cooling, about three parts are left in solution. Arsenic is soluble in hot HCl, in solutions of alkalies and of tartaric acid. Dissolved in acids it forms a binary compound of arsenic, as, for example, arsenous chloride when dissolved in hydrochloric acid. Dissolved in alkalies it acts as the negative element forming arsenites of the alkali metals, as K_2HAsO_3, potassium hydro-arsenite.

Locally, it acts as an escharotic, first destroying the vitality of organic structure, decomposition then ensuing.

It is a powerful antiseptic, retarding putrefaction to a marked degree.

Uses in dentistry: arsenous oxide is used to destroy the vitality of tooth pulps; it has also been used as an obtunding agent. It kills a tooth by causing irritation; there is increased flow of blood to the parts, the arteries are enlarged so that there is no return of blood through the veins, hence strangulation at apex of the tooth.

Toxicology: arsenic in doses of from one to two grains is a powerful poison. It is poisonous also even when locally applied. There is danger of absorption when arsenic is applied to the teeth.

The treatment of poisoning by this agent, when administered internally, is to provoke or promote vomiting by giving large quantities of hot milk and water or emetics, as sulphate of zinc (5 grains repeated in 15 minutes) or mustard (teaspoonful or two of ground mustard in water); subcutaneous injection of apomorphine hydrochlorate in doses of $\frac{1}{15}$ to $\frac{1}{10}$ of a grain will speedily bring about emesis. The *antidote* to arsenic is ferric hydrate, conveniently made by adding Aqua Ammoniæ to Tincture of Ferric Chloride. A brownish substance is formed which, separated from the liquid, may be given *ad lib.* The antidote should be given *after* vomiting has been brought about. Finally bland liquids, such as milk and eggs, should be given; sugar and magnesia in milk are highly recommended. When arsenic has been absorbed from local application it is of course useless to give emetics, etc., the only treatment possible being that of treating the symptoms as they appear, promoting elimination by diuretics as potassium nitrate, etc., etc.

Note: in making the antidote for arsenic let the precipitate drain on a wetted muslin strainer until most of the liquid has run off, gather up the cloth, press it with the hands until no more liquid can be squeezed out, then add water and administer. The official hydrate is made from solution of normal ferric sulphate.

264. **Phosphorus.—**

Symbol: P. *Atoms in molecule*: P_4. *Atomic weight*: 31. *Molecular weight*: 124. *Density*, of vapor: 62. *Specific gravity*: yellow 1.83, red 2.14. *How liquefied*: the yellow melts at 111° F. under water. *Solubility*: yellow is insoluble in both water and alcohol, but soluble in carbon disulphide, while the red is insoluble in the latter.

Occurrence in nature: does not occur native, but as phosphates, etc.

How made: from ash of burnt bones by treating with sulphuric acid, and heating with charcoal.

Properties: yellow is translucent, waxy, shines in the dark, readily oxidized, taking fire at 140° F. and must be kept under water. Becomes covered with red or white coat on exposure to light; poisonous. Red does not inflame readily, and is not poisonous. Phosphorus combines with most elements except C, N, and H, and reduces some metallic salts as of Cu, Ag.

Use in dentistry: phosphorus is of value as a deoxidizer in fusing refractory metals such as iridium, nickel, etc.

Toxicology. Carious teeth, swollen and inflamed gums, finally necrosis of the jaws, usually of the lower one, are often noticed in those who work in match factories. Most cases of phosphor-necrosis originate in unsound teeth or where the gums are kept away from the teeth by tartar.

About $\frac{1}{70}$th grain of phosphorus is contained in a match head. In the dipping and packing room the matches are handled the most, and in damp weather the fumes are given off so that no workman with carious teeth should work in these rooms. Alkaline mouth-washes should be used, and workmen should keep their hands clean and not eat in the work rooms. Good ventilation should be secured.

The use of *red* phosphorus instead of yellow is to be advised, as the former is not poisonous.

265. **Anhydrous Phosphoric Acid,** so called, is phosphoric anhydride, *i. e.*, phosphoric oxide or phosphorus pentoxide, P_2O_5, and is formed by the rapid burning of phosphorus in air or in oxygen. It is very deliquescent. It forms with water a solution of the glacial acid, HPO_3.

$$P_2O_5 + H_2O = H_2P_2O_6 = (HPO_3)_2 \text{ or } 2HPO_3.$$
Phosphoric   water.   Glacial phosphoric acid.
anhydride.

266. Hydrogen Phosphate or Phosphoric Acid.—

There are several kinds of phosphoric acid, but we shall here speak of two only:—

1. **Common Phosphoric Acid.**—*

Synonyms: tri-basic phosphoric acid, tri-hydrogen phosphate; (it is sometimes called ortho-phosphoric acid).

Theoretical constitution: H_3PO_4: may be regarded as mono-meta-phosphoric acid, *i. e.*, the acid obtained by removing one molecule of water from ortho-phosphoric* acid, Ortho-phosphoric acid has for its formula H_5PO_5, which formula minus H_2O becomes H_3PO_4, rationally $(PO)'''(HO)_3$. The acid contains, then, three atoms of hydrogen, one of phosphorus, and four of oxygen; by weight 3 parts hydrogen, 31 of phosphorus, 64 of oxygen. Molecular weight, 98. Its salts are *phosphates.***

Preparation: made by boiling phosphorus in dilute nitric acid, and evaporating to a syrupy liquid.

Properties: syrupy liquid, which, if evap-

---

* Phosphoric acid is tri-basic, and, therefore, three hydroxyl groups are assumed to be present in it, hence the rational formula is $PO(HO)_3$. The graphic formula is probably

$$PO \begin{cases} -OH \\ -OH \\ -OH \end{cases}$$

** Called often ortho-phosphates.

orated spontaneously over sulphuric acid, gives hard, transparent, prismatic crystals readily deliquescing. It does not coagulate albumin.

Acidum Phosphoricum, U. S. P., is a colorless, strongly acid liquid of sp. gr. 1.347. It does not fume and should not contain arsenic. It contains 50 per cent. acid to 50 of water. It is odorless.

Acidum Phosphoricum Dilutum, U. S. P., contains 10 per cent. of H_3PO_4, and is composed of 1 part of Acidum Phosphoricum, to 4 of distilled water.

Syrupy phosphoric acid: H_3PO_4, syrupy phosphoric acid, contains on an average, about 66 per cent. of H_3PO_4, and as sold by manufacturing chemists is not the glacial acid but merely a strong phosphoric acid of syrupy consistence. It is of different strengths according to the makers.

2. **Glacial Phosphoric Acid.**

Synonyms: mono-hydrogen phosphate, meta-phosphoric acid, di-meta-phosphoric acid, mono-hydrated phosphoric acid.

Theoretical constitution: HPO_3 or di-metaphosphoric acid, *i. e.*, derived by subtracting two molecules of water from ortho-phosphoric* acid. $H_5PO_5 - 2H_2O = HPO_3$. Its molecule, therefore, consists of 1 part hydrogen, 1 part

---

* Not what is usually called ortho-phosphoric acid, but the maximum hydroxide or normal acid of phosphorus.

phosphorus, and 3 parts oxygen; by weight 1 part hydrogen, 31 of phosphorus, and 48 of oxygen. Molecular weight, 80.

Preparation: it may be made by heating the ordinary acid, which loses a molecule of water and becomes the glacial acid.

$$\underset{\text{Phosphoric acid.}}{H_3PO_4} = \underset{\text{Glacial phosphoric acid.}}{HPO_3} + \underset{\text{Water.}}{H_2O}$$

It is sometimes made by calcining ammonium phosphate, but the product is then likely to contain ammonia.*

Properties: on cooling the platinum vessel in which the common acid, H_3PO_4, has been heated to redness, a vitreous mass, HPO_3, is seen, hard, colorless, transparent, not crystallizable, readily soluble in water, forming an intensely acid solution which is slowly converted into the ordinary acid. It coagulates albumin. In commerce it comes in the form of sticks or brittle cakes, odorless, sour to the taste and hygroscopic, more or less contaminated with pyro-phosphoric acid, and containing phosphates of sodium, calcium, magnesium, etc. Solution of the common acid in water when heated becomes first pyro-phosphoric acid, then (at red heat) glacial phosphoric acid.

Use in dentistry: the dilute acid is used as

---

* The formation of meta-phosphoric acid from ordinary phosphoric acid is represented thus:—

$$P \begin{cases} O \\ OH \\ OH \\ OH \end{cases} = P \begin{cases} O \\ O \\ OH \end{cases} + H_2O$$

a local application in caries, and has been given internally. It is liable to fungoid growth of a tenacious or mucoid character, diffusible, and of a yellowish-gray color; it loses strength on development of this growth, its specific gravity falling often below 1055.

TABLE 22—PHOSPHORIC ACIDS.

COMMON PHOSPHORIC ACID.	GLACIAL PHOSPHORIC ACID.
H_3PO_4. Called by some ortho-phosphoric acid.	HPO_3. Called metaphosphoric acid.
Syrupy liquid.	Solid.
Evaporated spontaneously yields prismatic crystals.	Does not crystallize, but forms an amorphous, glassy mass, coagulates albumin.
Does not coagulate albumin.	Slowly turns into the common acid.
Strong acid is called syrupy phosphoric acid.	Is volatile at red heat, and when boiled with water is converted into the common acid.
The official acid (50 per cent.) heated above 392° F. is converted gradually into the glacial acid and pyrophosphoric acid.	Abundant precipitate with solution of silver nitrate.
Little or no precipitate with solution of silver nitrate.	

---

* Rollins obtains it as a soft solid by the process given in section 201. It is said (*Zeitschrift f. anal. Chemie.*, VI. 187,) that really pure phosphoric acid makes a soft glutinous mass when heated, but on heating strongly for seven or eight minutes after the acid has begun to go off in white fumes a hard mass is obtained.

267. Nitrogen.

Symbol: N. *Atoms in molecule*: N_2. *Atomic weight*: 14. *Molecular weight*: 28. *Density*: 14. *Specific gravity*: 0.971, (air = 1). *Weight of one litre of gas*: 1.256 grammes. *Solubility in water*: 1 part of water dissolves 0.025 part by volume of nitrogen.

Occurrence in nature: nitrogen constitutes 79.07 per cent. by volume of atmospheric air.

How made: obtained from air by burning phosphorus in a confined space.

Properties: affinity for magnesium, borum, vanadium, titanium. Very inert chemically. Colorless, tasteless, odorless, transparent gas. Incombustible and does not support combustion. In combination found in nitroglycerine, poisonous alkaloids as strychnine, and in albuminoid substances.

268. **Ammonia.**

Theoretical constitution: H_3N or NH_3, one atom of nitrogen to three of hydrogen; by weight, 14 parts nitrogen to 3 of hydrogen. Molecular weight, 17; density, 8.5; specific gravity, 0.59 (air = 1).

Origin and method of preparation: it is a product of the putrefaction of animal matters. Artificially it may be prepared by heating sal-ammoniac and quicklime.

Properties: colorless gas, pungent odor, strongly alkaline, extraordinarily soluble in water, 1149 volumes of the gas in 1 of water. Very volatile.

269. **Nitrogen Monoxide or Laughing Gas.**

Synonyms: hyponitrous oxide, nitrous oxide, nitrogen protoxide.

Discovered by Priestly in 1776; first came into notice as anæsthetic in 1863; first used in dentistry by Wells of Hartford, in 1845.

Theoretical constitution: N_2O, hyponitrous

oxide or nitrogen monoxide; univalent nitrogen with bivalent oxygen—two atoms of nitrogen with one of oxygen; composition by volume, 2 parts of nitrogen to 1 of oxygen; by weight, 28 parts of nitrogen to 16 of oxygen. Molecular weight, 44. Density, 22. Sp. gr., 1.527. Weight of a litre, 1.98 gramme.

Preparation: made by *cautiously* heating ammonium nitrate, which is decomposed, yielding laughing gas and water:

$$\underset{\text{Ammonium nitrate.}}{NH_4NO_3} = \underset{\text{Nitrogen protoxide.}}{N_2O} + \underset{\text{Water.}}{2H_2O}$$

Properties: colorless, odorless, sweetish-tasting gas of neutral reaction, soluble in water 100 volumes of which dissolve 78 volumes of the gas, more soluble in alcohol. Supports combustion, the heat of burning bodies decomposing it and setting oxygen free. Condenses to a colorless liquid under pressure of 50 atmospheres and temperature of 45°F., specific gravity of the liquid, 0.908. Boiling point,—126°F., freezing point,—150°F.

When inhaled it causes exhilaration, anæsthesia, and finally asphyxia. It dissolves in the blood without entering into combination with it, and its action seems to be due partly to its excluding air and partly to its direct effect on the nervous system. The anæsthesia produced by it is of short duration and without an excitement stage. The sensation is usually one of agreeable intoxication; disagreeable after-effects are generally wanting. Vyman holds that the anæsthesia is a narcosis, but Wallian thinks with Ziegler that it is not merely an asphyxiating agent.

Use in dentistry as a temporary anæsthetic. Out of 121,709 administrations of the gas recorded from 1868 to 1881, there was not one which resulted fatally, nor produced serious ill-effects.

For anæsthetic purposes the nitrogen monoxide is liquefied and sold in wrought-iron cylinders provided with a stop-cock, on turning which the liquid is vaporized, and may be collected in rubber gas bags or small gasometers. When the gas is to be administered it may be inhaled from the gas bag or gasometer through a rubber tube and mouth-piece provided for the purpose. The advantages of the cylinder are that the gas may be kept for any length of time without loss of strength or volume.

270. **Hydrogen Nitrate or Nitric Acid.** — Synonyms: hydric nitrate, Glauber's spirits of nitre, spirits of nitre, fuming spirits of nitre, aqua fortis, azotic acid. Official name, Acidum Nitricum.

Known to the Arabs in the 8th century.

Theoretical constitution, HNO_3, an ox-acid whose molecule is composed of 1 atom of hydrogen, 1 of nitrogen, and 3 of oxygen. By volume it consists of 1 part of hydrogen, 1 of nitrogen, and 3 of oxygen. By weight, 1 part of hydrogen, 14 of nitrogen, 48 of oxygen. Molecular weight, 63.

Preparation: made by decomposing potassium nitrate (nitre) with sulphuric acid:

$$KNO_3 + H_2SO_4 = KHSO_4 + HNO_3$$
Potassium nitrate.   Sulphuric acid.   Potassium acid sulphate.   Nitric acid.

Properties: the pure acid is a colorless, fuming, corrosive, rather heavy, strongly acid liquid of sp. gr. 1.52. The official acid has a specific gravity of 1.42, and contains 69.40 per cent. of absolute acid to 30.60 per cent. of water. Exposed to air and light it is decomposed and becomes yellow. Nitric acid dissolves mercury, copper, silver, and bismuth, especially when warmed; *dilute* nitric acid dissolves iron, lead, and silver. Antimony and tin are attacked by the acid and oxidized, but not dissolved. Nitric acid has no action on gold, platinum, or iridium. It attacks and destroys vegetable and animal tissues, producing a yellow discoloration, especially on animal matters and products. Its stain on clothing can not readily be removed but ammonia prevents destruction of the cloth. Its salts are *nitrates*.

Acidum Nitricum Dilutum is one part of the official acid to six of distilled water. Its sp. gr. is 1.059, and it contains ten per cent. of HNO_3.

Use in dentistry: mixed with four parts of hydrochloric acid, it is used to dissolve gold. [The official mixture is four parts nitric acid by weight, to 15 of hydrochloric acid, and is called Acidum Nitrohydrochloricum].

Nitric acid is also used to dissolve zinc oxide in the preparation of the oxyphosphate cement. It is used in dental medicine as a caustic. It attacks the teeth, and hence, when used in any form in the mouth, care should be taken that it does not touch other tissues than the ones to which it is applied.

Toxicology: nitric acid is a violent poison turning the mucous membranes a bright yellow and then corroding them. The *antidotes* are alkalies or magnesia suspended in water, sodium bicarbonate in water, soap and water; bland liquids should be given and the patient's strength sustained. Burns should be treated like those from hydrochloric acid. (See section 181).

TETRADS.

271. The following is a list of important tetrads:

TABLE 23. TETRADS.

Aluminium.* Cerium.* Tin. Palladium. Platinum. Iridium.	Tetrads positive to hydrogen.
Silicon. Titanium. Carbon.	Tetrads negative to hydrogen.

272. **Aluminium.—**

Symbol: Al. *Latin name*: Aluminium or Aluminum. *Equivalence*: IV and $(Al_2)^{VI}$. *Specific gravity*: 2.50 to 2.67. *Atomic weight*: 27. *Revised atomic weight*: 27.009. *Electrical state*: +. *Fusing point*: 1292°F. *Length of bar*: etc.: 1.0022 (5th rank). *Wt. of cubic ft. in lbs.*: 166.8. *Tensile strength*: 12. *Tenacity*: like silver. *Malleability*: like silver and gold. *Ductility*: 7; (7th rank). *Conducting power (heat)*: 4; (4th rank). *Conducting power (electricity)*: better than that of iron. *Resistance to air*, etc.: tarnishes very slowly; not affected by sulphuretted hydrogen. *Solubility*: soluble in hydrochloric acid, and in aqueous solutions of alkaline hydrates; resists cold acids, mineral and vegetable (except hydrochloric). *Direct combinations*: with many metals and non-metals. Does not oxidize; is not attacked by sulphur compounds. *Color and appearance*: bluish white, brilliant. *Structure*: octahedral crystals. *Consistence*: hard as zinc. Very sonorous. *Compounds*:

---

* Both aluminium and cerium appear to be trivalent, but are really quadrivalent like the ferric compounds.

two atoms with equivalence of six like ferric salts. *Alloys*: aluminium bronze, solder, etc. Does not amalgamate. *Use in dentistry*: for making "plates."

Occurrence: the great mass of the earth is composed of aluminium, in combination with silicic acid, in silicated rocks, such as granite, feldspar, basalt, slate, mica, etc., and in the various modifications of clay. Every variety of clay contains it in quantity varying from 12 to 20 per cent.* The minerals known as corundum, ruby, sapphire, and emery are *aluminium oxide* in crystallized state.

Preparation: the usual process for obtaining aluminium has been to decompose the chloride by metallic sodium:

$$Al_2Cl_6 + 6Na = 6NaCl + 2Al$$

It will be noticed that aluminium acts as a pseudo-triad, $(Al_2)^{vi}$, in the chloride of aluminium.

The process is that of Deville. At the works of Morin in Paris, ten parts sodio-aluminium chloride, five parts of fluorspar or cryolite, and two parts of sodium, are mixed together and thrown upon the hearth of a reverberatory furnace, previously heated to full redness. A violent action takes place, great heat is evolved, and the liquefied mass of slag and metal collects at the back of the furnace. The latter is drawn off and cast into ingots.

Metallic sodium is very troublesome to handle, and its cost has been so high that the price of aluminium has been, in consequence of the difficulty and expense of the process, higher per troy ounce than that of silver. Recent improvements in process have been made in this country; one is to reduce the aluminous materials with sodium vapor, and to use the double fluoride of aluminium and sodium, or double chloride of aluminium and sodium, made at reduced cost; another is to prepare the

---

* The sapphire and ruby contain also a little oxide of iron; emery contains oxide of iron and also silica.

metal electrolytically;* another to reduce the aluminous earths with zinc ore. The price will probably be greatly reduced before long. Metallic magnesium has been reduced to one-fifth of its previous price, and, as this substance also is used in manufacture of aluminium, it will, probably, affect the price of the latter.†

273. **Value in dentistry and in the arts:**‡ aluminium is remarkable for its resistance to the air, and for its great lightness. It is said to be stronger than steel. It is four times lighter than silver, and seven or eight times lighter than platinum. Gas fumes and sulphur do not tarnish it. It is whiter than nickel, and makes a fine substitute for silver. Alloyed with silver and copper, it gives a non-tarnishing and non-corrosive quality to these metals, and greatly increases their tensile strength. Aluminium bronze is composed of 10 pounds of aluminium to 90 pounds of copper, and has a tensile strength of three tons per square inch greater than Bessemer steel. A solder has been invented which, it is claimed, will enable aluminium to be welded. [An alloy of aluminium and tin has been used, 10 parts tin to 100 of aluminium, for internal parts of instruments, as electrical instruments. The apex of the Washington Monument is of aluminium; its surface appears much whiter than silver, and is so highly polished as to resemble a plate glass mirror].

---

* The Cowles method consists in passing a powerful electric current through a mixture of mineral copper and carbon. A high temperature is obtained by which the mineral is reduced by the carbon.

† The Netto process involves the use of ingots of sodium.

‡ When aluminium is to be melted to make a casting, for instance, this must not be done in clay crucibles, since it reduces the silica contained therein to silicium, whereby it becomes gray and brittle. It must be melted in lime crucibles; or if clay crucibles are used, they must be lined with carbon or well-ignited cryolite. Graphite crucibles, however, are the best.

In prosthetic dentistry the use of aluminium has been urged, on the ground (1) that it is the only metal which can be used *pure* and unalloyed in the manufacture of plates, (2) that it is the lightest of the metals available for such a purpose. It is claimed by some that aluminium is unalterable in the mouth, and does not irritate the gums, hence is superior to caoutchouc. It is thought, therefore, that it will replace gold and platinum in prosthetic dentistry.* According to Palmer there is little or no galvanic action in the oral cavity when aluminium is used; a carpet tack may be held in the mouth, in contact with the aluminium, without unpleasant sensation.

274. Alloys of Aluminium.—

Aluminium solder is 6 parts aluminium, 4 copper, 90 zinc. Others have been devised as follows:

	No. 1.	No. 2.	No. 3.
Zinc	80	85	88
Copper	8	6	5
Aluminium	12	9	7

---

* Some have claimed that it is gradually attacked by articles used in diet, such as vinegar and solutions of common salt, and by alkaline solutions. Chandler's objection to its use is the difference in expansion between it and the vulcanite used in fastening the teeth. The heat of the mouth, hot drinks, etc., etc., cause a separation. Carbonate of lime is deposited from the saliva in the opening, until finally the space is perceptible to the tongue.

Aluminium may be soldered by coating it with copper as in electrotyping, then soldering as usual.*

275. **Compounds of Aluminium.—**
Alums:
Theoretical constitution: alums are what are known as "double salts." They are formed by the combination of aluminium sulphate with other sulphates. The formula for aluminium sulphate is $(Al_2)_2(SO_4)_6$ or $Al_2(SO_4)_3$, aluminium being a pseudo-triad. The formula for potassium sulphate is K_2SO_4, for ammonium sulphate $(NH_4)_2SO_4$. The formula for potash alum or potassium and aluminium sulphate is $K_2Al_2(SO_4)_4$, that is $K_2(SO_4) + Al_2(SO_4)_3$. Ammonia alum is $(NH_4)_2Al_2(SO_4)_4 24H_2O$. *Ferric* alum contains no aluminium at all, but is the double sulphate of ammonium and ferric iron, thus $(NH_4)_2Fe_2(SO_4)_4.24H_2O$. The official alum is potash-alum, $K_2Al_2(SO_4)_4.24H_2O$.

Official name: Aluminii et Potassii Sulphas.

Preparation and properties: alum is manufactured, on a large scale, by decomposing various silicates of aluminium with sulphuric acid, aluminium sulphate being formed. To this is added solution of potassium sulphate, if potash alum be desired, or ammonium sulphate, if ammonia alum is sought. On evaporation the alum crystallizes.

Potash alum occurs in form of regular octahedral crystals, white, efflorescent, soluble in 10 parts of cold water and

---

* A good solder for aluminium is said to be made by melting together 5 parts of zinc, 2 parts of tin, and 1 part of lead, and rolling this out into thin sheets. The aluminium surface to be soldered must be scraped clear of all oxide, and coated with paraffin. A piece of the solder is then placed upon each portion and heated This causes the paraffin to melt; on further heating the solder melts and unites with the aluminium. The two surfaces thus coated are then soldered together in the usual manner.

0.3 parts boiling, insoluble in alcohol; its solution has an *acid reaction* and an astringent, sweetish taste. By heating for several days at a temperature of 176°F., the water of crystallization is expelled and it becomes dried alum, **Alumen exsiccatum.** Alum is used in dentistry as an astringent, styptic, and, in connection with Labarraque's solution, as a bleaching agent.

Aluminium chloride: this substance, Al_2Cl_6, comes in colorless, deliquescent crystals, very soluble in water, of a sharp saline taste, antiseptic, disinfectant. It is made by passing chlorine gas over a mixture of charcoal and alumina at bright red heat:

$$Al_2O_3 + 3C + 6Cl = 3CO + Al_2Cl_6$$
Alumina carbon chlorine carbon monoxide aluminium chloride

It has been used to bleach discolored teeth.

The substance called *Choralum* contains the chloride of aluminium.

Aluminium permanganate: this substance is said to be a constituent of some disinfecting solutions.

Aluminium silicates: there are many silicates of aluminium. Clay is a hydrated silicate, usually mixed with excess of silica. Purer kinds of clay are derived from feldspar of the formula, $Al_2O_3K_2O, 6SiO_2$. On exposure to air the silicate of aluminium alone remains, the alkaline silicates washing away. Earthenware, bricks, and pottery are made from clay, porcelain and the better kinds of stoneware from the purest clay, and glazed with feldspar. Firebricks, crucibles, and the like are prepared from pure varieties of clay, free from lime, magnesia, or iron, but containing a large proportion of silica. Common clays have the formula, $Al_2O_3.2SiO_2$; some kinds of fire clay, $Al_2O_3.6SiO_2$. Silicate of aluminium is an ingredient of hydraulic cement.

Alumina is an oxide, Al_2O_3. Corundum and emery are nearly pure alumina.

276. **Artificial teeth:** teeth are composed of two portions, the *body* or *base* and the *enamel*. The constituents of the body are chiefly *silex, feldspar,* and *kaolin.* The enamel is composed principally of *feldspar.* Coloring matters are also used, and consist of various metals, in a state of minute division, or of metallic oxides.

277. **Feldspar** is a double silicate of aluminium and potassium, its composition being represented by the formula, $K_2Si_3O_7, Al_2Si_3O_9$. It also contains lime and oxide of iron. It is prepared for dental uses in the same way as silex. It is readily fusible.

278. **Kaolin** is essentially a silicate of aluminium. It usually contains oxide of iron and some other substances, as magnesia, potash, etc., etc. It is the result of the decomposition of feldspar. Relatively large proportions of kaolin give teeth an opaque and lifeless appearance; modern mineral teeth contain less kaolin and more feldspar. It is prepared for dental uses by washing, letting settle, decanting, letting settle, decanting again, and drying in the sun.

279. **Crown enamels** are composed of feldspar, as a basis, with various coloring matters, such as titanium, spongy platinum, oxide of gold.

280. **The dry method of preparation of**

gum-enamel as practised by Wildman and described by Essig, is divided into three stages: first, the preparation of the oxide; second, fritting, or, by aid of heat, uniting the metallic oxide with a silicious base; and, third, diluting the frit so as to form the desired shade. In this method the purple of Cassius (metallic oxide) is prepared in the dry way by fusing silver, gold, and tin with borax, removing borax glass formed, dissolving the silver with nitric acid, washing well and drying. The frit is formed by mixing the purple of Cassius thus made with a flux composed of quartz, borax glass, and sal tartar. Lastly, the frit is diluted with the proper amount of feldspar.

281. **Cerium.—**

Symbol: Ce. *Latin name*: Cerium. *Equivalence*: II and IV. *Specific gravity*: 6.62. *Atomic weight* (approx.): 140.4. *Atomic weight* (revised): 140.424. *Electrical state*: +.

The most important compound is the *oxalate*. (Section 435).

282. **Tin.—**

Symbol: Sn. *Latin name*: Stannum. *Equivalence*: II and IV. *Specific gravity*: 7.29 to 7.30. *Atomic weight*: 117.7. *Revised weight*: 117.698. *Electrical state*: +. *Fusing point*: 442°F. (According to some, 458.6°F.) *Length of bar at 212°*: 1.0023; (4th rank). *Weight of cubic feet in lbs.*: 455.1. *Tensile strength*: 2 to 3.5. *Tenacity*: 1.33 compared with lead; (9th rank). *Malleability*: 4; (4th rank). *Ductility*: 9; (9th rank). *Conducting power (heat)*: 7; (7th rank). *Conducting power (electricity)*: 83, (silver = 1000); (9th rank). *Resistance to air*, etc.: 3; (3d rank). *Solu-*

bility: soluble in dilute acids and alkalies. Resists corrosion of air, water, etc., better than iron or copper. Nitric acid converts it into metastannic acid. Dissolved in hydrochloric acid, stannous chloride is formed. In aqua regia, stannic chloride. *Direct combinations*: with oxygen when strongly heated, sulphur, chlorine. It does not combine chemically with mercury. *Color and appearance*: white, brilliant. *Structure*: crystalline in two systems, isometric and quadratic. *Consistence*: soft. *Compounds*: stannic (equivalence IV) and stannous (equivalence II). *Alloys*: pewter, brittania, queen's metal, solder, bell-metal, gun-metal, bronze, speculum metal, fusible metals, sterro-metal, type metal.

Occurrence: tin occurs chiefly in form of *tinstone*, stannic oxide, SnO_2. The ore is found in Cornwall, Australia, Bohemia, Saxony, Malacca, Banca, Siberia, Sweden, North and South America. Tin obtained from Malacca and Banca is known as *straits tin*, and is of great purity. The tin deposits of New South Wales cover an area of over 5,000,000 acres; tin ore is also very abundant in Queensland. In the United States tin ore has been found in West Virginia and adjoining parts of Ohio, in North Carolina, and in the far West, as in Utah, Dakota.

Preparation: the metal is easily obtained from the ore by heating the latter, after purification, with coal:

$$2SnO_2 + 2C_2 = Sn_2 + 4CO$$
Stannic oxide — Carbon — Tin — Carbon mon-oxide

283. *Pure tin*, in crystalline form, may be

thrown down by introducing a plate of tin into a strong solution of stannous chloride, on which water is floated. Another method by which tin, entirely pure, may be obtained is by evaporating a solution of stannous chloride to small bulk, and oxidizing by addition of nitric acid. Stannic oxide is obtained, which, after washing and drying, is exposed to a red heat in a crucible with charcoal.

284. **Tin in dentistry:** tin amalgamates readily with mercury, and in most cases there is condensation. Pure tin in form of foil is used as a filling, and also in connection with non-cohesive gold.

285. **Alloys of tin.—**
Pewter is an alloy of variable composition, usually tin, lead, copper, and antimony or zinc. Plated pewter is 7 antimony, 2 bismuth, 2 copper, 89 tin. A pewter often used is tin, 92, lead, 8.

Rees's alloy is tin 20, gold 1, silver 2.

Common Solder is an alloy of tin and lead. [Fine solder is 33.3 lead to 66.6 tin. Common solder is equal parts tin and lead; coarse solder is 66.6 lead to 33.3 tin].

286. **Compounds of tin.—**
Stannous Chloride:
This substance, known to the dyer as "tin salt," is made by dissolving metallic tin in hydrochloric acid. It may also be prepared by distilling tin filings with mercurous chloride. Its formula is $SnCl_2, 2H_2O$; molecular weight, 224.5. It is used locally. It is poisonous; the antidotes are baking soda, magnesia, milk, and white of egg. Tin dissolved in nitrohydrochloric acid yields

stannic chloride, SnCl$_4$. The two chlorides of tin in connection with auric chloride yield purple of Cassius. (See section 258.)

287. Palladium.—

Symbol: Pd. *Latin name*: Palladium. *Equivalence*: II and IV. *Specific gravity:* 11.80. *Atomic weight*: 106. *Revised atomic weight:* 105.737. *Electrical state*: +. *Fusing point*: lower than platinum, but requires oxy-hydrogen blow-pipe. *Length of bar*, etc.: 1.0010; (12th rank). *Wt. of cubic ft. in lbs.*: 736.6. *Tenacity*: 11½ (Lead = 1): (7th rank). *Malleability*: inferior to platinum. *Ductility*: 6; (6th rank). *Conducting power* (*electricity*): 184 (silver = 1000); (5th rank). *Resistance to air*, etc.: 1; (first rank). More oxidizable than platinum at red heat. *Solubility*: soluble in nitric acid; attacked by iodine; aqua regia best solvent. *Direct combinations*: cyanogen, iodine, hydrogen, sulphur, chlorine, phosphorus, arsenic. *Color and appearance*: like platinum, or a platinum-gold alloy. *Structure*: native, grains of fibrous appearance. *Consistence*: hard as platinum. *Compounds*: palladium (II) and palladic (IV). *Alloys*: salmon-bronze.

Use in dentistry; in amalgam alloys. (See section 223).

288. Platinum.—

Symbol: Pt. *Latin name*: Platinum. *Equivalence*: II, and IV. *Specific gravity*: 21.50. One of the heaviest substances in nature. *Atomic weight*: 197. *Revised atomic weight:* 196.700; (according to some, 194.8). *Electrical state*: +. *Fusing point*: above 3500° in oxyhydrogen flame, or coal-gas and oxygen flame. *Length of bar*, etc.: 1.0009; (13th rank, least expansible of the 13 metals). *Wt. cubic ft. in lbs.*: 1.344. *Tenacity*: 15, compared with lead; (4th rank). *Malleability*: 5; (5th rank). *Ductility*: 3; (3d rank). *Conducting power* (*heat*): 8; (8th rank). *Conducting power* (*electricity*): 180 (silver = 1,000): (6th rank). *Resistance to air*, etc.: 1; (1st rank). *Solubility*: dissolves slowly in aqua regia. Acted on by fused alkaline hydrates at red heat. *Direct combinations*: sulphur, phosphorus, arsenic, silicon, chlorine. Absorbs and condenses gases when in finely divided state. *Color and appearance*: white with tinge of blue, brilliant but less than silver. *Structure*: (native) rounded grains; sometimes octahedral crystals. *Consistence*: hard as copper. *Compounds*: platinous (II), and platinic (IV). *Alloys*: with most metals. Gold, silver, lead form easily fusible alloys with it.

Use in dentistry: in amalgam alloys, for plates of continuous gum teeth, for pins for fastening porcelain teeth to the rubber or celluloid plate. Metallic platinum does not amalgamate with mercury, but spongy platinum unites with the latter when triturated with it in a warm mortar or in contact with acetic acid. (See, however, Rollins's process, following below). In finely divided state it is used as a coloring matter for artificial teeth.

Preparation of platinum for coloring the enamel of artificial teeth.—

The ordinary platinum sponge is too coarse to produce the best results without much grinding. Rollins proceeds as follows: Dissolve twenty grammes of platinum in aqua regia and evaporate to a thick syrup, then add one hundred grammes of caustic potash and boil. To this mixture add fifty grammes of grape sugar and boil ten minutes. Wash thoroughly by decantation and dry the residue, which is platinum in an exceedingly fine state. To prepare what is to be called "Platinum Color" use feldspar eight grammes, this platinum five hundred milligrammes.

Mix and grind five minutes on slab. Use this mixture to add to uncolored spar for the enamel.

289. Platinum metals: these are platinum, rhodium, palladium, ruthenium, and iridium.

Occurrence: the chief supply of platinum, which, like gold, is found free, is derived from the Ural Mountains. The Russian platinum diggings are near Bogoslowsk, Miask, Newjansk, and Nischnei Tagilsk. It is also found in Brazil, Peru, Columbia, California, and Borneo. The Russian platinum is always associated with other metals: analysis showed in one specimen, 75.1 platinum, 1.1 palladium, 3.5 rhodium, 2.6 iridium, 0.6 osmiridium, 2.3 osmium, 0.4 gold, 1.0 copper, and 8.1 iron.*

Preparation: the platinum is dissolved in fused galena, a little glass is introduced to melt over the surface, and a quantity of litharge, equal in weight to the galena, is gradually added. Sulphurous acid gas, from the lead sulphide and lead oxide, is formed, leaving metallic lead in combination with the platinum, free from osmium and iridium. The lead-platinum combination is then treated in a *cupellation* furnace, that is, a furnace containing a *cup*, made of bone ash; the lead removed as

---

* The annual product is two or three tons, of which the United States furnish about 200 ounces. It is worth about $15 an ounce, and the price tends to rise in consequence of the demand for it for use in electric lighting.

an oxide, leaving the platinum in spongy state on the cupel. The spongy platinum is refined in a lime·furnace, by the heat of an oxy-hydrogen, or coal gas and oxygen flame.

290. **Compounds of platinum:** platinic chloride, Pt Cl_4, is formed when metallic platinum is dissolved in aqua regia. It is a reddish, deliquescent substance readily soluble in water and in alcohol.

291. **Iridium.—**
Symbol: Ir. *Latin name:* Iridium. *Equivalence:* II, IV, VI. *Specific gravity:* 21.1. *Atomic weight:* 192.7. *Revised atomic weight:* 192.651. *Electrical state:* +. *Fusing point:* fusible in oxyhydrogen blow-pipe; more refractory than platinum. *Resistance to air:* unalterable in air. *Solubility:* not soluble in aqua regia unless alloyed with platinum. *Direct combinations:* sulphur, chlorine, iodine, oxygen. *Color and appearance:* white, like polished steel. *Consistence:* very hard, brittle. *Compounds:* iridic, iridious, hypoiridious. *Alloys:* with platinum. *Value in dentistry:* for alloy with platinum in manufacture of plates and wire.

292. **Silicon.—**
Symbol: Si. *Latin name*: Silicium. *Equivalence*: II and IV. *Specific gravity*: 2.49. *Atomic weight (approx.)*: 28.2. *Atomic weight (revised)*: 28.1950. *Electrical state*: — *Solubility*: in melted zinc, etc. *Fusing point*: above melted iron. *Preparation*: made by action of sodium on potassium fluo-silicate.

Properties:· occurs in three forms somewhat resembling carbon. Is an amorphous, nut-brown powder. In combination, as silica, SiO_2, found in sand, rocks, etc.

293. **Compounds of silicon:** the most important is *silica*, SiO_2. Silica occurs in nature as quartz crystal and in sand. Is found in animal tissues. Compounds are

silicates. Insoluble in water or acids, infusible except by oxyhydrogen flame, sp. gr. 2.66. Percentage composition, silicon, 48.04, oxygen, 51.96. Used in manufacture of porcelain teeth.

Use in dentistry: dentists use silica under the name of *silex* in the preparation of artificial teeth. For dental uses it is prepared by heating to white heat, plunging into cold water, and grinding to a fine powder.

294. **Titanium:** titanium itself is not used in dentistry, and the only compound of interest is the dioxide, titanic oxide, TiO_2, which occurs native in several different forms, viz., as the minerals rutile and anatase, and as brookite.

Rutile is the most abundant, and is used, ground up, as a coloring matter for artificial teeth. If ground moderately coarse it imparts a yellow of redder cast than when ground fine. It is used for the yellow color of the body of porcelain teeth.

295. **Carbon.—**

Symbol: C. *Equivalence:* II and IV. *Atomic weight (approx.):* 12. *Atomic weight (revised):* 11.9736. *Electrical state:* —. *Fusing point:* infusible. *Properties:* affinity for oxygen, hydrogen, sulphur. Infusible, non-volatile, unalterable solid. Absorbs gases, disinfectant.

296. **Dental uses.—**In the form of charcoal, coke, and anthracite coal, carbon is used in the dental laboratory. In the form of animal charcoal and of wood charcoal it is used in dental medicine.

Charcoal is prepared on a large scale by burning wood in heaps with limited supply of air. *Carbo ligni* is the official preparation.

Coke is the substance left in retorts after coal has been distilled in the production of illuminating gas.

Anthracite coal is the result of the slow decay of vegetable matter. It often contains 96 to 98 per cent. of carbon.

Carbo animalis purificatus consists of carbon and several salts of calcium, notably the phosphate and the carbonate.

Charcoal, and especially *animal* charcoal, has the power of absorbing gases, of destroying noxious odors, and of filtering coloring matters from solutions of organic substances. One volume of wood charcoal at 212°F will absorb 90 volumes of ammonia gas, 55 volumes of sulphuretted hydrogen, and 9 volumes of oxygen. It is administered internally to counteract the effect of poisons, as, for example, strychnine, but should be removed by the stomach pump.

297. **Illuminating gas** is made by subjecting bituminous coal to the action of dry heat in retorts. The coal is heated to bright redness, and the products given off from it are passed through a series of upright tubes, in form of an inverted U, called *condensers*, where the tar, steam, and ammonia are condensed. The gas is then passed through a series of large boxes called *purifiers*, in which it is purified by coming into contact with various substances as fresh slaked lime or a mixture of sawdust and iron oxide, and then it goes to a large tub-shaped vessel called the *gasometer* to be stored until needed.

It is a mixture essentially of hydrogen and marsh-gas mixed with variable proportions of olefiant gas, acetylene, the oxides of carbon, etc., etc. [Much of the illuminating gas now used is the so-called "water-gas," which contains usually a considerable amount of carbon monoxide, and is made by decomposing steam and then carburetting the gases formed].

298. Compounds of carbon.—

Carbon forms two compounds with oxygen, namely, *carbon monoxide* and *dioxide*. Carbon monoxide, CO, is formed when carbon is burned in deficient supply of air. Molecular weight, 28; density, 14; sp. gr., 0.9678. Is a gas. Colorless, insipid, very poisonous, insoluble, combustible.

Called also "carbonic oxide gas."

Carbon dioxide, CO_2, is a product of combustions and of fermentation. Made by pouring an acid on a carbonate, as sulphuric acid on marble or limestone. Molecular weight, 44; density, 22; sp. gr., 1.529. Colorless, odorless gas, present in air, water, breath, heavier than air. Narcotic. Slightly acid taste. Very soluble in water. Compounds are *carbonates*.

Carbonic Acid gas, known to chemists as carbonic dioxide, or carbon dioxide, is a constituent of the breath, is found in small quantities in the atmosphere, and is a product of fermentation. It is not a true acid, as defined in this book, but an *anhydride*, carbonic anhydride, CO_2. The hydrated acid is not found, but its salts exist, as, for example, the various *carbonates*, like sodium carbonate, Na_2CO_3.

299. Carbon Disulphide.—

Synonyms: carbon bisulphide, carbon bisulphuret or bisulphuret of carbon. Official name, Carbonei Bisulphidum.

Theoretical constitution: CS_2, one atom of carbon and two of sulphur. Molecular weight, 76.

Preparation: made by passing fumes of sulphur over red hot charcoal.

Properties: mobile, colorless liquid of disgusting odor except when pure. Very volatile. Dissolves iodine, sulphur, phosphorus, oils, fats, caoutchouc, etc. Sometimes used as local anæsthetic.

Use in dentistry: to dissolve caoutchouc.

PENTADS AND HEXADS.

300. None of the pentads are used in dentistry except those classified as triads, when varying in equivalence. The following list shows *hexads* of importance:

TABLE 24. IMPORTANT HEXADS.

Manganese. ⎫
Iron.   ⎬ Hexads positive to hydrogen.
Nickel.   ⎪
Cobalt.   ⎭

Chromium.   ⎫ Hexad negative to hydrogen. ⎭

301. **Manganese.—**
Symbol: Mn. *Latin name:* Manganesium. *Equivalence:* II, IV, VI; also a pseudo-triad. *Specific gravity:* 8.01 to 8.03. *Atomic weight (approx.):* 53.9. *Atomic weight (revised):* 53.9060. *Electrical state:* +. *Properties:* grayish white metal of but little lustre, hard, brittle, and nearly as refractory as platinum.

302. **Compounds of manganese.—**
The only important compound for dental uses is the *dioxide*, MnO_2, which, in minute quantity, imparts a purple color to the frit, probably due to formation of an oxysilicate. A *silicate* is also used in enamels; it is a yellow amorphous powder turning brown on exposure to air and soluble in dilute acids.

Manganese dioxide occurs in nature as the mineral *pyrolusite*. It is a heavy, black, crystalline mineral insoluble in water. When heated to redness it liberates oxygen.

303. Iron.

Symbol: Fe. *Latin name:* Ferrum. *Equivalence:* II, IV,* VI. *Specific gravity:* 7.79 to 7.84. *Atomic weight:* 56. *Revised atomic weight:* 55.9130. *Electrical state:* +. *Fusing point:* 3500°F (wrought iron). Ordinary, 2900°F. *Length of bar:* 1.0012 (10th rank). *Weight of cubic foot in lbs.:* 489.4. *Tensile strength:* 29.0 (maximum). *Tenacity:* 27½, steel, 42, (1st rank). *Malleability:* 8; (8th rank). *Ductility:* 4; (4th rank). *Conducting power (heat):* 6; (6th rank). *Conducting power (electricity):* 168; (silver = 1000); (7th rank). *Resistance to air:* rusts in moist air. *Solubility:* soluble in hydrochloric and sulphuric acids; in dilute nitric. *Direct combinations:* chlorine, bromine, iodine, sulphur, and members of the phosphorus group except nitrogen. *Color and appearance:* depend on variety. Pure iron is white. *Structure:* white cast iron, crystalline; gray iron, granular; wrought iron, fibrous; crystals probably cubical. *Consistence:* pure iron is soft and tough. *Compounds:* ferric $(Fe_2)^{vi}$, ferrous (Fe^{ii}), and ferroso-ferric, $Fe^{ii}(Fe_2)^{vi}$. *Alloys:* Aich's metal, arguzoid, German silver plate, sterro-metal.

Use in dentistry: as steel, and in many ways.

Occurrence: the iron ores are very numerous and widely distributed; those used in the manufacture of iron are hæmatite (Fe_2O_3), magnetite (Fe_3O_4), limonite (a hydrate), and siderite ($FeCO_3$).

Preparation: the general process is to reduce with carbon, metallic iron and the oxides of carbon being formed. Sometimes the ore is first roasted to get rid of sulphur, carbonic

---

* Iron as a pseudo-triad in ferric compounds is really quadrivalent.

acid, water, etc. The ore, containing iron oxide, is then reduced, *i. e.*, deprived of its oxygen, in a blast furnace, which is filled at the top with alternate layers of coal, broken ore, and fluxes, such as limestone or silicates. Iron obtained by this method is known as **cast-iron,** and contains more or less carbon and slag, when drawn off into moulds to form **pig-iron. Wrought-iron** is made by subjecting pig-iron to the **puddling process,** during which the molten metal is thoroughly stirred in reverberating furnaces, where there is a free supply of air, so that the carbon of the pig-iron is burned and other impurities oxidized.

304. *Steel* is now made by the Bessemer process, by blowing air under great pressure into molten cast-iron, consuming the carbon; iron rich in carbon and manganese, termed *spiegel-eisen*, is then added to give the proper amount of carbon.

Malleable iron is steel which has undergone further treatment by heat and atmospheric air.

305. Dental uses of iron: chiefly in tools; iron is by far the strongest and yet one of the lightest of the metals; steel is the strongest and one of the hardest and most elastic of all materials; malleable iron possesses great strength and toughness, but is soft enough to be turned, bored, and punched, and, when heated, is easily wrought and without crack-

ing. Wrought-iron, at bright red heat, can be welded, that is, joined to another piece of metal, without the use of solder. Wrought-iron has the property of acquiring with great rapidity the properties of a magnet and of parting with them rapidly, hence is well adapted for use in the construction of electro-magnetic and magneto-electric apparatus. Cast-iron is easily melted, and can be made into castings, which may be readily filed or turned, or made so hard that no tool can affect them.

When cold, iron is the least malleable of metals in common use, but when heated, its ductility is such that it can be rolled into the thinnest sheets and drawn into the finest wire, which, when $\frac{1}{10}$th inch in diameter, will sustain a weight of 700 pounds. With exception of platinum, iron is the least fusible of the useful metals.

306. **Compounds of Iron:** compounds of **Iron** are chiefly of two kinds, ferr*ic* and ferr*ous*.

Ferric compounds: iron as a pseudo-triad. *Ferric* chloride, Fe_2Cl_6, per-chloride, sesquichloride, chloride of iron, Ferri Chloridum; orange-yellow, deliquescent, soluble. *Liquor ferri chloridi*, U. S. P., contains 37.8 per cent. of the anhydrous. "Tincture of Iron" is one part of the *Liquor* to about two of alcohol (Tinctura Ferri Chloridi, U. S. P.); hemostatic, strong chalybeate, styptic taste, acid reaction, stains teeth and acts on them. *Ferric Hydrate*, $Fe_2(HO)_6$, hydrated oxide, hydrated peroxide, peroxide, sesquioxide, red oxide. Precipitate ferric sulphate or ferric chloride by ammonia or by sodium hydrate. Reddish-brown powder used as antidote to arsenic; must be freshly made. *Hydrated oxide of iron with magnesia*, U. S. P., made by adding magnesia to a solution of ferric sulphate. *Ferric Sulphate*, $Fe_2(SO_4)_3$, in solution forming "solution of tersulphate of iron," U. S. P., color reddish-brown. *Ferric Subsulphate* (doubtful composition) $Fe_4O(SO_4)_5$, called "Monsel's solution," ruby-red; valuable as a hemostatic, may be taken internally. *Dialyzed Iron*, aqueous solution of about 5 per cent. of ferric hydrate with some ferric chloride. Ammonia is used in making it, and the ammonium chloride formed passed through a dialyzer.

Ferrous compounds: iron as a dyad. Ferrous salts are usually green, and alter in the air to -*ic* salts. *Ferrous chloride*, $FeCl_2$, protochloride; *ferrous iodide*, FeI_2, protiodide, green, volatile, deliquescent, soluble. *Ferrous sulphide*, FeS, protosulphide, sulphuret of iron, is used to make H_2S (sulphuretted hydrogen). *Ferrous sulphate*, $FeSO_4$, green vitriol, copperas; dissolve iron in 1½ parts H_2SO_4 diluted with 4 parts water: efflorescent, bluish-green crystals, acrid, styptic taste, soluble in water, insoluble in alcohol, astringent, irritant, disinfectant.

307. **Dental uses of compounds of iron:** ferric chloride is used externally, to arrest alveolar hæmorrhage, either in form of the deliquesced crystals or in solution. It is also applied to fungous tumors. It is given internally. Monsel's powder and solution are used to arrest hæmorrhages following extraction of teeth, etc., etc.

308. **Nickel.***—

---

*Nickel is one of the toughest of all metals, and is now used in manufacture of crucibles which to some extent are taking the place of platinum crucibles, as they cost only about one-tenth as much.

Symbol: Ni. *Latin name:* Niccolum. *Equivalence:* II, IV, (Ni$_2$). *Specific gravity:* 8.60 to 8.82. *Atomic weight:* 58. *Revised atomic weight:* 57.928. *Electrical state:* +. *Fusing point:* less than iron. *Weight of cubic foot in lbs:* 541.2. *Tensile strength:* same as iron. *Tenacity:* like iron, very great. *Malleability, Ductility:* very ductile and malleable. *Conducting power* (*heat*): about the same as iron. *Conducting power* (*electricity*): 131; (8th rank). *Resistance to air:* rusts less readily than iron; magnetic. *Solubility:* soluble in dilute mineral acids, especially nitric. *Direct combinations:* with chlorine, cyanogen, oxygen, sulphur, arsenic. *Color and appearance:* silver-white, with a slight yellowish tinge and very lustrous. *Consistence:* hard. *Compounds:* mostly nickelous. *Alloys:* arguzoid, electrum, German silver, tutenag.

309. **Cobalt.**—
Symbol: Co. *Latin name:* Cobaltum. *Equivalence:* II, IV, (Co$_2$)^{VI}. *Specific gravity:* 8.49 to 8.9. *Atomic weight:* 58.9. *Revised atomic weight:* 58.8870. *Electrical state:* +. *Fusing point:* less than that of iron. *Weight of cubic foot in lbs.:* 558.7. *Tensile strength:* like iron. *Tenacity:* like iron. *Malleability:* like iron. *Ductility:* like iron. *Resistance to air:* like nickel. *Solubility:* like nickel. *Direct combinations:* chlorine, oxygen, sulphur. *Color and appearance:* reddish-white; magnetic. *Structure:* has granular fracture. *Consistence:* hard. *Compounds:* cobaltous, cobaltic, and cobaltous-cobaltic like ferroso-ferric.

Compounds of Cobalt.—[*]

Impure protoxide of cobalt serves as a basis for the preparation of the colors of cobalt, among which are various blues. Oxide of cobalt is sometimes used for the blue color of points of porcelain teeth.

[*] The term "cobalt" is sometimes applied to metallic arsenic.

310. **Chromium.—**
Symbol: Cr. *Latin name*: Chromium. *Equivalence*: II, IV, VI, and pseudo-triad. *Specific gravity*: 7.01. *Atomic weight* (*approx.*): 52. *Atomic weight* (*revised*): 52.009. *Electrical state*: —.

311. **Compounds of Chromium. Chromic Anhydride.—**
Synonyms: chromic trioxide, chromic oxide, chromic acid. Official name, Acidum Chromicum.

Theoretical constitution: chromic "acid" so-called is not an acid but an oxide, CrO_3, composed of one atom of chromium to three of oxygen; by weight, 52 parts of chromium to 48 of oxygen. Molecular weight, 100.

Preparation: chromic anhydride separates in crystals from a mixture of potassium dichromate and sulphuric acid:

$$K_2Cr_2O_7 + 2H_2SO_4 = 2CrO_3 + 2KHSO_4 + H_2O$$

Potassium dichromate.   Sulphuric acid.   Chromic anhydride.   Acid potassium sulphate.

Properties: fine, red, very deliquescent,* needle-shaped crystals, which have strongly corrosive action on organic matter, and decompose certain substances with explosive violence, as alcohol, sugar, or glycerine. It forms dichromates with oxides of the alkali metals, as potassium dichromate with potassium oxide:

$$K_2O + 2CrO_3 = K_2Cr_2O_7.$$

Potassium oxide.   Chromic oxide.   Potassium dichromate.

The crystals are readily soluble in water, forming an orange yellow solution of strongly acid properties. Alcohol is inflamed by the crystals.

Dental uses, etc.: used in dentistry locally, for removal of tumors, morbid growths, etc., etc. If combined with glycerine, care must be taken not to mix too rapidly, but

---

*Absolutely pure chromic acid, wholly free from sulphuric acid, should not deliquesce when used as a caustic.

drop by drop to avoid explosion. It penetrates tissues deeply.

Toxicology: chromic acid is a poison, and a violently corrosive agent. Poisoning by it should be treated promptly and with vigor as in case of poisoning by sulphuric acid. Cause the patient to drink at once water containing 300 to 400 grains of magnesia, or else half an ounce of soap which has been dissolved in two quarts of hot water and cooled, or water with which wood ashes have been mixed, or a solution of sodium bicarbonate (150 grains in a pint of water). If nothing else is at hand, give milk or the whites of four eggs in a quart of water. Burns from it should be treated as in case of hydrochloric acid, and as promptly as possible.

Chromic oxide of formula Cr_2O_3, better known as the *sesquioxide*, is a green powder insoluble in water and in acids. It is obtained by heating potassium dichromate with sulphur. It is used as a coloring matter for porcelain teeth to modify or tone the bright yellow of the oxide of titanium in the darker shades.

CHAPTER IV.

CARBON COMPOUNDS OR ORGANIC CHEMISTRY.

312. **Theory.—**
1. *Organic Chemistry* is the chemistry of *carbon* compounds.
2. The *elements* found in organic compounds are, besides *carbon*, chiefly *hydrogen, oxygen,* and *nitrogen*, sometimes sulphur and phosphorus.
3. *The general properties* of organic compounds are as follows: combustible (except CO_2 and its salts); solids usually when carbon atoms predominate in their molecule; liquids or gaseous when hydrogen predominates; easily volatilized gases or liquids when a small number of atoms in the molecule; liquids of high boiling points or solids when the number of atoms in the molecule is large.
4. *Quantitative* analysis more important than qualitative to establish identity of organic compounds. If the elements of an organic substance are determined, the

analysis is called *ultimate* or *elementary*; if different organic substances when mixed together are separated, the analysis is called *proximate*.

5. The presence of *carbon* in a combustible form will prove a compound to be organic, hence, if a substance burns with generation of carbon dioxide (shown by passing the gas through lime-water) the organic nature of this substance is established. The presence of *hydrogen* may be shown by allowing the gaseous products of combustion to pass through a cool glass tube, when drops of water will be deposited. To show presence of *nitrogen*, heat with a mixture of two parts calcium hydrate to one part sodium hydrate; the nitrogen is converted into ammonia, recognized by its odor and action on paper moistened with copper sulphate solution.

6. A chemical *formula* is called *empirical* when it gives the simplest expression of the composition of a substance; this formula, however, does not necessarily denote the actual number of atoms in the molecule, which may be two or three times the number given in the empirical formula; thus, the empirical formula of acetic acid is CH_2O, but the actual molecular formula contains twice the number of atoms or $C_2H_4O_2$. Besides empirical and molecular formulæ, others called *rational, constitutional, structural,* or *graphic* are used. The molecular formula of acetic acid is $C_2H_4O_2$, but the formula $HC_2H_3O_2$ shows that acetic acid, like nitric acid, HNO_3, is monobasic, containing one atom of hydrogen, which can be replaced by an atom of a metal; hence $HC_2H_3O_2$ is called a *constitutional* formula.

7. *Radicals* or *residues*. These are expressions for unsaturated groups of atoms known to enter as a whole into different compounds, but having no separate existence. Water, H_2O, is a *saturated* compound, that is the one atom of oxygen—which is a dyad, and may be said therefore

to have *two* points of attraction—combines with two of hydrogen and therefore has both its points of attraction satisfied. If now one atom of H be taken from H_2O, there is left the group of atoms HO, which is called a radical, as it consists of an atom of oxygen, in which but one point of attraction is actually saturated, the second one not being provided for; moreover, this group HO occurs in many compounds—as, for example, in the hydrates, as potassium hydrate, KHO, etc. The *equivalence* of radicals depends upon the number of points of attraction unprovided for: carbon requires four atoms of hydrogen to provide for its points of attraction; therefore CH_3 would be a *monad*, CH_2 a dyad, CH a triad. (See Chapter II).

Radicals are *electro-positive* and *electro-negative*. The most important positive radicals are ammonium NH_4, the ethyl series of radicals (such as methyl CH_3, ethyl CH_4, etc.) and also of other series, phenyl, glyceryl, etc.

The most important negative radicals are *acid* radicals, as $C_2H_3O_2$, that of all acetates, C_2O_4 that of all oxalates, etc. HO the radical of hydrates and CN of cyanides are negative also.

8. *Chains:* the expression *chain* denotes a *series* of atoms, held together in such a manner that affinities are left unsaturated. The atoms of the series must have a greater equivalence than one, *i. e.*, must be dyad, etc. The existence of such an enormous number of carbon compounds is greatly due to the property of carbon to form these chains. Carbon is a tetrad, hence two atoms would form a chain as follows:—$\overset{|}{\underset{|}{C}}-\overset{|}{\underset{|}{C}}$—; each atom has four

bonds, one of which unites with one of the other, leaving in this particular chain six free affinities. Three atoms of carbon would be $-\overset{|}{C}-\overset{|}{C}-\overset{|}{C}-$; four, $-\overset{|}{C}-\overset{|}{C}-\overset{|}{C}-\overset{|}{C}-$, etc., etc. The free affinities may be saturated with various atoms or radicals, hence the almost unlimited number of possible combinations. Atoms are not always united by one affinity. When they are united by *two*, the expression for two atoms of carbon would be $\rangle C = C \langle$; if by three, $-C \equiv C-$. In the so-called *closed chain* of C_6 we have the atoms united partially by double and partially by single union:

$$\begin{array}{c} \overset{|}{C} \\ \diagup\diagdown \\ CC \\ \| \| \\ CC \\ \diagdown\diagup \\ \underset{|}{C} \end{array}$$

Benzine, C_6H_6, would then be represented as follows:

$$\begin{array}{c} H \\ | \\ H-C=C-H \\ | \| \\ C . C \\ | | \\ H-C=C-H \\ | \\ H \end{array}$$

It is easy to see from these two diagrams the origin of the term *skeleton*, which is sometimes used instead of chain.

9. *Homologous series.* Any series of organic compounds, the members of which preceding or following

each other differ by CH_2, is called a homologous series.*

10. *Types.* Most substances may be classified under the five following types;

I.	II.	III.	IV.
Hydrogen.	Water.	Ammonia.	Methane.

$$H-H \qquad H-O-H \qquad N{<}{H \atop H}^H \qquad {H \atop |} C {<}{H \atop H}^H$$

V.
Phosphoric chloride.

$$\begin{array}{c} Cl \\ | \;/Cl \\ P-Cl \\ | \;\backslash Cl \\ Cl \end{array}$$

Almost any compound may be classed in one of these types by replacing the constituents of these types by other elements or radicals of the same equivalence.

11. *Substitution.* Replacement of an atom or group of atoms by other atoms or groups: $C_6H_6 + HNO_3 = C_6H_5NO_2 + H_2O$. Here for one atom of hydrogen in benzine (C_6H_6) has been substituted the group NO_2. (See Chap. II).

12. *Derivatives.* Chloroform, $CHCl_3$, is a *derivative* of marsh gas, CH_4, because it may be obtained from the latter by replacement of three atoms of hydrogen by three of chlorine. The term is applied to bodies derived from others, by some kind of decomposition, generally by substitution. (See Chap. II).

13. *Isomerism.* Two or more substances having the same elements in the same proportions by weight, or having the same percentage composition, and yet being

---

* When the carbon remains the same but the hydrogen differs by H_2, the series is said to be *isologous*.

different bodies with different properties, are called *isomeric* bodies. When two or more substances have the same molecular formulæ they are said to be *metameric* with one another; thus CN_2H_4O is either urea or ammonium cyanate; hence, urea is said to be metameric with ammonium cyanate. Sometimes structural formulæ will serve to distinguish two substances metameric with each other. When a substance contains some multiple of the number of each of the atoms contained in the molecule of the other, it is said to be *polymeric* with it; thus acetic acid $C_2H_4O_2$, is polymeric with grape-sugar, $C_6H_{12}O_6$. (See Chap. II).

14. *Decomposition.* Organic bodies decompose readily under the influence of heat or chemical agents. Heat will volatilize some organic bodies without decomposition; whilst others are decomposed by heat with generation of volatile products. *Dry or destructive* distillation is the term applied to the process of heating non-volatile organic substances in such a way that the oxygen in the air has no access and to such an extent that decomposition takes place. (See Chap. II).

15. *Combustion and decay.* In common combustion, provided an excess of atmospheric air be present, the carbon of an organic substance is converted into carbon dioxide, the hydrogen into water, sulphur and phosphorus into sulphuric and phosphoric acids, and the nitrogen set free. In decay, which is slow oxidation, the compounds mentioned above are finally produced, but many intermediate products are also generated. Alcohol when burned forms carbon dioxide and water; exposed to the air, it undergoes slow oxidation, forming aldehyde first, then acetic acid.

16. *Fermentation and putrefaction.* An organic substance under favorable temperature and during the presence of moisture and of a substance termed a ferment, undergoes

a peculiar kind of decomposition, during which its molecule is split up into two or more molecules of less complicated composition.

17. *Difference between fermentation and putrefaction.* (See Ferments, section 476).

18. *Action of various agents on organic matter.* Chlorine and bromine usually remove or replace the hydrogen of an organic substance. Sometimes they combine directly with it, and sometimes, in presence of water, act as oxidizing agents by combining with the hydrogen of the water and liberating oxygen. Nitric acid either forms (i) salts with organic matter, (ii) oxidizes it, or (iii) substitutes NO_2 (nitryl) for hydrogen. In the latter case the additional quantity of oxygen added renders the compounds highly combustible or even explosive. Substances having a great affinity for water, as, for example, sulphuric acid, act on many organic substances by removing hydrogen and oxygen, leaving dark or black compounds consisting mainly of carbon. Alkalies may combine directly, form salts, form soaps, oxidize, or evolve ammonia from nitrogenous compounds. Reducing agents, especially nascent hydrogen, either combine directly, remove oxygen, or replace oxygen.

313. **Classification of organic substances:**

Organic substances of interest to the dentist may be classified as follows: *hydrocarbons* (ethyl series of radicals) *alcohols* (carbohydrates) *ethers, glucosides, fats, waxes, aldehydes, ketones, organic acids and salts, alkaloids, proteids, ferments.*

314. **Hydrocarbons.**

Group 1. Paraffines: the general formula for this series is $C_nH_{2n}\times_2$, which means that, however many carbon atoms a paraffine contains, it will contain *twice* as many hydrogen atoms and two more. Thus marsh gas, a member of this series, contains one atom of carbon; one multiplied by two and two added to the product equals *four*, therefore the number of hydrogen atoms is *four*, and the formula is CH_4.

American petroleum contains many members of this series. They are isolated from petroleum by *fractional distillation*. This process may be conducted in the following manner: the liquid to be distilled is placed in a retort, through the tubulure of which a thermometer passes to indicate the temperature at which the substance boils. The first portion, which distills over, will consist chiefly of that liquid which has the lowest boiling point, and, if the receiver be changed at stated intervals corresponding to a certain rise in the temperature, a series of liquids will be obtained, containing substances the boiling-points of which lie within the limits of temperature between which such liquids are collected.

315. **Petroleum or Mineral Oil.**—
This substance, known also as *rock oil* or *liquid bitumen*, is a natural product, consisting of a number of hydrocarbons,* together with small quantities of sulphuretted, oxygenized, and nitrogenized bodies. It contains about 85 per cent. of carbon, and 15 of hydrogen.

316. Among the products obtained from petroleum are *rhigolene, gasoline, naphtha, benzine, kerosene*.†

317. **Rhigolene:** one of the lighter products of petro-

---

* These are homologous derivatives of CH_4 up to about $C_{16}H_{34}$.

† In distilling the crude oil, naphtha, benzine, rhigolene, etc., being the lightest come over first; then at greater heat, *kerosene;* the residue is composed of the heaviest compounds which require high heat for their distillation: namely, lubricating oil, vaseline, paraffine, etc.

leum, sp. gr. from 0.590 to 0.625. Highly volatile, inflammable, boils at 70°F, colorless, odorless, when pure. It is used for producing local anæsthesia. Most specimens of it have a disagreeable odor of petroleum. It should be kept in a cool place, in a tightly stoppered flask, and should not be brought near a light nor used at all at night.

318. **Gasoline:** this substance is the lightest and most volatile portion of petroleum "naphtha," and is employed for napthalizing gas and air. Its specific gravity is from 0.650 to 0.665. It boils at 119°F.

319. **Naphtha** has a density of from 0.695 to 0.705, and is often an adulterant of kerosene.

Mineral Naphtha or **"benzine"**: this substance should not be confused with *benzene*. "Benzine" is a petroleum product, while benzene is a coal-tar product. The synonyms of "benzine" are petroleum spirit, petroleum naphtha, shale naphtha, benzoline.

It is a thin, colorless liquid of 0.69 to 0.74 sp. gr., inflammable, volatile. It dissolves gutta percha, napthalin, paraffine wax, and many similar substances. It is used as an illuminating agent in sponge lamps.

320. **Mineral burning oil or kerosene:** American petroleum yields from 50 to 70 per cent. of its weight of kerosene, which is also called refined petroleum, photogene, and paraffine oil.

It is a solvent of sulphur, iodine, phosphorus, camphor, wax, fats, many resins. It softens india-rubber to a glairy varnish. Its sp. gr. is from 0.78 to 0.82. Good lamp oil should neither be too viscous nor too volatile, and should have a tolerably high boiling point. Cold oil of good quality will not take fire, when a light is applied to it, nor should its vapor inflame. New York State law declares that oils used for illuminating purposes shall not give a vapor that will "flash" below 100°F., nor shall themselves ignite below 300 F.

321. Vaselene or vaseline.—
Synonyms: cosmolene, saxolene, petroleum jelly.

Theoretical constitution: *vaselene is a mixture of hydrocarbons,* consisting chiefly of those whose formulæ are from $C_{16}H_{34}$ to $C_{20}H_{42}$, together with some of the olefine series.

Preparations: vaselene consists of those portions of petroleum which, at ordinary temperatures, are soft or pasty. The last distillate or the undistilled portion is treated with superheated steam, and filtered through animal charcoal.

Properties and uses: colorless or pale yellow, odorless, translucent, slightly fluorescent, neutral, semi-solid. Its sp. gr., when melted, is 0.840 to 0.866, and it melts from 95°F. to 104°. It is insoluble in water, nearly in alcohol, freely soluble in ether, chloroform, benzene, carbon disulphide, and turpentine. It is miscible in all proportions with fixed and volatile oils. It forms an intimate mixture with glycerine. It dissolves sulphur, iodine, bromine, carbolic acid, atropine, strychnine, phosphorus, benzoic acid, and iodoform, the last best when warmed. *It can not be saponified, nor does it become rancid;* hence is a valuable agent in ointments. It is but little affected by chemical reagents. *It is a valuable substitute for lard in the preparation of ointments containing sulphur, the iodides, compounds of lead, zinc, and mercury.*

Use in dentistry: vaseline is used as an application to inflamed surfaces, as a dressing in periostitis, and as an emollient after devitalization or removal of dental pulps.

322. **Mineral lubricating oil:** the various products known by this title are obtained from the less volatile fluid portions of petroleum. It consists chiefly of higher members of the olefine series. Its color ranges from pale yellow, through all shades of red, brown, green and blue, to black. Good qualities have very little taste, and no marked smell, even when heated.

323. Group 3. Hydrocarbons of the *fourth* series. General formula, C_nH_{2n-4}.

[Hydrocarbons of the *third* series, C_nH_{2n-2}, are of no importance to the dentist]. Those of the *fourth* series include turpentine and a large number of oils, essential or volatile so-called. These different essential oils are mostly isomers or polymers, having for a formula $C_{10}H_{16}$, or some multiple of it.

324. **Oil of turpentine:** $C_{10}H_{16}$, called also **spirit of turpentine** and essence of turpentine, obtained by distilling turpentine or oleo-resinous juice, exuding from various kinds of pine.

It is a colorless, mobile liquid, having peculiar, aromatic and disagreeable odor; acrid, caustic taste; does not mix with water; soluble in alcohol; dissolves iodine, sulphur, phosphorus, fixed oils, resins, etc.; exposed to the air absorbs oxygen, becomes thicker, finally resinous. *After prolonged contact with air becomes ozonized.* Sp. gr., 0.864. Boiling point, 312°F. It is miscible in all proportions with ether, or at least very soluble in it, and in carbon disulphide, chloroform, benzine, petroleum spirit, fixed and essential oils. *It dissolves fats, waxes, resins, and caoutchouc.*

325. *Sanitas oil* is made by oxidizing oil of turpentine, floating on water, by a stream of heated air.

326. **Terpenes, terpin, terebene, etc.:** there has been great confusion in regard to the names of these substances.

Terpene is the general name for hydrocarbons having $C_{10}H_{16}$ or some multiple for their composition. Thus, for example, pure oil of turpentine, $C_{10}H_{16}$, is called a terpene. [*Camphene* has been used as a general term for terpenes, *but it is also used for a particular kind of terpene*].

Terpene is not the same as terpin or terpine; terpin is a *particular* member of the group to which the *general* name terpene is given. Terebene is a terpene. Terpenes are either natural or artificial: the natural terpenes occur in oil of turpentine; the artificial are camphene, terebene, menthene, cajuputene, etc., etc. The derivative from *French oil of turpentine only* is called terpene hydrate. Derivatives from any oil of turpentine are terpene hydrochloride, terpin hydrate, terpin, terpinol, etc., etc.

327. **Terebene:** this substance, $C_{10}H_{16}$, isomeric with oil of turpentine, is an artificial terpene produced by the action of sulphuric acid on oil of turpentine. *It is a molecular modification of essence of turpentine.* It is a clear, color-

less liquid and an agreeable remedy, having an odor like that of freshly sawn pine wood. It does not mix with water. It imparts a very distinct odor of violets to the urine.

Dr. Wm. Murrell, of London, has employed terebene for the last five years and has made experiments to ascertain its properties. In the proportion of one to five hundred it checks fermentation, and in one to one thousand prevents it.

It absorbs oxygen readily, and is a disinfectant, and antiseptic. It dissolves in the various essential oils, and is a solvent for gutta percha, iodine, and resins. It is soluble in 10 parts of alcohol. Its sp. gr. is 0.860, and it boils at 313°F. Most commercial terebenes are contaminated with resin, turpentine, and dioxide of hydrogen. It is, however, almost impossible to prevent the formation of hydrogen dioxide in terebene, which, so far as topical action is concerned, does no harm, but is of advantage. Iodol and terebene are now used together in proportions as follows: iodol, 10 grains, terebene, 1 fluid ounce.

Terebene is used in dentistry as an *antiseptic, disinfectant,* and stimulant.

328. **Terpin:** and **terpin hydrate:** the "terpin" used in medicine should preferably be called terpin hydrate, as it is not properly terpin. Nor is it by any means terp*ene* hydrate. The substance now used as an expectorant is $C_{10}H_{16}(H_2O)_2, H_2O$. It occurs in large, transparent crystals.

329. **Essential or volatile oils:*** theoretical constitution: most of the volatile oils of plants are *terpenes*, that is, hydrocarbons of formula $C_{10}H_{16}$; others are polymers of terpenes of

---

*Called *essential* oils because usually the fragrant essence of plants especially of the flowers.

formula $C_{15}H_{24}$. The hydrocarbons of plants are liable to change in contact with air or moisture, so that they are not found in the pure state, even when freshly obtained. Some essential oils consist mostly of certain ethers, some of aromatic aldehydes.

Preparation: the volatile oils of plants may be obtained either by *pressure*, as in case of oils of laurel, lemon, or bergamot; by *distillation* with water, or by passing a current of *steam* over the matter to be extracted; by *fermentation and distillation*, as with oils of mustard and bitter almonds; by *solution in a fixed oil*.

General properties: essential oils of plants are *liquid* at ordinary temperatures, but deposit solid matters in severe cold. Usually lighter than water, colorless or yellow, rapidly darkening and ultimately becoming resinoid, of marked and highly characteristic odor, readily combustible, *nearly insoluble in water, freely soluble in alcohol*, miscible in all proportions with carbon disulphide, fixed oils, turpentine, and petroleum spirit; as a rule not saponified nor acted on by alkalies, but destroyed by strong nitric or sulphuric acid. They may be separated from their alcoholic solutions† by addition of water or solution of

---

†An alcoholic solution of a number of these oils is called a *cologne*.

sodium sulphate. They are very often adulterated with alcohol, chloroform, oil of turpentine, and fixed oils. Cheaper essential oils are often mixed with the more expensive. Essential oils are gradually affected by exposure to air, some oxygen being absorbed, while at the same time a peculiar resin is formed. This oxidizing action is attended by development of ozone. If a spray of one of these oils be discharged into a room where there is plenty of sunlight, enough ozone is generated to purify the air.

It is likely that the oxidation and change of these oils is due to the presence of small traces of water. Mr. John Williams has obtained anhydrous essential oils, by means of apparatus in which the oils were distilled without presence of water.

330. **Anise oils:** the Saxon oil is the best, though the Russian is much liked. The official, Oleum Anisi, is colorless or yellowish, with the peculiar odor and taste of the seed. Its sp. gr. is 0.976 to 0.990, increasing by age. At 50°–59°F. it solidifies, but is fluid at 62°.6. It is soluble in an equal weight of alcohol.

331. **Bergamot:** Oleum Bergamii. It is of sweet, very agreeable odor, and of bitter, aromatic, pungent taste. In color the oil is pale green-yellow. The reaction is slightly acid. It is soluble in alcohol.

332. **Cajuput:** this oil is transparent, with lively, penetrating, camphor-like odor, of green color, and warm, pungent taste. The green color is due to copper, sometimes to chlorophyll. It is met with of a greenish color, even when no copper is present. A specimen of Paris oil contained, according to Guibourt, 0.022 per cent. of copper.

Cajuput oil is used in dentistry as a local application in odontalgia, and in neuralgia. Oleum Cajuputi is the official name.

333. **Caraway:** this oil, Oleum Cari, is somewhat viscid, pale yellow, becoming brownish with age, with odor of the fruit, and of aromatic, acrid taste. It consists of two liquid oils, *carvene* and *carvol*, is of neutral reaction, and soluble in alcohol.

334. **Carvacrol:** obtained by treating caraway oil with iodine, and washing the product with caustic potash. Pure carvacrol is a viscid, colorless oil, nearly insoluble in water, of an odor like creasote, and of strong, acrid, persistent taste. It is lighter than water. It is antiseptic, disinfectant, and escharotic. It is used in dentistry locally in odontalgia, where there is sensitive dentine, alveolar abscess, as an *antiseptic*, and in gargles. It dissolves Hill's Stopping and gutta percha.

335. **Cinnamon:** obtained by distillation from cinnamon, of a light yellow color when freshly prepared, becoming deeper by age and finally red. It has a pungent, hot taste. It is used in dentistry locally, for relief of odontalgia.

336. **Cloves:** the oil of cloves contains a *cedrene* or hydrocarbon having the formula $C_{15}H_{24}$, and called *caryophyllin*. It contains other substances, as tannin, resin, and an oxygenized oil called *eugenol*, or *eugenic acid*. Oil of cloves is clear and colorless when freshly prepared, but yellow and finally reddish-brown on exposure. It has a hot, aromatic taste, and the odor of cloves. Good Zanzibar cloves yield about 18 per cent. of oil. Oil of cloves is used to disguise the odor of

carbolic acid, creasote, etc. It is used in dentistry to relieve odontalgia.

337. **Eucalyptus:** the oil of eucalyptus is colorless or very pale, yellowish, of characteristic aromatic odor, and pungent, spicy, cooling taste, neutral in reaction and soluble in alcohol. The official name is Oleum Eucalypti.

338. **Eugenol:** $C_{10}H_{12}O_2$, an oxidized oil, prepared by decomposing potassium eugenate with sulphuric acid. It is properly an acid, and will be considered under the head of acids.

339. **Lavender:** this oil is obtained from the flowers of *Lavandula vera*, and is of a pale-yellow color.

340. **Oil of Gaultheria** is a stimulant, volatile oil from the leaves of *Gaultheria procumbens*, first colorless, gradually becoming reddish, and one of the heaviest of the volatile oils. About 90 per cent. of the oil is composed of the so-called methyl salicylate, $(CH_3(C_7H_5O_3)$. The formula of salicylic acid is $C_7H_6O_3$; that of methyl salicylate, $C_7 \begin{Bmatrix} H_5 \\ CH_3 \end{Bmatrix} O_3$.

341. **Mint:** oil of peppermint, Oleum Menthæ Piperitæ, is of greenish-yellow color, becoming reddish by age. It has a strong aromatic odor, and a warm, camphorous, pungent taste, succeeded by a sensation of coolness, when air is drawn into the mouth.

342. **Neroli:** the oil obtained from orange flowers is termed oil of neroli, and is a volatile oil of delightful odor.

343. **Pyrethrum:** the oil dissolved in ether is used in odontalgia. Pyrethrum or pellitory is a powerful local irritant.

344. **Rose:** this substance, known also as *attar* or *ottar* of rose, is nearly colorless, concrete below 80°F., liquid between 84° and 86°F. It has a powerful and diffusive

odor, is slightly soluble in alcohol, and of a slightly acid reaction. The official name is Oleum Rosæ. Probably all the oil of rose of the Turkish market is adulterated. It should, when slowly cooled to 50°F., deposit a crystalline substance, called a *stearopten*, free from oxygen.

345. **India-rubber:** caoutchouc or India-rubber is the dried, milky juice obtained from several trees growing in the tropics. When freshly obtained the juice is acid in reaction. It contains several hydrocarbons which are soluble in ether, benzole, carbon disulphide, chloroform, and turpentine, but insoluble in water and in alcohol. It is hard and tough in the cold, softens on heating, becomes elastic, melts, and, on cooling, is soft and viscid. It combines directly with sulphur, hardening, and forming **Vulcanized India-rubber;** carbon disulphide is used to facilitate the union. Mixed with half its weight of sulphur, **Vulcanite** or **Ebonite** is formed.*

Dental rubber: India-rubber is prepared for vulcanizing by incorporating with it either sulphur alone, or some of its compounds; a coloring matter is also added, in many cases mercuric sulphide (vermilion) but white clay, oxide of zinc, and calcium carbonate are also used. Para rubber is the kind used, the vermilion being added when a "red rubber" is desired, and the oxide of zinc or some form of

---

* Both India-rubber and gutta-percha resist the action of most chemical substances, and hence are dissolved with difficulty.

aluminium silicate, as white clay, when a "white rubber." "Black rubbers" are the result of vulcanizing the rubber directly with sulphur, no pigment being added. It is claimed that the various pigments, when in large percentage, produce soft, inflexible rubbers. Difference in shade of red is supposed to be due to difference in percentage and kind of vermilion used.

346. **Gutta-percha** resembles caoutchouc in chemical characters, and is the *hardened milky juice* of an Indian tree. It is *harder than rubber and less elastic*, but becomes quite soft in hot water, and can then be moulded. When purified it is brown-red, of a density of 0.979, electrified by friction, and is a very slow conductor of electricity. It has, at ordinary temperatures, *considerable tenacity*, is as strong as leather but less flexible. At 115°F., it is pasty and still very tenacious. At 103° and 104°F., it may be spread out into sheets, or drawn out into threads or tubes. Its suppleness and ductility diminish as the temperature is lowered, and it has not at any temperature the elastic extensibility of caoutchouc. Softened by heat, it may be worked by pressure into any shape. It is *soluble in carbon disulphide*, benzene, chloroform, in hot oil of turpentine. *It is insoluble in water*, in which it is best preserved, *resists alkalies, hy-*

drochloric acid, and hydrofluoric acid. Gutta-percha alters, and this fact must not be forgotten. If in thin sheets or threads, at a temperature of from 77° to 86°F., it gradually becomes useless and gives off a pungent odor. The change is due to oxidation.

Use in dentistry: gutta-percha is used as a plastic filling material. It is an ingredient of Hill's Stopping. Together with oxide of zinc, it is used as a filling material. According to Flagg it is easy to raise the gutta-percha to any reasonable degree of temperature at which it becomes plastic, by simply increasing the relative quantity of inorganic admixture, but this very increase is destructive to the value of the gutta-percha.

As found it is often adulterated, but owing to advanced knowledge pure gutta-percha can be more readily obtained than formerly. We have to distinguish between two forms of adulteration, those used for the purpose of fraud in weight,—that is, foreign substances such as small stones, sand, and pieces of bark; and, second, those that combine with it to injure its strength, –pitch, tar, etc. But, strange to say, none of these latter interfere with its hardness when cold. This last adulteration the dentist has to guard against, and therefore to test its strength it should be slightly warmed. The two best grades are known to the trade as "G. P. A." and "G. P. F." The G. P. A. is of a light-brown color, and the G. P. F., when sheeted, is a beautiful marbled white. (Meriam).

For dark-colored stopping Meriam uses G. P. A., and for light, G. P. F., and for medium, the two mixed.

For convenience they had best be bought sheeted, keeping in mind that the different forms in which it is offered do not indicate different varieties. The gutta percha should always be fresh, and feel soft and unctuous in handling.

The splint gutta percha, often called pure, which is occasionally recommended, is adulterated with tar or resin, and it can readily be seen that such adulteration must injure its fibre.

Pure gutta percha can be obtained by dissolving in chloroform, drawing off with a siphon, and then distilling off the chloroform, or dissolving in disulphide of carbon and filtering through animal charcoal. These methods need not be used to-day, as G. P. F. sheeted will be found white enough for all purposes. (Meriam).

Meriam uses oils for softening the surface.

347. **Artificial gutta perchas** are now made. According to Zingler copal resin, sulphur, petroleum, casein, tannin, and ammonia are the substances used in manufacture.

348. **Camphor.—**
Theoretical constitution: $C_{10}H_{16}O$. It is sometimes classified among the aldehydes, but for convenience will be considered among the hydrocarbons on account of its oils. Camphor is a concrete substance derived from camphor-laurel tree; soft, tough cakes, easily powdered on addition of a little alcohol; translucent, strong fragrant odor, aromatic bitter cooling taste, volatile, inflammable; lighter than water; slightly soluble in water, but soluble in alcohol, ether, chloroform; dissolved in alcohol forms *spirit of camphor*, from which it may be precipitated by water; dissolved in water, containing a little alcohol and a little magnesium carbonate, forms *camphor-water;* boiled with bromine, forms *mono-bromated camphor*, $C_{10}H_{15}BrO$. Gum-camphor has a rotatory movement on water

which is stopped by the least trace of fat. Camphor is a local irritant, stimulant, and poison. It is a constituent of celluloid.

Spirit of camphor is locally employed in dentistry to allay pain. With ether it is used as a local anæsthetic.

Taken internally, it is poisonous, although recovery from its effects are usual. The treatment consists in use of emetics and castor oil.

349. The official *Oleum Camphoræ* is made by heating camphor. It is a light reddish-brown fluid, of the taste and odor of camphor.

350. **Resins, Balsams, Gum-resins, etc.:** *resins* are *oxidized terpenes*, produced by the oxidation of the essential oils of plants. They are brittle, solid, transparent bodies, of no well marked odor or taste, soluble in alcohol, insoluble in water, combustible, yield a lather with alkalies.

Resins are employed in the manufacture of varnishes: copal resin is prepared by simple exudation.

351. **Guaiacum** resin is prepared by destructive distillation, and in other ways, from a tree growing in South America and the West Indies. It comes in large, irregular, semi-transparent, brittle pieces, externally of an olive or deep green color, internally red. It has a slight balsamic odor, and leaves a hot acrid sensation in the mouth and throat. It is wholly soluble in alcohol, partly soluble in water.

352. **Gum-resins** are resins *mixed with gum, sugar, etc., in plants*, and are insoluble in water, soluble in glycerine, turpentine, and strong alcohol. They are a mixture of several bodies, hence have not a definite chemical formula.

353. **Myrrh** is an exudation from an Arabian or African tree, and is a *gum-resin*. It is

of reddish-yellow or reddish-brown color, of fragrant, strong, peculiar odor, and bitter, aromatic taste. It is translucent, pulverizable, and brittle. It should dissolve in fifteen times its weight of water, when rubbed up with an equal weight of sal-ammoniac. It has a resinous fracture, and makes a light yellowish powder. Inferior kinds are darker, less translucent, and less odorous. The resin of myrrh is called *myrrhic acid*. Myrrh forms an emulsion with water, and is soluble in alcohol and in ether. An old tincture of it has been shown to have an acid reaction.* It is used in dentistry as a local application. The powder is also used in dentifrices.

354. **Gums** are non-volatile, colloid, almost tasteless bodies, occurring in the juices of plants. (See Carbohydrates).

355. **Sandarach:** sandarach is a substance composed of three resins, which are of different solubility in alcohol, ether, and turpentine. Sandarach comes in tears, which are small, and of a pale yellow or brown color, and more or less transparent: they are dry and brittle. Sandarach is inflammable, and melts on being heated. It is soluble in alcohol, ether, and warm oil of turpentine. It is used in dentistry, dissolved in alcohol, as a *varnish*.

The name sandarach is sometimes given to the disulphide of arsenic, which, however, has nothing to do with the resin sandarach, and should not be confused with it.

356. **Lac:** lac consists of resin, soluble coloring matter, lacin, wax, and salts. The resin is about 90 per cent. of

---

*Brackett.

lac. **Shell Lac** is one of the commercial varieties of lac, and is an exudate from several kinds of trees growing in the East Indies; it is caused by punctures of insects. It is prepared from the crude lac by melting, straining, and pouring on a flat, smooth surface. Shellac comes in thin, shining, hard, brittle fragments, odorless, insoluble in water, but freely soluble in alcohol, more so in warm alcohol. It is used in dentistry as a *varnish*.

357. **Naphthalene:** naphthalene or naphthalin, $C_{10}H_8$, or $(C_{10}H_7)H$, is a *coal tar product*, distilling from this substance between 356° F. and 428°. It crystallizes in large, white, rhombic plates, of silvery lustre, and characteristic odor, and of a biting, somewhat aromatic taste. It melts at 174.5° F., and boils at 420° to 428°. It volatilizes very sensibly, even at ordinary temperatures. It is *inflammable*, burning with a luminous and very smoky flame. Its specific gravity is 1.15. When melted, it dissolves sulphur, phosphorus, iodine, and indigo. It is insoluble in water, but soluble in hot alcohol, benzene, and ether, also in wood-spirit, chloroform, carbon disulphide, petroleum spirit, fixed and volatile oils. It is insoluble in alkaline or dilute acid solutions, slightly soluble in concentrated acetic acid. It is an *antiseptic* substance, and, when used as dressing, should be thoroughly purified by recrystallization from alcohol or by distillation with steam. It is not corrosive, and when *entirely* pure is odorless; it is, however, almost impossible to obtain it free from the characteristic odor, but the latter may be entirely overcome by adding a few drops of oil of bergamot to 4 oz. of the naphthalin. In powdering naphthalin, addition of a little alcohol greatly facilitates the operation. As an antiseptic, the best results have been obtained from use of it in powdered form. Combinations of this substance with iodoform and with boric acid should make valuable antiseptics. The naphthalin made in this country can be

reduced to a moderately fine powder; the pure, imported naphthalin cannot be reduced to powder except when very cold. Attention should be paid to the fact that it is *inflammable*.

358. **Naphthols:** $C_{10}H_7O$. There are a number of these compounds. What is commercially known as "hydronaphthol," is properly, *beta-hydro-naphthol*, has powerful antiseptic properties (1-7200 limit) and is *non-poisonous*.

[That which is called in commerce "beta-naphthol," is properly, according to Wolff, *betanahydro-naphthol*, and according to Bouchardat, Kaposi, Miner, Piffard, and others, is poisonous. To distinguish them dissolve in alcohol. Hydronaphthol (non-poisonous) dissolves in 10 parts alcohol, with a deep-brown coloration, while beta-naphthol dissolves without coloration].

Naphthol used medicinally crystallizes in thin, shining plates, readily soluble in alcohol, ether, chloroform, and fatty oils.

359. **Ethyl series of radicals, alcohols, and carbohydrates.**

Before considering the alcohols, it is well for the student to become familiar with the ethyl series of radicals.

TABLE 25. ETHYL SERIES OF RADICALS.

Compound Radicals.	Hydrides of, or Marsh Gases.
Methyl, CH_3	Methane, CH_3H or CH_4
Ethyl, C_2H_5	(marsh gas).
	Ethane, C_2H_5H or C_2H_6
Propyl, C_3H	Propane, etc.
Butyl, C_4H_9	Butane, etc.
Amyl, C_5H_{11}	etc., etc.
etc., etc.	etc., etc.

TABLE 25—*Continued.*

Oxides or Ethers.	Hydrates, or Alcohols.
$(CH_3)_2O$, or C_2H_6O, methyl ether.	CH_3HO, or CH_4O, wood spirit, methyl alcohol.
$(C_2H_5)_2O$, or $C_4H_{10}O$, ethyl ether.	C_2H_5HO, or C_2H_6O, ordinary alcohol.
etc.	etc.
etc.	etc.
etc.	$C_5H_{11}HO$, or $C_5H_{12}O$, amyl
etc.	alcohol, fusel oil.

360. Theoretical formation: the starting point in forming these compounds is with the *hydrates* or alcohols, and not with the compound radicals themselves. For example, when an alcohol, as C_2H_6O, is oxidized with *oxygen limited in amount*, there results what is called an *aldehyde* or dehydrated alcohol, as C_2H_4O, two atoms of hydrogen being withdrawn and *no oxygen* added.

If, however, the alcohol is oxidized with *plentiful oxygen*, an atom of oxyen is added in place of the two atoms of hydrogen withdrawn, and an *acid* is formed; thus, from C_2H_6O comes $C_2H_4O_2$, or acetic acid.

361. Tabular view of aldehydes and acids of ethyl series of radicals:

Radicals.	Alcohols.	Aldehydes.	Acids.
Methyl. CH_3	CH_4O	CH_2O	CH_2O_2 (forming acid).
Ethyl, C_2H_5	C_2H_6O	C_2H_4O	$C_2H_4O_2$ (acetic acid).
etc.			
etc.			

Compounds of the hydrocarbon radicals with chlorine, bromine, etc., are called *haloid ethers*, while salts proper of the hydrocarbon radicals are called *compound ethers*. Ethers are, in general then, compounds of the hydrocarbon radicals other than the marsh gases, alcohols, aldehydes, and acids. (See section 407).

362. **Alcohols:*** alcohols may be regarded

*It will be noticed that the chemist's conception of alcohols includes many substances, such as glycerine, which resemble little our ordinary alcohol.

as substances derived from hydrocarbons by replacing one or more hydrogen atoms by the radical hydroxyl, HO. Thus ethyl hydride, (C_2H_5) H, becomes ethyl alcohol, (C_2H_5) HO, by exchanging one atom of H for the radical HO. Alcohols are called monatomic, diatomic, or triatomic, according as HO replaces one, two, or three atoms of H in a hydrocarbon. *Ordinary alcohol is a monatomic alcohol*, diatomic alcohols are also called *glycols*, and of triatomic alcohols glycerine is a notable example.

The alcohols are *hydrates*, resembling the inorganic hydrates, as, for example, potassium hydrate, KHO; common alcohol is ethyl hydrate, C_2H_5 HO.

363. **Alcohol.—**

Synonyms: ethyl alcohol, common alcohol, ethyl hydrate, ethylic alcohol, Spirit of Wine.

Theoretical constitution: C_2H_5HO, hydrate of the radical ethyl, two atoms of carbon, six of hydrogen, and one of oxygen; formula sometimes written C_2H_6O. Molecular weight, 46. 24 parts by weight of carbon, 6 of hydrogen, and 16 of oxygen.

Preparation: alcohol is obtained by the fermentation of saccharine liquids, brought about by the growth of a microscopic plant called yeast.

Grape sugar or glucose yields alcohol when fermented:

$$C_6H_{12}O_6 = 2CO_2 + 2C_2H_6HO.$$
Glucose — carbon dioxide — alcohol

The fermented liquid is distilled, and a dilute alcohol obtained; repeated distillations will finally give an alcohol containing about 14 per cent. of water. To obtain alcohol, free from from water, the former must be mixed with half its weight of lime, and the alcohol distilled off from the mixture.

Properties: absolute alcohol containing no water is a transparent, mobile, volatile, colorless liquid of an agreeable, pungent odor, characteristic of itself, and a burning taste, boiling at 173° F., of a sp. gr. 0.794, and has never been solidified. It is neutral in reaction, inflammable, *burning with a non-luminous flame, dissolves resins, essential oils,* alkaline hydroxides, alkaloids, calcium chloride, mercuric chloride, and many other substances, but especially those rich in hydrogen. Mixed with water, a *contraction* of volume occurs, with production of heat. *Its attraction for water is very great; it absorbs moisture from the air and abstracts it from membranes, tissues, etc.* Shaken with pure, colorless sulphuric acid, it should not become colored. (Presence of fusel oil). It is poisonous.

364. *Absolute alcohol:* commercial usage accepts as

absolute, alcohol of not less than 99.5 to 99.7 per cent. of sp. gr. (at 60° F.) 0.7938, boiling at 172.4° F.

Alcohol, U. S. P., is 91 per cent. by weight of real alcohol, or 94 per cent. by volume, the rest being water.

Alcohol dilutum is 45.5 .per cent. by weight, or 53 per cent. by volume.

Spirit of wine (*rectified spirit*) is 84 per cent. by weight. *Proof-spirit* is 49 per cent.

Spirits are substances distilled from fermented liquors; brandy, whisky, rum, and gin are examples. They contain from 35 to 45 per cent. of alcohol by volume, although some specimens run as high as 50 per cent. (brandy, rum) and some as high as 60 per cent., (whisky).

Wines contain from 6 to 25 per cent., sherry and port being the strongest.

Beers average 4 to 5 per cent., though some are very weak, containing only 1 per cent.

Use in dentistry: alcohol is used in dentistry for various purposes, as styptic, antiseptic, obtunding agent, for drying cavities, in lotions, gargles, etc., etc., and as a solvent and preservative.

Toxicology: the stomach pump should be used in cases of poisoning by alcohol, and, if the bladder is distended, use of the catheter is indicated. Cold affusion to the head, fresh air, ammonia, and strong coffee are valuable, especially if the stupor be intense.

365. **Tinctures** are alcoholic solutions of the medicinal agents in plants, prepared by maceration, digestion, or percolation.

366. **Fluid Extracts:** these preparations are concentrated, and represent considerable drug-power in small bulk. Each Cubic centimetre represents a gram of the crude drug.

367. **Wood Spirit:** methyl alcohol, or wood spirit, is methyl hydrate, CH_3HO, called pyroligneous ether,

pyroxylic spirit; wood naphtha is largely composed of it. It is made by distillation from wood. It is a liquid of spirituous odor, and is inflammable.*

368. **Fusel Oil** is amylic alcohol, $C_5H_{11}HO$, hydrate of the radical amyl, called also *potato spirit*. Fusel oil proper is a mixture of several alcohols, of which amylic alcohol is one. It is made from residues left in the still, after common alcohol is distilled off. It has a peculiar, irritating odor, and is very poisonous. Is produced in the fermentation of grain, hence often an impurity in whisky.

369. **Glycerine.—**
Theoretical constitution: this substance is a triatomic alcohol derived from propane (C_3H_7) H, by substitution of 3HO for *three* atoms of H. The formula for propane may be written C_3H_8; take away three atoms of H and we have C_3H_5; add 3HO and there results C_3H_53HO, or $C_3H_8O_3$. Glycerine is, then, the hydrate of a radical, C_3H_5, called *glyceryl*, *trilenyl*, or *propenyl*. Hence the modern term for glycerine, namely, *trilenyl hydrate*.

Properties and uses: glycerine is obtained from fats by treatment with alkalies, **soap** being formed and glycerine liberated. The process is called **saponification.** Pure glycerine is a colorless, or light straw yellow, thick, syrupy liquid, unctuous, inodorous, of sharp, sweet taste; soluble in water, alcohol, and oils, but not in ether or chloroform. *It is valuable*

---

*Methylated spirit is composed of 9 parts ordinary alcohol to 1 part wood alcohol.

as a solvent for many medicinal substances, official solutions of which in glycerine are called glycerites. Glycerine is permanent and does not evaporate or dry at any temperature. Official **Glycerinum** has a sp. gr. of 1.25. It dissolves about fifty familiar substances used in medicine, among which are boric acid, borax, carbolic acid, creasote, potassium iodide, arsenic, alum, zinc salts, morphine salts, tannate of quinine.

Use in dentistry: its value in dentistry is as a solvent, and when combined with other substances, as an emollient and solvent. Teeth lotions contain glycerine, as for example the following: tincture of quillaia, eau-de-cologne, water, borax, glycerine, with coloring. Glycerine is found to be of service in the process of vulcanizing India rubber, giving the latter the property of resisting oils and fats. Glycerine may be used to detect carbolic acid adulteration in creasote. (See Creasote).

370. **Glycerites:** these are solutions of various substances in glycerine. Those most commonly used in dentistry are the glycerites of *carbolic acid, gallic acid, tannic acid,* * *sodium borate, starch, thymol,* and *pepsin.*

The glycerite of borax (sodium borate) becomes acid and unfit for use after a time.

371. **Boroglyceride :** boroglyceride, $C_3H_5 BO_3$, is *glyceryl borate,* or tritenyl borate, made by heating boracic acid, $H BO_3$, with glycerine, C_3H_53HO, or $C_3H_8O_3$:

---

*The glycerite of tannin is used as an application to spongy gums.

$C_3H_8O_3$ + H_3BO_3 + heat = $C_3H_5BO_3$ + $3H_2O$.
Glycerine.   boracic acid.   boroglyceride.   water.

6 parts of boric acid in fine powder and 9 of glycerine are heated together in a porcelain dish at 302° F., stirring well until aqueous vapors cease to be given off, and a homogeneous, transparent mass is formed, which becomes hard and tough on cooling. Care is taken not to heat the mixture too strongly, as that would render the product dark colored. Boroglyceride is a colorless, tough, solid substance, soluble in water, and in alcohol, odorless, tasteless, not poisonous. *It is used in dentistry as an antiseptic*, and, in combination with sodium sulphite, for bleaching teeth.

372. **Sodium glyceroborate:** this substance is made by heating equal parts of sodium borate with glycerine. Soluble, deliquescent, odorless, antiseptic.

373. **Calcium glyceroborate:** made by heating equal parts of calcium borate with glycerine. Soluble, deliquescent, odorless, antiseptic.

374. **Creasote:** creasote, **Creasotum**, is a mixture of substances, but consists chiefly of *creasol*, $C_8H_{10}O_7$, and *guaiacol*, $C_7H_8O_2$. *It is a product of the distillation of wood-tar*, occurring in the lowest layer of the distilled liquid. It is colorless, or faintly yellow, when fresh and pure, of sp. gr. 1.046, U. S. P., but usually varying from 1.040 to 1.090. It boils at 392°-410° F. *It is of disagreeable, penetrating, smoky odor, and burning, caustic taste.* It is soluble in 80 parts of cold water, and 24 of hot, and in all proportions in alcohol, ether, acetic acid, and carbon disulphide. Ignited, it burns with a white,

sooty flame. It forms a clear mixture with collodion; precipitates solutions of gum and of albumin. On growing old, it gradually becomes brownish in color. It may be distinguished from carbolic acid by not solidifying when cooled, by not coloring ferric chloride permanently, by its lower boiling point, and by being *insoluble in glycerine.*

A specimen of creasote, if pure, should leave no stain on paper, after being dropped on it and volatilized by heat. Mixed with equal volume of collodion, it should not cause the latter to gelatinize.

Creasote water, Aqua Creasoti, consists of one fluidrachm of creasote to one pint of water. Solidified creasote is made from 10 parts of collodion to 15 of creasote.

Use in dentistry: creasote is used as an obtunding agent, styptic, antiseptic, to counteract any acid in a tooth cavity, to harden the contents of dental tubuli and render them imperishable.

Toxicology: *creasote is poisonous*, in overdoses causing giddiness, obscurity of vision, depressed heart action, etc., etc.

The treatment consists in administration of white of egg, milk, wheat flour, and stimulants, as aromatic spirit of ammonia. An emetic should be first administered.

375. **Phenyl alcohol or carbolic acid.—**[*]
Synonyms: phenol, phenylic alcohol, phenic acid. Official name, Acidum Carbolicum.

Theoretical constitution; carbolic "acid" is really an alcohol, C_6H_5HO, or hydrate of the radical phenyl[†], C_6H_5, graphically

$$\begin{array}{c} CH-CH \\ / \quad \quad \backslash \\ HC \quad \quad \quad C-O-H \\ \backslash \quad \quad / \\ HC = CH \end{array}$$

It is by weight composed of 72 parts carbon, 6 of hydrogen, and 16 of oxygen. Molecular weight, 94.

Preparation: crude carbolic acid is obtained by distilling coal-tar between the temperatures of 302°F. and 374°F.

Official carbolic acid is a pure phenol, obtained by distilling crude carbolic acid between 338°F. and 365°, separating from other products, and purifying by repeated crystallization.

Properties: carbolic acid, in the pure state, forms needle-shaped, colorless, interlacing crystals, neutral in reaction, having a characteristic, slightly aromatic odor, and pungent, caustic taste; the taste is sweetish when the acid is

---

[*] Called "acid" because of its ready combination with bases forming carbolates or phenates, so-called.

[†] This radical phenyl belongs to the aromatic series.

slightly diluted. *It produces a white eschar on animal tissues, having a benumbing (caustic) effect.* When pure, carbolic acid is permanent in the air, and not affected by light, but the ordinary acid usually changes to pink or red. The color does not in the least impair the medicinal value of the phenol.

Water dissolves 6 per cent. of phenol, according to Squibb. Five parts of phenol dissolve in 1 part of alcohol; 4 in one of ether; 3 in 1 of chloroform; *7 in 2 of glycerine;* 4 in 7 of olive oil. It is also soluble in benzol, carbon disulphide, fixed and volatile oils. Variations in the melting and boiling points of phenol are due to the greater or less proportions of water in it. Phenol is liquid at ordinary temperatures, when it contains 8 to 10 per cent. of water. The best grades in the market contain at least 2 per cent. of water, and often over 4. *One volume of liquefied carbolic acid*, containing 5 per cent. of water, *forms, with 1 volume of glycerine, a clear mixture*, which is not rendered turbid by the addition of 3 volumes of water (absence of creosote and cresylic acid). Carbolic acid should have no odor of creosote nor of volatile sulphur compounds. A clean, sweet, phenol odor is one of the best signs of good quality in carbolic acid. It should also be hard and dry. An anhydrous acid, fused with from 4 to 5 per cent. of water, should, on cooling, become a solid mass of crystals again. The crystals become liquid at a temperature of from 96.8°F. to 197.6°. When reddened and liquefied, carbolic acid resembles creosote, but gives, dissolved in water, a *permanent* violet-blue with ferric chloride, *while creosote gives a blue which changes to green then to brown.* The crystals may be prepared, for antiseptic use, by warming the bottle till they liquefy, then adding a few drops of glycerine. *Carbolic acid is a valuable antiseptic.* It coagulates albumin and is poisonous. Death has followed external application of the acid, in large quantity, to extensive surfaces.

Use in dentistry: as an antiseptic, disinfectant, styptic, escharotic, obtunding agent, local anæsthetic, etc., etc.

Toxicology: carbolic acid is a powerful poison, being corrosive and also producing coma, the acid being rapidly diffused, and the odor of it, after death from poisoning, noticed everywhere throughout the body, even in the brain. The treatment is to give emetics, as, for example, apomorphine hydrochlorate subcutaneously, then raw eggs *ad libitum*, and magnesia suspended in a mixture of olive and castor oils; lime water with sugar is also recommended. The coma must be treated as in cases of opium poisoning, by artificial respiration, galvanism, etc., etc. Chances of recovery from poisonous doses of the acid are not good. The urine should be watched, when carbolic acid is being used, and if it becomes dark-colored, it is a sign that too much of the agent is being used.

376. **Various preparations containing carbolic acid.**

Robinson's remedy is composed of equal parts of caustic potash (potassium hydrate) and carbolic acid, mixed by trituration.

Chloral hydrate and carbolic acid, when mixed in proportion of 1 part of chloral to 1.7 parts of the acid, liquefy, and the liquid is soluble in water in all proportions.

377. **Phenates:** carbolic acid, with solutions of the alkalies, forms soluble compounds called phenates or phenylates, which are capable of dissolving large quantities of phenol.

378. **Phenol sodique or sodium phenate:** this substance, C_6H_5NaO, is also called carbolate of sodium, sodium phenoxide, Sodæ Phenas. It is made by the direct combination of carbolic acid with sodium oxide; caustic soda and a little water are used in the reaction, which is as follows:

$$C_6H_5HO + NaHO = C_6H_5NaO + H_2O.$$
Carbolic acid   sodium hydrate   sodium phenoxide   water

Sodium phenate occurs in form of acicular crystals of light pinkish color, liquefied by heat. It is used in dentistry as an astringent, styptic, disinfectant, etc., etc. It is freely soluble in water.

379. **Phenol terchloride:** this substance is of Russian introduction, and is extemporaneously prepared by mixing one part of a four per cent. solution of carbolic acid with five parts of a saturated solution of chlorinated lime; the filtrate is said to be 25 times more powerful than carbolic acid. According to some authorities it may be made by passing a stream of chlorine gas through pure melted carbolic acid, until a violet color is seen.

Dental uses: **Phenol terchloride** is used as an antiseptic and disinfectant. It is combined with iodoform, and used as a capping and filling material, incorporated with decalcified dead bone.

380. **Phenol-camphor*** is best obtained by heating

---

* Synonyms: Carbol-camphor, Camphor-carbol, Campho-Phenique.

pure crystallized carbolic acid (phenol) until it fuses, and then gradually adding gum camphor; a clear liquid is obtained which is characteristic on account of its permanence. In preparing this substance, use equal parts of camphor and carbolic acid: it remains liquid for an indefinite time, and does not solidify on being subjected to the low temperature of a frigorific mixture of snow and sodium chloride. Phenol-camphor [$C_8H_{11}O(?)$] is a limpid, colorless, volatile, refractive liquid, possessing the fragrant odor of camphor, entirely extinguishing the one of carbolic acid, and has a sweetish, camphoraceous, but biting taste, not as caustic as that of carbolic acid, somewhat benumbing the tongue. It is *soluble in alcohol*, ether, chloroform, and ethereal oils, but *insoluble in glycerine and in water*, being heavier than the latter. When ignited it burns with a smoky flame. There is reason to believe that it is a chemical compound.' Dr. Schaefer has used phenol-camphor as a *local anæsthetic* in tooth-ache, introducing it on cotton into the cavity of a carious tooth. This substance can be likewise used as an *antiseptic*. It mixes well with paraffin, cosmoline, and a number of oils. In impregnating cotton gauze (antiseptic gauze) phenol-camphor may be used as a substitute for carbolic acid. Phenol-camphor is less irritating, less caustic than carbolic acid, and has also the advantage of possessing a pleasant odor. It is used in dentifrices.

381. **Resorcin:** this substance has for its formula $C_6H_6O_2$, or better $C_6H_4\begin{cases} HO \\ HO, \end{cases}$ from which it will be seen that it differs from carbolic acid, in that the radical HO has been substituted for one atom of hydrogen, carbolic acid being C_6H_5HO, and resorcin, $C_6H_4 2HO$.

It is made from gum-resins, such as galbanum, extract of sapin wood, or Brazil wood, by fusing them with caustic potash. It occurs in the form of colorless crystals, of somewhat sweetish, slightly pungent taste, very soluble in water, less so in alcohol, ether, glycerine, and vaseline, insoluble in chloroform, and carbon disulphide. It is not so irritating as carbolic acid. It is said to be a disinfectant and local anæsthetic.

*It is used in dentistry as an antiseptic.** Strong solutions are caustic, but dilute ones merely astringent.

382. **Menthol:** this substance is really *menthyl alcohol*, $C_{10}H_{20}O$, and is found in peppermint oil. It is a white, crystalline solid of but slight peppermint-oil odor when pure, soluble in alcohol, and in the essential oils. It has been called peppermint camphor, Japanese camphor, peppermint stearescence, and stearoptene of peppermint, but, in constitution, is a monatomic alcohol. *It is an antiseptic and local anæsthetic.* It is used in dentistry as an obtunding agent, local anæsthetic, and antiseptic. Care must be taken in applying it, as small doses, taken internally, have been known to produce vomiting.

383. **Eucalyptol:** $C_{12}H_{20}O$, liquid, colorless, of aromatic odor. It is derived from the leaves of *Eucalyptus globulus*, and is sometimes called eucalyptus oil. It is but slightly soluble in water, but is soluble in alcohol. It is an efficient *antiseptic*, and is used in dentistry on this account, and as an astringent, styptic, and *local anæsthetic. It has solvent action on gutta percha.* The purest eucalyptol is as clear as water, of specific gravity 0.910 to 0.920 at 60°F., and boils between 338°F. and 343°. There is in the market an eucalyptus oil which differs from the genuine eucalyptol; 90 per cent. alcohol makes a clear solution of eucalyptol, while the eucalyptus oil is but slightly soluble in it.

Alantol: $C_{20}H_{32}O$. A liquid stearopten found besides helenin in the root of elecampane.

---

*Said to be a stronger antiseptic than carbolic acid, and not so poisonous.

384. **Myrtol:** myrtol is obtained from the distillation of the leaves of the myrtle; it is a liquid possessing the characteristic perfume of the plant. It is of less density than water, evaporates at the ordinary temperature, stains paper, but the stains disappear entirely. It has a warm, slightly acrid taste, soon followed by a sensation of freshness. It is said to be an excellent *disinfectant* and an energetic *antiseptic*.

385. **Safrol:** this substance is obtained by fractional distillation from crude oil of camphor. It has a strong sassafras odor and taste, and is used for disguising the taste of other substances.

386. **Thymol:** formula $C_{10}H_{14}O$. There are many thymols. The one found in essence of wild thyme is used in dentistry, and may be procured by treating the essence with potassium hydrate; insoluble in water, antiseptic. Freely soluble in alcohol. Used in dentistry, combined with glycerine, as an antiseptic.

387. **Carbohydrates:** these are substances containing six atoms of carbon, or a multiple of six, and twice as many atoms of hydrogen as of oxygen. They closely resemble the alcohols, and may be divided into three classes: *saccharoses, glucoses,* and *amyloses.*[*]

Of the saccharoses, cane sugar and milk sugar are important.

388. **Cane Sugar:** saccharose, cane sugar, beet sugar, $C_{12}H_{22}O_{11}$, does not occur in the body; white, inodorous, *very sweet*. Cold water dissolves three times its weight; insoluble in alcohol. Converted by ferments first into mixture of glucose and lævulose, called *invert* sugar.

---

[*]*Saccharin* is not a carbohydrate, but the sulphinide of benzoic acid. (See Benzoic Acid).

Blackens with H_2SO_4. (Glucose unites with the acid and does not blacken). Cane sugar occurs in the juices of many plants, fruits, flowers, and in honey. It is found also in the juice of the sugar cane, in sorghum, beet-root, and sugar-maple. *The most soluble sugar* as well as the sweetest and most crystallizable.*

389. **Milk-sugar:** lactose, sugar of milk, Saccharum Lactis, $C_{12}H_{22}O_{11}H_2O$, one of the constituents of milk of mammals; rarely found in vegetables. To prepare it, coagulate skimmed milk with a little acetic acid, heat, filter, concentrate filtrate by evaporation, let crystallize, dissolve in boiling water and re-crystallize. Odorless, white, *hard*, occurs in four-sided, rhombic prisms; *taste faintly sweet*, gritty between the teeth; soluble in seven parts cold water, one of boiling; insoluble in even 60 per cent. alcohol; not charred by H_2SO_4; not directly fermented by yeast, but easily when cheese is added; does not form a syrup with water. *Used in tooth powders and in triturating medicines.*

390. **Glucose:** $C_6H_{12}O_6$, is raisin sugar and grape sugar; it is also called dextrose and starch sugar. It is found in vegetables, fruits, and honey. Is white, inodorous, and soluble in its own weight of water. *Only one third as sweet as cane sugar.* Ferments directly with yeast, and when in contact with decaying animal matter. Made on a large scale from corn starch, by boiling with dilute sulphuric acid, neutralizing with lime, draining off clear syrup, evaporating, and allowing to crystallize. Fermented, it decomposes into alcohol and carbonic acid. *Valuable reducing agent.*

391. The **amyloses** are starch, dextrine, gum, etc. **Starch** is found in grains of cereals and in potatoes; is food of plants becoming sugar as they ripen. Insoluble

---

*Dissolved in water forms Syrupus Simplex, or simple syrup.

in cold water, alcohol, or ether; in boiling water it becomes gelatinous, but does not dissolve ; heated dry it becomes dextrine, which is converted into glucose by action of diastase (a ferment found in cross-spired barley).

Dextrine: is an amorphous, yellowish-white, soluble substance; does not give blue coloration with iodine; basis of mucilage. Reduces alkaline copper solutions.

The formula for dextrine is probably $C_6H_{10}O_5$. That of starch some multiple of $C_6H_{10}O_5$.

392. **Honey:** honey is practically a strong solution of dextro-glucose and lævo-glucose in water. Analyses show that the lævulose and dextrose are nearly equal in amount. Fictitious honey is sometimes manufactured from glucose and flavoring materials; the presence of glucose, as an adulteration, is indicated by increased proportion of ash, and by the presence of a notable amount of calcium sulphate. *Honeys* are preparations of medicinal substances in honey, the clarified article being used. *Honey of sodium borate* contains a drachm of borax to the ounce of clarified honey.

393. **Gums:** these bodies are probably carbohydrates. They are a peculiar class of bodies, occurring in the juices of plants. They are entirely non-volatile, of little or no taste, uncrystallizable, and colloidal. They are either soluble in water, or swell up in contact with it. They are not capable of being fermented by yeast and are insoluble in alcohol.

394. **Gum Arabic** is the dried exudation from the bark of various species of *Acaciæ*. Picked Turkey gum is the finest, and occurs in colorless lumps, full of minute cracks. It consists chiefly of calcium arabate, the calcium salt of arabic or gummic acid. It is inodorous, of feeble, slightly sweetish taste, and with water forms a viscid mixture, called a *mucilage*. The mucilage is used in dentistry as an emollient.

395. **Gum Tragacanth:** this is a white, or yellowish substance which is only very slightly soluble in water, and swells up in it. It contains usually about 60 per cent. of a substance which yields *pectic acid*, also 8 or 10 per cent. of soluble gum, probably *arabin*, the rest being starch, cellulose, water, etc., etc.

396. **Cellulose:** *Cellulin, lignin,* $C_6H_{10}O_5$, is an isomer of starch, and constitutes the essential part of the solid framework or cellular tissue of plants. Swedish filter-paper, linen rags, and cotton wool are more or less pure cellulose. Soluble only in a solution of cupric oxide in ammonia.

Absorbent cotton: consists essentially of cellulose.

397. **Collodion** is made by dissolving 4 parts of pyroxylin in a mixture of 26 parts alcohol and 70 of ether. Pyroxylin is prepared by steeping cotton in a mixture of nitric and sulphuric acids.

Flexible collodion is collodion to which 5 per cent. of turpentine and 3 per cent. of castor oil have been added.

Cantharidal collodion is made from powdered cantharides and flexible collodion, with sometimes addition of a little Venice turpentine, to prevent contraction on drying.

Iodized collodion is a solution of iodine in collodion, 20 grains to the ounce. *Iodoform collodion* contains 1 part iodoform to 15 of collodion.

Styptic collodion contains 20 per cent. of tannic acid.

Collodion is a colorless liquid, of ethereal odor, and very inflammable; exposed to the air it rapidly evaporates, leaving a thin, transparent, strongly contractile film of dinitro-cellulose, which is insoluble in water or in alcohol. It is precipitated by carbolic acid. Collodion is used in dentistry as a local application in alveolar abscesses, in combination with other agents in odontalgia, on cotton as temporary filling, as a styptic, etc., etc. A colored preparation of collodion is used to coat the surface of plaster models. Collodion, when thickened, may be rendered thinner by dilution with a solution of 1 part alcohol in 3 parts ether.

Cantharidal collodion is used as a counter-irritant in dental periostitis. A German preparation of cantharidal collodion has been proposed by Dieterich to contain—in 1,900 parts of collodion—3 parts of cantharidin and 97 of oil of rape. The German blistering collodion is stronger than the U. S.

398. **Celluloid:** pyroxylin is reduced to a pulp, mixed with camphor, oxide of zinc, and vermilion, subjected to immense pressure, and seasoned.

ETHERS, GLUCOSIDES, FATS, WAXES, ALDEHYDES, KETONES, ETC.

399. **Ethers** are derived, theoretically, by replacing the hydrogen atoms in water by hydrocarbon radicals; they are, therefore, *oxides*. Ethers are either *simple* or *mixed*, according as the hydrocarbon radicals are alike or different; thus common ether is a *simple* ether, $(C_2H_5)_2O$, that is, $C_2H_5-O-C_2H_5$, while methyl-ethylic ether is a *mixed* ether C_3H_8O, that is, $CH_3-O-C_2H_5$.

Haloid ethers are bromides, chlorides, etc., of the hydrocarbon radicals: thus, hydrobromic ether is C_2H_5Br, or ethyl bromide. *Compound ethers* are salts of the hydrocarbon radicals, as, for example: methyl acetate, $CH_3(C_2H_3O_2)$, or $CH_3-O-C_2H_3O$. *Fats* are compound ethers, in which the hydrocarbon radical is *glyceryl*—

in almost all cases; thus, stearin is stearate of glyceryl, $C_3H_5(C_{18}H_{35}O_2)_3$.

400. **Common Ether.—**

Synonyms: ethyl ether, ethyl oxide, vinic ether, sulphuric ether, Æther, Æther Sulphuricus.

Theoretical constitution: $(C_2H_5)_2O$, or ethyl oxide, derived from H_2O by substituting C_2H_5 for each atom of hydrogen; contains 4 atoms of carbon, 10 of hydrogen, and 1 of oxygen in its formula; by weight, 48 parts carbon, 10 of hydrogen, and 16 of oxygen. Molecular weight, 74. Graphic formula, C_2H_5—O—C_2H_5.

Preparation: sulphuric acid is used to etherize alcohol, hence the name sulphuric ether. There is not, however, any sulphuric acid in pure ether. 1 part of strong sulphuric acid and 6 or 7 of commercial alcohol are heated to 266° F., in a retort, and then alcohol is run in, slowly, by means of a funnel, while the temperature is kept between 266° F. and 284°, and the mixture distilled. The liquid resulting from the distillation contains on its surface crude ether, which, purified by washing, dried, and redistilled, is ready for the market. The reactions are as follows:

First stage,

$$C_2H_5HO + H_2SO_4 = (C_2H_5)HSO_4 + H_2O.$$
Alcohol   sulphuric acid   ethyl sulphuric acid   water.

Second stage,

$$C_2H_5HSO_4 + C_2H_5HO = (C_2H_5)_2O + H_2SO_4$$
Ethyl sulphuric acid — alcohol — ether — sulphuric acid.

The second equation shows that the acid is obtained again, hence a small quantity of sulphuric acid can be used to convert considerable alcohol into ether. Ether for anæsthetic purposes is further purified by shaking with water and contact with lime and chloride of lime.

Properties: pure ether is a mobile, very volatile liquid, colorless, limpid, and inflammable, of sweetish, characteristic odor* and burning taste. It should be kept in bottles closed by ground-glass stoppers, as it readily evaporates. It is soluble in 10 volumes of water, and in alcohol in all proportions. When *pure* it dissolves oils, resins, many organic bodies, iodine, bromine, sulphur, phosphorus, and mercuric chloride. Ether should not only be kept from the air, but also from the light. Its vapor is 2½ times as heavy as air, therefore flows, and will inflame with explosion from contiguous flame. The sp. gr. of ether is variously given as 0.720, 0.736, and 0.713; that of stronger ether, Æther Fortior, is 0.728. The latter contains about 94 per cent. of pure ether, and 6 per cent. of alcohol. Ether used for anæsthetic purposes should not effect blue litmus, should leave no

---

*Called *ethereal* odor.

residue when evaporated on a watch glass, and should not impart a blue color to ignited copper sulphate. Samples should be tested before being used.

401. Use in dentistry: ether is used as an anæsthetic, both by inhalation and locally; also as an anodyne, and in various conditions, as aphthæ, etc. *It is useful as a solvent.*

Toxicology: the treatment, in cases where dangerous symptoms appear, is to cease administering the ether at once, and, if the breathing begins to fail, to pull out the tongue, to apply electricity, the poles being placed over the phrenic nerves (on a line with the 4th cervical vertebra) and to try artificial respiration. In administering ether, the *breathing* should be watched.

402. **Ethyl bromide.—**

Synonyms; bromide of ethyl, hydrobromic ether, Ethyl Bromidum,

Theoretical constitution: C_2H_5Br, bromide of the radical ethyl, one molecule of ethyl and one atom of bromine, or two atoms of carbon, five of hydrogen, and one of bromine in its molecule. It is one of the so-called **haloid** ethers (see Ethers).

Preparation, properties, etc.: ethyl bromide is obtained by distilling potassium bromide with alcohol, water, and sulphuric acid. The resulting product is redistilled with calcium chloride,

Ethyl bromide is a very volatile, colorless liquid, of ethereal odor, strong, sweetish, pungent taste. It is heavier than water, and but slightly soluble in it; soluble in ether and in alcohol. It often contains bromoform as an impurity, and, if it acquires a disagreeable odor, becomes brown on standing, or is inflammable or explosive, it is not fit for use.

Use in dentistry: *ethyl bromide is an anæsthetic*, producing complete anæsthesia in a few minutes, followed by recovery of consciousness in from one to two minutes after it is withdrawn.

Toxicology: several deaths from its use as an anæsthetic were reported some time ago, and its use was discontinued. But of late, according to Asch of Berlin, the discovery has been made that the toxic effects were due to sulphur and arsenic impurities consequent on the old method of preparation. It is said that C. P. ethyl bromide, made by the modern method described above, has been used repeatedly without deleterious results.

403. **Compound ethers.—Ethyl nitrite,** $C_2H_5NO_2$, diluted with alcohol forms "sweet spirits of nitre."

Amyl nitrite: this substance is the nitrite of the radical *amyl;* its formula is $C_5H_{11}NO_2$.* Molecular weight, 117. It is made by heating equal volumes of purified amyl alcohol (fusel oil) and nitric acid, until the mixture boils. *It is a yellowish, ethereal liquid, having the odor of over-ripe pears, and an aromatic taste.* Its specific gravity is from 0.877 to 0.900. It is volatile and inflammable, soluble in alcohol; solution rapidly deteriorates. Several samples of amyl nitrite examined by Allen contained only 80 per cent. of real amyl nitrite. It is used in dentistry as an antidote for chloroform, being administered by inhalation, and for relief of neuralgia, epileptic attacks during extraction of teeth, etc., etc.

Toxicology: in administering amyl nitrite by inhalation,

---

*It may be obtained put up in glass bulbs holding a drop or two. The latter are to be crushed before inhalation.

care should be observed. The handkerchief should be withdrawn when the face becomes flushed and the heart excited.

404. **Glucosides:** these bodies are regarded as ethers of glucose.* Those used in dentistry are tannin and gallic acid.

Tannin, tannic acid, gallotannic acid, is $C_{14}H_{10}O_9$. The tannic acid used in dentistry is obtained from powdered galls. It forms light-yellow, amorphous scales, of faint characteristic odor, and strongly astringent taste, easily soluble in water and in dilute acids. Tannin unites with albumin, gelatin, etc., forming insoluble compounds. In the blood, it absorbs oxygen and becomes gallic acid. It is an active astringent and styptic, and is a valuable agent in dentistry as a local application in many disorders, as mercurial stomatitis, hemorrhage after extraction, etc. It is sometimes used dissolved in glycerine, *Glyceritum Acidi Tannici,* and also in the preparation known as **styptic colloid,** which is a saturated solution of tannin and gun cotton.

405. **Gallic acid,** $HC_7H_5O_5$, or $C_6H_2(HO)_3CO_2H$, is obtained by exposing moistened galls to the air for six weeks. A peculiar kind of fermentation takes place, and

---

* Because when treated by ferments or dilute acids they are decomposed and yield glucose among other products. They occur in plants, and are often accompanied by an albuminoid substance which may act as a ferment and turn them into glucose.

the tannic acid of the galls is converted into gallic acid. Gallic acid is a white solid, occurring in long, silky needles. It has an astringent, slightly acid taste, and is acid in reaction. It is not readily soluble in cold water; it is soluble in three parts of boiling water, in alcohol, and in ether. It is used in dentistry in form of a gargle, as astringent, antiseptic, and styptic.

406. **Fats and fixed oils:** these substances, as has been stated before, are compound ethers of glyceryl. Some are liquid and others solid. *Stearin* is the constituent of the more solid fats, *palmitin* of mutton, lard, and human fat; *olein* is the fluid constituent of fats and oils; fats treated with hot alkalies or with superheated steam, are saponified, as the term is, stearates, palmitates, and oleates of the alkalies being formed (**soap**) and glycerine.

407. *Cacao butter* is a concrete oil from the kernels of the fruit of *Theobroma Cacao*.

408. *Waxes* belong to the spermaceti group of oils. They do not yield glycerine when saponified.

409. *Bees-wax* is the material of which the honeycomb of bees is composed. It occurs as a compact, tough, solid substance of a yellow or brown color, almost tasteless, but of characteristic, aromatic odor. It is not greasy to the touch. On exposure to air in thin slices, it becomes decolorized. It may be bleached by nitric acid. It is insoluble in water, but soluble in the fixed oils, oil of turpentine, benzol, ether, and carbon disulphide. It is difficultly soluble in alcohol. Its specific gravity is from 0.959 to 0.969.

410. The yellow wax is **Cera Flava;** bleached, it is called **Cera Alba,** or white wax. The best method of bleaching is exposure to moisture and the rays of the sun. A new process is, first, to melt together 8 parts of

yellow wax and 1 to 1½ parts of rectified oil of turpentine, and then expose to air, etc. Grain wax may be bleached by dioxide of hydrogen. Other chemicals can not be used as they change its constitution.

411. **Croton Oil:** this oil belongs to the Castor Oil group of oils, distinguished for their very high specific gravity and viscosity. They are readily soluble in alcohol, and are strongly purgative. Both castor oil and croton oil are miscible with glacial acetic acid in all proportions. In drying character, they resemble the oils of the Cotton Seed Oil group.

It produces pustules, when applied to the skin, and is valuable as a counter-irritant.

Toxicology: in overdoses it has frequently proved fatal.

412. **Chloroform.—**
Synonyms: trichlormethane, dichlor-methyl chloride, formyl terchloride.

Theoretical constitution: $CHCl_3$, or methane, CH_4, in which three atoms of hydrogen have been replaced by three of chlorine. Chloroform has, in its molecule, one atom of carbon, one of hydrogen, and three of chlorine; by weight, 12 parts carbon, 1 of hydrogen, and 106.2 of chlorine. Molecular weight, 119.2.

Preparation: *commercial chloroform is usually made by the action of bleaching powder on alcohol;* in 24 parts of water 6 parts of bleaching powder are dissolved, the mixture strained into a retort, heated to 102°F., and one part of strong alcohol added. The mixture is then distilled. Bleaching powder is chiefly calcium hypochlorite, which with alcohol yields on distillation chloroform, calcium formate, calcium chloride, and water, through various intermediate stages.

Chloroform for anæsthetic purposes, *purified chloroform*, U. S. P., is prepared from the commercial by mixing with sulphuric acid, agitating, drawing off the chloroform, treating with sodium carbonate, and distilling over calcium oxide.

In a new process for making chloroform, alcohol is said to be dispensed with, and the chloroform made by distillation of wood and subsequent treatment of the distillate. Chloroform is also made from chloral hydrate, and by electrolysis, from chlorides of the alkalies in presence of alcohol, aldehyde, or acetone.

Properties: chloroform is a mobile, *colorless, volatile liquid* of bland, peculiar, *sweetish, ethereal odor*, and hot, aromatic, saccharine taste. Specific gravity of the purified is 1.5022, and boils at 142°F. The official chloroform of the U. S. Pharmacopœa contains a little alcohol, and its sp. gr. is 1.488. It is heavier than water and not soluble in it, but is freely soluble in alcohol and ether. *It dissolves a large number of substances,* among them camphor, fixed and volatile oils, many resins, fats, caoutchouc, sulphur, phosphorus, iodine, bromine, and many alkaloids.

Purified chloroform should not affect litmus paper, nor color green a mixture of chromic and sulphuric acids. Sulphuric acid should not color it brown, nor should potassium hydrate. Allowed to evaporate on the hand, no foreign odor should be noticed.

It is said not to be inflammable, but is combustible burning with a dull, smoky flame on application of a naked flame to it.

Spirit of chloroform contains an ounce of chloroform in two ounces of dilute alcohol.

Uses in dentistry: as *an anæsthetic*, both general and local, though, for the latter purpose, usually combined with other agents; as an anodyne, and antispasmodic. It is also an *antiseptic* and *styptic*. Applied to the skin, it acts as an irritant and vesicant, if evaporation is retarded.

Toxicology: deaths following administration of chloroform have been quite frequent. Paralysis of the heart, and, in some cases, exclusion of air from the lungs are the causes of death. In administering it, some air should be admitted along with it. It should never be administered to persons suffering from diseases of the heart or kidneys. At the slightest symptom of heart failure during administration of chloroform, the patient should be placed in a recumbent position, cold affusions applied, and artificial respiration, together with induced electricity, be resorted to. Inhalations of from three to five drops of amyl nitrite have been recommended.

413. **Iodoform:** this substance, CHI_3, is similar in theoretical constitution to chloroform, except that it contains iodine instead of chlorine. It may be made by acting on alcohol, aldehyde, and many other substances with iodine and potassium carbonate or hydrate. *It is usually prepared by heating together an aqueous solution of potassium carbonate, iodine, and alcohol,* until the brown color of the iodine has disappeared. It occurs in *small, lemon-yellow, lustrous crystals of an odor* not so bad at first, but soon becoming unsupportable.* It melts at 248°F., and volatilizes gradually at ordinary temperatures. *It is nearly insoluble in water* and in acids, but soluble in alcohol, ether, chloroform, disulphide of carbon, fixed and volatile oils. It is not, however, so easy to dissolve it, as many of the books would lead us to infer. It is neutral in reaction. Iodoform is not an escharotic, and is an *antiseptic, disinfectant,* and *anæsthetic.* It is now made by electrolysis from iodide of potassium dissolved in alcohol, through which a stream of carbonic acid is constantly passed. Iodoform is decomposed by sunlight (turning

---

* The odor is called "*saffron-like,*" and is not perceptible in the preparation known as *bituminized iodoform.*

violet). It loses 0.016 per cent. an hour, exposed in a thin layer to the air.

Use in dentistry: *it is used as an antiseptic*, and anodyne; dissolved in oil of turpentine, it is said to be a germicide. It acts chemically, by allowing escape of free iodine, and also mechanically, favoring cicatrization. In dentistry, iodoform is combined with numerous agents, among them eucalyptol, arsenic, creasote, carbolic acid, camphor, etc., etc.

The odor of iodoform may be disguised by mixing 1 part of cumarin with 25 of iodoform.* The odor may be removed from the hands, by washing them in an aqueous solution of tannic acid. A French antiseptic dressing containing iodoform is composed of equal parts of powdered iodoform, cinchona, benzoin, and magnesium carbonate, the latter being saturated with eucalyptol. Acetate of potassium should be given in cases of poisoning.

414. **Iodol**: tetra-iodo-pyrrhol, C_4I_4NH, made from pyrrole, a product of the destructive distillation of proteids. Light-yellowish-gray, micro-crystalline powder, *odorless*, almost tasteless, almost *insoluble in water*, soluble in three parts alcohol† (by weight), in 2 parts ether, and in 7 parts warm oil. *Contains nearly 89 per cent. iodine*, and

---

* Oil of sassafras is also said to be useful in disguising the odor.

---

† Alcohol must not be boiled when used as a solvent for fear of decomposing the iodol.

used as a *substitute for iodoform*. Used in dentistry as an *antiseptic*. Iodol *wax* has been used as a temporary stopping. Said not to be so toxic as iodoform.

415. **Aldehydes:** aldehydes lie midway between alcohols and organic acids; they have two less atoms of hydrogen than the corresponding alcohol.

Paraldehyde ($C_2H_3HO)_3$ or $C_6H_{12}O_3$, is used as a substitute for morphine, and is a liquid.

416. **Chloral hydrate.—**

Chloral is prepared by passing dry chlorine into absolute alcohol, until saturated, then adding sulphuric acid and distilling. The chloral thus obtained is a colorless liquid; if, now, this liquid be treated with a small quantity of water, it becomes a solid, $C_2Cl_3 HO.H_2O$, which is the well-known **chloral hydrate.** The latter is a colorless, transparent, crystalline solid, of aromatic, pungent odor and taste, soluble in water, very soluble in alcohol, ether, glycerine, fixed and volatile oils, neutral in reaction, melting at 136.4°F., and boiling at 203°. It has a bitter, caustic taste; it liquefies when mixed with carbolic acid or camphor. It volatilizes slowly at ordinary temperatures. It is decomposed by weak alkalies into chloroform, and a formate of the alkali metal; this change was thought to take place in the blood when chloral was taken internally, but recent investigations fail to support the theory.

In preparing chloral, 5 per cent. of ferric chloride is added by some to the alcohol, before the chlorine gas is introduced.

Use in dentistry: chloral hydrate is used in dentistry locally, for relief of odontalgia, etc. It is an antiseptic, and local anæsthetic, especially when combined with other agents. Chloral hydrate is familiarly termed "chloral."

Toxicology: the treatment, in cases of poisoning, consists of use of the stomach pump, and maintenance of respiration.

417. **Croton-chloral hydrate** is, chemically speaking, *butyl-chloral hydrate*. Its formula is $C_4H_5Cl_3O.H_2O$. It is made by passing dry chlorine through aldehyde cooled to 14°F. Butyl-chloral is obtained, and, on addition of water, butyl-chloral-hydrate. It occurs in the form of crystalline, micaceous scales, of pungent odor, sparingly soluble in water, readily in alcohol, and in hot water, nearly insoluble in chloroform.

418. **Ketones:** these substances are consequent on the first action of oxidizing agents on secondary alcohols, just as primary alcohols yield aldehyde when oxidized. Secondary alcohols contain the group of atoms CHHO, instead of CH_2HO, which is found in ordinary alcohol.

419. **Organic acids and salts.—**
Organic acids may be deemed to be built upon the water type, half the hydrogen, in one or more molecules of water, being replaced by a compound organic radical, always containing oxygen: for example, water is H_2O or H—O—H; replace half the hydrogen, that is, one atom, by C_2H_3O, a compound ·organic radical containing oxygen, and we have H—O—C_2H_3O or $HC_2H_3O_2$, acetic acid. It will be noticed that *this formula is the same as that of ethyl aldehyde, plus one atom of oxygen.* Alcohol, aldehyde, and acetic acid resemble one an-

other in a certain way. Thus, the formula for ethyl alcohol is C_2H_6O, that of aldehyde, C_2H_4O—or alcohol minus two atoms of hydrogen—and that of acetic acid, $C_2H_4O_2$, or aldehyde plus one atom of oxygen.

420. **Acetic acid**: its formula is $C_2H_4O_2$, or C_2H_3O—O—H. It is a monobasic acid, like nitric, hence its formula is conveniently written, $HC_2H_3O_2$, and the radical $C_2H_3O_2$ occurs in all acetates, the H (one atom) being replaced by some positive element, as K, Na, Pb, etc. Acetic acid is the result of the fermentation of saccharine fluids, *after* alcoholic fermentation is over. It is prepared, however, from the residuary liquid obtained in the distillation of wood.

Acidum Aceticum, U. S. P., $HC_2H_3O_2 = 60$, is a watery solution, composed of 36 per cent of hydrogen acetate, and 64 of water. It is a clear, colorless liquid, of a distinctly vinegar-like odor, a purely acid taste, and a strongly acid reaction. Sp. gr. 1.048 at 59°F. Miscible in all proportions with water and alcohol, and wholly volatilized by heat. *Acidum Aceticum Dilutum* has 6 per cent. of absolute acetic acid, and a sp. gr. of 1.0083. *Acidum Aceticum Glaciale*, glacial acetic acid, is nearly or quite absolute acetic acid: at or below 59°F., it is a crystalline solid; at higher temperatures, a colorless liquid. It is very corrosive.

Acetic acid dissolves resins, camphor, fibrin, and coagulated albumin; it precipitates mucin. It blisters the skin and is a corrosive poison: antidotes are alkalies, alkaline carbonates, soap, etc. Glacial acetic acid is used by dentists, externally, as a caustic.

421. **Acetates**: important acetates are those of ammonium, aluminium, and lead.

Spirit of Mindererus: ammonium acetate, $NH_4(C_2H_3$

O_2). To make it, saturate dilute acetic acid with ammonium carbonate and filter. Colorless, pungent, odorless liquid; should be freshly made.

Used in dentistry as a lotion, and internally as a refrigerant. Its formula is usually written $NH_4C_2H_3O_2$. It is completely volatilized by heat.

422. **Aluminium acetate:** a solution of it, known as Liquor Aluminii Acetatis, occurs in pharmacy and is used by dentists as an antiseptic, disinfectant, and deodorizer. It contains from 7½ to 8 per cent of basic aluminium acetate. ($Al_2(HO)_2(C_2H_3O_2)_4$, 324).

423. **Lead acetate** is known officially as Plumbi Acetas, $Pb(C_2H_3O_2)_2, 3H_2O = 378.5$. For pharmaceutical purposes it is made from oxide of lead, acetic acid, and water; $PbO + 2HC_2H_3O_2 + 2H_2O = Pb(C_2H_3O_2)_2 3H_2O$ Colorless, glistening, transparent crystals, efflorescent, soluble, of sweetish, astringent taste. Aqueous solutions become turbid from presence of carbon dioxide of the air, causing formation of carbonate of lead which is insoluble.

424. **Sub-acetate of lead:** the acetate and hydrate, basic acetate, $Pb(C_2H_3O_2)_2$, $Pb(HO)_2$. Colorless liquid, more poisonous than the acetate. Precipitated by solutions of gum. Used in Goulard's extract, *Liquor Plumbi Subacetatis*, a 25 per cent. solution of the sub-acetate.

425. **Lead water,** which is two fluidrachms of Liquor Plumbi Subacetatis in a pint of distilled water, is used in dental practice as a local application. It is known as Liquor Plumbi Subacetatis Dilutus.

Compounds of lead are poisonous, but chronic poisoning is more common than acute; in the latter case, emetics should be administered or the stomach pump used, large draughts of milk containing white of egg given, and sulphate of magnesium dissolved in **dilute** sulphuric acid.

426. **Trichloracetic acid** should really be considered

under the head of chloral hydrate, for it is formed when the latter is oxidized by nitric acid. It is called also trichloroacetic acid. Its formula is $HC_4Cl_3O_2$; it is a colorless, crystalline solid, soluble in water and in alcohol. It is a caustic and coagulates albumin. It is used in dentistry as a germicide and an antiseptic. According to Dr. Filippowitch it is a powerful antiseptic even in 0.2 per cent. solutions, while in 1 per cent. or 2 per cent. solutions it destroys all forms of organic life; in 5 per cent. it does not arrest the growth of yeast, but does that of bacteria and micrococci.

427. **Benzoic acid:** formula, $HC_7H_5O_2$. This acid may be obtained from benzoin, naphthalin, toluol, or from the urine of herbivorous animals. It is a solid substance occurring in lustrous blades, or needles, but slightly soluble in cold water, soluble in boiling water, more soluble in alcohol and ether. Borax added to it increases its solubility in water, as does sodium phosphate also. The acid is monobasic, like nitric acid. Most benzoates are soluble. Benzoic acid is an *antiseptic*, and is used in dentistry as such; also, as a local hæmostatic, in combination with powdered alum. It is one of the ingredients of Harris's Gum Wash.

Ammonium benzoate, $NH_4C_7H_5O_2 = 139$, is the benzoate most used. It occurs in the form of prismatic crystals, colorless, and transparent, or white and granular, soluble in 5 parts of water. It becomes yellow on long exposure to air. Benzoates, like benzoic acid, are antifermentative in action. Ammonium benzoate is administered in cases of phosphatic calculus, which, in time, it dissolves. *Lithium benzoate* has for its formula $LiC_7H_5O_2 = 128$.*

---

* A derivative of benzoic acid is the new sweet substance *Saccharin;* a white, crystalline powder, soluble in 250 parts water, easily soluble in alcohol and ether. *Said* to be 280 times as sweet as cane-sugar. Solubility increased by addition of alkaline solutions.

428. Eugenic acid.—

Synonyms: eugenol, caryophyllic acid, oxidized essence of cloves.

Theoretical constitution: $C_{10}H_{12}O_2$.

Occurrence: found along with a hydrocarbon in oil of cloves.

Preparation: crude oil of cloves treated with potash is distilled, and the residue is subjected to the action of a mineral acid. The substance may also be obtained from cinnamon leaves.

Properties: colorless oil of sp. gr., 1.07, of spicy, burning taste, soluble in water and in alcohol. Reddens litmus, and coagulates albumin. On contact with air, becomes darker and resinous.

Use in dentistry: as a germicide, obtunding agent, etc., etc.

429. **Hydrocyanic acid:** Acidum Hydrocyanicum, HCN or HCy, cyanhydric acid. Exists ready formed in juice of the bitter cassava; may be obtained from bitter almonds, kernels of plums and peaches, apple seeds, cherry laurel, etc.; clear, colorless, volatile liquid, of peculiar, pungent odor. The official acid contains about 2 per cent. of the anhydrous acid. Its compounds are cyanides, or *cyanurets*, as formerly termed.

430. Mercuric cyanide, HgCy or HgCN, has already been considered.

431. **Oleic acid:** formula $C_{18}H_{34}O_2$, or $HC_{18}H_{33}O_2$, or $C_{17}H_{33}COOH$, is of the fatty acid series, like acetic acid. It is found, in combination with glyceryl, in most animal fats and non-drying vegetable oils. Its salts are called *oleates*, and are definite chemical compounds.

Metallic oleates seem to exert an antiseptic action, not only on the fats with which they may be combined, but also on discharges from suppurating surfaces, etc., etc. The pure oleic acid is free from unpleasant odor or rancidity. Oleates of the alkaloids are prepared by dissolving the alkaloid in oleic acid. Important oleates are those of aluminium, arsenic, bismuth, cadmium, copper, iron, lead, mercury, silver, tin, zinc, and iron.

432. **Mercuric oleate** is of stable composition, as now prepared, and has all the therapeutic effects of mercury. It does not become rancid nor stain the linen. Its formula is $Hg(C_{18}H_{33}O_2)_2 = 762$. It is made from yellow mercuric oxide. The official U. S. P. oleate is a liquid.

PERCENTAGE OF METAL IN THE METALLIC OLEATES.

100 parts of oleate of	correspond to	Oxide	%
Aluminium		Al_2O_3	5.86
Arsenic		As_2O_3	21.55
Bismuth		Bi_2O_3	22.22
Copper		CuO	12.67
Iron (ferric)		Fe_2O_3	8.89
Lead		PbO	28.95
Mercury (precip.)		Hg	28.32
Silver		Ag_2O	29.77
Zinc		ZnO	12.90

433. **Oxalic acid:** $H_2(C_2O_4), 2H_2O = 126$.
Occurs in combination in *Oxalis* and in Rhubarb. Made from sawdust by action of caustic alkali. Colorless, transparent crystals, readily soluble, odorless, of intensely acid taste. Dangerous poison.

The treatment, in cases of poisoning, consists in giving lime, chalk, or magnesia in very small quantities of milk, and subsequently emetics if there is no vomiting.

434. The **salts** of oxalic acid are **oxalates,** and contain C_2O_4; the acid is dibasic, hence calcium oxalate would have CaC_2O_4 for its formula; potassium oxalate, $K_2C_2O_4$, etc., etc.

435. **Cerium oxalate** is $Ce_2(C_2O_4)_3.9H_2O = 708$.

436. **Lactic acid:** this acid is of importance

to the dental student in view of the experiments of Miller, Black, Magitot, and others in regard to caries.

Theoretical constitution: $C_3H_6O_3$

graphically
$$\begin{array}{c} CH_3 \\ | \\ CH\text{--}O\text{--}H \\ | \\ CO.O\text{--}H. \end{array}$$

Composed of 3 atoms of carbon, 6 of hydrogen, and 3 of oxygen; by weight 36 parts of carbon, 6 of hydrogen, and 48 of oxygen. Molecular weight, 90. Formula usually written $HC_3H_5O_3$, to denote the monobasic character of the acid.

Occurrence and preparation: lactic acid is the acid of sour cabbage and of sour milk. It is produced in these substances by the action of a special ferment called **lactic ferment.** It is found in several parts of the human body, namely, in the urine, intestinal juices, and in the gastric juice. It exists in many products after fermentation, as in beet juice, various vegetables, nux vomica.

437. It, or isomeric modifications of it, occurs in the fluids which permeate muscular tissues. A variety called **sarco-lactic acid** is found in the muscles and also in the hepatic cells. *Abnormally*, lactic acid is found in the blood, particularly in leukæmia, pyæmia, etc.;

it may be found in purulent discharges, in the saliva in diabetes, and in the urine, especially after phosphorus poisoning, in acute atrophy of the liver, leukæmia, trichinosis, and occasionally in rickets and osteomalacia.

438. On a large scale lactic acid is prepared by the lactic fermentation, so called, of cane sugar and glucose. Flour is treated with dilute sulphuric acid and its starch thus converted into glucose; the free sulphuric acid is neutralized with milk of lime and sour milk is added, which gives rise to a fermentation in the sugars. This fermentation is checked before the so-called butyric fermentation sets in, by heating to the boiling point. Calcium lactate is formed, and the hot solution, after filtration, is evaporated down and allowed to crystallize. From calciumlactate, lactic acid is obtained by saturation with sulphuric acid.

In the human body, lactic acid is possibly a derivative of sugar:

$$C_6H_{12}O_6 \quad = \quad 2(C_3H_6O_3)$$
Glucose.   Lactic acid.

It is decomposed in the system into carbonic acid and water, perhaps splitting up first into butyric acid, carbonic acid, and hydrogen.

The lactic acid found in sour milk is produced by the transformation of the sugar of milk into lactic acid, by the influence of decomposing casein:

$$C_{12}H_{22}O_{11} \quad + \quad H_2O \quad = \quad 4HC_3H_5O_3.$$
Milk-sugar.   Water.

Properties: the official U. S. P. lactic acid is a colorless, syrupy, odorless, strongly acid liquid containing 75 per cent. of lactic acid. Sp. gr., 1.212. It mixes readily with water, alcohol, and ether; is nearly insoluble in chloroform.

Lactic acid possesses the property of dissolving calcium phosphate. It has been shown, by Magitot and others, to be capable of decomposing the teeth; sections of dentine, placed by Miller in infected culture fluids, were decomposed by the lactic acid formed. Leber and Rottenstein found that solutions of lactic acid, 1 part in 100 of water, decalcified the teeth.

Miller's experiments tend to show that, during caries, lactic acid is formed in the teeth and in sufficient amount to destroy the dentine.

439. Lactic acid is a monobasic acid, $H(C_3H_5O_3)$; its salts are *lactates*, and are all soluble. Phosphates dissolved in lactic acid form *lacto-phosphates*. Calcium lactophosphate is made by the action of lactic acid on calcium phosphate.

440. **Salicylic acid:** formula $C_7H_6O_3$, or $HC_7H_5O_3$, or $C_6H_4(OH)CO_2H$. It is also called *oxybenzoic acid*. It forms a large percentage of oil of wintergreen, but is prepared on a large scale by the action of carbon dioxide on sodium phenate (carbolate).

Properties: odorless, white and lustrous masses of fine, small, colorless needles, soluble in boiling water and in alcohol; tasteless at first, but afterwards sweet and astringent, causing acridity of the fauces; soluble in cold water containing three parts of sodium phosphate. Antiseptic and disinfectant. Heated dry in a test tube, sublimes in beautiful needles before melting-point is reached, and at higher temperature is dissipated. It is soluble in alcohol, ether, and glycerine. Its salts are salicylates; it is a monobasic acid, $H(C_7H_5O_3)$, therefore, sodium salicylate, for example, is $NaC_7H_5O_3$. Salicylic acid is used in dentistry as an antiseptic, dissolved in water containing a little sodium phosphate or sodium sulphite, or in glycerine, or in ether. It, like many other acids, attacks the teeth slightly, hence is not suitable for mouth washes. It is acid in reaction.

441. **Salol:** this substance is the phenyl ether of salicylic acid, that is, phenyl salicylate, $C_6H_4OH.COO.C_6H_5$; empirically, $C_6H_5C_7H_5O_3$, one atom of hydrogen in salicylic acid being replaced by the univalent radical C_6H_5. It is a white crystalline powder, of mild aromatic odor, insoluble in water but soluble in alcohol. Used in dentistry as an antiseptic.

Betol is the salicylate of beta-naphthol, $C_6H_4OH.COO.C_{10}H_7$. Said to be freer from detrimental properties than alcohol, White, insoluble in water.

442. **Sozolic Acid** (formerly called **Aseptol***):

Formula, $C_6H_4(HO)SO_2(HO)$, orthoxy-phenyl-sulphurous acid, containing SO_2 in place of carbonyl (CO) of salicylic acid.

It is a reddish syrupy liquid, of sp. gr., 1.40, with a feeble and not disagreeable odor. It dissolves in water in all proportions. With ferric chloride it gives the same violet coloration as salicylic acid. Though a decided acid, it has not the corrosive action of phenol. It is said to arrest absolutely every fermentation, diastatic or fungoid, to a much greater degree than phenol and other well-known antiseptics. The advantages of sozolic acid lie chiefly in its great solubility and freedom from odor - qualities which, together with the absence of corrosive action, should make it suitable for toilet preparations in many cases.

---

* Aseptol is a 33½ per cent. solution of the acid.

It is a valuable antiseptic, according to D. F. Hueppe, and doubtless will partially replace carbolic acid as a disinfectant and antiseptic. It would seem destined to be of value in dentistry in treatment of fetor of the breath.

443. **Tartaric acid:** $H_2(C_4H_4O_6)$, Acidum Tartaricum. Occurs in grapes, pineapples, tamarinds, and other fruits, as a tartrate. Prepared from crude tartar. Colorless, transparent crystals, soluble in water. Solutions are strongly acid, and deposit fungous growth.

In dentistry it is used, combined with "chloride of lime," to bleach discolored teeth.

444. **Cream of tartar** or **potassium bitartrate:** potassium acid tartrate, $KH(C_4H_4O_6)$, made from argols or crude tartar, a deposit on the sides of wine casks; odorless, of gritty taste, white, almost insoluble in cold water, soluble in from 15 to 20 parts boiling.

445. **Rochelle salt:** potassium sodium tartrate, $KNa(C^4H^4O_6) \, 4H_2O$. Large, transparent, colorless, slightly efflorescent crystals, of mildly saline and bitter taste, readily soluble.

446. **Tartar emetic:** tartrate of **potassium** and a radical called **stibyl**; potassium antimonyl tartrate, $2(KSbO.C_4H_4O_6).H_2O = 664$, is prepared by boiling 4 parts of antimonous oxide with 5 parts of cream of tartar in 50 of water. It is soluble in 17 parts of water, but insoluble in alcohol. It is poisonous: treatment should consist in use of stomach pump or emetics, administration of tannin in form of tea, infusion of nut galls, oak bark, etc., and of stimulants.

447. **Other organic acids:** valeric or valerianic, $HC_5H_9O_2$; citric: $H_3C_6H_5O_7.H_2O$. A new disinfectant is oxynaphthoic acid, alpha: a white, odorless, micro-crystalline powder, nearly insoluble in water, soluble in alcohol.

ALKALOIDS.

448. **Alkaloids** *are artificial, natural, or cadaveric.* Artificial alkaloids are the various amines, as methylamine, ethylamine, etc. Methylamine is a gas, ethylamine a liquid, propylamine a volatile oil.*

449. **The natural alkaloids:** a class of substances chiefly of vegetable origin, often active principles of plants, supposed to be like *alkalies*, hence name. Those containing no oxygen are volatile; those having oxygen are non-volatile. As a rule, are soluble in alcohol, ether, chloroform; contain nitrogen, turn plane of polarized ray of light to left (with few exceptions), furnish with platinic chloride, double chlorides; have bitter taste, resemble alkalies in uniting with acids to form salts, of which the sulphates, nitrates, chlorides, and acetates are usually soluble, and the oxalates, tartrates, and tannates usually insoluble; in solution are precipitated by many re-agents, including iodine dissolved in iodide of potassium: very poisonous.

The alkaloids used in dentistry are for the most part *natural* alkaloids, as morphine, cocaine, etc., etc.

Cadaveric alkaloids, or *ptomaines*, are those found in putrefying animal or vegetable matter, and, in certain

---

* Many therapeutic agents have been discovered among the amines and their derivatives, *e. g.* antifebrin, a derivative of aniline which is itself, *phenylamine.*

pathological conditions, in the human body during life. Pyæmic fluid yields an alkaloid, which has been named *septicine*.

Most of the natural organic bases or alkaloids resemble the –amines or compound ammonias; an –**amine** may be regarded as formed by the replacement of one or more atoms in the ammonia (NH_3) molecules by positive or hydrocarbon radicals, thus:

$$N \begin{cases} H \\ H \\ H \end{cases} \quad N \begin{cases} CH \\ H \\ H \end{cases}$$

ammonia   methylamine.

Some of the alkaloids are more like ammonium compounds than like amines. The molecular structure of the vegetable alkaloids is, in most cases, but very imperfectly understood.

450. **Aconitine:** $C_{30}H_{47}NO_7$, is the alkaloid of aconite, *Aconitum Napellus*, occurring as a glacial mass or white powder, crystallizing with difficulty in rhombic plates. It is soluble in 150 parts of water, slightly soluble in ammonia water, soluble in benzol, soluble in 2 parts ether, soluble in 2½ parts chloroform. It has a sharp, pungent taste, and is one of the most powerful poisons known. It is fatal, probably, in doses of $\frac{1}{13}$th grain. Samples of aconitine vary in strength, some being wholly inert, others powerfully poisonous. Morson's and Duquesnel's *crystalized* aconitine have about the same solubility, and are of about the same strength. Duquesnel's is in form of large crystals usually, some weighing $\frac{1}{10}$th of a grain.

Oleate of aconitine contains usually 2 per cent. of the alkaloid.

Aconitine, in dental practice, is administered internally, for neuralgia of the fifth pair of nerves. The treatment, in cases of poisoning, should consist in administration of emetics, and of stimulants as ammonia, brandy, strong coffee, and tea. Liniments and friction to the limbs and spine should be used, mustard plasters applied to pit of stomach, and slight galvanic shocks through the heart administered.

Tincture of aconite is a valuable local application in dentistry, especially when combined with various agents, as iodine, chloroform, etc. Poisoning by tincture of aconite is to be treated as above; the chief symptoms are numbness and tingling, great sense of fatigue, muscular weakness, etc., etc.

451. *Napelline*, an alkaloid obtained by Duquesnel from aconite, is less powerful than aconitine, and has hypnotic properties.

452. **Atropine:** $C_{17}H_{23}NO_3$. This alkaloid is from *Atropa Belladonna*. The *sulphate* of atropine is used in dentistry. Its formula is $(C_{17}H_{23}NO_3)_2H_2SO_4$, and it is made by combining atropine with sulphuric acid and evaporating. [The hydrogen of acids is not replaced by alkaloids, when they combine with the acids; in this respect the compounds formed differ from compounds of the alkali metals and acids: thus, while atropine sulphate is $(C_{17}H_{23}NO_3)_2$, H_2SO_4, potassium sulphate is K_2SO_4.]

Atropine sulphate is a white, crystalline powder, or forms small, colorless, silky prisms. It is soluble in 3 parts cold water, and 10 parts, 90 per cent alcohol. *The concentrated solution should be neutral to test paper.** It is insoluble in ether, inodorous, of disagreeable, bitter taste, and is an active poison. In dental practice, it is used locally as an obtunding agent, etc., and also internally, for neuralgia, etc. The fatal dose is two grains; the treatment should consist in administration of emetics, and subcutaneous injection of pilocarpine or of morphine.

---

* In order to test atropine sulphate, drop a little of the dry powder on litmus paper, both red and blue, previously moistened with water. It should not affect either paper.

Dryness of the throat, diplopia, vertigo, and in serious cases, delirium, are among the symptoms of poisoning by this substance.

453. **Chinoline or quinoline:** C_9H_7N.

This substance is an artificial alkaloid,† and is not the active principle of any plant. It was first made from coal tar, then from cinchona, but now is made from nitrobenzole, aniline, and glycerine, to which sulphuric acid has been added, the mixture being heated and cooled alternately. It is a colorless, oily liquid, of sp. gr. 1.094, and boiling at 460° F. In chemical constitution it may be regarded as naphthalin, $C_{10}H_8$, in which *one* CH group is replaced by N.

Chinoline forms crystalline salts with acids. The one used in dentistry is the tartrate, $(C_9H_7N)_2 \, H_2C_4H_4O_6$, theoretically, but the real composition of German chinoline tartrate is said to be $3C_9H_7N.4C_4H_6O_6$, requiring 60.8 per cent. of tartaric acid. Chinoline tartrate forms (microscopic) columnar crystals; it is soluble in 75 parts of water at 60.8°F., and in 150 parts of 90% alcohol, and 350 of ether. Its taste is peculiar, somewhat burning, penetrating, and suggesting peppermint. It has a faint odor, slightly suggesting bitter almonds.

It is used in dentistry as an antiseptic, usually in 5 per cent. solution. It is sometimes combined with carbolic acid. Its aromatic odor is less pleasant than that of pyridine, which it resembles.

Chinoline enters into a definite combination with iodoform. One part of iodoform, dissolved in ether, is mixed with three of chinoline also dissolved in ether.

Salts of chinoline should be kept away from the light.

---

† *Antipyrine* is a derivative of chinoline; and is an antipyretic and anodyne.

454. **Cannabis Indica** products: the *tincture* of Cannabis Indica, diluted 3 to 5 times, has been used by A. Aaronson and others, as a local anæsthetic in extracting teeth.

455. **Cannabinum Tannicum** or cannabin tannate occurs as an amorphous, yellowish or brownish-gray powder, indifferent toward litmus, having a very faint odor of hemp, and a somewhat bitter, strongly astringent taste. When heated on platinum foil, it swells up and finally leaves minute traces of a white ash. It is almost insoluble in cold water, alcohol or ether, and dissolves but little on warming; but it is easily soluble in water or alcohol acidulated with hydrochloric acid.

456. **Cannabine:**[*] this is the name of an alkaloid recently prepared from Cannabis Indica. It appears as a viscid, brown substance, transparent in thin layers, of a strongly aromatic odor and a sharp, bitter, and somewhat scratching taste. It is insoluble in water, easily soluble in alcohol, ether, petroleum ether, chloroform, benzol, disulphide of carbon, ethereal and fixed oils. The solutions are golden-yellow when highly diluted, brown when concentrated. When heated on platinum foil it leaves no residue.

457. **Cocaine:** $C_{17}H_{21}NO_4$. This now famous alkaloid is prepared from *Erythroxylon Coca*, a shrub indigenous to certain regions in South America. It is found chiefly in Peru and Chili, and the alkaloid is extracted from the leaves. The process of extracting cocaine from coca leaves is given in full in Squibb's Ephemeris, Vol. II., No. 7; it is too long for insertion here.

Pure cocaine crystallizes in colorless, four or six sided monoclinic prisms, soluble in 704 parts of water at 53.6°F., easily soluble in alcohol, and still more so in ether.

---

[*] The pure alkaloid must be carefully distinguished from the resinoid called "Cannabin."

Cocaine melts near 197°F. Cocaine combines readily with dilute acids, forming easily crystallizable salts, which are more or less sparingly soluble in water, but soluble in alcohol. They are insoluble in ether, of bitter taste, and leave a transient sensation of insensibility upon the tongue.

The hydrochlorate, or muriate, of cocaine is the salt which has been most used. The *crystallized* hydrochlorate has for its formula, $C_{17}H_{21}NO_4,HCl. 2H_2O$, when crystallized from aqueous solutions. Dried and rendered anhydrous, its formula is $C_{17}H_{21}NO_4,HCl$.; crystallized from alcohol (B.P.), its formula is the same as the latter, for it is anhydrous. Hydrochlorate of cocaine occurs in the form of short, transparent, prismatic crystals, permanent in air. It is sparingly soluble in water, but readily soluble in alcohol, ether, and in vaseline.

The hydrochlorate is termed *hydrochloride* by some authors; the hydrogen of the hydrochloric acid is not given off in the combination, as is seen from the formula.

458. Other compounds of cocaine are the *hydrobromate*, $C_{17}H_{21}NO_4,HBr$; the citrate, $(C_{17}H_{21}NO_4)_3H_3C_6H_5O_7$; the oleate, $(C_{17}H_{21}NO_4)HC_{18}H_{33}O_2$, containing 5 per cent. of the alkaloid; the salicylate, $C_{17}H_{21}NO_4, HC_7H_5O_3$, the *phenate* or carbolate*, and the phtalate. *Salts of cocaine are used in dentistry* as local anæsthetics and anodynes, especially in alveolar pyorrhœa, extirpation of pulps of teeth, and that of hypersensitive dentine. They have also been used by injection, for extraction of teeth. Combined with menthol, and dissolved in alcohol, chloroform, or ethyl bromide, they are used as a lotion in neuralgia and odontalgia; for the same purpose, dissolved in oil of cloves. Toxic symptoms have followed injection

---

* The carbolate is a colorless mass of faint odor, very readily soluble in alcohol.

of 6 drops of a 20 per cent. solution into the gums; relieved by inhalation of amyl nitrite, 3 drops at a time, 3 inhalations.

The *purity of cocaine salts* is of the greatest importance. The permanganate test should be used for possible organic impurities.*

459. **Morphine:** morphine, morphia, $C_{17}H_{19}NO_3.H_2O$, exists as meconate of morphine in opium, which is the concrete, milky juice exuding on incising the unripe capsules of *Papaver Somniferum*, or white poppy. On account of the comparative insolubility of morphine, its *salts* are preferred for use in dentistry. Of these the acetate, hydrochlorate, and sulphate are official. They are all freely soluble in water.

460. *Morphine acetate,* $(C_{17}H_{19}NO_3)HC_2H_3O_2.3H_2O$, occurs in the form of a white or yellowish white, amorphous or crystalline powder of bitter taste. Soluble in both alcohol and water. It is known officially as *Morphinæ Acetas*.

461. *Morphine hydrochlorate,* $(C_{17}H_{19}NO_3)HCl.3H_2O$, also known as the hydrochloride or muriate, occurs in the form of snow-white, feathery, flexible, acicular crystals, of bitter taste and silky lustre, wholly soluble in both alcohol and water. Morphinæ Hydrochloras or Murias is the official term.

462. *Morphine sulphate,*† $(C_{17}H_{19}NO_3)_2H_2SO_4.5H_2O$, oc-

---

* To test the hydrochlorate (muriate) of cocaine, take 1½ grains cocaine muriate and dissolve in 80 minims of *distilled* water; add 2 drops of dilute C. P. sulphuric acid, then 1 drop of a 1 to 100 solution of potassium permanganate in distilled water. Instant discoloration, or in less than one minute, shows presence of organic impurities. The purest is said not to discolor in an hour. Comparative tests, that is of several samples at a time, are desirable.

† For hypodermic use, the *phtalate* of morphine is recommended. It comes in transparent, glassy scales, and is said not to be so liable to decomposition as the sulphate.

curs in form of crystals like the hydrochlorate, neutral in reaction, odorless, with bitter taste, soluble in both water and alcohol.

463. **In dentistry the salts of morphine**, especially the acetate and the hydrochlorate, are used in devitalizing mixtures and as obtunding agents, also for temporary relief of odontalgia, usually in combination with carbolic acid, oil of cloves, etc., etc. The acetate is used in nerve paste, rather than the sulphate, which latter is thought more irritating. Morphine is also given internally, in facial neuralgia, etc. The average fatal dose of the salts of morphine is 2 grains. Treatment of poisoning by these agents should consist in the use, by all means, of the stomach pump, washing out the stomach either with an infusion of coffee or green tea, or else with water in which finely powdered charcoal is suspended, using a fresh amount for each injection. If the pump is not used, vomiting should be encouraged, zinc sulphate in 5 grain doses, with fifteen minute intervals, being given, or *apomorphine hydrochlorate* subcutaneously, in doses of from 1-15 to 1-5 of a grain. Subsequently, 15 drops of tincture of belladonna, or 1-35 grain of atropine sulphate (subcutaneously), should be given. In the early stages of poisoning the above mentioned treatment is often all that is necessary. In later stages artificial respiration and use of the battery (Faradic current) are imperative. Enemata of strong coffee may be administered.

464. **Quinine**; $C_{20}H_{24}N_2O_2 + 3H_2O$. This alkaloid occurs in cinchona bark, together with a number of others of which cinchona, quinidine, and cinchonidine are the most important. Quinine (crystallized), is a white powder, of bitter taste and alkaline reaction. It is nearly insoluble in water. Quinine itself is seldom used. Salts of it are sulphates, hydrochloride, salicylate, tannate, hydrobromide, valerianate, citrate (of iron and quinine), hypo-

phosphite. The sulphate, disulphate, hydrobromide, hydrochloride, and valerianate, are official.

465. **Quinine Sulphates:** there are three of these, of which the diquinic sulphate $(C_{20}H_{24}N_2O_2)_2.H_2SO_4.7H_2O$, is the official sulphate. It occurs as long, brilliant needles, efflorescing to a white powder. It is but sparingly soluble in water: 1 in 780 parts; in alcohol, 1 in 65. It is readily soluble in dilute acids, but nearly insoluble in ether or chloroform.

The official *bisulphate* is obtained by dissolving the sulphate in dilute sulphuric acid. Its formula is $C_{20}H_{24}N_2O_2.H_2SO_4.7H_2O$.

There is another sulphate, obtained by dissolving quinine in excess of dilute sulphuric acid. Its formula is $(C_{20}H_{24}N_2O_2)2H_2SO_4.7H_2O$. It is not official. There is also a hypophosphite.

466. **The salts of quinine are used in dentistry** in the treatment of various facial and neuralgic affections and as ingredients of dentifrices.

467. . **The alkaloids of Nux Vomica:—**

Strychnine, Strychninum, strychnia, $C_{21}H_{22}N_2O_2$. Occurs in seed of Strychnos Nux Vomica, or poison-nuttree; also in Strychnos Ignatia, or St. Ignatius bean, found as strychnate or acetate.

Brucine is the other alkaloid, and is more soluble than strychnine.

The bitter taste of strychnine is perceptible in a solution containing but one part in 1,000,000. Strychnine sulphate $(C_{21}H_{22}N_2O_2)_2.H_2SO_4.7H_2O$, is official, and readily soluble in water. Salts of strychnine are very poisonous, ¼ of a grain having caused death. The treatment, in cases of poisoning, should consist in inhalation of chloroform, use of emetics, and, if possible, the injection into the stomach and withdrawal therefrom of powdered charcoal. Chloral hydrate and paraldehyde are sometimes administered as antidotes, and chloroform given internally.

468. **Veratrine:** $C_{37}H_{53}NO_{11}$, is an alkaloid found in *Veratrum sabadilla* and in *Cevadilla*, the seeds of *Asagræa officinalis;* also in *Veratrum album* or white hellebore, and *Veratrum viride,* or American hellebore. It occurs as a white, or grayish-white amorphous powder, of acrid taste; it causes violent sneezing, if inhaled. The *oleate* of veratrine is official, and is made to contain 2 per cent. of the alkaloid, and also ten per cent.

In dental practice, veratrine in form of ointment is used for neuralgia, etc.

469. **Other alkaloids:—**

Antipyrine, dimethyloxyquinizine, useful as an adjunct to cocaine in dental anæsthetization. Synthetic alkaloid. Formula, $C_{11}H_{12}N_2O$. White, crystalline, odorless, bitter tasting powder.

Antifebrin or acetanilide.

N $\begin{cases} C_6H_5 & \text{crystalline, odorless, solid;} \\ H & \text{slightly soluble in warm water;} \\ C_2H_3O_2 & \text{very soluble in alcohol.} \end{cases}$

Synthetic alkaloid.

Alstonine, the alkaloid of *Alstonia constricta.* White crystals.

Apomorphine, emetic.

Caffeine: a new compound is the *boro-citrate* of caffeine.

Cytisine, alkaloid of *Cytisus laburnum.*

Ditaine, $C_{22}H_{30}N_2O_4$, alkaloid of Dita-bark from Alstonica scholaris.

Erythrophleine from Erythrophleum bark; said to be a local anæsthetic.

Ethyl-oxy-Caffeine, $C_8H_9(O.C_2H_5)N_4O_2$, used as a local anæsthetic by subcutaneous injection.

Hyoscyamine from the black Hyoscyamus plant; *eserine* from calabar bean; *narceine* from opium.

Is-atropyl Cocaine, $C_{19}H_{23}NO_4$, obtained as secondary product in manufacture of cocaine and thought to be possibly the cause of toxical accessory symptoms consequent on the administration of even slightly impure cocaine.

Jerubebine, alkaloid of *Solanum paniculatum*.

Lamine from flowers of *Lamium album*; hemostatic.

Oxy-propylene-di-iso-amyl-amine: synthetic, alkaloid. Colorless liquid.

Ulexine, alkaloid from *Genista tinctoria*.

ALBUMINOUS SUBSTANCES.

470. **Proteids:** a certain amount of knowledge in regard to these substances is essential. *Proteid* is the general term given to *albuminous* compounds, which form the chief part of the solids of the organs, blood, muscle and lymph of animals, and seeds of plants. They are not crystalline, but colloid, do notid ffuse through animal membranes, and readily putrefy when exposed to the air. They are white, flaky or granular, amorphous, and difficult to obtain in the pure state.

Some are soluble, others insoluble in water; they are soluble in mineral acids and caustic alkalies, but almost insoluble in alcohol and ether. They have the peculiar property, however, of becoming insoluble either spontaneously, or after action of heat, or under influence of weak acids. They all yield what seems to be the same substance, *syntonin*, and, under the influence of the gastric juice, they are capable of generating peptones, or bodies easily assimilated and very nutritious. Proteids, when heated, do not volatilize, but, when burnt, they give off products having odor of burnt horn.

No accurate formulæ have been found for proteids, but they are known to contain carbon, hydrogen, *nitrogen*, oxygen, sometimes sulphur, sometimes phosphorus, and iron; in their ash, calcium phosphate is found. Their percentage composition, according to Wurtz, is carbon 52.7 to 54.5, hydrogen 6.9 to 7.3, nitrogen 15.4 to 17, oxygen 20.9 to 23.5, sulphur 0.8 to 2.2.

471. Proteids heated with a solution of mercurous nitrate, containing nitrous acid, assume a fine red color. On exposure to the air, proteids putrefy readily, fine granulations being developed in their interior, which change into vibrios, oxygen at the same time being absorbed, while **carbon dioxide** (carbonic acid gas), nitrogen, **ammonia, sulphuretted hydrogen**, hydrogen, ammonium sulphide, are discharged, and fatty acids, as butyric, **lactic acid,**—amines, leucin, tyrosin, etc., formed.

472. Proteids are classified by Hoppe-Seyler as follows:

1. Native albumins: soluble in water and precipitated by boiling; albumin of serum (blood albumin) and albumin of white of egg. Blood albumin is coagulated by a temperature of from 122°F. to 163°, but not by ether. Egg albumin begins to coagulate at 129°, coagulation increasing at 145° and 165°; it is precipitated by ether. Blood albumin, in solution, may be precipitated by concentrated nitric acid, citric or acetic acid plus potassium ferrocyanide, picric acid, and by many other substances.

2. Globulins: insoluble in water, soluble in 1 per cent. sodium chloride solution, but precipitated (except vitellin) by saturated solution of common salt or by addition of large quantity of water. The globulins are vitellin,

crystallin, fibrinogen, fibrino-plastin, myosin or muscle fibrin. Syntonin may be prepared from myosin by treating the latter with a very little HCl.

Fibrin: a white, elastic, more or less fibrillated solid, insoluble in water and dilute sodium chloride solutions, prepared by rapidly stirring freshly drawn blood with a bundle of twigs, and washing the coagulum with water. Neutral solutions of fibrinogen and fibrinoplastin, mixed, in presence of fibrin ferment, form fibrin. Fibrin does not dissolve in 1 per cent. solution of HCl, but swells, becoming soluble on addition of pepsin. Fibrin coagulates spontaneously on exposure to air.

4. Albuminates or derived albumins, sometimes called modified albumins: these are (1) acid albuminate, known also as syntonin, albumose, and parapeptone, and (2) alkali-albuminate found in blood corpuscles, blood serum, etc., and closely resembling casein.

5. Peptones: albuminous bodies are converted by the action of the gastric, pancreatic, and, doubtless, intestinal juices, into more diffusible and soluble bodies called peptones.

6. Amyloid substance or lardacein.

7. Coagulated albumin, as produced by action of heat on solution of serum albumin.

8. Special albumins found in cysts, dropsical fluids, etc. (Metalbumin, paralbumin).

9. Collagens: albuminous bodies which do not yield syntonin when treated with dilute acids. Hot aqueous solutions become jelly-like on cooling. The collagens are ossein, gelatin, chondrin, mucin, and elastin. Ossein is the proteid basis of bones, and contains 49.9 per cent. of carbon, 7.3 of hydrogen, 17.2 of nitrogen, 24.9 of oxygen, and 0.7 of sulphur. Chondrin is the proteid found in cartilages.

473. *Mucin* is found in several parts of the body and is

one of the excretion products of the protoplasm of epithelial cells lining mucous surfaces, and of the secreting mucous cells of the sublingual and submaxillary glands. Its average composition is 49.5% carbon, 6.7% hydr,ogen 9.6% nitrogen, and 34.2% oxygen. Dry mucin yields about 2.44% ash and contains no sulphur. In chemical constitution it is a nitrogenous glucoside and probably an albumin derivative. Mucin, when obtained in the free state, occurs in white or yellow, thready, tenacious masses. It swells in water and mixes with it, but does not dissolve. It is soluble in dilute HCl, in weak alkalies, but insoluble in alcohol, ether, chloroform, dilute acetic acid, very dilute mineral acids. Acetic acid makes it shrink; caustic potash makes it more thready at first, then dissolves it. Its solutions are precipitated by acetic acid, and, according to Oliver, by alcohol, dilute mineral acids, and all vegetable acids.

Elasticin or (elastin) is the proteid composing the fibres of yellow elastic tissue.

474. 10. Proteid derivatives: leucin, $C_6H_{13}NO_2$, or amidocaproic acid, is an important proteid derivative, and is a constant product of the decomposition of albumin and of nitrogenous substances. It is formed in decomposing cheese. Tyrosin, $C_9H_{11}NO_3$, is also a proteid derivative. Both are occasionally found in the saliva. Both unite with both acids and bases.

475. 11. Nitrogenized products of tissue metabolism: uric acid, sarkin, xanthin, guanin, etc., etc. **Uric acid,** $C_5H_4N_4O_3$, is found in calculi, blood, urine, etc., etc. It is very sparingly soluble in water. It forms urates, of which lithium urate is the most soluble. Compounds of lithium are, therefore, administered in cases of uric acid calculi.

476. **Fermentation:** according to Gautier, fermentation takes place whenever an organic

compound undergoes changes of composition under the influence of a nitrogenous, organic substance, called a *ferment*, which acts in small quantities and yields nothing to the fermented substance. In a word, *fermentation is the decomposition of carbo-hydrates into simpler compounds, by the agency of living microbes.*

Putrefaction is the name given to decomposition-fermentations in animal or vegetable organisms *rich in proteids;* in putrefaction, offensive odors are given off. Neither fermentation nor putrefaction is simply oxidation, but the presence of oxygen appears to be necessary to set up the change. The presence of water is also necessary to processes of fermentation.

477. **Ferments:** ferments are in general of two kinds (1) **soluble** or **unorganized** (enzymes, and (2) **organized.**

478. **Soluble** or **unorganized** ferments are proteid substances having the power, under favorable circumstances, of causing certain chemical changes in bodies with which they come into contact, whilst they themselves undergo no change. Several soluble ferments are of vegetable origin, and of these diastase is the most important; those of animal origin are pepsin, ptyalin, trypsin, etc., etc. They are soluble in water, very diffusible, and, although not precipitated by boiling, nevertheless lose their activity. They neither give to the bodies with which they are brought in contact nor take from

them. Their activity is destroyed by borax, but not by hydrogen dioxide. They do not reproduce themselves during the period of their activity.

479. *Diastase* (maltin) is the ferment formed in grains, at time of sprouting, from the gluten. It converts starch into dextrin and maltose. *Ptyalin*, the salivary ferment, has the same action; they act slowly on unchanged starch, but rapidly on cooked starch. The starch is first liquefied, then converted into dextrin, then into maltose. The amount of starch that can be transformed is anywhere from 2,090 to 100,000 times the weight of the ferment.

480. *Pepsin* is secreted in the glands of the stomach. It is obtained from the stomach of the pig by digesting the mucous membrane in hydrochloric acid, and precipitating by sodium chloride. It is a yellowish or grayish-white powder, insoluble in water, but soluble in water to which glycerine has been added. It is of peculiar odor, and bitter, nauseating taste. Heat of 230°F. decomposes it and renders it inert, but its solutions lose activity at much lower temperatures. The temperature most favorable for its activity is 98.6°F., and presence of a dilute acid as hydrochloric, lactic, phosphoric, etc., is required to develop its peculiar action. $\frac{1}{10}$th per cent. NaCl also favors its action, but half of one per cent. hinders it. Carbolic acid or excess of alcohol retards its action. In **dental practice, pepsin** is used in the treatment of putrid pulps, as an antiseptic and deodorizer.

It has been used and recommended by Coleman, of England, to digest dead pulp in inaccessible teeth, dilute hydrochloric acid being employed along with it.

481. **Organized ferments:** soluble ferments, as we have seen, are responsible for all physiological fermentations; on the other hand, pathological fermentations are caused by *organized ferments*, which are forms of low or-

ganisms, vegetable in origin, whose activity is greatest at temperatures ranging from 68°F. to about 104°. Their activity is retarded by temperature below or above these limits, and temperatures near 212°F. entirely destroy their activity, as does also hydrogen dioxide. The latter agent stops also the chemical change which is the direct result of the growth of the organized ferments. These ferments are remarkable in that a very minute quantity will grow and exert its action as long as appropriate nourishment is furnished it. Organized ferments have, then, powers of growth and reproduction, and the ferment power cannot be separated from the ferment organism by filtration or by any solvent. The chief food of organized ferments is ammoniacal salts and alkaline phosphates. The most important of the organized ferments are yeast (alcoholic ferment) acetic acid ferment, lactic and butyric acid ferment, the ferment of "thrush," and the putrefactive ferments.

482. *Yeast spores* are always to be found either in the air, or on fruit. Their chief action is to convert saccharose into grape sugar, and then to change the latter into alcohol and carbonic acid with a trace of succinic acid and glycerine. The equation of the change due to yeast would be:

$$C_6H_{12}O_6 + 2H_2O = 2C_2H_6O + 2H_2CO_3$$
Glucose.   Water.   Alcohol.   Carbolic acid,

Yeast is known as *Torula* (*Saccharomyces*) *cerevisiæ*.

483. The *acetic acid ferment* belongs to the bacteria family and grows in alcoholic solutions containing a little albuminous matter or various salts, as those of ammonium, or alkaline and earthy phosphates. It acts by oxidation changing alcohol to acetic acid, the *mycoderma aceti* acting as an oxygen carrier.

484. The *lactic acid ferment* grows in a neutral or alkaline medium and best without oxygen, at a temperature

of from 95°F. to 104°F. Various kinds of sugar and dextrine, under the action of *bacterium lactis*, are converted into lactic acid in the presence of a decomposing albuminous substance, especially casein, and water. The process is also favored by presence of chalk, or alkaline carbonates, which neutralize the lactic acid as fast as it is formed; were it not for this neutralization, the production of acid would prevent the continuance of the fermentation. The equation is as follows:

$$\underset{\text{Lactose.}}{C_{12}H_{22}O_{11}} + \underset{\text{Water.}}{H_2O} = \underset{\text{Glucose.}}{2C_6H_{12}O_6} + \underset{\text{Lactic acid.}}{4C_3H_6O_3}$$

also

$$\underset{\text{Glucose.}}{C_6H_{12}O_6} = \underset{\text{Lactic acid.}}{2C_3H_6O_3}$$

Lactic acid is, according to Miller, formed in the teeth during caries.

485. The *butyric ferment* goes hand in hand with the lactic. Lactic acid is split up by its agency into butyric acid, carbon dioxide, and hydrogen.

$$\underset{\text{Lactic acid.}}{2C_3H_6O_3} = \underset{\text{Butyric acid.}}{C_4H_9O_2} + \underset{\substack{\text{Carbon.}\\\text{dioxide.}}}{2CO_2} + \underset{\text{Hydrogen.}}{2H}$$

486. The *thrush ferment* is a fungus, which appears on the mucous membrane of the mouths of infants, especially of those brought up by hand. The saliva becomes acid and white spots appear, especially on the tongue, gums, and soft palate.

487. Various forms of bacteria cause *putrefactive fermentation* in proteids, by which the latter are decomposed into fats, tyrosin, leucin, ammonia, sulphuretted hydrogen, carbon dioxide, hydrogen, and nitrogen. *It is from the decomposition of proteids that the sulphuretted hydrogen in the mouth is formed.*

488. **Classification of Bacteria, etc.:** the term *microbe* is used, in general, to designate the minute organized

beings which are found on the borderland between animals and plants; in the majority of cases they may be regarded as true plants. Broadly, microbes may be divided into *parasitic fungi* and *moulds, ferments,* and *bacteria,* and to the last the term *microbe* in particular is usually applied.

489. **Fungi** are plants devoid of stems, leaves, and roots; they consist only of cells in juxtaposition, devoid of chlorophyll; they never bear a true flower and are simply reproduced by means of very minute bodies, usually formed of a single cell, called a *spore* and representing the seed. Among the parasitic fungi and moulds may be found the rust of wheat and grasses, the ergot of rye, mould of leather and dried fruit, potato fungus, mildew, the fungi of certain skin diseases as tinea, thrush, etc.

490. **Ferments** are closely allied to a variety of fungus called *microsporon,* but as they live in liquids or on damp substances they are classified by many among the Algæ, a species of water fungi. Ferments, however, differ from Algæ in not containing chlorophyll. Each plant of the ferment variety is usually composed of a single cell, spherical, elliptical, or cylindrical, formed of a thin cell-wall, containing a granular substance called *protoplasm**, which is the essential part of the plant. The cells have an average diameter of ten micro-millimetres; they grow and bud, and each divides into two parts. Among the ferments, we find those of wine, beer-yeast, bread-yeast, etc., etc.

491. **Bacteria** are alike in form and organization to ferments, but, as a rule, are of smaller size. Microbes or bacteria (Schizophyta or Schizomycetes) appear, under

---

* The composition of protoplasm is essentially proteids, water, certain mineral matters, fats, starch, and sugar.

the microscope, as small cells of a spherical, oval, or cylindrical shape, sometimes detached, sometimes united in pairs, or in articulated chains and chaplets. The diameter of the largest of these cells is but two micro-millimetres, and that of the smallest is a fourth of that size. A power of from 500 to 1,000 diameters is necessary to make them clearly visible under the microscope.

Morphologically, Dujardin-Beaumetz recognizes six forms: (1) Monad, micrococcus, or moner, immobile point-like microbes, often regarded as spores. (2) Bacteridia and bacillus, immobile, linear microbes. (3) Bacteriens, cylindrical mobile microbes, the end rounded, or the body indented in the centre, so as to form a figure of 8. (4) Vibriones, eel-shaped, undulating, mobile and flexuous microbes. (5) Spirilla and spirochœte, corkscrew-like, spirally moving microbes. (6) Capitated microbes, *Bacterium capitatum*, mobile rods, with one or both extremities long, globular, and more refractive than the rest of the body.

This classification has reference to the cells as seen singly or in very limited numbers; when aggregated so as to form colonies there are distinguished four forms:

1. Torula, in the form of a necklace, composed of micrococci.

2. Leptothrix, made up of bacteria, clustered end to end.

3. Mycoderma, immobile, composed of bacteria in sheets.

4. Zoöglœa, being masses of bacteria, immobile, inclosed in a sort of jelly which holds them together.

492. Varied conditions of existence influence the form taken by these organisms, so that distinctions into genera and species are not as yet made on precise data. The *microbe of acetic fermentation* is a true bacterium (bacter-

ien). The *microbe of lactic fermentation* is also a bacterium. The *microbe of butyric fermentation* is a bacillus.

493. In **putrefaction,** or fermentation of dead organic matter exposed to the air, the substances are first rapidly covered with moulds, they lose coherence, and after a few days give off carbonic acid, nitrogen, hydrogen, and fetid effluvia, due largely to carburetted, sulphuretted, and phosphoretted hydrogen, and to the circulation of decomposing organic particles. The microbes which appear simultaneously with the moulds, penetrate deeply into the tissues, disintegrate them by feeding at their expense, and the putrid condition increases; then the decomposition changes its nature and becomes less intense. The putrefied matter is finally dessicated, and leaves a brown mass—a complex mixture of substances combined with water and of fatty mineral substances, which gradually disappear by slow oxidation. (Gautier). In such putrefaction of animal matter in water are found microbes in the form of globules or short rods (*Micrococcus, Bacterium termo, Bacillus, etc.*), either free, or in a semi-mucilaginous mass to which the term *Zooglœa* has been given. These microbes deprive the liquid of all its oxygen. A thin layer on the surface absorbs oxygen; in the interior, albuminoid matter is changed into more simple substances, and the microbes on the surface change the latter into gases. A substance remains rich in fats, earthy and ammonical salts, and fit to serve as nutriment to plants.

494. **The microbes of the mouth** of a healthy man are numerous, and include (1) Spirochœte, (2) a species of Sarcina, and (3) more especially, a large organism called *Leptothrix buccalis* which is never absent from the rough surface of the tongue nor the interstices of the teeth. The saliva contains a *micrococcus* which may become exceptionally virulent.

The microbe of dental caries: according to

Miller, dental caries is chiefly due to the development of one or more species of bacteria. The microbe most common in decayed teeth is very polymorphic, *micrococcus*, *bacterium*, chains, and filaments are found, all different phases of the same plant, which is responsible both for acid fermentation in the mouth and for the formation of lactic acid.

495. **The microbe of pus**, as found in blood poisoning, is termed Micrococcus septicus: it may either appear free or in the form of chaplets (*vibrio*), or in the interior of the colorless corpuscles of pus, or embryonic cells, which, in form of *zooglœa*, it ruptures. The germs of Micrococcus septicus are introduced into the blood, and multiply there through the exposed surface from a wound or by agency sometimes of the instrument causing the wound. When bacteria multiply in the blood, they must necessarily have an irritating effect on the walls of the capillaries and the cells are transformed in consequence into embryonic or migratory cells which differ but slightly from the colorless blood-corpuscles and are pus-corpuscles. (Trouessart).

496. **Action of pathogenic microbes:** this is complex and is analyzed according to Trouessart as follows: (1) the action of a living parasite nourished by and multiplying at the expense of the fluids and gases of the system; (2) the formation by this parasite of a poisonous substance (ptomaine) the elements of which are derived from the organism, and it, the ptomaine, acts as a poison on this organism.

497. **Pus and suppuration:** acccording to Knapp, suppuration in every case depends on the action of microbes. Pus being defined as an albuminous, non-coagulable fluid

containing multitudes of leucocytes, suppuration is deemed to be the splitting up of living nitrogenous tissue into simpler compounds through influence of certain bacteria.

498. **Protection against microbes:** this is to be accomplished by what is, in general, called *disinfection*. Substances used for the purpose of preventing zymotic diseases, so-called, have been classified as follows:

1. *Diluents:* air and water.
2. *Absorbents:* dry earth and plaster of Paris.
3. *Destructive agents:* lime and sulphate of iron are most important. Under certain circumstances, permanganate of potassium, caustic potash, mineral acids.
4. *Antiseptics:* these check the development of the organism of putrefaction but do not necessarily kill disease germs. Most important: alcohol, sulphate of iron, borax. Commonly used: salt, saltpetre, carbolic acid.
5. *Germicides:* agents which have the power of killing disease germs; most important are chlorine and substances which contain it, as corrosive sublimate. All germicides are antiseptics, but the antiseptics proper are not germicides. Nearly all bacteria are destroyed in a very short time by high temperatures.

499. **Antiseptics are used in dentistry** for

moistening the pellet of cotton introduced into a cavity which is to be sealed: Harlan recommends carbolic acid, aseptol, creasote, terebene, resorcin, iodol, iodoform, beta-naphthol, eugenol, pheno-resorcin, eucalyptol, thymol, myrtol, menthol, boroglyceride, etc., etc., as antiseptics.

Disinfectants, or agents which will destroy foul odors by combining with them chemically, and will cleanse, purify, and destroy infection are used in the treatment of engorged antra, in and around the roots of teeth, in carious or necrosed bone, on buccal, pharyngeal, and laryngeal mucous membranes; in a word, wherever foul odors, infectious material, or decomposing matters are found. Harlan recommends Labarraque's solution, Condy's fluid, aqueous solution of zinc chloride, hydrogen dioxide, solutions of the acetate or chloride of aluminium, mercuric chloride, mercuric iodide, the hypochlorites, iodine, resorcin, trichlor-phenol, boracic acid, benzoic acid, etc.

Smith recommends corrosive sublimate dissolved in hydrogen dioxide. Abbott recommends half a grain of corrosive sublimate in twenty-one fluidounces of water.

Iodoform and eucalyptus, iodoform and oil of cinnamon, solutions of aluminium chloride, carbolic acid (with equal parts caustic potash—Robinson's remedy) salicylic acid, carvacrol, thymol (in glycerine) chinoline tartrate, creasote, eugenol, resorcin, Sanitas oil, Listerine, boro-glyceride, are antiseptics most commonly used by dentists in the treatment of various diseased conditions.*

In alveolar pyorrhoea Harlan recommends hydrogen dioxide and solution of zinc iodide.

500. In washing plates of artificial teeth, regard must be had for their metallic character; for example, a plate containing aluminium is said to be affected by a corrosive sublimate solution more readily than by carbolic acid.

A mouth wash containing 1 part of corrosive sublimate in 5000 can be made as follows: one grain of the perchloride of mercury and 1 grain of chloride of ammonium to be dissolved in 1 ounce of eau de cologne, and a teaspoonful of the solution to be mixed with two thirds of a wineglassful of water.

501. **Experiments of Miller:**

Experiments were made by Miller with various antiseptics, to ascertain which would answer best to retard or to prevent fermentation in the mouth. The following are the results:

The fermentative action is

	Prevented by 1 in	Arrested by 1 in
Corrosive sublimate	500,000	100,000
Silver Nitrate	100,000	50,000
Iodine (in Alcohol)	15,000	6,000
Iodoform	10,000	5,000
Naphthalin	9,000	4,000
Ess. Oil Mustard	5,000	2,000
Permang. Potassium	2,000	1,000
Oil Eucalyptus		600

* A coal tar substance called *creolin* is claimed to exceed carbolic acid in deodorizing efficiency. Its exact chemical composition is a trade secret. It is a powerful styptic and is said to be non-poisonous.

	Prevented by 1 in	Arrested by 1 in
Carbolic Acid	1,000	500
Hydrochloric Acid	1,000	500
Sodium Carbonate	200	100
Salicylic Acid	125	75
Alcohol, absol	25	10

These results are of considerable interest not only to dentists, but also for the preparation of efficient tooth powders.

Miller claims to sterilize the mouth, cavities in carious teeth, etc., by the following mixture:

Thymol	4 gr.
Benzoic Acid	45 gr.
Tincture of Eucalyptus	3½ fl. dr.
Water	25 fl. oz.

The mouth is to be well rinsed with this mixture, especially just before going to bed, since most of the damage by fermentative and putrefactive processes in the mouth is done at night during sleep.

Miller has suggested a number of formulæ, most of which contain eucalyptus; he thinks the presence of corrosive sublimate necessary to insure efficiency. His mixtures are intended to serve as *foundations* for mouthwashes, since many of them are not palatable and need agents to be combined with them which shall disguise the burning taste, especially of thymol and of eucalyptus.

502. Deodorizers :—

For fetor of the breath, etc., chlorinated lime solution, chlorine water, chlorinated soda, permanganate of potassium solution, phenol sodique are used; also certain vegetable substances, as orris root. Various oils such as safrol, oil of Pinus Picea, oil of anise, oil of rose geranium, impart a pleasing fragrance to the breath; a drop or two in a glass of water, thoroughly stirred, is all that is necessary. Many persons tire of the taste of the oils of wintergreen and of sassafras. The use of orris has also been carried to excess. The author has found Miller's mouth-wash an excellent deodorizer.

503. Antiseptics of more recent use.

Alantol, $C_{20}H_{32}O$, liquid, powerful internal antibacterial and antiseptic.

Alpha-naphthol, solid, 1 in 10,000 prevents alcoholic fermentation of glucose. (Maximowitsch). In same strength prevents propagation of typhoid and tuberculous bacilli.

Betol, $C_6H_4(OH)CO_2.C_{10}H_7$, salicylo-beta-naphthylic ether, white powder, crystalline; insoluble in water, soluble in boiling alcohol and warm linseed oil. (Kobert).

Bismuth oxyiodide, BiOI, brownish powder, insoluble. Used dry. (Lister, Reynolds, and others.)

Creolin already mentioned, section 499, foot note.

Cresylic acid, said to be superior in antizymotic action to carbolic acid. (Dujardin-Beaumetz).

Iodine trichloride, ICl_3, orange-red powder, strongly irritating odor; 1 in 1,000, in aqueous solution, destroys bacillus-spores. (Riedel).

Mercuric albuminate contains 4 parts mercuric chloride in 12 of albumin and 984 of milk sugar.

Mercuric Oxycyanide, said to have six times the bactericidal force of mercuric chloride. (Chibret).

Oxy-naphthoic acid, alpha. Said to have five times the anti-zymotic action of salicylic acid. White microcrystalline powder almost insoluble in water, more soluble in solutions of the bicarbonates.

Sodium silico-fluoride, non-toxic, surgical antiseptic. (Thomson).

Sodium sulphite, benzoated, non-toxic, surgical antiseptic. (Heckel).

Tribrom-phenol, made by action of bromine on aqueous carbolic acid, energetic and reliable disinfectant in purulent and gangrenous processes. (Grimm).

CHAPTER V.

THE TEETH AND THE SALIVA.

504. **Structure:** the chief mass of a tooth consists of a substance called *dentine*, in the interior of which is the *pulp cavity*. The crown of the tooth is invested by a substance called *enamel*, which extends some distance down the neck, but the fangs are covered by a substance known as *cement* (*crusta petrosa*). Before describing the dental tissues further, we shall pay attention for a moment to the chemistry of bone.

505. **Bone** consists of an organic substance called *ossein*, which we have seen is a proteid substance belonging to the collagens, intimately combined with a mineral substance called *bone earth*, in proportion of about 30 of ossein to 70 of bone earth. The latter is a mixture of various salts, as calcium phosphate, calcium carbonate, calcium fluoride, and magnesium phosphate, of which the most abundant in quantity are the calcium phosphate and carbonate. Bone contains also water and fat. The os-

310   DENTAL CHEMISTRY.

sein of bone resembles gelatin, and by boiling ossein with water it is changed into gelatin.

Hoppe-Seyler gives the general composition of normal, undried bone as:

    Water................ 50.00 per cent
    Fat .... 15.75 " "
    Ossein .... 11.40 " "
    Bone earth........... 21.85 " "

Most of the water is combined in the ossein. Expressing the composition of bone in order to show the relative percentage of organic and inorganic substances we find it, according to Heintz, as follows:

    Inorganic substances.... 69.53 to 68.88
    Organic substances...... 30.47 " 31.12

Analysis of the *ash* shows that of the inorganic substances tribasic calcium phosphate, $Ca_3(PO_4)_2$, constitutes from 83.89 to 87.70 per cent., calcium carbonate 8.9 to 13, 03, tribasic magnesium phosphate, 1.04 to 1.70 per cent., calcic fluoride and chloride, 0.76 to 4.90 per cent. Berzelius's analysis of bone resulted as follows:

    Ossein 32.17
    Calcium phosphate............. 51.04
    "   fluoride................ 2.00
    "   carbonate............... 11.30
    Soda with sodic chloride......... 1.20
    Magnesium phosphate.......... 1.16
    Vessels........................ 1.13

506. The inorganic constituents of bone increase slightly with age and the bone becomes more porous. The *marrow* of bones is of different composition, according to locality, but in the long bones (yellow marrow) is 96 per cent. fat, with some cholesterin, hypoxanthin, albumin and, occasionally, lactic acid. *Red* marrow contains a small proportion of fat, much albumin and salts, and an acid resembling lactic acid. In diseases of

bone the inorganic salts change in quantity, and the organic constituents in quality.

ANALYSIS OF BONE IN CARIES OF VERTEBRA.

Calcium phosphate......... 33.91
" carbonate.......... 7.60
Magnesium phosphate...... 1.93
Soluble salts, chiefly NaCl.. 0.61
Ossein, etc................ 19.58
Fat .... 1.22 (Valentin).

ANALYSIS OF BONE IN NECROSIS.

Calcium phosphate, etc..... 72.63
Calcium carbonate.......... 4.03
Magnesium phosphate...... 1.93
Soluble salts.............. 0.61
Ossein 19.58
Fat 1.22

507. Turning now to the chemical constitution of the **teeth**, we find that the *cement* has a structure resembling bone, and its chemical composition is almost the same, namely organic substances 30 parts, inorganic 70 parts; of the latter nearly 65 parts of the 70 are composed of *phosphates* of calcium and magnesium and *carbonate* of calcium, as follows:

Calcium phosphate 60.7
Magnesium phosphate. . 1.2
Calcium carbonate ..... 2.9 (Bibra).

508. The *enamel* of teeth is nearly all inorganic matter; in the enamel of some animals, as the dog, there seems to be no organic mat-

ter at all. In man, on an average, the inorganic constituents are from 95 to 97 per cent. in amount, the organic from 5 to 3; in the teeth of young infants, however, the inorganic matter is only from 77 to 84 per cent.

AVERAGE COMPOSITION OF THE ENAMEL.

Water and organic substances	3.6
Calcium phosphate and fluoride	86.9
Magnesium phosphate	1.5
Calcium carbonate	8.0

HOPPE-SEYLER'S ANALYSIS.

Calcium carbonate and phosphate, $Ca_{10}CO_3, 6PO_4$	96.0
$MgHPO_4$ (neutral phosphate of magnesium)	1.05
Organic substances	3.60

509. The *dentine* is more like bone than the enamel is, but less like it than the cement. It is composed of animal matter impregnated with earthy salts. It averages from 26 to 28 per cent. organic substances to 74 to 72 of inorganic matter.

ANALYSIS OF DENTINE.

	Woman.	Man.
Organic matter—ossein and vessels	27.61	20.42
Calcium phosphate	66.72	67.54

ANALYSIS—*Continued*.

Calcium carbonate	3.36	7.97
Magnesium phosphate	1.08	2.49
Other salts (NaCl, etc.)	0.83	1.00
Fat	0.40	0.58

ANALYSIS OF HOPPE-SEYLER.

$Ca_{10}CO_3, 6PO_4$	72.06
$MgHPO_4$	0.75
Organic substances	27.70

The organic matter of the dentine resembles the ossein of bone, but, according to Hoppe-Seyler, the walls of the canaliculi are invested with a body resembling *keratin* or *elasticin*. [Keratin is a proteid substance and is the chief component of epidermic structures. It is noticeable for the large amount of sulphur it contains. It is closely related to albumin, yielding leucin and tyrosin when decomposed. Its percentage composition is $C=50$ to 51.6, $H=6.4$ to 7.2, $N=16.2$ to 17.9, $S=0.7$ to 5.0, $O=20$ to 22.4. It is insoluble in alcohol and ether, swells up in boiling water, and is soluble in the caustic alkalies. It is not liable to decomposition, and melts when heated.

Elasticin is related to keratin, and is the substance composing the fibres of yellow elastic tissue. It is sometimes called *elastin*. It yields leucin but not tyrosin. Its percentage composition is $C = 54.32$, $H = 6.99$, $N = 16.75$, ash $= 0.5$].

Dentine contains 4 per cent. less water than bone. Its specific gravity, according to C. Krause, is 2.080. The walls of the canaliculi do not yield gelatin, but the ground substance of dentine may be transformed into gelatin, when heated in a Papin's digester. The globules of dentine are not convertible into gelatin, and resist the action of acids better than any other portions of the tissue do.

Of the three substances of which the teeth are composed we find that the enamel is the hardest, the dentine next, and the cement the least. The enamel is hard and brittle.

If the enamel be treated with dilute hydrochloric acid the calcium phosphate is dissolved, and there remain prismatic fibres which resemble epithelium and are not attacked by boiling water. If the cement be treated with an acid, its inorganic constituents are dissolved and there remains an organic residue which is said by Hoppe-Seyler not to yield gelatin; [according to some authors this substance *does* yield gelatin]. If the dentine be treated with acids, organic matter is left, most of which yields gelatin, but some does not. According to Bibra, molar teeth appear to contain more mineral matter than incisors.

510. Various analyses (tabulated for reference).

CEMENT OF TOOTH.

	Of ox (Fremy).	Of man (Bibra).
Ash (containing an average of) 67.1 per cent		70.58 per cent.
Calcic phosphate	60.70	"
Magnesic	1.20	"
Carbonate of lime	2.90	"

DENTINE OF TOOTH, (HOPPE-SEYLER).

$Ca_{10}CO_3, 6(PO_4)$	72.06
$MgHPO_4$	0.75
Organic substances	27.70

DENTINE (BIBRA).

	Adult woman.	Adult man.
Organic matter, ossein and vessels	27.61	20.42
Phosphate of lime	66.72	67.54
Carbonate "	3.36	7.97
Phosphate of magnesia	1.08	2.49
Other salts (NaCl, etc.)	0.83	1.00
Fat	0.40	0.58

ENAMEL OF TOOTH.

Water and organic substances............ 3.6
Calcic phosphate and fluoride............ 86.9
Magnesic phosphate.................... 1.5
Calcic carbonate....................... 8.0

It is thus given by Hoppe-Seyler:

$Ca_{10}CO_3 \, 6(PO_4)$...................... 96.00
$MgHPO_4$............................ 1.05
Organic substances.................... 3.60

ENAMEL AND DENTINE COMPARED—OX (AEBY).

	Enamel.	Dentine.
Organic substances and water....	3.60	27.70
Inorganic "	96.40	72.30

In 100 parts ash—

Calcic phosphate................	93.35	91.32
" carbonate	4.80	1.61
" oxide	0.86	5.27
Magnesic carbonate.............	0.78	0.75
Calcic sulphate..................	0.12	0.09
Oxide of iron...................	0.09	0.10

DENTINE, CEMENT, AND ENAMEL COMPARED.

	Ash.	Calcium Phosphate.	Magnesium Phosphate.	Calcium Carbonate.
Dentine......	76.8	70.3	4.3	2.2
Cement.......	67.1	60.7	1.2	2.9
Enamel.......	96.9	90.5	traces.	2.2

Minute amounts of chlorine and fluorine are found, especially in the enamel. (Fremy.)

CEMENT AND DENTINE COMPARED, (AEBY).

	Cement.	Dentine.
Calcium phosphate............	61.32	63.35
" oxide.................	5.27	0.86
" carbonate............	1.61	4.80
" sulphate	0.09	0.12

CEMENT—*Continued.*

Magnesium carbonate	0.75	0.78
Ferric oxide	0.10	0.09
Organic substances	27.70	26.00

ANALYSIS OF TEETH BY BERZELIUS.

Organic matter	28.0
Calcium phosphate	64.4
Magnesium phosphate	1.0
Calcium carbonate	5.3
Sodium " and chloride	1.3
Water, animal matter, alkali (traces)	0.0
	100.0

511. Action of Various Substances on the Teeth:— Owing to the solubility in acids of the phosphates and carbonates of magnesium and calcium, it stands to reason that a great part of tooth structure may be destroyed when brought into contact with substances either themselves acid or of strongly acid reaction.

According to many authorities as Westcott, Allport, Mantegazza, Magitot, Leber and Rottenstein, etc., the strong mineral and vegetable acids act promptly upon the teeth. Leber and Rottenstein found that in time a solution of *tartaric acid*, 1 in 1000 attacked the enamel, as did also *crushed grapes*, or a 1 in 1000 solution of *acetic acid*, of *oxalic acid*, or 1 in 100 solution of *alum*, or 1 in 1000 of *lactic acid*. According then to Leber and Rottenstein, as also to Westcott, Allport, and Mantegazza, all the vegetable acids without distinction attack the enamel of the teeth. It is well to bear in mind such substances in daily use as are either acids or have an acid reaction, and hence should not be allowed to come constantly into contact with the teeth; these are the *mineral acids*, as sulphuric, nitric, hydrochloric, phosphoric, etc., the *vegetable acids*, as oxalic, acetic, tartaric, lactic, benzoic, salicylic, tannic, etc., *many compounds of the metals*, as ferric chloride ("tincture of iron"), acid phosphates of calcium, magnesium, etc., etc., alum, arsenic, corrosive sublimate, zinc chloride, cream of tartar (acid potassium tartrate), the sulphate and subsulphate of iron, chromic anhydride (chromic "acid" so-called). Solutions of hydrogen dioxide are acid in reaction; some preparations of it contain much less acid than others.

C. A. Brackett has examined a number of substances used in dentistry and finds the following, among many other substances, to be acid in reaction:

Ordinary alcoholic tincture of myrrh (the specimen was some months old).

A solution of 1 part chloride of zinc to 2 parts glycerine.

Glycerine, 2 parts, tincture of aconite root, 1 part.

He found also, as might be expected, that the liquid portion of various "cements" was acid in reaction.

Among substances *but feebly acid* in reaction may be mentioned boracic acid.

Among substances which, *if pure*, should be neutral in reaction we find silver nitrate, carbolic acid. Among articles of diet which tend to attack the teeth may be mentioned acidulated drinks, foods readily becoming acid, and saccharine articles, shown by Miller to be converted into lactic acid.

512. **Chemistry of caries:** three theories have been advanced to account for caries, namely, *the chemical theory, the vital theory*, and *the germ theory*. According to the **chemical theory**, the substance of the tooth is decomposed by an acid; this acid acts more readily on

dentine than on enamel, hence the tendency to the enlargement of the cavity toward the internal portions of the tooth. The origin of the acids thus supposed to produce caries has been a subject of much inquiry. For a time the saliva was supposed to furnish them, but it was shown that decay occurred in mouths in which the saliva was habitually normal, and did not occur in some mouths in which the saliva was habitually acid. (Black). The hypothesis that the acid is furnished on the spot, through the decomposition of the food, seems much more feasible, and the production of the acid, if coming through fermentation, decomposition, or remoleculization of the substances lodged about the teeth, makes it easy for one to "glide from the old acid theory to the new germ theory." (Black).

The **germ theory** of caries sets forth, according to Miller, that no less than five different fungi exist in carious human teeth. These fungi have the power of causing fermentation in solutions containing fermentable carbohydrates and producing, as one of the products, optically inactive *lactic acid*. Free oxygen is not required for the production of this fermentative action, though it is probably accessory to the life and growth of the fungi. They have the power to invert sugar, that is, to convert infermentable cane sugar into fermentable glucose. When sound teeth are exposed to the action of these fungi, they are rapidly deprived of lime, and, on microscopic examination, large masses of bacteria will be found in the dental channels. The equation for the production of the lactic acid has already been given.

The **vital theory** supposed caries to result from an inflammation of the structure of the dentine, terminating in the final breaking down of the part; and as the structure is incapable, as is well known, of physiological repair, a cavity is the inevitable result. According to Black, it is still very uncertain whether any of the theories in regard to caries are correct, but the phenomena are explained by more than one with sufficient accuracy to be of great value, both in the prevention and treatment. Whatever may be the theories, it is claimed that the teeth deteriorate as an effect of mental overwork; among the hard-worked pupils of the Paris public schools, the teeth become deteriorated in a few weeks after entry. According to Parker, increased decay and increased sensibility of the dentine are apparent in men training for athletic trials. Williams has shown that any mental strain shows itself in the teeth in a short time.

THE SALIVA.

513. **The Saliva:** the saliva is the product of the combined secretion of the parotid, submaxillary, and sublingual glands. In the mouth these secretions are mixed together, and, also with it the mucus secreted in the oral cavity.

Physical characteristics of mixed saliva: *taste*, none; *color*, none; *odor*, none; *specific gravity*, 1002 to 1006; *reaction*, alkaline; *appearance*, generally turbid; *consistence*, glairy, viscid, frothy. On standing for some hours in a cylindrical glass vessel, an opaque, whitish deposit collects at the bottom, while the supernatant fluid becomes clear and of a faint, bluish tinge.

The *average daily amount* excreted has been placed at 1500 grams (about three pints); according to Ralfe this is probably too high, and 800 to 900 grams (less than a quart) is nearer the mark.

The specific gravity, according to some authors, may range normally as high as 1009. Saliva from different individuals may show a constant difference in alkalinity, but it varies only within narrow limits, and, while showing within certain limits in the same individual a constant degree of alkalinity, there is a decided and constant difference in different individuals, but no constant corresponding difference in diastatic action, according to Chittenden. (Charles). The *solids*, present in saliva, form only about one half of one per cent. of it; half nearly of these solids are salts, the rest proteids, namely ptyalin, globulin, and serum albumin.

The alkalinity would seem to depend on the presence of alkaline bicarbonates and phosphates with, possibly, help from a combination of the ptyalin with soda. The *sediment* consists of epithelial cells and salivary corpuscles—the latter resembling the colorless blood corpuscles and probably derived therefrom; under the microscope, they present the same appearance as lymph cells, which have become swollen in water and within their bodies, as long as they are uninjured, a lively movement of small molecules may be perceived.

514 **Chemical composition of saliva:** the most important constituents of saliva are the diastatic ferment or

ptyalin, as it is called, *mucin*, and the chlorides of sodium and potassium; in addition are found traces of albumin, fat, *potassium sulphocyanide*, sulphates and phosphates of the alkalies and alkaline earths, chiefly calcium phosphate, also calcium carbonate, and oxide of iron. Sometimes, even in normal saliva, urea and ammonium nitrite are found. Saliva contains small quantities of nitrogen and oxygen, and an abundance of carbonic acid. The following are analysis of the mixed saliva:

FRERICHS.

Water.............................994.10
Solids............................. 5.90
  Epithelium and mucus................. 2.13
  Fat..................................... 0.07
  Mucin and traces of alcoholic extract...... 1.41
  Potassium sulphocyanide................ 0.10
  Chlorides of sodium and potassium, phosphates of sodium, potassium, and oxide of iron................................ 2.19

JACUBOWITSCH.

Water............................. 99.51
Solids............................. 0.48
  Soluble organic bodies, ptyalin, etc........ 0.130
  Epithelium............................ 0.160
  Inorganic salts........................ 0.182
  Potassium sulphocyanide............... 0.006
  Potassium and sodium chloride.......... 0.084

SIMON.

Water.............................991.22
Solids............................. 8.78
  Ptyalin................................ 4.37
  Mucin.................................. 1.40
  Sulphocyanide 1.40
  Salts 1.40

BERZELIUS.

Water	992.9
Solids	7.1
Ptyalin	2.9
Mucin	1.4
Sulphocyanide	1.4
Salts	1.9

HAMMERBACHER.

Water	92.42
Solids	0.58
Epithelium and mucin	0.220
Ptyalin and albumin	0.140
Inorganic salts	0.220
Potassium sulphocyanide	0.004

IN 100 PARTS SOLIDS.

Epithelium and mucin	37.98
Ptyalin and albumin	23.97
Inorganic salts	38.03

IN 100 PARTS ASH.

Potash	45.71
Soda	9.59
Lime	5.01
Magnesia	0.16
Phosphoric anhydride	18.85
Sulphuric "	6.38
Chlorine	18.35

Enderlin gives in the 100 parts ash 92.37 as soluble and 5.51 as insoluble, of which sodium chloride (common salt) = 61.93, sodic phosphate = 28.12, calcium phosphate and carbonate = 5.51, and sodium carbonate = 2.31.

The **functions** of the saliva are mechanical and chemical: fats are feebly emulsified and soluble substances, as sugar, are dissolved in it. Starch is converted into sugar:

$3(C_6H_{10}O_5) + 3H_2O = C_6H_{12}O_6 + 2(C_6H_{10}O_5) + 2H_2O = 3(C_6H_{12}O_6)$
Starch   grape sugar   dextrin   grape sugar.

According to Mering the starch yields dextrin and maltose and later grape sugar.

515. **Parotid saliva:** the following is Hoppe-Seyler's analysis of human parotid saliva:

Water.. 99.32
Solids.. 0.68
   Mucin, epithelium and soluble organic bodies..................................... 0.34
   Potassium sulphocyanide................ 0.03
   Inorganic salts........................... 0.34

It is a clear liquid, not viscous, but slightly alkaline. It gives no reaction for mucin, but contains albumin, ptyalin, and sulphocyanide of potassium.

Among more or less peculiar constituents we find paraglobulin, caproic acid, urea, and traces of sulphates. The reaction of the first secreted parotid saliva is less alkaline than that secreted later, although according to Astachewsky, it has a faintly acid reaction that gives place to an alkaline reaction, when the mucous membrane of the mouth is slightly irritated.

On standing, the parotid secretion becomes turbid, owing to the escape of carbonic acid and the consequent precipitation of calcium carbonate. Parotid saliva varies in quantity during the day, less being secreted immediately after a meal. (Charles).

516. **Submaxillary saliva:** in the dog, this saliva contains 99.44 water and 0.59 solids. Of the latter, mucin and epithelium form 0.066 parts, soluble organic bodies 0.17, inorganic salts 0.43. The character of submaxillary

saliva depends on the exciting stimulus to its secretion; stimulation of the *chorda tympani* nerve causes a normal, rich alkaline secretion, as noticed when acids are applied to the surface of the tongue, but in it no pytalin is found; with long continued stimulation the organic solids diminish somewhat, though at first the mucin is especially increased; stimulation of the *sympathetic*, as on application of pepper or alkalies to the tongue, produces a strongly alkaline secretion, of high specific gravity, 1.007 to 1.018, but viscid, turbid, slowly flowing, rich in mucus and irregularly formed cell elements.

In *chordal saliva* (submaxillary), Heidenhain gives the solids as 3 per cent., 2.5 organic and 0.5 inorganic; but other authorities give 1.2 to 1.4 per cent. In *sympathetic saliva* (submaxillary) Heidenhain gives 5.8 per cent. solids, Eckhard 2.7 per cent. In paralysis of the nerves supplying the gland very watery saliva is found, containing little solids or mucus. *In general, it may be said of saliva that it contains a comparatively large quantity of mucin dissolved in an alkaline fluid, together with a sugar-forming ferment, and potassium sulphocyanide.* Submaxillary saliva is comparatively poor in ptyalin, while parotid is rich in it; submaxillary saliva is rich in mucin, while parotid is poor in it. The submaxillary saliva is more alkaline than parotid and more viscid. Its average specific gravity is from 1.002 to 1.003. It contains much more carbonic aciu than is found in venous blood, but is poorer in nitrogen. (Pflueger).

517. **Sublingual saliva:** this saliva is very viscous and thready, strongly alkaline, rich in mucus and salivary corpuscles, and would appear to be the richest in solids of all salivas. Heidenhain found 2.75 per cent. of solids in the dog. Traces of cholesterin and fat have been found. (Charles).

518. **Buccal mucus:** the amount of this is inconsid-

erable and it contains, according to Bidder and Schmidt, 99 per cent. of water. Its reaction is said to be acid; it contains numerous form elements, flattened epithelial cells, and salivary corpuscles. Claude Bernard found buccal mucus alkaline; the acid reaction would appear to be due to alteration.

519. **Circumstances favoring the diastatic action of saliva:—**

I. Quality of saliva (parotid acting more slowly than submaxillary); quality of starch.

II. Presence of acid *up* to 0.005 per cent.

III. Dilute alkaline solutions at 104 F.°

520. **Circumstances** *interfering with or suspending* **diastatic action:**

I. Strong alkalies, acids, temperatures above 158°F.

II. Temperature at or near freezing point.

521. **Changes in the saliva:** the *quantity* is not constant even normally. Its secretions may be excited by the sight or even thought of food, by the movements of mastication, by vapors of ether or acetic acid, or by electric excitation. If Jacobson's nerve be stimulated, a watery secretion occurs with diminished ptyalin, albumin, and salts; if there is stimulation of the sympathetic at the same time, a copious secretion is obtained, in which the organic constituents are in abundance, with a slight increase of the salts.

Circumstances which increase the quantity in twenty-four hours:

I. Dry food and tooth-filling.

II. Debility; confluent small-pox; at end of typhoid fever; ague.

III. Certain drugs: mercury, pilocarpine, eserine.

IV. Dentition.

V. Pregnancy.

VI. Hysteria; facial neuralgia; idiocy; hemiplegia from cerebral cause.

VII. Water-brash; organic diseases of the stomach or abdominal viscera.

VIII. Stomatitis; ulceration of buccal mucous membrane.

IX. Injury from mineral acids taken internally.

Among the drugs which have been known to produce salivation are bromine, arsenic, antimony, lead, prussic acid, nux vomica, gold, cantharides, digitalis, conium, belladonna, opium, iodide of potassium particularly, iodine, copper, croton oil, colchicum. In mercurial ptyalism, *fetor* of the breath and *sponginess* of the gums are common, but these characters have been observed in salivation from arsenic and bismuth. Extremely minute doses of mercury will, in some persons, rapidly bring on salivation.

Certain substances, as bark of pyrethrum, tobacco, etc., excite the buccal mucous membrane and lead to salivation.

522. **Circumstances decreasing the quantity of saliva:—**

I. Fevers and inflammatory diseases.

II. Certain drugs, particularly belladonna and atropine.

523. **Circumstances rendering the saliva acid in reaction:—**

I. Decomposition of organic substances in the mouth.

II. Diabetes. (Saliva acid when secreted, and sometimes contains lactic acid).

III. Catarrh of the mouth and intestinal tract.

IV. Acute rheumatism.

V. Mercurial salivation.

VI. Occasionally in carcinoma of the liver and in typhus fever, in muguet, and frequently in dyspepsia, though in the last possibly due to acid mucus. Changes in the reaction of the saliva due to decomposition of food in the mouth must be carefully distinguished from changes due to disease. In the former case the saliva may be secreted of alkaline reaction, but in the latter case it comes acid from the ducts.

524. **Circumstances giving rise to odor in the saliva:—**
I. Gingivitis.
II. Scurvy.
III. Mercurial salivation.
IV. Angina.
A fetid odor has been noticed in the above named diseases.

525. **Circumstances increasing the amount of solids in the saliva** or producing abnormal solid constituents:
I. Mercurial salivation.
II. Bright's disease, (urea abundant).
III. Hysteria, (leucin found).
IV. Phlegmasia.

526. **Circumstances decreasing the amount of solids:—**
I. Chlorosis, (water increased).

527. **Tartar:** while the secretions of the mouth remain alkaline, there is a tendency to deposit lime compounds on the teeth. This constitutes *tartar*, and, although it protects the body of the tooth, it has an injurious effect on the gums. When the secretions of the mouth become acid, tartar is no longer deposited, and the decay of the teeth usually hastened. (Leffman).

Soft tartar, such as is found at the necks, especially of the back teeth of youth, is destructive, holding acids *in loco*. (Chandler).

Tartar is of grayish, yellowish, or brownish color; *leptothrix buccalis* is found in it; it consists chiefly of calcium phosphate, with a little calcium carbonate, and phosphate of iron. According to Charles its average composition is as follows:

	Per cent.
Calcium phosphate	55 to 64
" carbonate	7 to 8
Ferric phosphate	1 to 3
Residue: organic matter, salts of alkalies, silica, etc.	24 to 28

Magitot held that tartar in the region of the parotid was almost wholly carbonate, other tartar, phosphate. Alfred Vergne on the contrary claims that molar tartar has less phosphate than incisor, but that the carbonate is about evenly divided.

528. Salivary Calculi: saliva exposed to the air becomes covered with a film of calcium carbonate. Concretions of this substance are often found in the salivary ducts, in which case they are known as *salivary calculi*. These are of an elongated form, dirty white color, and formed in concentric layers. They vary in size, appearance, and composition. They contain no *leptothrix*. Their average composition is, according to Charles, as follows:

	Per Cent.
Calcic phosphate	30 to 80
" carbonate	11 to 15
Organic matter	5 to 25

Magnesium oxide, iron oxide, sodium chloride, sulphates, and potassium sulphocyanide, have all been found in salivary calculi.

529. *Uric acid* calculi have been found in the ducts in patients of an uric acid diathesis. Acids dissolve the ordinary salivary calculi very rapidly, considerable gas being given off owing to the abundance of calcium carbonate present.

CHAPTER VI.

PRACTICAL WORK IN DENTAL CHEMISTRY PROGRESSIVELY ARRANGED.

SHORT COURSE OF SIMPLE EXPERIMENTS ILLUSTRATING PRINCIPLES OF GENERAL CHEMISTRY.*

530. 1. Drop a piece of *marble* into a test tube. Add to it 20 or 30 drops of *hydrochloric acid*. After a few minutes introduce a burning wooden tooth-pick. What happens?' Why? (Section 298).

2. Heat 15 or 20 grains of *potassium chlorate* in a test tube. After it melts and, gives off gas-bubbles introduce the glowing stick used in experiment 1. What happens? (Section 241).

3. Drop a small piece of *zinc* into a test tube and add 30 drops of *hydrochloric acid*. In a minute or two bring a lighted match to mouth of the tube. Equation? (Section 176).

4. Add a few drops of any *acid* as hydrochloric to a test-tube half full of water. Taste a drop of the liquid. Drop into it a slip of *blue litmus*. What happens? (Section 129, Definition 8).

---

*These experiments may be shown in the lecture room by the lecturer or performed by the class in the laboratory in the first week of the term.

SIMPLE EXPERIMENTS.

5. Add a few drops of *ammonia* to the same amount of water. Taste a drop of the liquid. What is the difference in taste from that of the preceding? Drop into the liquid a slip of *red litmus?* What happens? (Definition 9, page 55).

6. Dissolve *common salt* in water, taste it, and drop into it both red and blue litmus. What is the effect on the litmus? Does it resemble that of 5, or of 6, or neither?

7. Carefully pour into a test-tube containing water about twice as much *sulphuric acid*. What is noticed? (Section 240).

8. Pour *nitric cid* upon a copper cent. What is the blue liquid? What are the fumes? (Have a good draught to carry off fumes). (Section 270).

9. Dip a glass rod into nitric acid and touch the back of your hand with it. Sensation after a few minutes? Color of stain? Effect of washing the stain?

10. Pour a few drops of ordinary Aqua Ammoniæ into one tumbler and a drop or two of *hydrochloric acid* into another. Then invert one tumbler over the other. What is the result? What is formed? (Table 15, Page 110).

11. Procure an ignition tube and put into it a mixture of *oxide of copper* and *charcoal*, ten times as much by weight of the former as of the latter, and filling the tube not more than one-third full. Heat fully five minutes. Then remove, cool, pour out on paper and look for what? Why? Equation? (Section 209).

12. Put a *dime* into a dish and pour over it a mixture of *nitric acid and water*, in which there is twice as much water as acid. What will happen? (Section 270). N. B. Warm gently and notice what happens. Let cool. Take out any undissolved silver. Add as much water as was used in making the mixture with the acid, and immediately drop into the liquid a *cent*. Let stand. What will take place?

13. Obtain a rod of zinc. Polish it and drop it into a test-tube containing a freshly made solution of sugar of lead. Let stand. What takes place?

14. Dissolve chloride of gold in a little water, warm gently, and drop into it a small piece of phosphorus. (Section 252).

15. *Mix nitric and hydrochloric acids*, using four times as much hydrochloric as nitric. Now drop into the mixture a bit of *gold leaf.* What happens? Warm the mixture slightly. What happens? (Section 258). What gas is formed? Prove it by holding a piece of paper on which there is writing, still wet, over the tube and noticing what happens. (Section 247).

16. Warm a few crystals of *iodine* dry, in a test-tube, notice what happens and introduce into the tube, while still warming, a glass rod. What is noticed on the rod and what is the term used for the process and results? (Section 65, Chapter I).

17. Blow through a glass tube into lime-water. What happens? Now add a drop or two of acid and stir well. What happens? What was formed at first? (Section 187). In what is it soluble? In what is it insoluble?

18. Put equal parts of sulphuric acid and alcohol into a test-tube and warm over alcohol-lamp flame. What odor is noticed? What is formed? (Section 400).

19. Obtain some of the substance alluded to in experiment 18 and put a few drops of it on the hand. What is observed?

20. Dissolve some gutta-percha in carbon disulphide and filter through animal charcoal.

21. Obtain the *white of an egg* and drop it into *boiling water*. What results?

22. Treat half of the mixture obtained in experiment 21 with *nitric acid* and the other half with *ammonia*. What happens in each case?

23. Put equal quantities of *urine* into two bottles. Into one bottle put a pinch of *salicylic acid* but not into the other. Cork and let stand for several days and examine as to odor. What has been the action of the salicylic acid ?

LABORATORY COURSE OF SIXTY EXPERIMENTS ILLUSTRATING THE PRACTICAL APPLICATION OF CHEMISTRY TO DENTISTRY.*

531. **Objects of Laboratory work:**—first, to teach the dental student to observe correctly, free from unconscious inference. Second, to illustrate by experiment the chemical changes occuring in the mouth. Third, to impart a knowledge of the principles of chemistry.

Method of work: first, examine carefully all substances to be used; second, perform the experiment as directed; third, make a record of what has been done, using a notebook. Lastly observe all phenomena resulting from the operation performed and seek explanation by reference to known principles of chemistry as set forth in Chapter II.

Order of recording work:—Write down in note-book first the names (formulæ where possible) of substances used; second, a description of the operations performed; third, an account of the changes observed; fourth, the theoretical explanations. Use abbreviated language, write legibly, do not crowd the notes but leave plenty of space.

532. **Examination of a substance:**—in examining a substance the student should endeavor to answer the following questions in regard to its nature:

1. *Is the substance a solid, a liquid, or a gas?*

---
*Contributed by J. H. Salisbury, M. D., Professor of Chemistry in Lake Forest University, Dental Department.

2. If solid, does it possess crystalline form?
3. Does it contain water of crystallization?
4. Is it efflorescent, deliquescent, or permanent in the air?
5. Color?
6. Odor?
7. Taste? Test this by a drop of a *dilute* solution always.
8. *Is it soluble in water? Reaction of solution to litmus paper?*
9. When heated does it volatilize readily?

(Those questions in italics must be answered without fail. Others may be investigated according to the time and inclination of the student).

Experiment 1: examine metallic mercury.

To illustrate chemical combination. Multiple proportions. Quantivalence and the naming of binary compounds. See sections 115—117, 120, 123—125, rules 4—10.

2. *Examine iodine.*
3. *Combination of mercury and iodine.* Mix a quantity of mercury with a small quantity of iodine, adding a little alcohol to control the action by keeping down the heat.

Observe the phenomena and examine the product, (Section 236) mercurous iodide.

4. Mix a quantity of mercury with a larger quantity of iodine, adding a little alcohol.

Observe the phenomena and examine the product. (Section 235), mercuric iodide.

5. *Examine mercuric oxide.*
6. Place mercuric oxide in an ignition tube, (Fig. 1) provided with a cork, through which passes a bent delivery tube dipping under water; invert over the end of the delivery tube a test-tube filled with water. Heat the ignition tube to redness and collect the gas given off in the inverted test-tube.

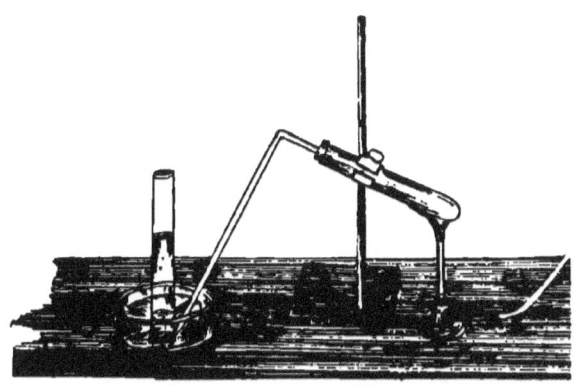

FIG. 1.

Notice a sublimate of metallic mercury on ignition and delivery tubes.
7. Examine the gas in the test-tube. Plunge into it a match which has been lighted and then extinguished leaving a glowing coal on the end.

(See Section 241, page 158).

Compounds of mercury with chlorine. Chlorine is a gaseous element which combines with mercury in two proportions, viz:

Calomel- Mercury, 200, and Chlorine 35.37.

Corrosive Sublimate=Mercury 200 and Chlorine 70.74. Name these two compounds (Section 123, Rule 5.)

8. *Examine Calomel.* (Section 233, Page 150).

N. B. To determine whether a substance is soluble in water; digest it with distilled water, filter, (Fig. 2), and evaporate filtrate to dryness (in this case over water-bath) on a glass slide, or piece of mica or platinum foil. If anything has been dissolved, a residue will be left on the glass, mica, or foil.

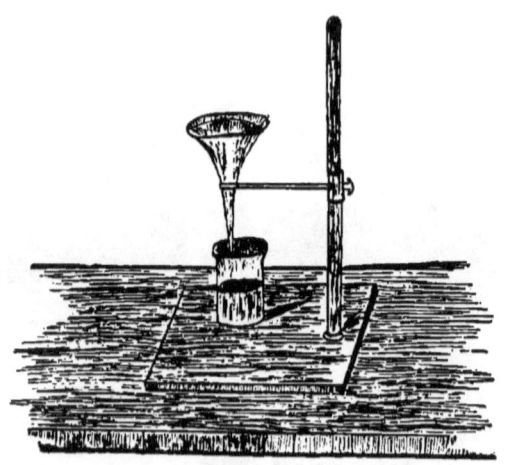

FIG. 2.

9. *Examine corrosive sublimate.* (Section 232, Page 148).

10. *Expulsion of mercury from its compounds by copper*, illustrating substitution.

Into a solution of corrosive sublimate put a piece of bright copper foil. Heat for a few moments. Take out the copper and notice that it is covered with mercury.

11. Dry the copper between folds of filter

paper. Put it into the bottom of a narrow glass tube, closed at one end, and heat the copper to redness. The mercury will volatilize and be deposited on the tube in microscopic globules. Under a low power of the microscope these globules appear round and opaque by transmitted light, but shine like stars by reflected light.

12. Insert into the mouth of the tube a small crystal of iodine, and stop up the mouth of the tube with wax. Leave for a day in a warm place The iodine will volatilize and combine with the mercury, forming a red compound.

13. Test an unknown liquid for mercury, as follows: add hydrochloric acid and drop in a small piece of bright copper, boil, then take out the copper, wash, dry, and heat in a tube as in the previous experiment.

14. *Mercury combined with other metals:*— amalgamate zinc by dipping it into mercury. Set aside the mercury, so used, for purification, labelling it "impure mercury."

15. Heat the amalgamated zinc in a tube and collect the mercury given off.

16. Drop a piece of ordinary zinc into dilute sulphuric acid. Notice that a gas is given off. The gas is hydrogen.

17. Drop a piece of amalgamated zinc into dilute sulphuric acid. Notice that little or no hydrogen is given off.

18. *Action of acids on metals:* examine zinc.

19. Examine hydrochloric acid.

20. Observe action of dilute hydrochloric acid on zinc.

21. Collect the gas given off and prove it to be hydrogen; (Section 176). This can easily be done as follows: fit to a test-tube in which the acid is acting on zinc, a cork or rubber stopper, through which passes a short tube. Hold an inverted test-tube over the end of this tube for a short time. The gas will partly fill the tube, and when brought mouth downward to a flame, will give rise to a sharp explosion. Hold the test-tube over the mouth of the tube a longer time. It will fill entirely with hydrogen, and when brought to the flame it will burn quietly up the tube with but a slight explosion.

22. Evaporate the solution to dryness and examine the salt formed.

23. Examine sulphuric acid.

24. Observe the action of concentrated sulphuric acid on zinc.

25. Observe the action of dilute sulphuric acid on zinc.

26. Observe the action of acetic acid on zinc.

27. Observe the action of dilute acids on silver, copper, tin, and lead.

28. *Action of hydric sulphide upon the metals of alloys.* Generate sulphuretted hydrogen from sulphide of iron and dilute

sulphuric acid (Fig. 3) and observe the properties of the gas.

Make a solution for further use. (Section 239 and 544).

29. Drop a drop of sulphuretted hydrogen solution on a surface of zinc; on one of copper, on one of silver; and on one of mercury. Observe results.

30. Put a piece of silver in a rotten egg, and observe the discoloration of the metal.

31. Expose an amalgam plug to the action of sulphuretted hydrogen, and also to the action of decaying food, such as would be found in the mouth.

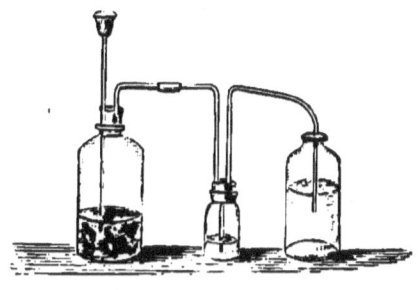

FIG. 3.

533. 32. *Experiments illustrating the composition and chemical properties of the teeth.* Examine calcic carbonate.

33. Treat calcic carbonate with hydrochloric acid and examine the gas given off. (Section 298).

34. Pass this gas into lime water and notice the deposition of calcic carbonate.

35. Continue passing the gas, until the carbonate at first thrown down is re-dissolved.

36. Boil the solution thus obtained and notice the precipitate of calcic carbonate.

This experiment illustrates the way in which water becomes hard, and also the deposition of carbonate and phosphate of calcium from the saliva, upon escape of the carbon dioxide which held it in solution.

37. Prove the existence of carbonates in teeth by treating the latter with hydrochloric acid and passing the gas given off through lime water.

38. *Phosphoric acid.* Burn phosphorus under a glass vessel, as a large beaker, and notice the snow-white powder produced.

39. Dissolve the powder in water. Notice the acid reaction and sour taste.

40. Boil the liquid, adding to it some ammonia and a solution of calcic chloride. Notice the precipitation of calcic phosphate.

41. Examine calcic phosphate.

42. Add to calcic phosphate dilute hydrochloric or acetic acid, heat, filter, and to filtrate add ammonia water. Notice that calcic phosphate which has been dissolved by the acid is precipitated by neutralization.

43. Dissolve teeth in hydrochloric acid, filter, and precipitate with ammonium hydrate. The precipitate is due to the presence of phosphates in the teeth

44. Add to a solution of a phosphate a

mixture of ammonic chloride, ammonic hydrate, and magnesic chloride or magnesic sulphate. Notice a crystalline precipitate proving presence of a phosphate. (Arsenates give the same reaction).

45. *Examine quick lime (calcic oxide).*

46. Slake quick lime and examine the resulting calcic hydrate. Make a solution and examine it.

47. Form calcic carbonate by double decomposition.

To form an insoluble substance by double decomposition we must remember that the substances put together should be soluble. One should contain the metal of the insoluble compound required, and the other the acid radical of the same compound. Further, the decomposition must not result in the formation of any substance capable of holding in solution the substance which we wish to form, else no change will occur. In this case it is required to form calcic carbonate. The metal of calcic carbonate is calcium, hence we must have a soluble compound of calcium. The acid radical of calcic carbonate is found in all carbonates, and we must take a soluble carbonate. This reduces us to a choice of two of a few compounds. Thus we have:

Soluble salts of calcium.
Calcic chloride,
" bromide,
" iodide,
" hydrate,
" nitrate,
" chlorate,
" acetate, etc.

Soluble carbonates.
Hydric Carbonate
Potassic "
Sodic "
Ammonic "

Any of these combinations may be used except that with hydric carbonate, which will form an acid which would hold the calcic carbonate in solution. Thus calcic chloride and carbonic acid will not form calcic carbonate, because hydrochloric acid would be formed at the same time.

48. Filter and wash precipitate until free from chlorides. We must determine when a precipitate is sufficiently washed by appropriate tests, instead of by guessing, as is frequently done. In this case the proper test is nitrate of silver added to a small portion of the filtrate, which will give a white precipitate of silver chloride, insoluble in nitric acid, as long as any chloride is washed away by the water which runs through the filter.

49. *Prepare pure calcic phosphate from bone ash* by dissolving the latter in hydrochloric acid, filtering, and precipitating the pure calcic phosphate by ammonia. This of course contains some magnesium.

50. *Form calcic oxalate* by precipitating a solution of calcic chloride with ammonic oxalate.

51. *Show the presence of calcium in teeth* by dissolving in hydrochloric acid. Filter, expel acid by evaporation, dissolve residue in water; add excess of ammonia, dissolve precipitate with the smallest quantity possible of acetic acid, and add solution of ammonic oxalate.

52. *Examine magnesium.*
53. *Examine magnesic sulphate.*
54. Form magnesic carbonate by double decomposition.

Ammonium carbonate cannot well be used because a soluble double salt of magnesium and ammonium is formed, which retains part of the magnesium in solution.

55. Examine magnesic carbonate.
56. Form ammonio-magnesic phosphate by adding to a solution of magnesic sulphate, ammonic chloride, ammonic hydrate, and sodic phosphate. The formula of the precipitate is $MgNH_4PO_4$.
57. Examine the precipitate thus formed.
58. This precipitate, after calcium and other metals, except potassium, sodium, and ammonium, have been removed from solution, forms a test for magnesium.
59. *Complete analysis of a tooth*, (Section 573).
60. *Examination of the saliva*, (Section 568).

LABORATORY WORK: METALS AND THEIR REACTIONS.

534. **If the substance to be examined is a metal or an alloy**, certain preliminary tests will give the analyst a hint as to what line of work is to be followed.

535. 1. Observe the **color, weight,** and

hardness; if the substance is very heavy, suspect *gold* or *platinum* as one of the constituents; if very light, *aluminium;* if brittle, *antimony,* or *bismuth;* if yellow or bronze in color, *gold* or *copper;* if grayish, *lead, cadmium, antimony, tin, bismuth;* if very white, *silver* or *nickel;* pour on a little nitric acid, and if the substance does not dissolve, but becomes a fine insoluble powder, *antimony* or *tin* is indicated.

2. Next study **the blow-pipe and its use.**

536. The blow-pipe, as commonly used, is a small, hollow, cylindrical, brass instrument, curved at the narrower end; it serves to conduct a continuous, fine current of air into a gas flame, or into the flame of a candle or lamp. [Various improvements on the ordinary instrument have been devised; for example, the trumpet mouth piece, so called, is used so that the muscles of the lip may not be fatigued. Fletcher's blow-pipe is highly recommended by Essig for work in the dental laboratory; in this instrument the air-tube is coiled into a light spiral, over the point of the jet].

537. If the ordinary blow-pipe is used, the beginner must practice blowing a steady current through the blow-pipe *with the cheeks and not with the lungs.* Distend cheeks, take the blow-pipe between the lips, and practice quiet breathing for some little time. When sufficient readiness in producing the current is thus acquired, bring the blow-pipe to a flame and practice on what are called the **reducing flame** and the **oxidizing flame.** Note: a flame of gas, candle, or lamp, consists of three parts, (a) a dark nucleus in the centre, (b) a luminous cone surrounding

nucleus, and (c) a feebly luminous mantle encircling the whole flame. Fig. 4.

538. **The reducing flame** is produced by keeping the jet of the blow-pipe *just on the border* of a tolerably strong gas flame, and driving a moderate blast across it: the resulting mixture of the air with the gas is only imperfect and there remains, between the inner bluish part of the flame, and the outer barely visible part, a **luminous and reducing zone,** of which the hottest point lies somewhat beyond the apex of the inner cone. This flame serves, under certain circumstances hereafter to be explained, *to take away oxygen* from a metallic compound, *i.e.* to reduce it.

539. **The oxidizing flame** is produced by lowering the gas, pushing the jet of blowpipe a little farther into the flame, and increasing the strength of the current. This serves to effect an intimate

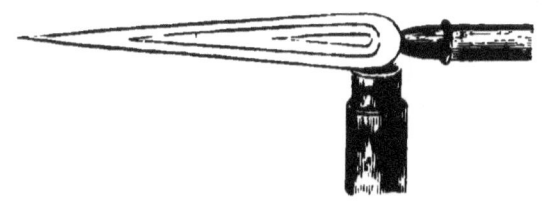

FIG. 5.   FIG. 4.

mixture of the air and gas, and an inner, pointed, bluish cone, slightly luminous towards the apex, is formed, and surrounded by a thin, pointed, light-bluish, barely visible mantle. The hottest part of the flame is at the apex of the inner cone. Difficultly fusible bodies are exposed to this part to effect their fusion; but bodies to be oxidized are held a little beyond the apex, that there may be no want of air for their combustion. For an oxidizing flame, a small spirit lamp will in most cases be sufficient. Fig. 5.

540. **Charcoal** is used for *reducing* processes: the substances to be operated on are put into small cavities in it, scooped out with a penknife, and the reducing flame of the blowpipe is directed upon them. The fusibility of bodies is also ascertained by use of charcoal as a support. *Incrustations* are often formed on the charcoal, composed of an oxide formed after reduction, when the metallic fumes pass through the outer flame, and become *re-oxidized*. Many incrustations have characteristic colors, leading to the detection of metals.

541. **Platinum wire** and sometimes **platinum foil** are used for *oxidizing* processes, and also when fusing substances with fluxes, in order to obtain what is called a **bead**, etc., etc. The wire is cut into convenient lengths, say 8 centimetres (a little over 3 inches) and twisted at both ends into a small loop. When required for use, the loop is moistened with a drop of water, then dipped into the powdered flux—if any is to be used, and the portion adhering fused in the flame of a gas or spirit lamp. When the bead produced, which sticks to the loop, is cold it is moistened again, and a small portion of the substance to be examined is put on, and made to adhere to it, by the action of gentle heat. The loop is then exposed to whatever flame is desired.

[Many kinds of supports have been devised, but when a small quantity of gold or silver is to be melted in the dental laboratory, the operation is usually performed on a support made of charcoal. Essig recommends that a good, solid, cylindrical piece of thoroughly charred pine coal be cut in halves vertically, by means of a saw. On the end of one half, a depression is cut for the reception of the metal to be melted, and on the flat side of the other half, extending to the end, the ingot mould is carved. The two halves are tied together with wire].

542. The simplest **self-acting blowpipe** is really the Bunsen gas-lamp, provided with a chimney. The flame is non-luminous, and burns without soot; Bunsen distinguishes six parts to the flame: the *base* near where the gas escapes from the burner, the *fusing zone* about one-third of the height of the flame from the bottom, and equidistant from the outside and inside, *the lower oxidizing flame* on the outer border of the fusing zone, *the upper oxidizing flame*, which is the non-luminous tip of the flame, *the lower reducing zone* in the inner border of the fusing zone, *the upper reducing flame* in the luminous tip of the dark inner cone. Many substances give characteristic tints to a colorless flame like the Bunsen. For instance, salts of sodium impart to flame a yellow tint, potassium a violet, lithium a carmine, etc., etc.

3. Having become familiar with the use of the blowpipe, the structure of flame, etc., etc., take a portion of the substance to be examined, place it with an equal weight of sodium carbonate in a little cavity in the charcoal, and expose for some minutes to the *inner* or *reducing* flame of the blow-pipe.

543. The following table* will serve to aid in the interpretation of results:

Cu.	Au.	Ag.
A red bead, somewhat difficult to fuse. No incrustation.	A yellow bead, easily malleable. No incrustation.	A white, malleable bead. No incrustation.

Pb.	Sn.	Sb.
Grayish-white globule, with yellow incrustation. Very soft.	White globules, not so readily reduced as Pb; malleable. Incrustation yellowish when hot, white when cold.	Gray, brittle globules which readily oxidize when hot. White incrustation.

*Oldberg and Long.

544. Short method for blow-pipe analysis.
I. Heat on charcoal equal weights of the substance to be examined and sodium carbonate. Use inner or reducing blow-pipe flame. Notice *odor, metallic globule, incrustation.* [If none, go on with II]. If a result is apparent, consult the following table:

Metallic globules.	Incrustation.	Probable metal.	Remarks.
Very brittle.	White.	Antimony.	Metal volatilizes.
None.	White.	Arsenic.	Garlic fumes.
Brittle.	Yellow.	Bismuth.	Metal easily fused.
Red, malleable.	Little or none.	Copper.	Difficult to fuse.
Soft, malleable.	Yellow.	Lead.	Marks paper.
Malleable.	Little or none.	Silver.	Not oxidizable.
Malleable.	Little or none.	Tin.	Easily oxidized and easily fused.
None.	Yellow when hot, white when cold.	Zinc.	Infusible, mass greenish-white.

Antimony gives off white fumes, and covers charcoal with incrustation. If **arsenic** is suspected, proceed as in V. If **bismuth** is apparently the metal, confirm as follows: heat a portion of the original substance on charcoal with a mixture of equal parts sulphur and potassium iodide: *bright red incrustation* on the cooler part indicates *bismuth.*

Copper may first be seen in the form of a reddish-brown substance, after heating in the inner flame. Now heat in the point of the blue inner flame, and a metallic globule of tough copper is obtained. If the substance is **brass,**

a yellow incrustation of oxide of zinc will be seen when the substance is hot, becoming white on cooling.

Lead may readily be recognized by its metallic globule of considerable size; the globule is soft, and may readily be flattened with a knife or cut. If the lead contain *silver*, the latter is detected by the use of bone-ash. Fill a bowl-shapéd cavity in the charcoal with finely powdered bone-ash, pressed down well so as to fill the cavity with a compact mass, smooth, and slightly hollowed on the surface. In this bone-ash place a small piece of the lead, hold the charcoal horizontally, and direct the extreme point of the *outer* (oxidizing) flame upon the metal. The bone-ash absorbs the lead oxide formed, leaving a metallic globule of silver; the latter may be covered with a thin film of oxide, showing rainbow tints. When the colors cease, and the globule no longer diminishes in size, it is pure silver. The process is hindered by presence of tin.

Silver is easily reduced, but not readily fused to a globule. Sharp heat is required to accomplish the latter. When the globule is once formed, it is easily distinguished from all other metals by the fact that it retains a bright metallic surface, when fused at the point of the outer (oxidizing) flame, and shows a characteristic white color.

If **tin** be suspected, take a fresh quantity of the original substance and heat with potassium cyanide instead of sodium carbonate. A very liquid slag is obtained, in which a large globule of tin may be formed without difficulty.

Zinc is so readily volatilized, i. e., converted into vapor, by heat that no metallic globule is formed, but merely a yellow incrustation. Moisten the latter with a dilute solution of cobalt nitrate, heat strongly, and a *green* compound (of zinc and cobalt) is formed.

11. If nothing be found by proceeding as

in I, take a very little of the substance, reduce to powder, heat on borax bead, in a loop of platinum wire, in the outer (oxidizing) flame. Note the color when hot, let cool, and observe the color. Now expose to inner flame, noting color when hot and when cold, as before. Then consult the following table:

Metals.	Outer Flame.	Inner Flame.
Chromium.	Yellowish green.	Emerald green.
Cobalt.	Blue.	Blue.
Copper.	Blue.	Brown or colorless.
Iron.	Brownish yellow.	Bottle green.
Manganese.	Purple or pink.	Colorless.
Nickel.	Brownish yellow.	Muddy gray.

III. If nothing distinct has been noted in procedure as by II, moisten a clean platinum wire with HCl, take a very little of the powdered substance on it, expose to inner blow-pipe flame. Observe any distinct color which may be imparted to outer flame. Consult the following table:

Metal.	Color imparted to outer flame.
Barium.	Green.
Calcium,	Red.
Copper.	Bluish-green.
Potassium.	Violet-blue.
Sodium.	Yellow.
Strontium.	Carmine.

IV. If no distinct color, other than yellow, be observed in III, proceed now as follows: heat a little of the powdered substance on charcoal at the point of the inner blow-pipe flame, until it leaves an infusible residue. Moisten this residue with a drop or two of cobalt nitrate. Heat strongly in point of inner flame. Consult the following table:

Metal.	Appearance.
Aluminium.	Blue mass.
Zinc.	Green mass.
Magnesium.	Pink mass.

v. Finally, if no color has been obtained by proceeding as in IV, mix a little of the powdered substance with dried sodium carbonate and a little charcoal, pour into a small tube closed at one end and heat. Consult the following table:

Metal.	Result.
Mercury.	Minute, gray globules, condensed on cooler part of the tube.
Arsenic.	Shiny, black sublimate.
Ammonium compounds.	Odor of ammonia given off. (Bloxam).

545. **Testing for metals by the wet way—apparatus, etc.:** procure a **test-tube rack,** preferably one provided with pegs on which the test-tubes may be inverted so as to dry, **two dozen test-tubes** of medium size, and a **test-tube brush** or two. Wash out the test-tubes before undertaking any tests, using the brush; take care not to force the brush through the closed end of the test-tube. Invert over the pegs, and let drain.

In order to filter, it is necessary to have glass **funnels, filter papers,** a **filter stand,** and a **receiving vessel** of some kind, as for example, a **beaker.** (See Fig. 2). Filter papers may be procured in packages already cut.

It is advisable to use the Swedish paper, in size suited to the glass funnel used. Take one of the papers from the package, fold it in halves, then fold again in halves, at right angles to the first folding. A funnel shape is thus given to the paper; fit it into the glass funnel, insert the funnel into the ring of the filter-stand, place the receiving vessel beneath the spout of the funnel, then pour the solution into the paper. If it be noticed that the liquid collecting in the receiving vessel is turbid, it will be necessary to filter again, using a fresh paper, as there was probably a break in the paper.

546. In order to make **hydric sulphide** (sulphuretted hydrogen) proceed as follows: put some lumps of ferrous sulphide into a bottle with a wide mouth; bore two holes, by means of a metallic cork borer, through a cork, and through one of the holes push a thistle tube, (long tube with cup-shaped extremity) and through the other hole a tube bent at right angles. (See Fig. 3). Fit the cork, thus equipped, into the bottle and slip some rubber tubing on the (right angled) delivery tube; connect the rubber tubing with a small piece of glass tubing, and cause the end of the latter to dip into distilled water, contained in a beaker. Now pour some distilled water down the thistle tube on the lumps of ferrous sulphide, until the lower end of the thistle tube is under water. Pour in a few drops of hydrochloric acid, and wait a few moments; if no bubbles of gas are seen to rise from the ferrous sulphide, pour in a few drops more of the acid. Gas will now be given off, pass out through the right angled delivery tube into the water in the beaker, revealing its presence by bubbling up through the water, and by a disagreeable odor, like that of rotten eggs. After it has bubbled ten or fifteen minutes, enough has been generated, if the bubbling has been vigorous. If not, more acid should be added *by degrees*.

547. **In making the various tests,** pour some of the solution to be tested into a test-tube—to the depth say of an inch or two—and add 15 or 20 drops of the solution (reagent) used to produce the precipitate—except in cases where the precipitate is soluble in excess (explained hereafter) when but few drops should be added. After the precipitate has formed, note its color and appearance, let it settle, pour off the supernatant liquid as much as possible, pour the precipitate remaining into two or more test-tubes, a little into each, and add the various solutions required for testing its solubility. In making the various tests numbered 1, 2, etc., it is understood that a fresh quantity of the solution to be tested is to be used in each case, unless otherwise specified.

548. Reactions of the more important metals.—

Silver:

1. Add to solution of a silver salt, hydric sulphide or ammonium sulphide: a black precipitate of silver sulphide is produced:

$$2AgNO_3 + H_2S = 2HNO_3 + Ag_2S.$$

2. Add hydrochloric acid, or any soluble chloride: a white curdy precipitate of silver chloride is produced, insoluble in acids, but soluble in ammonium hydrate:

$$AgNO_3 + NaCl = NaNO_3 + AgCl.$$

3. Add chromate or dichromate of potassium: a red precipitate of silver chromate or dichromate is formed.

Lead:

1. To solution of a lead salt, add hydric sul-

phide or ammonium sulphide: a black precipitate of lead sulphide is produced:

$$Pb_2NO_3 + H_2S = 2HNO_3 + PbS.$$

2. Add sulphuric acid or any soluble sulphate: a white precipitate of lead sulphate is formed:

$$Pb_2NO_3 + Na_2SO_4 = 2NaNO_3 + PbSO_4.$$

3. Add hydrochloric acid or any soluble chloride: a white precipitate of lead chloride is produced, which is dissolved on the addition of much water, as lead chloride is not entirely insoluble. For the same reason, the precipitate is not formed when the solutions are dilute.

Mercury:

Reagent.	Mercurous salts.	Mercuric salts.
1. Hydric sulphide or ammonium sulphide.	Black precipitate of mercurous sulphide. $Hg_22NO_3+H_2S = 2HNO_3+Hg_2S.$	Black precipitate of mercuric sulphide. (Precipitate may be white or gray, with an insufficient quantity of the reagent).
2. Potassium iodide.	Green precipitate of mercurous iodide. $Hg_2NO_3+2KI = 2KNO_3+Hg_2I_2.$	Red precipitate of mercuric iodide, soluble in excess.

Copper:

1. Add to solution of a copper salt, hydric sulphide or ammonium sulphide: a black precipitate of cupric sulphide is formed:

$$CuSO_4 + H_2S = H_2SO_4 + CuS.$$

2. Add sodium hydrate or potassium hydrate: a bluish precipitate of cupric hydrate, Cu2HO, is formed, which is converted into dark brown cupric oxide, CuO, by boiling.

3. Add ammonium hydrate; a dark blue solution is produced, containing an ammonio-copper compound.

4. Add potassium ferrocyanide; a reddish brown precipitate of cupric ferrocyanide is formed.

Gold:

1. Add hydrochloric acid to a solution of a gold salt: no precipitate is formed.

2. Add hydric sulphide to solution of the terchloride: a brown precipitate of auric sulphide is formed:

$$2AuCl_3 + 3H_2S = Au_2S_3 + 6HCl.$$

3. Add stannous chloride: a purple-brown precipitate is formed.

4. Add ferrous sulphate: a brown precipitate is formed. Wash, dry, heat to redness, and metallic gold is obtained.

Platinum:

1. To a solution of a platinum salt add hydrochloric acid: no precipitate is formed.

2. Add hydric sulphide: a blackish brown precipitate is produced, which is insoluble either in nitric or hydrochloric acid.

3. Add ammonium hydrate: a yellow, crystalline precipitate is formed.

4. Add sodium hydrate cautiously, and but little of it: a brown precipitate is thrown down, soluble on addition of more of the sodium hydrate (soluble in excess).

5. Add stannous chloride: a deep brown color, but no precipitate.

Zinc:

1. Add hydrochloric acid: no precipitate is formed.

2. Add hydric sulphide: no precipitate.

3. Add ammonium hydrate, ammonium chloride, and ammonium sulphide: a *white* precipitate is produced; the color may be *greenish-white*, if iron is present as an impurity.

Commercial samples of zinc sulphate sometimes give a light brown precipitate with ammonium sulphide.

4. Add ammonium hydrate cautiously, and in very small amount: a white precipitate is formed, soluble in excess.

5. Add potassium ferrocyanide: a white (or greenish-white) precipitate is formed.

Tin:

1. To a solution of a tin salt add hydrochloric acid: no precipitate.

2. Add hydric sulphide: a brown precipitate of stannous sulphide is formed (if the solution be a stannous one).

3. Add auric chloride to a diluted solution of stannous chloride: a purple precipitate (purple of Cassius) is formed.

Aluminium:

Same reactions as for **Zinc,** 1, 2, 3. Add ammonium hydrate as in **Zinc,** 4, and a precipitate is formed, **insoluble in excess.**

549. **Short scheme for qualitative analysis of ordinary metals.—**

I. Add hydrochloric acid: a precipitate may be:

Silver chloride, ⎱
Mercurous chloride, ⎬ White.
Lead chloride, ⎰

Add ammonia abundantly to all three precipitates and shake well: *silver* is dissolved, a *mercurous compound* blackened, *lead* not dissolved nor blackened.

II. If nothing with HCl, add hydric sulphide: a precipitate may be:

Insoluble in ammonium sulphide.	Soluble in ammonium sulphide.
Mercuric sulphide. ⎱	Arsenous sulphide, yellow.
Bismuth sulphide. ⎬ Black.	Antimonous sulphide, orange.
Cupric sulphide. ⎰	Stannous sulphide, brown.
Cadmium sulphide, yellow.	Stannic sulphide, yellow.
	Auric sulphide, brown.
	Platinic sulphide, brown.

A. In order to ascertain whether the precipitate is soluble or not in ammonium sulphide, throw on a filter, wash well, wash off precipitate from filter, by means of wash bottle, into a porcelain dish, let settle, pour off supernatant liquid, then add ammonium sulphide and stir well. If insoluble in ammonium sulphide, the original solution contained either lead, mercury(-ic), bismuth, copper, or cadmium. Cadmium is easily told by its yellow color, a mercuric salt by the change of color, on addition of hydric sulphide (reddish-yellow to black, with a mottled appearance). If neither of these be found, take a fresh amount of the original solution, and add ammonium hydrate: if it is copper, a beautiful blue color is seen at once. If none of the above tests are successful, it is probably bismuth, or a dilute solution of lead. To a fresh amount of the original solution, add potassium chromate: a bright yellow precipitate indicates lead. (*Dilute* solutions of lead may not be precipitated by hydrochloric acid, but yet may yield a slight precipitate of a dark color with hydric sulphide, verified by potassium chromate). If no lead be found, take a fresh amount of the original solution, and add hydric sulphide. A black precipitate, insoluble in dilute hydrochloric acid, indicates *bismuth*.

B. If the precipitate is soluble in ammonium sulphide, the color of the precipitate produced by addition of hydric sulphide will serve to distinguish *antimony*, which yields an orange precipitate in an acid solution. Arsenic and tin (stannic) yield yellow precipitates with hydric sulphide, but the arsenic in acid solutions is distinctly *lemon-yellow*. If there is any doubt, take some of the original solution and pour it into an apparatus from which hydrogen is being evolved and is burning at the mouth of the delivery tube. If arsenic is present, the flame will now deposit a stain on cold porcelain, soluble in sodium hypochlorite. Tin (stannous), gold, and platinum form brown precipitates, when hydric sulphide is added to solutions of their salts. To a fresh amount of the original solution, add stannous chloride: if *gold* is present, a purple color will be seen; if platinum, a brown; if tin, no change.

III. If there has been no precipitate with

hydrochloric acid and none with hydric sulphide, take a fresh amount of the original solution, add ammonium hydrate, ammonium chloride, and ammonium sulphide:

Ammonium hydrate and **sulphide** precipitate
Iron group and **earths:**
Ferrous sulphide, black.
Cobaltous sulphide, black.
Nickelous sulphide, black.
Manganous sulphide, flesh colored.
Zinc sulphide, white.
Chromic hydrate, green.
Aluminium hydrate, white.

If the precipitate produced by the ammonium sulphide is *black*, to a fresh amount of the original solution add potassium ferrocyanide: a blue precipitate indicates presence of salt of *iron*.

If the precipitate with ammonium sulphide is white or greenish-white, zinc or aluminium is the metal. Take a fresh amount of the original solution, and cautiously add a small quantity of ammonium hydrate, causing it to trickle down the side of the tube: if the precipitate formed is cleared, on addition of plenty of ammonium hydrate, it is *zinc*, if not, *aluminium*.

IV. If no precipitate has occurred in I, II, or III, take a fresh sample of the original solution, and add ammonium hydrate, ammonium chloride, and ammonium carbonate:

Ammonium carbonate precipitates **Alkaline earths:**

Calcium carbonate,
Barium carbonate, } White.
Strontium carbonate.

If ammonium carbonate produce a white precipitate, add to the original solution potassium chromate: a precipitate of yellow color indicates *barium*, rather than calcium. If there is no precipitate with potassium chromate, but a white one with ammonium oxalate insoluble in acetic acid, but soluble in nitric, it is *calcium*, rather than barium. Calcium, barium, and strontium are readily identified by flame reactions.

In solution are left: **alkalies** and **magnesium**:

Magnesium.
Potassium.
Sodium.
Lithium.
Ammonium.

Magnesium salts are recognized by yielding a white precipitate with sodium phosphate, after addition of ammonium chloride and hydrate: the precipitate is ammonio-magnesium phosphate, readily soluble in acetic acid.

Ammonium salts do not answer to any of

the preceding tests, but, if heated with potassium hydrate, the odor of ammonia is noticeable and fumes are seen, if a rod, moistened in hydrochloric acid, be held at the mouth of the tube.

Sodium and potassium are recognized by flame reactions. (See Section 542, III).

CHAPTER VIII.

LABORATORY WORK CONTINUED—CHEMICAL WORK IN THE DENTAL LABORATORY: REFINING GOLD, TESTING AMALGAMS, MANIPULATION OF VULCANITE, COMPOUNDING RUBBER, ETC., ETC.

550. **Refining Gold:** the separation of foreign metals from gold is a matter of great importance to the dentist, as can be inferred from page 169, on which the effects of the different metals on gold are discussed. Metals may be separated from gold in two ways, by the "dry way" and the "wet way." The object of the "dry method," or *roasting*, is to convert the metals into oxides, chlorides, or sulphides.

1. Plate-scrap or clippings, and plate-filings; these need usually only to be remelted, if of suitable fineness originally.

2. Mixed filings, and fragments containing solder and platinum; these should be either roasted, or reduced to gold by the "wet way."

3. Sweepings: these should be first well washed, then either mixed with class second, or separately refined.

A good method is to fuse 8 parts of sweepings with 4 of

common salt, 4 of impure potassium carbonate, 1 of potassium bitartrate, and one-half of potassium nitrate, in a crucible.

551. Separation of foreign metals from gold: the most troublesome constituents of gold alloys are tin, lead, zinc, iron, antimony, bismuth, etc., etc. Most of these are oxidizable, hence roasting with nitre is usually sufficient, but tin alloys may better be roasted with mercuric chloride, and if the alloy contain a number of the different metals, sulphide of antimony should be used.

Richardson recommends the following method:

1. Remove all traces of iron or steel by passing a magnet repeatedly through them.*

2. Place the fragments and filings in a clean crucible, lined on the inside with borax, and covered either with a piece of fire-clay slab, or broken crucible.

3. Place the crucible in a furnace, on a bed composed of mixed charcoal and coke.

4. Add small bits of borax and when the metallic mass is fluid, add the potassium nitrate (or whatever refining agent is used) in small quantities from time to time, and continue the roasting from half an hour to an hour, according to the coarseness of the alloy.

Roasting with nitre is usually sufficient, but

---
* Gold scrap sometimes contains traces of steel that should be removed by treatment in the " wet way."

sometimes effects partial separation only. In such a case proceed as follows :

1. Remove crucible from the fire, after roasting with nitre, and let cool gradually.

2. Break the crucible, remove the button of gold, separate from slag by use of hammer, put into a new crucible, and melt again.

3. Add any particular agent capable of uniting with any particular base metal known to be present; or, try, first, one refining agent then another, until sufficient separation is effected.

4. Pour the melted metals into previously warmed and slightly oiled ingot moulds.

5. Hammer, anneal, and roll the ingot, and if still brittle, melt again with mercuric chloride.

Another method, of advantage in a greatly impoverished alloy, is the following :

1. Melt the alloy in a large crucible, adding small quantities of native antimony sulphide, until three or four times the weight of the alloy has been reached.

2. A lead-colored alloy of gold and antimony is formed; place it in a clean crucible, melt, and blow a current of air, by means of a bellows, over its surface.

3. Blow gently at first; a current strong enough to produce visible fumes is all that is necessary. When the fumes cease, increase

the heat, and before pouring out the gold throw a forcible current of air on the surface.

In case the alloy be found now malleable, but stiff or elastic and of dull color, *platinum* is probably present and must be removed by the "wet method," which, in general, must be used when it is desired to reduce the alloy to *pure* gold, as is the case when the gold to be refined consists of very coarse filings, fragments of plates containing large quantities of solder, linings with platinum pins attached, particles of base metals, etc., etc. Proceed as follows by the method of Watt:*

1. Dissolve the alloy in aqua regia, using four parts of hydrochloric to one of nitric, C. P. acids being used. The chloride of silver is found as a grayish-white powder at the bottom of the vessel. Let settle, and pour off supernatant liquid.

2. Add gradually to the liquid poured off a clear, filtered solution of ferrous sulphate in distilled water. Gold is precipitated as a brown powder.

3. Let settle, filter, wash off from the filter paper, digest in dilute sulphuric acid, filter again, wash well, and the result is pure gold.

552. **To determine the carat of an alloy.**

Multiply 24 by the weight of gold in the alloyed mass, and divide product by weight of the mass. Take, for ex-

* Quoted by Richardson.

ample, a solder composed of 6 parts gold, and 3 of other ingredients: the weight of the gold is represented by 6, the total weight 9 ∴ 24 × 6 ÷ 9 = 16. The alloy is, then, 16 carats fine. When now the gold is not pure, attention should be paid to the number of carats, and deduction made accordingly. Suppose a solder contain 48 parts of 22 carat gold, and 28 parts of other constituents; here the true weight of the gold is not 48, but 44. (22 carat gold is one-twelfth alloy; one-twelfth of 48 is 4 and 48— 4 = 44).

553. **To reduce gold to a required carat:** multiply 24 by the weight of pure gold used, and divide the product by the required carat. The quotient is the weight of the mass when reduced, from which subtract the weight of the gold used, and the remainder is the weight of the alloy to be added. For example, reduce 10 ounces of pure gold to 18 carats: 24 × 10 ÷ 18 — 10 = 3.3 + ounces of alloy to be added. If the gold is not pure, allowance must, of course, be made by subtracting as in the previous rule.

554. **To raise gold from lower to higher carat:** Multiply the weight of the alloyed gold used, by the number representing the proportion of alloy·in the given carat, and divide the product by that number representing the proportion of alloy in the required carat; the quotient is the weight of the mass, when reduced to the required carat by adding fine gold.

For example, suppose it is required to raise 16 carat gold to 18 carats: in 16 carat gold there is 24 — 16, or 8, alloy; in 18 carat gold there is 24 — 18, or 6, alloy. The example, therefore, becomes 1 × 8 ÷ 6 = 1⅓; that is, add ⅓ of a pennyweight of pure gold to the 1 pennyweight of 16 carat gold, in order to obtain 18 carat gold.

If, now, instead of adding pure gold it be desired to add gold of some particular carat, it is merely necessary to subtract the numbers, as 16 and 18 above, from the carat instead of from 24. The example above would then become, if 22 carat gold were to be added, $1 \times 6 \div 4 =$ 1½, that is to each pennyweight of 16 carat gold, add ½ pennyweight of 22 carat gold.

555. Methods of preparing dental amalgam alloys.—
Take a Hessian or sand crucible, fuse in it enough borax to fill the crucible at least one-third full, melt the tin in it over the usual dental or smelting forge-fire and, after it is melted, add the granulated silver, which, preferably, should have been heated to a low redness. The silver soon fuses in the molten tin and after thoroughly stirring with an iron rod or clay pipe-stem of small size, the copper, in form of small pieces of wire, should be added. After it has melted, and the mixture has been stirred, the gold is added, melted, and all is thoroughly stirred. After fusion and mixing is complete, quickly pour the fused mass into a broad, open, flat, shallow receptacle of iron or soap stone, and let cool. (Flagg).

According to Flagg, *very slow cooling* is to be avoided, as it gives rise to almost complete separation of the silver from the tin, or in other words, the cohesion of like molecules overcomes the adhesion of unlike ones. The end sought for is to fix the molecules, as much as possible, in the position into which they are driven by the heat. Prompt cooling secures the greatest uniformity of distribution to components. (Flagg).

Essig prefers to melt the platinum and silver together first, in case platinum is used, so that oxidation of the tin may not take place at the instant of union with the platinum. After the platinum and silver have been melted, the tin and gold are to be added. Borax is to be fused in the crucible first and, lastly, a layer of broken charcoal should be placed over the mass before the heating.

556. Alloys and amalgams: tests: the tests by which good amalgam alloys are recognized are partly chemical, partly mechanical. The latter will not be considered in this work. The chemical tests include the quality of the mercury. Pure mercury, practically free from metallic admixtures, should be used.

557. Mercury may be freed from mechanical impurities by filtering it through a cone of paper, round the apex of which a few pinholes have been made. Lead may be removed from it by exposing the mercury in a thin layer to the action of nitric acid, diluted with two measures of water, which should cover its surface and be allowed to remain in contact with it for a day or two, with occasional stirring. Wash well with water, dry first with blotting paper, then by gently heating.

For effect of sulphuretted hydrogen on alloys, see Section 530, 31. Use a weak solution to note gradual discoloration.

558. **In testing an alloy** for constituent metals, first make a preliminary examination as follows: into a test tube drop some of the metal or alloy in form of clippings, or coarse powder, then pour in some C. P. nitric acid; convenient proportions are a few grains of the metal to a drachm or two of the acid; warm over an alcohol flame, being careful not to let the acid boil over out of the test-tube, as it is very corrosive and will burn hands, clothing, etc. Of the commoner metals, copper, silver, and zinc will be dissolved. If the copper is in any noticeable quantity, the solution may acquire a green or blue color. Tin, gold, antimony, and platinum are not dissolved, though traces of the last two may go into solution.

559. **Short method of qualitative analysis of amalgam alloys:** according to Eckfeldt and Dubois,* an idea

---
* Quoted by Flagg.

may be had of the presence of gold and platinum from the action of the tin, which is not dissolved; but, after the action of the acid is over, shows itself as a whitish precipitate, colored from light to deep purple, if *gold* be present, or dirty-blackish color, if *platinum* be present with or without gold. After some idea is thus gained, take more of the metal or alloy, say 20 grains, and dissolve in half an ounce of acid, using a *beaker*. It is advisable to use what is sold as C. P. nitric acid, strong. The beaker should not be brought into contact with the naked flame in warming; it may be passed to and fro through the flame, or warmed by dipping into boiling water. After the action is over, evaporate to dryness in a porcelain dish over the *water bath*, a copper vessel filled with water under which is the alcohol flame. The whole should be under a "hood" for carrying off the vapors, or in a well-ventilated room. The fumes of the nitric acid are very irritating, and should not be breathed. (I.) After the nitric acid mixture has well evaporated, which will take some little time over the water-bath, add distilled water, stir well, and filter. [Previous work has revealed the presence or absence of gold, platinum, and tin; there remain silver, copper, cadmium, and zinc to be looked for].

(II.) After filtering, add some dilute hydrochloric acid—a few drops of acid in a test-tube half full of water will be enough and, if *silver* is plenty, a white, *curdy* precipitate will be formed.

(III.) Filter again, and to a little of the filtrate (liquid which goes through the paper) apart from the rest, add a few drops of ammonia water (made by mixing one volume of *stronger* ammonia water with three volumes of distilled water); a blue color indicates *copper*.

(IV.) To the rest of the filtrate add sulphuretted hydrogen. After the sulphuretted hydrogen water has been added, a black precipitate of *copper sulphide* will result, unless modified in color by a large percentage of *cadmium.*

(v.) Filter, saving the filtrate, wash the precipitate off the filter paper into a porcelain dish, using the *wash bottle* (a flask with a perforated cork having two bent glass tubes passing down into the flask; blowing into one tube will force water out through the other in a fine stream). Boil the precipitate in the porcelain dish with sulphuric acid diluted with water (one part of acid, added very slowly and with constant stirring, to four parts of water, well mixed, allowed to stand 24 hours, and decanted).

(vi.) Filter, and add sulphuretted hydrogen water to the filtrate, and then a few drops of ammonia; a bright yellow precipitate will indicate *cadmium.* Suppose now that when testing for copper as above (iii.), no blue color appeared with ammonia, then test directly for cadmium, as in (iv), which, if present, will appear as a yellowish precipitate, on addition of the sulphuretted hydrogen; (*brownish-yellow* indicates that silver has not been completely removed by precipitation with HCl).

(vii.) Go back now to the filtrate saved in (v) and boil it down until nearly dry to expel sulphuretted hydrogen, then add a little pure water, and solution of sodium carbonate until neutral (shown by dipping a piece of red and a piece of blue litmus paper into the mixture which, when neutral, will not change the color of either paper). A white precipitate indicates presence of *zinc.*

The above described process will enable the beginner to test the various dental amalgam alloys for the presence of those metals usually found in them. The detection of *gold, platinum, copper, cadmium,* and *zinc* is of importance, for all the alloys contain silver and tin. It is desirable to procure a sulphuretted hydrogen apparatus, such as a Kip generator, and some Woulfe bottles; pass the gas generated through a Woulfe bottle, containing a little water, so as to *wash* it, then directly into the solution to be tested.*

560. Short method of quantitative analysis of the more common amalgam alloys.

1. Estimate the **mercury**—of an old amalgam, for example—by weighing, heating to redness, weighing again. The loss in weight indicates the weight of mercury which was present.

2. Estimate the **tin** by weighing, heating to *bright redness* with borax, adding potassium nitrate in small quantity, cooling, collecting button and globules, weighing again. The loss in weight indicates the weight of the tin.

3. Estimate the **silver** by rolling out the button (obtained by procedure as in 2) into a thin ribbon, boil in a platinum or glass vessel with at least two or three times its weight of concentrated sulphuric acid. Continue boiling until the acid no longer attacks the metal, let settle, pour off supernatant liquid, **save the residue.** Precipitate silver from the poured-off liquid, by dipping plates of copper into it. Collect the silver, wash well, heat, weigh.

4. Go back to residue obtained in 3, wash well, dissolve in aqua regia, drive off acid by evaporation, dissolve in a large quantity of distilled water, add oxalic acid, the **gold** is thrown down, let settle, pour off supernatant liquid and save it. Collect gold, wash, dry, heat to redness, weigh.

5. To the supernatant liquid obtained in 4, add ammonium chloride as long as there is any precipitate. Let

---

*To detect mercury in form of vapor given off from amalgam alloys, Haines and Talbot have used ammonio-silver nitrate, a drop or two of which, on *chemically pure filter-paper*, they find will detect, by discoloration, exceedingly small quantities of mercury. Whether fillings which respond to this test are hurtful to the patient or not, must be decided by clinical experience.

precipitate settle, filter, wash, dry, and weigh the precipitate. Every 100 parts contains 44.28 of platinum. (Essig).

6. Estimate the percentage of each metal present by dividing the weight of the metal found by the weight of the amalgam in the beginning, before anything was done to it.

561. **Tests for cements:** tests should be made both of the liquid and of the powder. The *oxyphosphate* cements consist usually of glacial phosphoric acid and oxide of zinc. Take the reaction of the liquid with blue litmus to show that it is acid. Pour a little of the liquid into a test tube, and holding the latter inclined, let an aqueous solution of a little egg-albumin gradually trickle down the side of the tube into the acid. If a zone of whitish turbidity is noticed at the juncture of the two liquids, it is glacial phosphoric acid, rather than the common acid. To prove that it is phosphoric acid rather than any other, as for example, lactic or hydrochloric, add to a little of it, solution of silver nitrate, and a *white precipitate* is produced; this does not tell it from hydrochloric, but further add *barium chloride* solution, and if glacial phosphoric acid is the one, a white precipitate will be produced. The tests, then, for glacial phosphoric acid are as follows:

1. Coagulation of albumin.
2. White precipitate with silver nitrate.
3. White precipitate with barium chloride.

[*All* these tests should be successful; hydrochloric acid gives two of them, (1 and 2) but not three if pure. Sulphuric acid is distinguished by the heat evolved on mixing it with water. Nitric acid coagulates albumin, but does not answer to tests 2 and 3. Common phosphoric acid, *when pure*, does not answer to test 1, nor when diluted to test 3, but if it contains sulphates as an impurity, will answer to test 3, and it may, if not pure, answer also to test 2. The "vegetable" acids like acetic, lactic, etc., etc., do not respond to test 1]. If the phosphoric acid is in form of crystals, dissolve in as little water as possible, or melt by *gentle* heat, and then apply the test as above. If the crystals are dry, drop one of them into a solution of egg albumin, and if a *cloudiness or turbidity* surrounds the crystal as it dissolves, test No. 1 is successful. At red heat the crystals should volatilize. As to the *purity* of the glacial acid: *commercial* glacial acid is a hard, glassy mass, but the pure is softer and wax-like.

The acid is deliquescent, and dissolves readily in water, and in alcohol.

To test the liquid of the *oxychloride of zinc* cements, it is necessary to show that it contains *zinc* and is a *chloride*. Take the reaction of the liquid, which should be acid. Pour a little of the liquid into a test tube, and add *hydrochloric acid;* no precipitate should be noticed. Next add *sulphuretted hydrogen,* either in gaseous form or in solution, and no precipitate should be noticed. Take a fresh amount, to which nothing thus far has been added, and add *ammonium hydrate* (Aqua Ammoniæ will do), *ammonium chloride,* and *ammonium sulphide;* a *white* precipitate should be noticed. N. B. The precipitate may be greenish white, if there is iron present as an impurity. Now take still another sample of the liquid, and cautiously add *ammonium hydrate,* letting it trickle down the side of the tube, and a delicate white zone of turbidity will be noticed. Shake it or add plenty of ammonia, and it will disappear. *All* these tests, if successfully obtained, show presence of zinc; confirm with blow-pipe. Next, to prove that it is a *chloride* of zinc. Take a fresh amount of the liquid, and add *silver nitrate* to it; a curdy, white precipitate becoming violet on exposure to light, and soluble in (plenty of) ammonium hydrate, shows the presence of a *chloride.*

In testing the *powder* used in both oxyphosphate and oxychloride cements, attention should be paid both to its ingredients and quality; first, prove that it contains zinc by dissolving in nitric acid, as dilute as possible, and testing as for zinc in the liquid, or by means of the blowpipe.

Next as to quality: its specific gravity should be 5.6, *it should turn yellow when heated in a test-tube, and become white again on cooling. Try to dissolve a little in water, and notice that it is insoluble; add to a mixture of it with water, a little nitric acid, and notice that it is dissolved completely. To the solution thus obtained in nitric acid, (1) add *silver nitrate:* no precipitate should appear; to a fresh amount of the nitric acid solution, (2) add *barium chloride:* no precipitate should appear. Now take a fresh amount of the powder, add water to it, and a few drops of *hydrochloric acid:* then add (3) *sulphuretted hydrogen:* there should be no discoloration; to a fresh amount of hydrochloric acid solution, add (4) *potassium ferrocyanide.* A precipitate appearing should not be colored green or blue. Test (1) is for chlorides, (2) for sulphates, (3) for lead, (4) for iron.

562. **Manipulation of vulcanite, etc.**: much in regard to this subject belongs properly to mechanical dentistry. When the rubber is ready for hardening or vulcanizing, the latter may be accomplished by submitting it for a time to the action of hot air, steam, or hot water. A strong boiler called a **Vulcanizer** is usually used, the metal of which should preferably be wrought.

563. **To improve the color of rubber,** Wildman advises exposing to action of alcohol in sunlight from six to twelve hours. **Bending** hard rubber may be accomplished after heating to the proper temperature as 240° to 280° F. Small pieces, *uniformly thick*, may be softened by oiling and holding over the flame of a spirit lamp. Large pieces or those of irregular thickness may be softened by immersing in oil in a vessel and raising to the required temperature.

---

*Determine the specific gravity according to Chapter I.

564. **Parting the plaster:** an ounce of castile soap (cut into thin shavings) dissolved in a pint of water, by boiling, is used for parting the plaster.

565. **Coloring plaster:** to color plaster add a little vermilion or burnt umber to the dry plaster.

566. **Hardening the plaster:** the operation may be hastened by mixing thick, adding common salt,* or using hot water, or by combining the three methods.

567. **Compounding rubber:** caoutchouc may be mixed with sulphur and the coloring matter, either by passing repeatedly between steam-heated rollers or by reducing the caoutchouc in the first place to a pulpy or gelatinous state (by the action of some such substance as carbon disulphide) and then mixing the sulphur and coloring matter with it. [Wildman prefers to soften caoutchouc in oil of turpentine or in equal parts of coal naphtha, or benzine, and oil of turpentine]. From 5 to 50 per cent. of alcohol should be added to the solvent, in order that the latter may be at least partially recovered after the caoutchouc has softened. Wildman levigates the coloring matter and sulphur in spirits of turpentine, first grinding the coloring matter to a fine powder, then adding the sulphur and grinding thoroughly. He next adds a little of the pulpy caoutchouc, mixes thoroughly, and so on.

568. **Substances used to color rubbers:** the natural color of hard rubber, composed of caoutchouc and sulphur only, is a dark brown. Red oxide of iron and also vermilion are used to make red rubbers; cadmium sulphide to make a yellow, and with oxide of zinc to make a lighter yellow. Ivory black is used to produce a black rubber. Various modifications of the different colors may be made by combining the coloring materials in different proportions.

569. **Testing rubbers chemically:** to ascertain whether

---
*Addition of salt is said to weaken the plaster.

metallic mercury is set free in the body of the rubber by the decomposition of the sulphide (vermilion) during vulcanization, a simple method is to digest the rubber in nitric acid, then test the solution for mercury in the usual way.* **Sulphuretted hydrogen** may be proved to be given off during vulcanization by heating a sample of the rubber to 320°F., for one hour and a quarter in a suitable receptacle, and collecting the gas in a solution of a lead salt. A black precipitate indicates formation of sulphuretted hydrogen.

*Prof. Salisbury says that some of his students have used the copper test for mercury in rubbers: no response to the test has been obtained *before* vulcanizing, but *after* vulcanization evidence of abundance of mercury has been obtained, showing a change to have taken place to a more soluble compound or to metallic mercury.

CHAPTER IX.

ANALYSIS OF SALIVA, TEETH, TARTAR, AND URINE.

570. A complete course in salivary analysis is as essential to the dental student as one in urinary analysis to the medical student.

I. Become familiar with the **physical characteristics** of the saliva: 1. Cause the patient to wash his mouth out thoroughly with a warm, dilute solution of sodium bicarbonate, and afterwards with cold spring water, if it can be obtained, or with cold distilled water. Brush the inside of the mouth lightly with a glass rod, moistened with a little dilute acid, when the mouth will be filled with a considerable amount of clear, viscid fluid. Cause the patient to expectorate into a cylindrical glass vessel, tapering at the bottom and provided with a lip, so that the sediment may be collected and examined with the microscope.

II. While it is settling, note the **color, odor, reaction, transparency, consistence, appearance of sediment, specific gravity:** color should be absent, so also odor; take the reaction with litmus paper, dipping both red and blue slips into the fluid at once; if neither change color, the reaction is *neutral;* if the blue is turned red, the reaction is *acid;* if the red is turned blue, the reaction is *alkaline.* A variety of litmus paper may now be obtained, which turns red in an acid liquid, and blue in an alkaline one. The transparency should not be great, for normal saliva is turbid; the consistence should be glairy, viscid, and there should be froth. Notice whether the sediment after standing some hours is opaque and whitish, or whether *stringy masses* are present in it. [The latter is not likely to be the case in saliva obtained as directed in (1) but is sometimes noticed in cases of chronic gastric catarrh].

N. B. In order to note the physical characters in detail, to collect and examine the sediment, and to ascertain the specific gravity, several specimens of saliva collected in separate beakers or cylinders should be conveniently procured, in order to save time. The first specimen may be set aside, in order that the sediment may settle in it; the second specimen may be used for observation of the color, odor, reaction, and also for the chemical tests; the third, in case of a scanty supply, may be set aside for dilution in order to ascertain the specific gravity by methods hereafter to be explained.

III. Next ascertain the specific gravity,

which can be done by means of the urinometer:

The urinometer consists of a glass float weighted below with a bulb of mercury, and with a stem graduated from 0 to 60 at intervals of one or two degrees; the instrument should sink to zero when floated in distilled water in the beaker, which usually accompanies it. If there is plenty of saliva, the specific gravity can be obtained at once by floating the urinometer in the saliva, and reading off the number on the scale at the level of the liquid. It should average from 1002 to 1006, or possibly, 1008 or 9. If the amount of saliva is scanty, the specific gravity may be obtained by dilution: take *one* part of saliva by volume (bulk), and add one part of distilled water to it so as to make enough liquid to fill the cylinder, or beaker used, say two-thirds full; take the specific gravity as before and multiply the last figure of it by 2, and the result is the true specific gravity of the saliva.

IV. Next proceed with **chemical tests,** first for the **normal** constituents, next for possible **abnormal** ones.

571. **A. Qualitative tests for normal constituents.—**

1. Boil a little of the saliva in a slender, long test-tube, held between thumb and forefinger by the closed end; heat the *upper part*

only of the fluid. A turbidity noticed indicates presence of *albumin*.

2. To a fresh supply of the saliva, add a drop or two of *ferric chloride:* a blood-red color indicates presence of sulphocyanide. This test is sometimes performed by means of prepared test-paper: immerse strips of paper in an amber-colored solution of ferric chloride, to which a few drops of hydrochloric acid have been added. Let dry. A drop of saliva will give a red spot on such paper. The red color is removed by addition of a drop of mercuric chloride.

[The test may fail altogether, in which case the saliva must be distilled with phosphoric acid and the first of the distillate tested].

3. Collect a plentiful supply of the saliva by chewing rubber, or by inhaling ether vapor into the mouth: add four times its volume of water, stir well, let settle, pour off the supernatant liquid from the sediment. Prepare some starch mucilage by rubbing a little starch into a thin paste, with a little cold water, then pouring into about half a pint of boiling water. Boil for five or ten minutes and when cool, decant the clear liquid. Pour some of the starch mucilage into a small beaker, add a little of the diluted saliva, lay aside for ten minutes in a drying oven where the temperature is about 95° to 104°; in default of a hot chamber, place

the beaker some time in water of temperature of 104°, or warm the mixture very gently in a test-tube over a flame, taking care by cooling with the hand that the temperature does not rise much above 95°. Apply the tests for starch and for sugar, and it will be found that the starch has disappeared wholly or in part, and that sugar has been formed, showing presence of *diastatic ferment* (ptyalin) in saliva.

[The test for sugar should be made as follows: procure what is known as Fehling's test-liquid, essentially an alkaline solution of copper sulphate, boil a little of it diluted with four parts of water in a test-tube, and if it does not lose its blue color on cooling it is fit for use. Now add a drop or two of the starch mucilage on which the saliva has acted, and raise just to boiling point again; *reddish-yellow precipitate* indicates presence of grape-sugar. Compare now the action of a weak solution of *iodine* in alcohol on the original starch mucilage, and on that which has been acted on by the saliva; with the original it should form a deep indigo-blue compound].

4. Fill a tall beaker with dilute acetic acid —say one part of the ordinary acid to two or three of water—and let the saliva drop slowly into it; *stringy flakes* indicate presence of *mucin*.

5. To show the inorganic acids, evaporate the saliva to dryness in a porcelain crucible; do not withdraw the heat till the residue is well blackened or darkened from charring of the organic matter; when it is so, remove, let

cool, and add a little distilled water, stirring well, and adding a drop of acetic acid. Filter and divide the filtrate into three parts; to two add a few drops of nitric acid, and to one a solution of silver nitrate; a turbidity indicates presence of *chlorides.* The precipitate thus formed should be soluble in ammonia. To the other add ammonium molybdate solution and heat; a yellowish color, becoming possibly a precipitate, indicates presence of *phosphates.* To the third add a drop or two of hydrochloric acid and some barium chloride solution; a white precipitate shows presence of *sulphates.*

6. To show the presence of *lime* and *magnesia,* take a portion of the filtrate obtained in 5, and divide it into two parts; to the first add ammonium oxalate solution: a white precipitate indicates presence of *calcium* (lime); to the second part add ammonia and sodium phosphate solution: a white precipitate indicates presence of *magnesium.* The calcium precipitate should be insoluble in acetic acid but soluble in nitric; the magnesium precipitate should dissolve completely in acetic acid on shaking.

572. B. **Quantitative analysis.—**

Ptyalin may be separated nearly pure by precipitating fresh saliva with dilute normal phosphoric acid and then adding lime-water; filter off precipitate and dissolve it in distilled water, from which it is to be precipitated by alcohol, collected on a filter, washed repeatedly with a mixture of alcohol and water, dried, and weighed.*

Mucin, obtained as in the qualitative method, can be collected on a filter, washed with alcohol, dried, and weighed. The weight of the saliva being known, the percentage of ptyalin, or of mucin, can be readily calculated by dividing each weight by the weight of the entire saliva used.

Fatty matters can be estimated as follows: a definite quantity of saliva being evaporated to dryness over the water-bath, triturate the residue carefully, scraping off any that may adhere, and exhaust thoroughly with boiling ether. Evaporate in a weighed platinum capsule † and the increase in weight of the capsule represents the amount of fatty matter present. The operation should be repeated often enough to obtain a reasonably constant result.

Potassium Sulphocyanide. Dissolve perfectly dry potassic sulphocyanide, 0.05 gram in water (100 C. c.), and add to it ferric chloride till no more intensity of color is produced; then measure the volume of liquid. This is the test solution a.

Now take a definite volume of the saliva, and place it in a small, graduated, cylindrical glass vessel; add to it a drop or two of hydrochloric acid and ferric chloride, with brisk stirring, until its maximum of intensity of color is obtained; call this b.

Having carefully noted the intensity of the tint b, place three or four cylinders similar to that holding the saliva beside it on a piece of white paper in a good light; then add to one of these by means of a graduated pipette a few C. c. of the ferric sulphocyanide solution (a); make it up

---

* In order to dry properly there is need of a *drying oven;* filters are conveniently dried and weighed by placing them between two watch glasses held together by a clamp. For weighing there is need of a delicate *chemical balance.*

† A nickel crucible may be used for this operation.

to the same volume as the saliva (*b*) using distilled water. After stirring well note the intensity of color by looking vertically downwards through the column of liquid, and compare it with that of the saliva. If not so deep a red tint, a fresh experiment must be made in the same way, but using more of the sulphocyanide test solution. We thus proceed till an equal intensity of color is obtained in the two columns of liquid. From the amount of the test solution *a* required, we can easily calculate the percentage of sulphocyanide in the saliva. (Charles).

Each C. c. of the test solution (*a*) contains .0005 grams sulphocyanide. If, therefore, 10 C. c. of the test solution are required, the amount of sulphocyanide in the saliva is .0005 × 10 or .005, and so on. Divide the amount of sulphocyanide found by the weight of the saliva, and the quotient is the percentage of sulphocyanide.

The **chlorides** may be estimated *volumetrically*,* that is by use of standard solutions, directly from the saliva after the removal of the organic constituents. Fifty cubic centimetres of saliva should be boiled and filtered. To the filtrate add an equal volume of saturated baryta solution (1 volume barium nitrate, 2 volumes barium hydrate, each a saturated solution); this precipitates the organic constituents and phosphates. Filter, and to the filtrate add, drop by drop, a standard solution of mercuric nitrate, of which 1 C.c. precipitates .01 gram of sodium chloride. The number of C.c. used shows the number of $\frac{1}{100}$ths of a gram of sodium chloride present. The filtrate from the baryta precipitate should be acidulated with a few drops of nitric acid, before the mercuric nitrate is added.

---

*In *volumetric* analysis the determination is in general brought about by adding to a weighed quantity of the substance to be examined a solution of some reagent of known strength, until the reaction is exactly completed. The operation is termed *titration*, and requires skill and practice. The student is referred to "Sutton's Volumetric Analysis."

573. **Special tests for constituents of oral secretions:** T. Storer How has arranged a series of **litmus tests of oral fluids** together with a system of nomenclature as follows: first take with the foil-pliers a piece of blue litmus, wet it with parotid saliva and put the wet piece on a leaf from a foil book. In like manner treat the sub-max. saliva, placing the wet piece on the leaf below the other. Thus also test between the teeth, in carious cavities, pulp cavities, roots, sulci, pus-pockets, under calculi, plates, bridges, etc. Make the same tests in the same order with red litmus. Fill up the blank with the other statistics, and then note and record either the unchanged color of both the blue and the red by the symbol **N**, neutral, or the change of the blue to red by the symbol **A** acid; or the change of the red to blue by the symbol **Ł** alkaline, as the case may be.

As abbreviations for the different reactions, How suggests the following:

Ł —Alkaline.
A —Acid.
N —Neutral.
I —Slightly, alkaline or acid.
L —Obviously, alkaline or acid.
U —Decidedly, alkaline or acid.
O —Excessively, alkaline or acid.

[Dr. Oliver, of England, has prepared for use in urinary analysis, litmus paper charged with a definite quantity of alkali so as to distinguish several grades of acidity in reaction, such as *sub-acid, acid, hyper-acid,* etc. It would seem as if these papers under certain circumstances might be of use in salivary analysis].

Detection of mercury in saliva: collect all the saliva possible in 24 hours, and acidulate it with dilute hydrochloric acid (1 part acid to 9 of water). The mixture is heated for two hours on a water bath, filtered, and filtrate marked (*a*), and concentrated to half its bulk over the water bath. Go back to the precipitate on the filter, place it in a beaker filled three parts full with dilute hydrochloric acid (1 part acid to 6 parts water), and heat the whole over a water bath, adding from time to time small quantities of potassium chlorate, and constantly stirring to dissolve the organic residue. When this is completely dissolved, filter, and add filtrate to the previous filtrate marked *a*. Concentrate the mixed filtrates to one-fourth their bulk. The solution contains as dichloride, any mercury that may be present. To prove the presence of mercury, (1) place a drop of the solution on a gold or copper coin, and touch with blade of knife; a bright, silvery stain will appear. (2) Place a few strips of *pure* copper-foil in a test-tube, and add a little of the solution, and boil; the mercury will be deposited on the surface of the copper-foil. Remove the strips and wash them with very dilute solution of ammonia, and dry them between blotting-paper. Then place them at the bottom of a narrow glass tube (German glass), and apply heat; the mercury will be volatilized, and deposited as a ring of minute globules at the upper end of the tube. The character of these globules can generally be recognized by the eye. If, however, they are too small, remove the strips of copper from the tube, and dissolve the ring by the addition of a drop or so of dilute nitro-muriatic acid, and gently evaporate the solution. Dissolve the residue in a little water, and divide into two equal portions: (*a*) tested with a drop of dilute solution of potassium iodide, it gives a red precipitate of mercuric iodide, soluble in excess of potassium iodide solution; (*b*) a drop added to solution of caustic potash gives a yellow precipitate of hydrated mercuric oxide, insoluble in excess of liquor potassæ. (Ralfe).

Microscopic examination of the sediment: let the saliva settle in a conical vessel as directed, and examine the sediment with a power of 400 to 500 diameters; note the salivary corpuscles, various kinds of epithelial cells. With higher powers bacteria, fungi, etc., may be studied.

574. Morphology of the human sputum: E. Cutter has made a partial list of the forms and substances found in the human sputum.

1. Mucous corpuscles.
2. Mucous cells swarming with the moving spores, probably of the leptothrix buccalis; not found in the mouths of healthy infants.
3. Mucous corpuscles distended with crystalline and other bodies.
4. Epithelia, ciliate and non-ciliate.
5. Spirillum.
6. Vibriones.
7. Micrococcus spores.
8. Bacilli.
9. Spirulina splendens.
10. Gemiasma verdans and rubra.
11. Alcoholic and lactic acid alcoholic yeast.
12. Vinegar yeast and lactic acid vinegar yeast.
13. Mycelial filaments of vinegar and lactic acid yeasts.
14. Leptothrix buccalis spores and filaments.
15. Papillæ of tongue, usually infiltrated with spores of 14.
16. Mucor malignans.
17. Hairs of plants and animals.
18. Vegetations found in croupal membranes.
19. Pus corpuscles.
20. Blood corpuscles, white and red.
21. Clots of blood.
22. Granular tubercular masses.
23. Elastic lung-fibres.
24. Inelastic lung-fibres.
25. Lumen of veins and arteries.
26. Carbonized tissue from lungs.
27. Partially carbonized vegetable tissues from smoke.
28. Oxalate of lime.
29. Uric acid crystals.
30. Cystine.
31. Phosphate of lime.
32. Triple phosphate.
33. Cholesterine.
34. Calculi, made up of one or more of 28, 29, 30, 31, 32, 33. These may all come under the appellation of "gravel of the lungs."
35. Other crystals whose names have not been made out.
36. Amorphous, organic, and inorganic matters, including dust and dirt inhaled from the atmosphere.
37. Portions of feathers of animals and insects.
38. Potato starch.
39. Wheatstarch.
40. Elements of animal food eaten, cooked and uncooked.
41. Elements of vegetable food eaten, cooked and uncooked.
42. Cotton fibre.
43. Silk fibre.
44. Linen fibre.
45. Wool fibre.
46. Woody fibres, pitted ducts, etc.
47. Asthmatos ciliaris.

575. **Analysis of teeth and tartar:—**

I. Qualitative analysis of the teeth.

1. **To show the presence of organic matter, ossein, etc.** Digest the teeth for a day or two in dilute hydrochloric acid (10 per cent). The earthy salts will be dissolved out, and what remains will be *soft* and *elastic*.

2. **To show the earthy salts:** place a few teeth in a clear fire and let them remain there until perfectly white. Powder, and dissolve in hydrochloric acid; dilute and add plenty of ammonia; a white, gelatinous precipitate occurs of *phosphates of lime and magnesia.* Filter, and to the filtrate add oxalate of ammonium: a precipitate of *oxalate of calcium* shows itself, indicating presence of lime not as phosphate; prove that there is *carbonate* by digesting powdered, uncalcined teeth in dilute hydrochloric acid, when an effervescence due to carbonic anhydride takes place.

II. Quantitative analysis of teeth: the teeth should be cleaned and reduced to powder in a mortar; weigh out 5 to 10 grams of powdered teeth, dry at 212° and then at 248°, until it ceases to lose weight. 1. The loss gives the **water.** 2. Take the mass thus obtained and calcine in a porcelain crucible at as low a temperature as possible; the loss in weight gives the **organic matter**, and the residue the **ash.** It is desirable to saturate the calcined residue with ammonium carbonate before weighing, and then to heat again to an elevated temperature. 3. Dissolve with the aid of gentle heat the ash obtained in 2, in as little moderately dilute hydrochloric acid as possible; add ammonia in excess to the solution; a precipitate is thrown down, chiefly of calcium phosphate, with a little magnesium phosphate and calcium fluoride. Filter, and wash the precipitate with water containing ammonia. 4. To the filtrate add ammonium oxalate to complete precipitation, boil, filter, dry the precipitated oxalate of calcium, ignite, and weigh; the result is the amount of **calcium carbonate.** 5. Go back to the precipitate obtained in 3, dissolve in strong acetic acid with the aid of heat (calcine any remaining undissolved, and estimate as pyrophosphate), and to the solution add ammonium oxalate; boil and lay aside for 12 to 24 hours; collect the precipitated calcium oxalate on a filter, wash, dry, and ignite both precipitate and filter. Care must be taken not to heat too strongly, and it is always advisable to moisten the precipitate with ammonium carbonate before drying at a moderate heat and weighing. The result is calcium carbonate. Calculate the total amount of lime by adding the figures obtained in 4 and 5, and making the following proportion:

$$100 : 40 = \text{weight obtained} : x$$
$$\text{CaCO}_3 \quad \text{Ca.}$$

6. Evaporate the filtrate of 5 to small bulk, and also the washings of 5, mix with excess of ammonia, stir well, boil, lay aside for 12 hours; collect on a filter, wash with water containing ammonia, dry, ignite to redness, weigh. Calculate the magnesia by the following:

$$174 : 80 = \text{weight obtained} : x.$$
Pyrophosphate   Magnesia.
of
magnesium.   (2 molecules).

7. To the washings and filtrate obtained in 6, add a mixture of magnesium sulphate, ammonium chloride, and ammonia, lay aside for 24 hours, filter, wash with water

containing ammonia, dry, ignite to redness, weigh. Calculate the phosphoric acid by the following:

1 : 0.216 = weight obtained : x.

576. III. Qualitative and quantitative analysis of tartar:

A. 1. Take a gram of tartar, calcine in air, dissolve residue in nitric acid; the part remaining undissolved is **silica.** 2. Boil the nitric acid solution for two hours with great excess of pure sodium carbonate, filter, and the bases, lime, magnesia, etc., remain on the filter as carbonate or oxide. 3. Wash the precipitate well, add ammonium chloride in excess, then ammonia. A precipitate shows presence of **iron.** Now precipitate the **calcium** by adding excess of ammonium carbonate. Filter. 4. To the filtrate add sodium phosphate, and a slight precipitate of ammonio-**magnesium** phosphate is obtained, which after 24 hours is complete. Calcination gives very slight residue, so that the magnesia may be reckoned as a **trace.**

B. 1. Now take a fresh supply of tartar, reduce to fine powder, weigh, treat with boiling water, which removes soluble alkaline salts and a part of the organic matter. Filter, evaporate filtrate to dryness, calcine, and the residue consists in the main of chlorides and sulphates and should be weighed.

2. Take the precipitate obtained in 1, dry, weigh, calcine in an open porcelain crucible, weigh. Loss is **animal matter.**

3. Take residue obtained in 2, boil in concentrated solution of ammonium chloride, which converts all the calcium carbonate into calcium chloride, filter, treat filtrate with calcium oxalate, wash the precipitate, dry, calcine, weigh, and the result is the **carbonate of calcium.**

4. Take precipitate obtained in 3, wash it off from the filter paper, dissolve in nitric acid; all is dissolved except a slight residue (silica); which should be washed, calcined, and weighed. The result is the amount of **silica.**

5. Add to the nitric acid solution obtained in 4, some ammonia—enough to overcome the acidity. The **phosphates** are precipitated. Now add acetic acid in excess; part of the precipitate is dissolved, part is not. Filter. Collect the precipitate on the filter, wash it off, calcine, and weigh. The result is **phosphate of iron**.

6. The filtrate contains the calcium phosphate: neutralize with ammonia, then add ammonium oxalate, filter, collect precipitate on filter, wash, calcine, weigh, and the result is calcium carbonate. Calculate the **lime** from this.

7. To the filtrate obtained in 6, add ammoniacal magnesium nitrate, and in 24 hours triple phosphate is completely precipitated; collect on filter, calcine, weigh, and calculate the **phosphoric acid** from the weight as pyrophosphate.

ANALYSIS OF URINE.

577. A. Note the *quantity* of urine voided in 24 hours, the *color, odor, specific gravity* (using urinometer, section 563), *reaction*, (using litmus, section 563, 11), *transparency*, and *consistence*. Normal urine is excreted in quantity about three pints in 24 hours, of straw-yellow color, aromatic, characteristic odor, 1015 to 1025 in specific gravity, clear, with slight mucous "cloud" settling as the urine stands; normal urine is an easily dropping fluid like water.

B. Get the urine perfectly clear by filtering, if necessary, through a number of filter-papers folded together, then test for *albumin*. Place clear, filtered urine to depth of an inch in a test-tube; hold latter inclined, and allow pure, colorless nitric acid to flow down side of test-tube into the urine. Use a nipple-pipette for delivering the acid. A clear-cut whitish band of coagulated albumin will be seen at the juncture of urine and acid, if the urine contains albumin. Confirm by taking fresh amount of clear, filtered urine and pouring into test-tube until two-thirds full; add a drop or two of acetic acid and heat upper part of column of urine, holding test-tube at the bottom between thumb and fore-finger. A turbidity seen in the heated portion indicates albumin.

C. Test for *sugar*, first removing albumin, if any is present, by boiling the urine to which a drop of acetic acid has been added, and filtering. Test the filtered urine for sugar as in section 569, A.3. Or boil the filtered urine with an equal bulk of Liquor Potassæ and a decided yellow coloration becoming darker indicates sugar. Pay no attention to "flocks" seen in the liquid, as these are merely precipitated phosphates.

D. Test for *bile* precisely as for albumin, test 1, using, however, nitrous acid instead of nitric. [Nitrous acid may be made by boiling nitric acid with a bit of wood as end of tooth-pick]. A set of colors will be seen at the juncture, if bile is present. Of the colors, *green* is the most constant and the first in order from above downward.

E. Let four fluidounces of the urine settle in a conical glass vessel covered over to keep out dust. After the sediment has well settled, pour off supernatant urine and test sediment chemically or examine with microscope. [Use of the latter is to be preferred, but will not be considered here]. Test for *urates* by warming a little of the sediment in a test-tube. If gentle heat dissolves the sediment, it is composed of urates. If not, add acetic acid, shake well and warm; if now it clears, *phosphates* are in the sediment. If no results thus far, take fresh amount of the sediment and add a drop or two of Liquor Potassæ; if the sediment become stringy, *pus* is present.

Blood may be recognized by the color imparted to the sediment, which does not clear on being heated. *Uric acid* is often recognized by the naked eye, as it occurs in the form of reddish grains on the side or bottom of the glass.

F. Estimate *urea* the chief normal constituent of urine,

(quantity 20 to 40 grammes daily). Use any of the convenient instruments, as Marshall's, Greene's, Doremus's, Squibb's, some of which may be obtained with full directions for use from the various dealers.*

---

*For further information on this subject, the reader is referred to the author's work on "Diseases of the Kidneys."

GLOSSARY.

Acid—Opposite of alkali. Section 129.
Acidify—To render acid.
Actinic—Name given to rays of sun-light having power to produce chemical changes.
Aeriform—Resembling air; term applied to gases and vapors.
Alcohol—Ethyl hydrate.
Algaroth—Compound of trichloride and trioxide of antimony.
Allotropism—Property of assuming different states and manifesting different chemical and physical properties.
Alum—Potassium aluminium sulphate.
Ammonia Alum—Double sulphate of aluminium and ammonium.
Ammonia—Ammonium hydrate.
Ammonia Gas—A compound of nitrogen and hydrogen.
Ammoniated Submuriate—Old term for mercur-ammonium chloride, "white precipitate."
Anæsthetic—Substance which for a time diminishes sensibility, as ether.
Anhydride—Anhydrous acid, that is acid without water; oxide of negative element.
Anhydrous—Containing no water.
Antiseptic—Preventing putrefaction.
Antozone—Name given by Schœnbein to an electro-positive oxygen, which with electro-negative oxygen (ozone) forms ordinary oxygen.
Aqua Ammoniæ—Ammonium hydrate solution.
Aqua Fortis—Nitric acid.
Aqua Regia—Nitrohydrochloric acid.
Argillaceous—Like, or containing clay.
Argol—Crude cream of tartar.
Arsenic—Arsenious anhydride.
Artiads—Atoms of even valence.
Asbestos—Incombustible substance occuring in nature and essentially a silicate of magnesium.

GLOSSARY.

Aseptic—Free from germs.
Auriferous—Gold containing.
Baryta—Old name for barium protoxide.
Base—Any substance which has one or the other of the two following characters: (a) of combining with acids, partially or wholly neutralizing them to form salts; (b) of playing the role of an electro-positive element in a combination.
Basicity—Property of playing the role of a base.
Bi-carbonate of Soda—Hydrogen sodium carbonate.
Bi-sulphuret of Carbon—Carbon disulphide.
Bleaching Powder—Calcium hypochlorite and chloride.
Blende—Native zinc sulphide.
Blue Vitriol—Copper sulphate.
British Alkali—Sodium carbonate.
British Gum—Dextrine.
Burnett's Disinfecting Fluid—Contains zinc chloride.
Butter of Antimony—Antimony terchloride.
Cadet's Fuming Liquor—Arsenical alcohol.
Calamine—Native zinc carbonate.
Calomel—Mercurous chloride. See section 233.
Caramel—Burnt sugar.
Carbolic Acid—Phenyl hydrate.
Carbonate of Soda—Sodium carbonate.
Carbonic Acid Gas—Carbon dioxide.
Carburetted Hydrogen—Marsh-gas.
Casein—Proteid found in milk; essential constituent of cheese.
Caustic Potash—Potassium hydrate.
Caustic Soda—Sodium hydrate.
Cellulose—Substance forming walls of vegetable cells.
Centigrade—Thermometric scale on which the freezing point is zero, and the boiling, 100°.
Chili Saltpetre—Sodium nitrate.
Chlorate of Potash—Potassium chlorate.
Chloride of Lime—See Bleaching Powder.
Chloride of Potash—Potassium chloride.
Chloride of Soda—See Labarraque's solution.
Chlorous—Having odor of chlorine.
Chrome-alum—Double sulphate of chromium and potassium.
Chromic Acid—Chromic anhydride.
Cinnabar—Native sulphide of mercury.
Colloid—Substance non-crystallizable and passing with difficulty through animal membrane.

Concentrated—With diminished proportion of liquid.
Copperas—Ferrous sulphate.
Corrosive sublimate—Mercuric chloride.
Corundum—Mineral containing oxide of aluminium.
Cream of Tartar—Potassium acid tartrate; potassium ditartrate.
Condy's Fluid—Contains potassium permanganate.
Cumarin—The crystallizable principle of Tonka bean.
Cupellation—A method of separating unoxidizable metals, as gold or silver, from oxidizable ones by use of cup-shaped vessels.
Cyanogen—A gas containing carbon and nitrogen.
Decomposition—Splitting up of molecules.
Deflagration—Phenomenon which takes place when two or more bodies reacting strongly on one another produce much noise and heat, melt together, etc.
Dialysis—Method of separating non-crystallizable (colloid) substances from crystallizable by diffusion of the latter through animal membrane.
Dilute—Not in full strength.
Dippel's Oil—Oily liquid from distillation of bones, etc.
Distillation—Process of separating the more volatile principles of a body from the less volatile, by means of heat.
Dragon's Blood—A resin.
Dutch Liquid—Ethylene chloride.
Ebullition—Boiling.
Electrolysis—Electro-chemical decomposition of a body.
Epsom Salt—Magnesium sulphate.
Fahrenheit—Name given to a thermometric scale on which the freezing point is 32°, and the boiling 212°.
Ferment—Body which, by mere contact with certain other bodies, sets up fermentation.
Fermentation—Splitting up of a body with evolution of gas, swelling up, and heat of the mass from no apparent cause.
Fluorescence—Appearance of emitted chlorine.
Fluor Spar—Calcium fluoride.
Fowler's Solution—A preparation containing arsenious oxide.
Fuming Liquor of Libavius—Stannic chloride.
Fusible Metal—Mixture of bismuth, lead, and tin.
Galena—Lead Sulphide.
Gangue—Miners' term for worthless matter containing useful metals.
Glauber's Salt—Sodium sulphate.
Glucoside—Substance found generally in nature in the vegetable kingdom and derived chemically from glucose—example, salicin.

Glycerole—Substance in which glycerine is solvent or vehicle.
Glycols—Diatomic alcohols.
Goulard Water—Solution of subacetate of lead.
Green Vitriol—Ferrous sulphate.
Green Salts of Magnus—An ammoniacal platinum compound.
Gypsum—Native calcium sulphate.
Horn-blende—A native double salt of silicic acid, magnesium and calcium with ferrous oxide.
Horn-silver—Native silver chloride.
Heavy-spar—Barium sulphate (native).
Hydrocarbons—Substances formed by the direct union of carbon and hydrogen, as spirit of turpentine.
"Hypo" or "Hyposulphite"—Sodium thiosulphate.
Isomerism—Isomeric bodies are those having the same elements in the same proportions by weight.
Kermes Mineral—Mixture of antimonous oxide and potassium sulphide.
Ketone—Substance formed by the action of oxidizing agents on secondary alcohols.
Kupfernickel—A mineral containing nickel and arsenic.
Liebig's Condenser—Apparatus for condensing steam.
Labarraque's Solution—Solution of chlorinated soda, sodium hypochlorite, and chloride.
Lactose—Sugar of Milk.
Laughing Gas—Nitrous oxide, nitrogen protoxide.
Lime—Unslaked, calcium oxide; slaked, calcium hydrate.
Litre—French unit of capacity.
Lithate—Old term for urate.
Litharge—An oxide of lead; lead protoxide.
Lunar Caustic—Silver nitrate.
Lugol's Solution—Contains iodine dissolved in solution of KI.
Magendie's Solution—Contains morphine sulphate.
Magnetite—Magnetic oxide, triferric tetroxide.
Magnesia—Magnesium oxide.
Microcosmic salt—Hydro-phosphate of sodium and ammonium.
Metaphosphoric acid—Term formerly used for glacial phosphoric acid.
Mindererus, Spirit of—Aqueous solution of ammonium acetate.
Monsel's Solution—Contains subsulphate of iron.
Mosaic Gold—Disulphide of tin.
Muriatic Acid—Hydrochloric acid.
Muriate of Morphia—Morphine hydrochlorate.

Muriate of Ammonia—Ammonium chloride.
Nitre—Saltpetre.
Nordhausen Acid—Fuming sulphuric acid.
Nurnburg Gold—An alloy of copper, gold, and aluminium.
Olefiant Gas—Ethylene.
Oil of Vitriol—Sulphuric acid.
Oxide—Binary compound, in which oxygen is the negative element.
Oxychloride—Term given to a chloride of an oxide.
Ozone—A very active form of oxygen.
Paris Green—Essentially an arsenite of copper.
Perissads—Atoms of uneven valence.
Peroxide of Hydrogen—Hydrogen dioxide.
Phosphor-iridium—Metal prepared by heating iridium ore with phosphorus (Holland). Combines with small quantities of silver forming the most flexible and resisting alloy of silver.
Phenacetine—An antipyretic, an acetyl compound of phenetidine.
Platinum-black—Finely divided platinum.
Platinoid—Kind of German Silver with 1 to 2 per cent tungsten.
Platinum-sponge—Platinum obtained by heating ammonio-platinic chloride.
Platinor—An alloy of platinum, silver, copper, zinc, and nickel.
Potash—Old name for potassium oxide.
Potash Alum—Double sulphate of aluminium and potassium.
Prussic Acid—Old name for hydrocyanic acid.
Prussian Blue—Ferrocyanide of iron.
Pyrites, Copper—Double sulphide of copper and iron.
Pyrites, Iron—Disulphide of iron.
Realgar—Native red sulphide of arsenic.
Red Precipitate—Mercuric oxide.
Red Prussiate of Potash—Potassium ferricyanide.
Robertson's Alloy—Gold 1, silver 3, tin 2.
Sal-alembroth—Double chloride of ammonium and mercury.
Sal-ammoniac—Ammonium chloride.
Sal-polychrest—Potassium sulphate.
Sal-prunelle—Fused nitre.
Saleratus—Potassium dicarbonate.
Sal-sodæ—Sodium carbonate.
Sal-tartar—Potassium carbonate.
Sal-volatile—Commercial carbonate of ammonium.
Salt Cake—Sodium sulphate.
Saltpetre—Nitre; potassium nitrate.
Salts-Epsom—Magnesium sulphate.

Salts-Glauber—Sodium sulphate.
Salts of Lemons }
Salts of Sorrel } Potassium dinoxalate.
Salts of Tartar—Potassium carbonate.
Silica—Silicon dioxide.
Soda—Old name for sodium oxide.
Soda Ash—Sodium carbonate.
Sphalerite—Zinc sulphide, (mineral).
Speculum Metal—An alloy of copper and tin.
Sub-acetate of Lead—Basic acetate of lead, acetate and hydrate of lead.
Sub-muriate of Mercury—Mercurous chloride.
Sub-nitrate of Bismuth—Bismuthyl nitrate.
Sulphuret—Old term for sulphide.
Sulphuret of Iron—Ferrous sulphide.
Sulphuretted Hydrogen—Hydric sulphide.
Sulphide of Tin—Stannous sulphide.
Sulphonal—Dimethyl-diethyl-sulphonyl-methane. Odorless, tasteless, crystalline solid. Hypnotic.
Syntonin—Parapeptone, acid-albumin.
Talc—Magnesium silicate.
Tartar Emetic—Potassio-stibyl tartrate.
Turnbull's Blue—Ferricyanide of iron.
Valence—Equivalence of atoms.
Vienna Paste—Contains calcium oxide and potassium hydrate.
White Precipitate—Mercur-ammonium chloride.
White Vitriol—Zinc sulphate.
Yellow Prussiate of Potash—Potassium ferrocyanide.

INDEX.

Absorbents	303
Acetanilide	290
Acetates	271
Acetic Acid	63, 271
Acids	53
Ox-Acids	53, 54
Sulpho-Acids	53, 54
Acid, Acetic	271
Arsenous	175
Benzoic	273
Boracic	175
Carbonic	118
Carbolic	247
Chromic	212
Citric	280
Eugenic	274
Hydrochloric	114
Hydrocyanic	61, 274
Hydrosulphuric	61, 55
Lactic	275
Nitric	186
Oleic	274
Oxalic	275
Oxybenzoic	278
Oxynaphtholc	280, 307
Phosphoric	180
Salicylic	278
Sozolic	279
Sulphuric	156
Tartaric	280
Trichloracetic	273
Valeric	280
Aconitine	282
Oleate	282
Tincture	283
Adhesion	3
Alantol	252, 307
Albuminoids	291
Albuminates	293
Alcohol	240
Absolute	241
Dilute	242
Alcohols	239
Alcohol	240
Aldehydes	269
Alkalamides	60
Alkaloids	281
Cadaveric	281
Natural	281
Alloys	87, 88, 89
Alstonine	290
Aluminium	85, 189
Alloys	192
Compounds	193
Aluminium, tests	357
Alumina	194
Aluminium	189
Acetate	272
Chloride	194
Permanganate	194
Silicates	194
Alums	193
Alpha Naphthol	307
Amalgam Alloys	147
Amalgam Fillings	148
Amalgams	138
" Antimony	139
" Cadmium	139
" Copper	139
" Gold	144
" Palladium	144
" Platinum	145
" Silver	146
" Tellurium	146
" Tin	146
" Zinc	146
American Weights	24
" Measures	24
Amidocaproic Acid	294
Amides	60
Amines	60
Ammonia Gas	101, 184

INDEX.

Ammonium Compounds 63, 100
  Benzoate 273
  Carbonate............101
  Chloride 101
  Hydrate............101
Amorphous............ 15
Ampère............... 22
Ampère's Law........ . 11
Amyl Nitrite 261
Amylose 254
Amyloid substance..... 293
Analysis 32
  Saliva............377
  Tartar............390
  Teeth............ 388
  Urine............391
  Volumetric............384
Anhydrous Acid 63
Anhydrous Phosphoric Acid 179
Anise Oil 228
Antifebrin 290
Antimony............ 172
  Butter of............173
  Tests for............348, 357
Antimony Amalgam.... 139
Antimony Oxychloride 173
Antipyrin 284, 290
Antiseptics 303
Apomorphine 288, 290
  Hydrochlorate.........288
Arsenates............. 58
Arsenic 175
Arsenites 58
Arsenous Anhydride... 175
  Tests for............357
Artiads 44
Artificial Teeth........ 195
Asbestos............... 130
Aseptol 279
Atmosphere 159
Atomic Weight......... 39
Atomic Weights........ 37
Atom.............1, 33, 34
Atomicity............. 38

Atoms............... 38
Atropine 283
Attraction.............
  Atomic............1
  Chemical............ 34, 73
  Molecular............1
  Of Mass............1
Auric Chloride 171
Auric Oxide............ 171
Avogadro's Law........ 11, 35
Babbitt metal.......... 135
Bacilli 300
Bacteria 299
Bacteridia............ 300
Bacterium............. 302
Balsams............... 235
Barium............... 115
  Chloride............115
  Compounds............115
  Nitrate............115
  Tests for............350, 360
Bases............... 55
Battery...............
  Galvanic............16
  Faradic............20
  Storage............19
Bases............... 55
Beers 242
Bell metal............ 135
Bending Rubber 232
Benzoates............. 273
Benzoic Acid.......... 273
Benzoin............... 273
Benzoates............. 273
Benzine............217, 221, 222
Bergamot Oil........... 228
Betol............279, 307
Bichromates 58, 212
Binaries............... 46, 47
Bismuth............... 160
  Alloys............162
  Compounds............161
  Oxyiodide............307
  Subnitrate............161
  Tests for........348, 357, 358

Blowpipe	344	Cannabinum Tannicum	285
Boiling Point	12	Capillarity	7
Bone	309	Carat	167
Boracic Acid	61, 174	Caraway Oil	229
Borates	58	Carbohydrates	253
Borax	99, 196	Carbolic Acid	247
Boric Acid	61, 174	Carbon	203
Boroglyceride	244	Compounds	214
Boron	174	Carbonic Acid Gas	205
Brass	135	Carbon Compounds	205, 214
Brittleness	4	Carbon Disulphide	205
Bromine	111	Carbonic Oxide Gas	205
Bronze	135	Carbonates	58, 205
Bronzes	136	Caries	317
Brucine	289	Carvacrol	229
Buccal Mucus	324	Cells	19
Bunsen Burner	347	Celluloid	257
Cacao Butter	263	Cellulose	256
Cadmium	130	Cement	119, 309
Cadmium Amalgam	139	Cements	
Cadmium Sulphate	131	Oxychloride	128
Caffeine Borocitrate	290	Oxyphosphate	127
Cajuput Oil	228	Oxysulphate	129
Calcium	115	Centigrade	31
Compounds	116	Cerium	196
Carbonate	117	Oxalate	275
Fluoride	119	Chains	216
Glyceroborate	345	Charles' Law	11
Hydrate	118	Chemical Arithmetic	71
Hypophosphite	121	Affinity	34, 73
Lactophosphate	278	Change	64, 65, 66, 72
Oxide	118	Effects, Light	17
Phosphate	120	Equations	69
Sulphate	116	Philosophy	32
Sulphite	120	Chemism	33
Camphene	225	Chinoline	284
Camphor	234	Chloric Acid	61
Mono-bromated	234	Chlorine	111
Oil	235	Compounds	113
Spirit	234	Chloroform	264
Water	234	Chloral	269
Cane Sugar	253	Chloral Hydrate	269
Cannabine	285	Chlorates	58
Tannate	285	Chlorinated Lime	120
Cannabis Indica	285		

Chromates	58	Corrugated Gold	167
Chromium	212	Coulomb	23
Compounds	212	Creasote	245
Tests for	359	Cream of Tartar	280
Chromic Acid	61	Creolin	305, 307
Chromic Anhydride	212	Cresylic Acid	307
Circuit	21	Croton Chloral Hydrate	270
Citric Acid	280	Croton Oil	264
Cinnamon Oil	229	Crown Enamels	195
Classification		Crystal Gold	165
Elements	74, 91	Crystallization	15
Organic Compounds	220	Water of	16
Closed Circuit	18	Crystalline Structure	80, 84
Cloves Oil	229	Crystalloids	15
Coagulated Albumin	293	Crystals	15
Cobalt	211	Systems	17
Compounds	211	Cupric Sulphate	136
Tests for	359	Current	
Cocaine	285	Electric	18
Carbolate	286	Induced	20
Hydrobromate	286	Cyanides	274
Hydrochloride	286	Cytisine	290
Phenate	286	Decay	219
Phtalate	286	Decomposition	67, 69, 219
Cohesion	3	Definite	
Cohesive Gold	167	Proportions	45
Collagens	293	Deliquescence	14
Collodion	256	Dental Amalgams	147
Colloids	15	Dental Rubber	231
Coloring Rubber	231	Dentine	309
Combustion	158, 219	Density	11, 45
Compound	33, 34	Deodorizers	306
Molecules	44	Derivatives	218
Compounds		Derived Albumins	293
Binary	46	Destructive Agents	303
Ternary	52	Dextrin	255
Compound Radicals		Dialyzer	15
(table of)	58	Dialysis	15
Compounding Rubber	231	Diastase	296
Compressibility	2	Diluents	303
Conducting Power	83, 84	Discoloration of Fillings	148
Condy's Fluid	96	Disinfectants	304
Constants		Displacement	7
Of the elements	37		
Copper	50, 133		
Alloys	135		
Compounds	136		

Distillation	13	Eugenol	230
Ditaine	290	Evaporation	13
Divisibility	2	Expansibility	380
Ductility	4, 80, 83	Extension	2
Dutch Gold	170	Fahrenheit	31
Dyads	41, 115	Farad	23
Dynamo	21	Faradic Battery	20
Effect of metals on gold	169	Fats	263
Efflorescence	14	Feldspar	195
Elasticity	3	Fermentation	219, 294
Elasticin	294	Ferment	
Elastin	294	Acetic Acid	297
Electricity	17, 21, 72	Butyric "	297, 298
Dynamic	21	Lactic "	297, 298
Galvanic	21	Thrush	297, 298
In the mouth	23	Ferments	295, 299
Static	22	Organized	296
Voltaic	21	Soluble	295
Electrodes	18	Unorganized	295
Electro-Motive Force	22	Dental	368*
Electrolysis	21	Ferric Compounds	209
Elements		Ferricyanides	58
Classification	74, 78, 91	Ferrocyanides	58
Negative	37, 40	Ferrous Compounds	210
Positive	37, 40	Fibrin	293
Table of	37	Fixed Oils	224, 264
Empirical Formulæ	215	Flames	
Enamel	309	Oxidizing	345
Energy	5	Reducing	345
Equations	69	Fluid	5
Equivalence	41	Fluid extracts	242
Erythrophleine	290	Fluorine	37, 42, 114
Eserine	290	Fool's Gold	170, 367
Essential Oils	226	Force	5
Ether	258	Formulæ	45
Sulphuric	258	Binary	47, 51, 61
Ethers	257	Empirical	215
Ethyl Bromide	260	Graphic	215
Nitrite	261	Rational	215
Oxy-Caffeine	290	Structural	215
Ethyl Series	238	Ternary	52, 61
Eucalyptus Oil	252	Forms of Cells	19
Eucalyptol	252	Foot Pound	5
Eugenic Acid	274	Formulæ	45
		Friction	7

Frits	196	Gum Enamel	196
Fungi	296	Gum Resins	235
Fusion	367, 12	Gum Tragacanth	256
Fusibility	80	Gutta Percha	232
Fusible Alloys	162	Hardening Plaster	375
Fusel Oil	243	Hardness	4
Gallic Acid	262	Heat	12
Galvanic Battery	18	Hexads	42, 206
Gas	5	Hill's Stopping	233, 229
Illuminating	204	Homologous Series	217, 238
Gasoline	222	Honey	255
Galvanic Battery	18	Horse Power	5
Galvanic Electricity		How Substances Act	73
In the Mouth	23	Hydrates	55, 56
Gay-Lussac's Law	65	Hydriodic Acid	61
German Silver	104	Hydrocarbons	220
Germicides	303	Hydrobromic Acid	61
Germ Theory	302	Hydrochloric Acid	61, 113
Glacial Phosphoric Acid	181	Hydrocyanic Acid	62, 274
Globulins	292	Hydroferricyanic Acid	62
Glucose	254	Hydroferrocyanic Acid	62
Glucosides	262	Hydrofluoric Acid	61
Glycerine	243	Hydrogen	105
Glycerites	244	Monoxide	106
Glyceroborates	245	Hydrogen Dioxide	109
Gold	162	Hydrogen Orthoborate	174
Alloys	169, 170	Hydrogen Phosphate	180
Crystal	165	Hydronaphthol	238
Cohesive	167	Hydrosulphuric Acid	61
Corrugated	167	Hyoscyamine	290
Compounds	171	Hypochlorites	58, 62
Pure	164	Hypophosphites	58, 61, 62
Refined	164	Illuminating Gas	204
Solders	171	Impenetrability	2
Tools	170, 367	Inclined Plane	7
Gold Aluminium Bronze	136	Induced Current	20
Gold Alloys	170	Insoluble Substances	68
Gold Amalgam	144	Iron	207
Gold Base Plate	170	Cast	208
Green Gold	170	Dental uses	208
Guanin	294	Pig	208
Guaiacum	235	Wrought	208
Gums	255	Iron Compounds	209
Gum Arabic	255		

India Rubber	231	Liquid	5
Vulcanized	231	Litharge	133
Iodine	110	Lithium	101
Trichloride	307	Lustre	80
Iodoform	267	Machine	5
Iodol	268	Magnesium	121
Iridium	202	Carbonate	121
Iron	50	Chloride	121
Is-atropyl Cocaine	291	Hypochlorite	121
Isomerism	218	Oxide	121
		Phosphate	121
Jerubebine	291	Magneto-Electricity	22
Kaolin	195	Magnesia	64
Kerosene	222	Magnitude	2
Ketones	270	Malleable Iron	208
Labarraque's Solution	100	Malleability	4, 80, 83
Lac	236	Manganese	206
Shell lac	237	Compounds	206
Lactates	278	Tests for	350, 359
Lactic Acid	275	Manganese Dioxide	206
Lacto-Phosphates	278	Mannheim Gold	170
Lamine	291	Mariotte's Law	11
Lardacein	293	Mass	1
Latin names of elements	37	Matter	1, 2, 33
Laughing Gas	184	Properties	2
Lavender Oil	230	Measures	24, 25
Lavoisier's Law	65	Melting Points	37
Laws		Mendeleef's Law	76
Avogadro's	11	Menthol	252
Berthollet's	11	Mercury	136
Charles'	11	" Tests	357
Of Fusion	12	Mercury and Copper	
Of Machines	6	Equivalence	49
Mariotte's	11	Mercuric Compounds	148
Lead	131	Albuminate	307
Acetate	272	Chloride	148
Sub-Acetate	272	Iodide	152
Compounds	133	Oleate	275
Tests for 347, 348, 349, 353		Oxide	152
Water	272	Oxycyanide	307
Leptothrix	300, 301	Sulphide	151
Leucin	294	Mercurous Chloride	150
Lever	6	" Iodide	153
Light	17, 72	Mercury	50, 136
Lime	64	Metalbumin	293
Lime Water	119		

INDEX. 407

Meta-elements	38
Metalloids	90
Metals	80
" . Properties 80, 81, 85, 86, 87	
Metric Equivalents	26
System	25
Meyer's Classification	78
Microbe of Caries	301
Of Pus	302
Microbes	301
Pathogenic	302
Protection Against	303
Micrococcus	300, 302
Milk Sugar	254
Miller's Experiments	305
Mint Oil	230
Mineral Lubricating Oil	224
Mixture	34
Mobility	3
Molar Motion	1
Molecule	1, 33, 34, 35, 38, 39
Molecular Motion	2
Monad	41
Morphine	287
Acetate	287
Hydrochlorate	287
Phtalate	287
Sulphate	287
Mosaic Gold	170
Motion	1
Atomic	2
Molecular	2
Mouth Washes	306
Mucin	293
Muriatic Acid	64, 113
Mycoderma	300
Myrrh	235
Myrtol	253
Naming Binaries	47
Napelline	283
Naphtha	222
Naphthalin	237
Naphthols	238
Beta-Hydro	238
Beta-Anhydro	238

Narceine	290
Native Albumins	292
Neroli Oil	230
Nickel	210
" Tests	350
Nitrates	58
Nitrites	58
Nitric Acid	61, 186
Nitrogen	184
Monoxide	184
Nomenclature (old and new)	63
Non-Metals	90
Ohm	22
Ohm's Law	23
Oil	224
Anise	228
Bergamot	228
Cajuput	228
Caraway	229
Cinnamon	229
Carvacrol	229
Cloves	229
Eucalyptus	230
Eugenol	230
Lavender	230
Gaultheria	230
Mint	230
Neroli	230
Pyrethrum	230
Rose	230
Sanitas	225
Turpentine	224
Oils	224, 226
Oleates	275
Oleic Acid	274
Olein	263
Oreide	170
Organic Acids	270
Organic Compounds	214
Organic Chemistry	214
Organic Formulæ	218
Organic Theory	214
Organized Ferments	295
Ox-Acids	54
Oxalates	63, 275

INDEX.

Oxalic Acid	63, 275
Oxybenzoic Acid	278
Oxychloride Cement	128
Oxygen	158
Oxynaphthoic Acid	307
Oxyphosphate Cement	127
Oxypropylene-di-iso-amylamine	291
Palladium	199
Palladium Amalgam	144
Palmitin	263
Paraffines	220
Paralbumin	293
Paraldehyde	269
Parotid Saliva	323
Parting Plaster	375
Peptones	293
Pepsin	296
Percentage Solutions	27
Periods	75
Perissads	44
Petroleum	221
Pewter	132
Phenacetine	398
Phenates	250
Phenol	247
Phenol Camphor	250
Phenol Terchloride	250
Phenol Sodique	250
Phenyl Alcohol	247
Phosphates	58
Phosphorus	178
Phosphor-bronze	136
Phosphor-iridium	398
Phosphoric acids	61, 180
Pinchbeck	170
Platinum	199, 346
Tests for	355
Platinum Amalgam	145
Platinum Metals	201
Polymorphous	15
Potassa	64
Porosity	2
Positive and Negative elements	37, 40
Potassium	93
Bicarbonate	93
Bitartrate	280
Chlorate	93
Chloride	93
Hydrate	94
Iodide	94
Nitrate	95
Permanganate	96
Tartrate	280
Tests for	350, 360, 361
Potential	22
Preparation of Dental Amalgam Alloys	139 to 147
Proof Spirit	242
Proteids	291
Prussic Acid	274
Ptomaines	281
Ptyalin	296
Pulley	6
Pulp Cavity	309
Pure Gold	164
Purple Of Cassius	172
Pus	302
Putrefaction	220, 295, 301
Pyrolusite	206
Pyrophosphates	58
Pyroxylin	257
Pyrethrum Oil	230
Quantity	22
Quantivalence	41
Variations	43, 49
Quicksilver	137
Quinine	288
Sulphates	289
Quinoline	284
Tartrate	284
Radicals	52, 215
Negative	58, 216
Positive	216
Reactions	66

INDEX.

Reading Binary Formulæ	51	Similor		170
Reagent	66	Soda		64
Red Gold	170	Sodium		96
Rees's Alloy	198	Sodium Compounds		96
Refined Gold	164	Bicarbonate	97	
Resins	235	Borate	99	
Resistance	22	Bicarbonate	97	
To air	84	Glyceroborate	245	
Resorcin	251	Hypochlorite	100	
Rhigolene	221	Hydro-Carbonate	97	
Robertson's Alloy	398	Silico-Fluoride	308	
Robinson's Remedy	249	Sulphite	308	
Rochelle Salt	280	Solders		90
Rose Oil	230	Solid		5
Rutile	203	Soluble Ferments		295
Safrol	253	Solubility		14
Salicylic Acid	63, 278	Solution		13
Salivary Calculi	328	Solvents		14
Saliva	319	Sozolic Acid		279
Salivary Analysis	377	Special Albumins		293
Salol	279	Specific Gravity		8, 80
Salt	56, 57	Of Elements	37	
Epsom	121	Heat	37	
Sandarach	236	Volume	28	
Sarkin	294	Speculum Metal		197, 136
Saturated Solution	14	Spiegel-Eisen		208
Screw	2	Spirilla		300
Septicine	287	Spirit of Mindererus		271
Series	217	Spirit of Wine		242
Homologous	217	Spirits		242
Sesqui	64	Spirochœte		300
Shellac	237	Sputum		387
Silex	203	Standard Pressure		12
Silica	203	Standard Temperature		12
Silicates	58	Stannous Chloride		198
Silicon	202	Starch		254
Compounds	202	States		
Silver	101	Of matter	5	
Alloys	104	Stearin		263
Amalgam	145	Steel		208
Chloride	105	Storage Battery		19
Nitrate	104	Strontium, Tests		360, 350
Oxide	105	Strychnine		289
Sulphide	105	Sulphate	289	
Tests	347, 349, 353			

Styptic Colloid	262	Terpenes	225
Sub-Acetate of Lead	272	Terpin	225
Sublimation	13	Tests for metals	353
Sublingual Saliva	324	" blow-pipe	347, 348
Submaxillary "	323	Testing alloys	367, 368
Substitution	218	Tests for cements	372
Sugar	253	Testing rubbers	375
Cane	253	Tetrads	42, 189
Grape	254	Thermal unit	12
Milk	254	Thermo-electricity	22
Sulphates	58	Thermometry	30
Sulphites	58	Thymol	253
Sulpho-acids	54, 62	Tin	196
Sulphocyanic acid	62	Alloys	198
Sulphonal	399	Compounds	198
Sulphur	154	Tests	347, 348, 349, 356, 357
Sulphurets	64	Tin Amalgam	146
Sulphuretted Hydrogen	154	Tinctures	242
In the Mouth	298	Titanic Oxide	203
Sulphuric acid	61, 156	Titanium	203
Sulphurous acid	61, 154	Tooth structure	309
Suppuration	302	Torula	300
Symbols	35, 7	Triads	41, 160
Synthesis	32	Tribrom-phenol	308
Syntonin	291	Trichloracetic acid	272
Systems of crystals	16	Turpentine	224
Talmi Gold	170	Type metal	173
Tannic Acid	262	Types	218
Tannin	262	Tyrosin	294
Tartar	327, 390	Ulexine	291
Emetic	280	Units	
Tartaric Acid	63	Electrical measurement	22
Tartar Emetic	280	Uranium oxide	133
Tartrates	63	Uric acid	294
Tellurium	153	Urates	294
Tellurium Amalgam	146	Valence	41
Tenacity	4, 83	Valeric acid	280
Tensile Strength	82	Vapors	5
Terebene	225	Variations	
Terminations of Binary and Ternary Compounds	61	In quantivalence	43, 49
		Vaseline	223
		Veratrine	290
Ternary Compounds	60	Vibriones	300

Vienna paste	95	Writing acid formulæ	54
Vital force	73	" binary "	47
Volatile compounds	68	" formulæ of hydrates	56
Volatile oils	226	Writing formulæ of salts	57
Volt	22	Xanthin	294
Volume		Yeast	297
Specific	28	Zinc	122
Volumetric analysis	384	Alloys	124
Water	106	Amalgams	146
Water of crystallization	16	Solders	124
Wax	263	Zinc and tin alloy	124
Bees	263	Zinc Chloride	125
Waxes	263	Oxide	127
Weber	23	Oxychloride	128
Wedge	7	Oxyphosphate	127
Weights	24	Oxysulphate	127
Wheel and Axle	6	Sulphate	129
Wines	242	Iodide	130
Wood spirit	242	Tests	348, 349, 351, 356, 359
		Zöoglœa	300

www.ingramcontent.com/pod-product-compliance
Lightning Source LLC
Chambersburg PA
CBHW030547300426
44111CB00009B/886